Descartes

Descartes

An Intellectual Biography

STEPHEN GAUKROGER

CLARENDON PRESS · OXFORD

1995

Oxford University Press, Walton Street, Oxford OX2 6DP
Oxford New York
Athens Auckland Bangkok Bombay
Calcutta Cape Town Dar es Salaam Delhi
Florence Hong Kong Istanbul Karachi
Kuala Lumpur Madras Madrid Melbourne
Mexico City Nairobi Paris Singapore
Taipei Tokyo Toronto
and associated companies in
Berlin Ibadan

Oxford is a trade mark of Oxford University Press

Published in the United States
by Oxford University Press Inc., New York

British Library Cataloguing in Publication Data
Data available

Library of Congress Cataloging in Publication Data
Gaukroger, Stephen. (b. 1950).
Descartes : an intellectual biography / Stephen Gaukroger.
Includes bibliographical references.
1. Descartes, René, 1596–1650. 2. Philosophers—France—
Biography. I. Title.
B1875.G38 1995 194—dc20 94-31924
ISBN 0-19-823994-7

1 3 5 7 9 10 8 6 4 2

Typeset by Graphicraft Typesetters Ltd., Hong Kong
Printed in Great Britain
on acid-free paper by
Bookcraft Ltd., Midsomer Norton, Avon

For my mother and father
Siobhan O'Connor and Herbert Wallace Sutcliffe Gaukroger

Preface

Every great philosophy has so far been the self-confession of its originator, a kind of unintentional, unconscious *memoires*. (Nietzsche, *Jenseits
von Gut und Böse*)

I have a vivid and happy memory of my first reading of Descartes, for
it was with unbounded enthusiasm that I devoured the *Discourse on
Method*, sitting in the shade of a tree in the Borghese Gardens in Rome
in the summer of 1970, just before I started studying philosophy at
university. But I cannot honestly say that my enthusiasm was fuelled
by my subsequent undergraduate courses on Descartes, which simply
followed the trade winds, in an obsessive but completely de-
contextualized way, through the tired old questions of the *cogito* and
the foundations for knowledge. So it was that my interest in the early
seventeenth century came to be stimulated by Galileo rather than
Descartes, and it was to Galileo that I devoted my main attention while
a research student at Cambridge in the mid-1970s. While there, however,
Gerd Buchdahl and John Schuster revealed to me a different Descartes,
a more authentic and vastly more engaging one, whom I only began to
explore properly ten years later. It is this Descartes who is the subject
of this book, and I warn readers—if 'warn' is the right word, as some
may breathe a sigh of relief—that it is not the Descartes from whom
philosophers have made such a good living for decades that they will
find here. But I have not simply set out to write the history of science
or cultural history. Descartes is, after all, the figure who stands at the
beginning of modern philosophy, just as Plato stands at the beginning
of ancient philosophy. While I shall argue that his philosophical achievements are much more intimately linked to his interest in what subsequently have been considered 'scientific' questions than is commonly
realized, my aim is not thereby to take Descartes out of the realm of
philosophy, but rather to throw light on how he did philosophy.

It is with some trepidation that I pursued this goal through the genre
of intellectual biography, even though my own early interest in philosophy had been fired by Simone de Beauvoir's incomparable intellectual autobiography. People read intellectual biographies with different
expectations, from the naïve attempt to understand, at a distance as it
were, how a 'great mind' works, to attempts to model one's own

thought and career on that of someone one admires. Perhaps the most famous example of modelling is Thomas Mann, who evidently tried to mirror in his own intellectual development the stages in Goethe's intellectual development, although I think there are very many less explicit cases, and that biography generally has played an important role in 'self-fashioning' since the nineteenth century. This makes it a rather delicate genre, both from the point of the view of the reader and from that of the writer. Self-fashioning is part of the rationale behind reading, and perhaps behind writing, intellectual biographies, but any self-fashioning will have to be very indirect in the present case. While the thesis of Jacques Le Goff, that modernity did not begin and the Middle Ages did not effectively cease until the French and Industrial Revolutions, is stronger than anything I would wish to argue in this book, I have no doubt that the culture in which Descartes lived and worked is much more remote from our own than is commonly recognized. This has consequences for biography, because a biography explores the emotional life of its subject, and the more removed from our own culture our subject is, the deeper the problems about how we are to succeed in this exploration. I have tried to be more responsive than my predecessors to the difficulties that these issues raise, with the result that there is much greater concentration on the culture in which Descartes worked than one finds in earlier biographies. But I am also very conscious of the problems of over-contextualization, and I have tried to make sure that neither the subject of my biography, nor his contribution, slips out of focus.

Anyone writing on Descartes cannot fail to acknowledge the excellent edition of Descartes' works by Adam and Tannery, which appeared in the first decade of this century, and more recently in a revised edition. I am grateful also to John Cottingham, Robert Stoothoff, Dugald Murdoch, and Anthony Kenny, *The Philosophical Works of Descartes* (3 vols., Cambridge, 1985–91), which has set the standards of clarity and accuracy in the English translation of Descartes. Although I have generally given my own translations, on a number of occasions I have found that I have not been able to improve on that of Cottingham *et al.*, and have followed theirs.

In the course of taking on the project, I have inevitably run up debts to too many people to acknowledge all those from whom I have learned. I have especially benefited from conversation and correspondence with Hans Aarslef, David Armstrong, Gordon Baker, John Bigelow, Keith Campbell, Desmond Clarke, John Cottingham, Jim Franklin, Helen Irving, Jamie Kassler, Tony Kenny, John Kilcullen, Katherine Morris, Lloyd Reinhardt, John Schuster, William Shea, Michael Shortland, John Sutton, and John Yolton. An earlier version of parts of chapter 4

Preface

appeared in the *Journal of the History of Ideas*, vol. 52 (1992); but as for my other writings on Descartes, I have changed my mind so significantly over the past two or three years that all of them are superseded by the present book.

Part of the work was done while I was a visitor at Corpus Christi College, Oxford, in the second half of 1991, and I would like to thank the University of Sydney for granting me study leave at this time, and the President and Fellows of Corpus Christi for the facilities they offered me. The project has been helped along enormously by three grants from the Australian Research Council, which assisted me in numerous ways, including allowing me relief from teaching in the second half of 1993, when the book was completed in draft.

S. G.

Sydney 1994.

Contents

Contents

Contents

Chronological Table

1596	Born at La Haye (now Descartes) near Tours at his maternal grandmother's house, on 31 March, third surviving child of Joachim Descartes, Councillor at the Parliament of Brittany, and Jeanne Brochard.
1597	Mother dies on 13 May. Brought up by maternal grandmother, Jeanne Sain, at La Haye, with his elder brother and sister.
1600	Father remarries. Descartes and his brother and sister remain with Jeanne Sain.
1606	Begins as a boarder at the Jesuit college of La Flèche at Anjou, where his elder brother was probably already a student.
1607	Father moves with his new family and Descartes' sister to Châtelleraut.
1610	Jeanne Sain dies (late 1609 or 1610).
1614	Leaves La Flèche, where from 1607 he has been looked after by the rector, Father Charlet, who has acted 'as a second father' to him.
1614–1615	Moves to a house just outside Paris, shutting himself off from others and quite possibly suffering a nervous breakdown.
1615–1616	Studies law, and perhaps some medicine, at the University of Poitiers, taking his baccalaureate and licence in civil and canon law in November 1616.
1616–1618	Descartes possibly spends late 1616 to the middle of 1618 in Paris.
1618	Goes to the Netherlands in the summer of 1618 and joins the army of Prince Maurice of Nassau as a gentleman soldier. In November he meets Isaac Beeckman, who rekindles his interest in scientific matters. He completes his *Compendium Musicae*, and presents it to Beeckman as a New Year's gift.
1619	Begins the year working intensely on mathematical and mechanical problems under Beeckman's encouragement and guidance. Extant writings from this period include fragments on the mathematical description of free fall, and an important treatment of hydrostatic paradoxes, which represents Descartes' first excursion into micromechanical explanation. Descartes leaves the army of Maurice and plans a journey through Germany to join the army of Maximilian of Bavaria, setting out in March. Early in 1619 he studies proportional compasses, and begins to formulate a theory of proportional

magnitudes which will ultimately lead him in the direction of algebra. Various notes from this period are collected in the fragmentary *Cogitationes Privatae*. During the course of 1620 Descartes has contact with Rosicrucians, including the Rosicrucian mathematician Johannes Faulhaber. He begins a mathematical treatise, *The Thesaurus Mathematicus of Polybius Cosmopolitanus*, which is soon abandoned, but it is likely that it was to be concerned with a 'universal mathematics', and an early draft of Rule 4 of the *Regulae* was probably composed at this time. He spends the later part of the year stationed at Ulm. Here he begins to formulate a general theory of method. Sometime in November he probably has a nervous breakdown, as well as his three famous dreams.

1620   The first six months of 1620 are probably spent at Ulm, but his movements after that are not known. He begins work on his *Regulae*, completing the first eleven Rules, then abandoning the project. In the course of 1620 he works intensively in geometry, probably completing a work on polyhedra and figurate numbers, *De Solidorum Elementis*, and in optics. In November he makes what he later refers to as 'a wonderful discovery', which is probably his solution of all problems resolvable in terms of cubic or quartic equations by means of a circle and a parabola.

1622–1623   Returns to France, his whereabouts in the intervening period unknown. On his arrival in Paris, he is challenged to defend himself against charges of being a Rosicrucian. He sells his property, left to him by his mother, in the process losing seigneurial rights and the title 'Seigneur du Perron', which he has held up to this time. The proceeds from the sale provide a regular but modest income. He considers a legal/administrative career. The *Studium bonæ mentis* may date from this period.

1623–1625   On 22 March 1623, he sets out on a journey to Italy, probably spending some considerable time in Venice. He returns in May 1625, and again considers (for the last time) a legal and administrative career.

1625–1626   Settles in Paris on his return from Italy. He has regular contact with Mersenne, who has published detailed criticisms of naturalism and is advocating mechanism as the appropriate natural philosophy for the new physics. In collaboration with others, Descartes works on geometrical optics, and he may have discovered the law of refraction as early as 1626.

1626–1628   Resumes work on the *Regulae*, possibly in the first instance by reworking Rule 8, and then going on to the new Rules, from 12 onwards. Here some of the philosophical consequences of his work in optics and algebra are explored, and the focus is now on questions of the mechanistic construal of perceptual cognition, together with the problem of legitimating mathematical operations. Probably in 1628, Descartes finally abandons the *Regulae*. During 1628 he makes visits to the Netherlands, with a view to settling there.

Chronological Table

In November, he attends a meeting on Aristotelian philosophy at the residence of the papal nuncio and gives a public announcement of his own work on method; he is encouraged in his researches by Cardinal Bérulle. At the end of 1628, he leaves for the Netherlands, where he will remain for the next 20 years, albeit with constant moves and intense secrecy about his address.

1629–1630   Begins work on a number of metaphysical questions, as well as devising a machine for grinding hyperbolic lenses. From August 1629 onwards, other projects are gradually abandoned as he tries to explain the meteorological phenomenon of parhelia (multiple suns), which by the end of 1629 has grown into an attempt to account for 'the whole physical world'. In October 1630 he writes a long abusive letter to Beeckman, accusing him of claiming the credit for being his teacher in the early years, and breaks off relations with him.

1630–1632   Descartes moves to Amsterdam at the end of 1630, lodging with his friend Villebressieu but generally avoiding visitors. The *Dioptrique* and the *Météors* are completed in draft, and Descartes makes what will be his last major contribution to mathematics, the solution of Pappus' locus problem. While in Amsterdam he visits butchers' shops daily to retrieve pieces for dissection. In May 1632 he moves to Deventer, partly to avoid interruptions to his work and partly to be near his first disciple, Henry Reneri. He is reconciled with Beeckman. He works intensely on physical optics, the laws of motion, and the outlines of a cosmology. The unfinished draft of the *Traité de la lumière* that has come down to us probably dates from late 1632.

1632–1633   Descartes turns to the *Traité de l'homme*, setting out a mechanistic physiology and a theory of the body as an automaton. Between July and November 1633, he prepares his treatises for publication, only to hear in November of the Inquisition's condemnation of Galileo, at which point, in obvious despair, he abandons plans to publish. In December 1633 he moves back to Amsterdam.

1634–1636   He prepares final drafts of the *Dioptrique* and the *Météors*, and starts to work on a preface to them, which will become the *Discours de la méthode*. In the Spring of 1635 he returns to Utrecht, where Reneri is about to provide the first institutional teaching of Cartesian natural philosophy. In August of 1635 his daughter, Francine, is born, her mother having been a maid at the house where Descartes stayed in Amsterdam. The *Discours* is written over the winter of 1635/6 and the *Géometrie* is put together from earlier drafts while the other treatises are being printed.

1637–1639   Descartes moves to Leiden in March 1636 to supervise publication of the *Discours* and the three *Essais*, which appear in June 1637. In August he moves to the coastal area around Haarlem, where he remains until November 1639. This is one of the happier periods in his life, the *Discours* and *Essais* having been generally well

xvi

received. He begins to take an interest in and possibly even spend time with his daughter.

1639–1640   Descartes works on the *Meditationes*, and begins to get involved in an acrimonious and very public dispute with Voetius, which raises a number of religious and ideological questions of the kind that he was always concerned to avoid. This is to be the first of a number of such public disputes that will dog him throughout the 1640s. He returns to Leiden in April 1640 to supervise a preliminary printing of the *Meditationes*. In September, Francine dies of a fever.

1641–1643   The *Meditationes* are published in 1641, together with six sets of objections and replies. Descartes moves to Endergeest, near Leiden. After giving up the idea of writing a dialogue (*La Recherche de la verité*), and setting out his metaphysics and natural philosophy in the form of an extended commentary on a standard scholastic textbook, he begins work on a comprehensive exposition of his philosophy in textbook form, the *Principia*, at the end of 1641. The second edition of the *Meditationes*, with a seventh set of objections and replies and a letter to Dinet, in which Descartes defends himself against attacks on the orthodoxy of the *Meditationes*, appears in 1642. In response to Descartes' long attack on him in the *Epistola ad Voetium*, published in May 1643, Voetius succeeds in having the council of Utrecht summon Descartes, and he is threatened with expulsion and the public burning of his books. He seeks refuge in the Hague, where is he able to use his influence to get the Prince of Orange to intervene on his behalf. In May 1643, he moves to Egmond du Hoef.

1643–1646   Descartes starts an affectionate and fruitful correspondence with Princess Elizabeth of Bohemia, focusing on his account of the passions. The *Principia*, four parts of its originally projected six complete, is published by Elzevier in middle of 1644. In May 1644 he travels to France, returning in November to the Egmond area, where he will be based until 1649. A good deal of his time is taken up with dissection of animals and studying the medicinal properties of plants. By 1646 he has a draft of the *Passions de l'âme* complete. Elizabeth moves to Berlin in August 1646, and Descartes is never to see her again, although their correspondence continues. At the end of 1646, Queen Christina of Sweden initiates a correspondence with Descartes through Chanut, a French diplomat attached to the Swedish court.

1647–1649   Descartes is condemned by Revius and other theologians at the University of Leiden in March and April 1647, and he travels in France from June to September 1647. While there he meets Hobbes, Gassendi, and Pascal. French translations of the *Meditationes* and the *Principia* are published in 1647, and his attack on his erstwhile disciple Regius, the *Notae in Programma*, appeared at the beginning of 1648. On 16 April 1648, he is interviewed on his philosophy by a young Dutch student, Burman, who keeps an invaluable record of the interview. In May 1648 he returns to Paris yet again, this time to take up a pension from the king, but Paris is in the middle of political turmoil, and he returns to the Netherlands in August.

1649–1650   At the end of February 1649, Descartes is invited to Sweden, to the court of Queen Christina, and he finally accepts in July, embarking on 31 August. The *Passions de l'âme* appears in November 1649. Early in the new year he contracts pneumonia, from which he dies, in Stockholm, on 11 February 1650.

Descartes as Faust. Frontispiece to Descartes, *Opuscula Posthuma* (Amsterdam, 1701).

Introduction

Since the eighteenth century, there has been in circulation a curious story about Descartes. It is said that in later life he was always accompanied in his travels by a mechanical life-sized female doll which, we are told by one source, he himself had constructed 'to show that animals are only machines and have no souls'. He had named the doll after his illegitimate daughter, Francine, and some versions of events have it that she was so lifelike that the two were indistinguishable. Descartes and the doll were evidently inseparable, and he is said to have slept with her encased in a trunk at his side. Once, during a crossing over the Holland Sea some time in the early 1640s, while Descartes was sleeping, the captain of the ship, suspicious about the contents of the trunk, stole into the cabin and opened it. To his horror, he discovered the mechanical monstrosity, dragged her from the trunk and across the decks, and finally managed to throw her into the water. We are not told whether she put up a struggle.

This story had a wide currency in the nineteenth and early twentieth centuries, at one stage being taken as a theme for a novel by Anatole France. It exists in a number of versions, some of them explicitly fictional, some purporting to be factual, and the detail varies quite considerably from version to version.[1] So far as I can tell, the story originates no earlier than the eighteenth century, and it received most attention in an era preoccupied with the theories of La Mettrie, the French Enlightenment *philosophe* who, in his infamous *L'Homme Machine* (1747), had extended the idea of animals being automata—developed by Descartes in his *L'Homme*—to human beings, offering a materialist account of the mind, and suggesting that Descartes himself had held such a view, but that judicious self-censorship had prevented him making the theory public.[2] There is, in fact, absolutely no evidence that any version of the story is true. Its origins are rather obscure, but by the second half of the eighteenth century it was a propaganda weapon in the fight against La Mettrie's materialism, Descartes himself being seen as the ultimate instigator of this pernicious doctrine. Given this context, the story has all the elements of propaganda, including that favourite propaganda weapon, sexual innuendo, and I have little doubt that it originated as a tool of the eighteenth-century struggle against materialism.

More recently, the charge that is made against Descartes is not that he was a closet materialist[3] but that he inaugurated, in the modern era, a disastrous separation of mind and body, which had the effect of relegating the body from serious philosophical consideration and isolating the mind in a purely intellectual realm. The mind/body separation has an enormous number of ramifications, and one to which some modern commentators have drawn attention is the way in which the mind/body distinction is intimately tied in with the reason/emotion distinction. The argument is along the lines that the emotional life, which depends upon the exercise of the passions (something that occurs when the body acts on the mind in Descartes' account), is absent from the rational mind; and because emotional questions were traditionally treated as part of the female domain, there was a corresponding assumption that reason was present to a lesser degree, or even absent, in women. As one recent writer puts it, 'we owe to Descartes an influential and pervasive theory of mind, which provides support for a powerful version of the sexual division of mental labour. Women have been assigned responsibility for that realm of the sensuous which the Cartesian Man of Reason must transcend, if he is to have true knowledge of things'.[4] On this reading, the image of man-machine is replaced, as it were, by that of woman-machine, for Descartes has not only excluded a whole realm of life from rational thought, but he has excluded women from rational thought in the same process, effectively treating them as mere bodies, that is, for him, machines. And, quite independently of this line of argument, Julian Jaynes has speculated that Descartes may have named his daughter Francine after the Francini brothers, who were responsible for creating the mechanical moving statues of gods and goddesses in the grottoes under the Royal Gardens at Saint-Germain.[5] This idea carries with it overtones of Descartes constructing his daughter on the model of a mechanical doll. And in a more explicit way, a late nineteenth-century biography of Descartes, in a popular 'Philosophic Classics for English Readers' series, makes the claim that Descartes' interest in his daughter (and by implication women generally) was purely scientific, maintaining that it was no accident that Descartes' daughter was conceived in 1634, the very year when Descartes was working on his treatise on the formation of the foetus, for this was simply part of a scientific experiment, whereby Descartes 'carried his theory of *bêtes-machines* a step higher than he confessed in public', and his sexual 'adventure' was 'merely the result of scientific curiosity'.[6] And commentators have not been content to limit his scientific curiosity in *bêtes-machines* to foetuses: as recently as five years ago, a writer on

Introduction

Descartes confidently tells us that he alienated his wife (Descartes was in fact never married) by experimenting on the family dog.[7]

Descartes' almost canonical status has led to his thought being assimilated to a range of very different philosophies, and put to a wide variety of different and often incompatible uses. More than any other modern philosopher, he has been fashioned according to the philosophies of the time and interpreted accordingly, a fashioning that places him at the roots of particular modern developments, and has often created images of a particular *persona*.[8] Although the idea of Descartes as the 'father of modern philosophy' is, I suspect, one that has its origins in nineteenth-century historiography of philosophy, it is undeniable that he has had a pivotal role in philosophical thinking since the middle of the seventeenth century. This pivotal role arises, however, at least in part as a result of various kinds of philosophical and other investments that later thinkers and teachers have made in him. Indeed, it is this, rather than new discoveries about Descartes or occasional lapses in scholarship (although both do occur), that goes furthest towards explaining why what will be treated as core Cartesian doctrines in one era will often be replaced by something quite different in another.

It is easily forgotten just how controversial, reviled, and celebrated a figure Descartes was, not only in his own lifetime, but for the next 150 years or so. Although there was no strictly Cartesian school after Descartes' death,[9] it is a striking fact that even in areas where Descartes had had little or nothing to say, his name and ideas were evoked; virtually anyone in virtually any area who considered themselves an innovator in France in the second half of the seventeenth century, for example, invoked Cartesianism in some way.[10] On the other hand, his writings were placed on the Index of Prohibited Books in 1663, Louis XIV renewed a ban on the teaching of Cartesian philosophy in 1685, and there was extensive opposition to Cartesianism in the universities in France right into the eighteenth century. Cartesians were excluded from the Académie des Sciences, and although the French authorities allowed Descartes' body to be returned to France, during the reburial service in June 1667 an order came from the Court forbidding the pronouncement of the funeral oration.[11] The French Enlightenment *philosophes* seized on him as their hero, d'Holbach in his *Système de la nature* of 1774 declaring that Descartes was rightly accused of atheism because 'he very energetically destroyed the weak proofs of the existence of God that he gave', and d'Alembert in 1778 seeing him as revolutionary, as 'one of the chiefs of the conspirators who had the courage to raise the banner against an arbitrary and despotic power, and who, in preparing a brilliant revolution, laid the foundations of a government more just and happier than any ever seen established'.[12]

Cartesianism was in fact developed into a specific social philosophy at an early stage, and François Poulain de la Barre, in his *Discours physique de moral de l'égalité des deux sexes, où l'on voit l'importance de se défaire des préjugez* (1673), applied the 'method of doubt' and the doctrine of clear and distinct ideas to the prejudices of the day, and unmasked the falsity of one of the greatest of these prejudices, the inequality of women, offering one of the first and most articulate defences of feminism in the early modern era.[13] Indeed, there was a group of women thinkers—which included Descartes' niece, Catherine—who in the 1670s developed a version of Cartesian philosophy in which Cartesianism was proposed as an alternative (with women particularly in mind) to the philosophies of the schools and Académie.[14] And while the use to which the Enlightenment thinkers put Descartes can be explained partly by their association of intellectual with political radicalism, the appropriation of Cartesianism in the cause of the Enlightenment idea of 'progress', if not quite as wild as it may seem[15], is none the less something that would have been alien to Descartes.

As well as in politics, Descartes' influence was evident in the arts, another topic on which he never published a word. In late seventeenth-century French art theory, the Academic school not only developed a theory of representation of facial expression based on the Cartesian theory of the passions,[16] but also defended the primacy of shape over colour on explicitly Cartesian grounds—extension being a real property of bodies whereas colour was not—and treated colour as a danger that could seduce one into turning away from the truth.[17] Even in areas such as architectural theory, various connections with Cartesianism were made,[18] and it is not too difficult to detect the influence of Descartes in Rameau's *Traité de l'harmonie* (1722), the fundamental textbook on musical theory of the eighteenth century.[19] Perhaps most surprising of all, given Descartes' strong adherence to Catholicism and his general avoidance of theological questions, is the use of Cartesianism by a number of Calvinist theologians in the second half of the seventeenth century.[20]

One area where he had published a great deal was natural philosophy, and his immediate influence here was immense: the *Essais* and the *Principia* formed the starting point for all serious work in this area in the middle decades of the seventeenth century.[21] There was a thriving Cartesian tradition, and Newton, the success of whose work was largely responsible for the demise of Cartesianism later in the century, was himself a Cartesian in the early 1660s, before he developed his own distinctive natural philosophy. Nevertheless, both Cartesian physics and Cartesian natural philosophy came under intense criticism from the later seventeenth century onwards. Descartes' theory of vortices, which provided a fundamental, mechanistic account of planetary orbits, was destroyed by Newton in Book II of his *Principia*, and his advocacy of a hypothetical method was increasingly criticized, especially by English natural philosophers in the wake of Newton's rejection of hypothetical reasoning in science.[22] A second feature of Descartes' approach, his commitment to mechanism, had a more complex reception. Mechanism in physics did not always mean the same thing to all writers. In its mid-seventeenth century manifestation it involved the reduction of dynamics to kinematics, and as areas of physics other than mechanics came to be studied closely in the eighteenth century, it also came to be interpreted as the reduction of all physical phenomena to mechanics. This was initially restricted to magnetism and then gravitation, but later came to cover areas such as electricity. Not every such attempt can be construed as Cartesian, but many were. In the eighteenth century, for example, there were a number of attempts to develop a Cartesian alternative to Newtonianism which tried to restructure Newtonian physics in terms of a broadly Cartesian natural philosophy.[23] These became less and less plausible as the century progressed and the fundamental nature of non-mechanical forces became apparent.[24] In physiology, on the other hand, where mechanism was almost exclusively associated with Descartes, it took the form of the mechanical modelling of biological entities and processes. Here Cartesianism, which in this area effectively became a type of materialist reductionism, was an immense success throughout the eighteenth and nineteenth centuries. As late as 1901, the British physiologist Sir Michael Foster could write that Descartes' account, with very little change in detail, 'and some of that hardly more than a change in terminology would convert that exposition into a statement of modern views'.[25]

By the end of the eighteenth century Descartes had begun to become, first, domesticated—the fact that this occurred around the same time as the beginnings of the idea of Descartes as the 'father' of modern philosophy is perhaps not wholly accidental—and then revered (as fathers tend to be). This came about as the result of the conversion of Descartes into a 'philosopher', that is, into an epistemologist, and into the founder of a philosophical school. The transformation occurred in a number of stages: Malebranche put a much more epistemological gloss on Descartes' doctrines than Descartes himself did, and he played a significant role in turning philosophy in the direction of epistemology in the late seventeenth and eighteenth centuries, particularly because British eighteenth-century philosophers tended to read Descartes very much through Malebranche.[26] This process was helped along by the contrast that Voltaire and others drew between Descartes and Locke, a contrast in which compatibility with Newtonianism, rather than epistemological and metaphysical questions in their own right, played the most significant role, although the doctrine of innate ideas formed a convenient dividing line. In the late 1720s, Voltaire wrote:

Our Descartes, born to unearth the errors of antiquity, and to substitute his own, spurred on by a systematising mind that blinds the greatest of men, imagined that he had shown that the soul is the same thing as thought, just as matter for him is the same thing as extension. He maintained that we are constantly thinking, that the soul comes into the body already endowed with all the metaphysical notions, knowing God, space, the infinite, having every abstract idea, in short full of learning, which it unfortunately forgets on leaving its mother's womb.[27]

This somewhat partisan summary, which focuses on the kinds of question that Locke took issue with in Descartes' work—the context is that of a letter on Locke—indicates clearly how Cartesianism was being read in the eighteenth century.[28] The decisive version of this transformation of Descartes' work occurred above all in the nineteenth century, however, in the work of Kuno Fischer, who supplied the definitive version of the modern account of the development of philosophy in the seventeenth and eighteenth centuries.[29] Basically, this account did two things. First, it identified philosophy since the seventeenth century as being fundamentally epistemology, whereas prior to the seventeenth century it had been fundamentally metaphysics. Secondly, it marked out the seventeenth century as beginning a new era in philosophy: the old Platonist/Aristotelian dichotomy (which Kant had worked with, for example) is replaced by a new one, reflecting the fact that a new beginning had been made. This new dichotomy was one between competing and mutually exclusive epistemologies, rationalism and empiricism, the former basing everything on truths of reason, the latter basing everything on experiential truths.[30]

In common with an increasing number of commentators, I shall not be following this historiographic model, for the identification of philosophy with epistemology would, I believe, have been wholly alien to Descartes. It serves both to mislead us as to what his intellectual concerns were, and as to the role epistemology plays in relation to his other concerns. An intellectual biography of Descartes has a special responsibility to take care over such questions of interpretation, for its aim is to reconstruct the development of his thought, not to reconstruct what he might have answered to issues on which had no views, either because these are peculiarly modern issues, or (more likely) because the context within which he was writing made certain approaches, which now seem to us promising, so wholly unsatisfactory as to be not worth pursuing. But having said this, I should warn that I am not advocating 'going native'. There are some situations in which hindsight proves

6

invaluable. One such case, I believe, is the development of Descartes' views on cognition. In the mid 1630s Descartes abandoned a naturalistic approach to questions of cognition in favour of one which was directed by a sceptically driven epistemology. He had never considered that his naturalistic account would tell the full story even in the case of perceptual cognition, and he had supplemented it with an account of perceptual cognition as the cognition of signs; but he never developed this beyond a few remarks in the first chapter of *Le Monde*, and the connection between his accounts of the psychophysiology of perceptual cognition and perceptual cognition as a kind of interpretation was never set out in a satisfactory way. Moreover, at no stage did he believe that human perceptual cognition, still less human behaviour, could be explained fully without reference to an immaterial intelligence. Nevertheless, what he offered in his writings of the 1620s and early 1630s was a strongly naturalistic account of perceptual cognition. From the *Discours* (1638) onwards, however, his account of human perceptual cognition was to change direction radically, and was to become largely dominated by questions deriving from the project of legitimation, a project driven by the idea that insight into questions of cognition was ultimately to be gained by considering the kinds of threat posed to knowledge by scepticism, and providing knowledge with a foundation that protected it from this.[31] This project gradually gathered momentum in subsequent philosophical thought, especially in eighteenth-century Britain, so that the naturalistic psychophysiology that characterizes Descartes' discussion of cognition in the 1620s and early 1630s was ignored, as the mind-body problem, particularly in the guise of the 'veil of perception' doctrine, took over. There is an irony here in that, in the twentieth century, two developments have occurred which have not only caused a reversal of the fortunes of traditional sceptically driven epistemology, but have resulted in the two areas that Descartes had begun to abandon in the 1630s being pursued with a new vigour. First, the question of interpretation received a new lease of life with the work of Frege, and then Wittgenstein and Husserl, to the extent that questions of meaning and interpretation came to usurp epistemology in attempts to understand our cognitive relation to the world.[32] Secondly, advances in understanding brain functions, 'artificial intelligence' (at least from Turing machines onwards), and the area of cognitive science generally revealed that avenues that would have seemed a dead end to seventeenth-century thinkers opened up the possibility of a genuinely naturalistic theory of cognitive functions.[33] In other words, projects that Descartes abandoned at least in part because the resources available to him made them look like dead ends have, with a change in resources, now come to look promising. This gives an urgency to the question of why exactly these were abandoned and why they were replaced with a sceptically driven epistemology, and prompts us to delve much more deeply into this question than we might have were we to see ourselves still in the tradition of a sceptically driven epistemology. The aim is not to show the extent to which Descartes was a 'precursor' of modern cognitive science—a pointless exercise, of no use in understanding anything—but to show why a particular approach, which we now have good reason to take seriously, seemed attractive to Descartes, only to be abandoned.

A biography, as opposed to simply a story about the life of someone, is something that explores the emotional life of its subject; and an intellectual biography is something that throws light on that subject's intellectual pursuits, not merely by trying to establish a sequence or chronological order in those pursuits, but by trying to establish a rationale for them both in terms of the subject's motivations and in terms of a specific cultural and intellectual context within which those motivations are shaped and bear fruit. I have tried to deal with three general questions in this biography. The first is that of the relation between Descartes' personal development and the cultural environment in which he lived and worked; the second, the relation between Descartes' personal development and his intellectual development; and the third, the relation between his intellectual pursuits and the cultural and intellectual environment in which they were pursued. In each case, it seems to me, what one must avoid is reduction or conflation. Descartes' personal and intellectual development are not the same thing, even though they are very closely related after late 1618. Nor can his intellectual achievements be treated simply as the products of a particular intellectual, cultural, and scientific environment, although I do believe that if one does not understand this environment, and in some depth, then no proper understanding of Descartes' work is possible. Finally, Descartes' own personal development is not *sui generis,* but nor is he simply a product of a particular kind of family, or of the Jesuit education system, or of Catholic gentlemen and scholars of his age, or whatever.

On the first question, biography, if pursued properly, can be a good genre for exploring some difficult questions about how the emotional and intellectual life of a subject are related, and thereby offering some insight into the nature of subjectivity. The genre of biography cannot remain untouched by the increased attention to the problems of subjectivity, which has made it both more a problematic and, I believe, more rewarding genre. A major problem is that a biography explores the emotional life of its subject, and the tools for the exploration of the emotions that we have were developed largely from the end of the nineteenth century onwards and, I believe, necessarily bear very deep and ineradicable traces of their cultural origins. If one is to be guided by the understanding of the emotions that psychoanalysis and related disciplines have yielded, the benefits are to be reaped not through the formulaic genre of psychobiography, but by using this understanding to raise questions that might not otherwise have occurred to us, and which alert us to dimensions of Descartes' character and personality that would otherwise remain hidden. I shall be concerned to give an account of Descartes' personal development principally in terms of the kinds of self-images that he forged for himself and tried to convey, both in his writings and in his personal conduct, and to examine the tensions in these self-images. But this is not a completely self-contained question, for such self-images, in Descartes' case, revolve around, and result in, intellectual questions. Descartes lived an unhappy and indeed, for some considerable periods, a rather disturbed life. This is something he made every effort to deny or disguise, and the means he chose were intellectual. His sources of pleasure were few, but intellectual achievements figure prominently amongst these, and these achievements were elevated into virtually the only form of worthwhile pursuit, in a way that goes well beyond a commitment to a 'life of the mind', for example. This provides a serious challenge to the biographer, as it poses in stark terms the question whether his intellectual development can be used to illuminate his personal development, and vice versa. Here we face a genuinely difficult interpretative problem. We are constrained to use largely the same materials, namely his writings and correspondence, to reconstruct both the thought of the philosopher and scientist, and the personality and personal development of a psychological subject who will inevitably have concerns not reflected in, and perhaps inexpressible in, his scientific and philosophical writings, and who may, indeed, have all kinds of personal beliefs in conflict with what he writes, arising from a variety of reasons, from the unconscious nature of these beliefs to self-censorship for religious or political reasons. What we have to set out, and take care not to run together, are these questions: What self-images were available in the culture in which Descartes lived? Which of these images did he take up and (in as much as it is possible to answer this question) why did he take up these? How are they expressed in his own writings, and to what extent do they shape his concerns?

But in raising these questions we have to exercise great caution, for we are making an assumption that, in understanding a subject's motivations, this understanding will ultimately take the form of an understanding of that subject's psychology. This may be an assumption requiring significant qualification in the case of a seventeenth-century figure. Let me explain what I mean. Recently I heard someone who teaches acting complaining about the difficulty that actors who have been brought up in a naturalistic tradition have in playing parts from the classical and the sixteenth- and seventeenth-century repertoire. What they do is to try to capture the psychology of the character, and then having built up an image of how the character thinks and behaves, they take on the *persona* of the character and play the part. But, while this may be the kind of thing needed for nineteenth- and twentieth-century drama, it does not always work with the drama of earlier periods. In the classical Greek drama, for example, the thing that primarily motivates the character's behaviour will be a violation of the natural order of things, and this is still an ingredient in seventeenth-century drama. Here we have something which loses all meaning if it is translated into a purely psychological struggle, so that what is written as a tragedy becomes a melodrama. There is a lesson to be learned from this. If a purely psychological interpretation of Racine's *Phèdre*, for example, fails to convey what it is that the play is about, making nonsense of the tragic elements, is it not possible that a purely psychological interpretation of the motivations of a biographical subject working in much the same culture as Racine will correspondingly fail to capture what is at issue? It is no answer to say that drama deals with fictional characters who can represent all kinds of things, whereas biography deals with actual historical figures, for there is surely some connection between how one conceives of what motivates one and how one represents motivations dramatically. If the purely psychological reading of Racine's play transforms Phèdre's tragic dilemma into something essentially no different from the personal traumas agonized over in a soap opera, do we risk transforming biography into soap opera in writing about Descartes' life as simply the life of his psyche? I think we do, and the biographer of Descartes has to be much more careful about where the line between 'public' and 'private' is drawn, and how sharply it is drawn, than the biographer of a twentieth-century figure, for example. 'Descartes' private life' is just not a topic that makes any sense beyond a certain very elementary point.

On the second issue, that of the relation between Descartes' personal and intellectual development, the question arises of the purpose of tracing his intellectual development. The neglect of philosophers' intellectual development in Anglophone philosophy is peculiarly selective: no one would run together early and late Plato, and most would distinguish early and late Aristotle after the pioneering work of Jaeger;[34] and no one would run together early and late Wittgenstein, or even early and late Russell. But in the case of seventeenth- and eighteenth-century philosophy, very little care is taken to understand the development of and changes in doctrine in the work of individual philosophers. Commentators on Descartes in the twentieth century, especially (but by no means exclusively) in Anglophone philosophy, have not taken much notice of Descartes' intellectual development, assuming that the *Discours de la méthode* (1638), the *Meditationes* (1641), and the *Passions de l'âme* (1649) somehow capture and sum up the whole of his thought.[35] And indeed, in an influential commentary, Martial Guéroult made the *Meditationes* into a canonical text against which all Descartes' other writings must be measured.[36] This homogenization of his thought has resulted in many misconceptions about what Descartes was trying to achieve and why he employed the means he did, as well as in a neglect of significant changes in his doctrines. At its worst, it may lead to a complete misunderstanding of the import of particular doctrines, which are read in terms of a general tradition rather than in terms of Descartes' aims in proposing them, aims that can be captured more accurately by looking at the genesis of the doctrine.

Let me mention three instances of this where, by following through the development of Descartes' thought in detail, I have been led to offer quite different interpretations from those current in the literature. In all three cases, the traditional interpretation relies on reading earlier developments in terms of later ones, and in each case this not only leads to a mischaracterization of the earlier doctrine, but serves to obscure the rather specific conditions under which the later doctrine is formulated, thereby completely missing the point of the exercise in the first two cases, and misunderstanding how the exercise was designed to be carried out in the third.

The first case concerns the question of the role of scepticism in Descartes' thought. Scepticism plays a dominant role in the *Meditationes*, and it is generally assumed that scepticism motivates Descartes' epistemology. But I have been unable to find any concern with scepticism before the 1630s, and the kind of epistemology that is pursued in the treatment of cognition in the *Regulae* and in *L'Homme* is naturalistically inclined, showing no concern at all with sceptical issues. Moreover, I have found no evidence that Descartes ever went through a sceptical crisis of any kind: he had plenty of intellectual crises, but none of them, so far as I have been able to tell, were sceptical. His interest in scepticism was relatively late, and took shape in the context of providing a metaphysical legitimation of his natural philosophy, a task which he never even contemplated before the condemnation of Galileo in 1633, and which was a direct response to that condemnation. Scepticism was simply a means to an end, and that end had nothing to do with certainty about the existence of the material world, but rather with establishing the metaphysical credentials of a mechanist natural philosophy, one of whose central tenets—the Earth's motion around the Sun—had been condemned by the Inquisition.

The second case concerns the way in which commentators have sought to clarify Descartes' physical doctrines by considering their metaphysical formulations as offered in late works such as the *Principia*. Part of the motivation for this undoubtedly lies in the assumption that the later the exposition the more it represents Descartes' considered view. But, in fact, the question of Descartes' 'considered view' cannot be approached in this way. In the early 1630s he formulated a physical theory, in *Le Monde* and related writings, which represents the final stage of his thinking on this topic. After 1633 his creative work in physical theory effectively comes to an end. What he was subsequently concerned to do was to legitimate his physical theory and the natural philosophy which he had used to articulate it. This legitimation was not something Descartes felt to be necessary because of any internal problems, but because of an external threat, and in fact it had to be met in a way that satisfied criteria and constraints that were in many ways alien to it. The only way to do this effectively, Descartes came to believe, was in terms of a vocabulary and a mode of presentation derived from scholastic natural philosophy and metaphysics, despite the fact that these were completely antithetical to his own natural philosophy. In other words, when Descartes discussed his fundamental physical notions in the vocabulary of substance, accidents, and modes, he wanted to demonstrate orthodoxy, not to provide a genuine elucidation of his physical theory and its consequences. Nothing could have been further from his mind: he not only deliberately tries on occasion to obfuscate such elucidation (e.g. in the completely spurious doctrine of the relativity of motion), but almost literally has a fit when his disciple Regius—starting a trend that will be followed by virtually all subsequent Cartesian natural philosophers—strips the *Principia* of its scholastic-metaphysical gloss and sets out the natural philosophy in a way that genuinely attempts to offer elucidation, and shows clearly the direction in which it is heading.

The third case concerns the way in which commentators have tried to shape Descartes' natural philosophy around conceptions of mechanism derived not from an examination of what form Descartes' own commitment to mechanism took, but rather from a consideration of later developments in mechanism. The mid-seventeenth-century tradition of Cartesian physics, the most illustrious representative of which was Huygens[37], interpreted Descartes' commitment to mechanism in terms of a commitment to kinematics, and, in its most extreme form, in terms of a reduction of physics to kinematics. But this ideal of a physical theory which eschewed force and made do solely with matter in motion was never, in fact, advocated by Descartes. On the contrary, a close reading of his early writings on hydrostatics shows that he developed a statical notion of force, as something like instantaneous tendency to motion, which he saw as capturing physical action in a way consonant with mechanism (because it does not violate the principle of the inertness of nature). Descartes' problems in physics arise not because he reduces physics to kinematics, but because he cannot do kinematics—to do kinematics one needs motions, and all Descartes has is a series of instantaneous tendencies to motion. The interpretative problems are compounded when commentators, unable to reconcile Descartes' instantaneous tendencies with their preconceived view of Cartesian physics as kinematics, then proceed to solve the 'problem' by construing the former as something which derives directly from the metaphysical doctrine that God recreates the universe at each instant. So now we are told that there is a discrepancy between the universe as conceived metaphysically, which consists of a series of discrete instants, and the universe as conceived physically, which consists of continuous motions. The only trouble is that Descartes is committed to the doctrine of instantaneous action from early 1619 onwards, whereas the metaphysical doctrine of the instantaneous nature of divine action first appears in 1640. The most elementary attention to the genesis of Descartes' doctrines would reveal that the theory of divine action is far more likely to be a metaphysical legitimation of a long-held physical theory. By paying attention to the precise stages at which various metaphysical doctrines entered into the argument, we should be able to decide when we are dealing a doctrine whose motivation and content is genuinely metaphysical (such as the doctrine of the creation of eternal truths), and when metaphysical arguments are simply being brought in because Descartes is writing for a particular audience who, he believes, have to be convinced by a metaphysical argument only because the natural-philosophical mode of argument, even if far more direct and clear, is so contentious that it would be counter-productive. Note, by the way, that this is not a question of different 'approaches' to Descartes, but a question of evidence: if we can establish (ideally) in the latter kind of case that the natural-philosophical doctrine is formulated first, that Descartes abandons the natural-philosophical mode of argument because of the 1633 condemnation of Galileo, that the doctrine reappears in a scholastic-metaphysical guise which not only adds nothing to it but actually obfuscates it, and that it is presented in the context not of a work directed towards those at the cutting edge of physical theory but in a textbook which is modelled on scholastic textbooks, then I suggest this is not incidental background material which philosophers can afford to ignore. It is a conceit of philosophers that they do not reflect sufficiently on the fact that explicitly 'philosophical' modes of argument can occasionally be used to obfuscate rather elucidate (even though a delightful antidote to this conceit is ready to hand in the form of Mr Flosky in Thomas Love Peacock's *Nightmare Abbey*).

The third question that I mentioned earlier, that of the relation between Descartes' intellectual pursuits and the intellectual and cultural environment in which they were pursued, is a complex one. A specific problem here, and one that has dogged the study of the development of the sciences in the early modern period, is the relation between philosophical, or more strictly speaking epistemological, concerns and the means by which physical theories are formulated. Alexandre Koyré, who more than anyone else was responsible from the late 1930s to the 1950s for transforming the history of science from a chronology of results into a serious intellectual discipline, devoted a lot of attention to this question in his writings. But ultimately, I believe, he did this at the cost of reducing scientific development to the development of epistemology: so, for example, he effectively put Galileo's success in astronomy and kinematics down to his having the correct epistemology (in this case, a Platonist as opposed to an Aristotelian epistemology). This philosophical reduction of science, even more of a problem in Descartes' case than in that of Galileo, is surely as misguided as the converse view which sees the two as separate developments. It is, I believe, very important that we be able to consider the emergence and development of scientific and philosophical disciplines wholly in the context within which that emergence and development occurred, without considering them simply as first attempts at something that can only be properly understood with hindsight. But I don't believe this aim is to be achieved by a 'grand theory' that purports to tell us in general terms what the relation between the two must be, and what their relation to their context of emergence must be. The lesson one must learn from previous attempts—the range of possibilities stretching from economic or social reductionism (an extreme form of 'externalism') to methodological and epistemological reductionism (an extreme form of 'internalism')—is that one must capture the specificity of these connections in particular contexts. An intellectual biography forces one to think in very specific terms, hopefully yielding a kind of understanding which historians of philosophy and science have missed because of their concern with taking a long-term, bird's-eye view.

I
'A Learned and Eloquent Piety'

Childhood, 1596–1606

In May 1645 Descartes wrote to Princess Elizabeth, to whom he acted as *de facto* personal confessor and adviser, to say that he had heard that she was suffering from a slow fever and a dry cough.[1] He offers condolences and advice. 'The most common cause of a slow fever', he tells her, 'is sadness.' Lest the remedy that he is about to propose seem too harsh, he prefaces it with a disclaimer: 'I well know it would be imprudent for me to want to convince someone to be happy when every day fortune inflicts new sources of annoyance on them; and I am not one of those cruel philosophers who wish their sages to be insensible.' Nevertheless, the solution to Elizabeth's problem is clear:

It seems that the difference between the greatest souls and those that are base and common consists principally in the fact that common souls abandon themselves to their passions and are happy or unhappy only according as the things that happen to them are agreeable or unpleasant; the greatest souls, on the other hand, reason in a way that is so strong and cogent that, although they also have passions, and indeed passions which are often more violent than those of ordinary people, their reason nevertheless always remains mistress, and even makes their afflictions serve them and contribute to the perfect happiness they enjoy in this life.

Elizabeth replies to assure Descartes than none of her doctors have prescribed such a salutary remedy.[2] Evidently encouraged, Descartes sets out the matter in more detail:

Consider a person who had every reason to be happy but who saw continually enacted before him tragedies full of disastrous events, and who spent all his time in consideration of sad and pitiful things. Let us suppose that he knew they are imaginary fables so that though they drew tears from his eyes and moved his imagination they did not touch his intellect at all. I think that this alone would be enough gradually to close up his heart and make him sigh in such a way that the circulation of his blood would be delayed and slowed down . . . On the other hand, there might be a person who had many genuine reasons for distress but who took such pains to direct his imagination that he never thought of them except under compulsion by some practical necessity, and spent the rest of his time in the consideration of things which could furnish contentment and joy. This would help him by enabling him to judge more soberly about the things that mattered because he would look on them without passion. Moreover, I do not doubt that this by

15

itself would be capable of restoring him to health, even if his spleen and lungs were already in a poor condition because of the bad temperament of blood produced by sadness.[3]

Then, after commenting further on the remedy for Elizabeth's condition, he turns to his own, in the only mention of his early childhood that, so far as we know, he ever made in his correspondence:

Further, I take the liberty of adding that I found by experience in my own case that the remedy I have suggested cured an illness almost exactly similar, and perhaps even more dangerous. My mother died a few days after my birth from a disease of the lung caused by distress. From her I inherited a dry cough and a pale colour which stayed with me until I was more than twenty, so that all the doctors who saw me up to that time condemned me to die young. But I have always had an inclination to look at things from the most favourable angle and to make my principal happiness depend upon myself alone, and I think this inclination caused the indisposition, which was almost part of my nature, gradually to disappear.[4]

A remarkable feature of this passage is that here, in Descartes' only extant reference to his mother, he gives the wrong date for her death. In fact she died on 13 May 1597, fourteen months after she had given birth to him. Why does he do this? It is most unlikely that he would never have known the real date of his mother's death, and still less likely that he had simply forgotten it or made a mistake. If we discount ignorance or carelessness, as I think we have to, then we must seriously consider the possibility that he is deliberately misleading his correspondent. But why would he want to do this? Descartes was intensely secretive, taking as his motto *bene vixit, bene qui latuit*—'he lives well who is well hidden'—but to hide information about himself by providing a false date for his mother's death would seem unduly duplicitous, even for Descartes. It is also true that he had forbidden his own birth date to be published in his lifetime because he feared it might give occasion to unsolicited horoscopes being cast for him,[5] but his fear of horoscopes being cast for his mother, if indeed he did have such a fear, would hardly explain the present case, for without a knowledge of his own date of birth, no horoscope could be cast for his mother either, on the information given here. The only explanation I can offer for the deception is that it is simply a means of indicating that he was raised without a mother: after all, he would be very unlikely to have any memory of her. But, considering the matter in psychological terms, to choose a means of indicating this fact which denies any contact with his mother is itself surely indicative of some strong feeling on the matter. It is not at all surprising that he should have strong feelings about such a distant event. There is a widespread view amongst psychologists that anxiety over separation from one's mother seems to affect the infant most greatly from about 13 to about 18 months, and his mother's death cannot have come at a worse time for Descartes, psychologically speaking. Unfortunately, we have little idea of what the content of this strong feeling was. If we had more information, if, for example, we knew that the cause of his subsequent very cool relations with his father derived from some resentment connected with his mother, then we might be in a position to assess some of the complexities in his relation to her. But we possess no information on such matters, and where we have possibly indirectly relevant material—for example, on the fact that Descartes appears to construct father-figures for himself in his adolescence and early adulthood (Father Charlet in his school-days, Isaac Beeckman in the period from 1618–1619) even though his father was still alive—the material itself is already so overdetermined, and its relation to the present question so unclear, that it would be reckless to offer an interpretation on the basis of it. Assuming the explanation of this matter needs to be (at least in part) psychological, we are, and are likely to remain, in the dark on the question of why Descartes should lie about the date of his mother's death.

But even more mysterious in some ways is Descartes' statement that not only Elizabeth's and his mother's illnesses were due to distress, but that his was too. It might seem at first that Descartes is saying that the distress from which he tells us he suffers is inherited from his mother, but in fact three factors are involved. First, he tells us that both he and his mother suffered from 'distress' (*quelques déplaisirs*). Second, he tells us that he inherited certain physiological concomitants of this distress. In his mother's case, these amounted to 'a disease of the lung', whereas in his case they took the form of a 'dry cough and a pale colour', although the seriousness of this, he tells Elizabeth, should not be under-estimated, as the condition could have led to his death. What kind of concomitants of distress are these? Well, Descartes describes his own illness as being 'almost exactly similar' to Elizabeth's, and he tells Elizabeth that hers is of a kind whose most common cause is 'sadness' (*tristesse*). So sadness or distress (the words seem to be used interchangeably) is the *cause* of the physiological state. Third, there is postulated what might loosely be called an attitude of mind which enables one to overcome the physiological symptoms, presumably because it is able to overcome the root psychological cause, although Descartes does not make this explicit.

What exactly is Descartes saying he inherited in these passages? Certainly the physiological symptoms, but presumably not a particular distress or sadness that his mother had, and which was the cause of her symptoms. Nevertheless, if distress or sadness were the cause of the illness, Descartes must have been subject to it. Part of the difficulty in describing the relation between physiology and psychology here is due to difficulties in Descartes' general theory of the relation between the intellect, and the passions and emotions. The passions are conceived as having their source in the body, and it is an important part of Descartes' account of action that the passions and emotions play a role in effecting actions, as opposed to the prevailing Stoic view that the relation between the intellect and the passions is one of straightforward conflict, so that the passions will only ever act to pervert judgement. The sophistication of Descartes' account allows him to accept the existence of psychosomatic and somatopsychic illnesses, but not to provide any really coherent formulation of them. Having said this, however, I do not think the unclarity here is to be explained wholly by a lack of clarity in his theory of the passions and emotions. The fact that he is describing his own case, and has already introduced an element of deviousness into his account, requires us to exercise some caution. His account of his mother's death is not the only respect in which we are entitled to have qualms about the accuracy of the information in the letter: he tells us, for example, that he always looks at things 'from the most favourable angle', whereas, as we shall see later, his behaviour is characterized by moodiness, misanthropy, and at times what can only be described as paranoia. Were Descartes simply describing symptoms from a distance, as it were, then the matter would be different. The fact that he clearly has some considerable psychological investment in what he is describing adds a significant degree of complexity to his account, and renders it more opaque.

As regards the question of what exactly Descartes is saying he suffered from, his use of the word 'sadness' (*tristesse*) is very indicative. The Latin term *tristitia* had traditionally been used to describe the symptoms of melancholia. Melancholia was, with phrenitis and mania, one of the traditional forms of madness. Phrenitis was an acute disease, accompanied by delirium and fever, whereas melancholia and mania were chronic diseases somewhat like what are now referred to as functional psychoses. By the Renaissance, melancholia had become a much-discussed topic. The nature of the illness also took on some rather distinctive social connotations. As one recent writer on melancholia has pointed out, 'with the Renaissance rehabilitation of Aristotelian melancholia as a character correlate of genius or being gifted rather than strictly as an illness, *melancholia, melancholie,* and *melancholy* came to be popular terms as well. In addition to denoting the illness, they were often used for almost any state of sorrow, dejection, or despair, not to mention respected sombreness and fashionable sadness'.[6] This social dimension to melancholia makes the question of its characterization somewhat complex. It is to be expected that

psychosomatic illnesses will manifest symptoms that are shaped cultur-
ally, but it also seems to be the case that particular cultural or social
malaises will be reflected psychologically. Certainly, a somewhat morose
sensibility was something fostered in Descartes' social and cultural
circles. *Tristesse* was a fashionable malady in cultured circles, and was
grouped with the disease of melancholia under the French word
merencolie.[7] It was a condition that was thought to endow one with
'intellectual acumen and profundity, with artistic ability, sometimes
with divine inspiration',[8] a view deriving from the pseudo-Aristotelian
Problemata, revived and popularized in the fifteenth century by Ficino.

It might seem eccentric to insist on describing Descartes' psychological state in terms derived from Classical and renaissance medicine. But
there are two main reasons why I believe serious attention to the phenomenology of melancholia is important. First, such a clearly psychosomatic condition is so closely bound up with the social and cultural
milieu which fostered it that, so long as we are not prevented from
identifying straightforwardly neurological or psychoanalytic conditions
that cannot adequately be described using the category of melancholia,
then, despite a loss of precision, we can benefit from the fact that it is
a category that includes such a broad and apparently heterogeneous
range of phenomena. Indeed, it is a remarkable feature of sixteenth-
and seventeenth-century accounts of melancholia that the term covered
everything from a socially acceptable, indeed perhaps socially induced,
form of sadness or despair, considered to be the natural concomitant
of a person of genius and inspiration, to quite severe disease involving
persistent hallucinations, epileptic fits, and lycanthropy.[9] Secondly, the
extremely close connection between genius, sensitivity, and melancholia was established in the aetiology of melancholia. Sixteenth- and
seventeenth-century accounts of melancholia were based on humoural
theory, which offered what might anachronistically be referred to as
a theory of personality types, explaining differences in temperament,
personality, ability, and so on in terms of the four humours. Ideally,
a balance between the four humours was what one aimed at, but this
was not achievable, so that one (or occasionally two) of the humours
predominated. Blood predominated in the sanguine personality, that is,
a person who was cheerful and friendly, but ill-suited to graver matters
and easily distracted by the senses. Phlegm predominated in the phleg-
matic person, someone lacking in feelings and backward. The bilious
or choleric person was quick-witted but lacking in profundity. A pre-
ponderance of the fourth humour, black bile, caused a melancholic
temperament, which ranged from genius to madness. There resulted an
assumption of a melancholic temperament amongst writers and artists,
ranging from the silly and affected, from the apparently self-induced

madness of Tasso, to the sensible and urbane form of melancholy espoused, for example, by Montaigne.[10] Melancholia forms an extremely powerful and pervasive ingredient in the images of a thinker and writer available in the culture in which Descartes worked, although the way in which it was incorporated into individual self-images was a function of both the psychological make-up of the subject and the fact that a very extensive range of attributes were covered in the term.

Three major factors play a role in Descartes' brief reflection on his own psychological constitution in the letter to Elizabeth: a possibly psychosomatic condition, a very general theory about the passions characterizing such conditions, and a number of social and cultural factors which may reinforce, encourage, or perhaps even create the psychosomatic condition, and which in any case shape its symptoms to a significant degree. It is worth pointing out from the outset that we will not be able to specify the precise contribution of these factors. It is in the nature of the case that they, and possibly other factors (like the precise nature of his relation with Elizabeth), will melt into one another. Nevertheless, there is a great deal that we can do, provided we have all the relevant information to hand, and provided we ask the right questions. To begin with, we need to supply as clear a picture as we can of the early years of Descartes' life.

We have very little information on the early childhood of René Descartes.[11] He was born on 31 March 1596, son of Joachim Descartes, who came from a predominantly medical family, his father and grandfather having been physicians, and Jeanne Brochard, whose family were merchants and later public administrators. His parents had been married in 1589 and René had two living siblings, Pierre, born in 1591, and Jeanne, born some time between 1590 and 1595. René was almost certainly named after his maternal grandfather, René Brochard, and he was probably born at the house of his maternal grandmother, Jeanne Sain, in La Haye,[12] Touraine, where she had retired upon being widowed in 1586. It is indicative of the poor state of our knowledge of his early life that we cannot even be absolutely certain of this, and another less likely but not implausible version of his birth has it that his mother, in travelling from her own house to her mother's for the confinement, went into labour before she could reach there, the philosopher being delivered in a ditch by the side of the road. When his mother died in 1597, René's father Joachim left the children with Jeanne Sain; his position as a Councillor at the *parlement* of Brittany required him to spend at least three (and later six) months a year at Rennes, and indeed, he had been at Rennes when René was born and also when his wife died in childbirth fourteen months later. René was brought up by Jeanne Sain until he entered the Jesuit college of La Flèche in 1606, and it seems to have been with her that he had his closest relationship until her death in 1609 or 1610.

In 1600, René's father remarried[13] and moved to Rennes. Despite the fact that he was only four at the time, René does not seem to have had much contact with his stepmother, and she is never mentioned by him. She and his father had four children from 1602 to 1611.[14] In 1607 the family made their home at an inn the father bought in a village near Châtelleraut, and Adam tells us that the family, including Pierre and Jeanne, but excluding René, was established there.[15] If this were true then it would be very interesting, as it would mean that Descartes was effectively alienated from the rest of his family at an early date. But Adam cites no evidence for the claim, and it is difficult to understand how Pierre could have been included in the family arrangements since he was a boarder at La Flèche with René from at least 1606, and perhaps as early as 1604. Moreover, we cannot say with any certainty what Descartes himself did between leaving La Flèche in 1615 (1613 on Adam's dating) and joining the army of Maurice of Nassau some time in 1618, except that he probably spent late 1615 to late 1616 at Poitiers. It cannot be ruled out that he spent some of this time with his family. In his first three years at La Flèche he was granted an annual one-month holiday (1 September to 1 October), which he would probably have spent with his grandmother. But between 1610 and 1615 he would have been granted three-, two-, and then one-week annual holidays,[16] and we have no reason to think that he did not spend these in his father's household.

Nevertheless, while the extent of his contact with his father's household is hard to gauge, his later silence on this question suggests that it cannot have been very considerable, although we do know that he was to correspond occasionally with his half-sister Anne in the 1640s.[17] One thing we can be sure about is that his domestic circle prior to 1606, when he went to La Flèche, consisted of his grandmother, his nurse, and his elder brother and sister. How different this circle would have been had his mother remained alive is of course a matter of speculation, but it is worth remembering that he would not have been likely to have had a great deal of close contact with her. As an infant he would almost certainly have been sent out to a hired wet-nurse for the first twelve to eighteen months, and thereafter children of his class would have been brought up mainly by nurses, governesses, and tutors, typically leaving home around the age of ten (as he did) to go to boarding school. René was close to his grandmother and his nurse, and, it would seem, to his sister (for whose daughter he was later to show great concern), and although no correspondence is extant, or even mentioned, it is very unlikely that he would not have corresponded with her. We do have a letter to Jeanne Sain,[18] and although it may be from René, it is much more likely the work of his elder brother, Pierre. Dated 12 May (1609?)[19] and written from La Flèche, it gives us a little extra insight into their family relations:

Mademoiselle Mother,

I have received your [letter] and, God be praised, you are in good health. As for my brother, thanks to God he has not been ill and at present is well, except for being a little thin; but it is only wickedness that prevents him from fattening up. There has not been very much illness here, except for my cousin, the younger Ferrand,[20] who has had his third fever in 15 or 16 days; but, with God's help, the doctors hope that he will come out of it soon. In closing, I thank you very humbly for the crown that you sent me, which I needed, and I shall do my best to study well so that those that you have yet to send me are not wasted, and may it please God,

Mademoiselle Mother,
to keep you in good health
Your very humble
and obedient son,
Descartes.

Despite its opening and closing words, the letter is not, of course, addressed to Pierre's mother, but to his maternal grandmother, Jeanne Sain. The expression *'ma mère'* was occasionally used for grandmothers —for example by Cléante in Molière's *Tartuffe*—but in this case there is a more personal explanation for the term; since the children were actually raised by Jeanne Sain, it is not surprising that they refer to her as their mother. Note, however, that the formal title 'Mademoiselle', reserved for noble ladies in the case of married women and widows, is used. This does not mean that the relationship was a formal one.[21] Indeed, from what we can tell from the letter, it was evidently quite relaxed: Pierre begins by referring to a single crown which he hopes his grandmother will send him, but crosses out the 'that' (*celui*) and writes 'those' (*ceux*) above it, obviously having decided, on reflection, to try his luck.

If René's later very businesslike relations with Pierre are any indication, there was not much warmth in their relationship. Pierre followed his father into the *parlement* of Brittany in 1618 and it is unlikely he and René would have had much in common, although they did correspond a bit in the 1620s on personal matters.[22] By 1640, their relations were such that Pierre did not even take the trouble to inform him of their father's death. René's later relations with his father were also to be very businesslike, and although soon after his father's death (20 October 1640) he does say that he has experienced tears and sadness at the recent deaths of two people who had been close to him,[23] I doubt if he is thinking of the death of his father: it seems to me more likely that he is referring to the deaths of two people to whom he was much closer, his sister Jeanne (shortly after October 1640), and his daughter Francine (7 September 1640).[24] His father had little sympathy with Descartes or with what he achieved, and he is reported as having said, on the publication of Descartes' first book, the *Discours* and accompanying essays, in 1637: 'Only one of my children has displeased me. How can I have engendered a son stupid enough to have had himself bound in calf?'[25]

This is really the extent of our knowledge of the facts of Descartes' early upbringing, and it should be noted that it was not at all exceptional or unusual. A historian of childhood writing specifically on seventeenth-century France has pointed out that a high mortality and remarriage rate introduced a complex kinship relationship into many French households at this period, with the authority of grandparents the effective one in three-generation families. Various problems affecting the stepmother-son relationship were also explicitly recognized, and occasionally rather drastic provision was made, such as when a remarried father was producing a new family at the same time and under the same roof as his son: there was a special provision in French law of the time to cover such cases, specifying that a father may kill his son if he finds him to have committed adultery with his stepmother.[26]

Descartes' autobiographical remarks in the first discourse of the *Discours de la Méthod* start with his education at La Flèche, and our information about his childhood derives in the main from the investigations of his first biographer, Baillet,[27] not from Descartes himself. If we are to be able to throw any light on Descartes' personality, we must find some way of rounding out our picture of him in his childhood and youth, despite the lack of direct information. There are, in fact, a number of indirect ways in which we can fill out the picture, in particular by exploring the kinds of self-image that would have been available to the young René. Three factors are, I believe, of special importance here. The first is the development of a particular kind of heightened religious sensibility in the sixteenth and seventeenth centuries, within both Catholicism and Protestantism, which has as one of its principal features what might be called an 'internalization' of religion. This had, amongst other things, far-reaching consequences for the issue of how subjectivity was to be conceived of, consequences that Descartes was amongst the first to draw out. But, more immediately, such considerations are rather important where we are concerned to elucidate features of his self-image, especially if we can give some detail as to the procedures whereby this internalization was effected, as I believe we can.

Secondly, there are a number of considerations touching on the socio-political milieu within which Descartes was raised. The Descartes family was part of a social élite that can loosely be referred to as the 'gentry' or 'upper bourgeoisie', a social class which, for all the difficulty there is in defining it, was seen by its members to be very different from both the ('lower') bourgeoisie, on the one hand, and the nobility on the other. This class had some distinctive features, and with its demise as an effective political force at the end of the sixteenth century, two features it comes to have in a very striking way are a generally misanthropic approach to life and a search for solace in the country-side. These are features that are very evident in Descartes, and while their specific psychological manifestation in him is doubtless due at least in part to personal factors, we cannot assume that the general features themselves are exclusively personal in nature: indeed, I shall show that Descartes' behaviour in these respects has significant precedents, and that it is at least as much a cultural phenomenon as a psychological one.

Thirdly, we need to look at the background to the kind of educational institution that Descartes was raised in. Descartes lived at the Jesuit *collège* of La Flèche from around his tenth birthday to the age of 19. The French *collège* was a combination of secondary school and, in its higher years, university: the French universities of the time, with the exception of the University of Paris, were really only specialized graduate schools for the study of law, medicine, and theology.[28] Descartes not only received everything he regarded as his institutional education there—his later year at the University of Poitiers studying law seems to have been little more than a formality—but it constituted his complete environment during his years there. There are some very distinctive features of the Jesuit education he received, but the novelty of this education has often been overestimated and precedents can be found in the earlier French municipal *collège* system.[29] This is of some importance because the municipal *collèges* were set up by the gentry with aims very different from those of the Jesuits, yet there were striking similarities in what was taught and how.

The three factors I have outlined are, as it turns out, not independent of one another, but I shall focus on the question of Christianity to begin with, as in some ways it is the most fundamental of the three.

The Christianization of Europe

Although medieval Europe was undeniably Christian, medieval Christianity differed somewhat from that which we find in both the Catholic and the Protestant churches from the sixteenth and seventeenth centuries onwards. Amongst the significant developments in the transition from medieval Christianity to the Christianity of the Reformation and Counter-Reformation, two are especially worth noting. The first is a shift from a very heterogeneous collection of practices which varied widely from region to region, as well as from individual to individual, to a uniform religious sensibility. The second is a corresponding general 'internalization' of religion, a shift from something public to something private. Certainly the former, at least, is to be explained partly in terms of Catholicism and Protestantism seeking to exercise better control of their congregations in the wake of the Reformation by providing distinctive teachings and by ensuring that these teachings were followed. But the second feature is, at a general level, common to both Catholicism and Protestantism, and in any case the first is a phenomenon which transcends the specific differences between the two denominations. While we do not find any explicit general rejection of medieval religious sensibilities and practices in the sixteenth and seventeenth centuries (although there are, of course, many criticisms of specific practices, such as the sale of indulgences), we do find a widespread sense that Christianity needs to be renewed, given focus, strengthened, and indeed, ultimately transformed in quite a radical way. As Delumeau had shown, the key ingredient in this process is a *contemptus mundi*, something originally developed and refined in the monasteries, and later transmitted to the whole of society, in the first instance through the mendicant orders, as 'a self-evident truth' which has three components—hatred of the body and the world, the pervasiveness of sin, and a sharp sense of the fleetingness of time.[30] There is a concern with self-reform, motivated by feelings of guilt and repentance, which we can find not merely in the devotional literature, but which is also reflected in the philosophical literature from Montaigne onwards, especially in writing on the passions and ethics. We shall see some evidence of this in Descartes' own case, in the way in which he sees consideration of ethics and the passions as being directed towards therapeutic self-reform.

At the propaganda level, there was a concerted campaign in the sixteenth and seventeeth centuries (on both sides of the denominational divide) against 'paganism'. This is a complex issue,[31] but one source of 'paganism' that we can identify without too much difficulty is that deriving from the local cultures to which Christianity often adapted itself, and which retained traits that, depending on such factors as the general religious climate, could be taken as antithetical to Christianity. Of considerable importance in this respect is the existence of quite local popular cultures which, depending on the religious and political

25

climate, could either not only be happily tolerated but incorporated into Christianity on the one hand, or be taken as antithetical to Christianity and condemned outright on the other. Here we can detect a very marked shift in the religious and political context starting from about the thirteenth century onwards, but reaching a peak in the late sixteenth and early seventeenth centuries, which resulted in a massive increase in vigilance on the part of the Church, and in the condemnation as 'pagan' of many previously tolerated and perhaps even sanctioned practices. Rather interestingly, what seems to happen is not so much that practices not previously considered alien to Christianity start to be seen as alien to it, but rather that practices which had always been, strictly speaking, outside Christian culture, and which had been recognized as such, now come to be seen as antithetical to it, as the understanding of what Christianity amounts to becomes both more all-encompassing and more exhaustively defined.[32]

The problem of popular local cultures is summed up well by Delumeau. Noting that ancient rites and beliefs co-existed along with Christianity, and indeed that there was a 'folklorization' of Christianity, in the countryside, he points out that this was tolerated largely because it was assumed that the non-Christian elements would gradually die out. Hence, for several centuries, 'the church spoke two languages simultaneously, a rigorous one directed at a narrow élite, and a language of compromise which was addressed to the masses. Christianity thus accepted the idea of integrating rural paganism. . . . As long as people did not rebel against the church they would be saved, despite their ignorance, thanks to their good will and the prayers of the clergy'.[33] Taking the matter very broadly, we can see this 'rural paganism' as a threefold phenomenon. First, there is the traditional Christian practice of taking over not just religious and philosophical precepts as its own, but also various rituals, festivals, and so on.[34] As Keith Thomas has pointed out, this process of assimilation 'was not achieved without some cost, for it meant that many of the purposes served by the older paganism were now looked for from nominally Christian institutions'.[35] Moreover, there was an immense propaganda value in such issues as the Christian appropriation of pagan feast days, and Hobbes, for one, was quick to draw on this.[36] Part of the solution to these kinds of criticism was the purging of such practices, a procedure followed by many Protestant sects; but, as Thomas has shown in detail in the case of sixteenth-century England, this had a number of unintended consequences, as the religious sensibilities that had traditionally underlain such practices were displaced into more explicit forms of superstition.[37]

Secondly, there is the related problem of the persistence of practices which were not sanctioned by the Church, but which medieval

Christianity had either ignored, turned a blind eye to, or tolerated. Part of the reason for this was that medieval Christianity was often as integrated into local customs as they were integrated into it. As one commentator has pointed out, 'churches were used as granaries, marketplaces, arenas for gaming and fighting. Priests kept taverns, and brewed their ale in the church building. Fairs and pagan celebrations were held in churchyards and even before the altar; from the thirteenth century on ecclesiastical councils condemned the singing, gambling and erotic dancing that frequently went on in holy places'.[38] Various attempts were made to abolish dancing, games, and commercial activities in cemeteries in an effort to undermine any familiarity between the sacred and profane worlds.[39] Again, purging seemed to be the answer, but there were many kinds and degrees of purging, and in any case the process could often only be a gradual one. Gambling, for example, does not seem to have been widely condemned as such in the seventeenth century, even in the case of schoolchildren, and only attracted serious moral sanction as late as the nineteenth century.[40]

Third, and far more dangerous than these two, especially for Catholicism, was the 'pagan' construal of Christian practices. Indeed, the most distinctive feature of this 'rural paganism' was a belief in magic. This was a belief reinforced in certain ways by Christian doctrine itself. The Church had a commitment to miracles on the grounds that they backed up its claims to be the sole bearer of truth, and this was a commitment it was unwilling to abandon. Keith Thomas sums up the situation nicely when he notes that the medieval church

acted as a repository of supernatural power which could be dispensed to the faithful to help them in their daily problems. It was inevitable that the priests, set apart from the rest of the community by their celibacy and ritual consecration, should have derived an extra *cachet* from their position as mediators between man and God. It was also inevitable that around the Church, the clergy and their holy apparatus there clustered a horde of popular superstitions, which endowed religious objects with a magical power to which theologians themselves had never laid claim.[41]

The upshot of this was the blurring of the distinction between the ritual of consecration and the utterance of magic words, between prayer and charms, which encouraged the view that various Christian practices had magical effects. The medieval church seems to have presented itself to popular consciousness as a vast reservoir of magical power, something capable of being deployed for a variety of secular purposes.[42]

Major programmes of reform were instituted by the Catholic Church in the sixteenth century, countering or matching those instituted by Protestantism, and the way in which this reform was instituted was, in one crucial respect, the same for the Catholic and Protestant Churches:

there was a concerted programme of 'Christianization', or perhaps re-Christianization, of the population. As Delumeau puts it, the problem 'was how to persuade hundreds of millions of people to embrace a severe moral and spiritual discipline of the sort which had never actually been demanded of their forebears, and how to make them accept that even the most secret aspects of their daily lives should thenceforth be saturated by a constant preoccupation with things eternal'.[43] This is the programme of 'internalizing' Christianity, and it was achieved through a virtue which was coming to the fore in a number of contexts in the later Middle Ages, a virtue which can generally be termed 'self-discipline' or 'self-control'.

The Civilizing Process

Self-discipline was not in itself something new. One of the principal 'quiet' virtues for the Greeks, for example, was 'moderation' (*soph-rosune*), and although in the pre-Classical era it was not especially highly valued,[44] it subsequently came to be seen as important in a number of areas. This is especially true of certain forms of political and military organization, where traditional values were counter-productive. The development of democratic institutions in Athens, for example, brought with it a move away from an ethos that can roughly be described as 'heroic' to a civic one. And the development of an efficient form of military organization in the form of the phalanx brought with it a severe curbing of the activities of the foot-soldier and the inculcation of a common, largely self-imposed discipline.[45] Moreover, I think it is fair to assume that there were traditionally a number of areas, especially those in which women played the major role, such as child-rearing, where patience and moderation would have been highly valued. Indeed, the establishment of some kind of civic, co-operative life in the *polis* may have drawn on such areas, although I know of no direct evidence that it did. However this may be, at the same time as the development of more co-operative virtues in specific spheres of daily life, there was the development of explicit philosophical reflection on the virtues and of the relative standing of the 'quiet' virtues, such as justice and moderation, from Socrates onwards. In the *Republic*, Plato presented a brilliant and detailed defence of these virtues, so that by the time of Aristotle it was no longer necessary to defend their value.[46]

With the development of Christianity, however, a new kind of focus on self-control comes to the fore. Christianity had always had a strong and distinctive interest in self-discipline. From its very earliest years, its adherents saw the need for a code of behaviour to mark themselves out as a distinctive group, and gradually a definite code of sexual deportment, ranging from continence to total renunciation (occasionally accompanied by self-castration) developed which provided Christianity with a very distinctive cultural identity. This was something quite different from, and indeed antithetical to, traditional Jewish and pagan practices, and it became all the more necessary after the persecution of Christians ceased and they began to be assimilated within what was still a largely pagan culture.[47] Sexual continence is not the only form of self-discipline, of course, and during the early development of Christianity other forms of continence, especially with respect to food and drink, were also widely practised. The important point is that self-denial, often of a particularly extreme kind, forms a central ingredient in early Christianity. It should be remembered, nevertheless, that self-denial is only a species of self-discipline, and while sexual self-denial is certainly the most striking feature of Christianity at this period, not all early Christians thought of self-control exclusively in terms of self-denial. A different kind of self-control is described in the *Paedagogus* of Clement of Alexandria. It was written explicitly to set out 'how each of us ought to conduct himself in respect to the body, or rather how to regulate the body itself', and it deals in some detail with questions of etiquette.[48] The *Paedagogus* is motivated by the belief that even the most mundane acts have a divine significance, and must therefore be regulated in an appropriate way. This theme, Stoic in its origins, was to pervade Christianity and help transform the discipline of self-denial into the more general discipline of self-control, which became a means of taking responsibility for oneself in a radical way.

In looking at the question of self-control in the early modern period, it will be helpful to have a focus for our discussion. The development of self-discipline in the educational institution is not only the most relevant for our purposes, but is also an area where one of the crucial features of the establishment of self-discipline, namely its development in tandem with the elaboration of procedures for the minute regulation of daily life, shows up with a striking clarity.

The minute regulation of classes seems to have begun with the schools of the Brethren of the Common Life, who, from the early to mid-fifteenth century onwards, initiated a number of educational reforms which were to be widely imitated by both Catholic and Protestant educators.[49] Instead of students of all ages and abilities being taught in the same class, they were now placed in a graduated system, with each class of about a hundred students being divided into groups of ten under the supervision of a *decurio* or *monitor*. Indeed the *decuriones* were themselves graded by achievement, so that there were, just at the student level, two forms of regulation: each *decurio* looked after the other nine students in his group, and he himself was a member of another group of ten, where again he had a fixed place in a hierarchy. In both capacities, he was subject to constant supervision and could be replaced immediately if he did not fulfil his duties adequately. These duties included spying on other students and reporting them, a common enough medieval practice, except that now the range of misdemeanours was radically extended; in many schools, for example, conversing with one's fellow students in the vernacular instead of Latin was taken particularly seriously.

These practices were largely common to both the *collèges* and the schools of the Brethren in the sixteenth century, and as the century progressed they received an elegant articulation in a number of theoretical treatises, by far the most popular being those of the Brethren's most illustrious pupil, Erasmus. Erasmus' educational programme is set out in a number of works first published between 1500 and 1530, including *De ratione studii* (1511), *De pueris instituendis* (1529), and *De civilitate morum puerilium* (1530). The general aim of the programme is quintessentially that of the Christian humanist, to produce in the student the Classical and Christian virtues of *humanitas* and *pietas* respectively. *Humanitas* is a translation of the Greek '*philanthropia*', a word covering everything from courtesy to sexual intercourse, but intended here in its general sense of a love for other human beings which derives purely from their human attributes. *Pietas*—piety, conscientiousness, pity, compassion are among its principal meanings—is conceived in specifically Christian terms, that is, in terms of qualities associated paradigmatically with the personality of Jesus. That the combination of these two types of quality should be the aim of a humanist education is not surprising. What is surprising is the minutely detailed account of the way in which they are to be inculcated. And the minute detail seems actually to be constitutive of the process of inculcation, rather than just a particularly developed form of it.

De civilitate morum puerilium libellus—a manual of 'civility for children'—is especially instructive in this respect. Although Erasmus himself thought it dealt with the lowest part of philosophy, this did not worry him, for as he explains in a letter to Budé, 'I do not write for Persius or Laelius, I write for children and for the unlettered'.[50] The book received a truly enormous circulation, going through 130 editions, appearing in English, French, Czech, and German translations, and even appearing in catechism form in 1534. Of the tasks required in instructing the young, Erasmus writes at the beginning of the work, 'the first and, therefore, the principal one is to inculcate in tender minds the seeds of piety; the second, to have them love and study the liberal arts; the third, to acquaint them with life's duties; the fourth, to accustom them from their first steps to courtesy in their manners'. The *De civilitate* is devoted above all to the fourth of these, and sets out the rules for an apprenticeship in propriety. To this end, he provides guidance for correct behaviour in a number of circumstances in a series of short chapters. The first (*De corpore*) deals with how people look and behave in general terms. As regards facial expression and countenance, some expressions remind him of animals and are to be avoided; more specifically, wide-eyed looks signify stupidity, staring signifies inertia, sharp looks signify anger, lively looks immodesty. Dress, deportment, and gestures are treated in a similar way in the next chapter (*De cultu*) and, in general, the lesson is that one's countenance and demeanour should show a calm mind and a respectful amiability. Erasmus continues with instructions on what to do and what not to do in church (*De moribus in templo*), how to serve at, and behave at, table (*De conviviis*), how to behave in meetings and in conversation (*De congressibus*), how to behave whilst playing (*De lusu*), and while in the shared bedroom (*De cubiculo*). While the *De civilitate* was certainly not without Classical precedents, the *Disticha moralia* attributed to Cato the Censor and Clement's *Paedagogus* standing out as the most likely models, Erasmus' work cannot be separated from a concern with 'civility', which played such an important role in the culture in which he operated.

The *De civilitate* was neither the only popular treatise on manners nor the first one in modern times, and the earliest modern work in this genre was Baldassare Castiglione's *Il Libro de cortegiano,* which had appeared a hundred years earlier. That the first manual should have been written by an Italian is not surprising, for it was in the urban centres of northern and central Italy, especially in Florence, that we find the first signs of the victory of 'civility' over ancient solidarities, and above all over the feudal system in which the privileges, immunities, and liberties of nobles were dominant. Such social change did not, of course, go unresisted. But it is often in apparently trivial incidents that the deep significance of the changes is most evident. In 1573, for example, the Venetian Inquisitors condemned a painting of the Last Supper by Paolo Veronese, one ground of complaint being that one of the apostles was shown eating with a fork. It was evidently felt that the Last Supper had been transformed into an exercise in civility, thereby challenging the identity between the social and the spiritual.[51] But things were changing, and in the second half of the sixteenth century we begin to find the ecclesiastical authorities taking rules of civility very seriously, and indeed providing their own. In the training of priests in the Catholic seminaries of the Counter-Reformation, for example, it was made clear that the priest should have a grave and reserved manner of deportment and gesture,[52] as a way of showing his difference from the laity.

The political significance of the provision of detailed instructions for the conduct of daily life has been analysed by a number of writers in recent years. Particularly important is the pioneering work of Norbert Elias on the nature of the 'civilizing process' in the transition from the medieval to the modern period.[53] One of Elias' broader theses is that the civilizing process that we find so marked from the early sixteenth century onwards provides above all a prototype for the conversion of 'external into internal compulsion'.[54] Elias argues this principally in the context of French Court society, showing in considerable detail how the absolutist monarchy was able to hold the warrior nobility in check by divesting it of military functions, requiring virtually constant attendance at Court, and inculcating 'courtly values' in this class. It forces the nobles into a single site of recognition, where their standing is something wholly subject to the king's discretion, and where the king functions as the paradigmatic and premier *gentilhomme*. It also serves to distinguish them from the bourgeois upper class, the gentry, who have no direct access to the Court. But it is clear that the point about the shift to internal compulsion is much more general, for in the course of the sixteenth century it comes to be manifested not just in Court but, much more significantly, in the schools; and this is especially true of the *collèges*, to which we now turn.

The Formation of a Gentilhomme

The *collèges* have a very explicit political dimension. They were above all the creation of the gentry, and a word about the nature of the gentry would be in order here. They are to be distinguished on the one hand from the nobles, and on the other from the lower bourgeoisie, such as merchants. Descartes is a good example. Up until the 1620s he sported the title 'Seigneur du Perron', such titles being common amongst those Frenchmen who considered themselves to be from the upper echelons of the bourgeoisie. They were usually attached to ownership of land, as indeed Descartes' was, he having been given the 'moderate fief of Perron' by his father, so Baillet tells us, 'out of the property of his mother', adding that he later sold the fief with its seigneurial rights.[55] Moreover, his father, being a regional parliamentarian, was exempt from taxation, and this was a privilege the gentry guarded jealously.[56]

The gentry, even the greatest parliamentary families, were spurned by the nobility—the courtiers and *gentilhommes des champs*—and the gentry in turn held the nobility in no less contempt, above all for their indolence, idleness, economic mismanagement, and gratuitous violence. Huppert[57] has drawn attention to an anonymous treatise, *Discours des querelles et de l'honneur* (Paris, 1594), which is of some interest in this context. It is devoted to the question of what, as a member of the gentry, one was to do when provoked and challenged to a pointless and possibly deadly duel by some ignorant noble, and it attempts to offer practical advice on this question. In the course of this, the author presents a mythico-historical argument in which the existence of a warrior nobility is traced back to the time of Hercules, who instituted a militia of *gentils* for the protection of the public from *vilains,* and the members of this militia received honours and part of the public revenue for their services. But, the author complains, times have changed, and this class is now doing violence to and extorting money from the populace. They are no longer the true *gentils,* and must be disbanded so that the gentry, who are the true *gentils,* can take control of the republic, as is their right.

The source of the nobility's failure is explicitly put down to their lack of self-control or self-discipline, and this is indeed the value that the gentry prize most highly. It is striking, for example, how that veritable bible of the gentry, Montaigne's *Essais*, is taken up as a basis for an understanding of self-control. The *Essais* had focused attention on the nature of the self, partly because the general thrust of Montaigne's arguments pointed in the direction of a life of self-absorption, but above all because it fostered a particular kind of thinking about the nature of subjectivity. As one commentator has put it, 'Montaigne focused attention on the single person as a complex and intriguing microcosm rather than as defined by his role in a larger structure—the church, the family, the status order, or the state'.[58] Montaigne's investigation of the self was immediately taken up by other thinkers, amongst the most influential of which was Charron, in whose *De la Sagesse* (1601) self-exploration is explicitly filled out in terms of self-control, and above all by the regulation of the passions by the reason and the will.[59] In the work of Montaigne and Charron we find the beginnings of a view of subjectivity which is peculiarly suited to self-control, and this is not a form of self-control which is necessarily subordinate to religious precepts, but one which is guided by the precepts of one's own reason.

In the literature of the gentry, it is the capacity for self-control that distinguishes them from the nobility on the one hand, and the lower bourgeoisie on the other. But it is also the capacity that marks them out as the class most appropriate to take political control and order society in a new and humane way. The key to the achievement of this aim seems to have lain in education. From the early sixteenth century onwards, the efforts of the gentry in trying to establish themselves as a distinct class turned largely on their ability to organize a comprehensive educational system at the secondary level, and the municipal councils gradually took control of secondary schooling in the course of the sixteenth century.

The municipally run *collèges* were explicitly based upon a humanist model, and they provided a largely secular education in which the philological study of classical literature played a major role. They were funded by the local burghers, in their role as leaders of the municipal councils, and they were staffed by (secular) masters—preferably University of Paris MAs—hand-picked by the local burghers. These *collèges*, whose programmes had become firmly established as early as 1530, inaugurated a radical cultural shift in sixteenth-century France in favour of literacy and a bookish culture. The contrast with medieval schooling is stark. On the one hand, some medieval institutions were so excessively disciplined that, as Montaigne put it, they were little more than 'jails for captive youth'.[60] On the other hand, in the University of Paris before the reforms of the mid-fifteenth century, students were unsupervised; they would occasionally live in accommodation shared with prostitutes, something shocking to sixteenth-century writers such as Pasquier,[61] although there is a case to be made that there was an element of communal regulation in their living arrangements which later critics chose to ignore.[62] In contrast to the indolence of medieval students, who often had to be bullied into learning, there is no shortage of references in the sixteenth-century literature to the over-zealousness of many students. Indeed, supervision was often required to contain such enthusiasms as reading by moonlight, and Dainville, in a careful search of contemporary records, has found that students of the age of 16 to 19 typically spent virtually all their paltry income on books (including expensive folio editions), leaving little for such items as clothing.[63]

The motivation behind the establishment of the *collèges* was not merely to improve on the quality of education available, but rather to provide a very different kind of curriculum to that provided in diocesan schools, by inaugurating a full-scale humanist curriculum. Nor was it merely to extend the educational process beyond the realm of intending clerics, for this itself required a radical rethinking of the aims of the schooling process, especially about the ultimate point of a broadly based secular education. The reform inaugurated by the *collèges* went far beyond a mere change in academic content. Indeed, it is difficult to understand the curriculum offered, unless we look at the humanist teaching programme in a much broader context.

A number of points should be noted here. First, those attending the *collège* were required to go through a process which removed them from the other children of the town, and which indeed foisted upon them a lifestyle completely different from that of those children with whom they had grown up prior to *collège*. They could normally have expected to enter into adult life sometime between the ages of 7 and 14, whereas in the *collège* they would have no adult freedoms or responsibilities. Second, the regime in the *collège* was one which regulated daily life in a minute way, something that went far beyond anything needed for the basic discipline required to teach effectively. Third, the burghers insisted upon a thoroughly Classical curriculum. Certainly learning in the sixteenth century was impossible without Latin, but a detailed study of Latin poetry and drama, not to mention the teaching of Greek, was hardly necessary for a grasp of Latin reading skills. In asking for an explanation of these features of the educational system, it must also be borne in mind that it was an extremely expensive system to set up and maintain. It required buildings, teachers (who could often command considerable fees), as well as involving significant administrative costs. It kept those attending the *collège* away from the daily work that others in the town would have been performing from an early age. Now one of the principal criticisms of the nobility that the burghers pressed again and again was what they viewed as their squandering of resources, and more generally their economic mismanagement. They clearly did not believe their own projects belonged in this category, but in that case we are entitled to ask what exactly their justification, economic or otherwise, was.

Huppert has argued that the creation of *collèges* gave institutional shape to the nurturing of a new class in society.[64] This is an important conclusion, for the cost-effectiveness of the *collège* system is questionable if one thinks of it in purely economic terms. What the process was ultimately meant to produce was something more directly political: in the briefest terms, a class able to articulate and advance its ideals and aims over those of the nobility. Amongst the more immediate consequences of this was the production of a generation of students who, at the end of the *collège* process, were able to express themselves in elegant French or elegant Latin, to argue persuasively on Classical models, as well as being familiar with Greek, mathematics, and maybe even some natural science. This put them on a powerful footing in disputes between the crown and the *parlements*. But no less important was the fact that regional centres were flourishing with an intellectual and cultural life which was not subservient to Paris in a way it had been earlier (and was soon to become again). The French towns were able to support theatres and publishing houses, and to produce a constant flow of drama and verse, as well as literature of a more political nature.[65] The threat to religious and political orthodoxy posed by printing was recognized by the Crown early on in the sixteenth century, and Francis I had even tried to suppress printing altogether in 1535.[66] In sum, there is a explicitly political edge to the situation: the *collèges* functioned as a means of fostering the values and aspirations of a particular class, the gentry, in the early stages of its development.

The Demise of the Municipal *Collège*

By the end of the sixteenth century, the French municipal *collège* was in a state of crisis. Pasquier, Montaigne, and others were complaining bitterly about the proliferation of *collèges,* and even more bitterly about the fact that the lower classes were leaving productive work and entering them, attracted by the lure of education, only to emerge, not more virtuous, but simply better qualified to enter training for the professions. This was certainly not the original intention, and the literary and cultural interests of the gentry increasingly came to be pursued, not in the municipal schools, but in their private retreats. The programme of moral elevation had failed, not so much because of the failure of teachers, but because of the incapacity of the vulgar to respond properly to a humanist programme; and Montaigne, who in his writings encapsulated the ideals of the gentry more than anyone else, even thought that the general populace should be refused access to the Bible because, no matter how well one had tried to educate them, they were not able to understand and make proper use of it. Combined with this there was the very marked failure of the gentry to achieve any of their political ambitions. Huppert sums up the situation as follows:

The creation of *collèges* had not served the cultivation of virtue, it had merely created opportunities for social climbing. The evangelical movement, instead of achieving religious reform, had created civil war. The gentry, in sum, had made a fundamental and fateful mistake. Thinking to create a following among the common people by allowing them to share its classical education and its reforming morality, the gentry had merely armed its enemy. Hordes of newly licensed lawyers stood ready to challenge the gentry's privileges, and armies of psalm-singing shop clerks were prepared to kill and burn in the name of the Lord. A generation of brutal social conflict, barely disguised as a religious crusade, taught the gentry that it stood alone in the world . . . The painful retreat from the world undertaken by the gentry during the Wars of Religion was more than a tactical withdrawal: it was a rout, a general *sauve qui peut* which sent the gentry back to their private libraries.[67]

The *collège* tradition did not disappear with the abandonment of the municipal *collèges* by the gentry, however. It was taken over and transformed by the Jesuits.[68] Although they rejected many of the secular values that the gentry had attempted to foster in the secondary system, and were concerned above all with making education the means of forming a Christian élite, not only did they continue the *collège* tradition of providing a uniform education for all their students—in opposition to the medieval system, codified in Gregory the Great's *Regula pastoralis,* whereby different types of education were to be provided for different social classes and groups[69]—but what they taught was strikingly similar to the curriculum that had been devised by the municipal authorities. The difference lay in the fact that the gentry had seen education as a means to taking political power, and correlatively as a means whereby the populace as a whole could be reformed, the qualities of self-control and a love of learning being fostered in them so that they would be fit to be governed in the kind of non-coercive, common-good regime envisaged by the gentry. The Jesuits, on the other hand, saw it as a means of spreading Christianity, of inculcating 'a learned and eloquent piety', as the Protestant educational reformer Sturm put it.[70] Moreover, the aim was not to provide an education for the general populace, but to make sure that those who were to take up positions of power in ecclesiastical, military, and civil life, were inculcated not only with the requisite Christian values, but with an articulate sense of the worth of those values and an ability to defend and apply them; and above all with an ability to act as paradigmatic Christian *gentilshommes.*

2

An Education in Propriety
1606–1618

In 1606, when he was 10 years old, Descartes left the house of his maternal grandmother, Jeanne Sain, to go to the Jesuit *collège* of La Flèche at Anjou, about 100 kilometres to the north east.[1] There he was to spend the next eight years of his life. René was a sickly child, and he had joined the college at Easter, rather than in January as was usual, because he had been too ill to commence his studies until winter had come to an end; moreover, it seems that he was regularly allowed to stay in bed late in the mornings because of his condition.[2] We know that his elder brother, Pierre, was there with him, and we know that the rectors of La Flèche knew the family. The first rector, Father Chastellier, was from Poitou, so would almost certainly have known the family well, and he was succeeded in 1607 by Father Étienne Charlet, who was also from Poitou and was closely related to the Brochard line of the family.[3] In a letter of 1645, Descartes writes to Charlet that he is particularly obliged to him because throughout his youth Charlet had acted as a second father to him.[4]

We know very little of a personal nature about Descartes in these early years at La Flèche. He presumably had school friends, for example, and Baillet[5] mentions the names of three—Chauveau, René le Clerc, and Mersenne—but he is certainly wrong about Mersenne, whom Descartes only got to know around 1622, and if Descartes was indeed a friend of the first two, there is no evidence that he kept up any contact with them.[6] However, we do know a good deal about what kind of social, religious, and intellectual environment he would have been raised in at the school, and the kind of education he received, as well as the subjects he studied and the texts used. Descartes looks back to his time at La Flèche and reflects upon it on a number of occasions throughout his life, and it was to play a pivotal role in his personal and intellectual development, for it was his home for eight formative years, as well as providing his only significant institutional education.[7]

La Flèche

The Society of Jesus was formed with a twofold aim, to engage in missionary activity to spread the faith in the non-Christian world, and to renew the faith in Christian countries by a concerted programme of secondary education. As regards the second aim, the Jesuits were the principal arm of the Counter-Reformation and, as one commentator has put it, 'the struggle against heresy completely determined the educational activity of the French Jesuits'.[8] The success of the Jesuits lay above all in their commitment and their organization, and in the latter regard the general view seems to be that the Society of Jesus was modelled on the army, although this cannot be accepted without qualification. The founder of the Society, Ignatius of Loyola, had himself been a soldier, and he thought of it as a kind of army, but we cannot assume that the discipline, minute control of behaviour, and constant supervision that he wanted to be exercised in Jesuit institutions were drawn from procedures that actually operated in his day. Armies in the sixteenth century were generally badly organized and disciplined, and when in the next century we encounter well-disciplined armies, the inspiration behind them comes in the main from Lipsius, who, as we shall see, derived a number of his organizational ideas from his own Jesuit education. Moreover, in many respects, such as the way in which discipline was to be enforced, the army would have been a particularly inappropriate model, since the Jesuits were opposed to coercion and corporal punishment, which had always been the stock-in-trade of military discipline. What the Society did have in common with the military was a centralized command structure. The aim, as far as recruitment of members of the Society was concerned, was to form a highly educated and highly motivated élite who would carry out the programme of the Society, which put itself exclusively at the service of the Church, obeying the Pope, as Ignatius put it, 'as if they were but corpses'.[9]

Jesuit colleges began in the mid-sixteenth century simply as houses where clerics could engage in individual study, but they were gradually transformed into teaching institutions, apparently, in the first instance, as a response to the need for clergy in Germany.[10] The Society offered no teaching at the primary level, and its tertiary teaching was almost completely restricted to seminaries. At the secondary level, it ran both seminaries and mixed schools for the clergy and the children of the nobility and professional classes. The seminaries became the principal centres of Tridentine reform, and their success in this area was complete when the Church's key seminary, the Collegio Romano, was turned over to them in 1565 (by which time it had been granted university status). They quickly staffed it with a number of able Spanish Jesuits, starting with the philosopher and theologian Francisco Toletus. The aim of these colleges was, in the words of Ignatius, to act like water towers from which Catholic educators and scholars would pour forth to preach and teach the word of God to the masses.[11]

The Jesuits were active in France in the second half of the sixteenth century, installing themselves in Paris under the protection of the king in 1561, despite fierce resistance from the *parlement,* the University, and the bishops. In 1595, however, they were expelled from Paris, following the attempted assassination of Henri IV, in which they were implicated because it was thought, amongst other things, that the writings on regicide of Mariana,[12] one of their most distinguished members, had influenced the assassins. In reality, this was only a pretext, and the reasons for the expulsion were certainly much more complex; in particular, their explicit allegiance to the Pope can only have raised loyalist suspicions. However that may be, Henri recalled them in 1603, allowing them to resume their teaching functions in a number of cities (although their important college of Clermont in Paris was shut down intermittently), and he continued the tradition, begun in 1575, of making a Jesuit (in this case a Father Cotton) his personal confessor. The Jesuits responded by becoming fervent defenders of the Bourbon monarchy.

Of the *collèges* they set up upon their return, the most prestigious was La Flèche, opened in 1604. The building, originally a palace, and

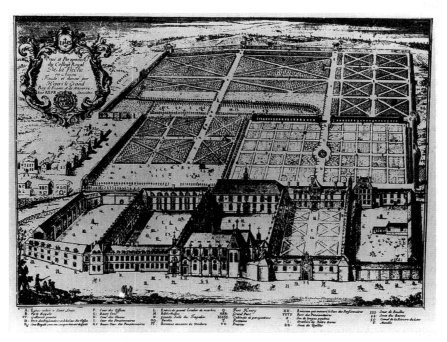

La Flèche. Seventeenth-century engraving by Pierre Aveline.

grounds were a gift from Henri. His mother had lived there when he was born, and his attachment to it was such that he left instructions that his heart and that of his wife be laid to rest in the College chapel. He had the palace renovated and turned into a college at his own expense, and issued detailed instructions on its running, his reforming zeal extending well into educational policy. Indeed, one can detect a shift in Henri's policy designed to regulate educational practices.[13] He had begun in the last decade of the sixteenth century by trying to intervene directly in the running of the municipal *collèges* by appointing regents and providing funds for teachers' salaries, but the opening of La Flèche marks the beginning of a new policy, namely the wholesale replacement of lay teachers by Jesuits, on whose unflinching support he believed (correctly, as it turned out) that he could rely. Gone were the days when provincial towns could run their own educational and cultural programmes: the kind of centralized control to which Jesuits were subject could, if properly harnessed by the monarch, be used to extend his absolutist power into a crucial area, thereby effectively destroying any political ambitions the gentry had left. And the Jesuits profited by the arrangement also, not only receiving significant endowments from suppressed abbeys and episcopal funds, but having the benefit, at least in the early years, of an effective monopoly on secondary teaching, and thus on the formation of a whole generation of political, cultural, and ecclesiastical leaders. The Jesuit education of the professional classes was part of the foundation of a new social order, and it is a role that they were well equipped to carry out. Just as the Society of Jesus had been the only group capable of putting into practice the teaching reforms of the Council of Trent in the education of the priesthood, so too it was the only real means by which Henri's policies could be implemented at the level of the education of the citizenry.

La Flèche may have begun life as a palace, but it had a relatively simple design, and it was added to extensively by the architect-general of the Society of Jesus, Martellange, enabling it to fit the Jesuit model approved by the Society. The basic model in the larger houses comprised three parallel quadrangles, the first for classes (usually with a chapel attached), the second, where the main entrance was located, for the lodgings of the Jesuits themselves, and the third for the lodgings of the boarders.[14] La Flèche deviated from this in having an extra courtyard on either side, but the simplicity of design, broken only by the royal gateway, and the central positioning of the Fathers between the teaching area and the boarders, evidently met the rather strict architectural requirements of the Society.

Like all Jesuits colleges, La Flèche was a 'total institution' in the sense that, while one was there, one's whole life revolved around the world of the institution. The rules governing daily life in these schools covered everything from the curriculum and the individual responsibilities of teachers to such details as the amount of salt to be used in cooking. The principal statements of the rules are to be found in the fourth book of the *Constitutions* of the Society and above all in the *Ratio Studiorum*, a set of rules developed and revised between 1584 and 1599, when the definitive version was produced. The enforcement of the rules was helped by the fact that boarders hardly ever ventured outside the college, and when they did it was usually on a supervised visit to one of the nearby Jesuit houses.[15] They had virtually no relations with their parents while in the college, being allowed to visit them only in the gravest cases, and they were subject to the exclusive authority of their teachers. In their early years, they were granted an annual holiday of four weeks, but this was gradually reduced to one week as they reached the senior years of the school. Severe constraints were also placed on day pupils; they were forbidden, for example, to attend any public celebrations and spectacles, although an exception was made for the execution of heretics.

On the other side of the coin, a very concerted effort was made to make the environment of the college a convivial one. Following in the tradition of the Brethren of the Common Life and Erasmus, corporal punishment, and indeed punishment of any kind, was frowned upon, although it was allowed in some cases. Rather than working within a punitive regime, a complex system of rewards was instituted to encourage students to perform better: termly prize-givings, and in exceptional cases crosses, ribbons, and insignia. These latter were based on Roman decorations, and the hierarchy of student *monitors* was named after ranks of the Roman republic, with classes themselves being divided into groups with names such as Romans and Carthaginians. It was a distinctive feature of Jesuit discipline that the students themselves were given a central role in the maintenance of discipline, and the *monitors* were charged with policing those under their control. Great emphasis was placed on emulation: of the saints, of model older boys, of those who won prizes, and so on. Teaching staff were required to take an interest in all students, to follow their progress, answer questions, and to provide sufficient time at the end of each class for individual difficulties to be dealt with. Prolonged, tiring study, as practised in the Benedictine schools, was rejected and, borrowing an image from Quintilian, the *Ratio studiorum* compares the mind of a child to the narrow neck of a bottle: if one tries to pour in too much, nothing ends up going in, whereas if one pours judiciously, one can fill it. The Jesuit attitude to games in school mirrors this. Rather than forbidding games, they assimilated them, specifying which were to be allowed and which were to be encouraged, and they were made part of the everyday activity of the school. Sports were actively encouraged, especially swimming, riding, and fencing. Dancing, including ballet, was practised by the boys, and it was thought to encourage good bearing. Theatrical entertainments (usually with ballet in the intervals) were similarly made part of school life, and as well as productions of classical drama, the Fathers themselves wrote a number of plays. In this way, the schoolchild was provided with a lifestyle which paralleled that of life outside the *collège,* but which followed detailed rules, and was closely monitored.

There was a curiously theatrical element in Jesuit education,[16] and this was nowhere more evident than in the funeral, and subsequent annual commemorations, of La Flèche's benefactor, Henri IV, who was assassinated on 14 May 1610. His heart was displayed in Paris until 1 June, and then it was taken on the three-day journey to La Flèche, accompanied by royalty, nobility, the clergy, and other notables, all in full mourning regalia. La Flèche was evidently draped wholly in black for the occasion, and one entered via a 27-foot triumphal arch covered in mourning cloth and illuminated by candles. The central courtyard was decorated with coats of arms, death masks of the king, and various tableaux of the king being carried to heaven by angels. A herald received the heart from one of the royal party on a stage in front of the altar, placing it in a gilded urn. The heart was then buried in a further elaborate ceremony,[17] in which Descartes himself participated, being one of the twenty-four pupils selected for this task. The event was subsequently commemorated annually in three-day celebrations that were even more elaborate than the original. On the first day, there was a procession from the church of St. Thomas to the chapel, with funeral orations being given in French and Latin. The events of the second and third days took place around a gigantic effigy of the king's heart, and as well as extensive readings in Latin, French, and Greek, there was, on the third day, an elaborate theatrical allegory. Not all the events on these occasions centred around the king's death, however, and the opportunity was taken to celebrate a number of different things, including (as we shall see below) the latest scientific discoveries. The purpose of such occasions seems to have been, as much as anything else, to provide a spectacular but uplifting form of entertainment, rich in pictorial and verbal iconography. Descartes was to retain an interest in such spectacles throughout his life, making detours in his travels to attend them.

As for teaching methods at La Flèche, these followed the procedures set down in the *Ratio* for all Jesuit colleges. There were four principal forms of instruction: *lectio, repetitiones, sabbatinae disputationes,* and *menstruae disputationes.* The *lectio* consisted of a reading of, and commentary on, a text; this was dictated to the students, but contrary to the medieval practice a significant amount of time was left at the end of each class (the classes ran for two hours in the morning and two in the afternoon) to clarify passages in the reading that remained obscure. Nevertheless, it should be remembered that classes in the first five years of study would have been very large, ranging from 150 to 200 students,[18] and it is hard to imagine that such periods can have been very useful. The *repetitiones* were a regular weekday event, held in the evening (at midday for day students) and presided over by a student. Students had to give an account of the lessons they had attended that day, and then there was extended discussion of any difficulties anyone might have with the material. The *sabbatinae disputationes* comprised a regular Saturday evening viva voce debate in the presence of a teacher. A *respondens* or *defendens,* nominated eight days in advance, expounded a thesis and defended it, and then an *argumentans* presented objections to it, with the *respondens* of the previous Saturday becoming the *argumentans* the next Saturday. The *argumentans* could put no more than three objections, and when the disputation was complete the assistants to each of the participants could claim the right to add further points. Finally, at the end of each month there was a similar disputation, the *menstruae disputationes.* Here the philosophy teachers and their pupils were present, and there was a *respondens* for each teacher, each *respondens* having two adversaries, one from his own class and one from a higher one. Such disputation was the principal form of assessment—written essays, for example, were rare—and it was conducted along quasi-military lines, with constant reference to the highly ritualized and bloody sport of jousting. Rules were set out for 'bearing arms' in philosophy, and those attending the disputations were free to applaud good arguments and clever distinctions. Such disputations had their medieval predecessors, of course, but the highly regulated way in which arguments were to be presented prevented the kind of violent excesses to which medieval disputes were occasionally subject.[19] Although not strictly part of this schema, we might add here the annual three-day literary competition, in which philosophical and literary dissertations, and prose and poetry in French, Latin, and Greek were read; these proceedings were open to the public, and evidently attracted large numbers of curious locals. After 1610 the competition was staged to coincide with the annual commemoration of the death of Henri, and it became the major public event, not just of the school, but of the whole surrounding area.

All teaching and disputation was carried out in Latin and talking to one's fellow students in the vernacular attracted punishment. The reasons for this went beyond the need to practise Latin thoroughly because it was the language of scholarship. It was also the language of the Catholic Church, and decidedly not the language of Protestantism, and there were politico-religious reasons behind the insistence on Latin being spoken. Amongst other things, the Church saw European nations as being a single family under the headship of the Pope, and Latin as the common language of this family. Its status was effectively that of a sacred language. The sixteenth-century humanist Juan Louis Vives, for example, argued that the diversity of languages was an effect of sin,[20] the implication being that there was something morally dangerous in the use of the vernacular. This commitment to Latin is reflected in the curriculum of the first five years of teaching, which was devoted almost exclusively to Latin, Greek, and Classical literature. When we bear in mind that many pupils left after the initial five years of lower school, and never went on to the study of philosophy and science offered in the later years, this is all the more striking, since for many students 'humane letters' comprised, not an introduction to higher things, but the whole of their education, and this was no oversight on the part of the Jesuits. Before we look at the content of this teaching, therefore, it would be of some benefit to determine what the justification and purpose of this apparent 'return to antiquity' was.

Christianity and the Classical Tradition

Ignatius, in common with writers such as Erasmus, Melanchthon, and Sturm, and with institutions such as the municipal *collèges* and schools of the Brethren of the Common Life, had a firm commitment to the humanist study of letters, and indeed made this the centre of the Jesuit programme of studies. Ignatius defends it in terms of the Augustinian doctrine of *exercitatio animi*,[21] whereby the mind, if it is to grasp spiritual truths, must prepare itself so as not to be blinded by the divine light, and the disciplines of grammar, rhetoric, and dialectic are advocated as means of accustoming one's mind to the contemplation of ideas, and of intelligible (as opposed to perceptible) reality.

The relation between Christianity and pagan literature in the sixteenth and seventeenth centuries was a vexed one. Calvin was resolutely opposed to pagan texts being studied alongside the Scriptures, whereas writers like Erasmus, Sturm, and Ignatius saw the works of Classical antiquity as being an essential preparation for educated Christians. There are two questions that we need to ask here. The first centres on what the acceptability of Classical philosophy and literature derived from. Was it not, after all, the product of a pagan culture that was in

45

many ways antithetical to Christianity? While it could be ransacked for passages and doctrines that not only conformed to Christianity but actually seemed to anticipate or support it, for every one such passage or doctrine one could easily find many incompatible with, or even subversive of, Christian teaching. Second, there is the question of why it was thought to form a necessary ingredient in a Christian education for these writers. It is one thing to try to show the compatibility of pagan authors with the teachings of the Church, but another altogether to make these effectively part of Christian teaching, not a part of Christian dogma, to be sure, but an indispensable part of its general teaching nevertheless. Was it that Christianity was completely lacking in these areas, and if so would it not be safer to develop something specifically Christian to make good the lack?

The answer to the first question is that Classical philosophy, in particular, had become so 'Christianized' by this period that it was hardly distinct from Christianity itself for many thinkers. In the Patristic period, we witness the gradual 'Christianization' of philosophy (metaphysics, natural philosophy, ethics, etc.), begun by the early Fathers and brought to completion by Augustine. In its early stages, the project is that of nurturing what is worthwhile in pagan thought in the nourishing atmosphere of Christian teaching. The approach of Clement of Alexandria is typical here. Presenting himself as Christ's gardener, he speaks in terms of cutting twigs from the rank, dried-back, and brittle bushes of pagan literature, and grafting them onto the stock of Christ's truth.[22] In its later development, especially in the writings of Augustine, the project amounts to nothing short of a total translation of all philosophy into Christian terms. Christianity is conceived of as the final form of philosophy. Using the language of the classical philosophers to formulate his theology, Augustine attempts to show that Christianity is able to answer all the questions of Classical metaphysics. In general terms, not only does Christianity supplement Classical philosophy here, it appropriates the teachings of this philosophy, denying that they were ever the property of the ancients in the first place, and it construes every philosophical question in terms of Christian teaching. This appropriation of earlier thought by Christianity made it possible for it to present itself as the final answer to what earlier philosophers were striving for, and in a number of cases it was strikingly successful in this respect: the great ease with which it transforms one of the central aims of Hellenistic philosophy, namely that of transcending the flux and disorder of life and the achievement of peace of mind (*ataraxia* or *apatheia*), into Christian terms, is quite remarkable.

In his discussion of Plato in Books 8 to 10 of the *De Civitate Dei*, Augustine speculated whether Plato could have had some knowledge of the Hebrew scriptures, and he suggests that the God of the Neoplatonists is the same as that of Christianity, and even that they speak, albeit in a confused way, of the Trinity. Yet, he tells us, these same Neoplatonists cannot know God. They mistakenly believe that they can reach Him by purely intellectual means, whereas in fact He can only be reached through the sacraments, which were instituted with the Incarnation of Christ. For Augustine, the superiority of Christianity over ancient philosophies and over the contemporary rivals of Christianity lay in the institution of the sacraments. But it is not so much that, for Augustine, Christianity is ancient philosophy plus the sacraments; a more accurate way of putting it would be to say that ancient philosophy is Christianity minus the sacraments. Christianity is the culmination of all previous philosophical reflection and religious belief, something that can be glimpsed by the appropriate allegorical readings of the ancient philosophers and sages just as much as it can by the allegorical reading of the Old Testament.

Such a reading of antiquity was prevalent well into the seventeenth century. As late as the second half of the seventeenth century, one can find a very orthodox and influential history of philosophy, Georg Horn's *Historiae Philosophicae* (Leiden, 1655), maintaining the view that all philosophy is to be traced back to Adam, the various philosophical schools or sects being simply a result of the Fall. And when one turns to works with a Hermetic inspiration, such as Cudworth's *True Intellectual System of the Universe* (London, 1678), one finds a much more elaborate attempt to read the whole of antiquity in Christian terms. These works are written at the end of, or at least towards the end of, a long tradition of interpreting the thought of Classical antiquity as being something which, in a fundamental way, presupposes Christianity. This being the case, it is difficult to talk of a straightforward incompatibility between Classical thought and Christianity, as if we were simply comparing two independent systems of thought.[23]

As regards the second question, the issue hinges on what kind of indispensable contribution Classical learning can make to the study of, or development of, Christian doctrine. At least in the first instance, the area that stood out most strikingly in this respect was Classical philology. During the Reformation, abuse within the Church stimulated a nostalgic desire for a return to earlier times when Jesus' simple message had been understood without the interpolations of medieval Christianity. The project was that of reconstructing Christianity on the basis of a reading of the New Testament that was free from the corruptions introduced by the interpretations of the medieval Church, and this meant reading the Gospels against the background of a more literal understanding of the Old Testament, an understanding occasionally

aided by reliance on the Rabbinic tradition,[24] but much more importantly, on Classical philology.

The concerted application of the principles of Classical philology to
the New Testament was initiated by Lorenzo Valla in the second quarter
of the fifteenth century, but the elevation of this project into a basis for
ecclesiastical reform began with Erasmus' Preface to his 1505 edition
of Valla's *Annotationes in Novum Testamentum*. Here we find the view
that the authentic teachings of Jesus are to be discovered by studying
the New Testament in its original language, using all the scholarship
of Classical philology, a view that was to be developed in detail in his
Novum Instrumentum of 1516. The response of the Council of Trent
was to make the Latin Vulgate the official version of the Bible, thereby
attempting to close off the possibility of extensive reinterpretations,
such as were beginning to be proposed by Protestant scholars on the
basis of a close reading of the Greek. This does not mean that the study
of either Greek or Classical philology was abandoned by the Catholic
Church. The Jesuits pursued both, although it is true that Greek was
not taught to anything like the same degree as Latin, and unlike Latin,
it was evidently not considered as having a value in its own right. Latin
was taught because good Latin style was considered essential for the
persuasive presentation of arguments, whereas Greek was taught above
all so that Protestants could be rebutted. As the *Ratio* puts it: 'It is
disgraceful to be defeated in this matter by the heretics [i.e. Protes-
tants], who, having been taught Greek from a very young age, scorn
Catholics ignorant of the language, making fun of their disgrace and
challenging them on the Greek sources of religion'.[25]

Res Literaria, 1606–1611

The first five years of the course at La Flèche comprised a year of
preparatory classes, then three years of 'grammar', and finally a year
of rhetoric. During this time the student acquired a good knowledge of
Latin and a reasonably thorough knowledge of Greek, as well as very
considerable familiarity with a wide range of classical texts, with Cicero
predominating. Texts were very rarely given in full, however, but almost always in the form of extracts, and Compayré has pointed out
that this is not so much the result of censorship as a consequence of
a desire to remove from ancient texts anything which shows them to
be distinctively of their epoch, anything which gives the text 'the stamp
of time, anything which gives it its own character'.[26] This is very much
in keeping with the general approach to Classical antiquity that I have
just outlined: it is deprived of any identity of its own as part of its

incorporation into Christianity. Indeed, it does not even have the right to be assessed in its own terms, and if it differs from Christianity in any way this is seen as a deficiency, to be made good by replacing, or trying to reconcile, the offending doctrines with Christianity. Such an approach was not unique to the Jesuits; on the contrary, they were working within a very firmly established tradition of interpretation.

The way in which the material was taught in class is interesting, for it seems that what the study of the texts was designed to yield was not so much an understanding and assessment of their content, but an appreciation of their style. There were strict and detailed rules governing the way in which material was to be presented, and the rules governing the exposition of the texts give us considerable insight into the nature of Jesuit teaching. The first part of the exposition was the *argumentum,* in which a general account of the passage under study was given. This was followed by an *explanatio,* in which sentences and phrases in the passage are paraphrased so that their meaning could be clarified. What then followed was not an investigation of the substance of the text, but rather a *rhetorica,* in which the way in which the rules of rhetoric, poetics, or even just grammar are applied in the text was examined and elaborated upon. This was often the longest and most detailed part of the exercise. Next came the shortest part, the *eruditio,* in which any historical facts necessary for an understanding of the text were given. Finally, in the *latinitas,* citations from other authors were provided to validate the grammar, style, imagery, etc. of the text. The principal aim of this type of teaching was language study, and in particular the ability to think, write, and speak fluently in elegant Latin. The models are very much what we would expect: Cicero (above all), Ovid, Virgil, Tibullus, and Catullus in Latin, with Aesop, Dio Chrystostomus, and others in Greek. In the fifth year, the moral writings of Cicero, Caesar, Sallust, and others, and the rhetorical writings of Cicero and Quintilian took up a major part of the curriculum, and in the study of Greek, Aristotle's *Rhetoric* and *Poetics* were studied alongside passages from Homer, Pindar, Demosthenes, Plato (the letters, not the dialogues), and the Greek Church Fathers.[27]

It is unlikely that the various rhetorical styles were presented in the classroom without preference, and although we can find some variation in the rhetorical styles of French Jesuit writers, there are a number of distinctive traits in their rhetorical writings, as Fumaroli has shown in his detailed analyses of the works of seventeenth-century French Jesuits.[28] Two of these are worth noting. In the first place, Jesuit writing showed a marked preference for a baroque style deriving from the second Sophistic, a form of display oratory typified in the works of the second-century writers Dio Chrystostomus, Aristides, and the earlier

Lucian.[29] It was characterized by the adoption and development of an 'Asiatic' prose style, which was initially associated with Isocrates and then Cicero in its milder forms, and was orotund and emotionally charged; its proponents aimed at virtuosity, but its detractors considered it merely affected. These features of the Asiatic style were exaggerated in the writing of the second Sophists. The 'Attic' style, in contrast, comprised short sentences which used a simple vocabulary and which had an air of informality, although its critics maintained it was artificial; its great exponent was Seneca, and it was a style strongly associated with, and defended by, the Stoics in antiquity.[30] What the Jesuits attempted to provide was some kind of balance between very curt Attic styles, such as that of Tacitus, taken up and defended by Lipsius in the sixteenth century, on the one hand, and excessively baroque styles on the other.[31] Descartes' position on these issues in later years is not at all straightforward. At times, he suggests that he has no interest in such questions, as when, reflecting on his early years at school, in the autobiographical part of the *Discours,* he tells us that he 'valued oratory and was fond of poetry; but I thought both of these were gifts of the mind rather than fruits of study. Those with the strongest reasoning who are most skilful at ordering their thoughts so as to make them clear and intelligible are always the most persuasive, even if they speak only the dialect of lower Brittany and have never learned rhetoric'.[32] But on one occasion, he apparently defends a rather baroque 'Asiatic' style, in an open letter of 1628 to one of the most famous Asianists of the seventeenth century, Jean-Louis Guez de Balzac, arguing that it has the correct balance. Moreover, writing to Mersenne about his *Géométrie,* in the same year that the *Discours* and the *Géométrie* were published, he compares his own achievement (which he rightly considered to be one of his greatest) with that of Cicero, telling us that: 'what I provide in the second Book [of the *Géométrie*] concerning the nature and properties of curved lines and the way of examining them is, it seems to me, as far beyond ordinary geometry as the rhetoric of Cicero is beyond the *abc*'s of children'.[33] Yet if one were to place Descartes' own style in either of these camps, one would have to say it was uncompromisingly 'Attic', with Seneca rather than Cicero as its model. I shall touch on these questions below when we come to look at his letter to Balzac, but it is worth nothing here that Descartes himself did not leave these questions behind when he left La Flèche, and we should be very cautious indeed about attributing to him a straightforward dismissal of rhetoric.

The second distinctive feature of Jesuit rhetorical writing is the preoccupation of much of it with emblems and symbols. Emblems and symbols were a major concern of court society, forming not just the basis for popular games, but a way of marking out court society from those who could not fathom the meaning of the symbols. Writing in the context of Florentine court society, Biagioli points out that 'emblematics was to court spectacles what etiquette was to court behaviour: it differentiated social groups and reinforced social hierarchies by controlling access to meaning'.[34] There was a strong current of concern with the educational value of emblems, and the solution of enigmas and interpretation of emblems and symbols was recommended as an exercise in the *Ratio Studorium*;[35] indeed, Fumaroli has drawn attention to the use made by a number of Jesuit writers of Philostratus' *Eikones,* which comprises exemplary exercises in the art of rhetorical description of paintings, in which the aim is to describe a painting (in Philostratus' case probably imaginary paintings) in sufficiently vivid terms as to make the reader feel he is seeing it.[36] What was at issue here was the traditional rhetorical theme of improvisation, particularly considered as a display of virtuosity. But very much part of this is a more general concern with the use of images, and this is a question of considerable importance. The rhetorical tradition was especially interested in the question of the vividness and particularity of images. In fact, a number of psychological and rhetorical concerns meet here, and the Roman rhetorical tradition—especially the writings of Cicero, the anonymous author of the *Rhetorica Ad Herennium,* and Quintilian— was to utilize elements from rhetoric, poetics, and psychology. Because it has so often been assumed that rhetoric is not something that played any role in Descartes' thinking after he left La Flèche, such considerations have been ignored. But rhetorical theory always carried with it a large amount of psychological theory, and indeed writers like Quintilian, who produced what was to become the most influential account of these issues, derived elements not only from Aristotle's *Poetics* and *Rhetoric,* but also from the theory of the psychological image in Book 3 of the *De anima.* The rhetorical/psychological theories of the image that he would have been familiar with from his reading of writers like Quintilian are, as I shall show later, a plausible source for many of Descartes' own psychological theories, including his key theory of clear and distinct ideas.

The Philosophical Curriculum

The majority of students left La Flèche after the fifth year. Not only had they received sufficient education to enable them to proceed to a professional course in a university by this stage, but many universities denied admission and graduation to the degrees of Master of Arts,

Medicine, and Theology to more advanced students of Jesuit colleges, such was the strength of feeling against the Jesuits at this time.[37] Descartes remained there to complete his education, and in 1611 he entered the first year of the 'philosophical' curriculum. The medieval education system had been loosely structured around a codification developed by the fifth- and sixth-century Latin encyclopaedists into the seven liberal arts, made up of the *trivium,* comprising the 'verbal arts', namely grammar, rhetoric, and dialectic (logic), and the *quadrivium,* comprising the 'mathematical arts', namely arithmetic, music, geometry, and astronomy. The curriculum at La Flèche reflects this ordering of material to some extent, albeit with significant revisions. In the first five years of the humanistic curriculum, the *trivium* was studied, with the exception of dialectic. In the second three years, the remaining liberal arts subjects were covered, although metaphysics, natural philosophy, and ethics were added. The way in which the 'philosophical subjects' were studied differed somewhat from the grammar and rhetoric of the earlier years. The range of authors was much more restricted, the use of commentaries was probably more widespread, and the works read were studied very much for their content, rather than for their style, contrary to what had been the procedure with the texts of the humanistic curriculum.

The restriction in the range of authors and the greater use of commentators reflects the fact that the topics of the philosophical curriculum were generally more contentious than those of the humanistic curriculum, and attendance at advanced courses in theology, as well as evidence of orthodoxy, were prerequisites for those teaching such courses. Some areas, such as metaphysics, were so contentious that they were either not taught at all (such as some of the theological parts of Aristotle's *Metaphysics*), or were taught on the basis of detailed commentaries where orthodoxy was followed closely. Ignatius had recommended the philosophy of Aristotle, as interpreted by Aquinas, to his followers. But this was not always an easy recommendation to follow. Aquinas' interpretation of Aristotle was being questioned by Paduan Aristotelians such as Zabarella, Pomponazzi, and Nifo from the late fifteenth century onwards, and they were offering a naturalistic reading of Aristotle which was very hard to reconcile with the use of his philosophy as a foundation for Christian theology. Moreover, although there had been a revival of Thomism in the early decades of the sixteenth century, and a corresponding decline in interest in his scholastic critics, such as Ockham and Scotus, what orthodox Thomism amounted to was not at all clear-cut. Various versions of Thomism were offered, often developed as responses to later criticisms, the most influential being those of Cajetan and Suárez. Cajetan deviated from Aquinas on a number of issues, including the metaphysical doctrine of analogy, a core doctrine because it purported to provide an account of the relation between human knowledge and divine knowledge. Suárez, while very broadly speaking Thomist, holds quite distinctive views on a range of metaphysical questions. As we shall see, Descartes was not taught 'pure Aquinas' any more than he was taught 'pure Aristotle'.

In some other areas, such as mathematics, there were two different kinds of problem. The first was not a problem of orthodoxy so much as an innate conservatism about the relevance of the *quadrivium* subjects. Although notionally on a par with the *trivium,* the *quadrivium* subjects had always fared badly in comparison, and some writers believed this was how things should be. Astronomy, arithmetic, and geometry had received renewed attention in the sixteenth century, however, because of a range of concerns, from calendar reform to ballistics, and there was a clear case for the teaching of these subjects at a college like La Flèche, where the nobility and the gentry were often expected to enter military and administrative careers on leaving the college. The second kind of problem turned on the role and status of mathematical arguments in areas like astronomy, where deeply held natural-philosophical views were at stake. Here questions of orthodoxy did arise, although this was not always evident before 1616, when Foscarini's attempt to reconcile Copernicanism and scripture led to the condemnation of the former by the Roman Inquisition.

Dialectic, 1611–1612

The *Ratio studiorum* recommends that the 'organon' of Aristotle form the core for teaching in dialectic, although it stipulates that material more relevant to metaphysics should not be included, nor should the later books of the *Topics,* and only extracts from the *De Sophisticis Elenchis* are recommended. This leaves us with the *Categories, On Interpretation, Prior Analytics* (first five chapters), *Posterior Analytics, Topics* (Books 1 and 2), as well as some material from the *De Sophisticis Elenchis.* These were supplemented by Porphyry's introduction to the *Categories* (the *Isagoge*), as was the usual practice. In the 1586 *Ratio* the commentary of Fonseca on the organon is recommended, and in the definitive 1599 version the *Introductio in dialecticam* of Toletus is added. Fonseca and Toletus were especially influential, and the very extensive series of commentaries on Aristotle put out by the Portuguese University of Coimbra in the 1590s was based in large part on their commentaries. It was these commentaries, written by Jesuits with a view to establishing a definitive reading of Aristotle, that provided the closest thing to an orthodox reading of Aristotle for the Jesuit schools, and it is by means of these commentaries that Descartes learned the vast bulk of his philosophy.

The Aristotelian texts chosen cover a range of topics, amongst the more important of which (if we exclude the metaphysical questions) are: the formal study of syllogistic, the application of syllogistic to scientific reasoning, and the discovery of appropriate arguments. However, the study of logic as a formal account of deductive inference had effectively come to an end by the early sixteenth century, and the Coimbra commentators dealt with logic in a highly psychologistic way, as a theory of the regulation of the functions of cognition, rather than as a theory of (for example) the formal features of valid inference patterns. This change in approach derives, at least in part, from rhetoric having taken over what had traditionally been conceived to be the concerns of logic. This is something I shall consider more fully in chapter 4, when we look at Descartes' early doctrine of clear and distinct ideas. For the moment, I want to concentrate on how the role of logic was seen in the Jesuit textbooks. Basically, it was thought to provide two things. The first was an account of scientific demonstration, a topic to which the *Posterior Analytics* was largely devoted. What was provided there was an account of the difference between syllogisms which, while formally identical, nevertheless differed in that some of them yielded conclusions that were merely descriptive, whereas others ('demonstrative' syllogisms) yielded conclusions that were genuinely explanatory. One of the main aims of Aristotle's theory of scientific demonstration was to provide a systematic account of what this difference lay in, but by the sixteenth and seventeenth centuries there was so much confusion and misunderstanding about what exactly the demonstrative syllogism was supposed to do, with many believing that the conclusion was (*per impossibile*) supposed to yield factually new information not contained in the premises, that it was rapidly becoming discredited.[38] The second thing that logic was thought to provide was a normative theory of thought, a set of rules for thinking correctly. Commentators in the Coimbra tradition tended to think of logic either in moral terms, as something which provides a norm morally binding on thought, or in medical terms, as something like a medicine that remedies the natural weakness of the mind.[39] The foundations for logic in the work of Fonseca and Toletus lie not in a theory of inference but in a synthesis of Aristotelian and Thomist psychology: logic provides us with an account of how the mind should function.

As we shall see, Descartes was to reject both these claims at quite an early stage in his career. He was one of the most fervent opponents of the Aristotelian idea of demonstration, considering it empty and fruitless.

But his rejection of the idea of logic as providing rules for the direction of the mind is no less important, both for his conception of scientific enquiry and for his general conception of epistemology.

Natural Philosophy and Mathematics,
1612–1613

The second year of the philosophical curriculum comprised a principal subject, natural philosophy, and a subsidiary subject, mathematics, which was taught for one hour each day. More time seems to have been devoted to the teaching of scientific subjects in Jesuit colleges than in, say, Protestant colleges, but practical and empirical subjects were taught in the subsidiary 'mathematical' part of the course.

The basic texts studied were Aristotle's writings on natural philosophy: the *Physics,* the *De Caelo,* the *De Mundo,*[40] and the first book of the *De Generatione.* The bare essentials of Aristotelian natural philosophy are much the same for Aristotle as for his sixteenth-century commentators. The fundamental distinction on which it rests is that between those things that have an intrinsic principle of change and those that have an extrinsic principle of change. Living things are the clearest case of intrinsic change: the acorn grows into the oak tree because of something internal to it, animals move not because they are swept along by something extrinsic but because they themselves direct their motions. The model for intrinsic change is a biological one, although it is central to Aristotle's conception of natural processes that the model be applicable to any kind of change, and he wants to conceive of inorganic processes in similar terms. He considers several forms of change, including change of one substance into another substance, change of the state of a substance in respect of some quality or quantity, and change in respect of place.[41] Change in respect of place, local motion, can be taken as an example. Take the case of an inorganic thing such as a stone. Aristotle considers that this can move in two different ways; either it can move due to some extrinsic principle, as when it is raised up, or it can move due to some intrinsic principle, as when it is subsequently dropped. The difference between the two cases is that, when the stone is raised, something extrinsic is needed, for left to its own devices, so to speak, the stone would have remained where it was; whereas when it is dropped from a height, no extrinsic action is needed; the stone moves of its own accord. Traditionally the fall of the stone would have been put down to the fact that it is made up of the element earth, which naturally moves downwards if unimpeded. Aristotle is not happy with this explanation, for it makes matter the source of change, something which he rejects. On Aristotle's account, everything is made up of matter and form, the form of the thing being what makes it what it is: the form provides the thing with both its essential and accidental properties or qualities, and indeed is constitutive of the thing as something that has determinate characteristics and a separate identity. Matter is merely a substratum, something that is pure potentiality until the imposition of form.

In sum, then, everything is comprised of matter and form, and it is the form of a thing, and not its matter as the ancient atomists had maintained, that is responsible for its properties. When a thing changes in some way, changes its position for example, and when this is due solely to its form, the source of change is intrinsic and the body is acting according to its nature. The aim of physical enquiry is to understand the natures of things, since in doing this we are able to explain their properties. But here a complication enters the picture, for if one considers the totality of what can be studied, it is not exhausted by corporeal bodies. What is distinctive about corporeal bodies, on Aristotle's characterization, is that they have an independent existence and are subject to change; but there are also categories of things that have an independent existence and do not change (namely God), as well as things that have no independent existence but do not change. This last category is that of mathematics. Its objects have no independent existence because they are abstractions. They form a different genus from corporeal bodies. This is important because the aim of scientific explanation for Aristotle is to determine what kind of thing something is by establishing its essential properties, and principles from one genus, that of mathematics, cannot be used in the establishment of principles in another genus, that of independently existing corporeal bodies. The mathematical (that is, for all intents and purposes, quantitative) demonstration of physical principles or results is therefore not only inappropriate, it is essentially misguided.

This much was accepted by both Aristotle and his sixteenth-century followers. But these are very general principles, and as soon as one tries to present a more detailed picture, any semblance of unanimity disappears. There are notorious problems even in Aristotle himself: he maintains that everything must comprise matter and form, yet seems to make exceptions in his doctrine of God as pure form and (perhaps) in his doctrine of 'prime matter', which is the ultimate kind of matter, devoid of all form; he sometimes thinks of form as being imposed on matter, rather like a shape is imposed on a substratum, whereas at other times (such as in his discussion of *energeia*) the form functions as something much more like an internal principle, and these are two conceptions which are likely to lead in two radically different directions;

and, although he rejects the use of mathematical principles in physical demonstrations, he discusses a category of 'mixed' or 'subordinate' sciences, such as optics, where it is admissible to use geometrical principles in one's account of a physical phenomenon, in this case the paths of light rays, although the status of this 'account' is unclear. Secondly, even where Aristotle presents an apparently unambiguous doctrine, it is subject to a variety of interpretations. His account of local motion was subject to fierce dispute as a result of the development of *impetus* theory, whereby the continuing motion of a projectile was explained, not in terms of the surrounding air propelling the body, as Aristotle himself had thought, but in terms of a force impressed on the body when it was first projected and which becomes 'internalized', so to speak. Although *impetus* theory had originally been proposed in the sixth century by Philoponus as a rejection of the Aristotelian account of motion, by the sixteenth century it was being accommodated without very significant revision to Aristotelian natural philosophy. The correctness of *impetus* theory was thus very much a dispute within Aristotelian natural philosophy in the sixteenth and early seventeenth centuries. But sometimes the reading of Aristotle was so liberal that one has good reason to doubt whether one was still within Aristotle's system. To give just one example, two of the most influential sources of Aristotelian natural philosophy in the seventeenth century were Johannes Magirus' *Physiologia Peripatetica* (1597) and Scipion Dupleix's *Corps de Philosophie* (1602). Both of these textbooks accept that the explanation of the properties of corporeal bodies must be in terms of their form and not their matter, but they both focus on the imposition of form on an original property-less substratum (the so-called 'prime matter'), and what results from this imposition of form is the differentiation of this matter into the four elements. These four elements are then used to do all the explanatory work in natural philosophy, and in some respects what results resembles the newer corpuscularian philosophies of the seventeenth century rather than traditional Aristotelian natural philosophy.

We shall have the opportunity to look at Aristotelian natural philosophy further below, and I shall not pursue any of these issues here. Nevertheless, it is worth drawing attention to two of its features that contrast sharply with the kind of natural philosophy that Descartes would do so much to establish, and which is more familiar to modern readers. The first is that Aristotle distinguishes three different genera of knowledge—physics, mathematics, and 'first philosophy' (metaphysics or theology)—and one cannot use principles drawn from one genus in the explanation of phenomena from another, the most important consequence of this being the rejection of a search for quantitative physical explanations. Secondly, the basic demarcation of Aristotelian natural philosophy is into those things that have within themselves an intrinsic principle of change and those that have an extrinsic principle. This is, above all, a distinction between natural objects and phenomena on the one hand, and artefacts and extrinsically produced change on the other. In particular it is important to note that organic and inorganic phenomena fall under 'physics', and that the model for physics is biological rather than, say, mechanical.

What was included under the rubric of 'mathematics' also differs considerably from what is now included under that title. The standard classification of mathematical subjects was that of the medieval *quadrivium*, namely arithmetic, geometry, music, and astronomy; but Clavius, whose mathematical commentaries were the standard ones in Jesuit colleges, also uses a second classification, based on a distinction between those disciplines studying things in abstraction from their matter (roughly corresponding to Aristotle's conception of mathematics), and those that study sensible objects mathematically (roughly corresponding to Aristotle's 'subordinate sciences'). In the first category are geometry and arithmetic; in the second are astrology, perspective, geodesy, music, calculation and practical arithmetic, and mechanics, as well as civil and military architecture.[42] This latter classification reflects the rationale for the introduction of teaching in mathematical subjects given by Clavius in his treatise, *On the Manner in which Mathematical Disciplines can be Developed in the Colleges of the Society,* which focuses on the usefulness of the mathematical sciences in understanding planetary and stellar orbits (Clavius is working within the geocentric theory); the multitude of angels; the astrological effects of stars; the infinite divisibility of continuous quantities; tides, winds, comets, the rainbow, and other meteorological phenomena; and 'the proportions of motions, qualities, actions, passions, reactions, and so forth' (which presumably refers to the quantitative classification of motions and the kinematics of impact).[43]

As regards the practical mathematical subjects, the seriousness with which they were pursued, and the general attitude that was taken to them in Jesuit schools, is a matter of dispute. Apologists for the Jesuit colleges understandably stress the very open atmosphere in which scientific questions were discussed, the scientific literature available to students, and the fact that considerable attention was paid to new scientific discoveries. Critics, on the other hand, have drawn attention to the small amount of teaching time devoted to such subjects, and Compayré has suggested that the Jesuit masters had little genuine scientific interest, but were concerned rather with novelties.[44] The first anniversary, in 1611, of the death of Henri IV is an interesting case in this respect. Among the sonnets presented to commemorate the king was one describing how God had made Henri into a celestial body to serve as 'a heavenly torch for mortals'; it is entitled 'On the Death of King Henri the Great and on the Discovery of some New Planets or Stars Moving Around Jupiter, Made this Year by Galileo, Celebrated Mathematician of the Grand Duke of Florence'.[45] Galileo's discovery of the moons of Jupiter was widely celebrated, and the Collegio Romano had supported theses defending Galileo in the same year.[46] But do we take the fact of the celebration of the discovery as the important thing, or the way in which it was celebrated? Scientific matters had been dealt with extensively in poetry in the Renaissance, where everything from the treatment of haemorrhoids to the structure of the cosmos had been put into metre,[47] but this kind of literature had usually reduced scientific questions to novelties. Interest in scientific discoveries turned around their value as novelties in this period—the Medici rewarded Galileo handsomely for his discovery of the moons of Jupiter not because of any scientific value that attached to the discovery but because of the spectacle provided thereby[48]—and there can be no doubt that the Jesuits encouraged a fascination with novelties in their students. Descartes was to be no exception. In the manuscript usually referred to as 'Observationes', dating from 1621, he describes with evident fascination how to create various optical illusions.[49] These in fact derive from Della Porta's *Magia Naturalis* (1589), and there is reason to think he was familiar with this from La Flèche, along with magical and mystical works by Lull and Agrippa.[50] On the other hand, there may be something to be said for the practice of encouraging interest in areas like optics through the use of novelties, and it must be remembered that two of the greatest researchers in optics of the first half of the seventeenth century, Descartes himself and Claude Mydorge, had been pupils at La Flèche. Nevertheless, the very marginal nature of these areas in the curriculum does indicate that they were not given any real prominence, and the evidence suggests that Descartes himself did not develop an active interest in these areas until the end of 1619, when Beeckman was to fire his imagination with mechanical problems derived from an altogether different tradition.

Metaphysics and Ethics, 1613–1614

The final year of the philosophical curriculum was also devoted to a principal and a subsidiary subject, in this case metaphysics and ethics respectively. Again, Aristotle provided the basic texts for the metaphysics lessons, parts of the *De generatione,* the *De anima* (excluding those passages dealing with anatomy and physiology), and parts of the *Metaphysics* (excluding any of the discussions of God) being the focus of attention. In many ways, such a course would have been a continuation of the lessons on natural philosophy of the previous year, with doctrines such as that of form being elaborated in greater detail. The commentaries used, those of Suárez, Fonseca, Toletus, and the massive ones of Coimbra, differed in significant respects from the corresponding medieval commentaries, however.[51] The difference arose in part from concern over the readings of Aristotle offered by Paduan philosophers, especially Pomponazzi, who had argued persuasively that Aristotle himself had elaborated a conception of the soul that was incompatible with the Christian doctrine of its immortality. The *Ratio* gave explicit instruction as to how these readings were to be dealt with; the teacher should 'not attach himself or his students to any philosophic sect such as the Averroists, Alexandrians [Pomponazzi] and the like, and let him not cover over the errors of Averroes or Alexander or the others, but on account of these let him more sharply attack their authority'. The response of the Collegio Romano was to seek to avoid such doctrines by reconstructing Aristotle's thought from first principles, so that from these true basic principles true consequences (corresponding to Christian teaching) could be derived. This, and a number of related developments, resulted in a new kind of commentary in the late sixteenth century. In contrast to the medieval commentaries such as those of Aquinas, which followed through the arguments in the order they were given in the text, the new commentaries, which were in the tradition of medieval *disputationes*, while they presented the full text, commented on it in a way which rearranged the material, and presented it in a way which purported to move from true first principles outwards to specific doctrines.[52] Indeed, at least for some of their proponents, such commentaries were not designed to supplement Aristotle but to supplant him.[53] And it is also worth remembering that some Jesuit philosophers were not even producing Aristotle commentaries at all: Suárez, who stands at the fountainhead of this movement, was more concerned to set out a systematic metaphysics rather than yet another Aristotle commentary, and this evidently gave his works a novelty and attractiveness which went some way to securing their success.[54] In the light of this, it is not at all surprising to discover that Descartes does not seem to have been very familiar with the writings of Aquinas until about 1628,[55] despite receiving an education that can, in broad terms, be called Thomist. The reason is that the kinds of problems that the Jesuits had to face as a result of disputes in the Collegio Romano over the interpretation of Aristotle, disputes centring on the question of whether Aristotle's philosophy could be used to defend key Christian doctrines such as the immortality of the soul and the existence of God, were resolved by a rewriting of Aristotle in such a way that those Christian truths demonstrable in natural theology could be derived from first principles. Aquinas had simply followed the order of Aristotle's arguments in his commentaries, and this now proved to be insufficient, hence the otherwise puzzling absence of many of these from the curriculum.

Aristotle's *Nicomachean Ethics,* together with the detailed Coimbra commentary on this work, formed the basis for the moral philosophy course, but there were in fact two different kinds of approach to ethics pursued, and the *Ratio studiorum* was particularly explicit in its insistence on a proper balance between the two. The first approach was that of speculative moral theology of the sort that one finds in Aquinas' *Summa Theologica.* The second was practical casuistry, which promoted a view of moral philosophy not in terms of adherence to general and universal principles, but rather in terms of developing practical guidance for resolving moral problems, guidance that may not be generalizable beyond the particular case. Such an approach had its origins in the writings of the Stoics, and its first full presentation in Cicero, and it fitted well with the kind of practical advice one might expect of a priest. The focus of such teaching was 'cases of conscience' and there were firm strictures against trying to resolve such cases from general principles. The cases themselves ranged from private matters of personal conduct to very public disputes: an important treatise in the latter category, Francisco Vitoria's *Relectio de Indis et de Jure Belli* (1539), for example, looks at the question of the status and rights of the indigenous peoples of Central and South America. There was no shortage of textbooks in the area of casuistry, both on specific issues and on the nature of casuistry itself, one of the most famous texts in the latter genre being Toletus' *Summa Casuum Conscientiae* (1569), and it is hard to believe that Descartes would not have been familiar with this, as the Jesuits made casuistry very much their own. Casuistry fell into disrepute (one from which it is only now beginning to recover) during the seventeenth century, principally as a result of the attacks of Pascal and the Port-Royalists on Jesuit casuistry, which they tended to construe as a kind of moral pragmatism;[56] but this was a later development. We have every reason to think, given the Jesuit focus on casuistry, that the young Descartes would have thought of morality above all in terms of casuistry, and a training in the subject would have served him well in the kind of political, administrative, or legal career that the Jesuits envisaged their students entering.

Le Bourgeois Gentilhomme: A Choice of Career, 1614–1618

Descartes left La Flèche around the middle of 1614, aged 18. He graduated in civil and canon law from the University of Poitiers in November 1616, and he had presumably spent the full academic year there, so we can reasonably suppose that he spent the bulk of the time between October or November 1615, and November 1616, when he completed his examinations, at Poitiers. He went to Breda, in the Netherlands, to join the army of Prince Maurice of Nassau as a gentleman soldier no later than the summer of 1618, and he remained there until early the next year. This leaves two periods unaccounted for, the summer of 1614 to the autumn of 1615, and the autumn of 1616 to the summer of 1618.

The first period, that between his leaving La Flèche and entering the University of Poitiers, is something of a mystery. Baillet tells us that much of the period was spent in a house in Saint-Germain-en-Lay, which was then a village just outside Paris.[57] Unfortunately, we have no way of corroborating this, and Baillet gets so many details from around this time wrong that we must be wary about the reliability of the account.[58] Nevertheless, in general outline this account looks plausible, and in the absence of any evidence to the contrary, I propose that we accept it. One question that arises if we do accept Baillet's version of events (in general outline) is why Descartes shut himself off from his friends and relatives for a prolonged period, perhaps of over a year. At least one commentator has maintained that Descartes 'suffered the first of several breakdowns' while there, but he offers no evidence for this.[59] Nevertheless, if Baillet's account is generally correct, then this is certainly a possible explanation, and one we must take seriously. Certainly Descartes' condition, in a mild form, seems to fit seventeenth-century conceptions of melancholia well. Summarizing the detailed and extensive records of Richard Napier, a seventeenth-century English clergyman and physician who treated more than two thousand mentally disturbed patients, one commentator has written:

Whether melancholy crept unprovoked upon the sufferer's affections or stormed into the void created by the death of a child, a spouse or a parent, its effect was to draw him away from normal involvement in the emotional and social world around him. Melancholy men and women lost the capacity to take pleasure from activities they had previously delighted in or to enjoy the social relations that gave happiness to others ... The alienation of melancholy men and women from the pleasures of everyday life was symbolized in literature and in descriptions of actual sufferers by their love of solitude ... Melancholy made men and women inner exiles.[60]

Automated figures in the grottoes of the Royal Gardens at Saint-Germain-en-Lay, from Salomon de Caus, *Les raisons des forces mouvantes avec diverses machines tant utiles que plaisantes ausquelles sont adjoints plusioeurs desseigns de grotes et fontaines* (Frankfurt, 1615).

The only form of recreation available in Saint-Germain would have been the Royal Gardens, which had recently been designed for the Queen by her fountaineers, the Francini brothers. As well as a marvellous series of fountains, the gardens contained grottoes in which hydraulically-powered statues moved, danced, played music, and apparently even spoke.[61] This is of particular interest for two reasons. First, we have seen that Descartes' education at La Flèche was such as to encourage an interest in what might loosely be described as scientific novelties. If he did indeed live in Saint-Germain, then there can be little doubt that he would have been extremely interested in the Gardens and their grottoes, although if his mental health at this time was indeed delicate, one wonders about the wisdom of regular attendance at a place which Jaynes has described as dark and subterranean, 'connected by stone vaneted corridors', with 'high gloomy echoing chambers, flickering with torch light on their sculptured ceilings and walls and often filled with eerie music from an hydraulic mechanical organ or mechanical singing birds'.[62] Second, it is possible that it is the devices here that Descartes will describe later in *Traité de l'homme*[63] in the context of elaborating the theory that animals are automata. How

63

early Descartes considered such a theory we do not know, but Beeckman reports in 1631 that Descartes had held this view for a number of years, and since it is not mentioned in their extant correspondence, it is possibly something that Descartes mentioned to Beeckman during their time together at the end of 1618, as they did not meet again between then and the late 1620s. This is, of course, all highly speculative, but when one puts the elements of the account together, I do not think anything fits the evidence, and answers the questions, better: we have no reason to doubt Baillet's general claim that Descartes lived in Saint-Germain (although the details are admittedly often incorrect), and if so it is almost inconceivable that he would not have visited the grottoes, in which case, as is clear from the *Traité de l'homme*, reflection on the mechanical figures he found there, at some time between then and, say, the mid-1620s, at least reinforced the plausibility of, and perhaps even initiated, the view that animals are automata, although we shall see below that he never considered animals to be literally machines.

The next stage of Descartes' career is better served by the evidence. We can be certain that he studied law at Poitiers and we know he completed his examinations on 9 and 10 November 1616. A number of commentators have speculated that he may also have studied some medicine while he was there. He does say in the *Discours de la méthod* that he had studied jurisprudence and medicine prior to 1619,[64] and the fact that neither of these were taught as such in Jesuit colleges, and that he groups them together, suggests Poitiers as the most likely place. By the late 1620s he had certainly picked up some skills in dissection, compatible with at least an elementary training in medicine. Indeed, why he did not study medicine formally, given the family precedents in this area, and given his later intense interest in physiology, is very puzzling. However that may be, the course in which he was examined, and in which he received his baccalaureate and licentiate, was law, and there can be little doubt that he had a legal career in mind. In a letter to his father of 24 June 1625 (no longer extant but reported by Baillet) he describes his attempts to negotiate for the position of lieutenant-general in Châtellerault, but is reticent about asking his father in case he thinks it is too late for him to enter a legal career.[65] That he could still contemplate a legal career at such a late date indicates that this was an option he took seriously, although it is likely that it never held any real attractions for him. In many ways, the study of law would have been rather like a continuation of his classes in rhetoric and casuistic ethics, and it is quite possible that his later unhappiness with these areas may derive not just from his studies at La Flèche, but also from his legal studies at Poitiers. The dedication of the theses he defended for his law degree, only recently discovered, tells us that he 'thirsted for the broader rivers of eloquence most ardently. But as they make one crave more knowledge rather than quench one's thirst, they could not satisfy me in the least'.[66]

We know little of Descartes' whereabouts or activities in the period between November and the middle of 1618,[67] but in the summer of 1618 he went to join the army of Prince Maurice of Nassau in the Netherlands. Although this was the army of the Protestant Dutch Republic, it is not at all surprising that a French Catholic *gentilhomme* should choose to join it.[68] In the first place, there was an unstable truce between the Dutch and the French, and the explicit policy of Henri IV, and later on Richlieu, had been support of the Dutch against the Spanish. It was a completely proper, and indeed patriotic, thing for a French *gentilhomme* to do. In the second place, it was the Netherlands, rather than France, that had been the centre of humanism from the 1570s onwards. The Dutch universities had scholars of the calibre of Lipsius, Scaliger, Grotius, and Vossius, and their pupils were soon to be found in all the universities of Europe. Oestreich has admirably summed up the distinctive features of Dutch humanism as follows:

This later phase of humanism is, of course, more than a class culture . . . more than a school of superior education, of critical method and brilliant philological conjecture. No education which was confined to formal aesthetics, antiquarian learning or linguistic scholarship would have been adequate to the exigencies of this age of confessional conflict or could have counted on an overwhelmingly favourable response. The aim of the Netherlands movement was comprehensive learning and influence, a firm philosophical ideal, the political and military transformation of the community, the educating of men for action in this community, self-control and involvement, and . . . a scientific approach to wide areas of practical life.[69]

Lipsius' aim was to foster the values of will, reason, and discipline, along largely Stoic lines, and he encouraged rulers to bring large areas of public life under the control of the state, and above all to adopt an educative role. His *Politicorum Libri Sex* (1589), which combined a commitment to the humanist ideal of civility with a commitment to the practical politics of administration, army organization, and state finance, set out a comprehensive concept of discipline to serve as the basis for military reform, and a revamped Roman Stoic ethical ideal as the basis for morality and ideology in the new army. It was the *Politicorum* that first stimulated Dutch army reforms, and Lipsius was to receive a considerable sum of money from Maurice of Nassau and his cousins on the completion of the last two Books, on external and civil war respectively.[70] Indeed, the influence of his teaching is nowhere more evident than in the army reforms of his pupil, Maurice of Nassau, who was remarkably successful in establishing strict discipline and a professional ethos amongst his officers; and he was the first exponent of the new kind of professional army that one begins to find in the seventeenth century, the most notable features of which are the constant daily drills, whereby soldiers are kept exercised and active when not fighting, and the replacement of an (often unsuccessful) imposed discipline with the ideas of self-discipline and of obedience as a *decorum*, something becoming in a soldier. In this connection, it is worth remembering that changes in the nature of fortifications, especially during the sixteenth century, had changed the nature of warfare from open battle to siege and skirmish, and the kind of expertise required of officers correspondingly changed radically: as Hale has put it, 'the notion of an institutionalised military education began to erode that of the well-born individual's right to command on the basis of birth and a familiarity with horse and sword'.[71] One can find various proposals for the education of officers from the 1530s onwards, but no one pursued this quest as seriously as Maurice. Education played a crucial role in his army, and learning the art of war under Maurice would, for Descartes, have followed on naturally in some ways from his education at La Flèche. Indeed, the programme of Lipsius that set the precedents for the organization of Maurice's army was in many ways based on Lipsius' own Jesuit education at Cologne,[72] and the values fostered in Lipsius' writings had a number of parallels in the Christian values nurtured at La Flèche. Regulated and supervised activity was central to both, and even the terminology of jousting and the 'rules for bearing arms' of the daily and weekly *disputationes* at Jesuit colleges, for example, are mirrored in the extensive military metaphors in Lipsius, with arguments introduced in the form of regiments, bearing military colours and led by playing bands.[73]

Moreover, Descartes would have pursued some of the mathematical sciences while attached to the army, especially in the area of military architecture and fortifications, for Maurice not only actively encouraged scientific research—it was, for example, to Maurice that the inventor of the telescope, the Dutch lens-grinder Hans Lipperhey, had applied for a patent in 1608—but he had employed one of the greatest scientists and engineers of his age, Simon Stevin, to oversee the education of his army. Descartes tells Beeckman in a letter of 24 January 1619 that he has been engaging in 'painting, military architecture, and above all Flemish',[74] in the time spent with Maurice (a temporary truce ensured that he was not required to fight). Stevin, showing the striking confidence of Dutch humanism, believed that Flemish, rather than Latin, was the original language from which all others had developed, his reasons for holding this lying in his belief that, more than any other language, it was Flemish that contained the Lipsian quality of comprising simple and modest words of infinite power.[75] That Descartes took the trouble to learn Flemish has inclined some commentators to suggest that he may have studied directly under Stevin, but the fact that he had to ask Beeckman to translate a mathematical problem from Flemish for him in November indicates that his grasp of Flemish would not have been nearly sufficient to enable him to follow lectures in Flemish at this time. But even given these language difficulties, he probably built up a renewed familiarity with applied mathematics in Maurice's army, and this is something he could easily have ignored since leaving La Flèche four years earlier.

Nevertheless, Descartes' stay in this army was short-lived. He was clearly unhappy, and at the end of his *Compendium Musicae*, written in December 1618, he describes himself, despite the daily activities of Maurice's army, as being 'idle', and as being 'in the midst of turmoil and uneducated soldiers'.[76] By January 1619 he had left Maurice's army to join the forces of Maximilian I, another army modelled along the lines of Lipsius' reforms.[77] But his short time in Breda was to be of lasting significance, for it was there that he met Isaac Beeckman, from whom he learned a model of natural philosophy that was to shape all of his subsequent thinking on the subject, and which ultimately ensured that he was not to follow the career of a lawyer or a soldier, but was rather to devote himself to natural philosophy.

The Apprenticeship with Beeckman
1618–1619

The Meeting with Beeckman

While stationed just outside Breda, Descartes met and subsequently began a collaboration with Isaac Beeckman which was to be a formative event in his intellectual life. Beeckman, who was seven years Descartes' senior, was born in Middelburg. He had studied theology at Leiden between 1607 and 1610, but he made his living making candles and laying water conduits. In 1618 he graduated in medicine from the University of Caen, but he never practised medicine. Rather, he took up teaching and educational administration, first, from November 1619, at the Latin School at Utrecht, then at the Latin School at Rotterdam, and finally in Dordrecht. Descartes and Beeckman first met in Breda on 10 November, 1618. Beeckman had gone to Breda in October 'to assist Uncle Peter, and for courtship as well', as he puts it in his diary.[1] The two men reputedly entered into conversation when reading a placard which set out a mathematical problem. The placard was in Flemish, and Descartes asked Beeckman to translate it for him.[2]

More discussion evidently ensued, for Beeckman, in a diary entry for 11 November, records that the previous day he had met 'a Frenchman from Poitou' who had tried to prove to him that an angle is actually nothing. The proof runs along the following lines (see Fig. 3.1). An angle (abc) is a combination of two lines (ab and bc) and a point (b). The angle can be cut by a line (de) which divides the point into two parts. But the definition of a point requires that any part of a point is nothing, so the angle itself must be nothing. Beeckman notes that the argument rests on a sophism, namely the idea that the point can be divided into two parts, whereas in fact it is not a 'real magnitude'.[3] The issue is not one of any great mathematical subtlety, and Descartes' 'proof' tells us more about his love of puzzles and conundrums than his mathematical skills. In fact, it has more the air of a probe to test Beeckman than that of a genuine mathematical conjecture. And the probe was to be successful, in two respects. First, Descartes and Beeckman quickly established that they had interests in common. Beeckman notes not only that they were 'the only two people in Breda to speak Latin',[4] but, more importantly, virtually on meeting Descartes,

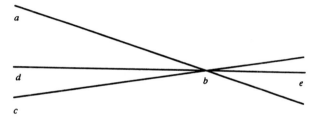

Fig. 3.1

he writes in his diary, under the heading 'Physico-mathematicians are very rare', that Descartes 'says he has never met anyone other than myself who pursues his studies in the way I do, combining Physics and Mathematics in an exact way. And for my part, I have never spoken with anyone apart from him who studies in this way'.[5] Second, the problem-solving mode provides the basis for the subsequent exchanges and collaboration between Descartes and Beeckman. Between November 1618 and early 1619, Descartes served what was effectively an apprenticeship with Beeckman. The routine seems to have been that, more often than not, Beeckman would set Descartes specific problems in mechanics and related areas, problems to which Beeckman himself sometimes knew the solution, and sometimes did not. But it was not just a teacher/pupil relationship. Beeckman was not an especially good mathematician, and he was keen to exploit Descartes' mathematical skills. Nevertheless, his contribution to the exercise was the more crucial, for he presented Descartes with a way of thinking about physical problems that was to form the basis for his own subsequent work in this area.

Beeckman's Micro-Corpuscularianism

Descartes worked with Beeckman on three extant projects during the brief period from November 1618 to early 1619. At this time, he also began independent work on the development and mathematical applications of different types of proportional compass, which we shall look at later in the chapter. A number of other topics were worked on in this period, principally mathematical problems, such as whether a chain hanging from two nails forms a curve describable by a conic section, or whether there is a method for giving a square equal to the root of another square. The three principal extant non-mathematical exercises deal respectively with the 'scientific' (as opposed to musicological or aesthetic) understanding of musical intervals, with the kinematic description of uniformly accelerated motion, and with problems in hydrostatics. In the case of the treatment of the first question, the approach is effectively one of mathematical reduction, with little attention to physical issues, and it forms by far the most conventional of the three exercises. The status of the work of free fall is more problematic, and there is some question as to whether the very significant problems that arise in Descartes' treatment derive from a mathematical reduction, or from an unsuccessful attempt to steer the exercise in the direction of dynamics. I shall suggest that the latter is in fact the case. The account of hydrostatics is above all else an example of the quantitative micromechanical explanation of a macroscopic phenomenon, and it marks the beginning of a serious and creative interest on Descartes' part in mechanical and natural-philosophical questions.

Before we look at these exercises some introduction to Beeckman's work may be helpful. His project can be summed up as the explanation of macro-geometrical regularities in terms of a micro-mechanical model, and he was almost certainly the first person in Europe to pursue this approach in detail. Largely self-taught, he seems to have developed his natural philosophy in a climate dominated by practical concerns—he had spent quite some time following his father's trade, laying water conduits for breweries, during the years between his graduation in theology and his time studying medicine at Caen—and by the time he came to study Aristotle's natural philosophy in 1631,[6] for example, he had already developed his own in some detail (not to mention setting up a *collegium mechanicum* to teach it to artisans), so that Aristotle can have looked to him little more than an historical curiosity. Nevertheless, his independence should not be exaggerated, for there was, from the late sixteenth century onwards, a Dutch tradition of practical mechanics, pursued in a mathematical vein, of which Stevin and Rudolph and Willebroed Snel were amongst the most illustrious representatives.[7] From this tradition derives Beeckman's insistence that macroscopic mechanical phenomena be explained in terms of microscopic mechanical processes which are essentially similar to them, in that they invoke entities and processes familiar to us from the macroscopic level,[8] as opposed to the Aristotelian procedure, which requires that the explanation invoke states or processes different in kind from those being explained. Mechanical processes, and physical processes more generally, have to be explained purely in mechanical terms, and this requires the postulation of a micro-mechanical level of explanation.[9] John Schuster has summed up Beeckman's approach admirably:

Apprenticeship with Beeckman, 1618–1619

No mechanic would appeal to teleological processes, occult virtues or immaterial causes to account for the functioning of a simple mechanical device. Explanations in the mechanical arts rested on the appeal to a clear picture of the structure and interaction of the constitutive parts of the apparatus. As simple mechanical and hydro-dynamical devices showed, only motion or pressure can produce the re-arrangement of parts and hence produce work, and, for theoretical purposes, the causes of motions and pressures are other motions, and pressures. What Beeckman demanded in natural philosophy was the application of the criteria of meaningful communication between mechanical artisans—the appeal to a picturable or im-aginable structure of parts whose motions are controlled within a theory of me-chanics. His central contention was that there is no point in talking about effects if you cannot imagine how they are produced, and the exemplar of imaginatively controlled efficacy is the mechanical arts where men do command nature at the macroscopic level. Beeckman's corpuscularianism reflected and reinforced these beliefs, because it permitted him to see on an ontological level that only motion need be asserted as the cause of motion, and that only displacement of parts need be asserted as the essence of change.[10]

There is shift from the macroscopic to the microscopic level here, and Beeckman shows an awareness of the mechanical problems involved in such scaling, for example, on the question of the significant change in the ratio of surface area to volume as the order of magnitude changes. But the context of his thought is very much that of a practical scientist rather than of a philosopher, and he ignores any metaphysical prob-lems about such scaling, such as whether redescribing macroscopic processes at the microscopic level, but in essentially the same kind of terms as one would describe them at the macroscopic level, can be said to have any genuine explanatory force. His approach was broadly in-strumentalist, and in this respect he was not unusual, for instrumentalism seems to have been the favoured view amongst mechanists (Descartes being, with qualifications, an exception), although Mersenne was, so far as I can tell, the only person in the first decades of the seventeenth century to mount an explicitly philosophical defence of it.[11]

Beeckman's natural philosophy is corpuscularian rather than straight-forwardly atomist, and it differs from traditional atomism in three respects. First, the atomism of Epicurus had been one that regarded the size and shape of atoms, and to a lesser extent the direction of their motion, as the features that carried explanatory weight: their speed, for example, carried no explanatory weight since atomic speed was the same for all atoms, irrespective of their circumstances. For Beeckman, and for seventeenth-century corpuscularians generally, it was above all speed and direction of motion that did the explanatory work. As often as not, atoms were thought of as invariant in shape, as spheres,[12] and while a few degrees of size were generally acknowledged, the different degrees were usually associated with distinctive properties which mirrored those distinctive properties of the traditional four elements to a greater or lesser extent. In Beeckman's case, this was to a greater extent, for he was keen to provide the theory of the elements with a suitable corpuscularian foundation. The reason for this, as Schuster has pointed out, is that it enabled him 'to de-emphasize atoms as explanatory elements in certain contexts'.[13] This brings us to the second difference between traditional atomism and Beeckman's corpuscularianism: whereas atoms have the ultimate explanatory role for the atomists,[14] as far as actually providing mechanical explanations is concerned it is conglomerations of atoms that provide the explanations for Beeckman (as they will, later in the century, for Boyle). Again, the reason for this derives purely from mechanical considerations. Atoms are perfectly hard, since they are by (implicit) definition simply regions of space fully occupied by matter. Perfectly hard bodies cannot rebound on impact, yet if any mechanical account of macroscopic phenomena is to be given purely in terms of microscopic parcels of matter in motion, then impact and elastic rebound must play a very significant role, for Beeckman is committed to the description of these microscopic processes purely in terms of the transfer of motion from one body to another as a result of impact. Indeed, the discovery of a satisfactory set of laws of impact was one of Beeckman's chief aims, something he returns to on a number of occasions in his diary. In an attempt to reconcile this approach with the inelasticity of atoms, he took elastic congeries of atoms and empty space as his fundamental mechanical entities.[15] These are Beeckman's corpuscles; it is these that possess the requisite mechanical properties, and it is to these that macroscopic phenomena are to be reduced in order that their properties be explained. Third, the very fact that speed and direction of motion were taken to be the basic explanatory features, rather than shape and size, indicates a significant difference in the style and difficulty of the explanations sought, and a shift to quantitative factors. Although shape and size are quantifiable in principle, shape was in fact never quantified at all, and size only in a rough and ready way, in the traditional atomist accounts, with the consequence that their 'explanations' invariably comprised highly qualitative reductions of macroscopic phenomena. Beeckman is committed to a genuinely quantitative account, and many features of traditional atomism, like surface features of atoms such as hooks, were as alien to his approach as anything in Aristotle.

Beeckman applied this corpuscularian natural philosophy in a number of areas, including hydrostatics, optics, gravitation, and acoustics. In each case the aim was to effect a reduction of the phenomena to a micro-corpuscular model in which impact was the sole form of action, and in which transfer of motion was the sole outcome of this action. Descartes may well have been thinking along the lines Beeckman was pursuing when he met him but, when one looks over the entries in Beeckman's diary from 1604 onwards, it soon becomes clear that it is extremely unlikely that Descartes, by the time of this meeting, would have reached anything like the comprehension of Beeckman's vision. It is also worth noting that this is a vision that he had already had some success in realizing, for from as early as 1613 we can find sophisticated discussions of inertia and free fall in the diary entries. This is important because of Descartes' later attempts to play down Beeckman's influence on his own thinking: there can be no doubt that Beeckman was far ahead of Descartes at their meeting and that, although he quickly caught up with and overtook his teacher/collaborator, Descartes did learn a great deal from him.

It is impossible to establish a strict chronology for the three roughly contemporaneous exercises that Descartes completed either with Beeckman or under his supervision, but we have some clues. We have a firm date of completion for the work on music, which was finished by the end of 1618. The fragments on falling bodies are, on internal evidence, the result of a very early collaboration between Beeckman and Descartes. In his statement of the problem of falling bodies, Descartes refers to Beeckman as 'a very ingenious man' whom he had 'met a few days ago',[16] and in Beeckman's report of Descartes' response in his diary he had originally left a blank, where he later filled in Descartes' name (wrongly spelled), suggesting that he did not know or could not remember it.[17] The manuscript on hydrostatics shows the influence of Beeckman to the greatest extent. I think it is impossible that it could have been completed before the work on falling bodies, assuming that this was written soon after their meeting; and I also believe that, had Descartes been aware of the micro-mechanical theories he deploys in the hydrostatics manuscript at the time he completed the *Compendium Musicae*, he would probably have been aware of Beeckman's micro-corpuscular theory of sound, whereas we know that he was not aware of this, adding a revision which takes the theory into account only after the completion of the manuscript. It would therefore seem reasonable to conclude that the hydrostatics manuscript was the last of the three to be written.[18] The relative priorities of the writings on music and free fall are somewhat indeterminate, as the latter could well have been written over a six-month period, whereas the latter was completed in 'a few days', as Descartes puts it. I shall treat the two more conventional exercises, on music and falling bodies, first, and then go on to consider the hydrostatics manuscript.

Compendium Musicae

The *Compendium Musicae* was presented to Beeckman as a gift for New Year's Day, 1619.[19] It is a short treatise, running to about thirty pages, and it may have been begun before Beeckman and Descartes met, but no earlier than the summer of 1618; and it was certainly completed during December 1618.[20] Beeckman, although familiar with little more than congregational singing, was intensely interested in the more scientific aspects of harmonic theory and acoustics.[21] He had developed a corpuscular theory of sound and a pulsation theory of its transmission during the 1610s; he was the first to offer a geometrical proof of the inverse proportionality between string length and frequency (1614/5); and he had offered an ingenious and elaborate explanation of consonance, in terms of his corpuscular theory of sound, by arguing that sound 'globules' were emitted from a vibrating string only intermittently, and that the periods of sound and silence coincided only when notes of the same frequency (pitch) were sounded together simultaneously, the two periods becoming less regular in relation to one another as the intervals between the two notes moved across the spectrum from consonance to dissonance.

Descartes, on the other hand, was something of a novice in the area. Like Beeckman, his practical musical skills were probably not great. Such skills would usually have been picked up in choral training, but La Flèche did not have a choir, the Jesuits having dispensed with them in their schools, although High Mass was sung on Sundays and feast days.[22] He says later that he cannot distinguish an octave from a fifth, which is a somewhat major musical disability (even when one takes into account that he is thinking of the 'sweeter' fifth of just intonation, rather than that of an equal-tempered scale). As regards musical theory, he had certainly studied some theory at school as part of the mathematical studies of the second year of the philosophical curriculum, and was familiar with the standard work of Zarlino. Indeed, the *Compendium* relies extensively on Zarlino, and it may be helpful to mention what his contribution was before we examine what Descartes does with it.

Although musical theory, considered as a scientific or mathematical discipline describing combinations of sounds, had been a part of the *quadrivium*, medieval musicians did not generally take much notice of its dictates, preferring instead to develop their own compositional rules. During the Renaissance, however, the situation changed, and the first major musical treatise in the new humanist genre was Giossefo Zarlino's *Istituzioni harmoniche* (1558), which, following the usual practice, offered an arithmetical account of musical intervals. The traditional theory of consonance—that of the Pythagoreans—had restricted consonances to the combinations produced by the ratios of string length within the first four numbers (the so-called *tetractys*), so that an octave is 1:2 (giving us the sounds produced by a full string and that string stopped exactly half way), a fifth 2:3, and a fourth 3:4. Zarlino enlarged the classification to include the first six numbers (the so-called *senario*), arguing that there was nothing sacred about the number four, as many Pythagoreans had believed. Rather, if any number had special properties it was the number six: six is the first perfect number (that is, it was the first number to be the sum of all the factors into which it could be resolved), the number of days taken by God to create the world, the number of zodiac signs always in our hemisphere, the number of the substantial qualities of elements, the number of species of movement, the number of directions, and so on.[23]

In the *Compendium*, Descartes provides an arithmetical account of consonance which follows that of Zarlino, rejecting some aspects of the reasoning behind the *senario*, but ultimately producing something that differs from it only in minor respects. He begins by maintaining that there are two principal attributes of sound, its duration and its pitch (*intensionis*), everything else coming in the domain of physics and being excluded from the treatise.[24] Consequently, what we are presented with (with one exception) is a purely mathematical account of consonance, and the principal respect in which Descartes goes beyond Zarlino lies in the representation of the mathematical ratios. Whereas Zarlino represents them in the form of numerals, Descartes presents them as segments of line lengths. This is a traditional form of representation of numbers, but it will take on an entirely new significance in Descartes, and the way in which he uses it here is of some interest. All senses, he tells us, are capable of experiencing pleasure, and this pleasure must be 'a proportional relation of some kind between the object and the sense itself'.[25] The more complex the proportional relation, however, the less pleasing it will be to the senses;[26] an object is perceived more easily when 'the difference between its parts is smaller', and this turns out to be the case where 'they are more proportionate to one another'. Then Descartes tells us about this proportion:

This proportion must be arithmetic and not geometric[27] because in the former there is less to perceive, as all differences are equal, and so in trying to perceive everything distinctly the sense will not be so strained. For example, the proportion that obtains between

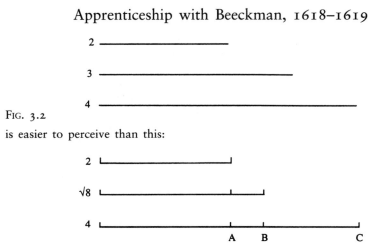

FIG. 3.2

is easier to perceive than this:

FIG. 3.3

for in the first case one only needs to perceive that the difference between any two [adjacent] lines is the same, whereas in the second example one needs to compare the incommensurable parts AB and BC, and therefore, I believe, there is no way in which they can be perceived perfectly at once, but only in relation to an arithmetic proportion, by realising that AB consists of two parts, whereas BC consists of three.[28]

What is of most interest here is the introduction of the question of clarity of representation right from the very start: a clarity which consists in our being able to grasp magnitudes at a glance. This ability to represent something to oneself so that it can be grasped at a glance is one which is going to figure very prominently in Descartes' subsequent thought, and its appearance here is worth noting.

In the present context, what the clarity is to reveal is the quantitative aspects of musical relations. When he gives musical examples, Descartes' labelling of the notes is at first puzzling. In discussing whole tones and semitones, for example, he gives the illustration reproduced as Fig. 3.4.[29] The letters here do not designate the names of the notes, but refer to the labelling of the divisions of a line length and have no musical connotation whatsoever. This is a revealing sign, and the whole aim of the treatise is a generally reductive, mathematical description of musical intervals. The principal way in which this is achieved is to associate each note of the scale with a number (Fig. 3.5).[30] Note that the numbers here do not represent something real, such as cycles per second, but something purely conventional, the base number being chosen simply on the grounds that it enables us to avoid fractions. Also, larger numbers represent lower pitches, because they are a notional measure of string lengths. The mathematical representation of an interval is then given by a ratio of the two numbers associated with the

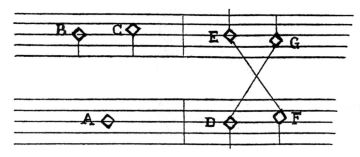

FIG. 3.4

Fig. 3.5

	♭ molle.	♮ quadratum.
E	la	72
D	sol	80 vel 81
C	fa	90
B ♭	mi	96
A	la re	108
G	sol ut	120
F	fa	135
E	mi	144
D	la re	160 vel 162
C ♯	sol ut	♯ 180
B ♭	fa	192
A	mi	216
G	re	240
F / E	ut	270 / 288
D		320 vel 324
C		360
B	&c. 405	384
A	432	432
G	480 vel 486	480
F	540	540

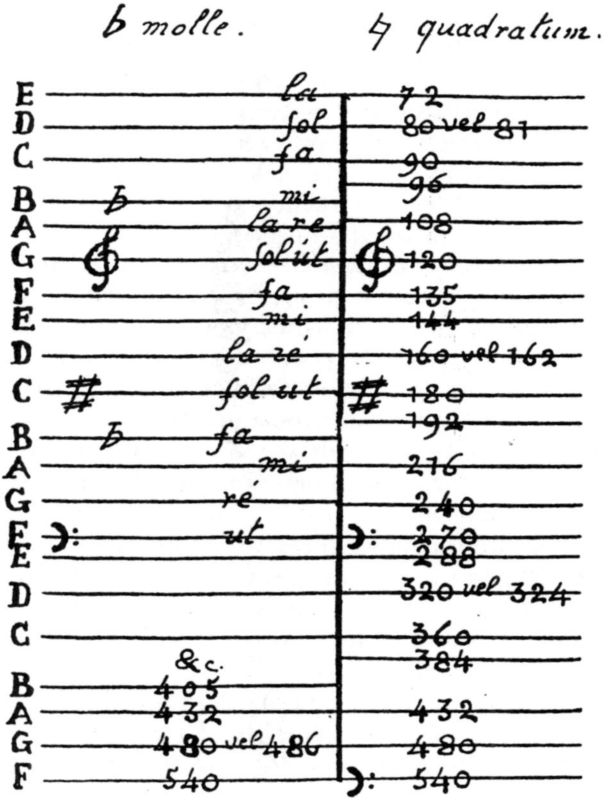

FIG. 3.5

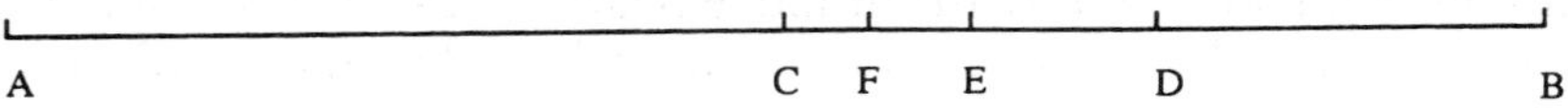

FIG. 3.6

notes, written with the lower number in the numerator. There is nothing here that goes beyond Zarlino, and, as Cohen has noted, the whole enterprise is very tradition-bound, blindly sticking to the diatonic scale, for example, with little or no appreciation of chromatic alteration.[31] But the procedure for generating intervals is different from that of Zarlino, and takes the form of continued bisection of a string AB (see Fig. 3.6).[32] The first bisection, at C, produces the octave, represented as AC-AB (1:2). Dividing CB at its mid-point D yields AC-AD, a fifth (2:3); and a further bisection at E yields the major third, AC-AE (4:5). What is interesting about this account is that Descartes introduces non-mathematical considerations to confirm a mathematical account. Note that only three intervals have been generated up to this point: the octave, the fifth, and the major third. Or rather, these are, in Descartes' terminology, the only intervals that have been 'properly' generated, for others have been 'accidentally' generated. In bisecting CB at D, two lengths are actually yielded: the one we seek, AC-AD, and a residual one, as it were, namely DB, which happens to be a fourth. Similarly, when we make the bisection at E, 'all remaining consonances' are yielded. At this point, Descartes justifies the distinction between 'proper' and 'accidental' in terms of the phenomenon of sympathetic vibration. When we pluck the string of a lute, he tells us, all higher strings which are at a fifth or a major third (or, of course, an octave) above the note will vibrate, but not those which are at a fourth or any of the other consonances (minor thirds, and major and minor sixths). Within limits, this does indeed happen.[33]

But this move into the physical realm is an isolated occurrence in the *Compendium*. Moreover, it is not followed up in physical terms. Rather, the reason he gives for the phenomenon is mathematical: 4 and 6 are simply multiples of 2 and 3, and, following Zarlino, he sees factors as having a special significance. It is true that, later in the *Compendium*, he does very briefly mention a physical explanation of sympathetic resonance in terms of the 'strokes' by which the sound strikes the ear,[34] but we now know this to be an addition to the completed manuscript made at the urging of Beeckman.[35] It is an anomalous addition to an otherwise mathematical account that really goes little way to solving the problems of Zarlino's original *senario* theory.

The *senario* account had the advantage that it allowed the inclusion of the major third (4:5), minor third (5:6), and major sixth (3:5). But this did not really capture the intuitive relative ranking of consonances, and Zarlino realized it was necessary to include the minor sixth, which could also serve as a consonance, even though it came outside the *senario*, since its ratio was 5:8. Even worse, if, as seems natural, one took the degree of dissonance to be directly proportional to the magnitude of the product of the integers making up the ratio, then the diminished fifth (5:7), which no one recognized as consonant, turned out to be more consonant than the minor sixth! Moreover, even if some way of mitigating these discrepancies could be found, why impose a restriction on the number of consonances in the first place? The postulation of an absolute discontinuity between the consonances and dissonances seems both contrary to what we actually hear and completely arbitrary. Worst of all, on Zarlino's account it remained a complete mystery how the mind was supposed to be aware of these ratios. The Pythagoreans had argued in terms of a numerological account which connected the ratios of the consonances with the properties of the mind, and in a similar way Kepler was arguing that consonances are derived from regular polygons inscribed in a circle, and that God had created the universe on geometrical archetypes and had implanted these in people's souls.[36] Zarlino was unattracted by such doctrines, but he provided no account at all of how the mathematical ratios defining the consonances could be translated into the psychological experiences of sweetness or pleasure by which the mind responded to them, still less of the more general question of how music is able to produce emotional effects in listeners.

Descartes does nothing to resolve these difficulties, except perhaps to abandon the numerological basis for the restriction of the number of consonances, although he himself works with a criterion which is arbitrary, since he has, for example, no theoretical reason to count diminished fifths or whole tones as dissonances.[37] In response to the increasingly recognized difficulties with Zarlino's treatment, the arithmetical account of consonance was being abandoned by thinkers like Benedetti, Vincenzo Galilei, and Beeckman, and replaced by the theory that consonance is due to coincidence in the vibrations of sound waves, or sound pulses, so that the traditional hierarchy of consonances in descending order of octave, fifth, fourth, etc., is due to the decreasing regularity of coincidences. The theory has the great advantage over the arithmetical account that it actually provides some explanation of our perception of consonances. Moreover, it does not impose any arbitrary restriction upon the number of consonances; instead, there is a gradual move from consonance to dissonance as the regularity of the coincidence decreases. Descartes is oblivious to such developments in the *Compendium*. He stays firmly within the realms of mathematics, evidently either unable or unwilling to make the crucial transition to a consideration of the problem in terms of the physical nature of sound.

Falling Bodies

Turning now to Descartes' treatment of free fall, the kinematic description of uniformly accelerated motion was an exercise in which a number of natural philosophers had engaged in the late sixteenth and early seventeenth centuries, and consideration of the topic goes back at least to the work of the Merton School in the first part of the fourteenth century.[38] It was widely recognized that free fall took the form of uniformly accelerated motion under some circumstances, most notably fall in a void, although Galileo was the first to establish this in detail in his *Two New Sciences* of 1638. The question had immense theoretical significance because quantitative mechanics up to this point had been largely restricted to statics, which deals with bodies in a state of equilibrium, whereas an account of free fall clearly involves the treatment of moving bodies, either in terms simply of an account of that motion (kinematics), or in terms of the forces responsible for it (dynamics). Beeckman had been concerned with the kinematic problem of free fall as early as 1613. He believed that bodies fall because they are attracted by the earth (although he did not understand the nature of this attraction), and he believed that this fall took the form of a uniform acceleration because (i) once a body has been set in motion it continues to move at the same rate, and (ii) at each instant of the fall there is a renewed attraction of the earth on the body, and so a new increment of speed is added to that which the body already has. But Beeckman was puzzled by the mathematics of the situation, and in 1618/19 he called upon Descartes' help.[39]

Beeckman asks Descartes how to determine the distance the stone will fall in one hour if one knows how far it will fall in two hours, assuming the principle that a moving body will move eternally in a void, and assuming that there is such a void between the earth and the falling stone. He then presents Descartes' reply in the following terms (see Fig. 3.7). Letting AC stand for two hours and AD for one hour, the distance covered in one hour will be, say, ADEF and that in two hours AFEGBHCD, where AFEGBHCD = ACB + AFE + EGB = ACB + 2AFE, and consequently:

if the moment is AIRS the proportion of space to space will be ADE with *klmn* to ACB with *klmnopqt*, that is, the double of *klmn*. Thus, since the proportion of space traversed consists in the proportion of the one triangle to the other, equal magnitudes being added to each term of the proportion, and since these equal

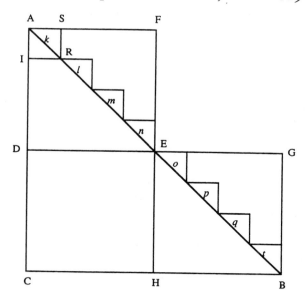

FIG. 3.7

added magnitudes decrease in proportion to the decrease in the moments of space, it follows that these added magnitudes will be reduced to zero. Now this is the moment of space traversed by the body. It remains, therefore, that the space traversed by the body in one hour is to the space traversed by it in two hours as the triangle ADE is to the triangle ACB. This was shown by M. Per[r]on [Descartes], when I gave him the opportunity by asking him if it could be determined how much space is traversed in an hour, if the space traversed in two hours is known, granting my principle *that, in a void, what is once set in motion continues in motion for ever*, and assuming that there is a void between the earth and the falling stone. If, then, in an experiment the body falling for two hours covered 1,000 feet, the triangle ABC would contain 1,000 feet. The root of this is 100 for the line AC, which corresponds to two hours. Bisection at D gives AD, which corresponds to one hour. To the double proportion AC to AD, which is 4:1, corresponds ACB to ADE, which is 1,000 to 250.[40]

In other words, it has been shown that, for a body falling in a void, the spaces traversed are proportional to the squares of the times. Before we look at what contribution Descartes actually makes to this solution of the problem, three points are worth noting about Beeckman's principle. First, Beeckman's formulation of the problem inquires how far a body will fall in one hour if we know how far it will fall in two, rather than asking how far a body will fall in two hours if we know how far it will fall in one, which might seem more natural to us. This suggests that he is following the traditional Aristotelian conception of

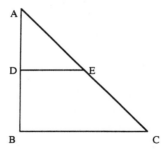

FIG. 3.8

motion as a process between two termini, so that in specifying the motion it is always necessary to specify its starting point and its end point, even though we have every reason to believe that he does not share the teleological conception of motion that motivates the process view. Second, the principle cannot be treated as a statement of the Newtonian principle of inertia because, as stated, it covers any kind of motion in a void, including circular motion, for example. Beeckman confines his attention to change of speed, and says nothing which indicates that he would treat change of direction as physically significant.[41] Third, the principle is also indeterminate in another respect. As it stands, it is compatible with two readings: on the first, a body will remain in uniform motion in a void in the absence of any forces acting on it; on the second, a body will remain in uniform motion in a void in the absence of any external forces, but the motion may be due to an internal force which is preserved in motion in a void. Descartes, as we shall see, will assume the second reading, but Beeckman does not seem to see that there is anything at issue here.

The first thing Descartes does in his response is to transform (apparently quite unwittingly) Beeckman's question from one about the relation between time and distance traversed into one about how one plots the trajectory of the body against its speed. He writes:

I have solved the problem. In the right angled isosceles triangle [see Fig. 3.8], ABC represents the space (the motion); the inequality of the space from point A to the base BC is the inequality of the motion. Therefore, AD will be covered in the time represented by ADE, and DB in the time represented by DEBC, it being noted that the smaller space here represents the slower motion. And ADE is one third of DEBC, so AD will be covered three times as slowly as DB. But the problem could have been posed in a different way: Suppose the attractive force of the earth remains the same as at the first moment, and that a new one is produced, the first remaining. In that case a pyramid [that is, a series of cubes rather than squares] would be the solution to the problem.[42]

What has happened here is that the problem has been reinterpreted in such a way that the line ADB, which for Beeckman represented (the square of) the time elapsed, is taken by Descartes to represent the trajectory covered. And ADE and ABC, which represent the 'moments' of space traversed (*momenti spatii*) for Beeckman, are interpreted by Descartes as the sums of the speed acquired, which he terms *minima* or *punctii motus*. Because of this, Descartes is led to the disastrous conclusion that, since the sum of speeds or 'total motions' is three times as great, the space DB will be covered three times as quickly. But this is wrong, for the 'total motions' do not increase as a linear function of the space traversed, and so cannot be represented by a triangle. However, just as Descartes had reinterpreted Beeckman's problem, so Beeckman, in considering Descartes' reply, reinterpreted this back into his own terms, apparently without even noticing what he was doing. He assumed that Descartes had plotted the increase in time along AD in Fig. 3.8, and the increase in speed along BC, so that the area traversed in one hour to the distance traversed in two hours is as the area of triangle ADE to triangle ABC. This yields the correct answer to his original problem!

At least part of the source of Descartes' misunderstanding here lies in the fact that Beeckman presents the problem as if it were a purely kinematic exercise, and Descartes, in his attempt to open up the question of the forces at work, is led to try to steer the problem in a different direction; but he is unable to do this successfully, and he ends up missing the crucial kinematic connection between distance traversed and time. Now in fact both Beeckman and Descartes have rudimentary dynamical models lying behind their accounts. In Beeckman's case, there is a micro-corpuscular model of the basis of his treatment. This becomes clear when we consider what he means by a 'moment'. It would be natural to assume that a moment is an interval of time, so that during each moment a constant tractive force acts continuously, resulting in an increase in speed, and consequently in the traversal of a greater distance than in the previous moment. But in fact, the way he conducts his discussion suggests that he is thinking of instantaneous increments of motion imparted *at the beginning* of each moment, and indeed, he does ultimately think of this tractive force as being caused by corpuscular collisions,[43] which would indeed result in discrete, as opposed to continuous, increments.

Descartes' terminology, on the other hand, suggests that he is concerned to incorporate into his account some treatment of the nature of the force responsible for the continued increase in motion. In the account in the *Physico-mathematica* manuscript, Descartes describes the situation in terms of the 'force' (*vis*) which, when added to the body at each moment, causes a new 'increment of motion' (*minimum motus*). Beeckman's principle of inertia stated that reiterated applications of a tractive force resulted in added increments of motion which were then conserved. Descartes thinks of this situation in terms of the reiterated addition of internal moving forces, where these forces are the causes, not just of the continued acceleration, but of the continued motion as such. Here Descartes appears to be following the version of *impetus* theory defended in Toletus and the Coimbra commentaries on Aristotle's *Physics* that he would have studied at La Flèche.[44] What he is invoking is the Aristotelian notion whereby a body will continue in uniform rectilinear motion only if there is a force (external in the strict Aristotelian case, internal in the case of *impetus* theory) maintaining that motion. Note, however, that this kind of explanation is not in conflict with the micro-corpuscularianism of Beeckman's account. As Beeckman's micro-corpuscularianism stands, there is no inconsistency in filling out the result of impact in the dynamical terms provided by *impetus* theory, although Beeckman himself would have been resistant to the explicit introduction of such quasi-Aristotelian notions.[45] Nevertheless, I doubt whether Descartes is thinking in terms of reconciling an *impetus* account with a micro-corpuscular model, for there is no evidence that he is even familiar with such an account here. Beeckman has not yet introduced him to his micro-mechanism, and when he does Descartes' whole approach undergoes a significant change of direction.

Hydrostatics

The hydrostatics manuscript, *Aquae comprimentis in vase ratio reddita à D. Des Cartes*, to give it Beeckman's full title,[46] is a response to a question from Beeckman, and is a good example of the style of collaboration between Beeckman and Descartes, the former setting the latter precise mechanical problems and offering guidance. The procedure pays off handsomely, and the result is something which not only goes well beyond anything in the *Compendium* or in the work on falling bodies, but lays down a procedure for dealing with mechanical problems that Descartes will subsequently reflect on, develop, and build upon. Indeed, it is a seminal text. As Schuster has pointed out, 'certain concepts and modes of argument appear in the manuscript which will constitute the essence of Cartesian micro-mechanism in optics, cosmology, physiology, and natural philosophy generally, after being refined over the next fifteen years through practice, criticism, and deliberate metaphysical reconstruction'.[47]

The four hydrostatic problems with which Descartes deals, at

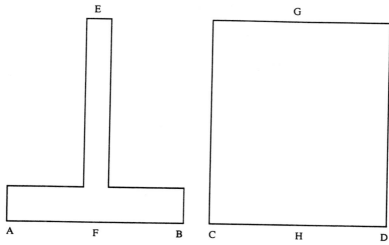

Fig. 3.9

Beeckman's instigation, all derive from Stevin.[48] We can restrict our attention to one of them, the so-called 'hydrostatic paradox', which shows that a fluid, by means of its pressure, can exert a total pressure on the bottom of its container that is many times greater than its weight. Consider two vessels (Fig. 3.9), EAB and GCD, having equal bases AB and CD, and equal heights EF and GH. GCD has ten times the capacity of EAB, and intuitively we might correspondingly expect that when the vessels are both filled, the first with, say, one pound of water, and the second with ten pounds, then the force the one pound of water exerts will be a tenth of that exerted by the ten pounds, on their respective bases, AB and CD. But Stevin shows that the force exerted will in fact be the same in the two cases, and he proves that the force is in fact proportional to the size of the base and the height of the water, or more exactly, that 'on any bottom of the water being parallel to the horizon there rests a weight equal to the gravity of the water, the volume of which is equal to that of the prism whose base is that bottom and whose height is the vertical from the plane through the water's upper surface to the base'.[49]

Stevin argues the case purely in macroscopic terms, following the traditional treatments of statical problems offered by the Alexandrian mathematicians. The core of the argument consists of an ingenious thought-experiment (see Fig. 3.10). He begins with a container, ABCD, full of water, and divides it up into portions, one of which, MIFE, he treats as if it were 'solid water'. Having shown that the body, whatever its shape, will remain in the water at equilibrium, irrespective of its

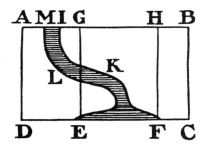

Fig. 3.10

position, he then shows that the water pressure in any channel in MIFE in contact with the base is independent of the shape of the channel and depends only on the height. In order to balance the pressure thereby exerted, a much greater quantity of water would be needed; and conversely, only a small amount of water is needed to support a far greater weight.

Descartes approaches the problem in a completely different way to Stevin. He accepts Stevin's demonstration, but he attempts to explain what happens, not in terms of a comparison of gross weights and volumes, as Stevin does, but in terms of the mechanical behaviour of the totality of 'points' making up the system. What he hopes to show is that the paradox is explained in terms of a demonstration that the force on each point on the bottom of the containers in Fig. 3.9 is equal, so that the force is equal over two equal areas.[50] He introduces three assumptions as a basis for this demonstration.[51] The first is that we can confine consideration of the water 'weighing down' to the weight of water on the bottom of the vessel, and the weight of the vessel and the water in it. Note, however, that when he comes to the demonstration, the weight of the water is not conceived in macroscopic terms as the weight of the whole minus the weight of the vessel, but rather as something more like the sum of all the forces exerted by the water at the base of the vessel on the base. In other words, there is either some kind of assumed translation between weight and force, or a reduction of weight to force. The second assumption supports the latter reading. We are told explicitly that 'weighing down' is to be understood as 'the force of motion by which a body is impelled in the first instant of its motion'. Even though the water 'weighing down' on the bottom of the vessel is not in motion, if the bottom of the vessel were removed the water would fall, and because of this Descartes is assuming that the water on the bottom of the vessel can be treated as being in virtual motion. The third assumption elaborates on the relation between weight,

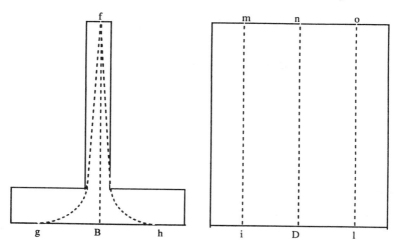

FIG. 3.11

motion, and force. It states that the 'weight', or force of motion of a body in its first instant of fall, is a function of both the 'quantity' of the body and its speed. Since the 'quantity' of a body is what would normally be considered its weight, it seems that Descartes is construing force of motion as a function of weight in this sense. Whatever the exact relation is, however, it is clear that weight is a form of virtual motion, and the crucial general point here is that apparently primitive, gross magnitudes are defined by a functional relationship, a relationship that is explicated in micro-mechanical terms.

What Descartes is seeking to show in these assumptions, and in the subsequent demonstration, is that weight is not a gross macroscopic given quantity but is rather a mechanical force whose operation can be described at the microscopic level. The nature of this mechanical force is not straightforward, however. In setting out the third assumption, he says that 'if one atom of water about to descend would be twice as fast as two other atoms, the one atom alone will weigh as much as the other two together', and not, as we might expect, 'if one atom of water descends twice as fast as two other atoms, the one atom alone weighs as much as the other two together'. This is not a grammatical idiosyncrasy on Descartes' part, but an indication of the fact that he is concerned not with motion but with an instantaneous tendency to motion. Indeed, his demonstration depends crucially on the representation of these tendencies to motion in terms of geometrical lines. Consider two containers, B and D, filled with water (Fig. 3.11). Descartes' aim is to demonstrate that the force on each point at the

87

base of B and D is equal, and since the areas of the bases are equal, the total force on the bases will be equal. The demonstration works by showing that there is a line connecting points on the surface with points on the base. This line (represented in the diagram by the dotted line) is a line of tendency to motion, a motion which would be propagated along the line by being transmitted from point to point:

I maintain that these points [g, b, H on the base] are pressed upon by an equal force, because it is evident that they are each pressed upon by what we can imagine as lines of water of the same length, from the top of the vase to its bottom. For the line fg should not be considered to be longer than fB or another line. It does not press down upon point g in respect to the parts by which it is curved and longer, but only in respect to those parts by which it tends downwards, in which respect it is equal to all the others.[52]

In the case of container D, it is plausible that each point on the surface should have a unique line of 'tendency to motion' to a point on the base, and that these should be of equal length. But in the case of container B, Descartes seems to be working on the assumption that the area at the base of the container is three times that of the top, and that for each point on the top there are three corresponding points on the bottom. Then, since the only physically significant component of this line is that which acts vertically downwards, and since the vertical component in fg and fB and fh is the same, the force given by the tendency to motion will be the same. But no justification whatsoever is given for the mapping from f to g, B, and h, and the subsequent demonstration depends upon this, for we are next asked to imagine the case where g, B, and h are removed; then 'point f alone would occupy a lower position just as equally as would the points m, n, o, if the three points i, D, l were expelled'. The demonstration is then given:

Therefore, point f alone presses upon the three points simultaneously with a force equal to that by which the three discrete points press the other three i, D, l . . . Therefore, the force by which point f alone presses upon the lower ones is equal to the force of the points m, n, o taken together.[53]

In other words, we are asked to imagine the point f descending through the fluid and out the bottom of the container, and the aim is to show that f will descend with equal ease through any of the three points on the base, in just the same way that m, n, and o descend along their unique paths.

As Schuster has pointed out, there is here what he terms a 'three-fold displacement from what we might consider the original terms of the problem'.[54] First, an *ad hoc* mapping is provided which represents the proposed 'tendencies to motion' as geometrical lines, which are then analysed to provide the solution. Second, a hypothetical void, which takes the form of the line representing the tendency to motion, is opened up in the fluid, and the point passes along this. Third, the part of the fluid not opened up is hypothetically solidified (in so far as it does not pour into the void that has just been opened up). We have a curious shift here between the geometrical representation of the direction of a force, and the physical passage of what can only be considered as a corpuscle through an evacuated tube. The physical passage is free fall in the case of vessel D, and also in the case of fB, and the argument seems to work on the assumption of free fall, but surely in the cases of fg and fh the corpuscle/point must be a rolling or sliding, and we get no account whatsoever of these motions, which are dynamically quite distinct from free fall (and from one another). Moreover, the direction of the geometrical line seems, in fact, to be determined by the physical end point of the tube, whereas if the 'demonstration' is to be at all convincing, then it is surely the tendency to motion that should determine the path. After all, we surely want to know why the point f has an effect on points g, B, and h, and not, say, on another three points, or on a different number of points. The 'demonstration' simply assumes what needs to be shown. And if that were not enough, what about the regions above g and h? No lines of force or tendency to motion are mapped from these, but surely corpuscles in these regions have weight and tend downwards: there is simply no reason why the upper surface on which f lies should be the only one from which lines of force or tendency to motion can be traced.

The exercise is, nevertheless, an interesting one. As well as providing a conception of weight as virtual motion, or more precisely instantaneous tendency to motion, which will play an important role in Le Monde, it has a more general significance: it attempts to combine a geometrical representation of a problem with a micro-mechanical model of it. Deficient as this combination might be in the present case,[55] what we have here is Descartes' first attempt to approach mechanical problems in a way that, with subsequent refinements, was to form the basis for his conception of physical explanation. Indeed, the cosmological optics of Le Monde would draw in a strikingly direct way upon this type of analysis.

Proportional Compasses and the Idea of a Mathesis Universalis

Beeckman left Breda just before the end of December 1618, but he and Descartes were in correspondence until the early 1620s, and there are five letters from Descartes to Beeckman extant, as well as a draft of one from Beeckman to Descartes, from the first five months of 1619. The letters provide invaluable information about Descartes' projects, and throw some light on his state of mind at this time as well as on his personal relations with Beeckman.

There is a genuine warmth in the letters. In the first extant letter, of 24 April 1619, he writes to Beeckman:

I have received your letter, which I was waiting for, and I was delighted to observe, right from the start, the notes of music in it: what clearer way could there be to show that you remember me? But I was expecting something else, more important, as well: what have you been doing, what are you doing now, and how are you? For I am interested not only in your studies but in yourself as well, and, take my word for it, not just in your mind, although that is the most important thing, but also in you in your entirety.[56]

The letter continues as one would write to a close friend. It is the Muses, he tells Beeckman, that have brought the two of them together 'in a bond of friendship that will never die'.[57] As the correspondence develops, however, Beeckman is cast more in the role of a mentor and confessor. In the next letter we have, dated 26 March, he tells Beeckman, for example:

As for my journeys, the last one went well, all the more as it seemed to be more dangerous, above all when I left your island. The first day, in Vlessingen, the winds forced us to return to port, but the following day, setting off in a much smaller boat, I encountered an even fiercer storm. Nevertheless, I was more pleased than frightened, for it was an occasion to prove myself. I have never attempted a sea crossing, and I made it without getting sick, becoming all the braver for the longer voyage.[58]

And further on in the same letter, he tells Beeckman that, in travelling to Bohemia, he will take along a servant and 'perhaps a few companions', and makes the point that he is telling him this so that Beeckman 'will not be afraid' for him.[59] In the letter of 23 April, he acknowledges his debt to Beeckman, telling him that he will acknowledge him 'as the initiator of my work and its first author', and he continues:

For you are indeed the one person who has shaken me out of my nonchalance and made me remember what I had learned and almost forgotten. When my mind strayed far from serious concerns, it was you who guided it back down the correct path. If, therefore, by accident I propose something which is not contemptible, you have every right to claim it for yourself.[60]

There is not a lot to go on here, but my own impression on reading the correspondence is that Descartes sees Beeckman as at least an older and wiser man, and perhaps even as a father figure, despite the fact that he was only eight years Descartes' senior: it is worth remembering here that the sheltered and very paternalistic upbringing he received at

Apprenticeship with Beeckman, 1618–1619

La Flèche would have meant that Descartes would have probably come to personal maturity relatively late. Ten years later, as we shall see, Descartes explodes at the suggestion that he ever owed anything to Beeckman, and addresses one of his longest and most vituperative letters to him. If it is in fact the case that Beeckman did act as a father figure, it would go some way to explaining the vehemence of Descartes' behaviour in 1629, since the episode would then inevitably have been overdetermined by associations with his natural father; but I cannot establish this, even to my own satisfaction, so I simply offer it as a suggestion, a proposed 'best explanation', that the reader might bear in mind, and make a judgement upon when we have looked more fully at the development of their relations over the subsequent years.[61]

The letters give details of Descartes' travel plans, and we can get the occasional glimpse of his feelings about engaging on the journey. He seems to have decided to join the army of Maximilian of Bavaria by the middle of March 1619 at the latest, for in the letter of 26 March he refers to the troubles in Germany having caused him to change his travel plans, and to proceed to Bohemia by a very circuitous route (Amsterdam, Danzig, Poland, Hungary, Austria).[62] He clearly feels great trepidation on setting out on such a journey, and this is understandable. Not only was the journey much more major than anything he had undertaken previously, but Europe was in a state of uneasy truce. As Descartes points out to Beeckman, there were persistent rumours of war, with many men under arms, and with the roads possibly full of pillaging soldiers. Yet the way in which he describes his projected journey suggests more personal reasons for trepidation as well. Quoting Virgil, he says that he no longer knows 'where destiny will lead me, or where it will bring me to rest'.[63] The context of the quote[64] is instructive, for here Aeneas and a few others who have survived the sack of Troy have received a divine instruction to search the world for a home in some uninhabited land. Descartes clearly has more in mind that furthering his military career in embarking on such a journey.

It is as a record of Descartes' intellectual life that his letters of this period are of greatest value. In the first letter (24 January) old ground is gone over, and he clarifies some issues of practical musical importance raised in the *Compendium*, such as the differences in the intervals that can be used in a single voice and those (a greater number) that can be used between voices. But thereafter, a number of new interests and discoveries emerge. To take a relatively minor example, he tells Beeckman that he has found 'a way of determining—no matter what my position is, and even if, while sleeping, I travelled for I do not know how long—how many degrees to the East or West I am away from another place known to me, solely by inspecting the stars', and, without

91

revealing the details of his discovery, he asks Beeckman whether this is an original discovery or not.[65] The problem Descartes is addressing here was one that was exercising Galileo, amongst others, at this time. It was known that latitude could be determined by the elevation of a star, or from the elevation of the sun at noon, but no procedure for determining longitude had been devised. We know what Descartes' own solution was because it is recorded in code in the *Cogitationes Privatae*, a code deciphered by Leibniz when he copied the entries out. The entry (with Leibniz's decipherments in square brackets) reads:

If leaving Bucolia [our starting point], we wish to head straight for Chemnis or any other port of Egypt [globe of the Earth], we must note carefully before leaving how far apart Pythius [the sun] and Pythias [the moon] are at the entrance of the Nile [starting point]. We shall then be able, in any location, to find our road by looking at Pythias and the servants of Psyche [the fixed stars] that accompany it.[66]

What Descartes has in mind is exploiting the corrections that had to be made at local times at different meridians. The moon rises later every day in the lunar month, and its position with reference to the fixed stars changes, allowing it to be used as quite an accurate clock registering short periods of time. If we are provided with tables calculated for time at standard meridian and a clock which gives us standard time, then comparing the difference between standard time and local time, we can determine our longitude.[67] The method is not original, Beeckman tells him, and it is clear from Beeckman's diary that he himself had developed it in 1614,[68] although he has the modesty not to reveal this.

Throughout this correspondence there are a number of references to Descartes writing a 'Mechanics' and a 'Geometry', and although Beeckman urges Descartes to complete the former, we have little idea what it would have contained at this stage. The project may well have been temporarily abandoned, for Descartes' efforts quickly became centred around mathematics. In the letter of 26 March, he breaks the news of a momentous mathematical discovery. During a period of intense work over six days, he says, he has 'found four extraordinary and completely new demonstrations by means of my compasses'. These discoveries mark the beginning of a new stage in Descartes' thought, and they were to shape his ideas not just about mathematics but also about the centrality of mathematics in any account of 'method', something that was soon to dominate his thought.

In his letter to Beeckman of 26 March, Descartes sets out his mathematical discoveries for the first time, and describes their ramifications:

I have been here for six days, and I've cultivated the Muses more assiduously than ever. In this short time, in fact, I've found four extraordinary and completely new demonstrations by means of my compasses. The first concerns the famous problem of dividing an angle into as many equal parts as one wishes [the traditional problem of 'trisecting' the angle]. The other three relate to three classes of cubic equation: the first class having the whole number, roots and cubes [$x^3 = \pm a \pm bx$]; the second, a whole number, squares and cubes [$x^3 = \pm a \pm bx^2$]; the third, a whole number, roots, squares and cubes [$x^3 = \pm a \pm bx \pm cx^2$]. I have found three demonstrations for these classes, each of which must cover the variable terms because of changes in + and − signs. I have not provided an account of everything yet; but I believe it will be easy to apply what I have found in the one case to others. And by these means it is possible to solve four times as many problems, and much more difficult ones, than one can with common Algebra. I allow thirteen different types of cubic equation,[69] whereas there are only three for common [that is, second-order] equations, namely between I$_δ$ and O$κ$ + ON [$x^2 = ax + b$], or O$κ$ − ON [$x^2 = ax − b$], or finally ON − O$κ$ [$x^2 = b − ax$].[70] And I am now looking for something different in order to extract roots of the sum of quantities which are incommensurable with one another.[71] If I find it, as I hope to, I will set the whole science to rights, provided I can overcome my natural laziness and fate allows me the leisure. Indeed, so that you are in no doubt as to the object of my enterprise, what I would like to present to the public is not Lull's *Ars brevis*, but a science with wholly new foundations, which will enable us to answer every question that can be put about any kind of quantity whatsoever, whether continuous or discontinuous, each according to its nature. In Arithmetic, certain questions can be solved by means of rational numbers, others by using irrationals, and finally others can be imagined[72] but not solved. In this way, I hope to demonstrate that, in the case of continuous quantity, certain problems can be solved with straight lines and circles alone; that others can be solved only with curves other than circles, but which can be generated by a single [continuous] motion and which can therefore be drawn using a new compass which I do not believe to be any less accurate than, and just as geometrical as, the ordinary compass which is used to draw circles; and finally, other problems can be solved only with curves generated by motions not subordinated to one another, curves which are certainly only imaginary, such as the quadratrix, which is well known. I do not believe one can imagine anything which could not be solved along similar lines: indeed, I hope to show that particular kinds of question can be resolved in one way and not another, so that there will remain almost nothing else to discover in Geometry. The task is infinite and could not be accomplished by one person. It is as incredible as it is ambitious. But I have seen a certain light in the dark chaos of this science, thanks to which the thickest clouds can be dispelled.[73]

This is tantalizingly compact, and provides us with little by way of detail. Fortunately, however, we do have another source of information on Descartes' mathematics from around the same time, the *Cogitationes Privatae*, which enables us to understand in some detail what his discoveries were.[74]

Before we can understand what Descartes' discovery consists in, however, we need to say a few words about the proportional compass. Various geometrical compasses had been constructed around the turn of the century to help with arithmetical or geometrical calculations.

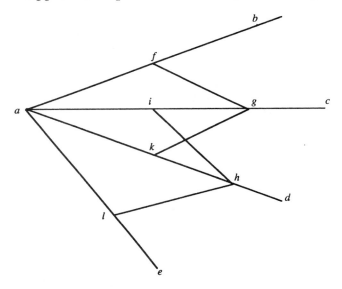

Fig. 3.12

Galileo, for example, had published a pamphlet in 1606[75] showing how various compasses or sectors can be used to compute compound interest, extract square roots, yield the mean proportional, and so on. The aim of the sector devised by Galileo, usually called a 'proportional compass', was to provide a quick and economical, practical means of solving mathematical problems whose solution would otherwise involve theoretical mathematical skills beyond the powers of the 'noble gentlemen' for whom the pamphlet was composed. Such proportional compasses had a widespread use in the early decades of the seventeenth century, and a noteworthy feature of them was that they were of use in dealing with both geometrical and arithmetical problems.

Descartes' work with compasses is distinctive, first, in the ingenuity with which he is able to devise and manipulate various forms of compass, and secondly, and more importantly, in his quite unprecedented attempt to provide the workings of the compass, especially its apparent indifference as to whether a problem is arithmetical or geometrical, with theoretical foundations through an algebraic theory. In the problem of 'dividing the angle into as many parts as one wishes', the task is accomplished by means of what we can call a 'trisection compass'.[76] The instrument and its operations are described in the *Cogitationes Privatae*. The compass (Fig. 3.12) comprises four main branches, *ab*, *ac*, *ad*, and *ae*, and the construction is such that, when the compass is opened, the angles between them remain equal. The sections *af, ai, ak,*

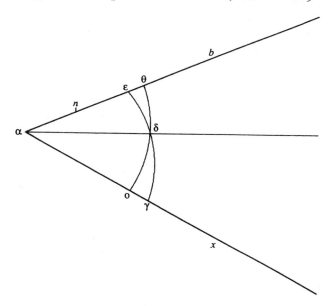

FIG. 3.13

and *al* are equal, and the connecting spokes *fg, gk, ih,* and *hl,* which are all of the same length as *af,* pivot around the points *f, g, i, h, k,* and *l,* and slide at *g* and *h.* To trisect an angle, one need only apply the compass to it. Let *xαb* be the angle to be trisected (Fig. 3.13), then the limb *ae* of the compass is placed over the line *αx,* and the limb of the compass *ab* drawn out so that it covers *αb,*

and the line will be described by point *g* like γδε. Then let *nα* be taken equal to *af,* and around point *n* the part of the circle θδo be drawn so that *n*θ be sure to equal *fg.* I say that the line αδ divides an angle into three equal parts. In this manner an angle can be divided into many if the compass consists of many limbs.[77]

The *Cogitationes Privatae* also show Descartes' interest in a number of other forms of compass, and he describes those for finding conic sections, and for finding cylindrical sections,[78] as well as mentioning others, such as the enlarging compass.[79] But by far the most important compass that Descartes used was the 'mesolabe compass', and it is from this instrument that his enthusiasm in the letter to Beeckman derives. The mesolabe was an instrument invented by the Alexandrian mathematician and astronomer Eratosthenes for finding mean proportionals between two given lines. The compass was used by Eratosthenes for dealing with the problem of 'duplicating the cube', that is, constructing the edge of a cube having twice the volume of a given cube using only a straight edge

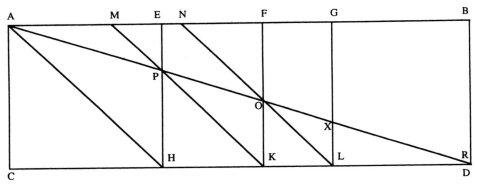

FIG. 3.14

and a compass. The proposed solution works in terms of a rigid plinth ABCD which has equal triangles AEH, MFK, NGL which have right angles at E, F, and G (Fig. 3.14). The triangle AEH is fixed and the triangles MFK and NGL are moved in parallel along the straight edges AB and CD. To find two mean proportional lines between AC and XL, let MFK and NGL slide such that P and O on the lines EH and FK respectively are in a straight line with A, X. Then:

$$\frac{AH}{PH} = \frac{AR}{PR} = \frac{AH}{PK} = \frac{HR}{KR} = \frac{PH}{OK} = \frac{PR}{RO} = \frac{PK}{OL} = \frac{KR}{LR} = \frac{OK}{XL}$$

which gives us:

$$\frac{AC}{PH} = \frac{PH}{OK} = \frac{OK}{XL}$$

which means that AC, PH, OK, and XL are in continued proportion. It follows that if AC and XL are two given straight lines, then PH and OK are the required mean proportionals.

The mesolabe compass that Descartes describes in the *Cogitationes Privatae* is a development of Eratosthenes' mesolabe, and Shea has offered an appealing reconstruction of how Descartes might have come across it.[80] The division of a string into equal semitones was a standard musicological problem of Descartes' time, and Zarlino in his *Istituzioni harmoniche*—a work Descartes was very familiar with, as we have seen—had raised the question of mean proportionals in the context of dividing the string in such a way as to produce equal tones. The octave is characterized by the ratio 1:2, and comprises twelve semitones, so what we must do is to take eleven mean proportionals, starting by taking two mean proportionals between the full length of the string and half its length. Zarlino knew this could not be done by a ruler and

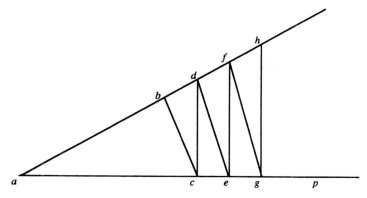

FIG. 3.15

compass, and he realized that Eratosthenes' mesolabe could be used to provide the required mean proportionals. It is possible that Descartes knew the mesolabe from a Classical source, as it was described by Pappus in the third book of his *Mathematical Collection*, translated in a widely circulated Latin version by Commandino in 1588; but we have no reason to think that Descartes was familar with the contents of this book at this time, and Shea's reconstruction strikes me as by far the most plausible route.

What is distinctive about Descartes' treatment of the mesolabe compass, however, is that he quickly moves from the question of finding mean proportionals into a much more mathematically sophisticated context, that of finding solutions to three types of cubic equation. His treatment of the first type of equation will suffice to indicate what is at issue. Putting the problem in modern notation,[81] the cubic equation he attempts to solve is $x^3 = 7x + 14$. He carelessly reduces the equation to $x^3 = x + 2$, but the important part of the exercise is the solution of $x^3 = x + 2$ by means of the mesolabe compass. The compass is described and illustrated (Fig. 3.15) in the *Cogitationes*, but neither the description nor the illustration is as clear as that given later in the second book of the *Géométrie*. Since the same instrument is being described, it is easier to follow the later account:

Consider the lines AB, AD, AF, and so on, which I assume to have been described with the aid of an instrument, YZ, composed of several rulers. [Fig. 3.16] These are so joined that when the one marked YZ is placed on the line AN, we can open and close the angle XYZ; and when it is completely closed, the points B, C, D, E, F, and H are all assembled at point A. But to the extent that we open it, the ruler BC, which is joined at right angles to XY at point B, pushes the ruler CD toward Z; CD slides along YZ, always at right angles to it, and pushes GH, etc. And we

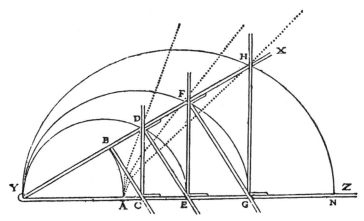

FIG. 3.16

can conceive of an infinity of others, which are pushed consecutively in the same way, half of which always maintain the same angles with YX and the others with YZ. Now as we thus open the angle XYZ, the point B describes the line AB, which is a circle, and the other points D, F, H, where the intersections of the other rulers occur, describe the other curved lines, AD, AF, AH, of which the latter are successively more complex than the first, and thus more complex than the circle.[82]

The similar right angles here give us these continuous proportions:

$$\frac{YB}{YC} = \frac{YC}{YD} = \frac{YD}{YE} = \frac{YE}{YF} = \frac{YF}{YG} = \frac{YG}{YH} = \ldots$$

If we then let $YB = YA = 1$, and $YC = x$, we obtain the continuous proportions of geometrical progressions, $1:x = x:x^2 = x^2:x^3 = x^3:x^4 = x^4:x^5 = \ldots$ Now, if we go back to the *Cogitationes*, we can translate the procedure easily into the terms of the figure given there (Fig. 3.15). We have $\dfrac{ab}{ac} = \dfrac{ac}{ad} = \dfrac{ad}{ae} = \dfrac{ae}{af}$, and $ae = \dfrac{ad^2}{ac} = \dfrac{ac^3}{ab^2}$. If we then put $ab = 1$ and $ac = x$, then we obtain $ce = x^3 - x$, which gives us $x^3 = x + ce$. Consequently, if we open the compass so that the value of ce is exactly equal to 2, we get $ac = x$ as a positive real root of the cubic equation $x^3 = x + 2$.

Descartes' achievement here is to have come to the fundamental realization that the representation of the roots of an irreducible cubic or biquadratic equation is equivalent either to the trisection of an angle or to the duplication of a cube. The credit for first having noticed this must go to Vieta, who remarked on it in his *Supplementum geometricae* (1593).[83] But Descartes' clumsy cossic notation, derived in all probability from Clavius' *Algebra*, which he had studied at La Flèche, indicates that he was not familiar with Vieta's work at this point, for Vieta's notation is clearly superior, and had he been familiar with it he could not have favoured that of Clavius. Descartes was obliged to rediscover these relations, to formulate the problems in his own terms, and to develop his own means to solving them, something he was to do in a way that went far beyond Vieta's pioneering work.

In more general terms, Descartes' discovery is that the key to the operations of the compass is the manipulation of proportional magnitudes, and that the compass could be used to resolve any question reducible to a problem about proportional magnitudes. He was beginning to realize that the manipulation of proportional magnitudes goes beyond the particular arithmetical or geometrical expression of the problems he was concerned with, in that the proportional magnitudes (in the form of line lengths) representing numbers or the numerical variables notated in cossic symbols, and the mean proportionals sought in the geometrical cases, can be similarly represented on the compass. Descartes begins to see the whole of mathematics in terms of the proportional compass, the aim now being, as Schuster has put it, to 'attempt to write equations as proportions and fit them into the architecture of the compass'.[84]

Such an enterprise initiates the investigation of what Descartes refers to as a *mathesis universalis* in the second part of Rule 4 of the *Regulae*, which was probably composed around the middle of 1619.[85] Describing how he had been puzzled as to why the ancients had taken mathematics so seriously, when all that mathematical writers presented were calculations and demonstrations that were quite superficial, he speculates that perhaps the explanation for this lies in the ancient mathematicians possessing a kind of mathematics very different from that which had been subsequently practised, and which, moreover, is not reflected in their own extant writings. He is convinced, he tells us, 'that certain primary seeds of truth naturally implanted in human minds thrived vigorously in that unsophisticated and innocent age—seeds that have been stifled in us by our constantly reading and hearing errors of all kinds'.[86] He can find traces of 'true mathematics' in the works of the Alexandrian mathematicians Pappus and Diophantus. But these writers, he has come to think, have:

with a kind of pernicious cunning subsequently suppressed this mathematics, as we know many inventors to have done in the case of their discoveries. They may have feared that their method, just because it was so easy and simple, would be depreciated if they had divulged it; so in order to gain our admiration, what they presented us with as the fruits of their method were some sterile truths demonstrated by clever arguments, rather than giving us the method itself, which would have dispelled our admiration. In present times some very gifted men have tried to revive this method, for it seems to me that this method is just the art that goes by the barbarous name of 'algebra'—or at least it would be algebra if the many numbers and incomprehensible figures that overwhelm it were discarded, and it had, rather, that abundance of clarity and simplicity which I believe true mathematics ought to have. It was these thoughts that made me turn from the particular studies of arithmetic and geometry to a general investigation of mathematics. I began my investigation by asking what exactly is meant by the term *mathesis* [mathematics or learning] and why it is that, in addition to arithmetic and geometry, sciences such as astronomy, music, optics, mechanics, among others, are called branches of mathematics. To answer this it is not enough just to look at the etymology of the word, as *mathesis* means the same as *disciplina* [discipline/learning], so they have as much right to be called mathematics as geometry has. On the other hand, it is evident to anyone with the most minimal education what pertains to mathematics and what does not in any context. When I attended to the matter more closely, I came to see that the exclusive concern of mathematics is with questions of order or measure, and that it does not matter whether the measure in question involves numbers, shapes, stars, sounds, or any other object whatsoever. This made me realize that there must be a general science that explains everything that can be raised concerning order and measure irrespective of the subject matter, and that this science should be termed *mathesis universalis*—a venerable term with a well-established meaning—for it covers everything that entitles these other sciences to be called branches of mathematics. How superior it is to these subordinate sciences both in usefulness and simplicity is clear from the fact that it covers all they deal with. . . . Up to now, I have devoted all my energies to this *mathesis universalis* so that I might be able to tackle the more advanced sciences in due course.[87]

Note that what is being advocated here is a revival of a traditional mathematical art, and not something Descartes considers to be completely new. In fact, the idea of a *mathesis universalis* had both a long history and a wide currency in the seventeenth century,[88] and the sources for the idea may have derived from such diverse figures as Aristotle and Proclus, although the most likely source is the sixteenth-century Belgian mathematician, Adrianus Romanus, who, in the second part of his *Apologia pro Archimede* (1597), developed the idea of a *mathesis universalis* in detail.[89] Note also that what Descartes is seeking is something that would cover arithmetic and geometry without distinction, in that it would comprise a level of abstraction, dealing with magnitudes in general, that went beyond specific arithmetical and geometrical content. We are given no idea about what this might amount to in the passage here, but we have seen that it was in his work on the mesolabe compass that Descartes had found what he believed to be the key, for here was an instrument that did indeed transcend the differences between the two (admittedly in a rather restricted range of cases) and the theoretical rationale underlying the compass seemed to be a theory of proportions. Such a theory Descartes proposed to develop, so far as we can tell, in a work provisionally entitled *The Thesaurus*

Mathematicus of Polybius Cosmopolitanus. The brief account of the contents of the proposed book are so close to the above passage from Rule 4, that the latter may have initially been intended as part of it. We are told that the work 'lays down the true means of solving all the difficulties in the science of mathematics, and demonstrates that the human intellect can achieve nothing further on these questions'. The aim of the work is to show the emptiness of the boasts of those who claim to 'show us miraculous discoveries in all the sciences', as well as 'those who squander their intellectual resources to no avail'. Who does Descartes have in mind here? The final sentence of the summary tells us that the 'work is offered afresh to learned men throughout the world and especially to the distinguished brothers of the Rose Croix in Germany'.[90]

What exactly was Descartes' attitude to the Rosicrucians, as they are better known, and why should Descartes bother to tell Beeckman in the letter of 26 March that he was not providing 'an *Ars brevis* of the Lullian variety', as if this were an obvious way to construe what he was doing? Two topics predominate in the correspondence between Descartes and Beeckman of the first part of 1619. These are the discovery of the proportional compasses, and the system of Raymond Lull. On the face of it, the topics could not be further apart. The first was an ingenious application of a very practical mathematical device to impose structure upon, and solve, a range of mathematical problems. The second was characterized by all the trappings of an esoteric art, replete with the delusions of grandeur that seem inevitably to accompany such an enterprise. Lull described his system, which is contained in various versions in about 260 works, as 'the art of finding the truth' (*ars inveniendi veritatem*). Its aim was to develop a kind of universal language which, by using an axiomatic system, could be used to generate truths from basic premises. Lull saw the specific purpose of the system in terms of convincing Muslims and Jews of the truth of the Christian doctrines of the Trinity and the Incarnation. Largely forgotten from shortly after his death, Lull's project, stripped of its evangelical purpose, was revived in the commentary on Lull's *Ars brevis* written by Cornelius Agrippa in his very popular *De Incertitudine et Vanitate de Scientarium et Artium* (1527). Agrippa's work, with its endorsement of the writings of Hermes Trismegistus, supposedly demonstrating a marvellous anticipation of Christianity by the ancient Egyptian *magus*, and its talk of a secret key to the whole of knowledge based on Lull's *Ars brevis*, subsequently came to form part of the basis for the mysterious 'Brotherhood of the Rose Cross'.[91] The Rosicrucians became a significant movement in 1619, sweeping across Germany and taking a leading role in the movement to install Frederick, Elector

Palatine, in Bohemia. The crushing of Frederick's army at the Battle of the White Mountain on 8 November 1620 led to the demise of the movement as a political force, but a concerted campaign was waged against it throughout the 1620s. Indeed, Baillet tells us that on his return to Paris from Germany in 1623, Descartes was called upon to defend himself against charges of being a Rosicrucian.[92]

By the time the *Discours de la Méthode* appeared in 1637, Descartes had completely dismissed Lull and his work.[93] But his attitude to Lull in 1619 was rather more ambivalent. On 23 April 1619 he writes to Beeckman:

Three days ago, I met a learned man at an inn in Dordrecht, and I discussed the *Ars Brevis*[94] of Lull with him. He claimed to be able to use the rules of this Art so successfully that, he said, he was able to elaborate on any subject whatsoever for an hour; and if he was then asked to speak for another hour on the same material, he would find something completely different to say, and so on for another twenty hours. . . . I asked him to tell me more precisely whether this Art consisted in an arrangement of the common places[95] of Dialectic, from which its arguments were taken. He acknowledged this to be the case, but added that neither Lull nor Agrippa had, in their books, revealed certain keys which according to him were needed to open the secrets of this Art. And I suspect he said this in order to attract the admiration of the ignorant rather than to speak the truth. All the same, I would like to look into this question if I had the book. But, as you have it, please examine it if you have the time, and let me know whether you find anything so ingenious in this famous Art.[96]

Beeckman replied in a letter dated 6 May, explaining the somewhat simplistic mechanism behind Agrippa's procedure, which derives from Lull. It consists in designating concepts by letters of the alphabet. Amongst the various devices Lull employs, one (the one Beeckman mentions) consists of concentric circles which are marked by these letters. The circles revolve and combinations of letters, representing new combinations of concepts, are thereby generated.[97] As Beeckman points out, 'thus, whatever the subject proposed, by combining these terms one can prolong a discussion for hours, almost indefinitely; but the speaker must be acquainted with many issues, and if he speaks for too long he will open himself up to ridicule, saying things which have no bearing on the subject, and finally it will become pure fantasy'.[98]

Whether this good advice ever reached Descartes, we do not know. More to the point, we may ask whether he ever needed it. I do not believe that there are any respects in which Descartes' interest in Lull can be said to have influenced his own thoughts in any significant way, but there are a number of parallels between 'the Lullian art' and his own concerns.[99] First, there was a concern amongst followers of Lull with a universal symbolism, conceived, it is true, as often as not on a numerological and Cabbalistic basis; but questions of symbolism were very important for Descartes in a mathematical context. Secondly, and more importantly, the Lullian art in the version of Agrippa had two fundamental characteristics which mirror those that Descartes is about to ascribe to his 'method'. These are, first, that it is a general and universal science, starting from absolutely certain principles, and establishing a secure criterion of knowledge; and secondly, that it is the science of all sciences, offering a key to the ordering of all knowledge.[100] However, these questions were not exclusively the concern of the followers of Lull, and it would be very misleading to think of Descartes' interest in them as being due to, or even significantly influenced by, Lullian doctrines. The first question had been discussed extensively from Ramus onwards, and was a common concern of all those interested in algebra, whether this concern was mathematically serious or not. The second question has an even longer history. Dialectic had been defined (following Aristotle's *Topics*, 101[b]3) in the works of Peter of Spain and Lambert of Auxerre as 'the art of arts, the science of sciences, possessing the path to the principles of all methods', and not only did the scholastic tradition thrive on this definition, but when Agricola took it up in his *De inventione dialectica libri tres* (1515), it also became a basic premiss for an important strand of humanist thought.[101]

It is of paramount importance here that we be clear about the fact that the latter concerns, about the ordering of all knowledge, are not features of *mathesis universalis* (as conceived in early 1619) for Descartes, for this deals with specifically mathematical topics. *Mathesis universalis* looks as if it has such a general coverage only because it is discussed together with general questions of 'method' in Rule 4, and method does indeed have such features. It is true that 'method' somehow seems to grow out of universal mathematics, but we should not identify the two, and above all we should not simply accept Descartes' claim, in the *Discours de la Méthode*, that method lies behind even universal mathematics. The move to the question of method, a move that inaugurates a major shift in Descartes' thought, appeared to him as a revelation, and to this revelation we now turn.

4
The Search for Method
1619–1625

Mirabilis scientiae fundamenta, November 1619

By the summer of 1619, Descartes had reached Frankfurt, where he witnessed the preparations for the coronation of Ferdinand II as Emperor. He was present at the coronation, which took place on 9 September, and which was by all accounts a magnificent spectacle, something an old pupil of La Flèche would have found hard to resist. The political situation surrounding the coronation was, however, an explosive one, and the Bohemians had already proclaimed a rival, Frederick V, as their king. Bohemia had long been the centre of Spanish power in the area, and Prague, its capital, had been the seat of Emperor Rudolph II. When the capital of the empire moved to Vienna, Bohemia held its central role, with the Bohemian king in all probability holding the casting vote in the election of the next emperor. An emperor sympathetic to, or even representative of, Spanish interests was something of great importance to the Spanish, for he controlled numerous areas of Italy and the Rhineland, as well as the strategically crucial Tyrolean passes, and under the weak Emperors Rudolph and Matthias, the able and forceful Spanish ambassadors Zúñiga and Oñate exercised effective control. Things changed radically in May 1618, however, when the Protestant nobility, responding to the refusal of the authorities to allow the building of Protestant churches in the towns of Klostergrab and Braunau—on the pretext that these were church and not royal properties, and thereby exempt from an earlier edict recognizing liberty of worship—followed the cherished Bohemian practice of political defenestration and flung three hispanophile Catholic ministers out of the window of the royal palace. Despite a fall of 46 feet, they all survived, something Catholics put down to angels supporting them in their fall, although Protestants tended to believe that their landing on a soft pile of rubbish may have been the significant factor. However that may be, a period of extreme tension ensued, brought to a head by the death of Emperor Matthias on 20 March 1619. Ferdinand was elected Emperor, but the Bohemians immediately deposed him as king and elected Frederick in his place.

The Search for Method, 1619–1625

The Catholic army of Maximilian was allied with France, so it is not surprising that Descartes should have attached himself to it, but we cannot say with any certainty how long he remained attached to it, or in what capacity. It is clear that he did remain in military service, however, and he spent the winter stationed at Ulm at Neuburg, while negotiations progressed. Ulm was at a strategic location, being on the road between Frankfurt and Vienna. It had a military engineering college, and while there he had a number of conversations with the mathematician Johannes Faulhaber, who seems to have been associated with the Rosicrucians, and who was indeed the first to publish a work addressed to the Brotherhood, the *Mysterium Arithmeticum* of 1615.[1] From 1604 onwards, Faulhaber had published a number of mathematical and scientific works, including treatises on mechanics, optics, and scientific and mathematical instruments,[2] and the orientation of his later work shows the influence of Agrippa. Descartes may not have been unresponsive to Rosicrucian ideas at this time, but we have no evidence that he learned anything specific either from Faulhaber himself, or from the *Arithmetica philosophica* (1604) of Peter Roth to which Faulhaber introduced him. But we cannot discount the significance for Descartes of meeting with someone who not only shared his range of scientific and mathematical interests—he had published a treatise on the proportional compass in 1610,[3] for example—but who was also a good mathematician. Unlike Beeckman, Faulhaber saw his projects in grander terms than a mere science of mechanics, and Descartes' philosophical interests may well have been re-awakened by the generality of Faulhaber's vision. Descartes was to share in something like the generality and indeed the delusions of grandeur of this vision, but (and here his philosophical background stood him in good stead) he filled the vision out not in the intellectually facile terms provided by Agrippa and the Rosicrucians, but rather in terms of an amalgam of elements drawn from virtually the whole range of his studies, from those in grammar and rhetoric to those in mechanics and algebra.

It is, I believe, this vision, which marks the beginning of his general theory of 'method', to which Descartes is referring in the statement that he has discovered the 'foundations of a marvellous science' (*mirabilis scientiae fundamenta*). The occasion, which Baillet dates to 10 November 1619, is described in the *Discours de la Méthode* in these terms:

While returning to the army from the coronation of the emperor, I was detained by the onset of winter in quarters where, having neither conversation to divert me nor, fortunately, cares or passions to trouble me, I was completely free to consider my own thoughts. Among the first that occurred to me was the thought that there is not usually as much perfection in works comprised of many parts and produced by many different craftsmen as in the works of one man.[4]

Descartes goes on to illustrate the point with reference to architecture, the establishment of laws, and religion, finally drawing the lesson for knowledge generally:

And therefore I thought that since the sciences contained in books—at least those based upon merely probable rather than demonstrative reasoning—are made up and put together bit by bit from the opinions of many different people, it never comes as close to the truth as the simple reasoning which a man of good sense naturally makes concerning whatever he comes across.[5]

But, unfortunately, we grow up of necessity ruled by our appetites and on the opinions of others, so that we cannot expect our adult judgement to be unclouded. To circumvent this problem what we must do is to get rid of our opinions and start again from foundations.

Now the *Discours* is not especially reliable as an account of the precise details of Descartes' development, and there are elements in his account that mix later metaphysical with earlier methodological concerns. But the main point is clear enough: knowledge generally needs to be placed on a different footing. Descartes' realization in 1619 was not just this, but also that he could perhaps develop some rules by which this might be done. Notice, however, the novelty of the project: up to this point, we have encountered nothing of this scope. The project of *mathesis universalis* was a purely mathematical one, whereas now Descartes is concerned with the whole of knowledge.

Baillet tells us,[6] on the basis of documents now lost, that Descartes, scorning company and even his usual solitary walks, devoted himself exclusively to his search, completely exhausting himself before he finally found what he was looking for. In a state of delirium, he experienced intense joy, and that evening he had three dreams which he interpreted as confirmation that he had reached a turning point in his life. The first was a nightmare, in which terrifying phantoms appeared. Trying to drive them away, he felt ashamed because of a great weakness in his right side which obliged him to lurch to the left. Suddenly caught up by a great wind, he was whirled around upon his left foot three or four times. He tried to drag himself along, terrified that he appeared to be faltering at each step. He managed to reach the chapel of a college that he came across, but before he could enter it in order to pray he realized he had just passed a man whom he recognized but had failed to acknowledge. Attempting to retrace his steps, he was thrown against the wall of the chapel by the wind. At the same moment, he saw someone else who called him by name and told him that if he wanted to seek out Monsieur N., he would give him something. He imagined this to be a melon which had come from a foreign country. The man was surrounded by people, who to his surprise were able to stand up straight whereas he was still only able to stand leaning to one side. Finally, he noticed that the wind was becoming less and less violent, and at that point he awoke, feeling a sharp pain in his left side.

Turning onto his right side, apparently in the belief that the dream had been partly due to his sleeping on his left side, he prayed for protection from the evil effects of the dream. Feeling that while he had not erred in the eyes of men, he may have erred in the eyes of God, he reflected on good and evil for a couple of hours before falling asleep again. He immediately had a second dream which consisted of what seemed to be a clap of thunder, and he opened his eyes to find his room full of sparks, not knowing whether he was asleep or awake. He had had the same experience on a number of previous occasions, and the sparks prevented him from seeing anything except those things which were very close. After blinking several times, he was able to get rid of the sparks, and he immediately fell asleep again, relieved.

In the third and final dream, he began by noticing a book on a table. He opened it and was pleased to see that it was an encyclopaedia or dictionary, which he believed might prove useful. At the same time, he also discovered a second book, a collection of poems entitled *Corpus Poetarum*. Opening this book, he chanced upon the words *Quod vitae sectabor iter?* (what road in life shall I follow?). As he was reading, a stranger entered and gave him some verses beginning with the words *est et non* (it is and is not). The man told Descartes of the excellence of the poem, and Descartes replied that he knew it well: it came from the *Idylls* of Ausonius, whose poems were included in the anthology on the table. He looked through the volume to find these poems, and the man asked him where he had got the anthology from. He was unable to tell him, and then noticed that the book had disappeared. It was now at the other end of the table, and the dictionary had changed into a slightly different one. He found Ausonius' poems, but not the one beginning *est et non*. Turning to the man, he told him he knew an even better poem beginning *Quod vitae sectabor iter?* On opening the book he noticed several copperplate portraits in it, which he thought he recognized. At this point, the man and the book both disappeared.

While remaining asleep, he asked himself whether he was imagining all this or whether it was real, and he began to ask about its significance. The dictionary is taken to represent all of the sciences, and the *Corpus* the union of philosophy with wisdom. Poets, he tells us, often have more profound things to say because of the divine nature of their inspiration, 'which makes the seeds of wisdom, which are found in the minds of men like the sparks of fire in flints, emerge with much more ease and clarity than can be accomplished by the reasoning of philosophers'. The words *Quod vitae sectabor iter?* he interprets as wise counsel, possibly even a moral maxim. At this point he wakes, but continues to interpret the dreams along the same lines. The *Corpus* represents revelation and inspiration,[7] while the *est et non* is interpreted as the 'yes and no' of the Pythagoreans, standing for truth and error. The third dream he sees as enlightenment about the future, the other two as a form of reprimand for his earlier life. The melon he takes to symbolize the charms of solitude.[8] The pain in his left side represents the devil trying to prevent him from going where he wants, and God does not let him enter the chapel because it is the devil who is pushing him there. The terror experienced in the second dream is a kind of remorse for his sins, and the thunderclap a sign that the spirit of truth is about to descend.

It is worth distinguishing between the reports of the first two dreams, which have the appearance of genuine dreams and which, if they yield anything, tell us principally about Descartes' psychological state, and the third dream, which is somewhat stylized, and is more likely to involve elements that reflect a conscious attempt to draw attention to the importance of his intellectual discovery. One factor that must be borne in mind in considering the third dream is that dreams were a standard literary device in which symbols could be deployed in a way that would be anomalous in other contexts. As well as very well-known Classical and biblical dreams which involve divine illumination, there is a Rosicrucian work, published in 1619, that has close parallels with Descartes' report of his dream. This is the *Raptus philosophicus* of Rodophilus Staurophorus. Here a young man dreams he is at a crossroads, and wonders which road to take, eventually choosing the straight and narrow one. After a number of adventures, he meets a woman who asks him where he is going, and she shows him a book in which all that is in heaven and earth is contained, but which is 'not ordered methodically'. The woman reveals that she is Nature, as yet unknown to scientists and philosophers. But I do not believe that the resemblance here shows Descartes to have been influenced by Staurophorus (after all, we do not know whether Descartes had read the work),[9] and there is nothing uniquely Rosicrucian about the ideas of a crossroads, following the right path, meeting a woman who can in some way be equated with wisdom, and so on. Even if one restricts oneself to the Christian tradition, one needs look no further than Boethius' *De Consolatione* to find precedents for these images, and the work of a writer like Dante is full of them. Indeed, it seems reasonably clear that Descartes and Staurophorus are both drawing on the same tradition of presenting material, especially that reflecting inspiration, whether poetic, or religious, or whatever, in the form of reports of dreams. This is not to say that Descartes did not actually have the dreams he reports, or in particular that he did not have the third dream: there do seem to be genuine dream elements in it. But he either had a very stylized dream (not an unusual phenomenon—patients undergoing analysis, for example, occasionally dream very 'Freudian' dreams), or he gives us a very stylized account of it.

When he was asked, Freud declined to speculate on the meanings of Descartes' dreams, pointing out that much of their content was symbolic in a way more characteristic of conscious processes than unconscious ones (something I am taking as more marked in the third dream), and that without some association of ideas on the part of Descartes, interpretation of the unconscious elements was not possible.[10] Some elements are, however, reasonably clear. The first and second dreams strongly suggest an internal conflict—being blown by a wind surely indicates some kind of internal struggle—and by Descartes' own account, it is a moral one, or at least one with moral overtones. He clearly has strong feelings of guilt. But I am not concerned here to interpret Descartes' dreams; rather, my concern is to understand what connection, if any, these dreams have with the intellectual discovery that this passage in the *Olympica* is otherwise devoted to.[11] The third dream suggests connections between his personal state and his intellectual pursuits, but, at least on the face of it, these connections tell us nothing at all about why guilt should be at issue, or how the intellectual discovery might play any role in resolving it. It is no answer to maintain that the dreams do not have to be connected, that, say, the first two might be primarily about guilt over some sexual matter,[12] whereas the third connects up much more closely with his intellectual discovery. This might well be true (we are not in a position to say), but the relevant fact is that Descartes himself includes all three dreams in his account of his intellectual discovery, an account that emphasizes its emotional and psychological aspects, rather than its specific content. We have every reason to believe that the dreams are each in some way connected with the catharsis that Descartes associates with the discovery.

The situation is a confusing one. In the *Discours de la Méthode*, Descartes tells us that, in settling down to think in his stove-heated room, he 'fortunately [had] neither cares nor passions to trouble me'. But in the *Olympica* we are told that the Demon 'had been exciting in him the enthusiasm with which, as he felt, his brain had been inflamed for several days'.[13] The *Olympica* is, so far as we can tell, a near-contemporary record made by Descartes, and I think we must prefer its version of events. If we do, then it seems that, far from having neither cares nor passions, Descartes was in fact in a state of considerable nervous anxiety, and awakening to see one's room full of sparks, not knowing whether one is awake or asleep, something which (Baillet tells us) Descartes was not experiencing here for the first time, is perhaps only a severe migraine, but it may well have been something far more serious. Indeed, it is quite possible that Descartes was suffering a nervous breakdown, almost certainly not his first. In this context it is worth comparing his dreams and his reclusive behaviour with the standard seventeenth-century medical description of melancholia, provided by André du Laurens. The 'melancholike man properly so called (I mean him that hath a disease in the braine)', he tells us,

is alwaies disquieted both in bodie and spirit, he is subject to watchfulnes, which doth consume him on the one side, and unto sleepe, which tormenteth him on the other side; for if he think to make truce with his passions by taking some rest, behold so soone as hee would shut his eyelids, hee is assayled with a thousand vaine visions, and hideous buggards, with fantasticall inventions, and dreadfull dreames; if he would call any to helpe him, his speech is cut off before it be halfe ended, and what he speaketh commeth out in fasting and stammering sort, he cannot live with companie. To conclude, hee is become a savadge creature, haunting the shadowed places, suspicious, solitarie, enemie to the Sunne, and one whom nothing can please, but onely discontentment, which forgeth unto it selfe a thousand false and vaine imaginations.[14]

What Laurens is describing here is the disease of melancholia, generally run together with the fashionable condition of *tristesse* in the seventeenth century; Descartes certainly tells us that he suffers from the latter (as we saw at the beginning of Chapter 1), but his general solitary behaviour and the dreams he describes have a striking similarity to the symptoms of the disease described here. And if the events of 10 November do signify a breakdown, then he may have experienced these symptoms rather severely. The feelings of guilt that accompanied the breakdown, and perhaps were instrumental in bringing it about, are only to be expected, even though we cannot determine their specific source. As I indicated earlier, the culture in which Descartes was raised was one in which the internalization of religion was part of an explicit programme of the Church, and this programme was carried out nowhere more enthusiastically than in the Jesuit colleges. Guilt played a crucial role in the 'Christianization' of the pupils, as did the constant self-imposed vigilance that was required with respect to one's passions. It would have been nothing short of remarkable if Descartes, clearly sensitive not only as a child and adolescent (perhaps feeling abandoned after the death of his maternal grandmother) but into his adult life also, had not felt the rigours of the Christianizing process more than most.

Nevertheless, we still seem to be left with two different events: the nervous exhaustion and excitement, and perhaps breakdown, that culminated in the dreams, and the possible recovery from this, on the one hand; and the intellectual discovery, which I am assuming to be the discovery of an account of 'method' (for reasons that will become clear below), which occurred at the same time and was symbolized in the third dream. One possibility is that Descartes suffered a nervous breakdown, recovered from it, and rationalized his recovery in terms of a great discovery. I think this is probably close to the truth. The discovery of a general method is something that will be set out in the early Rules of the *Regulae* shortly after the events of 10 November. What is set out there is certainly of great interest, and it marks a important step in Descartes' thought. But I do not believe it marks a turning point, and I think it is only with hindsight, above all with the optical and mathematical discoveries of 1625–6 and their subsequent reformulation in terms of 'method', and with the addition of the later Rules of 1626–8, which set out a path-breaking 'mechanization' of perceptual cognition, that the questions of 'method' raised in 1619/20 can be seen to be a major breakthrough. It might be objected that what is at issue is not so much whether it really marks a turning point, but whether Descartes himself thought at the time that it did so. In this respect it is worth remembering here that Baillet, in reporting Descartes' own account, tells us that 'his enthusiasm left him after a few days',[15] a surprising turn of events if one takes his word about how important the discovery was for him at the time. In the light of this, I find it difficult to believe that there was not a significant element of rationalization involved here. Indeed, I suggest that the events of the days surrounding 10 November probably constituted a mental collapse of some kind, and that the thoughts on method that Descartes had been pursuing at the time came to symbolize his recovery from this.

The Early *Regulae*, 1619/1620

Although the *Regulae ad directionem ingenii*, which were not published until after Descartes' death,[16] were once generally thought to have been composed in 1628, there have always been those who have believed that at least some of them were composed earlier, and following the detailed, pioneering work of J.-P. Weber,[17] there is now good reason to suppose that the *Regulae* were in fact composed between 1619–20 and 1626–8, and that a number of stages of composition are evident, some of the Rules comprising material composed at very different times. Following the general thrust of Weber's account (but not the details, which are often too fine-grained to bear the evidence), and adding revisions of Schuster's, the schedule of composition that I shall follow is one that recognizes two composite rules (4 and 8), and three stages of composition.[18] The first stage of composition is represented by what I have already referred to as Rule 4B, that is, the second part of Rule 4, where a *mathesis universalis* is discussed: indeed, significantly, this is the only place that *mathesis universalis* is mentioned in the whole *Regulae*. I have already suggested that this fragment, which may have initially formed part of the proposed *Thesaurus mathematicus,* dates from between March and November 1619. The exact dating is not crucial, only that it was composed before Rule 4A. The second stage of composition was 1619/20, the period after the events of 10 November. What seems to have been composed at this time were Rules 1 to 3, 4A, and 5 to 11, with the exception of parts of Rule 8. The *Rules* were then abandoned, and taken up again in a rather different vein in 1626–8, when the remainder, and the remaining parts of Rule 8, were composed. The three stages can be characterized briefly as follows. The fragment from the first stage envisages a general form of mathematics to which particular mathematical disciplines would be subservient. The material from the second stage sets out rules of method which go beyond specifically mathematical concerns, and it draws on areas as diverse as rhetoric, psychology, and dialectic. The material from the third stage is above all concerned with the mechanistic construal of cognition, although the final, incomplete, Rules return to more directly methodological concerns and appear to describe, in a general way, mathematical procedures that are set out much more fully in the *Géométrie*. The whole enterprise was finally abandoned in 1628.

Before we turn to the first eleven Rules, it might be worthwhile putting the question of method in perspective. Writing in 1565, the French classicist Turnebus tells us that the problem of method is the most discussed philosophical problem of the day. He is referring, amongst other things, to the problem of how one can be said to generate new and genuine knowledge of the facts if one starts by deducing first principles from the empirical phenomena, and then proceeds to demonstrate these empirical phenomena from the first principles. The problem derives from Aristotle's distinction in the *Posterior Analytics* (I. 3 and II. 8) between demonstration *quia* (to give it its Latin name), where the proximate cause is demonstrated from the sensible phenomenon to which it gives rise, and demonstration *propter quid*, where the sensible phenomenon is demonstrated from its proximate cause. The combination of the two procedures seems to be circular, yet precisely such a combination was thought to be required for the process of scientific discovery and demonstration, and the aim was to find some way of showing that the knowledge of sensible phenomena that one started with was different in kind from that which one had at the end of the process; in particular, that the knowledge one began with was only knowledge that something was the case, whereas the knowledge that one ended up with was a deeper kind of knowledge, namely knowledge of why something was the case. This problem was, however, really a symptom of a deeper and much more intractable problem, that of how deductive inference could be informative. The only model of scientific reasoning that had been transmitted to the Middle Ages and the Renaissance from antiquity was that of Aristotle,[19] and this model was almost universally misunderstood. Aristotle had concerned himself with two areas, the discovery of arguments by means of the 'topics', devices intended to show someone working in a scientific field how to organize the subject matter of the field so that the right kinds of questions could be asked, on the one hand, and the formal study of scientific inference and the nature of demonstrative arguments on the other. The first was Aristotle's 'method of discovery', the second was (in part) his 'method of presentation'. But in the later interpretation of Aristotle's theory, the method of presentation was mistaken for his method of discovery, and there was considerable confusion as to how the purely deductive process of scientific demonstration from first principles could possibly result in new empirical knowledge. This misunderstanding was compounded by the fact that his original method of discovery, the topics, had become lost or unrecognizable, for from late antiquity onwards they were used exclusively in a rhetorical context, and their use as a means of discovering scientific arguments was completely forgotten. The upshot of this was that the results of Aristotelian science had, by the Middle Ages, lost all contact with the procedures of discovery that produced them. While these results remained unchallenged, the problem was not apparent; but when, from the sixteenth century onwards, they came to be challenged in a serious and systematic way, they began to appear either as mere dogmas, or as the product of a hopelessly mistaken doctrine of method.[20] In other words, the empirical failure of Aristotelian science, a failure that had become manifest by the early decades of the seventeenth century, came to be seen as being due ultimately to a methodological failure, as arising either from a lack of method, or from the employment of a wrong method. It is in this context that we must consider Descartes' foray into the question of method,[21] for while his attempt to produce an account of it may have been stimulated by reflection on Rosicrucian attempts at method (not in the sense that he wanted to imitate these, but in the sense that he may have wanted to provide something at a similar level of generality but better), the question was one that was central to the philosophical tradition of thinking about natural philosophy.

This is evident in Rule 1, which sets out to establish the unity of knowledge. Descartes makes the claim there that 'all the sciences are so closely connected that it is much easier to learn them all together than to separate them from one another'.[22] Earlier in the Rule we are told that 'the sciences as a whole are nothing other than human wisdom'. This may be little more than a play on the word *scientia*, which had a much broader meaning than the modern idea of a 'science', covering both 'wisdom' and 'knowledge'. But the idea of the unity of knowledge marks a move away from the piecemeal studies that Descartes pursued with Beeckman, and a move towards the beginnings of philosophical reflection on the nature of scientific knowledge. Indeed, finding the right level of generality at which to approach and discuss natural philosophical questions is something that exercises Descartes more or less throughout his career from his work with Beeckman up until the mid-1630s, and it is interesting that the two extremes are broached within twelve months of one another: the extremely specific nature of the mechanical problems discussed under Beeckman's guidance at the end of 1618/early 1619 (although Descartes occasionally sought to broaden these, as in the case of free fall), and the extremely general level of discussion that we find in the early rules of method.

Having established the unity of knowledge in Rule 1, in Rule 2 Descartes sets out why we need a method if we are to succeed in our enquiries, holding up the mathematical sciences as models in virtue of the certainty of their results. Rules 3 and 4 then set out the two operations that method relies upon, namely intuition and deduction. The central topics here are the doctrines of intuition (*intuitus*) and deduction, and it is in these that the novelty of Descartes' account resides. Before we look at these, however, we should look briefly at the remaining Rules.

Rules 5, 6, and 7 provide details of how we are actually to proceed on this basis of the proposed method—they prescribe and explain what is meant by 'order', as Rule 8 puts it. Rule 5 tells us to resolve complex matters into simpler ones, and then build up our knowledge on the basis of the simple elements. The problem is how we recognize the simplest elements, and Rule 6 attempts to provide us with a criterion by which to do this, Descartes telling us that he considers this the most useful of all the Rules. The criterion rests on the distinction between 'absolutes' and 'relatives':

I call that absolute which contains within itself the pure and simple nature that we are considering, that is, whatever is being considered to be independent, a cause, simple, universal, one, equal, like, straight, and so forth. This absolute, this *primum*, I call the simplest and easiest of all, when it is of use in our further enquiries.[23]

The terminology of 'absolutes' here may seem to introduce a metaphysical note into the discussion. But in fact the phrase *de qua est quaestio* ('that we are considering') indicates that the absolute in question is relative to our enquiry, rather than to some basic metaphysical category, and the rest of the Rule bears this out. The list that Descartes provides is explicitly open-ended, and on the face of it is not exclusively mathematical, although it should be noted that his use of the term 'cause' in this context simply designates what comes first in a series, rather than a physical cause. His examples are exclusively mathematical, however, and if he does, as seems highly likely, consider the Rule as having a more general purview than mathematics, he is certainly modelling the rest of knowledge on mathematics. Finally, Rule 7 offers a view of the mind by which we are able to focus our attention on the totality of the elements that we are studying only by 'a continuous movement of thought', a topic we shall return to below.

Rules 8, 9, 10, and 11 elaborate on specific points relevant to the following of the proposed method. Rule 8, in the form we now have it, is in fact a complicated pastiche of texts which are not only not quite internally consistent but almost certainly date from different times.[24] The first two paragraphs alone would seem to date from 1619/20, and these merely tell us that we should not proceed in an enquiry beyond that of which we have a firm intuitive grasp. Rule 9 reminds us that we should dwell on the simplest cases, and seems directed against various naturalistic approaches to natural philosophy: so, for example, if we are concerned with whether natural powers can be transmitted instantaneously, we should confine our attention in the first instance to straightforward cases of motion such as the local motion of bodies, and not proceed any further until we have understood these, rather than immediately thinking in terms of the influence of the stars or the magnet, or the transmission of light. There can be little doubt that this was a very loaded way of raising this matter, despite its innocuous appearance, for, as we shall see in Chapter 5, there was a long tradition of taking light and magnetism as the model for the action of other forces, and such an approach could not be dismissed so easily. Rule 10 advises the reader to begin by exercising one's mental powers on problems already solved by others, and criticizes the attempt to discover truths by means of the syllogism. This last point bears on the question of the role of deductive reasoning in Descartes' method, as does the claim of Rule 11 that to see the connections between propositions we must run through them very quickly in our mind; and we can now turn to this core question in the *Regulae*.

Intuitus and the Doctrine of Clear and Distinct Ideas

'Deduction'[25] is a notoriously slippery term in Descartes; Desmond Clarke has drawn attention to contexts in which it is used to mean explanation, proof, induction, or justification, and on occasion it seems to do little more than describe the narration of an argument.[26] In Rule 2, Descartes makes a claim about deduction which at first makes one wonder just how he is using the term. He writes:

There are two ways of arriving at a knowledge of things, through experience and through deduction. Moreover, we must note that while our experiences of things are often deceptive, the deduction or pure inference of one thing from another can never be performed wrongly by an intellect which is in the least degree rational, though we may fail to make the inference if we do not see it. Those chains by which dialecticians hope to regulate human reason seem to me to be of little use here, though I do not deny that they are useful for other purposes. In fact, none of the errors to which men—men, I say, not brutes—are liable is ever due to faulty inference. They are due only to the fact that men take for granted certain poorly understood experiences, or lay down rash or groundless judgements.[27]

It is not too difficult to see why Descartes should want to maintain that we can never be mistaken about deduction, for he wants intuition and deduction to be the two trustworthy processes that we can use to lead us to genuine knowledge, and he makes the same claim about intuition, as we shall see. But to maintain that we can never make a mistake in deductive inference is a remarkable claim none the less. In order to find out precisely what he means, it is worth asking what precisely he is rejecting. What are the 'chains' by which the 'dialecticians' hope to regulate inference? These are presumably the rules governing syllogistic, those rules that specify which inference patterns are (formally) valid. The problem is to determine what it is that Descartes finds objectionable in such rules. The claim is certainly not that these rules are wrong and that others must be substituted for them, that new 'chains' must replace the old ones. Rather, the question hinges around the role that one sees these rules as having, since Descartes admits that they may 'be useful for other purposes'. What he is rejecting is their use as rules of reasoning, as something one needs to be familiar with in order to reason properly. If one looks at the logical texts with which we know him to have been familiar, above all those of Toletus and Fonseca, then we can identify the culprit with some degree of certainty: the Jesuit account of 'directions for thinking' (*directio ingenii*). As we saw when we looked at the logic curriculum at La Flèche, the Jesuit account of logic was one in which logic or dialectic was construed above all as a psychological process which required regulation if it was to function properly. In the light of this, one thing that we can take Descartes to be denying is that mental processes require external regulation, that rules to guide our thought are needed. This is made very clear in Rule 4(A):

[My] method cannot go so far as to teach us how to perform the actual operations of intuition and deduction, for these are the simplest of all and quite basic. If our intellect were not already able to perform them, it would not comprehend any of the rules of the method, however easy they might be. As for other mental operations which dialectic claims to direct with the help of those already mentioned, they are of no use here, or rather should be reckoned a positive hindrance, for nothing can be added to the clear light of reason which does not in some way dim it.[28]

This is an important point, for it is often implicitly assumed that the provision of such rules is just what Descartes is trying to achieve in the *Regulae*. But this cannot be the aim of the *Regulae*. Descartes' view is explicitly that inference is something that we, as rational creatures, perform naturally and correctly. What then do the 'rules for the direction of our native intelligence' do that is different from what the old rules of dialectic did? In fact, the difference seems to lie not so much in what the rules do as in what they rely upon to do it. Syllogistic relies on rules imposed from outside, in Descartes' view, whereas his rules are designed to capture an internal process which operates with a criterion of truth and falsity that is beyond question. This is that we accept as true all and only that of which we have a 'clear and distinct' perception. But the elaboration of this principle is largely confined to the discussion of 'intuition', and with good reason, for it soon becomes clear that deduction reduces, in the limiting case, to intuition.

Towards the end of Rule 3, Descartes tells us that 'the self-evidence and certainty of intuition is required not only for apprehending single propositions', but also for deduction, since in the inference 2 + 2 = 3 + 1, we must not only 'intuitively perceive that 2 plus 2 make 4, and that 3 plus 1 make 4, but also that the original proposition follows from the other two'. Here the first two perceptions are intuitions, whereas seeing the connection between them is a deduction. But the deduction seems in all important respects to be simply an intuition, albeit an intuition whose content is a relation between other intuitions. This clearly raises the question of the difference between an intuition and a deduction, and so Descartes sets out why he believes it necessary to distinguish deduction from intuition at all:

Hence we are distinguishing mental intuition from certain deductions on the grounds that we are aware of a movement or a sort of sequence in the latter but not in the former, and also because immediate self-evidence is not required for deduction, as it is for intuition; deduction in a sense gets its certainty from memory. It follows that those propositions that are immediately inferred from first principles can be said to be known in one respect through intuition, and in another respect through deduction. But the first principles themselves are known only through intuition, and the remote conclusions only through deduction.[29]

This is rather puzzling, given Descartes' example. Memory, in any genuine sense, would seem to play no real role in the deduction from 2 + 2 = 4 and 3 + 1 = 4 that 2 + 2 = 3 + 1. And why does he specify that *remote* consequences are known only through deduction? Could it be that the consequence in the example, which is far from being remote, is known not by deduction but by intuition? No: it is the example that Descartes himself gives of a deduction, and the only example at that. He seems concerned above all to restrict intuition to an absolutely instantaneous act, so that if there is any temporal sequence of any kind, no matter how brief, we are dealing with deduction rather than intuition. But this is the only difference, and even this difference is undermined in Rule 7, where Descartes elaborates on the question of how to make sure that deductions are reliable:

Thus if, for example, I have first found out, by distinct mental operations, what relation exists between the magnitudes A and B, then what between B and C, between C and D, and finally between D and E, that does not entail that I will see what the relation is between A and E, nor can the truths previously learned give me a precise idea of it unless I recall them all. To remedy this I would run over them many times, by a continuous movement of the imagination, in such a way that it has an intuition of each term at the same moment that it passes on to the others, and this I would do until I learned to pass from the first relation to the last so quickly that there was almost no role left for memory and I seemed to have the whole before me at the same time.[30]

In short, the more it approaches intuition, the more reliable deduction is. It is hard to avoid the conclusion that deduction is ultimately modelled on intuition, and that in the limiting case it becomes intuition.

Given this, the key notion is obviously that of intuition (*intuitus*). Intuition has two distinctive features: it is an instantaneous act, and it consists in a clear and distinct grasp of an idea. As regards the first feature, we have already seen how keen Descartes was to construe motion in terms of instantaneous tendencies to motion in the hydrostatics manuscript, and the importance of instantaneous acts or processes is something that he will make much of in his later writings. At this stage, however, we have so little to go on that we can do no more than note the fact that he seems committed to the idea of the instant, without providing any hint as to what the importance of instantaneous processes consists in. The notion of clear and distinct ideas, on the other hand, is something whose importance for Descartes we can understand, and the origins of the doctrine can be reconstructed.

Descartes is certainly not the first to employ the notion of clear and distinct ideas as a criterion for knowledge, the Stoics having operated with a similar criterion in their epistemology. Briefly, for the Stoics, our clear and distinct cognitive impressions provide us with a guarantee of the truth of these impressions. Descartes may have been familiar with this doctrine, and if he was it would have been from Book 7 of Diogenes Laertius' *Lives of the Greek Philosophers*, from Cicero's *Academica*, or from the very critical treatment in Sextus Empiricus. But I think it unlikely that he was simply taking over the Stoic doctrine, or even that he was influenced by the doctrine in its specifically Stoic form. For one thing, the Stoic doctrine is restricted in its application in the first instance to perceptual cognitive impressions, other cognitive impressions deriving their guarantee from these, whereas Descartes' paradigm case is that of a nonperceptual cognitive impression *par excellence*, namely mathematics: it is crucial to the Stoic doctrine that the fact that our impressions have an external source be taken into account,[31] whereas in Descartes' version of the doctrine the question of the source does not arise. Moreover, the Stoic doctrine, taken as one whereby we can inspect our cognitive impressions to determine whether they have the essential properties of clarity and distinctness, was subjected to severe criticism by Sextus, and one recent commentator has pointed out that it was so vulnerable that it is difficult to understand how the Stoics could have continued to defend it.[32] It is therefore unlikely that Descartes would simply have taken over the doctrine without at least trying to remedy defects that were pointed out in the expositions of Stoic teaching, especially since his own account, which focuses on properties of the image or idea, seems to rely on those elements that were most problematic for the Stoics and which they made the greatest efforts to go beyond by focusing on the external source of our impressions. In the light of this, I believe it is extremely unlikely that Descartes' account derives from the explicitly epistemological version of the doctrine offered by the Stoics, but rather that it derives from a more general and traditional version of it, which explicitly deals with qualities of ideas, impressions, or images in such a way that it is not their source that is at issue but the quality of the image itself, just as it is for Descartes. This is also a doctrine which we know with certainty that he would have been very familiar with.

And in fact Descartes' account of clear and distinct ideas has some rather striking parallels with a psychological theory of cognitive grasp that he would have been very familiar with from his studies at La Flèche. This theory, although Aristotelian in origin, is to be found not only in the Stoic version, but, in its most familiar form in the early modern period, in the writings of Quintilian. It may at first seem peculiar that Descartes should derive his criterion from a work which is, with Cicero's writings, the classic account of rhetorical invention. But this account was drawn upon extensively in the sixteenth and seventeenth centuries, and it is not at all surprising that Descartes should have taken such an account as his starting-point.

Rhetoric took over what had traditionally been conceived to be the concerns of logic in a number of areas. This is most evident in the case of 'invention', that is, the discovery of those arguments necessary to convince an opponent, starting from shared premises, of some case that one wants to establish. Aristotle had discussed this question in a broadly scientific context in the *Topics*, but the models for such conviction were drawn from rhetoric, especially from Quintilian, by the sixteenth century. Quintilian had devoted a great deal of attention to discovering those arguments likely to lead to conviction in areas such as legal argument and political oratory, and indeed if conviction were one's aim then such techniques are, it is true, more likely to be of use than an understanding of which syllogistic forms of argument are, say, formally valid. This does not mean that the espousal of rhetoric carried with it a disregard for valid arguments, for it did not: it just meant that validity was regarded merely as one ingredient in a good argument. Now, this is a fair point. Although Aristotle's syllogistic deals with probabilistic forms of argument, and accepts that arguments may be valid without being formally valid, it is above all a theory of formally valid inferences, and an understanding of formally valid inferences is not something that one is likely to find especially useful in trying to convince a recalcitrant opponent of some contentious conclusion.[33] It is far from clear that logic, understood as a theory of the nature of formally valid inferences, is of any use by itself in changing someone's mind about a conclusion, or that it is of any use in enabling us to understand why someone changed their mind as a result of being convinced by an argument.[34] The first question seems rather to fall under the category of techniques of persuasion, and the aim of rhetorical theories is precisely to capture and elaborate upon what kinds of techniques of persuasion are best fitted to different kinds of situation. This does not prevent logical considerations being brought to bear, but these will be paramount only in those cases where deductive certainty can be achieved, and such cases are not likely to be common.[35] The second question, that of how argument can change our beliefs, is much more difficult to deal with, but the rhetorical tradition, drawing on Aristotelian and occasionally on Stoic psychology, had tried to provide some account of how our ideas might be compared in terms of their vividness, for example, and it is not too hard to see how a notion such as 'vividness' might operate as a rudimentary criterion for the replacement of one belief by another. Although (so far as I can tell) this topic was not pursued in any detail in antiquity, there are explicit seventeenth-century accounts that show how the theory works. In Descartes' account of the passions, the body, acting by means of the animal spirits, stimulates a desire which the mind can counter by representing objects vividly to itself which, by the principle of association, halts the course of the spirits.[36] And Malebranche, when tackling the problem of how we are to resist a lesser good, by which we are tempted, in favour of a greater good, tells us that what we must do is to represent the greater good to ourselves as vividly as possible, so that it becomes more vivid in our mind than the lesser good, the suggestion being that once the balance of vividness has been tipped, we will automatically assent to or wish for the greater good. The ultimate source of such accounts lies, I suggest, in the rhetorical-psychological theories of the Roman rhetorical writers, especially Quintilian.

The Roman rhetorical writers took up elements from the psychological and poetic theories of their predecessors, as well as from their rhetorical works. Paramount amongst these earlier authors was Aristotle, and in the writings of Quintilian we can find elements not only from Aristotle's *Rhetoric* and *Poetics*, but also from the *Nicomachean Ethics* and the third book of the *De Anima*. In particular, Quintilian is concerned, as were earlier writers on rhetoric, such as Cicero and the author of the anonymous *Rhetorica ad herennium*, with the qualities of the 'image', with the search for and presentation of images that were distinctive in their vividness and particularity. A number of rhetorical and psychological concerns meet here, and it is a distinctive feature of Roman writers on rhetoric that psychological categories are used to provide a basis for rhetorical ones, this being nowhere more true than in Quintilian's *Institutio Oratoria*.

The very possibility of this whole approach derives initially from Aristotle's defence of the emotions in the third book of the *De Anima*. An important part of this account takes the form of a theory of the image-making capacity of judgement, something which Plato had a low opinion of, but which Aristotle is concerned to defend.[37] The imagination (*phantasia*), Aristotle tells us, functions rather like sense perception. It works with images that enable the mind to think, 'and for this reason, unless one perceived things one would not learn or understand anything, and when one contemplates one must at the same time contemplate an image (*phantasma*), for images are like sense perceptions, except that they are without matter'.[38] The Roman rhetorical tradition was especially concerned with such images, and above all with the question of what features or qualities they must have if they are to be employed effectively in convincing an audience. Whether one is an orator at court or an actor on stage, Quintilian tells us, our aim is to engage the emotions of the audience, and perhaps to get it to behave in a particular way as a result.[39] What one must do if one is to achieve this, in Quintilian's view, is to transform the psychological image, the *phantasma*, into its rhetorical counterpart, the *eikon*. Kathy Eden has drawn attention to a very interesting feature of this account, namely, that what Quintilian is concerned with above all is the *evidential* quality of images. What the orator needs to do is to *exhibit* rather than *display* his proofs: 'to perform its office, the image requires, even at the psychological stage, the vividness and palpability characteristic of real evidence in the law court'.[40] That there are parallels here with Descartes' doctrine of clear and distinct ideas is indisputable. Just as Aristotle and Quintilian are concerned with the vividness and particularity of the images employed by the orator, dramatist, or lawyer, so Descartes is concerned with the clarity and distinctness of the mental images he refers to as 'ideas'. In both cases there is some variation in terminology—Quintilian talks of both vividness and particularity, and vividness and palpability (amongst other variations), and Descartes of clarity and distinctness, clarity and vividness, clarity and simpleness, and so on—but nothing hinges on this. The question is whether the parallels are merely superficial, or whether they reflect a deeper shared concern.

One very important respect in which the context of the accounts of Aristotle and Quintilian and that of Descartes differ is that, in the former, conviction is conceived in discursive terms. In the case of Aristotle, this is as true of logic as it is of rhetoric, drama, and legal pleading. Aristotle conceived of the dialectical syllogism as being designed to induce conviction in an opponent, the demonstrative syllogism as being designed to induce conviction in a student, and so on. The context of argumentation is discursive in the sense that one is always arguing with someone on the basis of shared premises, for unless there were shared premises, the argument could not begin. In the rhetorical, dramatic, and legal cases, the situation is even more straightforward, for here what one is doing is directed towards an audience. And in Quintilian, where 'oratory' virtually takes over the whole question of inducing conviction, conviction is clearly directed at an audience.

Descartes' conception of conviction is different from this. For Descartes, the central task is to convince oneself, and only once one has done this does one try to convince others. The question that naturally arises here is whether a theory devoted to considering how, in general, one goes about convincing an audience of something, on grounds that may not always depend on the truth of what one is arguing, could possibly form the basis for a theory about what characteristics of ideas allow us to recognize their truth, even if we would have difficulty convincing others of that truth.[41] The answer is that it could. What we must focus on is the psychological content. Psychological theory about questions of judgement was transmitted to the modern era above all in the form of rhetorical theory, and of great significance here was Quintilian's treatise on oratory. There can be no doubt that this could have played a critical role in Descartes' thinking about judging the truth of theories in terms of the clear and distinct perception of ideas. On Quintilian's account, and here he follows Aristotle, vivid illustration (*evidentia*) of the facts 'goes beyond mere clarity, since the latter merely lets itself be seen, whereas the former thrusts itself upon our attention'.[42] But how do we achieve such *evidentia*? The answer is given as follows:

> If we wish to give our words the appearance of sincerity, we must assimilate ourselves to the emotions of those who are genuinely so affected, and our eloquence must spring from the same feeling that we desire to produce in the mind of the judge. Will he grieve who can find no trace of grief in the words with which I seek to move him to grief? . . . It is utterly impossible. Fire alone can kindle, and moisture alone can wet, nor can one thing impart any colour to another save that which it possesses itself. Accordingly, the first essential is that those feelings should prevail with us that we wish to prevail with the judge, and that we should be moved ourselves before we attempt to move others.[43]

Quintilian then goes on to ask how we generate these emotions in ourselves, and there follows his account of the evidential quality of images. The crucial point that I want to draw attention to here is that unless one is already convinced by one's own images, then one will not be in a position to use them to convince others. So self-conviction is a prerequisite for the conviction of others. And self-conviction, like the conviction of one's audience, depends on the qualities of the image, amongst which must figure clarity (*perspicuitas*) and vividness (*evidentia*).

This model of self-conviction, I am suggesting, is effectively that taken up by Descartes in Rule 3 when we are told that what we must seek is something we can clearly and evidently intuit (*clarè et evidenter possimus intueri*), and that the mind that is 'clear and attentive' will be able to achieve this. Although the early *Regulae* draws its model of knowledge almost exclusively from mathematics, the point is that the doctrine of clear and distinct ideas is exhibited paradigmatically in the case of mathematics, not that it is somehow derived from mathematics. It might seem peculiar that a conception based on such a strongly pictorial model of representation should find its paradigmatic manifestation in something as abstract as mathematics. But problematic though this is for Descartes, it is not especially surprising. As we saw in Chapter 2, the rhetorical exercises favoured by the Jesuit educators with whom Descartes studied at La Flèche were based, amongst other things, on Philostratus' procedure of describing an imaginary painting in such vivid terms that the reader was made to feel she was seeing it. And as we have also seen, in the earliest writing that we have from Descartes, the *Compendium Musicae*, clarity of representation, which amounts to favouring that pictorial form of representation in which differences can be detected at a glance—the representation of musical intervals not as a ratio of integers, but as a pairing of line lengths by arithmetic proportion—is a focal point of the treatise. Moreover, in the *Cogitationes Privatae*, which are roughly contemporary with the early *Regulae*, Descartes makes the image-forming power of the imagination the basis for the operations of reason, and indeed its power is extolled above that of reason:

> As imagination makes use of figures to conceive of bodies, so intellect makes use of certain sensible bodies to figure spiritual things, such as wind and light; by which, philosophizing more profoundly, we can draw our mind by cognition to the heights. It may seem remarkable that there are more weighty judgements in the writings of poets than of philosophers. The reason is that poets write with more enthusiasm and the force of imagination; there are within us, as in flintstone, sparks of the sciences which are educed through reason by philosophers but which are struck forth by poets through imagination.[44]

The idea of this image-forming power being at the centre of cognition was the dominant one for Descartes. Indeed, in his writings at this time Descartes does not use the term *imaginatio* and its correlates to indicate simple operations, but rather, to denote active, exploratory, investigative processes: visualizing geometrical constructions, visualizing the end of apparently infinite processes of division, applying mathematical constructs to physical problems, or the power by which a listener is able to synthesize a unity out of the discrete parts of a song.[45]

The Doctrine of Analysis

The theory of clear and distinct ideas is the crucial ingredient in the early *Regulae*, for it is this theory that enables Descartes to generalize his methodological considerations from mathematics to the whole of knowledge, in that it provides the key to modelling knowledge on mathematics. But what does this modelling consist in? When one thinks of the mathematical works of antiquity, one thinks of axiomatic systems. These are precisely what Descartes rejected in the early version of Rule 4—Rule 4B—and indeed, he accused the ancient mathematicians of duplicity, having discovered their results by a method which they then hid, and trying to mislead us by presenting the results as 'sterile truths demonstrated by clever arguments', that is, deductively or 'synthetically'. The point is repeated in 4A, where we are told: 'we are well aware that the geometers of antiquity employed a sort of analysis which they went on to apply to the solution of every problem, though they begrudged revealing it to posterity'.[46]

Descartes' advocacy of analysis at the expense of synthesis is an extremely important feature of his method, for it amounts to the advocacy of a problem-solving approach as the method of discovery, and the rejection of a deductive approach. Greek mathematicians, especially the later Alexandrian authors, had used two modes of mathematical argument, analysis and synthesis. Analysis consisted of techniques enabling one to find a solution to problems, either by establishing the truth of some theorem ('theoretical analysis') or by finding some unknown quantity or construction ('problematical analysis'). Such problem-solving techniques had a heuristic value, and they did not amount to proof. Synthesis, on the other hand, shows how a solution is to be derived from first principles. For the Greek mathematicians, both methods were needed, although the actual proof was conducted in the course of the synthesis, so it was usually only the synthesis that was presented. Now, like syllogistic, synthesis is a form of deductive demonstration. Descartes is rejecting as a means of discovery not just the former, but the latter as well. The uselessness of synthesis as a means of discovery may well have been compounded for Descartes by the attempt of Clavius to construe analysis in terms of syllogistic, thereby rendering the whole process, not just the synthetic part of it, deductive. Clavius' *Algebra* was Descartes' starting point for studies in the area, and he is still using Clavius' clumsy cossic notation at this stage. The *Algebra* proceeds synthetically, but in the first proposition of Book I of Euclid an 'analysis' is presented. This is not an analysis of the kind we find in Pappus, the kind that Descartes is trying to reconstruct, but an Aristotelian analysis which has nothing whatever to do with analysis in the sense in which Descartes is interested in it. Clavius simply decomposes the problem (the construction of an equilateral triangle on a given finite line) into three syllogisms, the first of which is of the form:

Every triangle having three equal sides is equilateral.
The triangle ABC has three equal sides.

Therefore, the triangle ABC is equilateral.

He then tells us that all other mathematical propositions can be similarly analysed, but that mathematicians do not usually bother to provide such analyses because the demonstration does not strictly require it, and can proceed more easily without it.[47]

What is happening here is that analysis is being made little more than a preparation for synthesis; it is simply an exercise in translating geometrical propositions into syllogistic form so that the deductive structure of geometrical demonstrations can be shown to be what it really is, namely an exercise in Aristotelian logic. If we bear this in mind, we can begin to understand the polemical edge in Descartes' attack on the 'sterile' demonstrations of the ancients, and his attempt to dissociate analysis from synthesis completely. The reconstruction of geometry in syllogistic terms would make it a thoroughly Aristotelian enterprise, and the point of trying to remodel knowledge along the lines of mathematics would be completely lost. Small wonder, then, that Descartes rejects the value of synthesis so decisively.

This was a view that Descartes never abandoned, as we shall see, and it takes little reflection to realize that it is completely at odds with the notion that a mathematical model for knowledge commits one to the discovery of knowledge by means of a deduction from first principles. If one still has any doubt about this, one only needs to look at the *Géométrie*. None of the axioms, theorems, etc., of Classical mathematics can be found there, nor a deductive system of any kind. Descartes does, it is true, present a few synthetic proofs, but it is the analysis that carries one along; and after a few preliminaries the reader is thrown into one of the most difficult mathematical problems bequeathed by antiquity, Pappus' locus problem for four or more lines, which Descartes proceeds to solve analytically without further ado. Problem-solving is what mathematics is about for Descartes, not axiomatic demonstration. And problem-solving, in the guise of analysis, is what he is concerned to foster in his account of method.

Fundamentum inventi mirabilis

The way in which Descartes describes his discovery of 'method' in the early *Regulae* might easily lead one to suppose that he was at the beginning of a period of new discoveries and synthesis of results. But in fact little seems to have come of the project. Indeed, he seems to have abandoned the *Regulae*. During 1620, he continued work in mathematics which shows no obvious connection with anything in the *Regulae*. He developed the connections between arithmetic and geometry in a number of ways, but none of them (despite his own later reconstruction in the *Discours*) seems to have any direct connection with 'method' in any general sense.

There are, in fact, a number of grey areas in this period, and even Descartes' movements during 1620 are something of a mystery. On 3 July 1620 a treaty between the Catholic League and the Protestant Union was drawn up at Ulm, and Descartes may have spent the month during which the negotiations were pursued at Ulm. It is quite possible, however, that he was no longer a serving soldier, and the circumstantial evidence indicates that he was probably not present at the Battle of the White Mountain outside Prague on 8 November, where the Catholic forces were victorious and Frederick was deposed.[48] Baillet tells us that he returned to France in February 1622, but his whereabouts between mid-1620 and then are unknown. 1620 seems to have been an intellectually productive year for Descartes, however, and he notes in the *Olympica* that on 10 November he had found the 'fundamental principles of a wonderful discovery' (*fundamentum inventi mirabilis*).[49]

What he is referring to here cannot be known with any certainty. The only extant work that we can date, even provisionally, to the period between the completion of the early *Regulae* at the end of 1619 or beginning of 1620, and the optical and mathematical researches that probably began around 1625, is the treatment of a number of problems in solid geometry and figurate numbers collected under the title *De Solidorum Elementis*.[50] There is some dispute as to the dating of the *De Solidorum*, but the most likely date of composition is some time in 1620, although it may have been as late as 1623.[51] The work is devoted to polyhedra, and in the first part of it Descartes tries to show how to extend results for plane figures to solid ones, extending Pythagoras' theorem to three-dimensional figures, for example. Most attention by commentators on this part of the work has focused on Descartes' supposed anticipation of the 'Euler formula' for convex polyhedra. Descartes offers the remark that 'there are twice as many plane angles as sides on the surface of a solid body, for one side is always common to two faces',[52] and some commentators have argued that this, combined with Descartes' claim that the number of plane angles equals $2\phi + 2\alpha - 4$ (where ϕ is the number of faces and α is the number of solid angles), yields a fundamental result, namely Euler's formula, $S - A + F = 2$ (where S is the number of vertices, A the number of edges, and F the number of faces); but Descartes does not put the two equations together, and the attribution is highly dubious.[53] Of some interest in understanding Descartes' general approach to mathematical problem solving is his attempt to prove that there cannot be more than five regular Platonic polyhedra, for here he takes a problem that had already been solved in geometrical terms (in Euclid's *Elements*, xiii. 18) and tries to give an algebraic proof of it. The procedure mirrors that of his work on hydrostatics, where he took a problem already solved in macroscopic terms and tried to solve it in microscopic terms, with the aim of providing a proper explanation of the phenomenon thereby; here the algebraic 'proof'—and it should be noted that it is not a full algebraic proof, but rather a somewhat intuitive sketch of an algebraic proof (mirroring the micro-reduction of the hydrostatics exercise)— is presumably supposed to replace the geometrical one in virtue of its greater generality.

Turning to the second section of *De Solidorum*, there are discussions of figurate numbers in the *Cogitationes Privatae* as well as in the *De Solidorum*, and Descartes evidently devoted considerable attention to them. Figurate numbers are integers that can be represented by a regular array of points. The number 20 can be represented by an array of equally-spaced dots—1, 3, 6, 10—for example, and since the dots form a triangle, the number is a triangular number. Triangles are the simplest form of polygon,[54] and Descartes is interested in the general case of polygonal numbers, which can be represented by the points making up a polygon, and polyhedral numbers, which can be represented by the points making up the three-dimensional version of the polygon, the polyhedron. He provides a means of calculating polygonal numbers by resolving them into triangular numbers, that is, by resolving the polygon into triangles. This then serves as a way into what appears to be the main task of the exercise, the calculation of polyhedral numbers, which are correspondingly resolved into pyramids. Descartes succeeds in calculating the polyhedral numbers for five regular and eleven semi-regular polyhedra.[55] Both Faulhaber and Roth had treated figurate numbers in some detail, and Faulhaber had given a detailed account of the polygonal and pyramidal numbers, from both a mathematical and a numerological perspective, in his *Numerus figuratus* of 1614, which there is every reason to think Descartes had read, given his friendship with Faulhaber.[56] The greatest interest in polyhedral numbers was exhibited by those with numerological or more generally mystical inclinations, and Kepler's *Harmonices mundi* (which falls into the latter category) devoted considerable space to the Archimedean semi-regular polyhedra.[57] Descartes' interest was certainly not numerological, and even given the odd rather exuberant sentence in the *Olympica*, it would be nothing short of ridiculous to ascribe mystical motives to him. The exercise does trade on relations between arithmetic and geometry, and in this respect might be thought to complement the project of establishing ties between arithmetic and geometry in terms of a theory of proportions, but in fact it is very difficult to understand what precisely the connection between the two enterprises would be at this level, and any parallels are probably superficial. His work on polyhedral numbers would seem to be unconnected with his other enterprises, and it may have been pursued simply because Descartes was keen to sharpen his mathematical skills in an area that was actively being pursued by his friend Faulhaber, much in the same way that he had taken on the mechanical problems that Beeckman had set him. Unfortunately, we do not know enough about his relation with Faulhaber to know whether there are any significant parallels with his relation with Beeckman, but he actively sought out problems from the latter and he may well have done so from the former.

It is unlikely that anything in the *De Solidorum*, assuming it to have been written in 1620, would merit the title 'fundamental principles of a wonderful science'. What, then, is Descartes referring to? Two possibilities have been suggested, neither of them reflecting anything extant, but there are indications in Descartes' extant writings of work on topics which seem to foreshadow developments that are only elaborated upon at a later stage, leaving open the possibility that the actual discovery was made at this early stage.

The first possibility is that Descartes discovered the sine law of refraction at this time. There is certainly no formulation of the law to be found in any extant writings of this period, but some commentators have suggested that it could have been derived from theories that he can plausibly be said to have held. Certainly Descartes had a very marked interest in optics. We have already seen that he was familiar with Della Porta's writings on optical illusions from his days at La Flèche, and he could not have failed to have been caught up in the widespread interest in theories of lenses in the wake of Galileo's telescopic discovery of the moons of Jupiter. The *Cogitationes Privatae* shows evidence of a reading of Kepler's pathbreaking work on optics, the *Ad Vitellionem*,[58] for at least one distinctly Keplerian doctrine— that the denser the medium the greater the motion of the ray of light— is to be found there. Certainly Descartes may have held assumptions from which the sine law of refraction can be derived, and Milhaud and Sirven, amongst others, have suggested that he did in fact discover it at this time.[59] As Sabra has shown, he certainly seems to have developed two principles which were subsequently to play a part in his physical explanation of the law. These are the principle of the direct proportionality of the force/speed of light to the density of the medium, which, as I have just indicated, probably derives from Kepler, and the principle of decomposition of the light ray into orthogonal components, also quite possibly deriving from Kepler.[60] We shall see how these principles operate when we come to look at Descartes' physical account of the law. For the moment, it is sufficient to note that, even given that Descartes was familiar with these principles in 1620, it is in fact highly unlikely that he discovered the sine law at this stage.[61] This is a topic to which we shall return in the next chapter. For the moment, we need simply note that while the discovery of the sine law of refraction was dated to 1620, this was by far the most promising candidate for the 'fundamental principles' that Descartes says he has discovered; but once this is discounted we are obliged to seek another possibility.

We do not have to look far. A number of commentators, including Liard and Hamelin, have argued that Descartes is referring to a mathematical discovery, and Milhaud and Sirven both accepted that some of the material presented in detail in the third Book of the *Géométrie* may have been developed in an embryonic form around

1620. The work that is picked out is the 'solution of all solid problems', that is, the construction of all problems resolvable in terms of cubic or quartic equations by means of a circle and a parabola. The evidence for the dating of this mathematical discovery is based above all on a statement by Lipstorp who, in his account of Descartes' life and work, *Philosophiae Cartesianae* (1653), tells us explicitly that, while at Ulm with Faulhaber in 1620, Descartes solved solid problems of the third and fourth degree by means of a circle and a parabola, referring us to Book 3 of the *Géométrie* for details of Descartes' account.[62] There is also an entry in Beeckman's diary dating from 1628–9 which describes Descartes' work since he left Beeckman at the beginning of 1619, which includes a description of a method for finding roots by means of the intersection of a circle and a parabola,[63] exactly the same procedure to which Lipstorp refers.

What Beeckman describes is an early version of the full treatment of Book 3 of the *Géométrie*. In the *Géométrie*, we are presented with an analytic procedure for construction of a parabola and a circle, and then a synthetic demonstration; whereas here we are only provided with the analysis, that is, with what Descartes considers to be constitutive of the mathematical enterprise. Beeckman begins his account of the solution as follows:

With the help of a parabola, to construct all solid problems by a general method, [which] D. des Chartes in another place calls a universal secret for resolving all complicated equations of third and fourth dimension by means of geometrical lines. I describe [this] word for word from his writings.[64]

The equation we are to solve is a quartic (sometimes called a biquadratic), so called because it is an equation of the fourth degree, that is, it involves terms of (and no terms higher than) the fourth power. Its general form, in the later notation of the *Géométrie*, is $z^4 = \pm pz^2 \pm qz \pm r$. In essence, what happened is that Descartes discovered that two mean proportionals could be found using only a circle and a parabola, and he realized that the procedure for doing this could be represented in a cubic equation; on the strength of this, he went on to ask whether all cubic and quartic equations could not be solved in a similar way. How Descartes first arrived at his solution is a matter of conjecture, but the most plausible reconstruction is that of Schuster, who has shown how reflection on the solution of the mean proportional problem by the mesolabe compass could have led Descartes in the right direction.[65]

Briefly, the reconstruction runs along the following lines. As we have seen in the last chapter, early in 1619 Descartes had solved the problem of the construction of mean proportionals using the mesolabe compass. The Alexandrian mathematician Menaechmus had also solved this problem. Descartes does not mention Menaechmus' solution in offering his own, and he may not even have been aware of it; but he seems to have become aware of it soon after. Menaechmus in fact offered two solutions, one requiring a parabola and a hyperbola, and the other requiring two parabolas. In reflecting upon the second of these in particular, Descartes may have wondered about the nature of the relevant curves defined by the motion of his compass. He knew that these curves were a circle and another curve that he had not been able to describe in the *Cogitationes Privatae*. Indeed, in the work of 1619/20 described in the *Cogitationes*, Descartes' approach was largely instrumental, and he was not particularly concerned with the analysis of the curves he was working with. But the discovery that his solution to the problem of mean proportionals was potentially simpler than that of Menaechmus—since he was able to solve the problem with the as yet unknown curve and a circle, whereas both Menaechmus' solutions required two conic sections[66]—may have been what guided his search for the nature of the curve. It was clear that its defining characteristic was a parabola, and the search was then on for a construction involving a circle and a parabola. Then, as Schuster points out, 'geometrical tinkering guided by simple algebraic analysis would have revealed the basic construction for $x^3 = a^2b$, and only two further basic constructive moves would have been needed to arrive at the solutions for $x^3 = \pm apx \pm a^2b$ and $x^4 = \pm apx^2 \pm a^2bx \pm a^3k$. The latter steps would have required only minimal geometrical adjustment guided by elementary algebraic insight'. There is a crucial move here, away from being completely guided in his constructions and equations by conformations of the compass, to an algebraic understanding of the curves generated by the compass. The gradual discovery of the means of solving solid problems is important above all because it points Descartes in a new direction, one in which, as Schuster puts it, 'the conformation of the compass matters less than the algebraic comprehension and manipulation of the curves generated', and towards the realization 'that algebra and geometry move hand in hand in the invention and specification of ever more complex constructions'.[67]

Descartes himself was certainly aware of the importance of his achievement. Reporting his discovery, Beeckman adds that Descartes 'considers this discovery so important that he grants that he has never discovered anything more outstanding and that no one else has ever discovered anything more outstanding'.[68] If the discovery can be dated to 1620, and no more plausible dating than this has been proposed, then it highly likely that this is what Descartes is referring to as his discovery of the 'fundamental principles of a wonderful discovery'.

Intermezzo, 1621–1625

1619 and 1620 were very productive years for Descartes, but there is no extant material that we can date with any confidence to the next four years, and it is possible that they were lean years intellectually. Indeed, these years are something of a mystery, and we cannot even be sure of Descartes' movements. Baillet tells us that Descartes returned to France in February 1622, possibly via the Netherlands and Flanders,[69] and remained there until 1623. We have a few isolated clues as to his whereabouts. There is a legal settlement signed by him at Rennes on 3 April 1622, in which he enters into an agreement not to sell certain property received from his brother Pierre (by this time a member of the Parliament of Brittany) for less than a certain price,[70] and we know that he was in Poitou on 22 May 1622, for Baillet reports a record of sale of his 'fief of Perron with seigneurial rights', as well as other properties.[71] The proceeds from these sales, which made up one third of his mother's estate, provided Descartes with an income which enabled him to live (modestly) without having to earn a living.[72] Baillet believed that he spent most of the time between February 1622 and March 1623 in Paris, and we have no reason to doubt this. We know little of Descartes' activities in Paris during this period. Baillet[73] reports work on a treatise *Studium bonae mentis*, now lost, which evidently covered the dispositions of mind required for scientific thought. We can provisionally date this to 1623, and it is possible that it was in the tradition of treatises on the passions,[74] which had been a popular genre since the 1590s. At this time, Descartes seems to have known, amongst others, Marin Mersenne and Claude Mydorge, both of whom had a great interest in mathematics. Mersenne had a very wide range of interests, and we shall be concerned with his formulation of mechanism and its influence on Descartes in some detail in the next chapter, but in the early to mid-1620s he had, amongst other things, a particular interest in mathematics, and in 1626 he compiled a large three-volume collection of the work of mathematicians (including both pure and applied mathematics), the *Synopsis mathematica*.[75] Mydorge was above all a mathematician, making important advances in the treatment of conic sections, although this interest came to be motivated principally by his interest in catoptrics (the optics of mirrors). Unfortunately, we do not know how well Descartes knew Mydorge at this period, or how familiar they were with one another's work.

In a letter to Pierre of 21 March 1623, Descartes tells his elder brother that he intends setting out to Italy, with the intention of being appointed Intendant of the army in the Alps. Baillet quotes from the letter, telling us that he says he 'ought to leave by post on the 22nd of the same month, after having sent word to his relatives that a voyage beyond the Alps would be of great use to him so that he might teach himself about business, acquire some experience of the world, and form habits which he had not previously had; adding that, if he did not become richer, he would at least become more able'.[76] So far as we can tell, he did make the trip soon afterwards, perhaps on the 22nd as planned. No record of the journey survives, although there are a few clues, and, as Adam has pointed out, the itinerary would to some extent have been modelled on Montaigne's travels in Italy[77] described in the *Journal* of his voyage, first published in 1581.

Baillet set out to reconstruct Descartes' probable itinerary, and it is likely that it is correct in general outline.[78] His route was through Basle, Innsbruck, over the Brenner pass, and down into the Adige valley in Venezia Giulia. The area around the strategically located Valtelline was occupied by French troops, and once through this area the short journey to Venice would have been straightforward. Baillet believes he was in Venice in 1624 to witness the annual celebrations in which, with great ceremony, a golden spear was thrown into the sea, to commemorate the Doge's bonds with the Adriatic, and these were held on the feast of the Ascension, which fell on 16 May. Immediately after his dream of 10 November 1619, he had promised to make a pilgrimage to Our Lady of Loretto, and he may have travelled to Loretto from Venice: it was a major place of pilgrimage, and it is unlikely that Descartes would have neglected to make a journey there. Over forty years earlier, Montaigne had made a similar trip, described in detail in the *Journal*, under similar spiritual circumstances, and given the place of Montaigne in the *gentilhomme* culture from which Descartes came, I do not believe there can be any doubt that Montaigne's model was taken very seriously.[79] Descartes returned via Tuscany and Piedmont, and although he travelled through Florence, where Galileo resided, he says in a letter of 11 October 1638 that he has never met Galileo.[80] After Piedmont, he travelled north-east, almost certainly crossing the Mount Cenis pass into France, for he shows some familiarity with Mount Cenis later on, maintaining that it is the best place for estimating the height of the mountains.[81] He probably crossed in May 1625, for in the *Météors* he tells us that he has seen avalanches in May while crossing the Alps.

Descartes may well have seriously considered staying in Italy, and in two later letters he discusses the advantages and disadvantages of living there.[82] The presence there of the greatest scientists attracted him, but evidently the very warm humid climate, and a serious crime problem, tipped the balance. And there were other kinds of trouble brewing. In 1616 the Roman Inquisition condemned a short treatise by Foscarini which attempted to show full compatibility between the Copernican theory and all scriptural passages, although an adherence to Copernicanism as a hypothesis was not forbidden.[83] This was the beginning of a gradual assault on Copernicanism, culminating in the condemnation of Galileo in 1633, which, as we shall see, was to have a great effect on Descartes. Even if he had been tempted earlier, Italy would certainly have lost any real attraction for him in the 1630s, as it gradually and tragically became transformed from a leading scientific and cultural centre into a backwater trading on an illustrious past.[84]

5
The Paris Years
1625–1628

Libertine Paris

By June 1625 Descartes had reached Poitiers, having travelled north via Lyons.[1] On his way there he had stopped in Châtelleraut, presumably to visit his family, and he had tried, whilst there, to negotiate for the position of Lieutenant-General of the area. This position was for sale as the incumbent had to relinquish it to buy another for his son, but the asking price was 16,000 crowns, which was 6,000 more than Descartes had. A friend, who Baillet tells us was the Sieur de Masparault,[2] offered to lend Descartes the extra money interest-free. Descartes then wrote to his father, who was in Paris, asking him for advice in making his decision. Evidently Descartes was afraid that his father would not consider him equal to the responsibility, having left it too late to enter the legal profession, and he offered to spend some time first as Procurator of Châtelet until he had learned enough about the duties involved. His plan was to go and see his father in Paris as soon as he heard from him.

We do not know what his father's response was, but we may surmise that it was not encouraging. Descartes was to remain in Paris, with occasional visits elsewhere, for the next three years, and he was never again to mention the possibility of a legal or administrative career, or indeed any paid career. From this time onwards, he was to live off the money that his mother had left him, at least some of which was invested in dairy farming.[3] He stayed initially at the house of a friend of his father's, Nicolas Le Vasseur, but left him suddenly without saying a word, and disappeared for five or six weeks. His host found Descartes, who had taken a room elsewhere, through a chance meeting with his valet in the street, and Descartes was apologetic,[4] but we have no explanation for this episode. From June 1626, Baillet tells us, he settled for a while in Faubourg Saint-Germaine, in the Rue du Four at *Les Trois Chappelets*, which appears to have served for a meeting-place for his friends.

The years spent in Paris, between the middle of 1625 and early to mid-1628, were the only ones in which we know Descartes to have worked in the company of a number of like-minded thinkers. The intellectual milieu of Paris at this time was conducive to new ideas, although on the face of it the contrary was the case. In the period between 1619, when Vanini was burnt at the stake for heresy in Toulouse, and 1625, there had been considerable repression of 'free thought', and in July 1623 the *parlement* of Paris ordered the arrest of four libertine authors of a collection of scurrilous verse, *Parnasse Satyrique*. Descartes admired the work of, and may well have known, one of this group, Théophile de Viau, who was condemned to banishment in 1625,[5] and he would doubtless have been familiar with this form of libertinage, which Pintard calls 'libertinage flamboyant'.[6] But the libertinage which flourished in this period in Paris was a much more general phenomenon than its 'flamboyant' variety, ranging from unorthodoxy or free thought to debauchery, deism, and Machiavellism. One of its fiercest critics, the Jesuit François Garasse, characterized libertinage as secretive, professing to believe in God while actually worshipping nature and submitting to the immutable laws of destiny, holding that the Bible offered both good and bad precepts, believing in neither angels nor devils, holding that animals may be superior to men in some respects, denying the Incarnation, and scepticism about the immortality of the soul.[7] Descartes' circle included both libertines, especially if one takes the term broadly to embrace any kind of unorthodoxy (remembering that orthodoxy was defined in a rigid and detailed way in this era), and critics of libertinage. Between 1623 and 1625 there had been a concerted campaign against libertinage, and in 1624 three anti-Aristotelian speakers—Jean Bituald, Étienne de Claves, and Antoine Villon—were exiled on pain of death from Paris for trying to hold a public meeting critical of Aristotle, which evidently attracted a crowd of eight or nine hundred, at which fourteen chemical/alchemical and atomist theses were to be debated.[8] The banishment of the authors was instigated by the Sorbonne, and on 4 September 1624 the *parlement*, on the advice of the Theology Faculty, prohibited anyone, on pain of death, from holding or teaching any theses 'contrary to the ancient approved authors, and from holding any public debate other than those approved by the doctors of the Theology Faculty'.[9] There followed a vicious campaign against various unorthodox philosophical and scientific views, which tended to centre around Hermeticism. The general paranoia about Rosicrucianism—'paranoia' because it was thoroughly defeated as a political force by this time—as well as the publication in France of the popular works of the English Hermetic philosopher Robert Fludd, created an atmosphere of near-panic amongst the orthodox. Conservatives like Garasse undertook a blanket campaign against libertinage *tout court*,[10] whereas more moderate writers like Mersenne tried to single out the threat to orthodoxy more precisely and to focus on that; sometimes, as in Mersenne's case, this was achieved using new and non-Aristotelian means.[11]

The combination of free thought and censorship in Paris in the 1620s needs to be understood in quite specific terms. In the seventeenth century France was able to re-establish the order that had broken down almost completely in the sixteenth, but the process of re-establishment was not complete until about 1660, and the intervening period was one in which there was a radical intellectual climate, not so much in that the political order was challenged, but in that public and private morality were separated and thought of in quite different terms. This separation, initiated by Montaigne, had a profound effect on both social and intellectual questions. Moral codes for individual action were developed which relied largely on Montaigne's assimilation of Stoic and Epicurean sources, and these differed considerably from the moral doctrines underlying the absolutist doctrine of the state. As one commentator has put it, 'it was taken for granted, by philosophers and magistrates alike, that individuals would observe their strict duty of obedience to the king and refrain from any public criticism of his behaviour, or any attempt to interfere in government. Within this constraint, moralists worked ingeniously to carve out a space for vigorous private action and individual achievement'.[12] The constraint was one that Descartes certainly adhered to publicly, and the first of the maxims of his 'provisional moral code' at the beginning of the third part of the *Discours* is to 'obey the laws and customs of my country, holding constantly to the religion in which by God's grace I had been instructed from my childhood, and governing myself in all matters according to the most moderate and least extreme opinions'.[13]

Much more influential than 'libertinage flamboyant' was what is usually referred to 'libertinage érudit', and this was to have a considerable impact on Parisian intellectual life in the 1620s. The programme of the 'erudite' libertines was to break with intellectual tradition and forge a new intellectual culture free from the accretions of the past. Although most of them were attached in one way or another to positions in the palace (principally through the patronage of Richlieu and Mazarin), many were freethinkers in political, theological, scientific, and philosophical matters. Taking their cue from Montaigne and Charron, they viewed themselves as free to follow their own lights, and as being very much an élite who, unlike the common masses, required no customs, established religion, or political authority to regulate them, although they were keen to support such institutions to maintain public order. They were sympathetic to scepticism and to empiricism, and were generally inclined towards atomism in natural philosophy. They ranged from publicists proclaiming the virtues of scepticism and free thought, such as Naudé and La Mothe Le Vayer, to natural philosophers concerned to defend atomism, like Gassendi; some, such as Naudé, may have been atheists or deists, whereas others, such as Gassendi, have a more complex position bordering on materialism.[14]

One did not have to be a libertine to enjoy and take advantage of the climate created by libertinage, and intellectual life in Paris at this time was clearly very active. Reporting from a letter, now lost, of Descartes to his elder brother, written from Paris and dated 16 July 1626, Baillet tells us that, having returned to Paris around June, Descartes 'did not find it as easy to enjoy his leisure as it had been previously. His old friends, particularly M. Mydorge and Father Mersenne, had so spread his reputation that he soon found himself overwhelmed by visits, and the site of his retreat became transformed into a meeting-place for discussion'.[15] Both Mydorge and Mersenne had been pupils at La Flèche, but there is no evidence that Descartes knew either of them there (although his elder brother, who would probably have been a contemporary of theirs at La Flèche, may have known them), and his friendship with them probably dated from 1625, or 1622 at the earliest. Amongst others whom Descartes counted his friends at this time was the anti-sceptical apologist Jean de Silhon,[16] whose *Les deux Veritez* (1626) had attempted to demonstrate the self-defeating nature of scepticism,[17] and the theologian Guillaume Gibieuf who was to publish a treatise on the liberty of God, *De libertate Dei et creaturae* (Paris, 1630), which he was working on throughout the 1620s, and which Descartes was familiar with, and would later cite approvingly. Also included was the polymath Claude Hardy, who lodged with Mydorge and produced a justly famous edition of Euclid with a Latin translation in 1625: Baillet tells us that Hardy knew 36 languages,[18] and Descartes will later make reference to his formidable linguistic skills.[19] We also know that Descartes was friendly with Étienne de Villebressieu, a chemist/alchemist, physician, and engineer to the King, and Jean-Baptiste Morin, a mathematician, astrologer, and, later, anti-Copernican propagandist. In the 1630s Mersenne was to try to form a group of mathematicians and scientists, whose core was taken from the Parisian circle of the mid-1620s, into an academy, meeting at the houses of Mersenne and the Abbé Claude Picot,[20] who was later to translate Descartes' *Principia* into French. He also would have had some contacts in the Hermetic circles that flourished in Paris in the mid-1620s, and he knew François du Sourcy, Sieur de Gersan,[21] a novelist and Hermetic philosopher; it was at his house that the aborted 1624 meeting of anti-Aristotelians was to have been held, and he evidently devoted his time to the search for potable gold, a form of gold in solution able to be drunk and reputed to have great therapeutic value. Descartes also kept up contacts with literary circles, and was on friendly terms with Jean-Louis Guez de Balzac, who was to be one of the greatest creators of elegant French literary prose.

In terms of immediate influence in 1626, however, Mydorge and Mersenne are the key figures. Mydorge was from one of the wealthiest and most illustrious families in France, and had served in various legal, administrative, and financial positions before effectively becoming a gentleman of leisure. This leisure was spent on the study of optics, particularly catoptrics, and geometry, where he made important advances in the study of conic sections. Marin Mersenne was the son of a labourer, who had obtained a scholarship to La Flèche when it opened in 1604, leaving in 1609, when he attended the Sorbonne. In 1611 he joined the order of Minims, returning in 1619 to Paris, where they had a convent. Mersenne made important contributions to acoustics, and his *Synopsis mathematica* of 1626 made available a number of very important mathematical texts, but his critical contribution of the mid-1620s was to natural philosophy, and it was he more than anyone else who forged a philosophical conception of mechanism. This was to have a profound effect on Descartes, but in 1625 and 1626 Descartes' interests seem to have centred on geometrical optics, and these interests he pursued with Mydorge and others.

The Discovery of the Law of Refraction

Some time before 1628, Descartes discovered the law of refraction, that is, the law describing the geometrical behaviour of light rays when they are transmitted from one optical medium to another. We cannot provide a precise, or certain, or even uncontentious dating for this discovery, and we can be even less sure of how it was made. We do know that Descartes had been interested in optical questions from his days at La Flèche, when optical illusions had commanded his attention, and in the *Cogitationes Privatae,* dating probably from 1619–21, there are a number of references to problems in optics. We know from later correspondence that Descartes was engaged in intense investigation of optics in the mid 1620s, and that he was familiar with key works in the perspectivist tradition in geometrical optics.[22] He carried out a number of experiments in optics with Villebressieu, with Mydorge, and probably with Guillaume Ferrier, a manufacturer of scientific instruments,[23] whom he would later consult on the cutting of hyperbolic lenses. One thing that Descartes and his co-workers were concerned with was discovering the anaclastic curve, that is, that shape of a refracting surface that would collect parallel rays into a single focus.

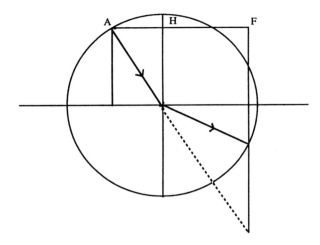

FIG. 5.1

The standard lens at this time was the simple biconvex lens, which did not do this, and the refracting telescope constructed with such a lens was subject to two serious problems as a result: spherical aberration, which occurs when rays incident at the periphery of the lens have a closer focus than those incident at the centre, resulting in an image which can never come into sharp focus; and chromatic aberration, which occurs when a distant white object, for example, will, because of the difference of focus, be represented as a series of images arranged in the order of colours of the spectrum. Although it is easy to show that spherical surfaces cannot represent axial point objects as point images, it was not easy to show what type of curve would represent them in this way; and the geometrical study of refraction hinged around these questions.

We are now generally familiar with the law of refraction as a law relating the sines of the angles of the incidence and refraction of the light ray (Fig 5.1), so that if v_i is the speed of light in the upper medium, and v_r its speed in the lower medium, then $v_r/v_i = k$ (a constant), and AH/HF or $\sin i/\sin r = v_r/v_i$. Now this is the form in which Descartes would give the law in the *Dioptrique,* but his demonstration of the law there, which is from basic principles of physical optics, is quite inadequate, to such a degree that most commentators now consider this an implausible route of discovery, and a number of attempts have been made to reconstruct a route which is independent of Descartes' own demonstration in the *Dioptrique.*[24] In particular, it seems likely that Descartes drew on the tradition of perspectivist optics and had a

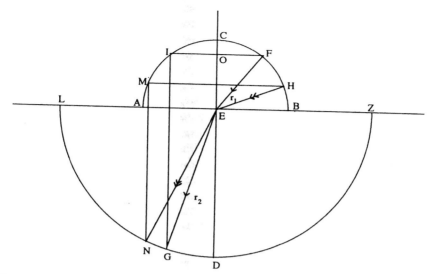

FIG. 5.2

geometrical proof of the law of refraction before he had formulated a
physical theory to account for it. How he made the discovery is an
open question, however. One very plausible reconstruction has been set
out by Schuster,[25] who notes the fact that, in the perspectivist tradition,
it is a cosecant rather than the trigonometrically equivalent sine version
of the law that is offered. The two earlier discoveries of the law
(unknown to Descartes), in the work of Harriot (c.1598) and Snel (mid-
1620s), result in the cosecant version, as does the account of Mydorge
in a letter to Mersenne of the early 1630s,[26] and this suggests that there
is a common starting point, perhaps in traditional writings on optics,
for their route to the discovery of the law. Indeed, Mydorge's account
of the law of refraction shows a reliance on the traditional procedure
for the location of image places, which suggests not only a specific
traditional source but a fairly plausible route of discovery. This is of
particular interest because Mydorge and Descartes worked together on
optical problems in the mid-1620s, and Mydorge's account possibly
provides an insight into Descartes' thinking at an earlier stage.

   In Proposition I of his report (see Fig. 5.2), that concerned with the
law of refraction, Mydorge sets out to show that, given an incident ray
(FE) refracted at a surface AEB and the refracted ray (EG), and so
being given the angle of incidence (CEF) and the angle of refraction
(GED), one can find the refraction of any other incident ray (HE).
First, one describes a semi-circle (ACB) of any radius (EB) around E,

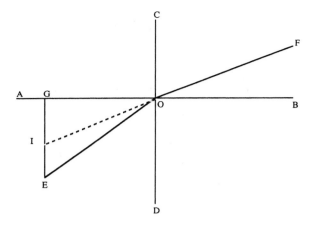

Fig. 5.3

the circumference cutting EF at F and HE at H. Then, IF is drawn parallel to AB, and from I, where IF intersects the semi-circle ACB, IG is dropped parallel to CE. IG will cut EG at point G. EG then acts as the radius of the semi-circle LDZ to be drawn around E. The way is now clear to finding the required refraction of HE: draw HM parallel to BA, and from point M, the intersection of HM and semi-circle ACB, drop a line parallel to CED. This parallel line MN will intersect LDZ at point N. The required refracted ray is then EN. The proof works on the principle of the constant ratio of radii of two unequal circles, and in its trigonometric form amounts to a proof that cosec i/cosec $r = r_1/r_2$.

Schuster's reconstruction of the route to the discovery of the cosecant law of refraction draws on two well-known traditional principles. The first is the principle of location of image places, which had been used since antiquity. Take two optical media separated by the surface AOB (Fig. 5.3), the lower medium being the denser. To locate the image of the point E one must extend the refracted ray OF into the lower medium and mark its intersection with EG, the normal from E to the surface AOB. The image is then to be found at I. The part of this technique that is of particular interest to us here is the construction of EG, named the 'cathetus'. The second principle derives from a feature of the refractometer, illustrated in the works of Ptolemy and Alhazen. Take the case of Ptolemy's refractometer (Fig. 5.4). This comprises a bronze disc ABCD, which has a fixed sight at E and movable sights at Z and H which are adjustable along the circumference. Imagine a case where one is concerned with refraction of a ray from water to air. The disc is placed on the surface of the water so that DEB lies exactly along

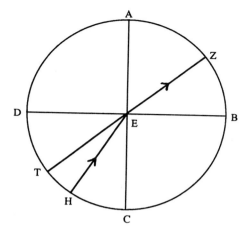

Fig. 5.4

the surface. Then one sights along ZE at an angle of incidence AEZ and moves H until it coincides with the line of sight. The path of the refracted ray emanating from the object point H is then given by ZE, EH.

Both the principle of image location and the principle behind the refractometer operate with the cathetus, and one of Ptolemy's figures supplies the cathetus. Moreover, the diagram illustrating the principle of the refractometer is such that it is easy to conceive of object points located on a circle equidistant from the point of refraction. The combination of these two is highly suggestive and may have prompted further investigation of the lines in triangle IOE (Fig. 5.3), which in turn may have been what caused Harriot, Snel, Mydorge, and perhaps Descartes to hit upon the constant ratio of OI to EO. The postulated route to the discovery of the law would, in Schuster's account, then involve the following elements: first, the assumption that the image rule is both valid and revelatory of the phenomenon of refraction; second, the plotting of empirical data on angles of incidence and refraction derived from Ptolemy via Witelo (we have a record of Descartes copying out Witelo's refraction tables[27]), or from new observations; third, the application of the image rule to the rays so plotted, 'thus leading to the discovery that if the object points are taken to lie on the circumference of a given circle about the point of incidence, then the calculated image places lie roughly on another smaller circle about the point of incidence'.[28] Mydorge's account in Proposition I of his report is quite consistent with his having come to the law by these means: not only is the law given in the form which employs the constant ratios of

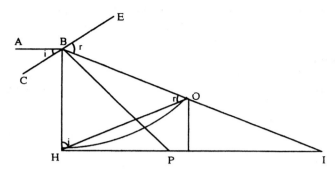

Fig. 5.5

two unequal circles, but it also constructs refracted rays by working backwards from their supposed image points.[29]

This reconstruction of Descartes' discovery of the law of refraction is not the only one, and Shea, following a suggestion of Costabel's, has offered an alternative reconstruction which is equally plausible and more direct, for it suggests that Descartes moved straight to the sine version.[30] Descartes was extremely reluctant to divulge the sine law to anyone, but in a letter to Ferrier of 13 November 1629 he tells him of a practical way of measuring refraction. Shea argues that this procedure might provide an indication of how Descartes discovered the law. The procedure that Descartes provides is also described in the *Dioptrique*: a ray AB enters a prism HBP and emerges along BI (Fig. 5.5). To measure the angle of refraction and incidence at B, Descartes would have added CE, the normal at B, which is perpendicular to BP. As Shea points out, it is a short step from this to the realization that HI is sin r and OI sin i. We simply join HO, and since BH = BO, HO is parallel to CE. AB is parallel to HI, and hence $\angle ABC = \angle OHB$, and $\angle EBI = \angle BOH$. Hence $\angle HOI = 180° - \sin r$. Since the ratio of the sines of two interior angles of a triangle is equal to the ratio of the sides opposite, sin HOI/sin OHI = HI/OI, or sin $180° - r$/sin i = HI/OI. But sin $180° - r = \sin r$, therefore sin r/sin i = HI/OI. In short, the constant ratio of refraction for a given material, its refractive index, is the ratio of the sine of incidence to the sine of refraction.

Descartes covered his tracks on the question of his discovery of the law, and we cannot establish any reconstruction with certainty, nor can we establish when the law was discovered, except that it was unlikely to have been before 1626 and was certainly before mid-1629. But there is now a consensus that Descartes' own account of how he discovered the law is not to be trusted, and that the physical underpinnings of his account came after he had discovered it, rather than before, as he would have us believe. The question of how far Descartes' thinking had progressed on the physical nature of light by this stage is an open one. The first part of *Le Monde* develops a comprehensive theory of light, and it relies upon a number of developments in Descartes' thought about the physical nature of light and its geometrical behaviour. By 1630, Descartes had not only formulated the sine law of refraction, but had also worked out a rudimentary physical optics. These were only presented in a published form in 1637, the former in the *Dioptrique*, and the latter in the *Météors*. An almost total lack of material makes it impossible to provide anything more than a speculative sketch of the development of Descartes' account of light between 1626 and 1630. As we shall see below, however, in the later version of Rule 8 of the *Regulae*, which may date from as early as 1626 and is certainly no later than 1628, he indicates that he already has an account of the physical nature of light.

We have two clues as to the nature of the account: his use of the term 'action' in referring to the physical nature of light in the *Regulae*,[31] and his attempt to explain his account of the nature of light using a statical analogy with a bent arm balance that he described to Beeckman, and which Beeckman describes in a short fragment in his diary entry for 8 October 1628.[32] 'Action' is a technical term in Descartes. In the *Dioptrique*, light is construed not as an actual motion, but rather as the *action* or tendency to motion of luminous bodies. There are a number of reasons why Descartes thinks of light in terms of a tendency to motion rather than as a motion, which we shall look at when we come to his account of physical optics in *Le Monde*. Such an approach suggests the modelling of the nature of light on statics, and hence it is not surprising that he should describe it in terms derived from statics to Beeckman. It is also worth noting that the Beeckman fragment suggests a sine version of the law, and it is possible that Descartes is trying to formulate a gross macroscopic analogy for this.[33]

The physical model of light that Descartes develops between 1626 and 1630 has a further distinctive feature. Like all mechanistic thinking in the first half of the seventeenth century, it works largely in terms of constructing plausible and striking macroscopic images and analogies of micro-mechanical processes. Many mechanists—Hobbes and Gassendi being among the most notable in this respect—had great difficulty going beyond such images, but Descartes did manage to do this. Nevertheless, such images still play a very critical role in his thinking, and his analogy of a tennis ball being reflected off a canvas, and penetrating a canvas and having its speed altered as a result, shaped his understanding of the physical processes involved in the reflection and refraction of light rays. This image stood in for a full physical theory until Descartes was able to develop one, and was in some respects mistaken for a physical theory. Consequently, when Descartes suggests in the *Regulae* that he has a physical optics lying behind his geometrical optics, we cannot assume that he has much more than some ingredients for a physical optics together with some very striking and plausible but essentially limited images modelling microscopic processes on macroscopic ones.

Mersenne, Mechanism, and the Problem of Naturalism

Around 1626, Descartes became concerned again with general questions of method. He had put his early attempts at the formulation of an account of method to one side in 1620. He returns to these with great enthusiasm in 1626 or 1627, adding to and reworking his earlier 'Rules', and transforming the whole exercise into something rather different from what he had envisaged in late 1619 and 1620. Indeed, one part of his new account would be something like a reworking of his early 'universal mathematics', albeit much transformed. That Descartes returned to the *Regulae* with greatly renewed vigour is evident, but why? There was no indication in 1620 that he intended to continue with it. Quite the contrary, having set out the Rules, Descartes simply abandoned them and devoted himself to specific studies in optics and algebra.

The later *Regulae* are devoted to the question of cognition. Descartes' concern in Rule 12, for example, is with perceptual cognition, and it might be thought that in this way he is following up his optical discoveries. I believe he is doing this, but it can only be part of the explanation, because his optical discoveries had been in geometrical optics, whereas in Rule 12 he is concerned to set out a speculative account of physical optics and to incorporate this into a no less speculative account of the nature of visual cognition. The motivating idea behind this, as we shall see, is mechanism: what Descartes is concerned to provide, above all, is an account of how our perceptual image of a mechanistic world is formed, and how the process by which this perceptual image is constructed can itself be accounted for in mechanistic terms. Descartes had been committed to a practical form of mechanism in 1619/20, in his work with Beeckman, and this took the form of a reconstruction of physical problems in micro-mechanical terms. That was something quite different from what was being envisaged here in the later Rules. Here he is concerned not with a piecemeal mechanism, but with the formulation of a general natural philosophy, an altogether more ambitious programme and, more importantly, one with very different aims, resources, and even to some extent motivation.

Mechanism as a general natural-philosophical position was developed in the mid-1620s by Mersenne, initially in two works, both of which appeared in 1623: *Quaestiones celeberrimae*, and (what is in effect a supplement to this) *Observationes et emendationes*.[34] The aim of these two treatises was to provide a detailed refutation of a number of heretical doctrines and practices, many of which had seen a revival in the Renaissance, including sorcery, cabbalism, naturalistic psychology, astrology, alchemy, and the doctrine of a world soul. The very fact that naturalistic psychology was included along with sorcery, for example, should serve to alert us to the fact that the contrast Mersenne wishes to draw is not between the scientific and the credulous (although he will criticize some specific areas, such as sorcery and cabbalism, as being credulous), but rather between the orthodox and the heretical.[35] Mersenne advocates mechanism not as an alternative to scholastic Aristotelian natural philosophy, but as a reaction to what can generally be referred to as 'renaissance naturalism'.

'Naturalism' is a term that covers a number of apparently disparate themes, and William Hine has pointed out that we should not run together renaissance naturalism, which is 'neo-Aristotelian, leans towards determinism, will have nothing to do with supernatural powers, and tries to explain miracles by appealing to natural phenomena', and renaissance magic, which is 'Neoplatonic, emphasizes man's freedom, too readily attributes events to angels or demons, and mixes in too much religious language'.[36] But the situation is not so straightforward. For one thing we must at least distinguish between supernatural and natural magic,[37] and the latter, which concerns itself with the activities and use of naturally occurring but hidden or occult powers (such as the power of certain combinations of herbs to heal wounds) comes firmly within the category of naturalism. And there is a deeper problem with this separation, for there is a sense in which both naturalism (taken as including natural magic) and supernatural magic derive from a particular kind of understanding of nature which is exactly what Mersenne is questioning. In as much as supernatural magic appeals to supernatural powers other than God—such as the stars in various forms of astral magic, for example—belief in it would, in Mersenne's view, simply be projecting supernatural powers on to things that do not have these powers, due to a general phenomenon that underlies both kinds of doctrine, namely a blurring of the distinction between the natural and the supernatural. In the one case this results in a tendency to deny the very existence of the supernatural, in the other to mistake the natural for the supernatural. In both cases, the root problem derives from a tendency to see nature as being full of all kinds of powers, and in both cases it results in the truly supernatural being effectively left out of the picture. Naturalism, broadly defined, is the doctrine that the truly supernatural (God alone) does not need to be invoked to explain a whole range of events in which it was traditionally thought to be required. Whether the explanations offered in place of traditional ones are naturalistic or quasi-supernatural is not the key issue for Mersenne: the key issue is the exclusion of the (genuinely) supernatural. This is the characteristic feature of naturalism for him, and it is this that makes it a threat to established religion, and hence something to be opposed as strongly as possible.

Mersenne saw that a return to the Aristotelian conception of nature that had so well served medieval theologians and natural philosophers was not going to be successful in countering these forms of naturalism. He did not reject scholastic Aristotelianism as such, and he wished to defend a number of tenets that it held dear, especially the clear separation of the natural and the supernatural, the personal immortality of the soul, and the rejection of determinism. All of these had been challenged in various ways by renaissance thinkers, the first most explicitly by those who, following neo-Platonic and Stoic sources, postulated the existence of a world soul; the second most explicitly by those who developed a strictly Aristotelian account of the mind; and the third by those accepted the claims of astrology, which took at least some of the responsibility for human affairs away from both God and human beings themselves. The trouble with Aristotelianism was that it had simply not been able to offer an effective answer to these troublesome doctrines, some of which had been explicitly condemned by the Lateran Council in 1513, and the problem lay largely in the fact that many of these doctrines were defensible on Aristotelian grounds. The two deepest challenges derived from the idea that nature, or more strictly speaking matter, was in some way essentially active. This had consequences for how nature was to be understood, and for how the human being was to be understood. On the first question, renaissance naturalism had undermined the sharp line that medieval philosophy and theology had tried to draw between the natural and the supernatural. Aristotle had thought of natural things and processes on a biological model, construing change teleologically, for example, and this gave natural processes an organic feel. The Stoics had gone further and offered a conception of the cosmos as a living organism, something which, while it was probably originally a development of Aristotelianism, later came to be taken over from the Stoics by neo-Platonists, and it was a conception that was part of many renaissance treatments of nature. It encouraged a picture of nature as an essentially active realm, containing many hidden or 'occult' powers which, while they were by definition not manifest, could nevertheless be tapped and exploited if only one could discover them. Such powers often acted at a distance—magnetic attraction was a favourite example—rather than through contact, and what one was usually dealing with were powers that brought to light connections and affinities that were not explicable in a traditional way, Aristotelian or otherwise. Take the case of the action of herbal remedies in healing wounds: what possible connection could some particular lower form of plant life have with human tissue such that it could heal it? The other side of the coin was a conception of God as part of nature, as infused in nature, and not as something separate from His creation: something like a pagan 'Mother Nature'. This encouraged highly unorthodox doctrines that tended in the direction of pantheism, the modelling of divine powers on natural ones, and so on. Worst of all, it opened up the very delicate question of whether apparently supernatural phenomena, such as miracles, or phenomena which offered communion with God, such as the sacraments and prayer, could perhaps be explained purely naturalistically, perhaps in psychological terms, as Telesio had been arguing. The problems were exacerbated by a correlative naturalistic thesis about the nature of human beings, which we can refer to as mortalism, whereby the soul is not a separate substance but simply the 'organizing principle' of the body, that is, something wholly immanent in the matter of the body. It did not matter much whether mortalism was advocated in its Averroistic version, where the intellect is in no way personal because mind or soul, lacking any principle of individuation in its own right, cannot be apportioned one to each living human body, or whether it was advocated in its Alexandrian version, where the soul is conceived in purely functional terms; in either case, personal immortality is denied, and its source in both versions is Aristotle himself.[38]

Mersenne sees the source of both naturalism and mortalism as lying in the construal of matter as being in some way active, and his solution is to offer a metaphysical version of mechanism, the core doctrine of which is that matter is completely inert. The threat to established religion posed by naturalism and mortalism is a radical one which has countless ramifications, and Mersenne's solution is to cut them off at the root, by depriving them of the conception of matter on which they thrive. If there is no activity in matter then the supernatural will have to be invoked to explain any activity. In criticizing the various forms of naturalism, Mersenne points to the credulity of many forms of renaissance thought, and he extols the virtues of mechanism for a quantitative understanding of nature; what is fundamentally at issue, however, is not the triumph of quantitative science over credulity, but the defence of the supernatural against appropriation by the natural.[39] This defence is undertaken by making the natural realm completely inactive, stripping it not merely of the various sympathies and occult connections postulated by naturalists, but also of the Aristotelian forms and qualities that provided the original inspiration for these.

The inertness of matter is the one characteristic feature of mechanism that will be generally adhered to in the seventeenth century. Other features of seventeenth-century mechanism that have been identified[40] are considerably less fundamental than the inertness of matter. The doctrines that all explanations must be in terms of the size, shape, and motion of corpuscles, and that occult qualities cannot be invoked in explanations, for example, both have their metaphysical rationale in the inertness of matter. Moreover, we cannot associate mechanism with a quantitative physics, for most mechanist natural philosophy in the first half of the seventeenth century was almost completely qualitative, consisting almost entirely in providing a plausible mechanist pictorial representation of natural processes (e.g. Hobbes and Gassendi), and, with the exception of Descartes' work (and Beeckman's very piecemeal writings), in the first half of the seventeenth century the two great contributors to mathematical physics are either explicitly naturalist and anti-mechanist (Kepler), or neutral on the issue (Galileo).[41] In short, despite the fact that mechanism promoted the ideal of a quantitative approach, it was neither necessary nor sufficient for a mathematical physics. Its core lies in its commitment to the inertness of nature, and this in turn is due to its ability to mark a clear separation between the natural and the supernatural.

When Descartes comes to investigate the metaphysical foundations of mechanism in his work of the 1630s and 1640s, his programme will be in many ways a detailed and sophisticated development of Mersenne's. In the later *Regulae*, however, he is not concerned with such metaphysical questions. But this does not mean that he treats mechanism merely as a preferred mode of solving problems in physics. On the contrary, he defends mechanism in a very general way, showing how a mechanistically conceived world could, despite appearances, give rise to our perceptual image of the world. In this respect he is in full agreement with Mersenne on the question of naturalistic construals of the world, and there are a number of implicit criticisms of naturalism. But he also treats cognition in a mechanistic way. Given that Mersenne's response to mortalism had been the same as that to naturalism proper, namely to establish the inertness of matter, it follows that many bodily functions that had previously been treated organically would now be dealt with in mechanistic terms, and in this sense Descartes' account is fully in accord with Mersenne's programme. But Mersenne had done little more than identify what he thought the root problem was in the case of mortalism, and he had given no indication as to how a mechanistic conception of the body might replace the elaborate organic conception that had traditionally been accepted.

On this traditional conception, one can distinguish between the 'organic' and the 'intellective' souls. The former, which was essentially embodied in physical organs, regulated life functions in both plants and animals, and, in the case of animals, regulated everything from respiration up to reasoning, memory, and cognition. The latter, which was generally considered not to require physical organs, was the seat of the intellect and the will.[42] The distinction had always been a problematic one in the sense that there was little agreement on the relation between the kind of cognitive grasp afforded by the corporeal organs and that afforded by the intellective soul. Aquinas, in particular, had tried to provide a detailed account of this relation, arguing that the material on which the intellect works must derive from our corporeal faculties: in other words, the body, via the senses, provides the material which is the basis for all knowledge. But so as not to make it wholly dependent upon the corporeal faculties, he argues that once the intellect has successfully applied itself to this material, it transcends the means by which it has arrived at it—namely the ratiocinative processes of imagining, remembering, and inferring—and understands it by means of a direct intuitive grasp, annihilating the corporeal origins of the material.[43]

The problems are, if anything, exacerbated with the attempt to replace the traditional conception with a mechanist one, and two new difficulties are added. First, the organic soul cannot be counted part of matter, since this would be to revert to naturalism, but nor can it be treated as pure mind, since this is the preserve of the intellective soul. Consequently, the organic soul must either be apportioned between the intellective soul and the mechanically-conceived body, or it must be absorbed into the body, or it must be abolished altogether. Secondly, the intellective soul tended to be identified with the soul of Christianity, which enjoys personal immortality. But there is a problem about where it is to be placed in Mersenne's schema of supernatural versus natural: this is problematic because the division, which mirrors the divide between the active and the inert, seems to allow the inclusion of God alone in the supernatural. If the mind is placed in the realm of the natural then it becomes passive and inert, whereas if it is placed in the realm of the supernatural it will be difficult to distinguish it from God. Both of these questions, and especially the issue of the intellective soul, turn out to be deeply problematic, and they arise because of the belief that mortalism and naturalism have a common source and need to be answered by the same doctrine, mechanism. Mechanism was devised specifically as a response to naturalism proper, however, and its concern to keep the natural and the supernatural distinct is not obviously relevant or appropriate to the question of mortalism.

Although he does not deal with the problem of the intellective soul in the later *Regulae*, Descartes will be concerned there with the extent to which the body can be construed mechanically. It is important to realize that this concern does nothing to further the programme of posing physical problems in a quantitative way, let alone solving them; it is quite irrelevant to the kind of practical considerations that motivated Beeckman's mechanism, for example. But neither can it be seen as part of some metaphysical enterprise in which Descartes is beginning to explore the mind/body problem, for no such metaphysical considerations are raised. What motivates Descartes' mechanization of the body in the *Regulae* is neither of these. It is, I try to show, something that is much more connected with the idea of the inertness of matter.

The Return to the *Regulae*, 1626

When Descartes abandoned the *Regulae* in 1620, he had drafted the first eleven Rules; but one of them, Rule 8, is in its final form a composite of material apparently written at different times, and it provides us with the join, so to speak, between the old Rules and the new. As Weber has shown in detail, it seems best to consider it as comprised of four parts: 8A, the first paragraph; 8B, the title and second paragraph; 8C, the next three paragraphs; and 8D, the remainder of the Rule.[44] Parts 8A and 8B are not quite mutually consistent and are therefore unlikely to represent a continuous text, but there is every indication that they date from the time of the early Rules, and the inconsistencies are of relatively minor interest. What is of much more interest is the shift from 8A/B to the mature parts of the Rule, for in this transition we can gain some insight into how Descartes' thinking underwent a very significant shift. The early Rules were dominated by methodological concerns, and above all with the question of what constitutes compelling evidence for something and how we come by such evidence. The first of these questions was dealt with largely in terms of the doctrine of intuition and that of clear and distinct ideas associated with it. These doctrines, as I have indicated, had their source in a rhetorical-psychological theory of cognition. It is on this central issue of cognition that the major developments now take place, as Descartes investigates the nature of cognition in much greater detail, focusing on how cognition occurs and what kinds of things can be cognized. As I hope to show, the rhetorical-psychological theory was not abandoned in the later *Regulae*. Far from it: its distinctive core idea of vivid and palpable representation becomes the basis for an elaborate theory of cognition.

Rule 8C offers two 'illustrations' of Descartes' method. The first construes the discovery of the law of refraction and the anaclastic in terms of his 'method'. Given what we have seen to be the probable route to the discovery of these, Descartes' own reconstruction is worth examining, not so much in order to show up his 'cover story' for what it is, but in order to try and throw some light on the thinking behind his construction of a method of discovery. He starts with the question of the mathematical discovery of the anaclastic (remembering that the anaclastic was of much greater immediate practical significance than the law of refraction on which it depends, because it had the potential to enable one to produce lenses free of the aberrations that had dogged the development of instruments such as the telescope). We can glean from Rules 5 and 6, he tells us, that 'the determination of this curve depends on the proportion that the angles of refraction bear to the angles of incidence'. But mathematics will not tell us what this proportion is, nor can one learn it from the writings of philosophers; nor, finally, from simple sense experience, for this last would violate Rule 3, which instructs us to rely only on those things that we can grasp clearly and distinctly.

Let us start with the question of how Rules 5 and 6 are supposed to help us realize that discovery of the anaclastic depends upon the nature of refraction. Rule 5 tells us that we must resolve complex propositions into simple ones. Certainly hindsight shows that the nature of the anaclastic is dependent on the nature of refraction, and anyone already knowledgeable in geometrical optics would understand this in advance; but Rule 5 clearly offers little help to the uninitiated, or to those who might think of the matter very differently, perhaps assuming something very different from the geometry of refraction to be the relevant simple proposition. And indeed, as we have seen, Descartes realizes this in the early Rules, especially Rule 10, advocating prolonged practice in dealing with problems that have already been solved, so that one has a model to follow, as it were.[45] This is also worth bearing in mind in the case of Rule 6, which goes over the same material, and which again looks very unhelpful if we assume that the Rule is directed to someone starting investigations in an area like optics from scratch. It is true that if we assume that these Rules are directed to those already familiar with the detailed work of others in the area, we still do not get the kind of guidance that would guarantee results, but there is no reason to think that Descartes is claiming this. Rather, he seems to be maintaining that it is only if one's investigations are in conformity with the Rules that one will succeed.[46] This certainly has some plausibility, but does it have any real bite? I think the best way to construe what is being claimed here is as follows: one must approach problem-solving by reducing complex problems to their simple ingredients, and one will learn how to do this by working through problems that others have already solved, but also one will learn to recognize the simple ingredients in many cases by virtue of having had the practice in problem-solving. In other words, recognizing the simple elements is a skill. If this kind of claim does have bite, it surely comes in Rule 9, where we are told that what was in fact the traditional naturalist construal of magnetism is mistaken, because it takes something as primitive, namely magnetic attraction, which is not in fact primitive at all. The case is an especially contentious one, for the naturalists tended to model natural phenomena generally on magnetic attraction (amongst other occult powers), thereby undermining any attempt to account for such attraction in terms of contact forces. Descartes' objection can be filled out as maintaining that experience in other areas of physics shows that something like a corpuscular-mechanical explanation of physical phenomena goes well beyond anything the naturalists were able to offer, and that such an approach, which involves understanding physical phenomena in terms of microscopic corpuscles exhibiting instantaneous tendencies to motion (the precise details do not matter), provides the real basic terms on which explanations must rest: the problem with the naturalists' account is that they have failed to reduce the problem to its simplest elements. This could be little more than a promissory note on Descartes' part, but the point is that a substantive claim can be made on the basis of apparently trivial Rules, although it is true that much of the work is done by the assumption that practical experience in problem-solving has yielded an understanding of the phenomenon of magnetism different from that of the naturalists.

After these methodological preliminaries, Descartes sets out how one might discover the anaclastic following his Rules:

Now take someone who does not limit his enquiries to purely mathematical issues, but, following Rule 1, seeks to discover the truth on any question that presents itself; if he is faced with the same difficulty, he will discover when he looks into it: [1] that the proportion between the angles of incidence and the angles of refraction depends on changes in these angles due to differences in the media through which the ray of light passes; [2] that these changes depend on the manner in which the ray of light traverses the whole transparent body; [3] that knowledge of the way in which this takes place presupposes a knowledge of the nature of the action of light; and [4] that this in turn presupposes a knowledge of what in general a natural power is—this being the last term in the whole series, and the most absolute. Once he has clearly apprehended this by intuition, he will, in accordance with Rule 5, return by the same steps taken in reverse order. If, at the second step, he is unable immediately to determine the nature of the action of light, he will, following Rule 7, enumerate all the other natural powers, in order that the knowledge of one of these other natural powers may help him to understand this one, at least by analogy, something I shall return to later. Having done that, he will investigate the way in which the ray traverses the whole transparent body, and running over the other points in order he will at last arrive at the anaclastic itself. Though this has long defied the efforts of many investigators, I can see nothing to prevent anyone who makes use of our method exactly from gaining an evident knowledge of it.[47]

On this account, then, one is led ultimately to an investigation of the general nature of a natural power (*potentia naturalis*), and Rule 9 makes it clear that this is to be spelled out in terms of the local motion of bodies, that is, in mechanical terms. The general suggestion is that one needs an understanding of the physical nature of light before the phenomenon of refraction can be fully understood, and the more specific suggestion is that this will have to take the form of a corpuscular-mechanical account of light. Now, as we have seen, the law of refraction can be elaborated without an understanding of the physical nature of light: it is a question of mathematics, plus empirical tables of refractions, although the route to the discovery of the law is aided by some very rudimentary hypotheses about the workings of refractometers. Indeed, for all we can tell, Descartes had no real understanding of the physical issues at this time, although he did have to hand a number of what were to be the ingredients of his final account. Ideally, an account of the physical nature of light, from which its geometrical behaviour could be deduced, would be needed, but at this stage Descartes probably has an account of its geometrical behaviour, together with a rudimentary and somewhat speculative account of its physical nature which hinges on little more than a suggestive analogy.

Later in the same Rule, Descartes provides an image that may be of help here. He compares his method with the procedure followed in the mechanical arts, where artisans must fabricate the tools they will need. A man starting up as a smith will use a large piece of stone or iron as an anvil, a small stone as a hammer perhaps, a shaped piece of wood as tongs, and so on. He will not then proceed directly to forging swords or helmets, but rather to making better tools, so that he can work his material better. I believe this provides us with a rather good understanding of how Descartes may have conceived of his reconstruction of the law of refraction. Telling us how we might discover the law, and the anaclastic, is analogous to telling someone how to forge a sword. Taking a ready-made hammer and anvil, one must imitate skilled workmen, and there are various rules and procedures one must follow if one is to forge something worthwhile. These rules and procedures can be set out with hindsight and are intended to be helpful in making swords, not to recount irrelevant biographical details about the various trials and tribulations that the smith actually went through in starting his trade from scratch. Similarly with Descartes' provision of rules: the aim is not to tell us how he himself found the law of refraction, but how, with hindsight, one should go about finding such laws. It is important that we do not conflate these two: no method of discovery, from Aristotle's topics, through the *regressus* theories of the Renaissance, to the inductivism of the nineteenth and twentieth centuries, ever do this, and we have absolutely no reason to think Descartes did.

An interesting feature of Descartes' reconstruction of the route to the anaclastic is the move from the level of geometrical description to the physical level. I have indicated that, from his earliest exercises in hydrostatics with Beeckman, Descartes employed a distinctive approach to problems. In the case of hydrostatics, he took a problem that had already been solved in macroscopic-geometrical terms as his starting point, and tried to provide a fundamental redescription in micro-mechanical terms. Later on, in the *De Solidorum Elementis*, we saw him doing something analogous in a purely mathematical case, taking an established geometrical proof that there can be no more than five regular Platonic polyhedra and attempting to provide a more general algebraic proof. Now, in the case of the law of refraction, we find the same kind of exercise repeated, except that the geometrical account of the behaviour of light that will form his starting point is something that he has developed himself, and what he is now trying to do is to go beyond this to an account of the physical constitution of light, something which he believes underlies its geometrically describable behaviour.

A central role here is played by the fundamental nature of micro-mechanical explanation. For Descartes, until the behaviour of light can be explained in such terms, we have no understanding of it. This is both a positive requirement that Descartes genuinely believes lies at the basis of any physical explanation, and a polemical weapon to be used against naturalists who believe that the nature of light can be understood without recourse to micro-mechanical explanations. But in neither case is he on especially strong ground. He has, as yet, no rigorously worked-out physical account of the nature of light that would stand up to detailed criticism, and he is nowhere near countering the naturalists' advocacy of magnetic attraction as a primitive (unanalysable) phenomenon with a micro-mechanical account of magnetism. Clearly some stronger guarantee of the superiority of micro-mechanical explanation would serve him better, and this is now the direction in which he starts to move.

Up to this point, Descartes' concerns remain much the same as those of the 1619/20 Rules; he just has a more powerful example. The move from the example of the anaclastic to his second example, however, marks a very significant shift.[48] The second 'example' is in fact not really an example at all. Descartes calls it the 'noblest example of all', but what he does is to move to the most general case of discovery, that where we set ourselves the task of examining *all* truths. Curiously, this topic is dealt with twice, in the remainder of 8C and in a much more elaborate form in 8D. Indeed, it is quite possible that 8C is actually a first draft of 8D: in support of this, it might be noted that in the Hanover manuscript of the *Regulae*, 8C is included at the end of the Rule, as a kind of appendix. The concern of 8C and 8D is with the question of cognition. Rule 8C argues that we must enquire into the workings of the understanding (*ingenium*) if we are to succeed in our task, and that once we have a grasp of the understanding we must turn to the other two instruments of knowledge that we possess, namely the imagination (*phantasia*) and sense (*sensus*). Since knowledge can only issue from the understanding, the other two faculties acting merely as aids to the understanding, it is of paramount importance that the respective contributions of the three be carefully distinguished. Once this has been done, it will be possible to distinguish soluble from insoluble questions, and to avoid wasting time on the latter, which go beyond the capacities of human reason.

This is a new direction in Descartes' thinking, and while it is embedded in a treatise on method, and indeed while it is explicitly said to follow the precepts of that method, it is very different in both content and aspiration from those Rules (including 8A and 8B) that I have identified as being of earlier origin. 8D leaves us in no doubt that the course of the *Regulae* is being fundamentally rethought and reorganized. It is no longer simply a question of studying the nature of the understanding and the faculties which aid the understanding (to which memory is now added), but of complementing this with a study of the 'objects' proper to each of these faculties. Moreover, a plan of the *Regulae* is now mapped out (and elaborated upon further at the end of Rule 12): the first twelve Rules will deal with an elucidation of simple natures, the second twelve with how to solve problems when we know the simple natures concerned, and the third twelve with cases where the relevant simple natures are not known, and must be discovered by analysis. The work to be done in completing the first part of the Rules now lies exclusively in Rule 12, the first complete Rule of the last stage of composition, and 8D effectively continues not with Rule 9 but with

Rule 12. Indeed, Rule 12 is in some respects an elaborate rewriting of Rule 8C/D.

The Nature of Cognition

Rule 12 opens with the statement that it 'sums up all that has been said in preceding Rules, and sets out a general lesson which has now to be explained in detail'.[49] But unlike the other Rules, it is exclusively concerned with the details of cognition, and traditional methodological issues of the kind we find in the earlier Rules play little part in the discussion. Moreover, it does not so much summarize and expand upon all the previous Rules, as Descartes maintains, but rather summarizes and expands upon Rule 8C/D. Descartes sets out its aim in these terms:

In dealing with knowledge of things, only two factors need to be considered: ourselves who know, and the things that we know. As for ourselves, there are but four faculties which we can use for this, namely, understanding, imagination, sense-perception and memory. The understanding alone is of course capable of apprehending truth; none the less, it has to be assisted by the imagination, sense and memory if we are not to omit anything that lies in our power. As to the things to be known, it is enough for us to ask three questions: (1) What is readily presented to us? (2) How may we know one thing by way of another? and finally (3) What conclusions can be drawn from each of these? I believe this list is complete, and omits nothing that can come within the reach of our human powers.[50]

Descartes tells us that important as it is for an understanding of the nature of the knower to provide an account of the question of what mind, body, and the relation between the two is, he cannot do this in any detail in the context of the present discussion. And not only is the detail missing, but so too is the metaphysical framework of the traditional treatment. He deals with it in terms of an account of perceptual cognition that draws on physiology, optics, and mechanistic natural philosophy. One gets the strong impression that Descartes thinks that questions that had traditionally been treated in metaphysical terms—and to some extent even theological terms—can be dealt with almost as scientific matters of fact. Certainly there were precedents for this in the medical tradition, but Descartes is going well beyond this tradition in introducing such detailed natural-philosophical considerations. And he is able to exclude certain questions that had been bound up with these questions in medieval and renaissance discussions, notably that of the personal immortality of the soul.

This indicates a novel mode of treatment of the question of perception—or rather perceptual cognition, for what we are really concerned with here is an account of how we arrive at knowledge by means of sense perception—and to understand what this novelty consists in, it will be of some help to look at the traditional Aristotelian account of perception first. Aristotle offered a comprehensive theory of perceptual cognition, one that unified physiology, psychology, metaphysics, and natural philosophy into a broad and powerful theory.[51] At the core of his account lay a theory that each sense organ has its own 'special sensibles', that is, things or properties or qualities that are perceived by one sense organ only, and to which that sense organ is naturally adapted. Colour, for example, is a 'special sensible' because it is perceived by vision alone. Now Aristotle holds that when the sense organs are perceiving their special sensibles, the perception is incorrigible. There are two connected reasons behind this. First, he has a thoroughly teleological conception of perceptual cognition. On Aristotle's account, we have the sense organs which we do because they naturally display to us the nature of the world. Each sense organ is fitted to perceive one specific kind of 'sensible', and the natural function of the sense organs is activated when they are actually perceiving their respective special sensibles. When each organ functions properly it fulfils its purpose properly, since otherwise nature would have made an imperfection in a fully developed organ. Indeed, at the beginning of Book 3 of the *De Anima*, Aristotle goes further, arguing that there can only be five senses, because it can be shown that these are sufficient to respond to the four elements from which everything is made. Secondly, perception of special sensibles is incorrigible for Aristotle because it is constitutive of the very notion of veridicality. Vision under optimal conditions is the only criterion we possess by which to judge whether something has a particular colour, for example: to view something under optimal conditions is to meet all the relevant conditions by which colour is to be determined. On this kind of account, to distinguish between something being really red, and its just looking red to someone with excellent eyesight who views the object under optimal lighting conditions, would simply make no sense.

Aristotle's account of what happens in visual perception is premised upon his account of the nature of substance. Substance is comprised of matter, which is a substratum having no properties in its own right, but which can become a definite substance when endowed with form; and of form, which is the bearer of properties and needs a substratum in which to inhere. What happens in the transmission of light is that the colours overlying the surfaces of visible bodies produce disturbances in the medium, which in turn acts upon the sense organ.[52] There is no physical movement of a corpuscle from the body to the eye, however. Indeed, there is no physical movement of any kind. Rather, what happens is that the transparency of the medium, which had previously been potential, is actualized by the luminous body, and then, once this has been achieved, a further qualitative change occurs in which the medium is actualized at a secondary level by the colour of the surface of the body, with the result that the body, which is separated from the observer, become visible. What happens when the perceiver perceives the colour is that the watery substance of her eye assumes the colour of the object perceived. Note the difference between this case of perception of a special sensible and the case of perception of a property that is not a special sensible, such as the visual perception of shape. When we visually perceive shape we do so by virtue of perceiving a colour bounded by that shape, for it is the colour that directly affects the eye, not the shape. Finally, in perception, the sense organ actually takes on the form of the object perceived, and the perceiver actually has the form of the object perceived, and hence its 'nature' (*phusis*), in her intellect.

Aristotle's account comprises a theory of the nature of luminous bodies, the transmission of light, and the action of perceived qualities on the eye, all incorporated into a general account of the function of visual perception. This is not an epistemological account of perception, in the sense of an account that tells us how the veridicality of our knowledge of the natural world can be secured. The teleology of the account obviates the need for such epistemological considerations: it is not just that the proper use of our sense organs automatically guarantees the veridicality of what we perceive, but rather that, given their proper use (i.e. the proper use of normal sense organs operating under optimal conditions) the question of our being mistaken simply makes no sense.[53] Of course, this only holds for the perception of special sensibles by the appropriate sense organ. But when we come to Aristotle's account of the perception of other kinds of sensible, liability to error is not accounted for in epistemological terms. Aristotle distinguishes two other kinds of sensible: common sensibles, which are those sensibles that are common to more than one sense, such as shape, which is common to sight and touch; and incidental sensibles, which are those sensibles that we perceive incidentally when we perceive a special sensible—for example, when I hear or see Diares, I am seeing and hearing special sensibles, and by virtue of this I am seeing and hearing him, but he himself is not a special sensible. Our degree of liability to error in the perception of common sensibles is greater than in the case of perception of special sensibles only because more conditions have to be fulfilled for the requisite optimal circumstances to obtain. The veridical perception of shape, for example, requires that both optimal visual and tactile conditions hold, and that both our sense of touch and vision are operating normally. Once these conditions do hold, then we have a similar situation to the perception of special sensibles by the appropriate organ. In the case of the perception of incidental sensibles, the kind of problem that we might encounter when we perceive a white thing as the man Diares is that of not being able to see clearly who it is. If distance is the problem here, the solution lies in our moving closer so that we can see clearly who it is; if lighting is the problem, we illuminate the object, and so on.

The account of perception that Aristotle provides is basically descriptive rather than legitimatory, and Descartes appears to be offering a descriptive doctrine in response. That is, he is concerned to describe the empirical processes that result in the formation of our perceptual image of the world, and while his account, unlike Aristotle's, will be constrained by a commitment to mechanism, this is in no way an epistemological constraint: it is not something designed to secure the veridicality of perceptual experience.

Dividing his discussion of perception in Rule 12 into a consideration of knowers and objects known, he begins his account of the former with a disclaimer: the assumptions he will make do not detract from the truth, and are designed simply to help one to see that truth more clearly. In other words, what he is offering is a hypothetical reconstruction. He proposes the following account:

First, in so far as our external senses are part of our body, sense perception is properly speaking merely passive, even though the application of the senses to an object involves an action, namely local motion, and it occurs in the same way that wax takes an impression from a seal. I am not just using an analogy here: the external shape of the sentient body must be thought of as being really changed by the object in just the same way that the surface of the wax is altered by the seal. And we must admit that this is so, not just in the case where we feel the body to have a shape, or to be hard, or rough to the touch etc., but also in the case where we have a tactile perception of heat, or cold, etc. The same is true of the other senses: thus the first opaque membrane of the eye takes the shape impressed upon it by the many colours of the light; and in the ears, nose, and tongue, the first membrane that is impervious to the passage of the object thus takes on a new shape from the sound, the smell, and the flavour respectively.[54]

This looks very much like the traditional atomist account of perception, with its insistence on local motion being the immediate or proximate cause of the change in the sense organ. Moreover, the non-Aristotelian nature of the account is reinforced when, in the next paragraph, Descartes goes on to take shape as his core case, on the grounds that 'the concept of shape is so simple and common that it is involved in everything perceivable by the senses'. The upshot is that rather than our perception of shape being dependent on our perception of colour,

our perception of colour is made dependent upon our perception of shape:

Whatever you may suppose colour to be, you will not deny that it is extended and so has shape. So what troublesome consequences would follow if—avoiding the useless assumption and pointless invention of some new entity, and not denying what others have said on the subject of colour—we simply abstract every feature of colour except its shape, and conceive of the difference between white, blue, red etc. as being like the difference between these or similar figures:

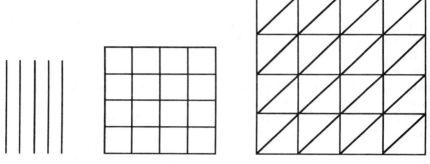

Fig. 5.6

The same can be said about everything that can be perceived by the senses, since we can be sure that the infinite multiplicity of figures is sufficient for the expression of all the differences in perceptible things.[55]

Descartes is not just reversing Aristotle's priorities here, making a common sensible prior to a special sensible on the grounds that it is common. Nor can he be redefining the function of the senses, so that they no longer work independently but collectively, the core case being something that they can all perceive equally. For while we might be able to see and feel shape, we can neither hear, nor taste, nor smell it. Consequently, it is not common to all the senses in the way in which what Aristotle would call a common sensible is common to the senses.

Descartes' claim that whatever we can perceive can be represented by shapes is motivated by three sets of considerations. The first is his doctrine of clear and distinct ideas, in which vivid pictorial representation still plays a key role, and where representation in terms of line lengths is the key to quantitative understanding. If we want a quantitative understanding of the world, we need a quantitative way of representing the world to ourselves; and, for reasons that will become evident in Rule 18, the only way of representing something quantitatively that meets both mathematical requirements and those dictated by his doctrine of clear and distinct ideas is by means of line lengths. Secondly, his account clearly extrapolates from the case of vision to other forms of perception. Descartes treats the retinal image as two-dimensional, and a two-dimensional image clearly limits the means of representation, though of course it does not exclude representation by colours, and indeed there are no optical considerations that require us to abandon the idea that our retinal image is coloured: Kepler, for example, quite consistently advocates such a view in his account of the formation of the retinal image. But representation by colours is clearly unwarranted if one wants the means of representation to be the same for all the senses, and here the third set of considerations—a commitment to the mechanistic construal of nature—enters. The assumptions that Descartes invites us to make help us to picture nature as if it were comprised exclusively of (spatially) extended magnitudes.

But can we actually do this on the basis of the account provided in the case of visual perception? We can, perhaps, imagine all colours being represented in terms of a variety of patterns of lines, but what is being asked of us is far more than that. The line patterns must not only represent differences in colours, but also differences between colours, temperatures, tastes, smells, and so on. It cannot be that there is a variety of shapes to which each sense organ responds in a different way, so that the first figure Descartes portrays represents, for example, a particular colour for sight, a particular temperature for touch, a particular odour for smell, and so on, for the obvious reason that, if it did, we should experience each of these every time we perceived that shape. There must at least be different kinds of shapes for each sense organ; and the idea of there being an infinite number of possible shapes does not help here, partly because it suggests that sense organs can distinguish infinitely complex shapes, which we have no reason to believe,[56] but more importantly because what we need to know is not how many shapes there can be but how the relevant kinds of shapes are distinguished. Remember also that some sense organs can distinguish many kinds of things at the same time: I can feel that something is round, hard, slimy, has a smooth surface, is very close to me, and so on. Again, surely different kinds of shapes would be needed here.

Alternatively, it might be argued that what is represented in the imagination is not what the body looks like, what it feels like, and so on. In other words, the representation in the imagination does not have distinguishable sensory ingredients: the visual and tactile information is not represented separately in the imagination, but rather has already been integrated in the common sense, allowing a representation of the body to be built up which draws on sensory information but which is not itself sensory. It is simply corporeally instantiated information, the form of instantiation being line lengths. I think this is more the kind of thing that Descartes needs, and the idea of the contents of the imagination being information is more like the kind of view he will move to in *L'Homme*, where the commitment to the requisite form of instantiation being in terms of line lengths will be weakened somewhat.

Whichever reading we prefer, however, we should not lose sight of what the mechanistic construal of perceptual cognition is aimed at achieving, and above all we should not over-interpret Descartes here. In particular, we should not read Descartes as suggesting (i) that there are only geometrical properties, and not real physical properties, in the world, or (ii) that qualities of physical objects such as colours, for example, do not really exist. The account we are offered here maintains that differences in colours and other perceptible qualities are represented in the imagination by differences in linear patterns. But this is not to tell us that differences in colours are actually just differences in linear patterns. Descartes' aim in Rule 12 is to give an account of how various physical properties and qualities can be accounted for on the assumption that whatever we are aware of perceptually is represented to us in terms of plane geometrical figures. Unless something can be represented to us in this way we will not perceive it. But to say that we perceive colour by means of plane geometrical figures is not to say that we do not perceive colours at all, that all we perceive are the plane geometrical figures. Nothing in the *Regulae* entitles us to such a reading. At this stage such questions must remain open. However, it is worth pointing out that Descartes will never treat colours as mere perceptual responses, as psychic additions of the perceiving mind, as Galileo had done and as later Cartesians such as Malebranche would do. The account he will offer is in fact a dispositional one, in which the colour of a body is not a property like its shape, but, like its weight, is something real nevertheless.

Having completed his account of how the sense organs represent the external world in terms of two-dimensional shapes—line lengths—Descartes provides an account of the transmission of these to the common sense, that corporeal faculty in which the impressions received by the various senses are brought together. This transmission is instantaneous, we are told, and an analogy is drawn with a man writing with a pen: as he moves the nib, the far end of the pen moves simultaneously, 'without anything real passing from one end to the other'. Does anyone think, Descartes asks, that the parts of the body are not more closely connected than the parts of the pen? This is disingenuous: the connections between the eye and the brain could take a number of forms, many of them less closely connected, if by this is meant something like 'less solid', than the parts of a quill pen. And the quill has, after all, a good deal of freedom of movement since it is in the air. Trap the

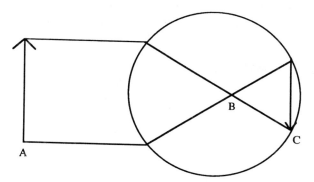

FIG. 5.7

quill between muscle and bone and one may well find that the only motion mirrored at the end of the pen is a longitudinal one and that any transverse motion is impossible.[57] The next stage in the process is the transmission of the information-cum-representation from the common sense to the imagination or phantasy, which is a corporeal organ, located in the brain, and which as well as receiving these representations is able to store them in the form of memories. Once the representations have reached the imagination, it can activate different motions in the nerves, for the nerves are connected to the imagination. This activation does not take the form of motions in the imagination being duplicated in the nerves; rather 'it has certain other images which enable these movements to follow on'.[58] Again the analogy of the moving pen is used, but now in a way that clearly reveals the optical model behind Descartes' thought. The end of the pen, he tells us, does not move in exactly the same way as the nib: it has a different, opposite (*diverso et contrario*) motion. In other words, if I make a mark with the nib which goes from left to right, the other end of the pen will move from right to left, and depending on where I am holding the pen, the latter movement will either be greater than, the same as, or smaller than the former. Now Descartes knew that the retinal image could be smaller than, or (rarely) the same size as, or (rarely) larger than the object, that it was an inverted image, and that it was topographically isomorphic with the object.[59] In this respect, the light ray and the quill act in the same way (see Fig. 5.7). Light rays coming from the arrow at A are refracted by the lens of the eye to the focus B, and form a smaller, inverted, topographically isomorphic image at C. If we imagine the path of the ray as being like the pen, then the focus will correspond to the point at which the pen is gripped, and the movement of the nib will be translated into a larger/equally-sized/smaller, inverted, topographically isomorphic image at the other end of the pen. This indicates that the formation of the retinal image is taken as a model for the perceptual process as a whole, and if we imagine the retina at C being a mirror, then the light rays striking it would follow the same path out: they would be re-inverted and the rays would follow the same path that they entered. This is what happens when the imagination redirects the motions it receives, except that, instead of passing these back along the same route, it now redirects them along the nerves, thereby causing the muscles to expand and contract. And this account, Descartes tells us, 'enables us to understand how all the movements of other animals can come about, even though we refuse to allow that they have any cognition (*cognitio*) of things, but merely grant them a purely corporeal imagination; and it also enables us to understand how there occur within ourselves all those operations that we perform without any help from reason'.[60]

What we are provided with here is, then, not just an account of perception, but also an account of how perceptual information is transformed into bodily action. On the question of whether this process can be said to be cognition of any kind, Descartes hedges his bets. Although he tells us that the process he is describing occurs in animals, where we do not allow any cognition or knowledge (*cognitio*), he immediately appears to qualify this in telling us that, in introducing the intellect, he is now turning to cognition properly speaking (*per quam res propriè cognoscimus*). This suggests that the process just described is in fact a kind of cognition, and indeed it is the kind of cognition that would traditionally have been described in terms of the activity of the organic soul. On the one hand, then, Descartes does not appear to be denying that there is some kind of cognition involved here; that is, he is not denying that animals have cognition; only that it is not the kind of cognition that he is interested in, namely human cognition.[61] But, just as clearly, he cannot account for the former kind of cognition in the traditional way. If we think of the matter in traditional terms, and there is no indication here that Descartes is not still thinking like this, then what distinguishes the two kinds of cognition is that the former involves no exercise of the intellect or will, whereas the latter does.[62] But to say that a form of cognition which we can term corporeal cognition because it necessarily involves the exercise of corporeal organs, does not involve the intellect or the will, still leaves it with recourse to a number of faculties: memory, imagination, and even ratiocinative reasoning. Animals, who are restricted to corporeal cognition, will therefore lack a will and pure intellect, which is certainly to say that they will not be able to exercise free will or reflect upon and make judgements about their own mental processes, but he does seem to allow a sense in which they reason, for example. This is implicit in his comment in Rule 2 that 'none of the errors to which men—men, I say, not brutes—are liable is ever due to faulty inference'.[63] Animals, as well as men, reason or make inferences, but animals are prone to errors of reasoning, whereas men, because their reasoning is guided by the natural light of reason, are not. It appears from this that Descartes is collapsing the traditional functions of the organic soul into the body, but in doing this he is not eliminating these functions: rather, he is explaining them in mechanistic terms. The kinds of process that can be explained in purely bodily terms, that is, in terms of an inert matter conceived mechanistically, are radically extended, in that functions previously construed organically—in terms of the organic soul—are now explained mechanistically. In other words, the animal lacks none of the functions it had when it was conceived as an organic soul animating matter, it is just that these functions are now to be explained in a radically different way. While it would be unwise to read too much into two short qualifications, made in passing, in the *Regulae*, it is very important that we do not start off on a wrong footing with Descartes' treatment of how the behaviour of animals—and by extension our own purely corporeal processes—is to be accounted for. It is an illegitimate reading of anything that Descartes says in the *Regulae* to attribute to him the view that animals are like bodies deprived of the organic soul: rather, his general project is to describe the organic functions in mechanist terms. This is strongly supported in his anatomical and physiological writings, as we shall see.

Descartes now turns from the kind of cognition we find in animals and occasionally in our own bodies, to cognition properly speaking, that is, cognition guided by the intellect. However, before we turn to the details of how the intellect operates, which are provided in Rule 14, we should look briefly at the other question dealt with in Rule 12, namely the objects of knowledge. Again the discussion is preceded by a disclaimer. Assumptions will have to be made which are like the 'imaginary circles astronomers use to describe the phenomena they study'.[64] Descartes begins by making a distinction between how things must be considered in relation to our knowledge of them, and how they must be considered in relation to how they are in reality. In the latter respect, for example, the one material body is something corporeal, it is extended, and it has a shape, yet it is in no sense a composite of these, since the three must always coexist. But in the former respect it is a composite, because we must understand 'corporeal', 'extended', and 'shape' before we can we can judge that the three of them invariably go together. There is something fundamental about our ideas of these. In elaborating on the sense in which these 'simples' are fundamental,

Descartes argues that what makes them so is the fact that our ideas of them are so clear and distinct that we cannot further subdivide them into others that are more distinctly known. We can even 'abstract from' these simples and they will still remain simples. For example, we can abstract the notion of 'limit' from that of shape, but this does not make it simpler than shape, because other things, such as duration, also have limits, and so we must have abstracted the notion from these also. 'Hence', Descartes tells us, 'it is something compounded out of many very different natures, and the term "limit" does not have a univocal application in these cases'.[65] In other words, I may have a clear and distinct idea of spatial limit, and a clear and distinct idea of temporal limit, but these are different ideas because, although the same word is used, something different is designated in the two cases. And of course a clear and distinct idea of spatial limit just is a clear and distinct idea of shape. Now simples can either be intellectual (such as our ideas of knowledge and the will), material (such as shape and extension), or common to both corporeal and spiritual things (existence, unity, and duration). The last category is especially puzzling. After all, Descartes has just told us that 'limit' is not a simple because it is not univocal, yet now we are told that existence and duration are simples, even though they apply to both spiritual and corporeal bodies. But surely if 'limit' is equivocal because it covers both spatial and temporal limits, then duration is equivocal because it covers both spiritual and corporeal duration. It is difficult to avoid the conclusion that what Descartes is seeking to establish here goes well beyond the arguments that he has at his disposal. But at least it is now clear what exactly it is that he is seeking to establish, namely that the notions taken as basic by mechanism, notions such as shape and extension, are genuinely basic, not in the sense that they are not further analysable, but in the sense that they are not further analysable into something that is as clear and distinct as they are.

The general argument of Rule 12 is an attempt to establish two things: that of those notions appropriate to body, some, such as extension and shape, are genuinely primary in that we cannot have a clearer or more distinct grasp of them than we have; and that we can represent everything we perceive in terms of extension and shape. In Rule 14, Descartes provides a crucial and extremely ambitious addition to this, namely an account of what the cognition of the corporeal world, construed in terms of extension and shape, consists in.

Rule 13 provides a lead-in to Rule 14. It tells us that, if we are to understand a problem properly, we must construe it in terms which allow us to compare the 'simples' common to the objects concerned, and this requires us to free our subject matter from any reference to particular things, so that, in the case of corporeal bodies, we deal with magnitudes in general. This is filled out in more detail in Rule 14:

We should think of all knowledge whatever ... as resulting from a comparison between two or more things. In fact the business of human reason consists almost entirely in preparing for this operation. For when the operation is straightforward and simple, we have no need of any technique by which to intuit the truth of what the comparison yields; all we need is the light of nature. We should note that comparisons are said to be simple and straightforward when the thing sought and the given data participate equally in some nature; preparation is needed for other kinds of comparison because the relevant common nature is not equally present in both, but only by way of other relations or proportions that imply it; and the principal part of human endeavour consists simply in reducing these proportions until an equality between what we are seeking and what we already know becomes clearly visible. We should also note that nothing can be reduced to such an equality unless it admits of greater and lesser and falls under what is called magnitude; and consequently, when the terms of a problem have been abstracted from every subject in accordance with [Rule 13], then we must understand that all we are now dealing with are magnitudes in general. And finally we should note that, if we are to imagine something, using not the pure intellect but rather the intellect aided by images depicted in the imagination, then nothing can be ascribed to magnitudes in general which cannot also be ascribed to any species of magnitude.[66]

There are two questions here. The first concerns Descartes' suggestion about what problem-solving consists in, the second the use of the imagination in problem-solving.

He gives as an example of elementary problem-solving[67] the inference 'all A is B' and 'all B is C', therefore 'all A is C'. Here A is the thing given and C the thing sought, and they are compared with respect to their both being B. There is, of course, no skill involved in making the connection between A and C here, either for Descartes or for those who accept the syllogistic form. Descartes tells us again that the syllogistic form is of no help in grasping the truth, but proponents of the syllogism would insist that the skill comes in discovering the requisite 'middle term': the B that genuinely links A and C. And Descartes' own procedure seems to be very close to this. Why, then, is he so critical of syllogistic? The answer is that syllogistic also purports to explain what the correctness of the inference consists in, whereas for Descartes there can be no such explanation: we grasp inferences by means of the 'natural light of reason' and, as we saw in examining the early Rules, this is beyond further discussion. Problem-solving consists in reducing everything to a form in which we can grasp it in an *intuitus*. Here Descartes does not go beyond the doctrine of the early Rules.

The second question, that of the role of the imagination, is an altogether different matter, for here Descartes introduces a new and potentially very powerful doctrine. The heading of Rule 14 spells out what this amounts to: 'The problem should be re-expressed in terms of the real extension of bodies and should be pictured in our imagination entirely by means of bare figures'.[68] Now Descartes insists in Rule 14 that we need both the intellect and the imagination in comparing 'simples'. But unlike the Thomist account, where the corporeal faculties such as the imagination play no further role once they have presented information to the intellect, in Descartes' account the imagination continues to play an indispensable role. This is a very distinctive feature of his account, and it is important to appreciate the precise way in which the intellect and the imagination act.

The imagination is needed because this is where 'the images of particulars are depicted', and what the intellect does is to abstract from these. Descartes insists that knowledge must begin with what he calls 'simple natures', which are those things that are not further analysable and which we can grasp in a direct and intuitive way. Such simple natures can only be grasped by the intellect, although in some cases the imagination is needed as well. He sets out the connection between the intellect and the imagination in these terms:

By 'extension' we mean whatever has length, breadth and depth, leaving to one side whether it is a real body or merely a space. This notion does not, I think, need further elucidation, for there is nothing more easily perceived by our imagination ... For even though someone may convince himself, if we suppose every object in the universe annihilated, that this would not prevent extension *per se* existing, his conception would not use any corporeal image, but would be merely a false judgement of the intellect working alone. He will admit this himself if he reflects attentively on this image of extension which he tries to form in his imagination. For he will notice that he does not perceive it in isolation from every subject, and that his imagination of it and his judgement of it are quite different. Consequently, whatever our intellect may believe as to the truth of the matter, these abstract entities are never formed in the imagination in isolation from subjects.[69]

Now whereas 'extension' and 'body' are represented by one and the same idea in the imagination, this is not true of the intellect. When we say that 'number is not the thing counted' or 'extension or shape is not body', the meanings of 'number' and 'extension' here are such that there are no special ideas corresponding to them in the imagination. These two statements are 'the work of the pure intellect, which alone has the ability to separate out abstract entities of this type'.[70] Descartes insists that we must distinguish statements of this kind, in which the meanings of the terms are separated from the content of the ideas in the imagination, from statements in which the terms, albeit 'employed in abstraction from their subjects, do not exclude or deny anything which is not really distinct from what they denote'.[71]

This distinction between the two kinds of proposition is perhaps most clearly expressed in the distinction between their proper objects, that is, the objects of the intellect and the objects of the imagination respectively. The proper objects of the intellect are completely abstract entities and are free of images or 'bodily representations'. But the intellect can also apply itself to 'ideas' in the imagination. In doing so it also carries out an operation which is proper to it, but which the imagination cannot carry out, namely, that of separating out components of these ideas by abstraction. It is here that the necessity for the imagination arises, because the intellect by itself has no relation at all to the world. Entities conceived in the intellect are indeterminate. The imagination is required to render them determinate. When we speak of numbers, for example, the imagination must be employed to represent to ourselves something which can be measured by a multitude of objects. The intellect understands 'fiveness' as something separate from five objects (or line segments, or points, or whatever), and hence the imagination is required if this 'fiveness' is to correspond to something in the world. What we are effectively dealing with here, as far as the intellect is concerned, is algebra. It is in so far as the objects of algebra, the indeterminate content of which has been separated out by the intellect, can be represented and conceived symbolically as lines and planes that they can be identified with the real world. Algebra deals with completely abstract entities, conceived in the intellect, but these abstract entities must be represented symbolically, and thus rendered determinate, which requires the aid of the imagination. The imagination thereby represents general magnitudes (abstract entities) as specific magnitudes (which are not distinct from what they are the magnitudes of).

However, not any kind of specific magnitude will do here. The privileged specific magnitude that Descartes wishes to single out is spatial extension. There are two reasons for this. First, algebraic entities can be represented geometrically, that is, purely in terms of spatial extension. Secondly, Descartes has already argued in Rule 12 that when we consider the physiological, physical, and optical aspects of perception, it turns out that we lose nothing if we suppose that the world is represented to us exclusively in terms of plane geometrical figures. It is important to note here that both the contents of the intellect *and* the contents of the world must *both* be represented in the imagination. The purely abstract entities of the intellect are represented as lines and line lengths, and the corporeal world is represented purely in terms of spatially extended magnitudes. The former, which are effectively measures of extended magnitudes, are mapped on to the latter, which are extended magnitudes. In other words, the pure thought characteristic of algebra in which the intellect engages does not map directly onto the corporeal world: it could not do so because it is indeterminate. Rather, a representation of it in the form of proportions depicted by line lengths maps onto a representation of the corporeal world, the latter representation consisting exclusively of two-dimensional shapes.

Because of the role that the imagination plays, our carrying out of mathematical operations, and the application of mathematics to the corporeal world, take place in the imagination. The imagination (which, it must be remembered, is a corporeal organ), drawing on both the intellect and the information gleaned from the sense organs, is effectively our mind as far as perceptual cognition is concerned. This is important because it means that there is direct cognitive awareness of both mental and physical states, and I suggest that we think of the matter in terms of the imagination representing to itself the contents of the world and the contents of the intellect, and perceptual cognition as taking place when it maps these on to one another.

The Representation of Algebra

It is because of the way in which mathematical operations are represented in the imagination that we are able to grasp them clearly and distinctly, for what more vivid and palpable—or 'clear and distinct'—form of representation could there be than representation in the form of line lengths? But it is on this very question that Descartes' project will now begin to fall apart, as the development of his algebra begins to come into conflict with the attempt to justify mathematical operations in terms of their clarity and distinctness, an attempt which carries with it the requirement that these operations be represented as operations on line lengths.

Descartes' rethinking of the nature of algebra is evident in the later *Regulae,* and we do not have any other account of his mathematical thinking at this time. This is unfortunate, because the treatment of algebra in the *Regulae* is embedded in an account of the cognitive role of the imagination which imposes constraints on it that are actually counter-productive. We shall return to these constraints, and the question of why Descartes finds it necessary to impose them even though he is fully aware of their problematic nature, below. For the moment, I want to disregard them, and extract an account of the nature of mathematical entities which he must have developed before completing the account of the *Regulae,* and which may well have been formulated around 1626.

The most significant aspect of Descartes' thinking about mathematics at this time is the very abstract way in which he conceives of numbers. In ancient mathematics, arithmetic is a form of metrical geometry.[72] This is evident in Aristotle's attempt to provide a conceptual and metaphysical basis for the conception of number current in his time, and he construes numbers as (purely intellectual) line lengths, subject in their manipulation to all the strictures on the manipulation of concrete line lengths. Indeed, when Aristotle, and Greek and Alexandrian mathematicians generally, talk of numbers in one dimension, plane (two-dimensional) numbers, and solid (three-dimensional) numbers, they mean what they say. Geometry does not merely provide the notation for arithmetic, and no Greek or Alexandrian author ever talks of numbers merely being *represented* geometrically. This kind of geometrical construal of number is clear in Greek and Alexandrian mathematical practice. Arithmetical propositions (see, for example, Books 7 to 9 of Euclid's *Elements*) are stated in terms of line lengths, not because this is how numbers are represented but because this is what they are. The most striking evidence for this is to be found in the way in which arithmetical operations are performed. Consider, for example, the case of multiplication. In multiplication, we multiply line lengths by line lengths. If a, b, and c are line lengths, for example, $a \times b$ is a rectangle having sides of length a and b, and $a \times b \times c$ is a solid figure of sides a, b, and c. Even though we are dealing with abstract numbers, we are always multiplying numbers of something by numbers of something, and consequently there is a dimensional change in multiplication, something indicated by the fact that we cannot multiply more than three numbers together, since the product of three (linear) numbers is a solid, which exhausts the number of available dimensions.[73] Finally, this extraordinarily constrictive conception of number was paralleled by an equally constrictive conception of arithmetic and geometry, whereby the point of the exercise was to compute a determinate number or construct a determinate figure respectively. For the mathematicians of antiquity it was only if such a determinate number or figure could be computed or constructed that one could be said to have solved the problem. And in the case of arithmetic, only natural numbers were allowable as solutions: negative numbers, in particular, were not, and were regarded as 'impossible' numbers.[74]

In Rule 16 of the *Regulae*, Descartes explicitly sets aside both the constrictive conception of arithmetic which limits it to computing determinate numbers, and the constrictive conception of number which, retaining the intuitive spatial elements of geometry, construes multiplication as a procedure in which products are always automatically of a higher dimension. The first he dispenses with as follows:

It should be noted that while arithmeticians have usually designated each magnitude by a plurality of units or by some number, we are abstracting here from numbers themselves, just as we abstracted above [Rule 14] from geometrical figures and from everything else. We do this not just to avoid the tedium of a long and superfluous calculation, but above all to make sure that those parts of the problem which make up the essential difficulty always remain distinct and are not obscured by useless numbers. If, for example, the problem is to find the hypotenuse of a right-angled triangle whose given sides are 9 and 12, the arithmetician will say that it is $\sqrt{225}$ or 15. But we will write a and b for 9 and 12, and shall find the base to be $\sqrt{a^2 + b^2}$. In this way the two parts a and b, which the number runs together, are kept distinct.[75]

He continues, dealing with the question of dimensional change in operations such as multiplication:

We should also note that those proportions that form a continuing sequence are to be understood in terms of a number of relations; others try to express these proportions in ordinary algebraic terms by means of several different dimensions and shapes. The first they call the *root*, the second the *square*, the third the *cube*, the fourth the *biquadratic*, and so on. These expressions have, I confess, long misled me ... All such names should be abandoned as they are liable to cause confusion in our thinking. For though a magnitude may be termed a cube or a biquadratic, it should never be represented to the imagination otherwise than as a line or a surface ... What, above all, requires to be noted is that the root, the square, the cube, etc., are merely magnitudes in continued proportion, which always implies the freely chosen unit that we spoke of in the preceding Rule.[76]

In other words, the cube of a, for example, is not designated a^3 because it represents a three-dimensional figure, but because it is generated through a proportional series with three relations: $1 : a = a : a^2 = a^2 : a^3$. He concludes:

We who seek to develop evident and distinct knowledge of these things insist on these distinctions. Arithmeticians, on the other hand, are content to find the result sought, even if they have no grasp of how it follows from what has been given, but in fact it is in this kind of grasp alone that science [*scientia*] consists.[77]

These are important developments, and Descartes shows a very clear and explicit awareness of the direction that his algebra is moving in. He is now beginning to consider both geometry and arithmetic in terms of a theory of equations, thereby showing a grasp of mathematical structure well beyond that of any of his contemporaries. The power of algebra, as Descartes construes it, is as a problem-solving technique which he identifies with the ancient art of analysis. It works by construing unknowns in terms of knowns, by providing a symbolism for them which enables them to be slotted into equations tying knowns and unknowns together in a systematic way. This procedure has immense advantages over the traditional geometrical proofs, and Descartes believes that an algebraic demonstration reveals the steps involved in solving the problem in a completely transparent way. Indeed it is the

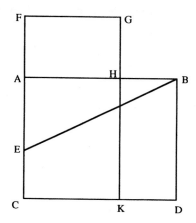

Fig. 5.8

transparency of its operations, as much as its abstractness, that Descartes finds of the greatest value in his new algebra. Boyce Gibson and Schuster have both given revealing examples of the way in which algebraic operations are more transparent than geometrical ones,[78] and we can take the case that Schuster looks at—the geometrical and algebraic solutions of a problem in Euclid II.11—as an example. Euclid's account of the problem and its solution (see Fig. 5.8) run as follows:

Let AB be the given straight line; thus it is required to cut AB so that the rectangle contained by the whole and one of its segments is equal to the square on the remaining segment. Let ABCD be described on AB; let AC be bisected at point E and let BE be joined; let CA be drawn through F, and let EF be made equal to BE; let the square FH be described on AF and let GH be drawn through to K. I say AB has been cut at H so as to make the rectangle contained by AB, BH equal to the square on AH. For since the straight line AC has been bisected at E and FA added to it, the rectangle contained by CF, FA together with the square on AE is equal to the square on EF [by Prop II.6]. Therefore the rectangle CF, FA together with the square on AE is equal to the square on EB. But the squares on BA, AE are equal to the square on EB, for the angle A is right [by Prop I.47]. Therefore the rectangle CF, FA together with the square on AE is equal to the squares on BA, AE. Let the square on AE be subtracted from each. Therefore the rectangle CF, FA which remains is equal to the square on AB. Now the rectangle CF, FA is FK, for AF is equal to FG, and the square on AB is AD. Let AK be subtracted from each; therefore FH which remains is equal to HD; and HD is the rectangle AB, BH for AB is equal to BD; and FH is the square on AH. Therefore the rectangle contained by AB, BH is equal to the square on HA. Therefore the given straight line has been cut at H so as to make the rectangle contained by AB, BH equal to the square on HA.[79]

Now consider how we would solve the problem algebraically, along Descartes' own lines. First we would assign symbols to knowns and unknowns, labelling AB as a, and AH, the unknown line, as x. The conditions of the problem are then translated into an equation:

$$x^2 = (a - x)a$$

We can then deduce the solution in what Descartes calls 'an easy and direct' way:

$$x^2 + ax = a^2$$

$$x^2 + ax + \frac{1}{4}a^2 = a^2 + \frac{1}{4}a^2$$

$$(x + \frac{1}{2}a)^2 = a^2 + \frac{1}{4}a^2$$

$$(x + \frac{1}{2}a) = \sqrt{a^2 + \frac{1}{4}a^2}$$

$$x = \sqrt{a^2 + \frac{1}{4}a^2} - \frac{1}{2}a$$

As Schuster notes, the algebraic notation records and makes it easy to grasp the chain of deduction involved in finding the solution, whereas the geometrical solution 'issues in a complex diagram, which records, but does not *reveal* the steps involved in unravelling the difficulty', and the algebraic demonstration makes clear what has been done to the known and the unknown quantities at each step.[80]

This 'transparency' of algebraic operations is what marks them out as being completely certain, and there can be little doubt that Descartes has identified an important and powerful feature of algebraic demonstration here. But he goes further, for what this transparency amounts to in philosophical terms for him is 'clarity and distinctness'. Moreover, it brings with it all the connotations of pictorial vividness which, I have argued, are such a crucial part of the doctrine of clear and distinct ideas as it figures in the early *Regulae*. Not only is the idea of validation by means of pictorial vividness still active eight years later in the later *Regulae*, but it is present in the most striking and unexpected context. Having established the highly abstract, structural features of his new algebra, its concern with magnitudes in general rather than particular numbers and shapes, the basis for its notation in a series of continued proportions rather than spatial imagery, Descartes proceeds, in Rule 18, to validate it in terms of intuitive obviousness, terms which are unashamedly spatial and, indeed, pictorial. Having set out arithmetical operations in algebraic terms, he continues:[81]

From these considerations it is easy to see how these two operations are all we need for the purpose of discovering whatever magnitudes we are required to deduce from others on the basis of some relation. Once we have understood these operations, the next thing to do is to explain how to present them to the imagination for examination, and how to display them visually, so later on we may explain their uses or applications. If addition or subtraction is to be used, we conceive the subject in the form of a line, or in the form of an extended magnitude in which length alone is to be considered. For if we add line *a* to line *b*,

FIG. 5.9

we add the one to the other in the following way,

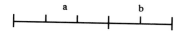

FIG. 5.10

and the result is *c*:

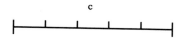

FIG. 5.11

And so on for subtraction, multiplication, and division. The case of multiplication illustrates the quite regressive nature of the representation of arithmetical operations required by Descartes' validating process:[82]

Again, if we wish to multiply *ab* by *c*,

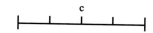

FIG. 5.12

we ought to conceive of *ab* as a line, namely:

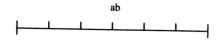

FIG. 5.13

in order to obtain for *abc* the following figure:

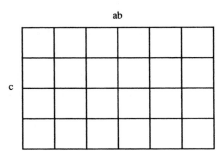

FIG. 5.14

There is clearly a discrepancy here between the concern to represent the operations of arithmetic algebraically, in structural terms, and the concern to provide a vindication of arithmetical processes in terms of operations so clear and vivid that one cannot fail but assent to them. The irony is that, having paid this high price for vindication, Descartes almost certainly realized that it would not succeed anyway, for in the uncompleted Rules 19–21 he extends his account to a set of problems—problems that must be set up in terms of several equations in several unknowns—that can be dealt with algebraically but which cannot be legitimated in the way proposed: and at this very point he abandons the *Regulae*.

Although Descartes only wrote out the titles of Rules 19–21, these provide straightforward descriptions of the proposed content. Moreover, we can fill out some of the details with confidence, since Rules 16 to 21 are mirrored in the early pages of the *Géométrie*. Rule 19 deals with setting up equations, telling us that we need equations for all the unknown lines (i.e. quantities); Rule 20 tells us that we should divide rather than multiply when we have a choice, because, as the *Géométrie* indicates, the former gives us the simplest terms to which the problem can be reduced[83]; and Rule 21 tells us that we should reduce many equations to a single one, an equation of all the equations, as it were.

The problem Descartes comes up against in trying to represent algebraic operations in terms of the manipulation of line lengths is brought out clearly in an entry for October 1628 in Beeckman's *Journal*, where he reports a 'specimen of Descartes' algebra'.[84] Here Descartes is showing how to solve an algebraic problem using line lengths and plane surfaces (see Fig. 5.15). The square *ab* has sides representing an unknown magnitude *x*. We are told that $x^2 = 6x + 7$. If we let *ae* and *ac* equal 3 units, then *fc* and *gb* each equal $3x$. If we then imagine *fc* and *gb* to be removed from the square, we may subtract $6x$ from *ab*,

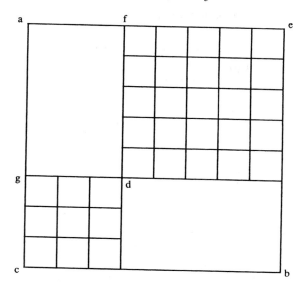

FIG. 5.15

but to do this is to subtract the square *dc* twice, in which case we will only have taken $6x - 9$ from *ab*. Consequently, the remaining square cannot consist of 7 units, but must consist of $7 + 9 = 16$ units. Then the root of *de* (which equals *fe*) is obviously equal to 4, and adding $af = 3$ we obtain $x = 7$ as the side or the root of *ab*.

The problem is how general this procedure is. A moment's reflection shows it to be very restricted. For a start, the procedure has only yielded one root, and the other root, -1, cannot be represented at all. And how would Descartes have managed if the problem had not contained a perfect square? He is aware of the problems. Beeckman reports that irrational numbers cannot be represented in this way but require a parabola (referring to Descartes' technique for general solutions of equations of the third and fourth power using a parabola and a circle[85]), and also that Descartes has a category of imaginary roots that are not constructable at all. The problem here is that the procedure is supposed to represent algebraic operations in terms of the manipulation of line lengths, and thereby provide them with a legitimation in terms of clear and distinct ideas, but except in the simplest case we end up at best invoking complex geometrical constructions, and at worst being unable to provide any construction at all. Neither of these latter cases yield the requisite 'clarity and distinctness'. And it is precisely such cases, namely higher-order root extractions, that arise in Rules 19–21. Descartes can argue for his procedures in purely mathematical terms—in terms of the theory of continued geometrical proportions, for example—but his attempt to justify mathematics as such in terms of the theory of clear and distinct ideas collapses.

What does the attempt at justification in the later *Regulae* amount to? Descartes' attempts to legitimate mathematics are not, I believe, a response to scepticism, for there is simply no evidence of any interest in scepticism in his writings at this period. How then are we to explain the attempt to legitimate or justify something as fundamental as mathematics? Who but a sceptic would believe that mathematics *tout court*— as opposed to certain contentious branches of mathematics (such as transfinite arithmetic in our own time)—was not justified or without legitimation? And why should anyone try to provide a legitimation of mathematical operations *tout court* unless they were responding to a general sceptical challenge? In response to the second question, we must ask who these sceptics were. Sextus Empiricus had challenged geometry on sceptical grounds,[86] but I know of no example of a sceptical challenge to mathematics *tout court* in the 1620s, and Sextus' interest in this area seems to have been universally ignored. But if Descartes was not responding to a sceptical challenge, what was he doing? I suggest that he was not trying to legitimate mathematics so much as to discover what its (unquestioned) legitimacy consisted in. The reason why he wanted to do this in the first place is simply that, like virtually everyone else with an interest in developing natural philosophy, he was attempting to provide the physical sciences with the kind of legitimacy and certainty that was universally ascribed to mathematics; and to do this, he had to discover what this legitimacy consisted in. Unlike others who reflected on mathematics, geometry in particular, and who saw its axiomatic-deductive structure as being the key ingredient, Descartes, as we have seen, had rejected this as early as 1620. Synthetic proof is, for Descartes, something that can only result in sterile truths and cannot be a source for the discovery of new truths. The certainty and legitimacy of mathematics is something that he fills out in terms of the immediacy of its operations, and he already has a well-developed version of a traditional rhetorical-psychological theory with which to think through this problem. The trouble is that in the later Rules, as we have now seen, this theory comes to appear less and less equal to the task.

Descartes must have been very disappointed at this failure, and his work on and interest in mathematics wound down very noticeably; and while he would turn again to mathematical questions in the 1630s, his fundamental work had been completed in the 1620s and his enthusiasm was largely gone. When visiting Beeckman in Dordrecht on 8 October 1628, he told him that he had 'nothing more to discover in arithmetic and geometry', for he had made as much progress as was humanly possible in the last nine years;[87] and eighteen months later he wrote to Mersenne that he was tired of mathematics and held it in such low regard that he could not be bothered solving the problems that Mersenne had sent him.[88]

The Final Year in Paris

In a letter to Mersenne of 15 April 1630, Descartes writes:

You may find it strange that I have not persevered with the treatises I began while in Paris. The reason is that, in the course of working on them, I acquired a little more knowledge than I had when I started, and when I tried to take this into account I was forced to start upon a new project, more extensive than the first. It is as if one were to start building a house and then acquired unexpected riches, so that one's position were changed and the building one had begun was now too small.[89]

The new project that Descartes is to start upon is *Le Monde,* as we shall see. The one he abandons is, I suggest, the *Regulae.*[90] We have already looked at some of the problems inherent in the *Regulae,* and these were sufficiently serious to halt progress. It is clear that Descartes had also begun to think in terms of a new project, although we do not have any evidence of his working on this until his arrival in the Netherlands. We do, however, have some idea of Descartes' interests and activities in his last year in Paris, 1628. In March he spent at least some time in Brittany,[91] and he had promised his friends a 'History of my Mind', quite likely what would become the biographical material of the *Discours de la Méthode.* He wrote a defence of Balzac's rhetoric around March, and we have a report of a meeting which Descartes attended and spoke at, probably towards the end of 1628. Let us look at these in turn.

Some time early in 1628, no later than the end of March, Descartes wrote an open letter to an unknown correspondent—'A Judgement on some Letters of Monsieur de Balzac'—defending Balzac's *Lettres* of 1624.[92] As I indicated earlier, Descartes studied rhetoric very intensely at La Flèche, and the French Jesuits developed a particular style of rhetoric which tried to provide a balance between very curt Attic styles and the baroque Asiatic style of the Second Sophistic. In so far as the Jesuits failed to achieve this balance, they tended towards a more Asiatic style. This was also a tendency exhibited in one of their students, Balzac, a friend of Descartes, and one of the most famous of the seventeenth-century French stylists. Balzac's critics thought that his style had been corrupted by the language of court, and the disputes that surrounded his work turn on the question of a 'natural' style, the opposing view being, essentially, that a style as elaborate and full of hyperbole as Balzac's cannot be counted as 'natural'.[93] In his open letter, carefully composed in Suetonian Latin, Descartes defends Balzac's style as capturing the correct balance, and even appears to offer it as a model:

In the case of M. de Balzac, however, everything that he undertakes to say is explained with such sound arguments and is illustrated with such fine examples that its most admirable feature is a certain stylistic vehemence and natural passion, unbroken by his careful skill, and that, with the elegance and ornamentation of modern times, he retains the vigour and majesty of the eloquence of ancient oratory. He does not abuse the simplicity of his readers, but generally uses arguments that are so clear that they easily gain credence among the common people, and for all that they are so certain and so true that the better the mind of the reader the more sure they are to convince, especially when he wishes to prove to others only what he has already persuaded himself of.[94]

Descartes' defence of Balzac's very florid rhetorical style is not quite as surprising as it may at first seem, for Balzac, like Descartes, is adamant that such style is not something that can be learned from manuals.[95] The point remains, however, that what is apparently being defended is a baroque style explicitly deriving from Classical rhetorical practice.

Or is it? As one commentator has pointed out, the Balzac whom Descartes praises is 'a Balzac revised and corrected along Cartesian lines'.[96] What Descartes is concerned to defend above all is an ideal of eloquence in which the conviction that the speaker or writer is speaking or writing the truth can be conveyed. This is also very much Balzac's concern. More specifically, what Descartes finds to agree with in Balzac is a rejection of 'arid' styles, a rejection of forms of eloquence that conceal the absence of arguments, and above all the priority of persuasion over style. But he also finds much he rejects, including the more traditional rhetorical skills, which Balzac does not completely ignore, such as the use of ornament to convince, even if it disguises or degrades the truth, and the practice of display oratory which has no persuasive value or intent.[97] On closer examination, then, Descartes is not so much concerned to defend traditional rhetoric as to identify those features of rhetorical practice that he finds valuable, and these are those which induce a heightened 'attentiveness' on the part of hearers or readers,[98] with the result that they are better able to grasp things clearly and distinctly. This is very much what we would expect given his account of clear and distinct ideas, and the fact that Descartes advances his own conception in the context of an explicitly rhetorical account is further evidence that his doctrine of clear and distinct ideas is still being thought of in terms deriving from rhetorical theory.

The Paris Years, 1625–1628

Very little of the detail of Descartes' stay in Paris has been recorded, and the only event of a personal nature that we know of is a reputed duel he is said to have fought over a lady, although he is said to have remarked, evidently around the same time, that he had never found a woman whose beauty was comparable with that of truth.[99] One event that was to have some significance for Descartes is also set down by Baillet, however. This is the public meeting at which Descartes refuted an anti-Aristotelian speaker, and was subsequently encouraged by Cardinal Bérulle to pursue his interests for the benefit of humanity. Although the story is, along with Descartes' dreams, just about the most-reported event in his personal life, there is much we are in the dark about concerning both the meeting itself and the subsequent events. There is some doubt as to when the meeting took place, for example, whether it was late in 1627 or in December of 1628.[100] The latter is the date suggested by Baillet's original account, and although Descartes had been in the Netherlands in October, he probably returned to Paris in November, not actually moving permanently until the beginning of 1629.[101] I will therefore take the later date as the correct one,[102] although nothing hinges on it. We may well ask why the papal nuncio, Bagni, who had been named a cardinal *in petto* in August 1627 and was to be proclaimed a full cardinal in November 1629, should invite scholars to his house to hear a lecture attacking Aristotle. Bagni was to appoint the libertine Naudé as his secretary in 1630, and evidently moved in libertine circles, although he cannot himself be called a libertine,[103] which suggests either that the intolerance and censorship of the mid 1620s had diminished to such an extent that public criticism was now again allowed, or that such discussion was a least sanctioned in the case of an elite.

Descartes attended the meeting with Villebressieu, and Morin and Mersenne were also in the audience, as was Cardinal Bérulle, founder of the Oratory, and the moving force behind the reform of the religious orders.[104] The speaker was a chemist/alchemist named Chandoux, an expert in base metals, who was later to be executed for counterfeiting. Chandoux propounded a new chemical philosophy, and he criticized the Aristotelian basis of existing chemical philosophy. Although we do not know what he defended, it would appear to have been broadly in line with the mechanist thinking of the time.[105] The talk was evidently received enthusiastically, but Descartes was less impressed, and when asked why by Bérulle, he apparently got up and spoke against the lecture, praising Chandoux's rejection of Aristotle, but criticizing him for putting in its place something that was merely probable. On being challenged whether he had anything better to offer, he proposed his own 'more true and natural principles'.[106] The only thing to be found in any extant writing of Descartes' from this period that could be described as 'true and natural principles' is his doctrine of clear and distinct ideas. But what is it being offered as an alternative or answer to?

Although it is widely assumed, especially following Popkin's attempts to reconstruct Descartes' career at this point in terms of a general Parisian 'sceptical crisis', that Descartes' concern with certainty here is as an answer to scepticism (and indeed marks the beginning of his concern with scepticism), it must be remembered that questions of the status of our understanding of the natural world had been raised in a natural-philosophical context of mechanism as well as in the epistemological context of scepticism. Popkin treats the Chandoux meeting as 'the microcosm of the plight of the whole learned world',[107] and tells us that

> the evidence of the autobiographical sections of the *Discours* and of Descartes' letters, indicates that around 1628–9 he was struck by the full force of the sceptical onslaught, and the need for a new and stronger answer to it. It was in the light of this awakening to the sceptical menace, that when he was in Paris Descartes set in motion his philosophical revolution by discovering something 'so certain and so assured that all the most extravagant suppositions brought forward by the sceptics were incapable of shaking it'.[108]

But I can find nothing in the *Discours* or the correspondence from this period to indicate any interest in scepticism on Descartes' part at this time, nor can I find any evidence at all that Descartes was motivated by an interest in scepticism before the 1630s. We must, therefore, seriously consider the possibility that his concern with certainty derives from natural-philosophical rather than epistemological considerations.

This would fit in with the tenor of the later *Regulae*, where questions of cognition are not raised in an epistemological but rather in a descriptive and psychological way, mechanism rather than any epistemological doctrine providing the motivation and constraints. Moreover, when we consider that Chandoux's talk was on the unsatisfactory nature of Aristotelian natural philosophy as a basis for chemistry, it is surely reasonable to assume that any philosophical questions that were at issue are much more likely to have been natural-philosophical ones rather than sceptical ones. The questions of hypotheses and probability were part and parcel of the discussion of mechanism. For example, although Mersenne—like Galileo, Kepler, and many others in this period—held up mathematics as a model for knowledge, because of the certainty of its results, when it came to an understanding of the natural world he had made human science strictly separate from divine science, only the latter being able to tell us how things are in reality.[109] More generally speaking, the rejection of Aristotelian essences led to a form of instrumentalism that was common amongst mechanists, and, particularly for Mersenne, mechanism is very much a hypothetical natural philosophy.

Could it perhaps be, then, that Descartes is advocating that mechanism can be provided with the requisite certainty through the doctrine of clear and distinct ideas? Such a project would certainly be developed throughout the 1630s (albeit on the basis of a very different doctrine of clear and distinct ideas from the one we have seen Descartes operate with until now), but if that is what is being advocated here, it is little more than a promissory note on Descartes' part, for not only is the mechanism of the *Regulae* explicitly hypothetical, but that of *Le Monde* is also. But this is not unduly worrying, for it would certainly not be the first promissory note on Descartes' part; and the Popkin interpretation has a similar problem, for, so far as I can tell, no one suggests that Descartes had provided an answer to scepticism at this time. Of more moment is the question why Descartes should want to provide certainty, if not for epistemological reasons to do with a wholesale sceptical threat to knowledge. One reason is that if other natural philosophies—especially scholastic Aristotelianism and naturalism—were being put forward on a realist basis, it might have seemed that mechanism was deficient in some way if it could be defended only instrumentally: and this would have concerned Descartes more than most because he had not just used it to account for natural phenomena but had actually started building it into a theory of cognition. Closely connected with this was the general question of the standing of mathematical and mechanical disciplines that Descartes was pursuing. These were considered not to deal with the real causes of phenomena, and consequently were not entitled to yield a physical interpretation of their system, but merely hypothetical constructions.[110] This was clearly something that Descartes had to counter if his project was to be viable. Another reason why he might have been concerned with certainty is that he knew of the condemnation of Copernicanism on 5 March 1616, in which Copernicus' *De Revolutionibus* was suspended until it had been 'corrected', that is, had been formulated more hypothetically. In a letter to Mersenne, written at the end of November 1633, in which Descartes reveals his dismay at the condemnation of Galileo, he writes that Copernicanism is so interwoven in every part of *Le Monde*, which he has just completed, that 'if it is false, so too are the entire foundations of my philosophy, for it can be demonstrated from them quite clearly'.[111] He would prefer not to publish *Le Monde* at all rather than publish it in a mutilated form, he tells Mersenne, for 'there are already so many views in philosophy that are merely plausible and maintainable in debate that, if my own views are no more certain and cannot be accepted without controversy, then I don't want ever to publish them'.[112] If Descartes' work was to secure an audience, his natural philosophy had to have a degree of certainty at least as great as the systems he was rejecting. The real targets of Descartes' natural philosophy were naturalism and scholastic Aristotelianism, not scepticism. This was the case in 1633, after the completion of *Le Monde*, and it was also the case in 1628 just as he was about to embark on it.

Finally, my reading of Descartes' concerns in the dispute with Chandoux as being natural-philosophical rather than sceptical is, I believe, confirmed by the report we have of his subsequent meeting with Cardinal Bérulle. Bérulle had asked Descartes to call on him to discuss further the questions raised at the meeting and his own intervention,[113] whereupon Descartes pointed out to Bérulle the practical advantages his method might have for medicine and mechanics, and Bérulle strongly encouraged him to pursue his researches.[114] Natural philosophy was charged with theological and metaphysical questions for Bérulle,[115] and one of Descartes' first tasks on arriving in the Netherlands was to be to work on metaphysical and theological questions.[116]

6

A New Beginning
1629–1630

The Retreat from Society

Descartes moved to the Netherlands at the end of 1628 or the beginning of 1629,[1] taking with him a Bible and a *Summa* of Aquinas[2] but apparently little else,[3] and he was to remain there for the next twenty years. Although several explanations have been proposed for his move, we do not really know exactly why he went there. The fact that he went from a Catholic country to a liberal Protestant one may suggest that he found the Netherlands more conducive to his interests than Catholic France. But whatever his sympathies with the religious and political regime in the Netherlands, Descartes was to resist all attempts to convert him to Protestantism,[4] and whatever he may have believed about the liberal climate in the Netherlands, it would turn out in fact that he would be persecuted much more vigorously by Protestants (especially Calvinists) than by Catholics.[5] It might also be noted that the Netherlands had very liberal printing laws and it was possible to publish work there that could often not be published elsewhere; but Descartes' move cannot be explained in terms of a desire to avoid censorship, for he would not publish anything that would fail to get past Parisian censors. Another possibility is that, as Descartes himself indicates in his correspondence and in the *Discours*,[6] he made the move in order to pursue his work without interruption. Although he had benefitted from collaborative efforts up to this point, it is quite possible that he now felt a new confidence in his ideas, and a desire to develop them in detail, something more easily achieved in the peace and quiet of the Netherlands. But the trouble with this explanation is that it is not clear why he could not have achieved as much peace and quiet in the French countryside as in the Dutch,[7] and in any case he was to spend much of his time in the first few years in the Netherlands in the cities. Moreover, despite the fact that the Netherlands had claim to being the scientific and cultural capital of Europe in this period,[8] and especially as somewhere where Copernicanism was widely accepted,[9] his work was in some ways clearly hampered by his isolation from Paris. In June 1628, for example, he wrote to Ferrier virtually begging him to come and help him in his optical researches, although by the

beginning of 1630, when he heard from Morin that Ferrier was planning to come to stay with him after all, he went out of his way to
prevent Ferrier's journey, asking Mersenne to tell Ferrier that he 'is
going out of this country and that he might not find me here'.[10] This
was a complete fabrication on Descartes' part,[11] possibly devised because his old friend Villebressieu may well have joined him by this
time, and he no longer wanted to be bothered with Ferrier, whom he
treats rather shabbily on a number of occasions.[12] As well as company,
he would miss some of the advantages of living in France, notably
French cuisine and the comfort of French furniture, and would find
little to admire in the Dutch educational system compared to the
French.[13] Finally, Descartes changes his address with startling regularity for someone who wants peace and quiet to get on with his work,
and at least some of his constant changes of address were dictated by
the desire to be near friends. At least one of these changes of address,
his move to Deventer in 1632, was due, at least in part, to his desire
to be near his first follower, Reneri, who began teaching Cartesian
natural philosophy at the University of Utrecht in 1636. In this connection, it is worth reminding ourselves that Descartes had some interest
in making sure that his own ideas were disseminated in the Netherlands:
not the behaviour we would expect of a recluse.

Nevertheless, it is hard to avoid the conclusion that Descartes' move
to the Netherlands is a kind of retreat, not so much a retreat to
the country (although he will spend a great deal of time living in the
country in the 1640s, and in 1629 he describes himself as living 'in the
wilderness'[14]) but as simply a retreat; for even when he is in the city,
he tells Balzac, he can go unnoticed since everyone is busy in his trade,
and 'I can walk out each day in the bustle of the crowds with as much
freedom and ease as you have in your paths, and I pay no more
attention to the people I meet than I would to the trees in your woods
or the animals that graze there'[15]. Since the idea of a retreat from society
is part of the *gentilhomme* culture in which Descartes and his Parisian
friends thrived, it may be worthwhile investigating whether this culture
can throw any light on Descartes' move. Montaigne had made the
retreat to the countryside almost mandatory for the true *gentilhomme*.
Although, like Descartes, Balzac had travelled in Italy and especially in
the Netherlands[16], he was the epitome of a *gentilhomme*, spending most
of his time at his estate near Angoulême—suffering from some unspecified ill-health—but making regular literary forays, and indeed
writing for the court. Descartes too would write at a distance, in an
important sense, following his move to the Netherlands; for although
he was to have friends and followers there, his intended audience would
always be predominantly a French one, and he never took advantage

of the liberal publishing laws of the Netherlands, for example, to publish material that might be subject to censorship in France, or indeed in any Catholic country. And when he was to write in the vernacular, it would of course be French, not Flemish. It is in this sense that we can treat Descartes as writing as an exile, from a retreat.

One factor that must be taken into account here is Descartes' lack of a patron. Sarasohn has defined patronage succinctly as 'a system of personal relationships between individuals, of unequal and varying degrees of status and power, who were bound together as benefactors and servants for the mutual advantage of each party'.[17] Many of the libertines in the 1620s had Richlieu and Mazarin as their patrons, but in the 1620s and 1630s the pre-eminent French patron of natural philosophers was Peiresc; unfortunately Peiresc already had a favourite, Gassendi, and Descartes never took to playing second fiddle to anyone. Still, Descartes would depend on scientific networks that Peiresc organized, and French natural philosophers, including Mersenne, relied on the patronage of Peiresc in numerous ways.[18] Patronage in the seventeenth century was a complex phenomenon, and clients as well as patrons generally benefited greatly from it.[19] It often imposed some constraints on research, but these were generally insignificant compared to the kinds of constraints, for example, that the Catholic Church imposed, or tried to impose. The simple fact is that patrons were not particularly concerned to uphold orthodoxy; they were far more concerned with having their standing or status enhanced by being associated with new scientific discoveries. They were able to offer protection from accusations of unorthodoxy, within limits, and, where needed, they were able to establish their clients in financially secure positions where they could pursue their research interests. It is hard to explain why Descartes took the unusual step of working outside the patronage system. In particular, I cannot see that his personality precluded his working within this system successfully any more than did Galileo's, who played the system brilliantly until 1633. His disputes with the Dutch authorities in the 1640s, arising from his quarrel with Voetius, show he was not short of the kind of political cunning that was occasionally required in the court intrigues to which patrons subjected their clients. And if someone like Gassendi, who associated with the libertines and was openly advocating Epicurean atomism, could be protected under Peiresc's wing, so certainly, could Descartes. However, the more important point in the present context is not so much why Descartes avoided the patronage system, but how one functioned outside it, when it provided contacts, funding, and protection. In eschewing patronage, Descartes was to a large extent placing himself outside the community of natural philosophers (in the way that a physicist or mathematician working privately outside the university system now would be), and having done this, the move to the Netherlands begins to look a little more natural. We cannot tell whether, at this stage, Descartes would have entered the patronage system had he found a conducive patron (as he was to do at the very end of his life, when he accepted the patronage of Queen Christina), but his failure to enter it at this time would have isolated him to such an extent that, while patronage and exile do not exhaust the possibilities, they certainly give one a fair idea of the nature of the choice.

Descartes' interests in 1629 begin to move in a new direction, and the years 1629 and 1630 are both especially crucial ones, and especially complicated in terms of his changing interests and the changing relations between them. Some guidance, however schematic, will therefore be of help, and, although it is impossible not to stray from them when we come to the detail, I propose that we think in terms of three periods. The first is that lasting from his arrival in the Netherlands at the end of 1628 to the autumn of 1629. In these months, he was to continue to pursue his work in optics, and he would begin to work on metaphysics, on the existence of God, and on the immortality of the soul. The next period lasts roughly from the winter of 1629 to the autumn of 1630. It is initiated by a letter in August asking for an explanation of parhelia, and a study of an isolated meteorological phenomenon was to grow rapidly into a major project of explaining 'all natural phenomena'. Descartes abandoned work on other projects, but was worried because his physical work was inevitably tied up with metaphysical and theological questions which he could not resolve. Finally, the third period lasts from around November 1630, when he gave up (at least in part) the attempt to reconcile his physical account with metaphysical and theological doctrines, and pursued a general account of material bodies that includes not just physics and cosmology, but also physiology. This project, which we shall look at in the next chapter, was pursued until 1633, when its completion and plans for publication were abandoned on his hearing of Galileo's condemnation by the Roman Inquisition.

Grinding the Anaclastic

When Descartes first arrived in the Netherlands he spent a short time in Amsterdam, and some time at Dordrecht visiting Beeckman, before settling in Franeker, where he registered at the university there as a student in April 1629, this probably being a formality which provided him with some kind of proper legal status in the Netherlands. His interests in the course of his first year in the Netherlands centred, by his own account, on metaphysics, but his extant correspondence from 1629 covers, as well as metaphysics, the grinding of lenses, music, optical illusions, and natural philosophy.

His brief treatments of optical illusions and music bring to light his attitude to the reductive aspects of mechanism in an interesting way. On the question of optical illusions, in which he still shows a keen interest, his approach is predictably deflationary: the illusions produced by magicians, allegedly with the help of demons, can in fact be produced simply 'by the air and light'.[20] And he offers a similarly deflationary account of cameos and talismans in a letter to Mersenne of 8 October.[21] But in the case of music, where we might expect the replacement of his early mathematical reduction by a more fully-fledged mechanist reduction—explaining consonance not in terms of ratios but in physical terms, as Beeckman and Mersenne had been doing—we find a move in exactly the opposite direction. He is now interested in the psychological effects of music. So, for example, the reason why one cannot move from a third directly to an octave is not explained reductively at all, but in terms of what the mind anticipates when it is aware of various intervals;[22] and the explanation for the ways in which various voices may move lies in a psychological theory about the emotional concomitants of various musical progressions and the ability of these progressions to stimulate our attention.[23] In general, his approach to music at this time indicates that harmonic and psychological considerations are now paramount; as we shall see below, within a couple of years he was to have taken this sufficiently far as to eschew any attempt to understand music in reductionist terms. What blocks off reduction in the case of music here is almost certainly the beginning of an awareness of where mechanical explanations might no longer be appropriate, something that would increasingly command Descartes' attention.

The project which, next to his work on metaphysics, apparently took up most of his time was the devising of an apparatus capable of grinding hyperbolic lenses; for he was convinced that the anaclastic was a hyperbola, that is, that a lens with a hyperbolic surface would refract incoming parallel rays cleanly to a single point, thus ridding lenses of the various aberrations that had hindered the construction of optical instruments up to this point. But there were formidable problems involved in grinding aspherical lenses. Descartes had approached Ferrier about this problem as early as 1626, and on 18 June he wrote to him that he had solved the practical problems involved[24] and insisted that Ferrier join him in Franeker, providing him with details of the route, and telling him that they would 'live like brothers', Descartes seeing to all his financial and other needs.[25] Ferrier was not to come to Franeker, however, and Descartes subsequently writes to him describing what he has in mind so that the latter can construct the apparatus needed in Paris. In two letters to Ferrier, Descartes writes in some detail about the construction of his lens-grinding machine, giving us some insight into the complexity and practical sophistication of what he has in mind. He sets out details of revisions to a machine that he had described to Ferrier in Paris, indicating how the blades that will do the grinding are to be cut, what material they are to be made of, and so on. Ferrier responds with a list of queries: how various parts can move without obstructing one another; how the machine is to cut convex lenses; whether the blades will need to be cut from two plates or whether one is enough; how identical moulds are to be made, one for rough-forming and one for finishing off; what kinds of material can be used to grind glass cleanly, without leaving a deposit that would interfere with smooth grinding; how to balance the softness of the grinding materials needed if they are to grind smoothly against the fact that if they are softer than the glass then the glass will grind them rather than vice versa; and so on.[26] Descartes replies in detail, showing what materials the different parts of the machine must be constructed of, the exact sizes of components, how the machine must be fixed to the rafters and joists to minimize vibration, how to avoid scraping or gouging the lens during cutting by performing the whole operation at an angle; in addition, he deals with more mathematical problems, providing details of how to cut a lens so that it has a predetermined focal length without losing any of the thickness of the glass, and how to trace a hyperbola using only a compass.[27] The account that Descartes gives of the grinding of aspherical lenses in these letters would form an unrevised basis for the definitive version given nine years later in Discourse 10 of the *Dioptrique*, where an illustration of the same machine is provided (Fig. 6.1).

The correspondence on grinding hyperbolic lenses is important because it reveals an insight into Descartes' working habits that is rare, for special circumstances require that he set out very practical matters in some detail. His exchanges with Ferrier show him to have some basic engineering skills with, for example, a good appreciation of practical questions concerning friction, vibration, and the qualities of different types of grinding materials. But these exchanges also indicate a grasp of the sine version of the law of refraction. Descartes does not actually set out the sine law, probably because to do so would be to allow Ferrier to pursue his optical researches independently of Descartes' guidance, and perhaps even to take credit for these: as we shall see below when we look at Descartes' dispute with Beeckman, he is very sensitive on such matters of priority.

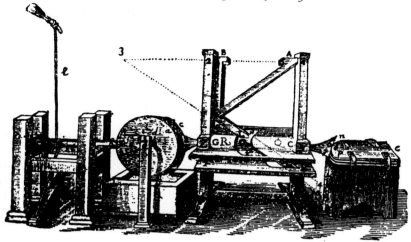

FIG. 6.1

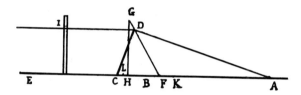

FIG. 6.2

In his letter to Descartes of 26 October 1629, Ferrier writes:

You have taught me that the [prism] can be made with any angle one wishes; I cannot demonstrate this, for all the prisms I have at present are the same, and I beg you to resolve this point for me.... M. Mydorge proposed a means that he has of tracing the required line so as to burn at a point he will determine for any given lens without knowing anything of its diameter or its thickness at its centre, and he says he alone has discovered this. I know that this secret is not unknown to you, and that all the said gentleman knows of it he has learned from you. If you decide that I could understand it, you would oblige me greatly by communicating it at your convenience.[28]

Descartes replies to the first question as follows, setting out what is in effect a method for determining the refractive index of a glass prism (see Fig. 6.2):

Let the line of your quadrant be AE, and let the glass prism be applied above it be FGH, which can be of any size provided that the line GH falls from it at a right angle to AE, so that the sun's ray passing through the pinnule I travels straight to

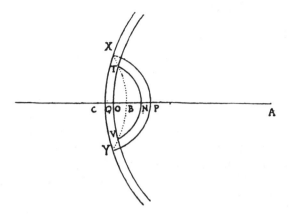

FIG. 6.3

D and is not refracted when it enters the lens but only when it leaves it, namely at point D. Note then the line GDF, which represents the inclination of the lens in which the refraction occurs, the point D, at which it is cut by the sun's ray, and the point AS, where the sun's ray IDA cuts the line of your quadrant. You then have the angle ADF. Now, from the point D draw another line DC so that the angle FDC is equal to the angle ADF, and consequently so that the whole angle ADC is double the angle ADF. Note the point at which the line DC cuts your quadrant, and when you have found this draw the line CK equal to CD, and the line AL equal to AD. Then find the mid point between the two points K and L, namely B. And having the three points A, B, and C, which give you the proportion between the lines AB and BC, you have then only to do as follows. This proportion will always turn out the same, no matter what glass triangle you take, provided they are of the same transparency.[29]

Descartes then proceeds to show Ferrier a simple way of tracing a hyperbola with a compass using A, B, and C as his reference points (Fig. 6.3). One opens the compass with the point at B and marks off points O and N equidistant from B. Then, taking A as centre, we trace the arc TOV, and from C as centre and CN as radius, we trace out the arc VNT which intersects TOV at V and T. We can find 'an infinite number of points in this way', Descartes tells Ferrier, simply by repeating the operation, for example by opening the compass a little further and starting with two points equidistant from B, namely P and Q. This will give us two larger arcs XQY and YPX. The hyperbola will lie along the points of intersection of the arcs, having B as its vertex.

This letter contains enough information for someone with a grasp of the fundamentals of geometrical optics to derive the sine law, as Descartes realizes, telling Mersenne that he is not afraid of anyone publishing the law before him unless 'they draw it from the letters that

I sent to Ferrier'.[30] He clearly knew the sine law by this time, and he was able to show Beeckman how to apply the law to lenses when he visited him in October 1629, demonstrating that an elliptical lens was anaclastic when constructed in a certain way, although Beeckman does not record the proof of this.[31] We do not know when he discovered the sine law, however. It was perhaps as early as 1626, for in setting out the account that we have just looked at, Descartes prefaces it with the comment that Ferrier has forgotten some of what he taught him in Paris.[32] The first time he sets out the sine law explicitly is in a letter to Mersenne of June 1632, where he tells him: 'as to my way of measuring the refraction of light, I compare the sines of the angles of incidence and the angle of refraction, but I would be happy if this were not made known as yet'.[33]

The Formulation of a Metaphysics

It is evident from his correspondence that although Descartes devoted considerable time to questions in dioptrics in the first part of 1629, his principal concern was with metaphysics. When he registered at the University of Franeker as a student in April 1629, he signed himself as 'Renatus des Cartes Gallus, Philosophus'. Baillet tells us that Descartes began a treatise on divinity in 1628,[34] while he was still in Paris, although we do not know what became of it. By 1629, however, he was certainly thinking seriously about at least two metaphysical questions: the existence of God and the immortality of the soul. He mentions that he had begun on 'a little treatise' in a letter to Gibieuf in July 1629,[35] and a later letter to Mersenne indicates that this was a treatise on metaphysics in which he 'set out to prove the existence of God and of our souls when they are separate from the body, from which their immortality follows'.[36] These were the two traditional questions that Parisian philosophers of the 1620s had been concerned with: Mersenne had devoted attention to both of them and Silhon had explicitly singled them out (along with God's providence) as the key issues in Les deux veritez. Both Mersenne and Silhon had been concerned with a form of religious scepticism which would deny these doctrines, but in Mersenne's case there is also an explicit awareness that naturalism needs to be rebutted if either doctrine is to be defended fully. We cannot ascertain whether Descartes was concerned with a naturalistic challenge to these doctrines or with a sceptical challenge at this time. Yet despite the paucity of material, we are not completely in the dark. From the scraps of information he gives on the content of his treatise, we can offer a reconstruction, albeit a speculative one, of the issues he deals with and of the direction in which his metaphysical thought was moving.

In a letter to Mersenne of 25 November 1630, he writes:

> The quickest way that I know of to reply to arguments which he [unknown author] brings against Divinity, and to the arguments of all atheists, is to find an evident proof which will convince everyone of God's existence. I can boast of having found one myself which satisfies me entirely, and which shows me that God exists with more certainty than with which I know the truth of any proposition of mathematics; but I do not know whether I would be able to make everyone understand it the way I do, and I think it is better not to deal with this matter at all than to deal with it imperfectly.[37]

The first question we must ask is why he thinks it necessary to add to the numerous proofs of God's existence that had already been adduced. It is important here that we recognize that the term 'atheist' in the seventeenth century is a term of abuse rather than something with a precise meaning. In fact one precise meaning it does not seem to have had is a literal belief that there is no God. What might well have been included in the term as Descartes uses it in this letter can perhaps be brought out by looking at how Mersenne uses the term in his *L'Impiété des deists*. Mersenne identifies Charron, Cardano, and Bruno as the principal atheists of his time,[38] but the fact that each of these believes in God is evident from Mersenne's own discussion of them. Charron believes that the existence of God cannot be proved by reason, but can be known only through faith; Cardano also denied that fundamental dogmas—the immortality of the soul, divine providence, creation *ex nihilo*—can be demonstrated by reason, and, Mersenne finds, he supports determinism, but he certainly believes in the existence of God; and Bruno argued that God's omnipotence was limited because, although infinite, He was necessarily caught up in finite things.[39] Mersenne is not interested in thinkers who genuinely did not believe in the existence of a God—he would have been extremely unlikely to have found any, if indeed there were any such people in the sixteenth and early seventeenth centuries.[40] Nor was he interested, for example, in Islam or (except in the case of the Cabbala) Judaism, or even Protestantism: his concern is with various forms of heresy within the Roman Church. What was at stake was not the existence of God *per se*, even the God of Christianity, but whether there was a compelling form of rational argument, independent of faith, which showed the existence of *the right kind* of God.

Now it is clear from the rationale behind Mersenne's advocacy of mechanism that one thing the right kind of God had to be was a God who was transcendent, in the sense of being independent of His creation. The traditional Scholastic arguments had attempted to prove God's existence from manifest features of His creation, such as the harmony in nature. Such demonstrations did not distinguish between an immanent God and a transcendent one, but this had now become the key issue, as Mersenne's anti-naturalistic writings testify. Such a transcendent God is not only not part of His creation, but not in any way dependent upon it. Therefore, if transcendence was to be guaranteed from the outset, a proof of God was needed which did not tie His existence in any way to His creation. Bearing this in mind, we can ask what Descartes' 'evident proof' might have been.

His remarks on eternal truths in the letters to Mersenne of April and May 1630, which we shall look at below, strongly suggest that, if He has a proof of the existence of God, it is one which makes God completely independent of anything He has in fact done. What later became known as the ontological argument fits the bill here, for this argument does not infer God's existence *a posteriori* from anything He has in fact created, but rather infers the necessity of His existence *a priori* simply from our concept of God. But in the record of his conversation with Burman of April 1648, Descartes distinguishes between the argument for God in the third Meditation and that in the fifth Meditation. In the former, he looks for some effect of God in order to deduce the existence of God as cause, and finds that the only effect which will support such an argument is his idea of God; he can attribute his ideas of other things to various sources, but his idea of God is such that the only thing he can conceive of as being responsible for it is God Himself. The argument of the fifth Meditation, on the other hand, he refers to as the *a priori* argument, *a priori* because it does not start from an effect. In brief, this argument (the 'ontological' argument) reflects on the idea that God is defined as that being which has every perfection, and since it is more perfect to exist than not to exist, if something has every perfection then it must exist. Now Descartes tells Burman that this *a priori* argument comes later than the causal argument because of 'the order in which the author discovered the two proofs'.[41] But we are not obliged to conclude from this that Descartes actually discovered the proofs in this order: his remark may simply reflect the fact that the general structure of the argument in the *Meditationes* requires him to show that my idea of God is caused by God before he can proceed to the *a priori* proof of God's existence, whereas in the *Principia*, for example, a different mode of exposition allows him to provide the *a priori* proof first.

In fact, however, what matters is not so much the actual chronological sequence as whether Descartes had the *a priori* argument worked out in some form in 1630. Unless his confidence in his demonstration is completely misplaced, I think we have to assume that he did, for there can be no doubt that this is the argument he needed if he was to establish transcendence definitively. Both arguments provide some indication of transcendence, but the *a priori* argument is in a stronger position to guarantee it because it relies on no creation whatsoever. The difference is that the causal argument moves from a particular idea considered as an effect to the ultimate cause of that idea, whereas the *a priori* argument reflects on the content of the idea and considers the implications of that content for what the idea refers to. It may be pointed out that in both cases the proof depends on the existence of the idea: in the causal argument it depends on the very fact of my having the idea, in the *a priori* argument on the nature of the content of the idea. The point is, however, that the *a priori* proof is designed to reflect a feature of God which He would have even if He had created nothing, whereas the causal argument is not. We need to have an idea of God to be able to go through the *a priori* proof, but God's necessary existence is not dependent on my ability to prove it, and hence not dependent on the existence of my idea of God, or indeed the existence of anything other than Himself, whereas the proof of His existence as cause depends on His having caused something, and hence on something other than Him existing.

There is a sense in which Descartes' proof of the existence of God is tied in with the very general metaphysical programme, outlined above all by Mersenne in his anti-naturalistic treatises of the mid-1620s, which proposes countering various forms of naturalism by providing a natural philosophy which allows a clear separation to be made between the natural and the supernatural, the former being construed as inert and the latter as completely transcendent. When we looked at Mersenne's account, however, I noted that his treatment of naturalism also included consideration of a second question, mortalism. He treated as part of the same general problem both the doctrine that nature is a realm of active powers, and the doctrine that the soul is simply the form of the body and cannot persist after the death of the body. His reason for treating these as part of the same general problem was that he thought of them both as arising from a blurring of the sharp separation between natural and supernatural, so that both nature generally and the human body were given active powers which, if extended as far as some renaissance naturalists were inclined to extend them, would have rendered the genuinely supernatural (namely God) redundant. The philosophical root of these dangerous tendencies was the Aristotelian doctrine of form, which could be used to support all kinds of occult powers in nature and to support the doctrine that since the soul is the form of the body, and since forms always need to be attached to something (the core of Aristotle's rejection of Plato), the soul must perish when its substratum, the material body, does. But if one grants that mechanism provides a satisfactorily sharp distinction between the natural and the supernatural, the problem still remains whether the requisite notion of the soul can be captured in this way. It can be included in the natural realm only at the expense of being made inert, which would surely be to deny it consciousness and will, a thing which neither Mersenne nor Descartes could do. But if it is included in the supernatural, it must be distinguished from God, if only because God has created it and consequently it must stand in a relation of dependence on Him.

The second question dealt with in the 'Little Treatise' is the immortality of the soul. We have very little on this question before the composition of the *Discours,* probably in the winter of 1635–6, and I believe that we must be very circumspect indeed about reading the discussion of mind in Part 4 of the *Discours* back into the 'Little Treatise'. But there is obviously some continuity. The 'Little Treatise' had examined the question of 'the existence of our souls when they are separate from the body'. In Part 4 of the *Discours,* the basis for this separate existence is laid out: 'Accordingly this "I"—that is, the soul by which I am what I am—is completely distinct from the body, and indeed is easier to know than the body, and would not fail to be whatever it is, even if the body did not exist'.[42] The traditional Thomist view had centred around the defence of the resurrection of the body at the Last Judgement. Descartes concerns himself neither with the Last Judgement nor with the resurrection of the body. In fact, this is only to be expected, as studies of the literature and iconography of death between the fourteenth and seventeenth centuries show that the body-and-soul resurrection becomes progressively ignored both by theologians and the general populace, as the image of death comes to focus on the decomposing cadaver, and the judgement of each individual soul immediately after death is accentuated.[43] Certainly if one did not accept the doctrine of the resurrection of the body at the Last Judgement, a doctrine which seems to have gone out of theological fashion by the seventeenth century and which Descartes clearly does not hold, then the soul would have to be independent of the body if it were to be immortal. But the way in which Descartes sets out the independence of the soul with respect to the body has a striking similarity to his account of the independence of God with respect to His creation. The soul, like God, transcends material things and is not dependent upon them: like God, the soul would not fail to be whatever it is, even if the body did not exist. In Part 4, the principal difference between myself considered as a soul and God seems to be that God has all perfections whereas I do not. In short, the parallels between the way in which God is distinguished from matter and the way in which mind is distinguished from matter suggest that Descartes sees them as being part of the same kind of exercise: a consideration dictated by mechanism.

The general rationale behind the 'Little Treatise' is presented briefly in a letter of 15 April 1630 to Mersenne:

As for your theological question, it is beyond the capacity of my mind, but it does not seem to me to be outside my province, since it does not concern anything that depends on revelation, which is what I call Theology in the strict sense; rather, it is a metaphysical question to be examined by human reason. I think that all of those to whom God has given the use of this reason are obliged above all to use it to know Him and to know themselves. It is with this that I tried to begin my studies, and I can say that I would not have been able to discover the foundations of physics if I had not looked for them along that road. It is the topic I have studied more than any other and in which, thank God, I have not completely wasted my time; and I think I have at least found a way of proving metaphysical truths that is more evident than the proofs of geometry—in my own opinion that is, for I do not know whether I shall be able to convince others of it. During my first nine months in this country I worked on nothing else.[44]

What does Descartes mean here when he tells Mersenne that he has found a way of proving metaphysical truths that renders them more evident than geometrical proofs, and that it is metaphysics that has enabled him to discover the basis of his physics? The former claim may at first seem especially obscure. I do not think that we should take 'geometrical proof' here to mean synthetic proof, that is, the deduction of theorems from first principles. Descartes has challenged the point of such kinds of proof, and he has developed his own procedure for rendering geometrical theorems evident in Rules 16 onwards. But, as we saw, this procedure, which is one for legitimating geometrical proofs in terms of clear and distinct ideas by representing the operations involved in the proof by operations on line lengths, came to grief once one moved beyond the simplest cases. Consequently, it would not be surprising if Descartes began to have some doubts about the centrality of mathematics. Nothing indicates, however, that he is not still concerned to employ the doctrine of clear and distinct ideas as the procedure by which one renders truths evident. Quite the contrary, his commitment to the criterion is as strong as ever. In a letter to Mersenne dated 20 November 1629, for example, Descartes raises some questions about 'a proposal for a new language' which Mersenne had sent him for discussion. The proposal took the form of a Latin prospectus containing six propositions, arguing for the merits of a new artificial language.[45] Descartes is not impressed by the proposal, but he does not reject the idea of an artificial language *tout court*:

I do believe that one could devise something over and above this, for making up primitive words and their symbols in this language, so that it could be learned very quickly, and by means of order, that is, by establishing an order among all the thoughts that can come into the human mind which is the same as that which naturally holds between numbers. And just as in a single day one could learn to name every one of the infinite series of numbers, and to write them down in an unknown language, even though this involves an infinite number of words, so one could do the same with all the other words needed to express all the other things that can come into the human mind. If this secret were discovered, I am certain that the language would soon spread throughout the world; for there are many people who would be willing to spend five or six days in learning how to make themselves understood by everyone. But I do not think your author has thought of this, as much because there is nothing in his propositions to suggest it, as because the discovery of such a language depends on the true Philosophy; for it is impossible otherwise to number and order the thoughts of men, or just to distinguish in them those which are clear and simple, which to my mind is the greatest secret in acquiring true science/wisdom [*scientia*]. And were someone to have explained correctly what are the simple ideas in the human imagination out of which all human thoughts are composed, and if his explanation were generally accepted, I would then dare to hope for a universal language which was very easy to learn, speak and write. Most of all, such a language would assist our judgement by representing matters so clearly that it would be almost impossible to go wrong. As it is, almost all our words have confused meanings, and men's minds have become so accustomed to them that there is virtually nothing that they can understand perfectly. Now I hold that such a language is possible, and that the knowledge [*scientia*] on which it depends can be discovered. It would make peasants better able to judge the truth about the world than philosophers are now. But do not hope ever to see such a language in use. For that, the natural order would have to change so much that the world would have to become a terrestrial paradise, and this happens only in fiction.[46]

The universal language proposed by Descartes here seems quite artificial. But it is premised on our ability to recognize which of our ideas are 'clear and simple', and this is something in which we are guided by the natural light of reason. Because of this, there is a sense in which the universal language that Descartes is advocating is something he thinks of as the only truly natural language, and that everyday languages are in some way artificial. There are some interesting parallels between Descartes' account of a universal language here and his account of the corruption of eloquence in his open letter to Balzac written eighteen months earlier.[47] In as much as we can reconstruct Descartes' thinking in this earlier letter, such a 'pure' language was that originally spoken, but it has been lost due to the perversions of eloquence, and if 'the emotions of the transparent soul' are once again to be expressed language must be remodelled using the criterion of clear and simple/distinct ideas provided by the natural light of reason. More generally, the 'language' in which we think is no longer reflected in that in which we speak and write, but this latter could in principle (but not in fact) be reformed so that it could once again capture our thoughts directly and transparently.[48]

Descartes' thinking about language in 1629 shows a continued commitment to reform in line with his doctrine of clear and distinct ideas, the reform now being one of language itself rather than just the sciences. Moreover, clear and distinct ideas still appear to be something deriving from a natural faculty. If they are such, then this is the last time they will be considered in this way (at least outside a mathematical context, where special considerations now apply, as we shall see), for developments in Descartes' thinking early in 1630 begin to make resort to such a natural faculty highly problematic, and clear and distinct ideas, which up to this point had provided a straightforward guarantee, now themselves begin to require legitimation if they are to continue to provide such a guarantee. In particular, the paradigm application of the doctrine would move from mathematics to metaphysics, and the development that inaugurates this change is, I shall suggest below, Descartes' formulation of a theory about the nature of God's powers.

As for the second claim, that it is metaphysics that has enabled him to discover the basis of his physics, there are a number of things this could mean. It could mean that Descartes believes he has provided metaphysical foundations for physics in the sense of being able to derive his physical theory from metaphysics, for example, or it could simply mean that he has uncovered metaphysical principles that enable him to distinguish true from false claims in physics. I know of no reason why we should construe what he says in the first sense—Descartes will never use metaphysics to generate physical truths, contrary to a popular misreading[49]—and the latter interpretation fits in with what we can establish about his intellectual development. I suggest that we think of the claim as indicating that Descartes now believes he has a way of determining the truth of his physical theories that relies on something metaphysical, and I suggest that this 'something metaphysical' is a metaphysical criterion of clear and distinct ideas. In very general terms, the doctrine of clear and distinct ideas, following the failures of 1628, gradually becomes transformed from a doctrine about the evidential value of images into one about our cognitive relation to the external world. The former doctrine, as we have seen, is ultimately derived from the rhetorico-legal tradition; the latter is metaphysical and has no such Classical precedent. The first relies on what Descartes refers to as 'the natural light of reason', and is indeed in many respects constitutive of the natural light of reason, something which, like conscience (to which it bears many resemblances and on which it may even have been modelled), is an ultimate resort. The second relies on a divine guarantee, and far from the criterion of clear and distinct ideas being something human beings have forged for themselves, it now becomes something that God has explicitly provided us with, and which He guarantees. Both versions of the doctrine are centred around the key question of self-conviction, but the former is concerned with compelling representation, whereas the latter is concerned with absolute certainty. The whole point of the doctrine, and the resources it draws upon, are completely transformed.

Descartes had certainly not made this transition fully in 1629, but it seems highly likely that what we are getting in the letter to Mersenne are the first traces of it. If this is indeed the case, then we can ask what the sources of this change might have been. Certainly the failure, in the case of geometry, of his rhetorico-psychological theory must have played a role in stimulating Descartes to look for a new basis for his doctrine. But it is far from easy to say what metaphysical considerations shaped the new version. One set of metaphysical considerations are singled out in a letter to Mersenne of 15 April 1630, however, and these turn on the nature of God's powers.

In his letter to Mersenne, Descartes writes:

In my treatise on physics I shall discuss a number of metaphysical topics and especially this: that the mathematical truths that you call eternal have been established by God and are completely dependent upon Him, just as any other of His creations are. To say that these truths are independent of Him is to talk of Him as if He were Jupiter or Saturn and to subject Him to the Styx and the Fates. . . . We cannot comprehend the greatness of God . . . even though we know it. . . . It will be said that if God had established these truths then He can change them, just as a king changes his laws, to which I reply that He can, if His will can change. 'But I understand them to be eternal and immutable'—and I would say the same of God. 'But His will is free'—Yes, but His power is beyond our grasp. Generally, we can assert that God can do anything that is within our grasp, but not that He cannot do anything that is outside our grasp; for it would be rash to think that our imagination extends as far as His power. I hope to put this in writing within the next fortnight in my physics.[50]

The question that I ultimately want to focus on here is whether this doctrine of God's power could have played any role in his move from a rhetorico-psychological account of clear and distinct ideas to the metaphysical doctrine. But before we can ask this, we need to know what exactly Descartes' doctrine is and why he proposes it.

The doctrine is originally theological in motivation and can be seen as a reaction to two currents of thought about the relation between our and God's knowledge. The medieval discussion can be seen as starting from a dissatisfaction with the account of Aquinas, which was effectively a compromise. Aquinas' problem was to defend the traditional doctrine that the attribution of properties to a transcendent being like God, and attribution of those properties to His creation, must be equivocal: that is to say, to speak of God as 'good' and to speak of a person as 'good' must involve some equivocation, because what it is for a perfect creator to be good, for example, must be different from what it is for a created, imperfect person to be good. But Aquinas did not want to accept the *via negativa* whereby we could say nothing at all about God, except that He is not this and not that. There must consequently be some bridge between God and His creation, and Aquinas supplies this bridge in terms of the doctrine of analogy. The theory which underlies the doctrine of analogy is exemplarism, whereby divine ideas are construed, in traditional Augustinian (and Neoplatonic) fashion, as exemplars, or patterns, or models on which God created the world, but which are only imperfectly exemplified in the world. Marion has shown how the ontological basis of exemplarism subsequently came to be replaced by an epistemological emphasis,[51] with the result that eternal truths, for example, were no longer construed as exemplars proper, patterns on which creation is modelled, but rather as something to be known by both God and us. In this way exemplarism becomes transformed into the problem of whether our ideas can represent these eternal truths, and in this changed context a new problem came to the fore, one which undermined the adequacy of the Thomist response. It was Duns Scotus who pointed out that analogy cannot be sufficient because we are concerned in metaphysics with being-*qua*-being, and for this to be possible we must have a unitary conception of being that is logically prior to the distinctions between created and uncreated being, finite and infinite being, and so on. Clearly such a conception of being cannot be elucidated by the doctrine of analogy, but must actually be prior to it.

The crucial response to this problem came with Suárez. Suárez was the Jesuit metaphysician *par excellence*, and Descartes was familiar with his writings from La Flèche. Indeed, Descartes may well have been familiar with the whole problem of the nature of God's powers principally through Suárez' discussion. Suárez allows that the ascription of some properties or qualities to God must be univocal, and he deploys analogy in a restricted range. In particular, he accepts the intuitively appealing view that there are general constraints on representing things to any intellect, whether human or divine. In Suárez' account, the key feature is not analogy, as it was in that of Aquinas, but univocity.[52] It is this account that Descartes explicitly rejects. So, for example, in a letter to Mersenne of 6 May 1630, Descartes writes:

As for eternal truths, I say that *they are true or possible only because God knows them as true or possible, and they are not known as true by God in any way that would imply that they are true independently of Him.* And if men understood the meanings of their words properly, they could never say without blasphemy that the truth of something is prior to the knowledge that God has of it.[53]

The words in italics here are in Latin in the original, in a letter mainly in French, which suggests a quotation or quasi-quotation. And indeed Descartes sticks closely in terminology and in some cases even syntax to Suárez' *Disputationes Metaphysicae*. For example, in the case of the above sentence, the corresponding sentence in Suárez reads, 'These propositions are not true because they are known by God, but rather, they are only known because they are true, independently of whether one could explain why God knows them to be true'.[54]

Descartes' doctrine about God's creation of eternal truths advances the claim that God not only made things so that certain propositions were true of them, He also created the true propositions and, because He created their content, He could have made the truths of mathematics, for example, different from what they are:

God was free not to make it true that the radii of the circle are equal—just as He was free not to create the world. And it is certain that these truths are no more necessarily attached to His essence than are other created things.[55]

Given the context of Descartes' statements about the inability of our finite minds to grasp God's infinite power, we must take this to mean not merely that God could have created a world in which all the radii of a circle were not equal, but that He could have created a world in which the radii of a circle were unequal but which was identical to the present one in *every* other (geometrical and physical) respect. It is difficult to imagine the first (though not too hard for us in the twentieth century: we just have to imagine the requisite non-Euclidean space), but impossible to imagine the second. What Descartes is claiming in the second is that God could have created exactly the same world as the one we have and yet have made different things true of it. No wonder that he is wary of saying even that he can know that 'God is the author of eternal truths':

I say that I know [*savoir*] this and not that I conceive [*concevoir*] it or grasp [*comprendre*] it; for it is possible to know that God is infinite and all-powerful even though our soul, because it is finite, cannot grasp or conceive Him. In the same way we can touch a mountain with our hands but we cannot put our arms around it as we could put them around a tree or something else that was not too large for them. To grasp something is to embrace it in one's thought; to know something it is sufficient to touch it with one's thought.[56]

What is being offered here is an extreme view of God's powers. The key to understanding why Descartes should offer such a strong doctrine lies in the question of transcendence. Just as the force of his *a priori* proof of God's existence turns on its ability to establish His transcendence, so too his account of eternal truths turns on God's transcendence in that, again, what is at stake is God's separation from His creation. God not only need not have created the things He did, but He need not have created them in the way He did. God is not constrained by His conceptual truths any more than He is by His empirical truths. But God's transcendence cuts both ways. It can make us completely dependent on Him, or it can make Him so distant and remote from us that our dependence on Him begins to lose content. Take the case of God's grasp of eternal truths. We cannot have any insight into how God knows 'eternal truths' to be true: when God grasps an eternal truth something very different occurs from when we grasp an eternal truth. God makes things true by fiat, and can change such truths if He so wills. He is not omniscient but cognitively omnipotent: He knows all truths because a truth is simply something He wills to be true. We cannot understand what such a grasp would consist in, and there is a sense in which such truths cannot be the same for us as for God. Questions that we settle by fiat we do not normally think of as truths at all, and consequently it is hard for us to understand how things that we regard as truths can be truths for God. A cognitively omnipotent God might well be able to divide sentences into those that we regard as true and those that we would regard as false, but unless He had an independent understanding of truth, a grasp of the point of the exercise, He might as well designate these 'T' and 'F', or '1' and '0', for they simply do not connect up with what we see as being the point of the exercise, which involves the idea at least of finding out about how things are.[57]

Such arguments are, perhaps, more familiar in a moral context than in a cognitive one. The parallel moral argument is that things are good because God has chosen to designate some things good, and not because of some intrinsic worth they may have. In this case, we are inclined to counter that acting in obedience to a law or code whose rationale we cannot have any grasp of—or indeed which does not have a rationale at all, if it is an arbitrary fiat of God—is not to act morally in that it robs morality of what we normally think to be its whole point, which is that moral behaviour at least reflects the intrinsic worth either of particular kinds of goods or, more problematically, of particular modes of behaviour (such as acting in accordance with one's duty).[58] If God simply legislates what is good and He is free to change His mind for no reason, then we have to say that our grasp of what is moral bears no relation to His.

So 'truths for God', like 'goodness for God', are quite different from 'truths for us' and 'goodness for us'. The problem is how we bridge this gulf. We seem to have nothing in common with God, on Descartes' construal of transcendence. We cannot be completely independent of Him in our cognitive operations, however, for He created us with the faculties and cognitive apparatus that we have: while He might have created us with different ones, and while we may not know why He created us with the ones we have, we cannot assume that how we experience things is an arbitrary choice on God's part. And in any case, if we did argue that our cognitive organs provide us with something that is so unlike divine cognition that we can only treat it as independent, this would be tantamount to naturalism.

Now worries over transcendence were not peculiar to Descartes, and the nascent Augustinian revival in France had already begun to draw attention to a number of related issues. It was Bérulle, more than anyone else, who had been instrumental in the revival of the Augustinian view. Augustinianism was clearly an option open to Descartes, and Bérulle had possibly mentioned it to him at their meeting.[59] In the Augustinian tradition, we can never know anything unless we are aided by divine illumination: just as we cannot see an object unless it is illuminated by a source of light, so we cannot grasp truths unless they are illuminated by God. Bérulle explicitly uses the doctrine of divine illumination to explicate the nature of eternal truths, thinking of them as being like light rays from the sun: these are our bridge with God, as He is manifest in these truths, and uses them to illuminate His creation.[60] Descartes explicitly denies this model in the letter to Mersenne of 27 May: 'I do not conceive [eternal truths] as emanating from God like rays from the sun'.[61] What the Augustinian position requires is a far more radical dependence on God than Descartes is prepared to allow, and it is worth remembering here that divine illumination is achieved not through intellectual enquiry but by being in a state of grace, something that would destroy Descartes' natural theology. So, some compromise had to be found between complete independence of God and the kind of dependence offered in the doctrine of divine illumination. In thinking about this question, it helps to translate the problem into the terms of the doctrine of clear and distinct ideas. Descartes' earlier doctrine of clear and distinct ideas relied on the 'natural light of nature' or 'natural light of reason' to guide us, and this faculty was conceived along lines quite compatible with naturalism: it was an exclusively human faculty which required no divine guarantee or intervention. Such a doctrine is no longer tenable, not just because it has failed to provide the requisite legitimation of higher mathematical operations at the end of the *Regulae*, but also because, in a metaphysical context, it provides the wrong kind of response to God's transcendence, making us independent of God. On the other hand, it would be no better to adopt an Augustinian approach and simply make clear and distinct ideas depend on divine illumination, because this ultimately makes them independent of anything we might have discovered about the nature of cognition, for example. Descartes needs some middle ground between these two. The solution he provides in the letter to Mersenne is that eternal truths 'are all inborn in our minds'.[62] That is, they derive from God, but are common to all human beings, irrespective of their state of grace.

In considering what is involved here, it is worth noting a further parallel between the moral and the cognitive cases, namely the way in which we ultimately rely on conscience in moral decisions, and the way in which we rely on the 'natural light of reason' in the case of cognition. Descartes wants to keep the idea of relying on something like the natural light of reason, but he does not want to construe it in exclusively humanistic terms any longer. The analogy with conscience is revealing here. I doubt if anyone in the seventeenth century would have treated conscience as a faculty completely independent of God, and there is clearly no point in making it dependent on divine illumination, for those who have received direct divine illumination presumably are those least reliant on conscience; after all, one's conscience is there to guide one when there is some ambiguity or difficulty in a choice, but someone who had access to God's direct illumination would simply not encounter such ambiguities or difficulties. Conscience was generally recognized as a faculty given to us by God so that we might exercise our moral judgement in accordance with His will. Similarly, the natural light of reason could be construed as a faculty given to us by God so that we might exercise our cognitive judgement in accordance with His will, recognizing as true what He has decreed to be truths.

The advantage of this approach is that it allows Descartes to reject a divine model for cognition on the one hand, and provide the ultimate metaphysical legitimation for knowledge, namely a divine one, on the other. On the first question, since God's grasp of truths is completely inscrutable, it cannot act as a model for our own cognitive powers. This provides a straightforward answer to the traditional cognitive problem of how to reconcile the belief that reasoning processes in human beings depend on the kind of corporeal organs we have, with the belief that there are pure spirits, such as God and the angels, who apparently reason yet do not employ corporeal faculties. It is a consequence of Descartes' account that we can say nothing at all about those creatures who reason without recourse to corporeal faculties (or even corporeal faculties sufficiently like ours). This is a radical move, and one quite different from that employed, for example, by other thinkers in the forefront of the seventeenth-century scientific revolution. Kepler, Galileo, and Mersenne all thought that our knowledge of mathematical truths, for instance, was the same as that of God, the difference being that whereas God knew all mathematical truths, we only know a few. Such a view not only provided a legitimation of mathematics, but the impetus to develop a mathematical physics. But for Descartes our grasp of mathematics cannot be like that of God, and consequently a different kind of legitimation of knowledge—whether mathematical or otherwise—is needed. Indeed, one consequence of this is that, contrary to its role in the late *Regulae*, where mathematics forms the connection between the deliveries of the intellect and the deliveries of sense perception, providing a legitimation in the process, it no longer has any special role or priority in the programme of legitimation; and we shall see that when it comes to metaphysical legitimation from now onwards, mathematics effectively drops out of the picture as having no special significance.

As regards the second question, the divine guarantee, on the face of it Descartes is not revising his original doctrine very much. It might seem that he is simply guaranteeing something that already acts a criterion, and after all, the original 'natural light of reason' could have been manifested in the form of innate ideas. But in fact the difference between the two doctrines is vast. The original 'clear and distinct ideas', as they figure in the *Regulae*, are constitutive of the natural light of reason: it is crucial to the way in which they work that they are self-legitimating. They bear their legitimacy on their face, so to speak, for what is at issue is our ability to represent an idea to ourselves in such a way that it is so vivid and striking that it compels assent. To provide further legitimation for such ideas destroys, or rather, completely changes their function and rationale.

However, one major qualification must be made to this assessment of the changes in Descartes' thinking about the doctrine of clear and distinct ideas. Although his interest in mathematics diminished after the collapse of the legitimatory project of the *Regulae*, he did continue to pursue some mathematical questions between 1628 and the early 1630s, and the way in which he pursues them is interesting for it indicates that he has not completely abandoned the legimatory project of the *Regulae*. Indeed, the ideal of clear and vivid representation of mathematical operations, as part of a quasi-pictorial doctrine of clear and distinct ideas, remains right up until the *Géométrie* of 1637. This may seem to conflict with what I have just argued, about the doctrine of clear and distinct ideas beginning to shed its criterion of vivid representation and beginning to become a metaphysical doctrine from the time of the 'Little Treatise'. But what happens is that while the doctrine develops in an explicitly metaphysical direction, with an abstract metaphysical guarantee of clarity and distinctness replacing the quasi-pictorial one, it is nevertheless an important part of the shift from the quasi-pictorial doctrine to the later one that mathematics ceases to provide the model and resources for the doctrine. When in later writings such as the *Meditationes* Descartes invokes mathematics as a model, what will be invoked will be a metaphysically tamed mathematics which does not reflect the real validatory problems Descartes faced in his practical mathematics. Mathematics, now beginning to be cut off from the thrust of Descartes' methodological and metaphysical concerns, harbours residual problems which turn on the question of representing proofs to ourselves in such a way that they bear their evidence on their face.

The Pappus Problem and the Classification of Curves

These problems are nowhere more evident than in the question of the classification of curves.[63] In 1619 Descartes had distinguished geometrical from non-geometrical curves on the basis of whether they could be constructed by manipulation of his mesolabe compass. The degree of simplicity of a curve, as measured by the ease with which it could be constructed by a continuous motion of the limbs of the compass, was not mirrored in the degree of the equation, however, and curves produced on the compass can be algebraically very complex. As Descartes' mathematical thinking developed, the equation became a much more important consideration than the degree of simplicity with which the curve could be constructed with the compass, but it was this latter that reflected its degree of clarity and distinctness. Both notions provided criteria—which we can refer to as algebraic criteria and instrumental criteria respectively—for classification of curves, but they provided different and in many ways incompatible criteria, and Descartes was extremely reluctant to recognize this.

The algebraic criterion ruled that a curve is properly geometrical if each and every point on it can be related to a rectilinear coordinate through a finite number of algebraic operations. The best example of Descartes' algebraic treatment of curves at this point is his solution of the 'Pappus problem'. When he enrolled at the University of Leiden in June 1630, Descartes registered himself as a student of mathematics. Jacobus Golius, professor of oriental languages since 1624, had taken up the chair of mathematics in 1629, his special area of interest being the ancient theory of conic sections, especially the work of Apollonius of Perga. At the end of 1631,[64] he sent a problem from Pappus to Descartes, Mydorge, and others.

In a commentary on Apollonius' *Conics*, Pappus notes a locus problem which none of the ancient mathematicians had completely solved.[65] A locus problem is one in which the aim is to find a set of points which satisfy a given condition: for example, to take a simple case, if we are asked to provide the locus of a set of given points in a plane that are all at the same distance from a given point in the plane, then we will find that the required locus is a circle. The problem that Golius set had initially been posed by Apollonius in terms of a three- or four-line locus problem, which he had solved in Book 3 of the *Conics*. Essentially, what is at issue is this. In the case of the three-line problem, we are given three lines with their positions, and the task is to find the locus of points from which three lines can be drawn to the given lines, each making a given angle with each given line, such that the product of the lengths of two of the lines bears a constant proportion to the square of the third. In the case of the four-line problem, we are given four lines with their positions, and we are required to find the locus of points from which four lines can be drawn to the given line, such that the product of the length of two of the lines bears a constant proportion to the product of the other two. Apollonius, who knew that the loci in these two cases were conic sections, had stopped at four lines, however, whereas Pappus generalizes the problem further, to five and six lines. Here, the requisite ratio is formed out of a rectangle contained by two lines and a solid by three lines, the point that makes the locus lying on a line that transcends the solid locus. But why stop at six lines? The answer is that after six lines we hit a very basic problem; as Pappus puts it, in the case of more than six lines, 'we cannot say whether a ratio of something contained by four lines is given to that which is contained by the rest, since there is no figure of more than three dimensions'.[66] The dimensional constraints of ancient mathematics block off any further developments, although Pappus, with great ingenuity, tries to overcome the problem by means of compound ratios, and is able, by these means, to pose the problem for *n* lines.

For the details of Descartes' solution of the Pappus problem we must turn to the *Géométrie*, although it is clear from his letter to Golius that the later published version simply goes over the solution he had already reached in the winter of 1631/2. His treatment of the question is algebraic and completely general, allowing us to express relations between the lines using only two variables. His approach is to show how the problem, explicitly solved for four lines but in a way which is theoretically

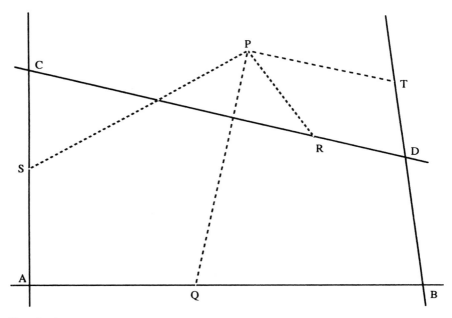

FIG. 6.4

generalizable to *n* lines, can, like all geometrical problems, be reduced to one in which all we need to know are the lengths of certain lines. These lines are the coordinate axes, and the lengths give us the abscissae and ordinates of points. Descartes' own diagram obscures this because he accommodates the axes to the problem rather than the other way round, thereby keeping the proportions he is dealing with simple and visible. This has the result that the axes are not perpendicular to one another, which is at first confusing to those not used to this way of proceeding, so it will be helpful just to set out the four-line problem in more familiar terms[67] and then turn to Descartes' treatment. Essentially what is at issue is this. In Fig. 6.4, we are given four lines in position AB, BD, CD, and AC. We have to find the locus of points P from which the lines PQ, PR, PS, and PT can be drawn to the four lines, each always making the same angle with the line it meets, such that PQ·PR is always in a given ratio to PS·PT. The locus is a conic that passes through the four intersections (A, B, C, D) for the four given lines.

The four-line problem is presented by Descartes as in Fig. 6.5.[68] Here the full lines are the given lines and the broken lines those sought. Descartes takes AB and BC as the principal lines and proceeds to relate

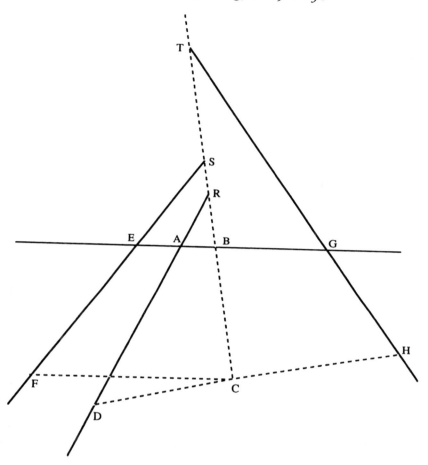

Fig. 6.5

all the others to these. Their lengths are x and y respectively, and in fact AB is the x axis, and BC the y axis. The solution proceeds as follows. The angles of the triangle ABR are given, so the ratio AB:BR is known. If we let this ratio be z/b, then BR $= bx/z$, and CR $= y + bx/z$ (where B lies between C and R). The angles of the triangle DRC are also known, so representing the ratio CR:CD as z/c, then CR $= y + bx/z$ and CD $= cy/z + bcx/z^2$. Moreover, since the positions of AB, AD, and EF are fixed, the length k of AE is thereby given; therefore EB $= k + x$ (where A lies between E and B). The angles of the triangle ESB are also given, and hence so is the ratio BE:BS. If we now let this ratio be z/d, then we obtain BS $= (dk + dx)/z$ and CS $= (zy + dk + dx)/z$ (where B is between

S and C). Since the angles of the triangle FSC are given, the ratio CS:CF is known. This ratio is z/e, so we obtain CF $= (ezy + dek + dex)/z^2$. Letting 1 denote the given length of AB, we have BG $= 1 - x$; and if we let the known ratio BG:BT in the triangle BGT be z/f, then BT $= (fl - fx)/z$ and CT $= (zy + fl - x)/z$; and, finally, if we let CT:CH in the triangle TCH be z/g then CH $= (gzy + fgl - fgx)/z^2$.

To understand what this solution amounts to, consider the simple case of the locus problem for a circle. I said above that the locus of a set of given points in a plane that are all at the same distance from a given point in the plane is a circle. If we denote this distance by r, then we can give the equation of the locus (in this case the circle) as $x^2 + y^2 = r^2$. What Descartes has done in the case of the much more complex Pappus locus problem is to show that, no matter how many lines of given position we are dealing with, the length of a line through C making a given angle with these lines can always be expressed in three terms of the form $ax + by + c$. For three or four fixed lines, the equation will be a quadratic equation, and this means that, for any known value of y, the values of x can then be found using only ruler and compass, and a sufficiently large number of values will enable us to trace the curve on which C must lie. For five or six lines the equation is a cubic, for seven or eight a quartic, for nine or ten a quintic, and so on, rising one degree with the introduction of every two lines.

To provide the equation, however, does not strictly solve the problem: one has to use the equation to construct the curve. The curve is constructed by choosing an arbitrary value for y (BC) and then constructing geometrically the corresponding value for x (AB). We repeat the process, gradually building up a set of points to give us the required locus. But here we hit a problem. Descartes also employs an instrumental criterion determining which curves are properly geometrical and which are not. His basic criterion is that a curve is properly geometrical if it can be constructed as a continuous line by manipulation of the limbs of his mesolabe compass. This was the criterion he had devised in 1619. It explicitly specifies continuous curves, and just as explicitly rules out 'pointwise' constructions such as the quadratrix and the Archimedean spiral. Take the example of the quadratrix. The construction of a quadratrix requires two independent motions (see Fig. 6.6). In the standard Pappus account of the construction,[69] we construct a square ABCD, and BED, a quadrant of a circle with centre A. The quadratrix is constructed by two simultaneous motions: the uniform motion of the line BC from BC to AD (always remaining parallel to BC), and the uniform revolution of the radius AE from AB to AD. In moving to AD, where they arrive simultaneously, AE and BC will, through their intersections, determine a range of points, and the locus

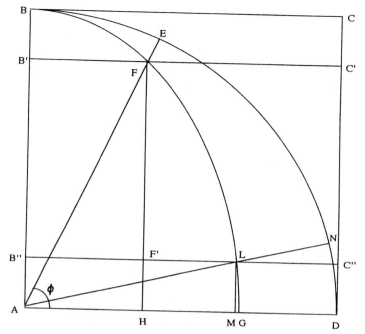

Fig. 6.6

of these points is the quadratrix. The trouble is that, in order to construct a quadratrix in this way, we would need to know the exact ratio of the speed of BC and AE, but this is precisely what we cannot do, because this ratio is a function of the circumference to the radius, which is 2πr, and π cannot be expressed as a whole number or a fraction.[70] So we can aim at greater and greater approximations to the quadratrix (by continued bisection of EAN or NAD) but we have no procedure that will yield a precise curve, only a series of points. Descartes will not accept this as a legitimate geometrical construction. But surely his own solution to the Pappus four-line problem is a pointwise construction! Descartes realizes this, of course, and in the *Géométrie* he distinguishes between his own geometrically legitimate construction of a locus and the geometrically illegitimate construction of a quadratrix. He tells us that we can only accept pointwise constructions in which every point can be constructed in principle, as with the conchoid. A quadratrix does not meet this criterion. In the case of the construction of a conchoid one can choose points indifferently, whereas in the case of the quadratrix, because the points are determined by reiterated bisection, one cannot do so: the point can only be where one bisects.

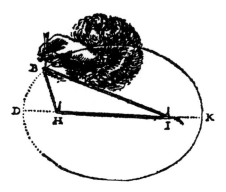

Fig. 6.7

It is difficult to understand why this difference should be so significant. It seems an arbitrary stipulation. But it is reasonably clear that
the context that throws it up is one where Descartes is desperately and
unreasonably trying to match algebraic and instrumental criteria for
the classification of curves. This becomes clearer when, in Book 2 of
the *Géométrie*, Descartes allows a third kind of representation of curves,
namely 'string constructions'. String constructions play a role in the
Dioptrique, where we are told that gardeners use them to give their
flower beds the shape of an ellipse or an hyperbola.[71] For example,
Descartes gives an illustration of how to construct an ellipse (Fig. 6.7):
two ends of the string BHI are tied together and placed around stakes
H and I. The string is stretched by a tracing pin B that is moved around
H and I, the string being kept taut. String constructions are eminently
instrumental rather than algebraic, and Descartes does not allow that
they are geometrically proper because they introduce the essentially
unknowable ratio between straight lines and curves. Why, then, does
he even bother mentioning them? The answer is because of their clarity
and distinctness. For all its failings, the string construction renders the
nature of the ellipse 'more comprehensible than either the section of a
cone or a cylinder'.[72] Just at the point where one might expect Descartes
to concentrate on algebraic criteria for the classification of curves, we
are back with a clearly instrumental criterion, motivated by the need
to legitimate the construction in terms of what might be called pictorial
clarity.

Descartes will not give up the attempt to match algebraic and instrumental criteria, or rather, he will not give up giving the reader the
impression that he has already accomplished this impossible task. In
Book 3 of the *Géométrie*, we are told that 'by the simplest curves we
must understand not only those that are easiest to describe, or make

the construction or the demonstration of the proposed problem easier, but mainly those that are of the simplest kind that can be used to determine the quantity that is sought'.[73] This is unhelpful in the extreme. Descartes never faced up to the incompatibility between his instrumental and his algebraic criteria for the classification of curves as geometrical, and the question we must ask is why he falls back on instrumental criteria, given that (i) he has perfectly good algebraic criteria for classification which he is not willing to renounce, even when they are incompatible with the instrumental criteria, and (ii) the instrumental criteria seem to rely on a notion of clarity and distinctness which had caused Descartes great problems in the later *Regulae* of 1628, and which he had abandoned in favour of a metaphysical criterion in the *Discours*, which accompanied the *Géométrie*. The answer lies, I believe, in the fact that Descartes realizes that the metaphysical criterion is simply too broad and general to be of use in understanding the nature of mathematical demonstration. For all its faults, and even though he has no way of filling out the idea, Descartes is unwilling to abandon the notion that what makes a mathematical demonstration compelling is ultimately the fact that it can be represented in terms of an operation on line lengths, something which has a completely intuitive and obvious compulsion about it.[74]

We shall return to some of these questions when we look at the *Géométrie*, but the *Géométrie* systematizes and refines rather than covering new ground. With the exception of his methods for finding tangents to curves, the working out of algebraic classifications of curves and the solution to the Pappus problem for *n* lines was Descartes' last real mathematical innovation, and so far as we call tell everything else of real substance in the *Géométrie* had been worked out by this time.

Parhelia and the Origins of *Le Monde*

In October 1629, Descartes wrote to Mersenne seeking fuller information on a particularly striking appearance of 'false' or 'mock' or 'multiple suns'—parhelia—observed at Rome on 20 March. Parhelia, along with rainbows, halos, and various streaks or columns of light collectively referred to as virgae, are meteorological phenomena that had been recognized since antiquity, and had commonly been thought to be of use in forecasting the weather. They are formed when the sun's rays are refracted through a thin cloud of hexagonal ice crystals, resulting in the formation of at least one circle with a red exterior and a blue centre. The astronomer Christoph Scheiner observed a particularly spectacular parhelion at Frascati, just outside Rome, which had three

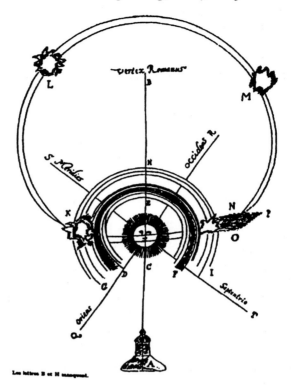

FIG. 6.8

circles and four patches of shimmering light, and his account was sent
to Cardinal Barberini, who sent it to Peiresc, who in turn distributed
several copies to scientists (see Fig. 6.8, which comes from Beeckman's
copy). One of those to whom copies were sent was Gassendi, who
provided Reneri with a copy, and Reneri showed it to Descartes. In the
two months between receiving the report and writing to Mersenne for
further information, Descartes had become quite excited about the
question, and realizing that the first two circles bore a striking similarity
to rainbows, dropped other projects, including the 'Little Treatise' on
metaphysics.[75] He tells Mersenne that he has been working on meteorological questions generally, and that his interest has outgrown a
concern merely to explain parhelia. He has resolved 'to write a small
treatise on [meteorology] which will contain the explanation of the
colours of the rainbow, which has given me more trouble than all the
rest and, in general, all sublunary phenomena'. But this will be no
ordinary treatise, 'for I have decided to exhibit it publicly as a sample

of my Philosophy, and to hide behind the canvas to listen to what people will say about it'.[76] The topic is one of the best he could choose for this purpose, he tells Mersenne, and he promises to send him the manuscript for publication when it is complete, as he would prefer that it be published in Paris. By November, the project has grown even further:

I should tell you that it will be more than a year before it is ready. For since I wrote to you a month ago, I have done nothing at all except sketch its argument, and instead of explaining a single phenomenon, I have decided to explain all natural phenomena, that is, the whole of physics. And the plan gives me more satisfaction than anything previously, for I think I have found a way of presenting my thoughts so that they satisfy everyone, and others will not be able to deny them.[77]

The move from parhelia, first of all to meteorological phenomena, then to the whole of the physical world, is a huge one, and it had taken shape in Descartes' mind over a period of no more than four months, between August and November 1629. I believe we can give some indication of why it should be meteorology that points Descartes in the direction of a general physics, and also why he should feel confident in providing a general physics, despite the very specific nature of most of his physical enquiries up to this point.

On the first question, we might note the opening paragraph of *Les Météores*, the final version of this work on meteorology:

It is natural for us to have more admiration for things that are above us than for those that are on the same level or below us. And although the clouds are scarcely higher than the summits of some mountains, and often it is even possible to see some that are lower than the pinnacles of our steeples, nevertheless, because we must turn our eyes towards the sky to look at them, we imagine them to be so high that poets and painters even make them into God's throne, and picture Him there, using His own hands to open and close the doors of the winds, to sprinkle the dew upon the flowers, and to hurl lightning against the rocks. This leads me to hope that if I explain the nature of the clouds here, in such a way that we will no longer wonder at anything that we see of them, or that descends from them, we will find it easy to believe that it is likewise possible to find the causes of everything that is most admirable above the earth.[78]

The point of the exercise is to show how purely natural explanations can be provided for sublunary phenomena, contrary to the approach that had been taken, with few exceptions, up to this point. Boyer has drawn attention to a good example of this earlier approach, the account given in the *Récréations Mathématiques* of the Jesuit writer Jean Leurechon, a popular work which appeared in 1624 and 1626, and which Descartes knew well.[79] Leurechon admits he is baffled as to how to proceed experimentally in investigating the rainbow because it lasts for such a short time, whether one observes the phenomenon in the sky, or using a spray of water droplets, or bubbles. Plato, he tells us, was right when he said that the rainbow 'is a sign of admiration, not of explanation. And he hit the nail on the head who said that it is the mirror in which human nature has had a full view of its ignorance; for all the philosophers and mathematicians who for so many years have been engaged in discovering and explaining its causes, have learned nothing except that they knew nothing but a semblance of truth'.[80] Boyer is surely right that this is a challenge that Descartes could not have resisted. And in meeting the challenge his aim is to show the mettle of mechanism, the rainbow thereby providing a way into general questions about the nature of physical explanation.

As for the second question, Schuster has very plausibly suggested that Beeckman may well have discussed his interests and progress with Descartes at their meetings at the end of 1628 and beginning of 1629, and perhaps shown him his notebooks, which reveal that from the middle of 1628 onwards Beeckman had been reading Kepler's astronomical writings carefully and attempting to provide a mechanistic celestial mechanics.[81] In a manner that he often pursued, and which Descartes learned from him, Beeckman works through Kepler not with a view to questioning his results but rather with the aim of reconstructing those results on a firmer basis. Beeckman was not concerned with observational questions or with the question of elliptical orbits, but rather with translating Kepler's celestial forces and powers into micro-corpuscularian terms. He notes that Kepler had thought of stellar influence along the lines of verbal warnings or other kinds of sign, but rather than rejecting this mode of action he seeks to mechanize it. Verbal warnings, he points out, require some mechanical interaction between cause and effect, so even if one accepts Kepler's model one is obliged to provide the requisite account of how the cause conveys its causal activity to the object affected; and Beeckman, unlike Kepler, assumes, of course, that this must take the form of contact action.[82] Like Beeckman, Descartes would show little interest in the observational or mathematical problems of celestial mechanics but, again like Beeckman, he would be very concerned to provide a fully mechanistic account of how celestial motions occur. What Kepler's work shows, and what Galileo's work at this time was showing even more forcefully, was that there was no longer any reason to separate terrestrial and celestial mechanics, in the traditional Aristotelian way, for both realms were amenable to the same kind of mathematical and physical treatment. What Beeckman and Descartes are concerned to do is to appropriate this unification, as it were, and to bring it to fruition by showing how a micro-mechanical natural philosophy can be shown to underpin both realms. But Descartes now has a much broader understanding of mechanism than Beeckman; he has gone beyond simply thinking of mechanism as providing a way of representing physical processes in micro-corpuscularian terms, and has begun to develop it as a systematic natural philosophy, as applicable, for example, to internal physiological processes as to external physical ones.

Consequently, although his physical enquiries had been rather specific up to this point, and indeed had centred on optics, he had had a very general concern with natural-philosophical questions since taking up the *Regulae* again around 1626, and his correspondence shows an increasing interest in detailed questions of natural philosophy. In a letter to Mersenne of 8 October 1629, for example, Descartes makes the passing remark that 'I agree with the doctor, and now share his views on the whole foundations of Philosophy, except perhaps that I do not explain the aether as he does'.[83] The reference is to Sebastien Basso,[84] a physician, whose *Philosophiae naturalis adversus Aristotelem Libri XII*, which was published in Geneva in 1621, did a great deal to popularize atomism in the early seventeenth century. Basso's atomism does not include a commitment to the void, however, and he postulates a 'universal spirit' which fills all the spaces between the smallest atoms.[85] Consequently, it is not as surprising as it might at first seem that Descartes should have agreed with the 'whole foundations' of Basso's philosophy. Indeed, like Basso, at the level of practical physics, Descartes will treat the very fine matter that separates bodies as a kind of void, and in his next letter to Mersenne, of 13 November, he discusses both the fall of bodies and the vibration of a string *in vacuo*.[86]

In Part 5 of the *Discours*, Descartes sets out the details of the treatise he was working on in the period from mid-1629 to 1633. He writes:

Since I tried to explain the principles in a Treatise which certain considerations prevented me from publishing, and I know of no better way of making them known than to set out here briefly what it contained. I had as my aim to include in it everything that I thought I knew before I wrote it about the nature of material things. But just as painters, not being able to represent all the different sides of a body equally well on a flat canvas, choose one of the main ones and set it facing the light, and shade the others so as to make them stand out only when viewed from the perspective of the chosen side; so too, fearing that I could not put everything I had in mind in my discourse, I undertook to expound fully only what I knew about light. Then, as the opportunity arose, I added something about the Sun and the fixed stars, because almost all of it comes from them; the heavens, because they transmit it; the planets, comets, and the earth, because they reflect light; and especially bodies on the earth, because they are coloured, or transparent, or luminous; and finally about man, because he observes these bodies.[87]

Two posthumously published texts, the *Traité de l'homme* (published as *L'Homme*, 1662) and the *Traité de la lumière* (published as *Le*

Monde, 1664), both parts of what is ostensibly a single work, form the backbone of this treatise, but it included more material. Some of this material is extant, namely the *Météors* and the *Dioptrique*, both subsequently published in 1637 along with the *Discours* and the *Géométrie*. There are also indications that Descartes had originally intended including other material, including material on music, for example, although this is not extant and may never have been developed in a systematic way.

From 1629 to 1630, the problem that Descartes faced was that of building up his general knowledge of physics and related areas, sorting out what he should and should not concentrate upon, and finding a guiding thread by which to organize the argument of his treatise. The first and second problems took up a great deal of his time. In his letter to Mersenne of 15 April 1630, he complains that his 'work is going very slowly, because I take much more pleasure in acquiring knowledge than in putting into writing the little that I know' and that he is 'now studying chemistry and anatomy simultaneously'.[88] But the third problem evidently gave him no less trouble. Later in the same letter he tells Mersenne that 'all these problems in physics that I told you I have taken on are all so interlinked and depend so much on one another that it is not possible for me to give a solution to one of them without giving a solution to all, and I cannot do that more quickly or more succinctly than in the treatise I am writing'.[89] And later in the same year he tells Mersenne that he has 'countless different things to consider all at once' and that he is trying to find some 'basis on which to give a true account without doing violence to anyone's imagination or shocking received opinion'.[90]

There is some evidence that *Le Monde* was proceeding in fits and starts in 1630, and that work on it was taking its toll on Descartes. In a letter of 15 April, for example, he asks Mersenne not to confirm to anyone that he is writing his treatise on physics but rather to give them the impression that he is not, for 'I swear that if I had not already told people that I planned to do so, with the result that they would say that I had not been able to carry out my plan, I would never undertake the task'.[91] By the end of the year he shows himself to be in very poor spirits, exacerbated by an acrimonious dispute with Beeckman.

The Dispute with Beeckman

When Descartes returned to the Netherlands in the autumn of 1628, he told Beeckman that he had not met anyone with whom he could converse about science to the same extent. The two agreed to revive their collaboration, but in October 1629 relations cooled considerably owing to a letter from Beeckman to Mersenne in which he said that he had told Descartes ten years earlier what he 'had written about the causes of the sweetness of consonances'.[92] Mersenne evidently reported this remark, in a letter which is no longer extant, to Descartes, and Descartes took it as either an intimation of plagiarism, or at least of priority on Beeckman's part. He writes:

I am very obliged to you for calling the ingratitude of my friend to my attention; I think the honour I have done him of writing to him has dazzled him, and he thought that you would have an even better opinion of him if he wrote to you that he had been my master ten years ago. But he is completely mistaken, for what glory is there in having taught a man who knows very little and freely admits this, as I do? I will not mention anything of this to him, since this is what you wish, although I would have plenty with which to make him ashamed, especially if I had his letter.[93]

Even without knowing precisely how Mersenne reported Beeckman's remark, we can safely say that Descartes over-reacted to a harmless (and correct) statement by Beeckman. The intensity of Descartes' reaction is quite out of proportion to the incident, even on his own reading of it, and very unfair to Beeckman. Far from plagiarizing Descartes' work, as Descartes claims, Beeckman was in fact extremely scrupulous and modest about recording his results, not only recording what he had learnt from nameless boys and girls in his diary, but showing delight on learning that Galileo had published discoveries that he himself had recorded in his diary ten years earlier.[94] There can be no doubt at all that Descartes was very indebted to Beeckman, and not only in the specific orientation of his work but right down to details of its presentation, which also derive from Beeckman. For example, in the early *Olympica*, *Praeambula*, and *Experimenta*, we find a number of distinctive Beeckmanian idiosyncrasies: beginning sections with grand titles and moral and biblical maxims, leaving blank pages (a rare practice at this time), adding notes on personal matters to scientific papers, adding later marginal summaries, and so on.[95]

By the end of 1629, Descartes had demanded his *Compendium Musicae* back from Beeckman and had cut off correspondence with him. Here matters rested until the middle of 1630, when Mersenne paid a visit to the Netherlands. While there Beeckman showed him his Journal, and Mersenne realized that Beeckman did indeed deserve the credit for a number of advances he had attributed to Descartes. Beeckman subsequently wrote to Descartes pointing out that Mersenne had spent days reading his Journal and had learned that some views he had ascribed to Descartes had in fact been first developed by Beeckman.[96] At this point Descartes explodes, and in the second half of September he writes a vituperative letter to Beeckman, explaining that any expressions of gratitude in his early letters to Beeckman were mere French civility, that Beeckman lacks manners in bragging that others owe things to him, especially when it is the other way around, and that he has learned as much from Beeckman as he learned from ants and worms.[97] Beeckman replied, in a letter now lost, probably setting out the topics which he believed Descartes had learned from him, and basing his claims on his Journal. In response, Descartes sent Beeckman one of the longest extant letters he ever wrote, full of self-justification, abuse, and vindictive disparagement of Beeckman.[98] He treats Beeckman like a schoolboy, putting his behaviour down to 'illness'. It is just not possible to take Descartes' side in this dispute, just as it is difficult not to agree with Cohen here that 'it is a really classic example of psychological projection, for clearly the obsession with "praise" and "being taught" is Descartes' own, not Beeckman's'.[99] But also, as I suggested earlier, there is evidence that Beeckman had acted as a father figure for Descartes in 1618/19, and it is possible that his reaction to Beeckman may be overdetermined by his relation to his father. It is at least the case that the nature and depth of the antagonism here reflects the former closeness of his relation with Beeckman. Within a year the row had blown over, and they became reconciled, although they apparently saw little of one another, and the relationship never returned to its former warmth. Indeed, Descartes shows himself to have been quite unmoved by Beeckman's death in 1637.[100]

7
A New System of the World
1630–1633

From the winter of 1630/1 to May 1632, Descartes was based in Amsterdam, making a number of trips to Leiden and to Dordrecht, and visiting Denmark in the summer of 1631. He moved to the town of Deventer at the end of May 1632 and stayed there until the end of November 1633. We know little about his living arrangements, but it is quite likely that he shared accommodation with Villebressieu, his friend from his Paris days, for at least some time during his stay in Amsterdam, as he writes to Villebressieu in the summer of 1631 that he will find him at 'our lodgings' in Amsterdam, where he 'will wait for' him. Descartes generally avoided French visitors assiduously,[1] refusing to reveal his address even to friends such as Mydorge, but Villebressieu seems to have been an exception. Descartes had been friends with him since the mid-1620s, and his interests coincided with Descartes' own concerns at this time, for Villebressieu was working in the theory of matter, which was coming to play a central role in Descartes' thought, and his mechanical theory would remain very dependent upon a hydrostatic/hydrodynamic model. We also know that, in Amsterdam, Descartes was friends with a physician, Plempius, an Aristotelian in natural philosophy and a Galenist in physiology until he became a late convert to Harvey: he was to remain on friendly terms with Descartes until 1638, but by the 1660s, when Cartesianism had become a significant force in Dutch universities, he became one of its fiercest opponents.

Descartes' move to Deventer was in part due to a desire get away from interruptions at Amsterdam[2]—this is a time of intense work on *Le Monde*—and in part to be near Reneri, who had moved to Deventer to teach at the recently founded École Illustre there. Villebressieu had left to return to France, and Descartes probably felt the need to be near someone with whom he could discuss his scientific interests.[3] Reneri had originally studied theology at the Catholic University of Louvain, only to convert to Protestantism on reading Calvin, and then studied medicine.[4] He was to be the first to provide institutional teaching of Cartesian natural philosophy, and Descartes' move to Deventer in 1632 seems to have been made with the purpose of teaching him some physics. Whether Descartes and Reneri shared accommodation we do not know, but they were clearly close, and Descartes would move to Utrecht to join Reneri in 1635. There was a very overt element of hero-worship in Reneri's relationship to Descartes,[5] and in the light of his obsession with 'praise' and 'being taught' in the letter to Beeckman, we may surmise that this is something to which Descartes was not averse.

The Structure of *Le Monde*

In a letter to Villebressieu written in the summer of 1631, Descartes congratulates him on discovering that:

there is only one material substance which receives its action, or ability to move from one place to another, from an external agent, and that it acquires from this the different shapes or modes which make it into the kind of thing we see in the primary compounds we call elements. Moreover you have observed that the nature of these elements or primary compounds—called Earth, Water, Air, and Fire—consists simply in the difference between the fragments, or small and large particles of this matter; and that the matter changes daily from one element into another, when the larger particles change into finer ones as a result of heat and motion, or into base substances, when the finer particles change into larger ones as the action of heat and motion ceases. You have also seen that the primary mingling of these four compounds results in a mixture which can be called the fifth element. This is what you call the principle of the most noble preparation of the elements; because it is, you say, a productive seed or a material life which takes specific form in all the noble particular individuals which cannot fail to be an object of our wonder.[6]

We can in fact take this as summing up, in a very general way, the programme of *Le Monde*, which is premissed upon a conception of matter as uniform and homogeneous. Such a conception is not only a necessary condition of the laws of motion that Descartes will offer, but also of his account of the transmission of light, and his mechanistic account of the vital functions of organic beings.

Le Monde and *L'Homme* together constitute the most ambitious systematic project that Descartes ever undertook and, for all its many flaws, it is a brilliant achievement. The text went through a number of redraftings, not just with respect to the detail of the arguments but also with respect to what should be included in the treatise and, as I indicated in the last chapter, the project that Descartes abandoned in 1633 included not only *Le Monde* and *L'Homme*, but also material which was subsequently to appear in the *Météors* and the *Dioptrique*. From the account given in Part V of the *Discours*, it seems that the original project was designed to cover three topics: inanimate nature, animals and especially the human body, and the 'rational soul' or mind.[7] The descriptions of the first and second parts correspond closely to what we have in *Le Monde* and *L'Homme* respectively, but the third part of the project is not extant, and may never even have been drafted at this time,[8] although it is safe to assume that it would have drawn on material in the abandoned treatise on metaphysics. As for the order of composition, we know that Descartes worked on *Le Monde* between 1630 and 1632. On the assumption that he wrote the chapters in the order in which they appear in the extant draft, he was up to Chapter 5 by the end of February 1630[9] and had completed the material for Chapters 6 to 8 in the first three months of 1632,[10] the remaining chapters being drafted between then and late 1632. From late 1632 he concentrated on *L'Homme*.

The text of *Le Monde* falls into three parts. The first five chapters form a kind of introduction, suggesting that matter and motion are sufficient to explain natural phenomena, and proceeding to set out the theory that the material world consists of nothing but matter (in particular, does not have any empty regions), and that this matter can be considered as comprising three sizes of corpuscle. The defence of mechanism offered starts off in the first three chapters as a very general and intuitive one, appealing to common-sense examples, although two deep and difficult questions are raised almost in passing: the nature of perceptual cognition in chapter 1, and the distinction between motion and direction of motion in chapter 2. The remaining chapters of the first part shift to a more contentious version of mechanism, as Descartes moves from a consideration of the nature of liquidity and hardness to a micro-corpuscular theory of elements and a rejection of an inter-corpuscular void. Chapters 6 to 14 then use this micro-corpuscular theory of matter, combined with a number of laws describing the motion of the corpuscles, to set out a mechanistic cosmology which includes both a celestial physics and an account of the nature and properties of light. The text ends abruptly with an unfinished Chapter 15; but what might have been included in the remaining chapters can be gleaned from the description in the *Discours*, from a letter to Mersenne of April 1632 where material that would naturally fit into the later chapters is set out, and from the *Principia*, where a later but essentially similar account to *Le Monde* is presented in a systematic way.

Descartes had taken a serious interest in anatomy and physiology in the late 1620s. He tells Mersenne in a letter of 18 December 1629 that he has taken up the study of anatomy,[11] and during his first winter in Amsterdam he would visit the butcher daily to watch the slaughtering of cattle, and would take parts he intended to dissect back to his lodgings.[12] He seems to have kept up an interest in these topics throughout the period of composition of the first part of *Le Monde*. By late 1632, when he stops this work to devote himself to *L'Homme*, he has already done a considerable amount of work in physiology. He tells Mersenne that he will 'speak more about man than I had intended to before, because I shall try to explain all of his principal functions. I have already written about those that pertain to life, such as the digestion of food, the beating of the pulse, the distribution of nutrients etc., and the five senses. Now I am dissecting the heads of different animals in order to explain what imagination, memory etc., consist of. I have seen the book *De motu cordiis* [of Harvey] of which you spoke to me earlier, and find I differ only a little from his view, which I came across only after I had finished writing about this matter'.[13] From this time until mid-1633 he appears to have devoted himself to physiology.

A Corpuscular Theory of Matter

In terms of its strategic place within the whole, the function of the first chapter of *Le Monde* is to show that our perceptual images need not resemble what they represent. In the course of showing this Descartes raises, almost in passing, deep questions about the nature of perceptual cognition. I shall postpone treatment of these for the moment, restricting our attention here to the rejection of a resemblance account of the perceptual image. The way in which Descartes puts the issue is to say that a sensation need not resemble the cause of that sensation and, although his concern is with light, visual perception is not a straightforward case, so he offers an example which is straightforward, and indeed intuitively striking. This is the case of someone who believes that he has been injured in a battle because he experiences a pain that he believes is caused by a wound. He calls a surgeon, who discovers that the cause of the pain is a strap caught under his armour, and, as Descartes points out, 'if, in causing him to feel this strap, his sense of touch had imprinted an image of it on his thought, there would have been no need of a surgeon to show him what he was feeling'.[14] The thrust of the argument goes beyond the claim that the world may be different from our perceptual image of it, however, and what Descartes is really trying to steer us towards is the idea that our perceptual image may not even be a guide to how the world is. In particular, Descartes suggests that light may be 'different in objects from what it is in our eyes'.

In the next stage of the argument, presented in the second chapter, he starts out on the task of establishing this. Turning directly to the nature of light, he points out that there are only two sorts of bodies in which light is found, namely the stars, and flame or fire, the latter being the more familiar and hence the best starting-point. The aim is to show how a macroscopic phenomenon can be accounted for plausibly in micro-corpuscularian terms, and fire is a good example for Descartes' purposes. Whereas the Aristotelian account of fire would distinguish between the form of fire, the quality of heat, and the action of burning,[15] Descartes tells us we need only look at a piece of wood burning to see that this is quite unnecessary. We can see that the fire moves the subtler parts of the wood and separates them from one another, transforming them into fire, air, and smoke, and leaving the grosser pieces as ashes. All we need to postulate to account for the burning process is the motion of parts of the wood resulting in the separation of the subtle parts from the gross parts. This might seem somewhat short on detail, but in mitigation it should be said that Descartes himself probably does not think that he has explained the nature of fire, simply that a micro-corpuscularian account should provide all the materials needed for an explanation. The challenge is to the reader to show that there really is a need for something other than matter and motion—such as a (non-reductive) theory of elements, or Aristotelian qualities and forms —in explaining the nature and action of fire.

In the course of his discussion of fire, Descartes tells us that he is not concerned with the direction of motion, for 'when you consider that the power to move and the power that determines in which direction the motion must take place are completely different things, and can exist one without the other (as I have explained in the *Dioptrique*), you will easily see that each particle moves in a way that is made less difficult for it by the disposition of the bodies surrounding it'.[16] Since when something moves it always moves in a direction, motion would appear to have both speed and direction, these being two inseparable components of the same thing. But Descartes sees matters differently. For him, the power by which something moves and the power which determines its motion as being in one direction rather than another are different powers. The relevant section of the *Dioptrique*, a section presumably complete by this time, makes the basis for his distinction a bit clearer. It begins with an account of reflection, using the model of a tennis ball being struck at A (see Fig. 7.1) and meeting the surface of the ground CBE at B, 'which stops its further passage and causes it to be deflected'. We are told that we need not consider the power that keeps the ball in motion after it has left the racquet, but that we need only note

that the power, whatever it may be, that makes the ball's motion continue is different from that which determines it to move in one direction rather than another. This can be seen easily from the fact that the movement of the ball depends on the force with which it has been impelled by the racquet, and this same force could have made it move in any other direction as easily as towards B; whereas it is the position of the racquet that determines it to tend towards B, and

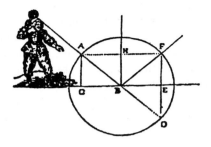

Fig. 7.1

this could have determined the ball in the same way even if a different force had moved it. This already shows that it is not impossible for the ball to be deflected on encountering the ground, and therefore for the determination that it has to tend towards B to be changed, without there being any change in the force of its movement, for these are two different things.[17]

Because the tennis ball and the surface are inelastic, if force and direction of motion were the same thing then the ball would first have to stop before it changed direction, and if it stopped a new cause would be needed for it to move again. But there is no such new cause available: therefore, its force is not affected in the impact, only the direction of its motion, which is changed.[18] He then goes on to show how the 'determination to move' of the ball from A to B can be resolved geometrically into two motions, one along the line AHF and the other from AF to CE. And since the collision with the ground can only hinder the second of these, not the first, the first component continues to act uninterrupted. The details of what happens can only be spelled out once we have been given the laws of motion, but what we are interested in here is not the details but rather the conceptual basis for the distinction between the power by which something moves and its 'determination' (*determinatio* or *détermination*). 'Determination' is something that both depends on the force or speed of the body and directs that speed or force.[19]

The geometrical configuration of other bodies can alter this determination, and Descartes goes on to tell us that the actual path of a moving body is determined by each part moving 'in the manner made least difficult for it' by surrounding bodies. No justification is given for this: we are simply told that this is a fact that we easily recognize when we consider it. But if we think of motion in traditional atomist terms, our recognition of this 'fact' will not be so easy. In a void, each direction will be as impediment-free as any other. If we imagine a body in a void, and ask in what direction it will move, we might be inclined to say that it will continue moving in the direction it is already moving, or alternatively, that it will move in that direction in which it is being moved. The direction of its motion would not be a function of surrounding bodies at all. In other words, there is a clear assumption in Descartes' discussion that moving bodies will always be surrounded by other bodies, and this is tantamount to the denial of the existence of a void. Even in a plenum, of course, we still do not have to accept that moving bodies will always take the 'easiest' route. This is on the assumption that we have a clear idea of what the 'easiest route' is in the first place. For example, we would need to know how and why a body will move in cases where those of the surrounding bodies affording the easiest passage would require an oblique change of direction in the body, whereas surrounding bodies lying along the path that the body is already following afford only a very marginally more difficult passage. According to the present principle it should presumably take the oblique path, but the later rules of collision set out in the *Principia* suggest that where it encounters a smaller body it would continue along its present path, simply pushing the matter which offers resistance in front of it,[20] and this does seem the most plausible route: indeed it is necessary if light corpuscles are to be refracted upon meeting a transparent surface. In the case where it cannot continue along the path it is already following, and must follow one of many oblique paths which are at different angles and which offer different resistance, we have no way of determining the resultant path; presumably the body will neither turn through a greater angle than it needs to nor overcome a greater resistance than it needs to, yet we have no way of making resistance and degree of obliqueness of angle commensurable. Ease of passage requires some kind of quantification—to take the form of something like a principle of 'least action'—if it is to do the work that Descartes requires of it.

At the beginning of chapter 3, Descartes explains that 'there are infinitely many diverse motions that endure perpetually in the world',[21] and that 'there is nothing anywhere that is not changing'.[22] He includes in this all the varieties of change that Aristotelian natural philosophy concerned itself with: celestial phenomena which produce the years, seasons, days etc., sublunary or meteorological phenomena such as the formation of clouds, terrestrial phenomena such as the flow of rivers and the decay of buildings, and the growth and subsequent decay of plants and animals. The total amount of motion in the universe is conserved, although this motion may be redistributed among bodies. Descartes, in common with his contemporaries, almost certainly derived the idea of the need for a conservation principle from the dynamically closed systems studied in statics, and it is impossible to do quantitative mechanics without conservation principles. While it is worth noting that essentially qualitative and organically modelled systems of natural philosophy, such as Aristotle's, do not require conservation principles at all—neither motion nor even matter need be conserved in Aristotle's natural philosophy—and that Descartes provides no justification for his principle of conservation of motion, I doubt if anyone at this stage in the development of mechanics would have found it contentious. Also, given his principles of conservation and the transfer of motion between bodies, his statement that he is not concerned with the causes of motion becomes relatively unproblematic in mechanist terms, for the question is not one of what the cause of a particular body's motion is: this can be given simply by specifying that a particular body moves in a particular way because some other body has transferred a deterministic quantity of motion to it. Rather, it is a question of what is the origin of motion—that is, the total quantity of motion—and on this question 'it is enough for me to suppose that [bodies] began to move as soon as the world began to exist'.[23]

Descartes' account of the difference between hard and fluid bodies in chapter 3 forms a bridge between a very general statement of the mechanist position, most of which would have been common ground to mechanists, and a specific version of micro-corpuscularianism which was both more distinctive and more contentious. The general principle from which Descartes works is that, given that all bodies can be divided into very small parts, a force is required to separate these parts if they are stationary with respect to one another, for they will not move apart of their own accord. If the very small parts of which the body is constituted are all at rest with respect to one another then it will require significant force to separate them, but if they are moving with respect to one another then they will separate from one another at a rate which may even be greater than that which one could achieve by applying a force oneself. The former bodies are what we call solids, the latter what we call fluids (*corps liquides*), and in the extreme cases they form the ends of a spectrum on which all bodies can be ranked, with rigid solids at one terminus and extremely fluid bodies at the other.

This ranking on a spectrum of fluidity provides the basis for Descartes' theory of matter, for it enables him to reduce the properties of matter to the rate at which its parts move with respect to one another. At the extreme fluid end of the spectrum comes, not air as one might expect, but fire, whose parts are the most obviously agitated, and whose degree of corpuscular agitation is such that it renders other bodies fluid. It turns metals into liquids and causes the smaller parts of the wood to fly away in the form of smoke.[24] So far so good, but if it is the motion of its parts that make flames burn, why does air, which is next along the spectrum of fluidity, not also burn, albeit to a lesser degree? To this

Descartes replies that we must take into account not merely the speed of the motion but the size of the parts, for 'it is the smaller parts that make the more liquid bodies, but it is the larger ones that have more force to burn and in general to act on other bodies'.[25] The explanation that he offers—qualitative and pictorial in the extreme—is as follows. Both air and flame consist of parts of various sizes. But flame must have a greater range of sizes than air. It must contain more larger parts than air because the larger the parts the more effect the body has on us, and flames have an effect on us whereas we can hardly feel air at all. These large parts of the flame must move very quickly compared to the large parts of the air, however, because the power to burn depends on the transfer of very rapid motion to the body burned. On the other hand, flames must contain more smaller parts than air: this 'may be conjectured from the fact that they penetrate many bodies whose pores are so narrow that even air cannot enter'.[26]

The discussion of the nature of air in chapter 4 opens with the question of the existence of imperceptible bodies. Descartes tells us he is clearing away a prejudice which we have from childhood, that the only bodies that exist are those that can be sensed, and that air is so faintly sensible that it cannot be as material or solid as those we perceive more clearly. All bodies, whether fluid or solid, are made from the one kind of matter. Descartes argues that the degree of fluidity of a body cannot be proportional to the amount of vacuum that exists between its consitutent parts. It is not clear who he has in mind as having argued this. On the traditional atomist model it was assumed that fluid bodies contain significant interstitial vacua whereas solid bodies do not, and that this is what makes the former rarer or less dense. It is possible that Descartes is wrongly running together fluidity and density and assuming that the atomist claim holds also for fluidity. However this may be, he tries to establish that there must be more space between the parts of a solid than between those of a liquid, because the moving parts of a liquid 'can much more easily press and arrange themselves against one another' than can the parts of a solid. But it is hard to imagine how motion could affect the space between those parts. And even if one were inclined to accept his account, Descartes immediately ruins his argument by giving an obviously misleading example: namely, that if one pours a powder into a jar then one can shake and pound it to make more room, whereas a liquid will arrange itself in the smallest space. An atomist would have no trouble answering this case, simply pointing out that a powder and a rigid solid body are quite different: the powder contains much more vacuum than the solid, and anyone who has pulverized a solid knows that the powder takes up much more space. The intuitively obvious atomist explanation of this is that the powder contains many more empty spaces between the pieces. Moreover, it is misleading of Descartes to treat a powder as a solid and not a fluid, when his original criterion for something's being a fluid was the ease with which it could be penetrated or cut. Indeed, it is hard to avoid the conclusion that he is conflating solidity and density here.

Descartes also refers us to unspecified experiments designed to prove the non-existence of a vacuum,[27] but his main conclusion is that if there is a vacuum anywhere it cannot be in fluids but must be in solid bodies, and he is more concerned to make sure that we accept that there are no interstitial vacua in fluids than to show the absence of such vacua in solids. This is because his account of the basic structure of the universe effectively subsumes it under fluid mechanics, and hence his interest is really in fluids. This begins to become evident in the subsequent discussion, where the question of the non-existence of a void is discussed in terms of the motion of fluids, and it becomes part of a question in fluid mechanics. Can one really believe, he asks, that water in a well will rise merely to fill a void in the pump, or that rain will be drawn from the clouds simply to fill in spaces here on earth? Rejecting such possibilities, he proceeds to tie the question of why liquids move to that of how they move. In particular, the question arises of how bodies can move at all if there is no empty space for them to move into, and the answer Descartes gives is that 'all the motions that occur in the world are in some way circular'.[28] With circular motion, matter could move in a plenum by means of a large-scale displacement: a region of matter will then be able to move when contiguous matter in the direction of its motion ('in front of it'), and contiguous matter in the opposite direction ('behind it'), also move in the direction of its motion, and when the same conditions hold for these contiguous pieces of matter, so that in the end a continuous loop or ring of matter is displaced. Descartes invokes two examples to show the plausibility of this. The first is the case of a fish swimming in water. When the fish is near the surface, there is a disturbance of the surface (showing that water is being moved out of the way), but when the fish is not too close to the surface of the water, there is no motion at the surface, showing that it is not all the water that is being indiscriminately displaced, but rather that 'it pushes only the water that best acts to perfect the circle of their movement and to occupy the place that they vacate'.[29] The second example is that of wine in a cask, which will not flow out of the bottom when the hole in the top is sealed. The reason for this is not 'fear of a vacuum', which suggests that the wine is able to 'fear' things, but rather that the region of air that the wine would displace were it to leave the vat would have nowhere to go, whereas when one

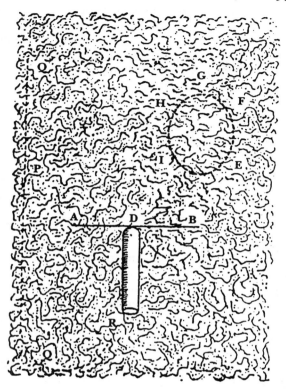

FIG. 7.2

opens the top of the vat one opens up a circuit, and the air at the bottom can move, pushing other air upwards in a circular column that replaces the region vacated at the top of the vat by the wine; although we must remember all the while that this must be a strictly instantaneous process if a void is not to be opened up.

The principle behind the vat example is set out in a letter to Reneri of June 1631.[30] Reneri had written to Descartes posing him two questions: why doesn't the great height of the atmosphere result in the earth under it being crushed, and why does mercury, when poured into an open pipe, not flow out when the pipe is inverted and its upper end sealed off? The latter question raises exactly the same issue as the vat of wine, but Descartes approaches it in a different way, reversing the order of the explanation. In his reply, Descartes proposes a model in which the air is like wool and the aether in its pores is like 'whirlwinds moving about in the wool' (see Fig. 7.2). The air at the bottom is pushed down by the air at the top and is therefore heavy: the air at

235

point O, for example, has the weight pressing down along QPO and it would require a great force to lift it because of this. But we do not notice this weight, because if we push the air at E, for example, towards F, then the air at F will move in a circle in the direction GHI and return to E. The situation is like that of rolling a perfectly balanced wheel: we do not feel the weight. The principle of circular displacement underlying this is then applied to the case of mercury in a closed tube. The mercury can only pour out of the tube if the air at R pushes the air at O, which in turn pushes the air at P and Q, forming a circuit ROPQD, but it cannot do this because the tube is sealed at D, and so the air around R remains stationary and no circuit is formed.

Whereas in *Le Monde* the account of circular motion is given as a prelude to the theory of elements, here in the letter to Reneri it is filled out in terms of that theory. And whereas in *Le Monde* the plenum is invoked to show the necessity of circular motion, here it is not. In fact, the account in the letter allows us to appreciate the connection between the account of circular translation and Descartes' earlier exercises in hydrostatics. As in the 1619 exercises, the problem is set out in micro-mechanical terms, and 'solved' in terms of tendencies to motion, the line ROPQ representing the line of tendency to motion of the mercury: this is also the line that must be raised if the mercury is to fall at R. But as Schuster points out, Descartes has altered the favoured mode of analysis by potential descents employed in the hydrostatics manuscripts, partly because of added complications occasioned by an explicit commitment to a plenum, but also partly because of the nature of the problem at hand.[31] After all, what needs explaining is what holds the mercury in when R is open, and this question was not one that arose in the 1619 exercises. The column of mercury has a tendency to motion, and this is greater than the tendency to motion of the surrounding air, this being the only explanation for why mercury falls in air on Descartes' principles: why then does it not move? The explanation offered is that the column of air particles QPO would have to be displaced. The explanation is not quantitative, but nor is it merely a natural-philosophical account which simply relies on the impossibility of motion without circular displacement in a void. It is a mechanical account, relying on an extension of hydrostatical principles conceived in micro-mechanical terms. This is Descartes' preferred form of explanation, something obscured by the mode of presentation in *Le Monde*.

In *Le Monde*, the doctrine of elements immediately follows the account of circular translation. We should not be misled by the nomenclature of fire, air, and earth that Descartes invokes, for he is not seeking to rescue part of the traditional doctrine of elements by showing, for example, how this doctrine can be filled out in mechanist terms as simply involving three different sizes of corpuscle. This would not explain why there are only three elements, for the traditional fourth element, water, could be similarly construed. And it goes without saying that the postulation of three elements is not the result of an empirical discovery. Why, then, are there only three elements?

The answer lies in the fact that Descartes is writing a treatise on *light*. At an intuitive level, three kinds of process are involved, namely the production of light, its transmission, and its reflection and refraction.[32] Descartes' model of light is one drawn from fluid mechanics and derives ultimately from hydrostatics, as we have seen. It is something that acts by means of mechanical pressure, and what needs to be explained is how this mechanical pressure is generated in the first place, how it is propagated, and why light so construed behaves in particular geometrically defined ways when it encounters opaque and transparent bodies. Light is generated by fiery bodies, transmitted through the air, and is refracted and reflected by terrestrious bodies. The traditional elements of fire, air, and earth have, then, a cosmological analogue. These three elements are for Descartes simply three different sizes of corpuscle: very fine, fine, and gross respectively. They are the kinds of matter Descartes believes one needs for a physical theory of light, and become unashamedly hypothetical by the end of the chapter, where Descartes tells us that he is going to 'wrap his discourse up in the cloak of a fable'.[33]

The Laws of Nature

Chapter 6 of *Le Monde* begins with Descartes' construction of a hypothetical world on the basis of the theory of matter set out in the first five chapters. The ultimate aim is to show that a world constructed in this manner is indistinguishable from the actual world. What is explicitly supposed to mark out the theory of matter as an appropriate basis for a reconstruction of the world is that it invokes nothing that cannot be grasped clearly and distinctly. Implicitly, it is just as important that it be consonant with the basic principles of a mechanist natural philosophy. We must also not lose sight of the fact that the working out of the theory of matter has evolved on the model of fluid mechanics. Water has not been included as one of the elements, but there is a sense in which it is the basic or ultimate element, for hydrostatics and hydraulics provide much of the basis for fundamental physical notions that Descartes' cosmology will operate with.

We are invited to imagine a universe of limited but, for practical purposes, indefinite extension. This is a limited region of the actual universe, and Descartes had checked on the theological acceptability of such a supposition when beginning work on *Le Monde* in December 1629. He had written to Mersenne asking 'whether there is anything definite in religion concerning the extension of created things, that is, whether it is finite or infinite, and whether there are real created bodies in what is called imaginary space, for although I have been afraid to touch on this question, I believe that I shall have to go into it'.[34] We do not have Mersenne's reply, but both were theologically vexed questions. As regards the infinity of the world, Descartes holds that an infinitely extended universe is within God's power, but he is happy to assume here that his imagined world is simply spatially indefinite. This is a distinction that he will later claim, in conversation with Burman, to have been the first to formulate,[35] but it does not solve the problem and the topic is one that will exercise Descartes explicitly on a number of occasions later in his career. The question of 'imaginary spaces', even though hypothetical in the present case, was also problematic. The medieval discussion of the plurality of worlds had focused on a number of different cases: were temporally successive different worlds possible? was it possible for there to be other worlds in the stars, planets, or even within the earth? was it possible for there to be a world completely outside this one, that is, outside our cosmos, which existed in an 'imaginary' space? Oresme had argued for the possibility of all three, and had devoted special attention to the last, but he had established its possibility by challenging a number of central ingredients in Aristotelian and Thomist natural philosophy,[36] and Descartes was wise to tread carefully in this minefield.

Descartes tells us that his hypothetical universe does not contain forms, such as 'the form of earth or the form of fire', or qualities, such as 'the qualities of being hot or cold, dry or moist, light or heavy, or of having some taste, or smell, or sound, or colour, or light, or other such quality whose nature is such that there might be said to be something which is not known clearly by everyone'.[37] Why does Descartes disallow all kinds of things that we naturally think we know from acting as a basis for pursuing natural philosophy, and what grounds does he have for maintaining that we cannot conceive of them 'clearly'? There is some sense in which he must be considering these forms and qualities not to be real or essential properties of bodies. The ensuing discussion suggests that he does not consider them to be essential properties. But even if it were granted that they were not essential properties, this does not preclude our being able to perceive them clearly. Note that the issue here is different from that discussed in Rule 12 of the *Regulae*. There, a question had been raised about the differences in colours and other perceptible qualities being represented in the imagination by differences in linear patterns, and Descartes had been concerned to show that what we perceive when we perceive a colour is something that can be represented in the imagination by a linear pattern. But there is nothing special about colours in this respect, for nothing can be represented in the imagination on this account unless it is represented in the form of a two-dimensional linear pattern, partly because the imagination is the two-dimensional surface of a corporeal organ, the pineal gland, and partly because such linear representation is necessary if something is to be grasped clearly and distinctly. But how things are represented in the imagination tells us nothing about the reality or otherwise of the colours that we perceive. In particular, it does not tell us that differences in colours are actually differences in linear patterns, only that, in the imagination, we represent differences in colours by means of differences in linear patterns. The discussion in the *Regulae* has no bearing on the question of whether colours are real or essential properties of bodies. Consequently, it cannot be the fact that colours are represented in the imagination by linear patterns that makes our knowledge of them unclear. In the context of the account in *Le Monde*, then, we need to ask what makes our knowledge of colour unclear.

It might at first seem that it is not 'clarity' that is doing the work, but mechanism. There is no evidence of a workable notion of 'clarity' which would provide a basis for Descartes' claim. On the other hand, there is no shortage of evidence that he wants to exclude the forms and qualities he mentions because they could not form part of a properly mechanist explanation. The task of the first five chapters has been to set out the kinds of entities and properties that Descartes wants to invoke in his account, and he has prepared the ground by trying to show that they have the requisite qualities of clarity and evidence. But nothing in the argument has indicated why these are the only things having this quality, which is what Descartes is now effectively claiming. On the other hand, while the aim of the exercise is indeed to provide a mechanist account, Descartes is concerned to secure the credentials of mechanism, and the notion of 'clarity' is supposed to achieve this. Is it possible to read Descartes, when he says that colour is not something 'that is clearly known by everyone', as maintaining that someone could conceivably be mistaken about what colour something was? And if so, is it possible to ascribe to him the converse claim that we know something clearly only when we cannot be mistaken about it? Such a claim is not part of the doctrine of clear and distinct ideas as it figures in the *Regulae*. That doctrine was about compelling evidence, not about freedom from error, but it is perhaps not too difficult to understand how, given the right circumstances, the move from one to the other could be made. And if it were made, Descartes would be operating with a notion of clarity that might just fit the bill. What is interesting about the present passage is that a notion of clarity is being evoked to provide the basis for mechanism, but it is a notion which cannot be filled out in terms of any discussion of clarity in Descartes up to this point. We are given no details as to how it is to be filled out, and it is quite possible that Descartes had not reformulated his criterion epistemologically at this stage. The need for a reformulation is perhaps now becoming evident, however.

The traditional conception of a world without qualities and forms would have been in terms of the Aristotelian doctrine of 'prime matter'. Descartes tells us that this is not what he wants to advocate. On the traditional conception, what results when one strips matter of all properties and forms is a propertyless substratum, which Aristotle himself seems to have conceived as a limiting case which could never actually be achieved (in principle), but which later thinkers took to be a genuine substratum underlying forms and qualities.[38] Descartes does not want to conceive of his world in these terms if for no other reason than because he does not want to allow that a world stripped of the forms and qualities he mentions would be propertyless: on the contrary, there is a presumption that in removing these, we would be left with its genuine properties. Descartes' new world is to be conceived as 'a real, perfectly solid body which uniformly fills the entire length, breadth, and depth of the great space at the centre of which we have halted our thought'.[39] This perfectly solid body is 'solid' in the sense of being full and voidless, and it is divided into parts distinguished simply by their different motions. At the first instant of creation, God provides the parts with different motions, and after that these motions are regulated by the 'ordinary' laws of nature; that is, He does not intervene supernaturally to regulate their motions.

The spatial extension of matter seems to be constitutive of it:

the quantity of matter I have described does not differ from its substance any more than number differs from the things numbered. Nor should they find it strange if I conceive of its extension, or the property it has of occupying space, not as an accident, but as its true form and its essence.[40]

The rationale for the identification of matter and space is the clarity it confers on the notion of matter, and the rationale for this in turn is that, if one starts off by restricting oneself to what one can conceive clearly and distinctly, then one protects oneself against hidden contradictions in one's reasoning. Consequently, the 'laws of nature' are simply the laws of this material extension.

These laws of nature are designed to describe the collisions of corpuscles. In imagining such collisions, it is tempting to picture them in terms of atoms colliding in a void, for in Descartes' account the collisions of corpuscles of gross third matter, and even collisions of the subtler second matter, all occur in a sea of first matter which has little effective density. But we must exercise care in allowing ourselves to think in these simplified terms, for we naturally think of atoms moving in a void as continuing for long stretches without collision, whereas for Descartes there is constant collision. This is important because the counterfactual situation in which a body moves in the absence of external constraints is not so immediately relevant to Descartes' analysis as it would be to a straightforwardly atomistic account, where the obvious way to proceed would be from the simple case of unconstrained motion to how the motion is changed by various constraints. This is the essence of the kinematic approach,[41] but it is far from clear that Descartes' approach is kinematic. His model seems rather to be taken from hydrostatics, and the point seems to be not so much to analyse the behaviour of a body under various kinds of constraint in terms of how it behaves when not under constraint, but rather to account for what happens when a body moves from one system of constraints to another, where the constraints that Descartes is interested in are collisions.

The three laws of nature that Descartes provides are designed to describe the behaviour of bodies in collision. But before we look at these laws, it is important that we make sure that we are able to distinguish the two components of a motion, namely the power of moving and the 'determination' of the motion. If we return to Descartes' example of the tennis ball reflected off a canvas, we can simplify matters by taking the initial motion as one in which the ball is given a speed and a direction of motion by the racquet. The ball then encounters the canvas, its speed remaining unchanged, but its direction altered. Descartes' laws of nature deal quite separately with the power of moving and the determination of a body. The first law tells us that a body conserves its motion except in collision, when, the second law tells us, the total motion of the colliding bodies is conserved but may be redistributed amongst them. It is left to the third law to tell us about direction, and according to this law, because a body's tendency to move is instantaneous, this tendency to move can only be rectilinear, because only rectilinear motion can be determined in an instant: 'only motion in a straight line is entirely simple and has a nature which may be grasped completely in an instant'.[42] Motion in a circle or some other path would require us to consider 'at least two of its instants, or rather two of its parts, and the relation between them'.[43] What path the body will actually take, however, will be a function of the collisions to which it is subject: in the simplified case of the tennis ball, for example, the path is determined by the initial collision with the racquet and the subsequent collision with the canvas.

Having set out the terrain, so to speak, let us look at the three laws in more detail. The first law states that certain states of bodies are conserved: they will remain unchanged unless something acts to change them. Among these are a body's size, shape, its position if it is at rest, and also its motion, for once a body has begun to move 'it will always continue in its motion with an equal force until others stop or retard it'.[44] This rule of conservation of state has always been considered to hold for the first three items, and many others, Descartes tells us, but not for the last, 'which is, however, the thing I most expressly wish to include in it'. It is certainly true that motion had been treated very differently from the others, and in the Aristotelian tradition it was considered that terrestrial motion was a process in which a body engaged in order to achieve some end, and that once this end had been achieved the motion ceased. This accorded well with experience, since terrestrial bodies never continued to move for very long, always coming to rest. Restricting our attention to the straightforward case of inanimate bodies, it was because local motion was thought to result from an external force acting on the body that there was no way in which a body could conserve its motion. Equally important was the fact that causation was not 'conserved', so to speak, in Aristotelian physics. Aristotle's picture of the consequences of an event is not one of chains of cause and effect interwoven in a nexus extending to infinity, but rather, in an analogy of David Balme's,[45] one resembling the ripples caused by the throwing of a stone into a pond, which spread out and combine with the ripples caused by other stones, but eventually die away and come to nothing. And conversely, Aristotle argues that there are fresh beginnings (*archai*), not confined to human agency.[46] The notion of causation as something fixed and conserved appears to have originated with the Stoics,[47] who had a very holist conception of a cosmos as an integrated system in which everything was deterministically linked with everything else and in which causes act inexorably, neither coming into nor going out of existence. In sum, then, the Aristotelian insistence on the decay of motion derives from empirical considerations indicating that terrestrial motion does always in fact die out, and natural-philosophical considerations about the external nature of the force responsible for motion and the nature of causation, as well as a view of causal activity as something local rather than global. The local nature of causal activity is doubtless encouraged by Aristotle's biological model and the anti-Platonist metaphysics that accompanies this, whereby individual substances are the source of all activity. Although Descartes does not mention the empirical question of motion dying away here, he does offer an explicitly holist model of causation, similar to that of the Stoics in that it is apparently deterministic and allows of no exceptions. Because of the close relation between causal activity and motion, we might expect the conservation of causation to be set out in terms of the conservation of motion, and this will be done in the second law.

In defence of the first law, Descartes spells out the conception of motion that it employs and contrasts this with the Aristotelian conception. The objection to the latter seems to be that it is so complex as to be unintelligible, and the assumption is that something as simple and straightforward as motion can surely be characterized in a simple and straightforward way. This is somewhat disingenuous, as the Aristotelian account not only builds an explanation of motion into its description of it, but the explanation is part of a more general account of change—including, for example, the coming into existence ('generation') and going out of existence ('corruption') of animals and plants—and so is necessarily complex, whereas the account Descartes offers is purely descriptive. His account is geometrical, and his model is that of the geometrical procedure of generating a line from the motion of a point and a surface from the motion of a line, a motion in which 'bodies pass from one place to another and successively occupy all the spaces in between'.[48] In other words, motion is simply to be equated with change of place, what I have been calling translation.

The second law of motion is, as I have indicated, a law of the conservation of motion (or perhaps a law of conservation of the total 'force of motion') in collisions. It states that 'when a body pushes another, it cannot give the other any motion except by losing as much of its own at the same time; nor can it take away from the other body's motion unless its own is increased by the same amount'.[49] In its defence, Descartes points to its advantages over the traditional accounts of continued projectile motion. Aristotelians were in disagreement amongst themselves about how to account for the continued motion of projectiles, and their accounts were premised upon a distinction between terrestrial and celestial motions. Descartes changes the question, so that it now becomes that of explaining why the motion of the projectile decays rather than why it continues to move, and the answer he provides, an answer Beeckman had given to the same question seventeen years earlier,[50] is the air's 'resistance'. This is not going to convince an Aristotelian, of course, and it is little more than a promissory note on Descartes' part, since what he refers to as the air's resistance is a complex phenomenon which he cannot explain. Indeed, he writes to Mersenne that it is so complex as to fall beyond the bounds of scientific explanation:

Now as for this resistance that you ask me to specify, I hold that it is impossible to reply *et sub scientiam non cadit* [and that it does not fall within science]; for its being hot or cold, dry or humid, clear or cloudy, and a thousand other factors can affect the air's resistance; and in addition, whether some body is of lead, or iron, or wood, whether it is round, or square, or has some other shape, and thousands of other things can change this proportion, and this is generally true of all those questions where you speak of the resistance of the air.[51]

Nevertheless, the proposed explanation certainly has no less empirical content than the Aristotelian one, and Galileo was able to show, contrary to Descartes' pessimism, that quite a good (kinematic) account of air resistance can in fact be given.[52]

When Descartes sets out the second law he talks about motion being conserved, but in subsequent elaboration he reformulates it in terms of conservation of 'force of motion':

The motion of a body is not retarded by collision with another in proportion to how much the latter resists it, but only in proportion to how much the latter's resistance is overcome, and to the extent that, in obeying the law, it receives into itself the force of motion that the former gives up.[53]

To understand what this 'force of motion' is, we need to recall a few general features of seventeenth-century accounts of the forces involved in collision. Alan Gabbey has summed up the situation admirably:

Taking seventeenth-century dynamics as a whole, insofar as this is permissible, it can be said that the great majority of its practitioners understood force in its functional sense as that concomitant of a body—expressed in terms of its whole speed and corporeal quantity—which could be identified with the body's relative capacity to overcome a similarly understood resisting force, whether potential or actual, irrespective of the speed and corporeal quantity in terms of which the contrary force was expressed. Interactions between bodies were seen as contests between opposing forces, the larger forces being the winners, the smaller forces being the losers: a conception of evidently anthropomorphic origin.[54]

This conception underpins Descartes' discussion of collision, and it suggests two kinds of case: either the motive force is greater than the resisting force, in which case there will be an exchange of motion, to be envisaged as the stronger body winning over the weaker one, with the result that the former pushes the latter; or the motive force is less than the resisting force, in which case the body with the motive force is the weaker and it will rebound off the resisting body.

This helps somewhat in understanding how Descartes' 'force of motion' operates, but not in understanding what exactly it is. In closing his discussion of the first two laws, Descartes tells us that they both derive directly from the immutability of God. It is because God always acts in the same way that He conserves the same amount of motion that He put in the universe at the first instant, and bodies retain or

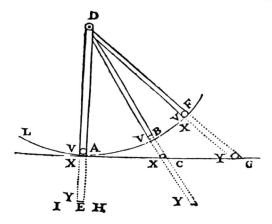

Fig. 7.3

transfer their motions, 'according as they have the force to do so', because God causes them to do this.[55] Descartes appears to be maintaining here that motion is conserved (that is, the total quantity of motion is conserved) because force of motion (that is, total quantity of force of motion) is conserved, and the force of motion of a body seems to be a direct expression of God's causal activity. Because of the difficulties in separating out what exactly is physical and what is divine in Descartes' account of causation and force, it is difficult to say whether causation is something physical, or whether it has both a divine manifestation and a physical manifestation in the form of force of motion, or whether force of motion is a physical expression of something that is non-physical.[56] But whichever of these we opt for, motion is conserved because force of motion is conserved, and force of motion in some way expresses or manifests God's causal activity. It is ultimately because causation is conserved—a conservation that Descartes puts in terms of God's immutability—that motion is conserved.

As I have indicated, whereas the first two laws deal with the power of motion, the third deals with what Descartes regards as a separate issue: the direction of motion. It asserts that, whatever the path of a moving body, its tendency to motion, or *action*, is always rectilinear. The evidence presented for this is (i) that a stone released from a sling will not continue to move in a circle but will fly off along the tangent to the circle, and (ii) while in the sling the stone will exert a force away from the centre, causing the string to stretch, and showing 'that it goes around only under constraint'. As an illustration, we are given the case of a stone moving in a sling (Fig. 7.3) along the path AB. At the instant it arrives at point A, it has an instantaneous tendency—an *inclination*—to move in the direction of C. Now this all looks eminently kinematic, contrary to what I said above about Descartes' analysis being derived from statics rather than kinematics, for the idea seems to be that rectilinear motion is 'natural' in the sense that a body will follow a rectilinear path in the absence of external constraints. But matters are not so straightforward.

The trouble is that while the third law as stated in chapter 7 would seem to establish the uniqueness of rectilinear motion as an inertial motion, when he elaborates further on the law in chapter 13, he apparently counts a circular component in the motion of the stone as inertial as well. He has already noted in chapter 7 that, as well as exerting a force at a tangent to the circular path, the stone pulls on the string. He now asks what causes this pull on the string. We have to imagine that the tendency to motion from A to C is not a primitive tendency but arises from two others: one along the circle AB and the other radially along the line DAE. We know that its inclination to travel along AB is 'in no way impeded by the sling', but the motion of the sling does impede the radial tendency away from the centre, and this is why the stone pulls on the sling.[57] Since the motion that carries it along the circle AB is in no way impeded by the sling, this suggests that the motion is being treated as inertial. In other words, as well as accepting rectilinear inertia, Descartes also seems to accept circular inertia. And this is not an isolated oversight, for later, in a letter to Ciermans of 23 March 1638, he explicitly treats rotational motion as being unproblematically inertial.[58]

It is not difficult to understand in terms of classical mechanics where Descartes has taken a wrong step. Instead of treating the circular motion as being a resultant of an inertial motion along AC and a centripetal force, which in this case constrains any motion so that the stone is always the same distance from a central point D, he thinks of the stone as possessing a centrifugal force, acting away from the centre. As a result he fails to arrive at the classical Newtonian understanding of inertia.[59] But the question is whether he is trying to arrive at such an understanding, and, if he is, why, after giving a clear statement of rectilinear inertia and providing an explanation of why rectilinear motion is the only inertial motion in terms of its 'simplicity', does he appear to blatantly contradict this? The answer is that a statement of a principle of inertia does not seem to be the main point of the exercise. He does not seem particularly concerned to specify how a body behaves in the absence of forces, for example, because the bodies he deals with always move within a system of constraints, just as in statics: the aim is to understand the instantaneous collisions of non-elastic bodies. One does not ask what would happen if the forces were removed, because the understanding of the action of these forces is the point of the exercise.[60]

Descartes' treatment of the motion of a stone in a sling in chapter 13 should be considered in this light. He singles out three tendencies— a tangential rectilinear tendency, a radial rectilinear tendency, and a circular tendency—and if we think of what he is doing as an attempt to give an account of inertia, then we do indeed end up treating circular motion as being as 'natural' as rectilinear motion, even though he seems to recognize clearly that the circular motion is constrained. But it is clear from the context that Descartes is not interested in trying to explain what causes the body to follow a circular path, but is rather trying to describe the tendencies that characterize a body already moving in a circular path. More generally, it is important to appreciate a feature of Descartes' account which has been widely misunderstood. On a standard reading of *Le Monde*, what Descartes is trying to do in his physical theory is to reduce the whole of physics to kinematics, thereby construing all physical events in terms of matter in motion, simply eliminating force at a stroke.[61] But this is not Descartes' aim at all. Force is built into his account at the most fundamental level, for his aim is not to reduce physics to kinematics, but rather to model it on hydrostatics: to employ the resources and procedures, and even some of the concepts (such as instantaneous tendencies to motion) of hydrostatics to think through physical problems generally. Descartes' treatment of circular motion strongly indicates that he is thinking primarily in terms of equilibrium: circular motion is a form of equilibrium in his account, and he appears to slide from this to treating it as a form of inertial motion. Indeed it is difficult to understand why commentators have been so committed to the view that Cartesian physics is kinematics, for his indifference to kinematics is very evident in his discussion of the laws of motion, where he shows almost no interest in the behaviour of unconstrained bodies, something central to kinematics. Descartes does not want to eliminate forces, he wants to account for them in a way that is compatible with the inertness of matter, something he tries to achieve in terms of an analysis of instantaneous tendencies to motion derived from hydrostatics. Indeed, I believe it is this reliance on hydrostatics rather than kinematics that explains Descartes' commitment to the notion of a plenum because, in his hydrostatic model, bodies always move in a system of constraints provided by the surrounding medium, the point of the exercise being to understand how these constraints operate. Later on, Descartes will try to provide metaphysical arguments against the possibility of a void, and because these arguments are reminiscent of Aristotle, who also rejected the idea of a void, it has occasionally been assumed that Descartes is following Aristotle here. But he is not: his rejection of Aristotelian natural philosophy would naturally push him—as it had pushed other mechanists—in the direction of atomism, and it is not metaphysical considerations that prevent him moving in this direction, for the plenum appears long before he has formulated any metaphysical views. Physical processes must occur in a plenum for Descartes because his mode of analysis derives from an area in which systems of constraint are constitutive of the physical behaviour that one is investigating, in the sense that it is the effects of the system of constraints on what is constrained that the theory seeks to explain.

Finally, the justification provided for the third law may at first seem puzzling. Descartes seems to want to derive the simplicity of rectilinear motion from its direct dependence upon God, who seems to act by means of instantaneous acts. This deepens the mystery rather than clarifies anything, for to justify the 'natural' status of rectilinear motion by appealing to a contentious metaphysical doctrine about the nature of God's action[62] seems an extremely uneconomical way to proceed. What we must remember again, however, is that the point of the exercise is to characterize moving bodies at discrete instants of their motion, very much on the model of statics. Descartes has an account of the nature of God's action which allows him to shore up his punctiform analysis by providing it with a metaphysical rationale, and we cannot take seriously the idea that he might have arrived at his punctiform analysis of motion by reflecting on the nature of God's activity, when his whole approach to mechanics from 1620 onwards has been in terms of instantaneous tendencies. But this is not to say that God is an 'added extra', as it were: far from it. God is the ultimate causal agent, and He acts through forces. If we take Descartes' talk of force of motion seriously then we have to say that God acts, not by means of motions, but by means of tendencies to motion. When He acts to change the positions of things, He does not simply locate them in different places, He acts by means of a force which gives bodies a tendency to motion which, depending on the disposition of surrounding bodies, causes them to move in a particular path. The responsibility for the actual path of the stone is shared between God and the surrounding bodies, God being responsible for all motions in so far as they are rectilinear, and the various dispositions of matter making them 'curved and irregular'.[63] Indeed, Descartes draws a parallel between God's action and His will: 'So the theologians teach us that God is also the author of all our actions, in so far as they exist and in so far as they have some goodness, but that it is the diverse dispositions of our wills that can render those actions evil'.[64] God provides the power or force necessary for a body to move in the first place, but it is the diverse dispositions of surrounding bodies that are responsible for the paths of those bodies. Of course, God knows what the dispositions of surrounding bodies are, just as He knows what the dispositions of our wills are, and Descartes presumably wants us to draw the orthodox conclusion that, just as the fact that God knows the dispositions of our wills does not mean that He is responsible for what we do, so too, just because He knows the dispositions of bodies this does not mean that He is responsible for their particular motions, as He would be if the corporeal world followed some divine plan down to the last detail. We can postpone discussion of these questions, however, for Descartes gives us no details of his understanding of the operations of the will until much later.

The Construction of a New World

In May of 1632, Descartes wrote to Mersenne:

If you know any writer who has made a special collection of the various accounts of comets, please let me know. For the last two or three months I have been quite caught up in the heavens; and have satisfied myself as to their nature and the nature of the stars we see there, and many other things which a few years ago I would not even have dared hope to discover; and now I have become bold enough to seek the cause of the position of each fixed star. For although their distribution seems irregular, in various parts of the universe, I have no doubt that there is between them a natural order which is regular and determinate. The grasp of this order is the key and foundation of the highest and most perfect science of material things that men can ever attain, for if we possessed it we could discover *a priori* all the different forms and essences of terrestrial bodies, whereas without it we have to be satisfied with guessing them *a posteriori* and from their effects.[65]

Chapters 8 to 12 of *Le Monde*, using the theory of matter and laws of nature already elaborated, set out the details of this cosmology in the form of an account of an hypothetical 'new world', from the formation of the sun and the stars (ch. 8), the planets and comets (ch. 9), the earth and the moon (ch. 10), and finally weight or gravity (ch. 11) and the tides (ch. 12).

The key to this whole cosmology is Descartes' account of vortices. Because the universe is a plenum, for any part of it to move it is necessary that other parts of it move, and, as he has explained earlier, the simplest form of motion which takes the form of displacement is going to be a circle (or, more generally, a closed curve), although we have no reason to think that the universe turns around a single centre: rather, we may imagine different centres of motion. The matter revolving nearest to the centre will be the smallest or least agitated, that furthest away will be the largest or most agitated. The reason for this is that the latter—which Descartes refers to as 'the strongest'—will describe the greatest circles, because it will have the greatest capacity to realize its inclination to continue motion in a straight line. Whatever differences in size and agitation we may imagine there to have been in the early stages of the universe, however, except for the large clumps of third element, we can imagine that the constant motion and collision caused the difference in sizes of matter to be reduced, as 'the larger pieces had to break and divide in order to pass through the same places as those that preceded them'.[66] Similarly, differences in shape gradually disappear as repeated collisions smooth off the edges and all matter (of the second element) becomes rounded, 'just as grains of sand and pebbles do when they roll with the water of the river'.[67] Some pieces of matter are sufficiently large to avoid being broken down and rounded off in this way: these are what Descartes refers to as the third element, and such pieces of matter form the planets and the comets. Finally, the collisions yield very small parts of matter, which accommodate themselves to the space available so that a void is not formed, and these move at great speed because 'having to go off to the side through very narrow passages and out of the small spaces left between the parts of the second element as they proceeded to collide head-on with one another, [the first element] had a longer route to traverse than the second in the same time'.[68] But the first element is formed in a greater quantity than is needed simply to fill in the spaces between pieces of second and third element, and the excess naturally moves towards the centre because the second element has a greater centrifugal tendency to move to the periphery, leaving the centre the only place for the first element to settle. There it 'composes perfectly liquid and subtle round bodies which, incessantly turning much faster than and in the same direction as the parts of surrounding second element, have the force to increase the agitation of those parts to which they are closest and even, in moving from the centre towards the circumference, to push the parts in all directions, just as they push one another'.[69] These concentrations of first element in the form of fluid, round bodies at the centre of each system are suns, and the pushing action that Descartes describes is 'what we shall take to be light'.

The universe, as Descartes represents it, consists of an indefinite number of contiguous vortices (see Fig. 7.4), each with a sun or star at the centre, and planets revolving around this centre carried along by the second element. For example, our system, whose limits are marked by FFFFGG, has S as its sun. The outermost bodies in the system rotate the fastest, but this holds only for the region between the limit FFFFGG and the sphere KK, where Saturn is located. Since it was known that

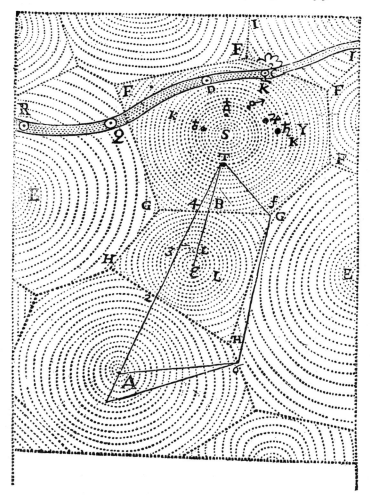

FIG. 7.4

Saturn rotated more slowly than Mercury, which is closer to the Sun,
speed of rotation could not simply be a function of distance from the
Sun. In an attempt to account for this, Descartes argued that those
planets closer to the Sun than Saturn are 'agitated by' the Sun's motion, which makes them move more quickly.[70]

The large clusters of third matter usually form planets (including
their satellites, which Descartes treats as planets), but their motion may
be such as to carry them outside their particular solar system altogether. They then become comets, an example being marked by the

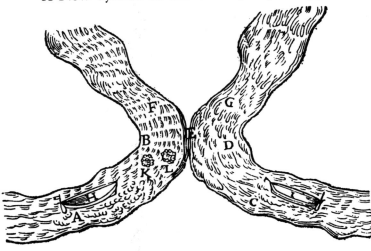

F<small>IG.</small> 7.5

path CDQR in Fig. 7.4. The difference in the behaviour of planets and comets is explained by analogy with the case of two rivers which meet, as in Fig. 7.5. The two rivers ABF and CDG come from different directions and meet at E. Boat H has sufficient bulk and speed to pass through E towards G; unless, that is, it meets boat I there, in which case the 'larger and stronger will break the other'. Lighter bodies, such as scum and leaves, initially at A, may, however, be carried along away from E towards B, where the flow of the water is not so strong (since the flow there is 'along a line that less approaches a straight line'[71]). By analogy, the heaviest bodies composed of third matter are pushed by centrifugal force to the periphery, and they follow a course through different solar systems. Less massive ones eventually enter into stable orbits—the less massive they are, the closer to the centre—and once in this orbit they are simply carried along by the celestial fluid in which they are embedded. The stability of their orbits arises because, once a planet has attained a stable orbit, if it were to move downwards (that is, inwards) it would immediately meet smaller and faster corpuscles of second element which would push it upwards; and if it were to move upwards it would immediately meet larger corpuscles which would slow it down and make it sink downwards again.[72]

This accounts for the motions of comets and the motion of planets proper around the Sun, but how are we to explain the motions of planetary satellites, or the diurnal motion of a planet like the Earth? Descartes has assumed up to this point that the planets are carried along at the same speed as the celestial fluid in which they are embedded,

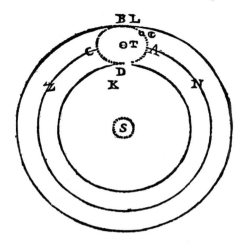

Fig. 7.6

which is a function of the size of the corpuscles of the second element from which that layer of fluid is composed. Reverting back to his analogy of the boat in a stream, he notes that large objects move more slowly than light ones in a river, and he now makes planetary speed also depend on the size of the corpuscles of third element making up the planet. This enables him to offer an ingenious account of both the lunar orbit around the Earth and of the Earth's diurnal motion.

The Earth, T in Fig. 7.6, is a massive body and correspondingly does not move as fast as the layer of second element in which it is embedded. Because the second matter at A moves faster than T, which it pushes towards Z, it is diverted towards B.[73] But in going from A to B, it causes T to turn around its centre, and this in turn carries the celestial fluid from B around to C, and then to D and A, and in this way it forms 'about the planet a particular heaven, with which it must thereafter continue to move from the direction that is called "west" to that called "east," not only about the Sun but about its own centre'.[74] The Moon, which moves in the same layer of celestial fluid, but is smaller and therefore faster (on the river analogy), will also be deflected towards B on arrival at A, and will be carried around the earth by the celestial fluid.

Descartes next turns to consider what the weight (*pesanteur*) of the Earth consists in, that is, 'what the force is that unites all its parts and makes them all tend towards its centre, each more or less according as it is more or less large or solid'.[75] We have seen that in the hydrostatics manuscript of early 1619, Descartes had rejected the idea of weight as

253

an intrinsic property, and was already defining it as 'the force of motion by which a body is impelled in the first instant of its motion'.[76] It is not surprising, therefore, that he has no hesitation in offering a similar account here in *Le Monde*. The principle is the same in both accounts, but now the question of how a body acquires its force of motion is described in terms of the different speeds of celestial matter. The vortex ABCD in Fig. 7.6, for example, contains celestial matter which is moving at a greater speed than, and with a greater centrifugal force than, the Earth. A body which is released above the surface of the Earth will consequently not be able to keep up with the celestial matter and will be pushed downwards.

Finally, the phenomenon of the tides—a key to the defence of the heliocentric theory for Galileo and one of the most intractable problems of seventeenth-century physics, defeating even Newton—is explained using the same materials. As Shea notes, a theory of the tides has to account for four cycles: '(1) the *daily cycle* with high and low tides recurring at intervals of twelve hours; (2) the *monthly cycle* whereby the tides lag behind 50 minutes each day until they have gone round the clock and are back to their original position; (3) the *half-monthly* cycle with high tides at new and full moon and low tides at quadratures; and finally, (4) the *half-yearly cycle* with greater tides at the equinoxes than at the solstices'.[77] All of these are explained by Descartes in terms of the vortical motion of celestial matter around the Earth. We are asked to imagine (Fig. 7.7) that the Earth is surrounded by a circulating layer of celestial matter ABCD, that its surface is covered by water 1, 2, 3, 4, and that this in turn is enveloped by air 5, 6, 7, 8. Because there is less space between o and 6 than between B and 6 the celestial matter has to pass a little more quickly between o and 6, and as a result the Earth is pushed a little towards D, so that its centre T moves away slightly from M. Because the air and water surrounding the Earth are fluid bodies, the force that moves the Earth slightly away from M will also move them towards T, acting on them from sides 6, 2 and 8, 4. This causes a compensatory rise at 5, 1 and 7, 3, and 'thus, because the surface EFGH of the Earth remains round, because it is hard, that of the water 1234 and that of the air 5678, which are fluids, must form an oval'.[78] Since the Earth rotates counterclockwise once every 24 hours, points 5, 1 and 7, 3 will move, giving rise to two high and two low tides daily. This explanation of the daily cycle of tides is confirmed, Descartes tells us, by reports of sailors that travel from east to west is easier than that from west to east, for travel from east to west follows the predicted bulges at 5, 1 and 7, 3, whereas travel in the opposite direction requires one to push against the bulges.

This theory also accounts for the monthly and half-monthly cycles,

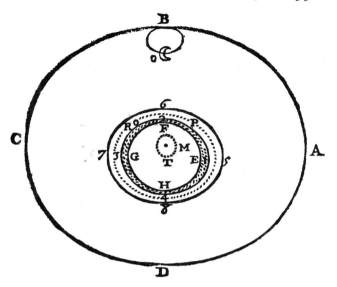

Fig. 7.7

although Descartes ignores half-yearly cycles.[79] Monthly cycles are put down to the fact that the Moon makes a full rotation around its axis once every lunar month, so that every six hours it makes 1/120th of its circuit; 'hence, these waters do not change precisely every six hours, but rather lag behind by approximately the fifth part of an hour each time as do those of our seas also'.[80] Finally, because the axis BD is slightly shorter than the axis AC, the moon moves more rapidly at B, where it is full, and at D, where it is new, than at A and C, when it is at quadrature.[81]

Descartes was especially pleased with his account of the tides. He wrote to Mersenne at the time that accounting for the tides had given him a great deal of trouble, and that while he was not happy with all the details, he did not doubt the success of his account.[82] And although he was to revise it over the next ten years, he would not alter its fundamentals. Indeed, the theory of the tides is really the first genuinely quantitative ingredient in Le Monde, but the fact that the earlier material is not quantitative should not blind us to the significance of Descartes' success in presenting a thoroughly mechanist cosmology which takes as its foundations a strictly mechanist conception of matter and the three laws of motion. Le Monde presents a fully mechanist alternative to Aristotelian systems, one which effectively derives heliocentrism from first principles, which offers a novel and apparently viable conception of matter, and which formulates fundamental laws of motion

—laws that are clearly open to quantitative elaboration. Moreover, it does this by relying on one of the few areas of physical enquiry that had been given comprehensive quantitative expression, namely hydrostatics, and whatever the pitfalls of this way of proceeding, Descartes had at his disposal a rigorous, mathematically developed discipline to draw upon. The discipline of hydrostatics was not in question, and so the issues hinged on the legitimacy of its application to cosmology, and Descartes' ingenuity here is beyond doubt. But the jewel in the crown of *Le Monde* is the theory of light set out in the last three chapters, for, especially if we read these together with Descartes' general work in optics at this time, we have an empirical, quantitative account of a physical question whose explanation derives directly from his mechanist cosmology.

The Nature of Light

The full title of *Le Monde* is *Le Monde ou Traité de la Lumière*—'The World or Treatise on Light'—and both its original aim and its final triumph is the theory of light. Descartes' purpose is to show how the behaviour of light rays can ultimately be explained in terms of his theory of the nature of matter and the three laws of motion. Indeed, the theory of matter turns out to be motivated directly by the requirements of Descartes' physical optics, for the first element makes up those bodies that produce light, namely suns and stars; the second element makes up the medium in which light is propagated, namely the celestial fluid; and those bodies that refract and reflect light, such as the planets, are made up from the third element. Moreover, it is the laws of motion that underpin and explain the laws of refraction and reflection of light, and the accounts of phenomena such as the rainbow and parhelia that are based on these. So, in terms of Descartes' original plan, one works back from parhelia and the rainbow to the laws of optics, and then to the physical underpinning of these laws. Let us look first at the physical underpinning, and then at how the physical optics actually works.

Chapter 13 of *Le Monde* begins with an analysis of the motion of a stone in a sling and, as we saw, Descartes singles out three tendencies: a tangential rectilinear tendency, a radial rectilinear tendency, and a circular tendency. This analysis is then applied to the corpuscles of second element making up the celestial fluid which rotates around a sun (Fig. 7.8). Corpuscles at E have a tangential rectilinear tendency towards P, but the matter beyond E restrains them just as the sling does the stone and it gives them a circular tendency towards R; they

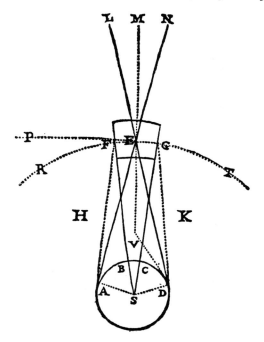

Fɪɢ. 7.8

also have a radial rectilinear tendency towards M. The latter is due in part to the restraint exercised by the matter beyond E, in part by the rotation of S, and in part by action of the matter between S and E. The result is that there is a pressure upwards on E; not all the matter in this region will have such a pushing effect, however, but only that included in the cone AED, for, given that nature will always take the shortest route and that motion will tend to continue in a straight line, the most economical way for nature to fill a hypothetical void at E would be for the cone AED to move into that vacated space.[83]

In other words, the laws of motion show us that, given the rotation of the sun and the matter around it, there is a radial pressure which spreads outwards from the sun along straight lines from its centre. This pressure is manifested as 'a trembling movement', a property which is 'very suitable for light'.[84] Indeed, the inhabitants of Descartes' proposed new world 'have a nature such that, when their eyes are pushed in this way, they will have a sensation which is just like the one we have of light'.[85] There are two key questions here: first, does this model account for the known properties of light? and second, what exactly is the relation between the physical agitation of matter that results in a stimulation of the eye, and the visual cognition that we have as a result of this? The first of these questions is dealt with in chapter 14 of *Le Monde*, but the account given there needs to be supplemented with the discussions of reflection and refraction in the *Dioptrique*, and the account of the formation of the rainbow in the *Météors*, both of which were completed by this time, in order to show the real strength of Descartes' overall approach. The second question is actually dealt with in the first chapter of *Le Monde*, but to appreciate its full import it is best considered when we have set out the account of light, and of the physiology of perceptual cognition given in *L'Homme*.

The 'principal' properties of light which a theory of light must account for are set out in chapter 14 as follows:

(1) that it extends in every direction around those bodies that are called 'luminous', (2) to any distance, (3) instantaneously, (4) and ordinarily in straight lines, which must be taken as rays of light; (5) that several of these rays while originating from different points can be collected at the same point, (6) or, originating from the one point, can go out to different points, (7) or, originating at different points and going to different points can pass through the same point without impeding one another; (8) and sometimes they can also impede one another, namely when their force is very unequal and that of some of the rays is much greater than that of others; (9) and finally they can be diverted by reflection, (10) or refraction, (11) and that their force can be increased, (12) or diminished by the different dispositions or qualities of the matter that receives them.[86]

Descartes then proceeds to show that his account is not only compatible with all of these, but can actually explain them. As regards (1), because the action that we call light arises from the circular motion of luminous bodies, it will of necessity extend in all directions. As regards (2) the plenum is a great leveller of distances, for any motion in a particular direction will automatically result in matter further out in that direction being moved. No one doubted (1) or (2), so the point was simply to account for them. The instantaneous transmission of light was a different matter, and Beeckman for one made it clear to Descartes that he doubted whether anything corporeal could move at infinite speed: indeed, he and Descartes tried (unsuccessfully) to agree on an experiment to determine this in August 1634.[87] The question is a key one for Descartes—he writes to Beeckman that the infinite velocity of light 'is so certain that if it could be proved false, I am ready to confess that I know nothing in all of philosophy'[88]—and he virtually treats the question here as an *a priori* one, maintaining that since all the parts of the second element between AF and DG in Fig. 7.8 'touch and press one another' then it is just like the case where 'the force with which one pushes one end of a stick passes to the other end in the same instant'.[89] The image of the pushed stick is one which Descartes will

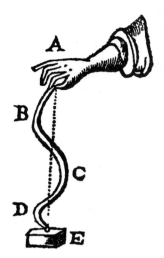

Fig. 7.9

use again, and not surprisingly, for it is a striking and compelling image. When a rigid stick is pushed at one end, not only do we not see any motion being transferred along its length, but conceptually (in pre-Relativistic physics) it seems intuitively obvious that all the parts of the stick will move simultaneously: no matter how distant the far end of the stick is, it will move at the same instant as the end which is pushed. Moreover, and here we come to point (4), it does not matter whether the stick is straight or twisted: the motion is transmitted in a straight line even if the parts transmitting it are arranged so that they are never lined up in such a way as to form an exactly straight line (Fig. 7.9). And the parts of the second element will rarely in fact be so aligned, because they consist of spheres which are normally packed, not one on top of the other, but in layers where the upper ones will fit into the space created at the sides of the lower ones. Points (5) and (6) are also dealt with by an analogy, for we can have several cords hanging from a pulley (see Fig 7.10). We can pull on these cords marked 1 to 5 each in a different way, but all the forces 'will come together' in the pulley. Conversely, 'the resistance of this pulley extends to all the different hands that are pulling those cords'.[90]

Meeting point (7) requires Descartes to postulate that the spheres of the second element 'can receive several motions at the same time'. Again we are given an analogy. We can push air through the pipe illustrated in Fig. 7.11 from F to G, from H to I, and from K to L, through the three tubes FG, I, and KL, even though they are all joined

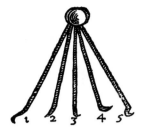

FIG. 7.10

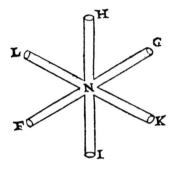

FIG. 7.11

at N so that air passing along any of them must necessarily pass through the middle of the other two. But one can see how a very strong blast of air through F will tend to impede air travelling from H to I, or from K to L. A similar account is given to deal with points (11) and (12), where it is pointed out that the force of light at some region is a function not only of the number of rays making it up but also of the dispositions of the bodies in the places through which it passes.

The really crucial points, however, are (9) and (10), and Descartes tells the reader that he has already dealt with reflection and refraction elsewhere. And indeed he has, in the *Dioptrique*. We have already looked briefly at the physical model used to deal with reflection, where an analogy is drawn with a tennis ball striking a canvas and being reflected off its surface. Refraction, a more complex phenomenon, is dealt with using the same model. The difference is that, in refraction, the analogy is with a ball that breaks through the canvas. It is struck at A towards B (see Fig. 7.12), and on reaching the canvas CBE at B it loses half its speed. To find the path of the ball, we trace three straight lines AC, HB, and FE at right angles to CBE, such that the

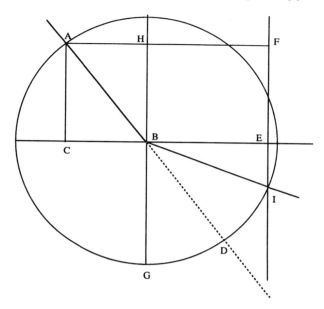

FIG. 7.12

distance from FE to HB is twice that from HB to AC, which shows that the ball tends towards I. The reason for this is that, since the ball loses half its speed in going through the canvas, it must take twice as long to reach a point on the circumference below CBE. But its loses none of its determination to advance to the right, so that, taking twice the time it took to move from AC to HB, it will travel twice that distance, that is, from HB to FE, and I is the only point below the canvas where FE and the circle intersect.[91]

The next step is to replace the canvas by water, so that the ball is travelling through air from A to B and through water from B to I. The same considerations apply.[92] But when we turn to light rays moving into a more dense from a less dense medium, we find that the deflection is not away from the normal, as in Fig. 7.12, but towards the normal, as in Fig. 7.13. To account for this in terms of his tennis-ball model, Descartes postulates that the ball is struck again with the racquet on reaching B, so that its force of motion is increased by one-third—corresponding to the greater ease with which light penetrates a denser medium—and it now covers in two moments the distance it had pre-viously covered in three. The analogy here, Descartes maintains somewhat hopefully, is that 'the same effect would be produced if the ball encountered at B a body which was such that it would pass through

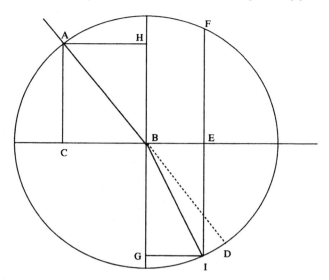

FIG. 7.13

its surface CBE a third more easily than through air'.[93] Consequently, if we take BE to be 2/3 BC, and draw the perpendicular FE which cuts the circle at I, we have the path of the refracted ray BI. The key ratio here is that between CB and BE. Since CB = AH and BE = GI, sin i = AH/AB and sin r = GI/BI, where AB = BI = 1, the ratio gives us the sine law, in a form where we can see easily what it is that has to be measured.[94]

What Descartes is doing in the present case is trying to show that the sine law can be demonstrated purely by considering the geometry of the situation. But just as important is his physical model of light, and it is in his account of the optics of meteorological phenomena that the physical and geometrical aspects of his conception of light are best appreciated. Such an account is his treatment of the rainbow which was to appear in Discourse 8 of the *Météors*, although we can be certain that the account had been developed by 1632.

Descartes begins by establishing the rainbow's terrestrial nature firmly, pointing out that rainbows are formed not only in the sky, but also in fountains and showers in the presence of sunlight. This leads him to formulate the hypothesis that the phenomenon is caused by light reacting on drops of water.[95] To test this hypothesis, he constructs a large glass model of a raindrop—a goldfish bowl, to all intents and purposes—and fills it with rainwater. Then, standing with his back to the sun, he holds up the sphere at arm's length in the sunlight, moving it up and down

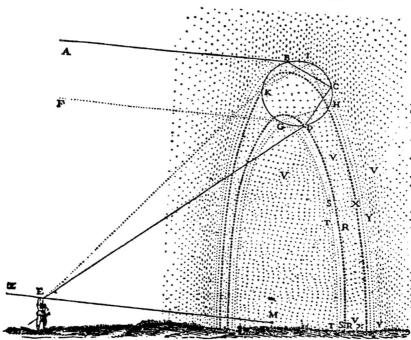

FIG. 7.14

so that colours are produced: this is a procedure that was well known, and Leurechon, for example, had recommended holding a glass of water up to the light. If we let the light come

from the part of the sky marked AFZ [see Fig. 7.14], and my eye be at point E, then when I put this sphere at the place BCD, the part of it at D seems to me wholly red and incomparably more brilliant than the rest. And whether I move towards it or step back from it, or move it to the right or the left, or even turn it in a circle around my head, then provided the line DE always makes an angle of around 42° with the line EM, which one must imagine to extend from the centre of the eye to the centre of the sun, D always appears equally red. But as soon as I made this angle DEM the slightest bit larger, the redness disappeared. And when I made it a little bit smaller it did not disappear completely in one stroke but first divided as into two less brilliant parts in which could be seen yellow, blue, and other colours. Then, looking towards the place marked K on the sphere, I perceived that, making the angle KEM around 52°, K also seemed to be coloured red, but not so brilliant as D.[96]

In an atmosphere packed with raindrops, red spots would appear on all of them that made an angle of 42° and 52°. More generally, what is produced is a primary rainbow at 42° which has red at the top and violet at the bottom, and a fainter secondary rainbow at 52° with the spectrum inverted.[97]

The next stage in the argument is to discover what the path of the light ray is; how, for example, is a light ray coming from A affected by passing through the raindrop? Placing a black sheet of paper between A and B, and then between D and E, he finds the red spot at D vanishes. It also vanishes when the paper is placed between B and C and then between C and D. However, he found that if he covered the whole globe, but left openings at B and D, the red spot was quite visible. Ignoring the refraction by the glass from which the bowl was made, he concludes that this means that the ray from A is refracted on entering the water at B, and travels to C, where it is internally reflected to D and is then refracted again on emerging at D. The secondary rainbow is formed similarly, except that, as well as the two refractions at G and K, two internal reflections are needed to account for it, at H and I.

So far so good. But why is the primary rainbow produced at an angle of 42° and the secondary bow at an angle of 52°? What determines the angles? The answer is: the refractive index of water in relation to air. It is because of this refractive index that a light ray coming from air into water at a particular angle of incidence will be bent at a particular angle, and it is this refractive angle, together with the internal reflections, that will determine at what angle the colours will be seen. Refraction is the key thing, and Descartes now moves to focus on refraction by showing that neither curved surfaces, nor internal reflections, nor multiple refractions are needed, for the phenomenon can be produced with a single refraction. It can be produced with a glass prism, for example, which is of especial interest because each part of the surface of the sphere can be regarded as a minute prism. Consider the prism MNP, illustrated in Fig. 7.15. When sunlight strikes the surface NM directly so that there is no appreciable refraction, and passes through a narrow aperture DE on an otherwise darkened face NP, the colours appear on the screen PHGF, red being towards F and violet towards H. For this, a single refraction is needed, for when NP was parallel to NM so that there was no appreciable refraction at all, then the colours were not produced. Descartes also notes that some limitation of the light was necessary, for if the aperture DE was too large the colours only appeared at the edges, the centre remaining white, while if it was removed altogether then no colours at all were formed.

He now sets out to explain why the colours are formed on the screen PHGF, and 'why these colours are different at H and at F, even though the refraction, shadow, and light concur there in the same way'.[98] To explain this, he invokes his account of matter, and asks us to consider

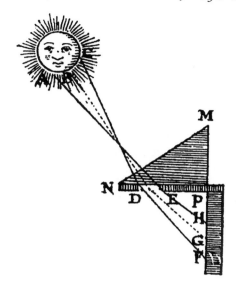

FIG. 7.15

the small spheres of air (second element) which transmit the pressure from the sun. These spheres initially have only a motion in the direction of their propagation, but on striking the refracting surface obliquely they acquire a rotary motion; thenceforth, they all rotate in the same direction or sense, and can either all rotate at the same speed, or neighbouring spheres can accelerate or retard their rotation; and this change in speed of rotation is invoked to explain changes in colour. What causes the differences in rotary speed can only be the contact with the shade at D and E, since the spheres all have the same motion initially, and without the shade around the aperture DE colours are not formed. Descartes speculates that the spheres in ray EH encounter spheres moving more slowly, which retard their own motion, and the spheres in the ray DF encounter spheres moving more quickly, which accelerate their own motion. He illustrates what happens in terms of a sphere 1234 (see Fig. 7.16) that is pushed obliquely from V to X: air to water, for example.[99] It acquires a rotary motion on reaching the surface YY because at the first instant part 3 is retarded while part 1 continues with undiminished speed. Hence the ball is compelled to rotate following the route 1234, that is, clockwise. Rotation occurs, then, simply as a result of the sphere passing from one optical medium to another. Next, Descartes turns to the question of how different speeds of rotation are produced (resulting in different colours). We are asked to imagine sphere 1234 being surrounded by four other similar

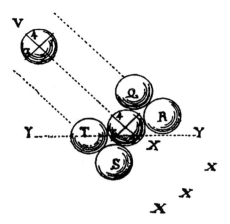

Fig. 7.16

bodies, Q, R, S, T. Q and R move 'with more force' towards X than does 1234, whereas S and T have been retarded. Q and R will accelerate 1234, because their translational motion will act to push parts 4 and 1 in a clockwise direction: they will give it a greater clockwise spin. S and T, on the other hand, will have no effect on it, 'because R is disposed to move towards X faster than 1234 follows it, and T is not disposed to follow 1234 as quickly as 1234 precedes it'. This, Descartes tells us, 'explains the action of the ray DF'. It explains it because what happens is that the corpuscles which skirt the edge of D will be retarded by their contact with this edge, and they will act as S and T do. Corpuscles further away from the edge will act as do Q and R, tending to accelerate the corpuscles in the path DF. At E, the converse process occurs, and the corpuscles in the path EH are retarded.[100] This results in the production of red at F and blue or violet at H.[101] Intermediate speeds are produced in the same way, the translational motions on either side of them being different, and causing changes in their rotational velocity accordingly.[102]

   This account of the production of colours rules out a traditional distinction between 'real' and 'apparent' colours, held for example by the Coimbra commentators,[103] who distinguished between the 'real' whiteness of swans and the blackness of crows, and the apparent and transitory colours formed in rainbows. It is ruled out because 'the entire true nature of colours consists only in their appearance' and so 'it seems to me to be a contradiction to say both that they are false and that they appear'.[104] The claim that the true nature of colours consists 'only in their appearance' could presumably be made also of light in Descartes' account, for here colours are no more or less real than light, the former being a translational motion, the latter a translational motion with a rotary motion added. But just what account we are to give of the 'reality' of this is something we shall consider below when we examine his account of visual cognition.

For the moment, I want to concentrate on what his treatment of the production of colour in the prism contributes to our understanding of the production of colour in the rainbow. Descartes tell us that at first he doubted whether the mechanism could be the same, for the prism requires shadows, whereas:

I did not notice any shadow which cut off the light [in the case of the rainbow], nor did I understand yet why they appeared only under certain angles. But when I took my pen and calculated in detail all the rays which fall on the various points of a drop of water, so as to see under what angles they would come toward our eyes after two refractions and one or two reflections, very many more of them can be seen under the angle of 41° to 42° than under any lesser one, and none of them can be seen under a larger angle. . . . [Similarly for the secondary bow at 51° to 52°] . . . So that there is a shadow on both sides, cutting off the light which, after having passed through an infinity of raindrops illuminated by the sun, comes towards the eye under the angle of 42° or slightly less, and thus causes the primary and most important rainbow [and similarly for the secondary rainbow].[105]

The calculations depend on a knowledge of the refractive index from air to water, which he determined to be 250/187, an accurate figure. His procedure is as follows (see Fig. 7.17).[106] Rays coming from the sun, marked S, are parallel, but the ray EF, for example, is refracted. The ratio FH:FC is the sine of the angle of incidence i for the ray EF. When FH = 0, its value when it coincides with AH (which is not refracted), i will be zero. Letting the radius of the drop be 10,000 units,[107] then when FH = 10,000, that is, when it just grazes the drop, the angle of incidence is 90°. When EF penetrates the drop and is refracted at K, it can either emerge at K or be reflected internally at K and then be refracted at N to the eye at P, or internally reflected again to Q and be refracted to the eye at R. The path FKNP, which produces the primary bow, involves one reflection and two refractions, and the path FKNQR, which produces the secondary bow, involves two refractions and two reflections. For the primary bow, we have to determine the size of the angle ONP, and for the secondary bow the angle SQR. Descartes calculates the angle ONP for the values of FH from 1,000 to 10,000 (Fig. 7.18). The calculation is based on the fact that at F the deviation δ is equal to $i - r$ (angle of incidence minus angle of refraction) measured by the angle GFK; at K the deviation is $180° - 2r$, and at N it is $i - r$. The total deviation is therefore $180° + 2i - 4r$, and since the angle ONP is $180° - \delta$, it is $4r - 2i$. Fig 7.17 represents the case where FH = 8,000. Here, i is about 40°44′.

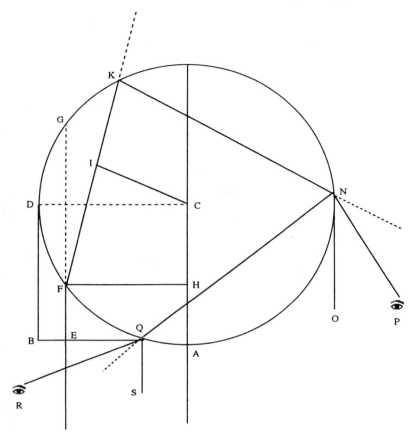

FIG. 7.17

What the calculations, as shown in Fig. 7.18, demonstrate is that, whatever the angle of entry of the ray, it will exit so as to make an angle no greater than 40° 57′ with the original path of entry. In fact, as Descartes shows in carrying out more precise calculations in the range FH = 8,000 to 9,888, there is a clustering such that a large number of rays are refracted at an angle of around 41° 30′. Allowing 17′ for the apparent radius of the sun, Descartes argues that the maximum angle of the interior rainbow must be at 41° 47′ and the minimum angle of the outer one at 51° 37′. This account is quite compelling. It shows not only why the bows appear at the angles they do, but also why the outer boundary of the primary rainbow is more sharply defined than the inner edge of the secondary one.

LA LIGNE HF	LA LIGNE CI	L'ARC FG	L'ARC FK	L'ANGLE ONP	L'ANGLE SQR
1000	748	168.30	171.25	5.40	165.45
2000	1496	156.55	162.48	11.19	151.29
3000	2244	145. 4	154. 4	17.56	136. 8
4000	2992	132.50	145.10	22.30	122. 4
5000	3740	120.	136. 4	27.52	108.12
6000	4488	106.16	126.40	32.56	93.44
7000	5236	91. 8	116.51	37.26	79.25
8000	5984	73.44	106.30	40.44	65.46
9000	6732	51.41	95.22	40.57	54.25
10000	7480	0.	83.10	13.40	69.30

FIG. 7.18

There are nevertheless a number of problems with Descartes' account of the formation of colours. He is unable to explain the reverse order of colours in the secondary bow, for example, and although his account of the constitution of colour in terms of rotational velocity is a major advance on earlier theories—which tried to explain colours in terms either of a mixture of light and darkness or of a mixture of what were considered to be primary colours—he gives no means by which this rotational velocity can be measured. But his general account is a milestone in optics, and it is not surprising that he will later hold it up as a sample of his method.[108] It is a model of mechanistic mathematical physics of the kind that no other mechanist was anywhere near achieving: no other mechanist—Hobbes, Gassendi, Mersenne, or Beeckman—had even approached such a successful quantitative approach, and where physical problems had been posed and solved quantitatively, as in the work of Kepler or Galileo, it was not within the context of mechanism.[109]

A Mechanistic Physiology

L'Homme follows much the same course as the treatise on light that forms the first part of Le Monde. It does not purport to describe the physiology of real human beings, but of 'statues or earthen machines' that God could have created, just as *Le Monde* describes an imaginary world and not the real one. At the end of each work the aim is to establish that if we compare the imaginary constructs with the real thing we will find in both cases that they are indistinguishable, and although the text breaks off before this point in *L'Homme*, Descartes writes to Mersenne that he has discovered nothing in his extensive dissections that he cannot explain, that is, that he cannot explain in micro-mechanical terms.[110] The only difference is that a full account of human beings would also include their souls, whereas Descartes is concerned only with their bodies here, the third section of *Le Monde*— on the soul—never having been completed, or perhaps even begun. In terms of the traditional distinction between the vegetative soul (which controls growth, nutrition, and reproduction), the sensitive soul (which controls perception, appetites, and animal motion), and the rational soul (which is the seat of the intellect and the will), what Descartes wants to show is that the first two can be dealt with in mechanistic terms. His listing of the questions dealt with in *L'Homme* makes this clear:

I should like you to consider, after this, all the functions I have ascribed to this machine, such as [*functions of the vegetative soul:*] the digestion of food, the beating of the heart and arteries, the nourishment and growth of members, respiration; and [*functions of the sensitive soul:*] waking and sleeping, the reception by the external sense organs of light, sounds, smells, tastes, heat, and all other such qualities; the imprinting of the ideas of these qualities in the organ of common sense and imagination; the retention or imprint of these ideas in the memory; the internal movements of the appetites and passions; and finally the external movements of all the limbs, movements that so properly follow not only the actions of objects presented to the senses but also the passions and impressions that are found in the memory, that they imitate perfectly the movements of a real man.[111]

Descartes undertook extensive anatomical investigation from the early 1630s to the late 1640s,[112] and this work shows him to have been a thorough and careful observer, although not an innovator; and indeed, he tells Mersenne that he has assumed nothing in anatomy which is not generally accepted.[113] The physiology of *L'Homme* is even more derivative, and it is based on three main sources: Hippocratic and especially Galenic treatises, Scholastic writers on medicine and commentaries on the biological writings of Plato and Aristotle, including Coimbra commentaries,[114] and biological and medical writers from the mid-sixteenth century onwards.[115] He builds up this material into a general account of physiology, and then tries to construe this physiology in mechanist terms. The exercise of taking already-developed material and reconstructing it along mechanist lines is one that we have seen

Descartes engage in on many previous occasions in areas such as statics and meteorology, where gross macroscopic results are taken as a starting-point and then accounted for in micro-mechanical terms. In *L'Homme* the project takes on its most ambitious form: the elaboration of a mechanist physiology. Although its findings had been summarized in the *Discours* in 1637, when it was published in 1664 *L'Homme* had an immediate impact. It was one of Descartes' most controversial and widely-read texts in the seventeenth and eighteenth centuries,[116] being taken as ammunition both by his detractors and admirers. Its two principal features are the construal of the body as a machine, and the attempt to explain physiological processes in terms of the behaviour of microscopic corpuscles. In fact, neither of these was new. The comparison of animals with clocks, for example, had been made by Aquinas, and in 1544 a Spanish physician, Gomez Pereira, had explicitly modelled animals on machines.[117] When Mersenne mentioned Pereira's work to Descartes, he was dismissive, saying he hadn't looked at it and had no wish to.[118] We have seen that Descartes was often reluctant to acknowledge the work of others, but I believe that there is something more to this dismissal than that. Despite the importance that the question of automata later took on, the machine analogy is made in passing in *L'Homme* and was really just a means to an end: namely, a means of clearing the ground for a mechanist physiology. What really mattered was Descartes' ability to construe physiological processes along mechanist and micro-corpuscularian lines.

Animal physiology is introduced right from the start as the workings of a machine.[119] The digestion of food is described in a mixture of mechanical and chemical terms. The food is first broken down into small parts and then, through the action of heat from the blood and that of various humours which squeeze between the particles of blood, it is gradually divided into excrementary and nutritive parts. The heat generated by the heart and carried in the blood is the key ingredient here, and Descartes devotes much more attention to the heart and the circulation of the blood than to functions such as digestion and respiration. He accepts that blood circulates throughout the body, but, like most of his contemporaries, rejects Harvey's explanation of circulation in terms of the heart being a pump,[120] preferring to construe the motion as being due to the production of heat in the heart.[121] The heart is like a furnace, or rather like the sun, for it contains in its pores 'one of those fires without light',[122] which are comprised of the first element that also makes up the sun. In fact, Descartes really had little option but to reject Harvey's account. To accept that the motion of the blood was due to the contractive and expansive action of the heart would have required providing some source of power for its pumping action, and it was hard to conceive how he could do this without recourse to non-mechanical powers, whereas at least he can point to phenomena such as natural fermentation in defending his own account of thermogenetic processes creating pressure in the arteries. As Hatfield has pointed out, 'the episode with Harvey may perhaps be seen as an example of how Descartes picked and chose—from among the available descriptions of vital phenomena and conceptions of vital functioning—those most suited for translation into the mechanistic idiom'.[123] The most important features of the circulation of the blood from the point of view of Cartesian psychophysiology, however, is the fact that it carries the 'animal spirits', which it bears up through the carotid arteries into the brain. These are separated out from the blood and enter the brain through the pineal gland, at the centre of the cerebral cavities. This is a mechanical procedure in that the animal spirits are the subtlest parts of the blood and hence can be filtered into the pineal gland through pores too fine to admit anything larger.[124]

Having dealt with the heart—the heat of which is the 'principle of life'—and the circulation of the blood, Descartes turns to the nervous system. The nervous system works by means of the animal spirits, which enter the nerves and change the shape of the muscles, which in turn results in the movement of the limbs, an analogy being drawn with the force of water in fountains. He sets out his programme as follows:

I wish to speak to you first of the fabric of the nerves and the muscles, and to show you how—from the sole fact that the spirits in the brain are ready to enter into certain of the nerves—they have the ability to move certain members at that instant. Then, having touched briefly on respiration and other such simple and ordinary movements, I shall say how external objects act upon the sense organs. After that I shall explain in detail all that happens in the cavities and pores of the brain, what route the animal spirits follow there, and which of our functions this machine can imitate by means of them. For, were I to begin with the brain and merely follow in order the course of the spirits, as I did for the blood, I believe what I have to say would be much less clear.[125]

The pineal gland is also responsible for the discharge of the animal spirits to the muscles via the nerves, which are hollow tubes with a double membrane continuous with the brain's pia mater and dura mater.[126] In general terms, what happens is that external stimuli displace the peripheral ends of the nerve fibres, and a structural isomorph of the impression made on the sense organ is transmitted to the brain. This results in changes in the patterns formed by the animal spirits in the brain, which can produce changes in the outflow of spirits to the nerves. At the muscle, a small influx of spirit from the nerve causes the spirits already there to open a valve into its antagonist. Spirits then flow from the antagonist which causes it to relax, as well as causing the first muscle to contract.

Descartes deals in turn briefly with the control of breathing, swallowing, sneezing, yawning, coughing, and excretion, before turning to 'automatic motions', which we shall look at below. He then deals with the external senses, concentrating on vision, before turning to an account of the internal senses, where he attempts not only to explain traditional areas such as imagination and memory in corporeal terms, but also provides a sketch of various temperaments in terms of animal spirits. The treatment of the latter simply translates various temperaments and humours into their supposed microscopic correlate in an intuitive but extraordinarily simplistic way. For example, generosity, liberality, and love are attributed to abundance of animal spirits; confidence and courage are attributed to strong or coarse animal spirits; promptness, diligence, and desire are attributed to unusually agitated animal spirits; tranquillity is attributed to the exceptionally uniform action of animal spirits; on the other hand, malice is attributed to lack of animal spirits, timidity to weak animal spirits, tardiness to lax spirits, and so on.[127] Various conditions such as sneezing and vertigo are explained in a similarly primitive way, as is the difference between the sleeping and the waking state: the brain in a waking state is characterized as having all its fibres tense and its animal spirits strong, whereas the sleeping brain is characterized as having lax fibres.[128]

Some parts of Descartes' account do go beyond this simplistic picturing of micro-corpuscularian mechanisms, however, and memory, for example, is given a rather more elaborate and interesting treatment. What memory does, in Descartes' account, is to enable previous representations on the pineal gland to be formed again, without the existence of the objects to which they correspond.[129] Descartes' account of both storage and retrieval of memory is organized around ease of accommodation to a mechanistic model, and this dictates what questions he is and is not concerned with. He shows no interest at all in the traditional practical questions of memory which had dominated sixteenth-century discussions, which centred around mnemonics[130]; but nor does he show much interest in the details of localization of memory, which had played such a crucial role not just in the anatomical tradition but in the late Scholastic treatment of memory also. Rather, he is concerned with *how* memory is stored, and the account he offers has two distinctive features. First, just as in his account of visual cognition, no resemblance between experience and memory is required, and this gives the account a significant degree of flexibility. Descartes does not require that the pineal patterns—ideas—be stored separately and faithfully, but just in a way that enables the idea to be presented again

FIG. 7.19

on the pineal gland. And this suggests a dispositional model, in which patterns are stored only implicitly and do not have to be kept in the same form between experiencing and remembering.[131] Secondly, storage and retrieval are accounted for in exclusively physical terms. Storage is effected through bending and rearranging of brain filaments, and retrieval is helped by repetition of recall. An analogy is drawn with a linen cloth which has several needles repeatedly passed through it (see Fig. 7.19).[132] The holes in the cloth will mostly remain open after the needles have been withdrawn, but those that do not will still leave physical traces which can easily be reopened. The importance of this is that the associative basis of Descartes' account of recall can be captured, as total recall as a result of partial input can be accounted for: 'if I see two eyes with a nose, I at once imagine a forehead and a mouth and all the other parts of a face, because I am unaccustomed to seeing the former without the latter'.[133]

There is a significant degree of sophistication in Descartes' account of memory, and real work is being done at the reductive level here. But the greatest sophistication is achieved—not surprisingly, given the attention he has already devoted to the phenomenon—in his account of vision. Here he provides a detailed account of ocular anatomy and physiology, showing how the lens refracts light rays, how its shape is adjusted, and how the size of the pupil is adjusted to control the amount of light entering.[134] This account includes a comprehensive theory of how shape, position, and distance are gauged. The most challenging of these questions is distance perception, and in the course of *L'Homme*, Descartes offers four criteria[135] by which we are aware of distance in visual perception. The first two of these—distinctness of outline or of colour, and inference of size from past experience—are traditional. But the third and fourth are not. The third is the degree of curvature of the lens: it is a matter of elementary optics that the lens must be flatter the more distant the object, and since the shape of the lens is controlled by the lens's muscles, which in turn are controlled by the degree to which the pores admitting spirits to the nerves which control these muscles are open, there will be a significant difference between focus on close and on distant objects. How we are aware of this difference is not specified, and Descartes simply tells us that 'the soul will be able to know the distance'.[136] Note, however, that even though the images on the retina are two-dimensional, whenever we look in a particular direction we have available a number of such two-dimensional representations depending on how we focus the lens of the eye, and this series of two-dimensional images provides us with snapshots of different depths, as it were. So we have access to a three-dimensional representation by means of a series of two-dimensional images.

The other means of determining distance is the most ingenious, and the most important of them all from the point of view of mechanism. The criteria just mentioned simply tell us how we judge distance, without explaining how it is possible in the first place that we might see things with which we are not in contact. Mechanism restricts all action to contact action, and this is, at least in the first instance, a problem for distance perception such as that which occurs in vision. Naturalism had no such difficulty, and in Kepler's Neoplatonically and Hermetically inspired account, for example, phenomena such as light and magnetism provide paradigmatic examples of ways in which a body can exercise influence throughout the cosmos. The action of a body is not restricted to the spatial region defined by the boundaries of that body in this naturalistic account, but of course it is in mechanism. Consequently, on a mechanist account, the only thing that can act on our sense organs is a body immediately in contact with it. Now in a plenum everything acts on everything else instantaneously, and everything is connected with everything else indirectly if not directly, so there is a sense in which things that we are not in direct contact with can nevertheless affect us immediately. But how do we account for the phenomenology of distance perception? In visual perception, we not only see distant things, we see them (within limits of precision) as being at a particular distance: how is this possible when our eyes are stimulated simply by corpuscles in contact with them? Here the fourth criterion,

FIG. 7.20

Descartes' theory of the eye's 'natural geometry', is crucial because it is designed to tell us how something in contact with the eye can convey information about the distance of its source. Descartes compares our distance vision to a blind man holding out two sticks so that they converge on an object (Fig. 7.20), and calculating the distance of the object from the base angles of the triangle so formed, where the base is simply the distance between the sticks in the man's hands. The blind man does not know the lengths of the sticks, but he can calculate this by means of a 'natural geometry' from the length of the base and the base angles. Analogously with the eyes (Fig. 7.21): here the base angles are given by the angles at which the light rays strike the eye, and an apparently innate 'natural geometry' enables us to calculate the distance of the object in the same way that the blind man does. This doctrine, which is fully in accord with the account of the nature of light and its action offered in *Le Monde*, secures both the restriction of all influence to contact action, and the possibility of genuine distance vision.

Automata and Perceptual Cognition

Having shown in the first part of *Le Monde* how a mechanistic conception of matter can underpin one part of the corporeal realm, including even such apparently intractable phenomena as fire and light, Descartes was concerned in *L'Homme* to show that it also underpinned the other part, organic bodies. One way in which he hopes to achieve this is by

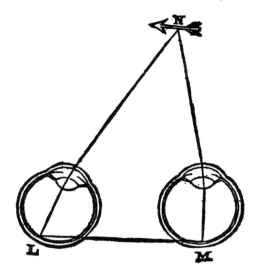

FIG. 7.21

providing details of the mechanisms by which sensory excitations and subsequent movements occur. Animal spirits play a key role here, for the whole sensory and motor process works in terms of animal spirits, carried in the nerves, reaching the brain and being sent from the brain to external members. The mechanist construal of the nerves as tubes is straightforward, but the introduction of animal spirits may seem more problematic.

In the Galenic tradition, the idea of nerves acting in their motor and sensory functions by means of a subtle fluid was commonplace,[137] and there had even been earlier attempts to mechanize this account, most notably in the work of the sixteenth-century naturalist Telesio, who had made the animal spirits completely corporeal and had envisaged them moving through hollow tube-like nerves. But the roles of the various kinds of 'spirits' were complex, and making them material was not such a straightforward procedure.[138] The trouble with animal spirits was that they had a rather complicated history and were expected to do a large number of things.[139] In medieval and renaissance discussions, for example, animal spirits were often used to bridge the gap between the soul and the body. It was common to see spirit treated as matter which is so tenuous that it has become soul, and therefore sentient, on the one hand, and on the other to see it treated as soul which is so gross as to have become matter. As Telesio pointed out, whichever way one argues, the implication is that there is only a difference of degree between mind and matter; and in that case the notion of spirit is superfluous, since its function is to connect two qualitatively different categories, but the very fact that it can bridge them shows that they are not qualitatively different after all. Consequently, Telesio does not use the term 'spirit' as a bridging concept, but to develop a form of naturalism in which everything is both sentient and extended, and his approach is designed to account for centralized systems of activity, particularly people and animals. By means of these spirits, Telesio's aim is to account for the organic unity of nearly all human functions and activities, both bodily and mental.

Given this background, it might seem that the risk Descartes faces is that of accounting for too much by corporeal means, and ultimately making the soul corporeal. But the problem was, I suggest, quite different from this. Many psychophysiological functions had always been construed corporeally. It was part of the medieval Christian tradition that the soul could not be localized, but it was widely accepted in this tradition that the functions of the mind could be.[140] Ventricular accounts, for example, persisted throughout the Middle Ages and, despite strong criticism by Vesalius, continued to be the dominant theory of cerebral localization of mental functions throughout the sixteenth and seventeenth centuries. Indeed, there was even an orthodox tradition, dating back to the Church Fathers, of construing thought in corporeal terms, a tradition which the 'theologians and philosophers' who compiled the sixth set of objections to Descartes' *Meditationes*, describe explicitly and approvingly as the 'soul thinking . . . by means of corporeal motions'.[141] Descartes' aim was to show that a number of psychophysiological functions *that had always been recognized as being corporeal* could be accounted for in a way which did not render matter sentient. He did not risk accounting for too much by corporeal means because he completely rejects the idea of matter being sentient, and because no one in this era would have thought the mind reducible to inert matter.[142] It would simply have been unimaginable to him that one's free will and reflection on one's own cognitive states, for example, could be captured physiologically. This is clear from Part V of the *Discours*, where, in summarizing *L'Homme*, Descartes maintains that there are two ways in which we can distinguish between human beings and animals. First, human beings have language, whereas animals do not, which 'shows not only that animals have less reason than men, but that they have none at all'.[143] Secondly, because we have reason, which is a 'universal instrument', we can respond to an infinite variety of circumstances, whereas animals 'require some particular disposition for every particular action'.[144]

What is original about Descartes' project is not that it construes the faculties in corporeal terms, for they had traditionally been so construed, but to show that construing them in corporeal terms did not contradict the central tenet of mechanism that matter was inert. The question is whether this results in a reductive or an eliminativist account of the organic. Is Descartes' point that the explanation of the constitution of organic bodies is different from that usually given, or is it that organic bodies themselves are completely different from how we normally think of them? Is he saying that the structure and behaviour of bodies are to be explained in the same way that we explain the structure and behaviour of machines, or that bodies actually are machines? Does he want to show how (a form of) genuine cognition occurs in animals and that this can be captured in mechanistic terms, or does he want to show that cognition does not occur at all, that *instead of* a cognitive process we have a merely mechanical one? In short, does he want to explain animal cognition or explain it away?

Crucial to Descartes' comparison of psychophysiological functions with the workings of machines is his account of automatic movement, where sensory input is directly correlated with motor response, a category of movement that includes both reflex movement and habitual response.[145] An example of this is the case of the man-machine in Fig. 7.22. His foot, B, is next to a fire, A, and because the parts of fire move very swiftly they displace the area of skin that they touch, pulling the end of the thread c which is there. When this is pulled the pore de, which is located in the brain where the thread terminates, is opened simultaneously, just as happens when one pulls a cord and the bell at the other end rings simultaneously. The entrance to the pore de being opened, the animal spirits from cavity F enter and are carried through it, 'part into the muscles that serve to withdraw this foot from the fire, part into those that serve to turn the eyes and head to look at it, and part into those that serve to advance the hands and bend the whole body to protect it'.[146] Such automatic motion is completely mechanical, and Descartes at one point compares the mechanical control of muscular motion to the operations of a church organ:

If you have ever had the curiosity to examine the organs in our churches, you know how the bellows push air into receptacles called (presumably for this reason) wind-chests. And you know how the air passes from there into one or other of the pipes, depending on how the organist moves his fingers on the keyboard. You can think of our machine's heart and arteries, which push the animal spirits into the cavities of its brain, as being like the bellows, which push air into the wind-chests; and of external objects, which stimulate certain nerves and cause spirits contained in the cavities to pass into particular pores, as being like the fingers of the organist, which press certain keys and cause the air to pass from the wind-chests to particular pipes. Now the harmony of an organ does not depend on the externally visible arrangement of pipes or on the shape of the wind-chests or other parts. It depends solely on three factors: the air that comes from the bellows, the pipes that make

Fig. 7.22

the sound, and the distribution of air in the pipes. In just the same way, I would point out, the functions we are concerned with here do not depend at all on the external shape of the visible parts that anatomists distinguish in the substance of the brain, or on the shape of the brain's cavities, but solely on three factors: the spirits that come from the heart, the pores of the brain through which they pass, and the way in which these spirits are distributed in these pores.[147]

The organ simply produces the music as a result of an input: it does not represent the notes to itself, in the way that the organist might. Is there any indication in Descartes' discussion that he intends his account of automatic motion to be a full account of the functioning of corporeal faculties?

We must distinguish here between four kinds of case: (1) a stimulus which results in an immediate motor response and which requires no representation, (2) a stimulus which results in an immediate motor response but which requires recognition of the stimulus, (3) a stimulus which results in a delayed motor response, and (4) a stimulus which results in no motor response. The response of an organ to the depression of the keys and the pumping of the bellows is of the first kind, as is the case of the man-machine in Fig. 7.22, where the response to the pain seems to be completely automatic. Indeed, it is unclear whether the process that Descartes describes in this case even involves the pineal gland.[148] In the illustration of automatic motion in Fig. 7.22, it is very tempting to construe the cavity F as the pineal gland, but the illustration is not Descartes' own but one drawn for the posthumously published text, so we cannot place too much weight on how things appear in the illustration. More importantly, Descartes never talks about the pineal gland being a cavity, whereas he tells us explicitly that F is a cavity; this suggests one of the cerebral ventricles rather than the pineal gland, which is what we would expect if the pineal gland is the surface on which things are represented and if the automatic response to being burned, which has to be automatic and immediate if it is to be effective, involves no representation.

But Descartes allows the other three kinds of case, which do involve the pineal gland, in animals. What happens in these three latter cases is that the stimulus is represented to the cognitive organs in some way. Take case (4): there are a number of instances in which Descartes describes the operation of faculties such as memory, where there is a sensory input but no motor output at all. Such cases seem to be straightforwardly cognitive: it is difficult to know how one would describe them otherwise. Case (3), where the need to store the stimulus in some form arises, is not explicitly mentioned, but there is no reason to think that Descartes excluded it, especially since it requires only as much as (4). Case (2) involves a sensory input and an immediate motor output, but because it requires recognition, it involves a representation of the stimulus. It is in fact difficult to see how animals could not have representations if we are to talk about visual cognition, for if they are going to engage in visual discrimination then surely they must have some way of picking things out visually. The animal could respond directly to the corpuscular action that makes up light without actually *seeing* anything, as a genuine machine might, but this is not how Descartes describes the visual process in automata either in this letter or in *L'Homme*. In *L'Homme*, he tells us that the 'figures traced in the spirits on the [pineal] gland, where the seat of imagination and common sense is, should be taken to be ideas, that is, to be the forms or images that the rational soul will consider directly when, being united to this machine, it will imagine or will sense any object'.[149] This indicates that there are representations on the pineal gland of the automaton, but Descartes is clear that the automaton has no awareness of them as representations. He tells one correspondent that it is wrong to suppose that 'animals see just as we do, that is, are aware or know that they see.' On the contrary, animals do not see as we do when we are aware that we see, but only as we do when our mind is elsewhere. In such a case the images of external objects are depicted on our retinas, and perhaps the impressions that they make in the optic nerves cause our limbs to make various movements, although we are quite unaware of them. In such a case we too move just like automata.[150]

The ability to reflect upon on one's cognitive representations is a necessary condition for judgement on them and Descartes rules out the possibility of such states in animals, for this is part of what is involved in the action of the rational soul. Although the problem is not confined to perception—animals have memory, imagination, perceptual powers, and, as we saw in the *Regulae*, even a kind of ratiocinative process (not guided by 'the light of nature'), and passions, as we shall see later— perceptual cognition is clearly the key to the question, and it is here that Descartes provides most details. What form would such perception without awareness take? How could an organism have—and, more importantly, act upon—representations without an awareness of these representations? The answer lies, if anywhere, in the first chapter of *Le Monde*, for not only is it established there that visual perception requires nothing over and above corporeal organs, but we are also given some account of what such visual perception without awareness would consist in.

When we looked at *Le Monde* above I left one question to one side, that of the relation between the physical agitation of matter that results in a stimulation of the eye, and the visual cognition that we have as a result of this. This is the question to which we now turn. In chapter 1 of *Le Monde*, Descartes offers an account of visual cognition which, on the face of it, could not be further from that which he set out in the *Regulae*. Simplifying somewhat, in the *Regulae* his account focuses on getting the 'perceptual' part of perceptual cognition right, whereas here he concentrates on the 'cognition' side of the question. The account of cognition in the *Regulae* is little more than a mechanist reworking of medieval faculty psychology: the perceptual process involves stimulation of the external sense organ, which in turn conveys motions or 'agitations' to the common sense, and then to the memory and finally the imagination. The account presented in the first chapter of *Le Monde* is quite different from this. Perceptual cognition is not thought of in causal terms, and it is not thought of as a multi-stage process. Rather, the treatment focuses on the question of how we are able to respond to certain properties or events as information.

The traditional Aristotelian account had focused on the cognition side of the question, and its treatment of the perceptual process was subordinated to this in as much as it was conceived in teleological and functional terms. It was assumed from the outset that we have the sense organs we do because they naturally display to us the nature of the world, and the account of what occurs in perception is shaped around this. So, the task was to understand how, given that (in optimal circumstances) our perceptual image of the world exactly resembles how the world actually is, the perceptual process works so as to secure such a resemblance. The account of the physical and physiological processes involved is strictly constrained by an understanding of the function of sense perception. The doctrine that, if genuinely veridical perceptual cognition is to take place, then what we grasp is something exactly resembling the object, provides the basis on which we subsequently ask questions about what kind of physical and physiological processes are involved. Now one reason why the Aristotelian account of perception came to fall apart at the beginning of the seventeenth century was that its account of the processes involved in perceptual cognition, particularly in respect to the optics of vision, was shown to be flawed, and flawed in a way that could not be easily corrected within the confines of the general understanding of vision. Kepler showed decisively in his *Ad vitellionem* (1604), for example, that the visual image is formed on the retina and not in the crystalline humour, and that it is an inverted image. Kepler restricts his attention to the formation of the retinal image, telling us that what happens after this is something quite different from the question that he is dealing with.[151] The thrust of his argument seems to be that the important thing is to get the details of the optical and physiological processes right, and perhaps that other questions about the nature and function of perception will then fall into place. For someone who wanted to build mechanism into these processes, it would seem even more imperative to let the nature and function of perception depend on one's account of the physical and physiological processes, rather than the other way around—Hobbes' account in his 'Little Treatise' (ca. 1630) is a good example of a case where the nature of perception is supposed simply to follow on from a causal story about the perceptual process, where the restriction of all processes to contact action is the paramount consideration.[152]

Yet in the first chapter of *Le Monde*, where Descartes is about to introduce a mechanistic cosmology and theory of light, virtually the first thing he does is to suggest that we conceive of visual cognition not in terms of the mechanical-causal process involved in perception, but as a single unified act of comprehension. In the *Regulae*, Descartes had worked with a visual model, for even though perceptual information does not take the form of images resembling what they represent, but rather takes the form of etched lines on a two-dimensional surface, the means of representation are still pictorial. We are now presented with a completely different non-pictorial type of model, a linguistic one:

Words, as you well know, bear no resemblance to the things they signify, and yet they make us think of these things, frequently even without our paying attention to the sound of the words or to their syllables. Thus it may happen that we hear an utterance whose meaning we understand perfectly well, but afterwards we cannot say in what language it was spoken. Now if words, which signify nothing except by human convention, suffice to make us think of things to which they bear no resemblance, then why should nature not also have established some sign which would make us have the sensation of light, even if the sign contained nothing in itself which is similar to this sensation? Is it not thus that nature has established laughter and tears, to make us read joy and sadness on the faces of men?[153]

There is one respect in which the linguistic model has immense advantages over the pictorial model of the *Regulae*. Rules 12 and 14 were primarily concerned with how visual information is conveyed, and the causal account of the transmission of light and the perceptual process offered there is one in which mechanism provides the guidance; but Descartes also had to deal with the question of how visual information is represented, and here he is on weaker ground. A commitment to mechanism, combined with an attempt to render mathematical operations completely clear and distinct by construing them in terms of operations on line lengths, constrained him to argue that whatever we can perceive can be represented by two-dimensional arrangements of line lengths. As we have seen, this is hopelessly implausible. By the time of *Le Monde*, however, Descartes has realized that there are immense problems with the attempt to legitimate mathematical operations in this way, and he abandons this highly problematic constraint here. But if the problem of representation cannot be solved by two-dimensional figures of potentially infinite complexity, how can it be solved? Language fits the bill perfectly. Given a finite number of syllables, an infinite number of ideas can be represented. Moreover, such an account meets the constraint of mechanism, as would have been generally recognized amongst mechanists. Mersenne, for example, in his detailed arguments against the Cabbalist belief that words signify the essences of things, explicitly invokes mechanism: the word is merely a *flatus vocis*, a purely conventional sign, an emission of air, which can be accounted for exhaustively in terms of acoustics and physiology.[154] And as we have seen, Beeckman, in his diary entries for the second half of 1628, where he criticizes Kepler's construal of stellar influence along the lines of verbal warnings, does not so much reject the whole model as point out that in the case of verbal warnings we still need an account of the mechanical interaction between the cause and the effect.

If we distinguish between the question of how perceptual information is conveyed, and the question of how perceptual information is represented, then we can see that Descartes had subordinated the second to the first in the *Regulae*, whereas here he is giving them some degree of independence. He is retaining a causal-mechanical model for the first, and advocating a linguistic model for the second. On the linguistic model, we grasp an idea in virtue of a sign which represents that idea to us. So, in the case of a conventional linguistic sign, when we know sufficient English, the word 'dog' conveys to us the idea of a dog. And just as conventional signs do not resemble what they signify, so too natural signs do not resemble what they signify either. Descartes tells us that there is in nature a sign which is responsible for our sensation of light, but which is not itself light, and which does not resemble light. All there is in nature is motion. In the case of a natural sign like motion, provided we have the ability to recognize and interpret it, when we grasp motion what it will convey to us is light. Light is what we will experience when we respond in the appropriate way to the sign. As examples of natural signs, Descartes tells us that tears are a natural sign of sadness and laughter a natural sign of joy. One of the things that distinguishes signs from causes is that whether a sign signifies something to us—that is, whether we can call it a sign in the first place—depends on our ability to recognize and interpret the sign, and it is this ability on our part that makes the signs what they are. Causation is clearly different from this, for causes do not depend in any way upon our ability to recognize them. The question is, what makes natural signs, signs? It cannot be, or cannot merely be, something in nature, for something cannot be a sign for us unless we can recognize it, so it must be something in us that makes tears, or laughter, or a particular kind of motion into signs. This something in us must be an acquired or an innate capacity; and Descartes' view is that it is an innate capacity which, it will turn out, God has provided us with. There would be no natural signs unless we had the capacity to recognize them as such.

One question which arises here is whether such innate capacities are part of our corporeal organs or our minds. One only has to note the fact that automata are able to see, that is, perceive light, whereas disembodied minds are not, to recognize that the capacity to grasp various kinds of translational and rotary motion as light must naturally reside in corporeal organs. Descartes never suggests that automata cannot respond to natural signs; indeed, such functions as nutrition in higher animals, where the appropriate kind of food has to be sought out visually or olfactorily, clearly require such recognitional capacities. And if we do not conceive of the capacity to 'decode' natural signs as something built into corporeal organs, then in the case of human beings we will have to make the mind responsible for this. Such a move would be a disaster, for to do this is merely to introduce what can only be called a decoding homunculus (perhaps to replace a more traditional seeing homunculus), and then we have to ask in turn of this homunculus what its decoding capacity derives from, so that we would soon find ourselves in an infinite regress, having to postulate yet another homunculus to explain the decoding ability of the first one, and so on. Descartes' account was indeed interpreted in this way by some of his successors, and it was on the basis of such an interpretation that Malebranche was later led to reject the linguistically-modelled account of perceptual cognition altogether.[155] But the interpretation that I have offered is far simpler and more consonant with what I take to be his overall programme of explaining, rather than explaining away, animal cognition.

In sum, there is an element of reciprocity in perceptual cognition as linguistically modelled which we do not find in the causal-mechanical account. The linguistic model enables us to grasp what perceptual understanding consists in, whereas the causal-mechanical account describes what physical-cum-physiological processes must occur if this understanding is to take place.

This idea of there being two complementary levels of description involved when accounting for perceptual cognition is something that we find in a related context, music, and indeed it may have been in his reflections on music that Descartes came to see that a causal-mechanical story was not sufficient to account for some aspects of cognition. Mersenne had been trying to explain and rank consonances in terms of the overtone series, that is, that series of tones which naturally accompany a sound and determine its timbre.[156] Since these tones seemed to correspond to what many researchers in acoustics, and musicians, took to be a natural ordering of degrees of consonance—the octave, the fifth, the fourth, the major third, minor third, etc.—it seemed that something purely physical could explain sensory-aesthetic differentiations. In the correspondence with Mersenne on music in 1630 and 1631, Descartes not only completely rejects any reduction of music to the sounds making it up, but also rejects any attempt to account for phenomena such as consonance in purely acoustic terms:

As regards the sweetness of consonances we must distinguish two questions: what makes them simpler and more accordant, and what makes them more agreeable to the ear. As far as what makes them more agreeable is concerned, this depends on the places where they are employed; and there are places where even diminished fifths and other dissonances are still more agreeable than consonances, so that it is not possible to say absolutely whether one consonance is more agreeable than another.[157]

The point is reinforced in another letter, when he complains to Mersenne that 'in asking me how much one consonance is more agreeable than another, you annoy me as much as if you were to ask me how much more agreeable I find eating fish than eating fruit'.[158] Descartes is concerned to make a distinction between two kinds of project, one which ranks the intervals in terms of their position in the overtone series, something which has a physical-arithmetical basis, and the other which explains the effect of various intervals in terms of their functional role in a piece of music.[159] In this he is surely right.[160] But the more general point to which I want to draw attention is his general awareness of the need for two different kinds of treatment. There is a level at which we can describe what is involved in understanding a piece of music, and there is a different level at which we can describe the mechanism by which we respond to sounds.

Now understanding language and understanding a piece of music involve the intellect: these are not things that animal automata are capable of. And at this point we must bear in mind that the linguistic modelling of perceptual cognition is just an analogy. For animals are as capable of perceptual cognition as we are, and they do not have intellects. The idea that there are two levels of description appropriate to accounting for perceptual cognition applies to animals as well as humans, and therefore makes no essential reference to the intellect. There are forms of visual understanding—visual recognition, visual discrimination—in which animals engage. These can be characterized in purely causal-mechanical terms, but they can also be characterized in a different way which is appropriate to describing the exercise of higher-order functions. In sum, two features of Descartes' account are worth drawing attention to. First, when he offers an account of what we might call sensory stimulation and perceptual understanding, he is *not* offering an account of two separate processes, but an account of a single act which can be characterized in two ways, in terms of a causal-mechanical process and a significatory process. Secondly, it is because the causal-mechanical process occurs that the significatory process occurs: we cannot treat the latter as if it were independent of the former,[161] but nor can we ignore the fact that being fitted out with the right responsive mechanisms—the right innate capacities—is necessary for the former process to yield the latter. And note that these responsive mechanisms are corporeal: so long as the questions of awareness of one's cognitive processes or judgements on these processes are not raised, we are resolutely at the corporeal level.

In what sense then are automata 'machines'? First, we should not let ourselves be misled by the term 'automaton', which in seventeenth-century usage meant little more that a 'self-moving thing'; Cottingham has reminded us in this context that Leibniz, 'defending his claim that we possess "freedom of spontaneity" speaks of the human soul as a "kind of spiritual automaton", meaning no more than that its action-generating impulses arise solely *ad interno*, and produce effects without the intervention of any external cause'.[162] If my account is correct then, as least as Descartes describes them in *L'Homme*, animal automata are unlike mechanical constructions such as clocks and organs in that they are able to have genuine perceptual cognition, in the form of a grasp of representations of perceptual stimuli, something which requires nothing over and above corporeal organs. What is mechanical about automata is the fact that their functioning can be described wholly in mechanical terms; in particular, no separate mental substance need be invoked, and nothing other than completely inert matter need be invoked. But this does not make them exactly like clocks, any more than the fact that the workings of a clock can be explained in purely corporeal terms makes clocks exactly like the wood and metal from which they are constructed. The addition of degrees of complexity brings with it significant qualitative differences—emergent properties—although, on Descartes' account, no such increase in degree of complexity could ever transform an automaton into a human being.[163] The common assumption that on Descartes' account 'animals have no souls, no thoughts or experiences', as one commentator puts it,[164] is at best misleading, as it suggests that animals are devoid of cognitive states of any kind. Descartes' claim is that their thoughts and experiences are not like ours, not that they do not have any thoughts and experiences at all.[165] The difference is spelled out in a letter to Fromondus in the claim 'that animals do not see as we do when we are aware that we see, but only as we do when our mind is elsewhere'.[166] There are general problems, which are not restricted to Descartes' account, in trying to describe the cognitive and affective states of creatures different from us—we can imagine an animal's mental states as being like a confused or inattentive version of ours[167], yet surely it is unhelpful as a general characterization to picture the behaviour of a dog, say, as being permanently confused or inattentive—and we might be led to believe that little determinate sense can be given to the idea that animals have such states, 'but not like ours'. But for Descartes it is an empirical question whether animals have rational souls, and the cognitive and affective states that go with this. He tells Gassendi that whether we say an animal can think or not is something that can only be settled by *a posteriori* investigation of its behaviour[168]; and to More he writes that 'though I regard it as established that we cannot demonstrate that there is any thought in animals, I do not thereby think it is demonstrated that there is not, since the human mind does not reach into their hearts.'[169] Indeed, I am inclined to agree with the view that Descartes continually confines himself to the negative consideration that we cannot demonstrate the presence of rational souls in animals, that his main positive claim on this question is that the traditional justifications for attributing consciousness to animals were vacuous, and that, as one commentator has put it recently, 'the most accurate way to characterize Descartes' view is to say that he was cautiously agnostic on the whole question.'[170] The important point is that we should not let difficulties (deep difficulties, and ones that will affect any non-eliminativist account of animal cognition) in characterizing the cognitive and affective states of animals lead to us to the conclusion that they cannot have such states. Difficult as they may be to characterize individually, we simply must recognize, on empirical grounds, degrees of cognitive sophistication. Descartes' aim is not to eliminate experience and thought from the animal realm, but to show that they can be accounted for, not merely in purely corporeal terms, but in a way that construes this corporeal substance purely mechanistically.

It is worth noting in this context that even naturalists were not strict eliminativists: the Paduan naturalists, in particular, had not maintained that all features of human thought could be accounted for completely in corporeal terms. Telesio is an interesting case in this respect, because his qualms about the completeness of naturalism were, as far as I can tell, widely shared in the sixteenth and seventeenth centuries. In Telesio's system, 'spirit' does all the ordinary, practically-orientated feeling, perceiving, and reasoning. His account is wholly naturalistic in all epistemological matters, and in everything that concerns natural philosophy. But as regards religious and what might loosely be called psychological issues, here Telesio finds it necessary to introduce the traditional notion of the soul. He argues that people are persistently desiring and seeking things that go beyond their mere preservation and pleasure, that they are always anxiously, restlessly looking for what is far beyond these, for useless knowledge, for God, for eternity. He believes that no naturalistic picture can account for this, much less explain it, and here we must go beyond naturalism. The argument holds *a fortiori* for materialist (that is, in the present case, mechanist) reductions: materialism did not look remotely plausible before the 1860s, when Helmholtz began his pathbreaking work on cognition. There was simply no way of achieving a completely corporeal account of mental functions without either moving in the direction of naturalism or materialism, and neither of these held any attraction for Descartes. Now one might accept the genuineness of the kind of worries that Telesio raises, but argue that it is mistaken to think that they are to be answered by providing the correct kind of account of mind. This seems to me to be the right response, but I doubt whether such an approach would have seemed to the point in an era in which such questions were intimately bound up with the nature of the soul, and the nature of our existence in the afterlife. Moreover, the kinds of things that Telesio thinks people desire differentiate them from animals in a sharp and intuitively appealing way, for animals manifestly do not seek useless knowledge or eternity. And what better way is there to explain this, given that we do not appear to be anatomically or physiologically different from higher animals in any sufficiently significant way, than to envisage something over and above the corporeal faculties that underlies the difference?

One significant difference between Telesio and Descartes, however, is that Telesio's naturalism only breaks down once we go beyond the question of cognition, whereas Descartes thinks that a number of aspects of human cognition which Telesio treats naturalistically must be accounted for by introducing a separate mental substance. Because *Le Monde* breaks off before reaching the third part, on the rational soul, we do not know much about what exactly its role in cognition is, but it is clear from *L'Homme* that it plays a distinctive role in human cognition. The pressing question is whether the rational soul simply takes experiences as given and reflects on them, makes judgements about them, etc.; or whether the fact that one has a rational soul completely transforms one's experiences, so that perceptual judgements, for example, are integrated cognitive acts, not simply reducible or analysable into perceptions plus judgements. Although there is the occasional intimation that the latter is Descartes' view, any answers to these questions must remain speculative in the context of *Le Monde*, because although Descartes tells us in the *Discours* that he had reached the end of his treatise in late 1633 and was beginning to revise it and put it in the hands of a publisher,[171] we do not know whether he had even started on the third part.

The Condemnation of Galileo and the Abandonment of *Le Monde*

At the end of November 1633, Descartes wrote to Mersenne:

I had intended to send you *Le Monde* as a New Year gift . . . but in the meantime I tried to find out in Leiden and Amsterdam whether Galileo's *World System* was available, as I thought I had heard that it was published in Italy last year. I was told that it had indeed been published, but that all copies had been burned at Rome, and that Galileo had been convicted and fined. I was so surprised by this that I nearly decided to burn all my papers, or at least let no one see them. For I couldn't imagine that he—an Italian and, I believe, in favour with the Pope—could have been made a criminal, just because he tried, as he certainly did, to establish that the earth moves.... I must admit that if this view is false, then so too are the entire foundations of my philosophy, for it can be demonstrated from them quite clearly. And it is such an integral part of my treatise that I couldn't remove it without making the whole work defective. But for all that, I wouldn't want to publish a discourse which had a single word that the Church disapproved of; so I prefer to suppress it rather than publish it in a mutilated form.[172]

Galileo's *Dialogue on the Two Chief World Systems* was originally entitled *On the Ebb and Flow of the Sea*, because of the way in which the tides were used to support the Copernican hypothesis. The title was considered too contentious, however, and the Inquisition had required that it be changed, and for a time there looked to be a good chance that other similar compromises could be reached. But a shift in political circumstances resulted in its condemnation in Rome on 23 July 1633.[173] Descartes was certainly correct in thinking that his own account in *Le Monde* had parallels with Galileo's—although he didn't actually see a copy of the *Dialogue* until August 1634[174]—but why was he so concerned about his own case? There is no doubt that he could have published in the Netherlands, where Copernicanism was widely accepted,[175] although in the circumstances this might have given ammunition to anti-Catholic forces there and Descartes would have wanted to avoid that. But he could have published in France, for not only was there was no Inquisition in France, but there was a good deal of sympathy with Galileo. Adam very plausibly suggests that Descartes wanted circulation for *Le Monde*, and he would have been worried that it would have been forbidden in French classrooms; and in any case there would have been little point in publishing something that would have got him into trouble in some circles and would not have furthered the Copernican cause because it would be largely unread. But in fact, Adam points out, Descartes was probably mistaken in this respect, for the response in Paris had been different to that of Rome, and there was some possibility that it would have had a significant circulation.[176] We must remember here that there was considerable dispute at the time as to the wisdom, legitimacy, and standing of the condemnation, and even about its relevance outside Italy.[177] Descartes himself asks Mersenne about the standing of the condemnation:

To the best of my knowledge neither the Pope nor a Council has ratified the condemnation that was made by the Congregation of Cardinals established to censor books. I would be happy to know what view is held in France, and whether their authority was enough to make it an article of faith.[178]

Yet for all his inquiries, Descartes did nothing. It was remarked of Descartes in 1637 that he was a zealous Roman Catholic who feared the displeasure of the Church above all else,[179] and he showed extreme caution in this matter. He almost certainly had more scope for man-oeuvre than he imagined, but wanted nothing to do with public controversy, telling Mersenne that his motto was 'he lives well who is well hidden',[180] and that from that point on he would instruct only himself, not others.

But whether he assessed the situation correctly or incorrectly, the fact remains that he was clearly devastated by the condemnation. The outcome of this crisis is a new direction in his work. Although we have seen that he took some interest in metaphysics, Descartes had primarily pursued natural philosophy up to this point. Galileo's principal weapons in the establishment of Copernicanism had been the theory of the tides, the movement of sunspots, and a doctrine of inertia in which motions in which one shares (such as the Earth's orbital and diurnal motions) were undetectable. These natural philosophical arguments were under-mined by the 1633 condemnation not because they were thought to be inadequate but because they were thought to be inappropriate: mere natural philosophy could no longer be used to establish Copernicanism. Descartes rises to the challenge. His creative period in natural philo-sophy comes to an end, and a creative period in legitimatory metaphysics begins. He certainly does not abandon interest in natural philosophy, and to the end of his life continues to think it has been his most im-portant contribution,[181] but his interest in it is now confined largely to polemics and systematization. His central concerns lie elsewhere, as he begins to follow up the question of the legitimation of knowledge in a new and radical way.

8
The Years of Consolidation
1634–1640

In December 1633 Descartes returned to Amsterdam, and he remained there until the Spring of 1635. He lodged with the family of a Thomas Sargeant, who was ten years Descartes' senior, and a master in the French school at Amsterdam.[1] Early in 1635, Descartes got to know Constantijn Huygens properly (they had first met in 1632). Huygens, who was an exact contemporary of Descartes, came from a family of diplomats and was secretary to Frederick Henry, Prince of Orange, and was to be a powerful and enthusiastic supporter of Descartes. An important correspondence developed out of this friendship, ranging from questions in optics (Huygens had a keen interest in scientific questions) to personal matters: indeed, the letter of condolence to Huygens on the death of his wife, if a little baroque by modern standards, is a moving testimony to their friendship,[2] and Descartes reserved his most personal correspondence for Huygens, who acted as a kind of confessor to him. Descartes was also to show an interest in the education of his son Christiaan in the 1640s, and Christiaan was to become one of the most brilliant mathematicians and physicists of the seventeenth century, pursuing a mechanistically conceived programme of kinematics of the kind that came to be associated with Cartesianism in the mid-seventeenth century. Descartes also took a pedagogical interest in his manservant, Jean Gillot, teaching him mathematics: indeed, he subsequently became an able mathematician and director of the school of engineering at Leiden.[3] We know a little of the social circles in which he moved from a report of Samuel Hartlib, who mentions that Descartes spent some time during the winter of 1634/5 at the house of Elizabeth Stuart, Electress Palatine, Queen of Bohemia.[4] Elizabeth was the wife of Frederick V, whose forces had been routed at the Battle of the White Mountain. Frederick and his family (comprising nine surviving children by 1630) went into exile in the Hague, stripped of his lands and of much of his income. When he died in 1632, his family remained in the Netherlands, beset by severe financial problems, despite the fact that his mother and his uncles provided them with a winter house in the Hague and a summer house near Arnhem, as well as some income.

Elizabeth, who was born in the same year as Descartes, was daughter of James I of England and Anne of Denmark (she was second in succession to the English throne at the time of her marriage to Frederick), and was an intelligent and cultured woman who became a symbol of the Protestant cause in Europe. Whether Descartes had regular contact with the family is impossible to say, and his later close friendship with Elizabeth's daughter, Princess Elizabeth of Bohemia, seems to be quite independent of this early acquaintance with the family, and should not be taken to suggest that he kept up relations with them.

Despite having abandoned *Le Monde* and written that he would thereafter teach only himself and not others, Descartes evidently decided to present some of his work—notably the *Dioptrique*, which was probably complete in draft by this time, and the *Météors*, also probably complete in draft—quite early on, and devoted some time in 1634–5 reworking these for publication. His *Anatomica* indicates that he also continued to work in anatomy, and his correspondence throughout the 1630s touches on anatomical, physiological, and medical matters. At this time, we find the first hard evidence of an interest in scepticism, and this will flower into a striking and novel formulation of the problems of epistemology over the next couple of years.

But let us begin with an event of a more personal nature. During his time at Thomas Sargeant's house, Descartes engaged in what Vrooman has aptly described as 'the only relationship in his life where by his own admission the sexual act played a significant role'.[5] He records the conception of his daughter by the serving maid at the house on Sunday 15 October.[6] We know the Christian name of the maid, Hélène, and the name of her father, Jans, from the certificate of baptism of the child dated 7 August 1635, but little else about her. She corresponded with Descartes (although no letters are extant) so she could presumably write,[7] and the fact that the child, Francine, was baptized in a Protestant church indicates that she herself was a Protestant. The encounter may have been unique, and it did not continue: Descartes will tell Clerselier in 1644 that it is ten years since he had been rescued by God from his 'dangerous relationship' with her and that, by God's grace, he had not fallen back into temptation.[8] He acknowledged paternity of Francine, as is clear from the baptismal records, but we do not know whether he was present at the baptism. Except for the admission to Clerselier, so far as we know he never revealed his relationship with Hélène to his friends, and the only time he refers to Francine he calls her his 'niece'.[9] It is possible, however, that he made arrangements for some kind of support for Hélène and Francine, possibly arranging for Hélène to stay in Deventer during her confinement, although his commitment—what commitment there was—was to Francine rather than to Hélène herself, who continued to work as a domestic servant. The unknown addressee of the letter of August 1637 clearly knows Hélène, and may have been Descartes' friend Cornelius van Hogelande, a Catholic physician who lived in Leiden near to Hélène.[10] Descartes entrusted his personal papers to Hogelande when he left for Sweden in 1649, and it is just possible that he may have entrusted the welfare of Hélène and Francine to him in this period. Although there is no evidence that he saw them for a couple of years after Francine's birth, he does seem happy in the letter of August 1637 at the prospect of Francine coming to stay with him. Nevertheless, neither Hélène nor Francine play any discernible role in Descartes' life before 1637, and it is hard to believe that this is simply the result of the secrecy surrounding his relationship with them.

From around 1635, Reneri was beginning to teach 'Cartesian' natural philosophy, and when he took up the chair of philosophy at the newly founded University of Utrecht in 1636, he was quickly able to build up a keen Cartesian following among the students.[11] This may have put some pressure on Descartes to set out his views in a form that would cause no offence to the Church, and in the first instance this took the form of a revision of the *Météors* and the *Dioptrique*. As I have indicated, a good deal of time in 1634 and 1635 was probably devoted to reworking the *Météors* and the *Dioptrique*. We can deal with these treatises briefly here, focusing on the structure of the finished products since we have already looked at most of the material they contain, principally in the discussion of *Le Monde*.

Of the three essays that will eventually accompany the *Discours* in 1637, the *Météors* is the most straightforward, the most conventional, and the one most suited for adoption as a textbook, which was clearly Descartes' intention. Meteorology had traditionally dealt with the sublunary realm and, following Aristotle, it had been divided into four areas, depending on which of the four elements was principally at issue. Many meteorological phenomena had traditionally been regarded as inexplicable, or had been explained in supernatural terms, and the area was a good one for mechanism to show its mettle.[12] Moreover, unlike astronomy and cosmology, it was an area where there was little religious or ideological resistance to new accounts.

The first move that Descartes makes is to undermine the doctrine of the four elements by carrying out a micro-corpuscularian reduction. Using his own three sizes of corpuscles, he then proceeds to account for meteorological phenomena exclusively in terms of these. But whereas his treatment of light depends on spherical corpuscles whose behaviour is described in terms of the laws of motion, most of his account here harks back to a much more qualitative, traditional form of atomism, in which intuitive and qualitatively conceived surface features of the corpuscles play the major explanatory role. So, for example, the shape of parts is invoked to explain fluidity and adhesion: water is made up of parts that are long and smooth, and because of this they never hook together, thus 'explaining' why water flows; other bodies have parts that are of very irregular shape and they become very closely intertwined like the branches of a tree, bodies such as earth and wood being formed; and finally air and very light fluids such as oils are formed when corpuscles simply lie on top of one another in layers.[13] The flexibility or rigidity of the parts is invoked to explain various other properties: rigid and unbending parts form various species of salt, whereas spirits which never freeze are made up of parts that are so subtle that they can easily be bent by the first element.[14] This is much more typical of the qualitative picture-building that we find in mechanists like Gassendi and Hobbes, rather than the genuinely quantitative and experimental approach that Descartes has shown he can provide in his account of light; but such picture-building, for all its lack of precision and empirical backing, does meet a genuine need. It provides us with some idea of what an alternative to an Aristotelian account would look like. Heat, for example, is to be explained in terms of the agitatory motion of parts,[15] light by translational agitation, and various processes such as freezing and evaporation by imagining rearrangements in the micro-structure of matter. And if the hypothetical details fall by the wayside in trying to fill out this alternative in more precise, empirical terms, then at least we have a picture to guide us. While Descartes does little more than set out such a picture for us in the bulk of the discourses of the *Météors*—in his accounts of vapours (Discourse 2), salts (Discourse 3), winds (Discourse 4), clouds (Discourse 5), snow, rain, and hail (Discourse 6), thunder and lightening (Discourse 7)—in the last three discourses, on the rainbow, coronas, and parhelia, he presents an account which, as we have seen, is both quantitative and experimental, and indeed was, for all its faults, the best available model of how to do quantitative mechanist natural philosophy.

The *Dioptrique* is above all a practical treatise, designed to show how optical instruments are to be constructed on the basis of a reasonably comprehensive geometrical optics. Descartes summarizes his programme as follows:

Since the construction of the things of which I shall speak must depend on the skill of the craftsman, who is usually uneducated, I shall try to make myself intelligible to everyone; and I shall try not to omit anything, or assume anything, that requires knowledge of the other sciences. This is why I shall begin by explaining light and light rays; then, having briefly described the parts of the eye, I shall give a detailed account of how vision occurs; and after noting all the things that can improve vision, I shall show how they can be aided by the inventions that I describe.[16]

Although general questions about light are raised in the *Dioptrique*, physical optics is only touched on in passing, and the cosmology to which it is so closely tied in *Le Monde* is completely absent.

In the first Discourse, a micro-corpuscular model of light is proposed and its transmission is described in terms of Descartes' favourite analogy of a blind man feeling his way around by means of a stick; and in filling out more precisely how light is transmitted he uses the analogy of wine in a vat, showing how the 'action' or tendency to motion of light can be accounted for in these terms. The basis for colours is set out in a concise way: we see black when the surface of a body completely destroys the light ray, white when the ray is reflected without any alteration, and the colours proper are formed when the ray is otherwise altered on being reflected off the surface, although details of how this happens are reserved for the *Météors*. The next Discourse sets out Descartes' account of refraction in some detail, building the geometrical optics on the basis of a physical account of what happens to the light ray as it passes from one optical medium to another. The tennis-ball analogy plays a key role here, and Descartes argues that the bending of the light ray results from the unequal speed of light in the two media, just as the tennis ball is deflected when it is slowed down as a result of breaking through the canvas surface. The theory that light travels faster in denser media, which Descartes probably took over from Kepler, is explained in terms of the texture of rarer bodies hindering the ray because the interstitial matter that is more extensive in rarer bodies is less responsive to the action of light. Much depends here on the ease of picturing the processes Descartes describes, and he trades a good deal on our intuitions in this respect. This much was the stock-in-trade of mechanism at this time. But Descartes has another string in his bow. He makes his account of the sine law of refraction appear to follow on from his account of the physical nature of light. And it is from the fact that he makes his intuitively appealing picture yield a secure and invaluable law in geometrical optics that the overall plausibility of his account derives, and he will not abandon it, even under serious pressure from Fermat and others, as we shall see later.

The next four Discourses—3 to 6—deal with vision, passing from ocular anatomy to the formation of the retinal image, and the mechanics of distance vision. Considerable attention is devoted to the inadequacies of the resemblance theory of perception, but although a representational theory of perceptual cognition is set out, we get no detail of what this cognition actually consists in, as we did in the first chapter of *Le Monde*, for example. Discourse 7, on the 'improvement of vision', is a transitory chapter, linking the account of vision with his account of optical instruments in the last three discourses, an account which is the avowed aim of the treatise. Vision depends, we are told in Discourse 7, 'on the objects, on the internal organs that receive the impulses of these objects, and the external organs that dispose these impulses to be received in the appropriate way'.[17] The first is easily corrected, by changing the distance of the object or its illumination, for example, and the second cannot be corrected since it is not possible to make new organs, although Descartes acknowledges that physicians may be able to help in some cases. This leaves us with the case of the external sense organ, and Descartes gives an account of the transparent parts of the eye and the appliances that can be interposed between the eye and the object. Vision is optimal under four conditions: (1) the rays travelling towards the extremities of the optic nerve should all come, as far as is possible, from a single part of the object, otherwise the image will not be distinct and will not resemble the object; (2) the image formed on the retina should be as large as possible; (3) the rays which produce this image must be strong enough to excite the fine threads of the optic nerve, but not so strong as to injure them; (4) it should be possible to form images of as many objects as possible so that we might see as much as possible at the same time.[18] The first condition is met in the normal eye, but it frequently happens that either the shape of the eye is problematic, or the ability to adjust the curvature of the lens is impaired, and he shows how concave and convex lenses can correct such problems to a limited extent. After discussing various impractical ways of dealing with the second problem, Descartes shows how it can be met by what is in effect a telescope, and in dealing with the third condition various properties of, and ways of improving, the telescope are discussed. Finally, he points out that the fourth condition cannot be realized by any optical means.

Discourse 8 deals with the shapes to which transparent material must be cut to improve vision. Showing that spherical lenses will not bring all divergent rays to converge at a single focus, Descartes investigates which curves do have this property, and which species of such curves have shapes which make it possible for them to be cut. He demonstrates that ellipses and hyperbolas have the requisite properties, he sets out the geometry of these curves and gives details of how they are to be cut, concluding that hyperbolic lenses are, in the final analysis, preferable to elliptical lenses for precision optics. The ninth Discourse then looks in more practical detail at the properties of lenses suitable for telescopes and microscopes, dealing with such questions as the shapes of the eyepiece and the object lenses, and the materials of which they should be made. Finally, in the tenth Discourse, following the details set out earlier in his 1629 letters to Ferrier, which we have already looked at, he specifies the procedure by which hyperbolas are to be drawn, and sets out how hyperbolic lenses are to be ground.

The *Météors* and the *Dioptrique* together give a fairly good account of Descartes' work up to this time, with the exception of his work in cosmology, geometry and algebra, and metaphysics. We have already looked at his reasons for not publishing the first, and we shall consider the question of metaphysics below. He planned to supplement the *Météors* and the *Dioptrique* with an account of his algebra and geometry, but left it until the last minute—the spring of 1636, while the *Météors* was being printed[19]—and then seems to have cobbled it together from various earlier writings. The reason for this, I believe, is that while he was keen to put on record his achievements in this area, he no longer had much active research interest in it, and given the intrinsic difficulty of the material, it would have been a considerable effort to master it again and set it out afresh. He may well have known that Fermat had grasped the fundamental principles of analytical geometry by the mid-1630s. Descartes was antagonistic towards Fermat and refused to recognize his achievements. It is possible that this was because he associated him with his mentor, Beaugrand, towards whom Descartes had good reason to be antagonistic, as we shall see below. But he may also have feared that Fermat would beat him into print, and take credit for something in an area in which Descartes believed he had nothing to learn from anybody.[20]

Although it was composed after the *Discours*, the *Géométrie* marks the end of an earlier project, and is best considered along with the other *Essais*. We have already looked at a number of the questions that it deals with, and we can restrict our attention here to its general design. It comprises three Books, the first dealing with 'problems that can be constructed using only circles and straight lines', the second dealing with 'the nature of curves', and the third with the construction of 'solid and supersolid problems'. From its title, which indicates that it concerns only those problems which utilize straight lines and curves in their construction, one might expect the first Book to contain the traditional material, and the others to contain the new material. After all, Euclid had given a reasonably exhaustive account of problems which can be constructed using only straight lines and a circle. But in fact the purpose of Book I is, above anything else, to present a new algebraic means of solving geometrical problems by making use of

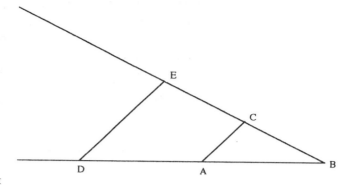

Fig. 8.1

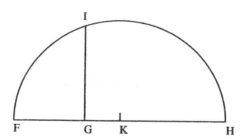

Fig. 8.2

arithmetical procedures and vice versa. In other words, the aim is to show how, if we think of them in algebraic terms, we can combine the resources of the two fields.

Book I opens with a direct comparison between arithmetic and geometry.[21] Just as in arithmetic the operations we use are addition, subtraction, multiplication, division and finding roots, so too in geometry we can reduce any problem to one which requires nothing more than a knowledge of the lengths of straight lines, and in this form the problem can be solved using nothing more than the five arithmetical operations. Descartes therefore introduces arithmetical terms directly into geometry. Multiplication, for example, is an operation which can be performed using only straight lines (see Fig. 8.1). If the task is to multiply BD by BC, we let AB be taken as the unit and join the points A and C, drawing DE parallel to CA. BE is then the product.[22] If we wish to find a square root, on the other hand, we require straight lines and circles (see Fig. 8.2). In order to find the square root of GH, for example, we must 'add, along the straight line, FG equal to one unit; then, dividing FH into two equal parts at K, I describe the circle FIH about K as a centre, and draw from the point G a straight line at right angles to G extended to I, and GI is the required root'.[23]

Descartes next points out that we do not actually need to draw the lines, but can designate them by letters. He instructs us to label all lines in this way, those whose length we seek to determine as well as those whose length is known, and then, proceeding as if we had already solved the problem, we combine the lines so that every quantity can be expressed in two ways. This constitutes an equation, and the object is to find such an equation for every unknown line. In cases where this is not possible, we choose lines of known length arbitrarily for each unknown line for which we have no equation, and:

if there are several equations, we must use each in order, either considering it alone or comparing it with the others, so as to obtain a value for each of the unknown lines; and we must combine them until there remains a single unknown line which is equal to some known line, whose square, cube, fourth, fifth or sixth power etc. is equal to the sum or difference of two or more quantities, one of which is known, while the other consists of mean proportionals between the unit and this square, or cube, or fourth power etc., multiplied by other known lines. I may express this as follows:

$$z = b$$
or
$$z^2 = -az + b^2$$
or
$$z^3 = az^2 + b^2z - c^3$$
or
$$z^4 = az^2 - c^3z + d^4, \text{ etc.}$$

That is, z, which I take for the unknown quantity, is equal to b; or the square of z is equal to the square of b minus a multiplied by z ... Thus all the unknown quantities can be expressed in terms of a single quantity, whenever the problem can be constructed by means of circles and straight lines, or by conic sections, or by a curve only one or two degrees greater.[24]

This is a novel approach to the question. Algebraic equations in two unknowns, $F(x,y) = 0$, were traditionally considered indeterminate since the two unknowns could not be determined from such an equation. All one could do was to substitute arbitrarily chosen values for x and then solve the equation for y for each of these values, something that was not considered to be in any way a general solution of the equation. But Descartes' approach allows this procedure to be transformed into a general solution. What he effectively does is to take x as the abscissa of a point and the corresponding y as its ordinate, and then one can vary the unknown x so that to every value of x there corresponds a value of y which can be computed from the equation. We thereby end up with a set of points which form a completely determined curve satisfying the equation. This procedure is exemplified in Descartes' resolution of Pappus' locus problem for four or more lines, the key problem of the *Géométrie*, which is now set out along the lines we have already examined.

In Book II of the *Géométrie*, Descartes extends his treatment of the Pappus loci for three or four lines by distinguishing the curves corresponding to equations of the second degree, namely the ellipse, hyperbola, and parabola. This treatment is fairly exhaustive, but he considers very few cases corresponding to cubics, maintaining (somewhat optimistically as it turns out) that his method shows how these are to be dealt with. Going beyond his treatment of the Pappus problem, he tells us that properties of curves depend only on the angles which these make with other lines (that is, on their equations).[25] When we are able to capture the relation between all the points on a curve and all the points on a straight line in the form of an equation we can easily discover the relation between points on the curve and all other given lines and points, and from these relations we can find the diameters, axes, centres, and other lines and points to which each curve will have some relation. The aim is then to choose and describe those relations which are simpler and more specific than it has to others, such as those expressed by equations of its tangents, normals, and so on. More generally, any property a curve has depends solely on the angle it makes with other lines: this is what makes coordinate geometry possible. Now the key thing, as Scott notes in his detailed commentary on Book II, is that 'the angle formed by two intersecting curves is no more difficult to measure than the angle between two straight lines, provided that a straight line can be drawn making a right angle with each of these at the point where it is cut by the other. Therefore, if we can discover a method of drawing a straight line at right angles to a curve at any arbitrarily chosen point upon it, we have accomplished all that is required in order to begin the study of the properties of curves'.[26] This is precisely what Descartes now does, demonstrating a method for finding normals to curves, which he describes as 'not only the most useful and most general problem in geometry that I know, but even that I have ever desired to know'.[27] The procedure enables us to find the normal to an algebraic curve at a fixed point P on the curve by taking a second variable point Q (see Fig. 8.3)[28], and then finding the equation of the circle which has its centre on the coordinate axis AG and passes through P and Q. Then, by setting the discriminant of the equation that determines the intersections of the circle with the curve equal to zero, the centre of the circle where Q coincides with P can be found. And once we have this centre, finding the tangent and the normal to the curve is straightforward. Descartes shows the mettle of this procedure by applying it to the ellipse, and maintains that it can be applied 'to every curve to which the methods of geometry are applicable'. With this powerful, if complex and somewhat clumsy, procedure behind him, he turns to a difficult class of curves, the ovals,

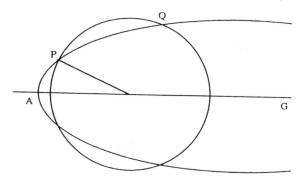

Fig. 8.3

which he views as a natural extension of ellipses and hyperbolas, and he uses what is sometimes called the 'inverse method of tangents' in dealing with them; that is, rather than moving from the curve to its tangent, which he has just set out a procedure for, he moves from the tangent to the curve. The rationale for his detailed treatment of ovals is not geometrical, however, but optical. He is concerned to provide a general geometrical treatment of anaclastic curves, indicating that much of Book II is motivated by considerations in optics. Indeed, his discussion of these is somewhat out of keeping with his treatment of topics in the rest of the *Géométrie*, for he provides no equations for his optical ovals, generating them all by pointwise constructions.

In Book III, solid and supersolid problems are examined, and Descartes sets out a number of important findings in the theory of equations—more specifically, he shows us how to discover rational roots, how to depress the degree of an equation when a root is known, how to increase or decrease the roots of an equation by any amount, how to determine the number of positive and negative roots, how to find the algebraic solution of cubic and quartic equations—as well as providing a notation which was far superior to that used to date. The former marks an important advance beyond the Alexandrian mathematicians, who only recognized constructions making use of curves other than straight lines and circles with reluctance, and the category of solid problems was never systematically thought through. Here Descartes extends his algebraic analysis far beyond the concerns of mathematicians of antiquity. The most striking feature of his approach is that, in order to preserve the generality of his structural analysis of the equation, he is prepared to allow not only negative but also imaginary roots, despite the otherwise completely counter-intuitive nature of these. Here we find a remarkable demonstration of Descartes' ability to abstract from particular numbers and shapes, as he had put it in the *Regulae*, and go straight to the mathematical core of the problem, which hinges on structural considerations brought to light in his algebraic notation. As regards concrete results, however, Descartes was far too optimistic in thinking that his procedures were capable of solving equations of any degree, and by the 1670s doubts had begun to be raised as to whether equations of the fifth degree and higher could be construed in terms of compound proportions at all.[29]

An Exercise in Autobiography, 1635–1636

The 'preface' to the three *Essais*—the *Discours*—provides us with a glimpse of the new metaphysical system that Descartes was constructing. Now it is likely that his interest in metaphysics was given a new urgency with the condemnation of Galileo. The condemnation raised the question of how natural philosophy was to be legitimated, and in particular how it could be raised above the level of the hypothetical. The need for metaphysical foundations was more urgent than ever, and Descartes now begins to pursue his metaphysics both directly, and by means of consideration of the epistemological questions raised by scepticism. The first mention of an interest in scepticism on Descartes' part occurs in a report by Samuel Hartlib on the meeting at Elizabeth's house in the Hague in the winter of 1634/5. Present at the meeting was the Scottish pastor and reformer John Dury, who offered a version of the millenarian response to scepticism by appeal to biblical prophecies, an approach which was evidently very common at this time.[30] It seems that Descartes challenged Dury, 'complaining of the uncertainties of all things' as Hartlib puts it. Just how general the discussion was we do not know, yet around this time, Descartes had almost certainly begun to think of the strategy that he was to employ in the *Discours*, of using a radical form of scepticism to clear the ground for a metaphysical legitimation of his natural philosophy.

In the spring of 1635 Descartes moved to Utrecht to join Reneri, who, as we have seen, was beginning his attempt to build up a following for Cartesianism, and Descartes evidently joined him in Utrecht to instruct him in his natural philosophy. In the period from late 1634 until his arrival in Utrecht, Descartes seems to have engaged in very little correspondence. This may have been due to his work on the *Météors* and the *Dioptrique*, or because of difficulties arising from the fact of Hélène's pregnancy. But on arriving in Utrecht, Descartes becomes an active correspondent again, and it is at this time that he worked on the *Discours*. The composition of the *Discours* is a vexed issue, and there can be no doubt that Descartes put it together from material written at different times. This is does not necessarily mean that the material was unrevised, however, and work on the final draft seems to have started in the winter of 1635–6. Since the *Discours* was designed for publication, initially as a prefatory essay to the *Météors* and the *Dioptrique*, the situation is quite different from that of the *Regulae*, which was never designed for publication, with the result that materials composed at different times are simply attached to one another without any regard for overall coherence. Nevertheless, some commentators have argued that the *Discours* is a composite work, and two kinds of evidence have been presented, one focusing on the apparent inconsistency between the criticisms of Stoicism in Part I and the advocacy of a kind of Stoicism in Part III, and the other on the apparently arbitrary way in which the six parts of the *Discours* are organized.[31] But as Curley has shown recently, neither of these points is convincing,[32] the first because it is far from clear that the comments in Part I about 'ancient pagans who deal with morals' are directed against the Stoics, in which case the alleged inconsistency between Parts I and III disappears, and the second because there is a natural way to make sense of the structure.

It is true that, at first glance, the organization of the material in the *Discours* does seems arbitrary and somewhat illogical. Part I and the first half of Part II are autobiographical. Then in the rest of Part II a rather abrupt transition is made to the question of method, which finishes, no less abruptly, with Part III launching immediately into morals. Part IV has no apparent substantive connection with this discussion, for it covers metaphysics. Part V provides a summary of *Le Monde* and *L'Homme*, while Part VI is an introduction to the *Météors* and the *Dioptrique*. And the content does indeed look somewhat arbitrary, for morals and metaphysics are not touched on in the essays to which the *Discours* is an introduction, so why include them? Curley proposes that we make sense of the content and organization of the *Discours* in autobiographical terms, arguing that it is not just the explicitly autobiographical sections but the whole of the *Discours* that is intended as an autobiography. I do not doubt that this is a better way to account for peculiarities in the structure and content of the text. We do not have to follow the chronological details that Descartes provides, as we have already seen that these details are often questionable, involving a degree of rational reconstruction on his part. But in as much as the *Discours* presents us with a picture of what Descartes thinks is important and significant in his life up to this point, it is of course of great interest.

The first question we must ask is why Descartes should have chosen to write an autobiographical introduction to his essays. The reason he gives is that, rather than teach others 'how to direct their reason', which he considers presumptuous, he will instead reveal how he has directed his own, so that others may imitate what they think worthwhile.[33] But this hardly requires the full autobiography that he provides. We have seen that he had promised a 'history of my life' to Balzac and other friends as early as 1628, and the fact that it was promised to friends suggests that it is not simply the basic facts of his life that were wanted, since they would presumably have known those. Autobiography is seen as a moral tale, as it had been seen, albeit in different ways, by Augustine in the *Confessiones*, by Cardano in his *De vita propria liber*, and by Montaigne in his *Essais*. It functions as a didactic genre in which lessons are implicitly contained in the story that is set out. But it is also a public exercise in self-knowledge, which for Descartes is a prerequisite both for knowledge more generally and for instruction of others, something closely connected with the idea, which we have already looked at, that self-conviction must precede any attempt to convince others. Because of this, we should not expect an account of the intimate details of Descartes' life so much as a stylized reconstruction. Indeed, Descartes himself characterizes his autobiographical material in the *Discours* as a story (*histoire*) or fable (*fable*) which contains some examples worthy of imitation.[34]

Part I, which covers his life up to 1619, when he joined the army of Maximilian, presents a picture of someone who has received the best education available, but who nevertheless finds it necessary to travel and observe, and must rely wholly on his own resources (Beeckman is not even mentioned), in order to free himself 'from the many errors that obscure the natural light of reason' so that, 'after I had spent some years pursuing these studies in the book of the world and trying to gain experience, I resolved one day to undertake studies within myself too and to use all the powers of my mind in choosing the paths I should follow'.[35] At this point we come to Part II, which contains his discovery of a 'method' as set out in the (early) *Regulae*, where he gives his famous account of being shut up in a stove-heated room, 'with no cares of passions to divert me', where he was 'completely free to converse with myself about my own thoughts'.[36] The project remains an essentially personal one however for, he tells us, 'my aim has never gone beyond the reform of my own thoughts, and to construct them on a foundation which is all my own', and he advises that few if any should take it upon themselves to imitate him in this respect, for it can lead to precipitate judgements.[37] The four rules of method that he sets out recapitulate those of the *Regulae*, and they are (1) to accept nothing that is not evidently true, (2) to divide the difficulty into as many parts as are needed, (3) to start with the simplest problems, and (4) to be so comprehensive as to leave nothing out.

Until one has rebuilt knowledge on this basis, however, a provisional code has to be followed, introduced at the beginning of Part III as follows:

Before starting to rebuild your house, it is not simply enough to pull it down, to make provision for materials and architects . . . ; you must also provide yourself with some other place where you can live comfortably while building is in progress. Likewise, lest I should remain indecisive in my actions while reason obliged me to be so in my judgements, and in order to live as happily as I could during this time, I formed for myself a provisional moral code consisting of just three or four maxims.[38]

In conversation with Burman, Descartes explains that he included a 'provisional morality' out of caution: since he was recommending a method that called everything into doubt, he had to protect himself against the charge that he was subverting conventional morality.[39] This is certainly plausible, and it is supported by the maxims of his provisional morality. The first of these is 'to obey the laws and customs of my country, holding constantly to the religion in which by God's grace I had been instructed from my childhood, and governing myself in all other matters according to the most moderate and least extreme opinions'.[40] As we saw in chapter 5, this is a classic statement of 'public morality' of the kind we find in French seventeenth-century libertinage, and it is more like an oath of allegiance than something with any private moral import or relevance in libertine culture. And in fact it simply rephrases Balzac's statement, in his *Dissertationes Chrestiennes et Morales*, Dissertation V (dedicated to Descartes), that 'I do not want to believe anything to be more true than what I have learned from my mother and my wet nurse'.[41] The second maxim is 'to be as firm and resolute in my actions as I could and to follow even the most doubtful opinions, once I had adopted them, with no less constancy than if they had been quite certain'. Combined with the first maxim, this prescribes a rigid adherence to social and moral conventions. The third maxim— 'to change my desires rather than the order of the world'—reinforces this. The fourth is less a maxim than an autobiographical aside. Descartes tells us that he 'decided to review the various occupations of men in this life, so as to try and choose the best . . . [and] I thought I could do no better than to continue in that in which I was engaged, and to devote my life to cultivating my reason'.[42]

A question that naturally arises here is the sense in which this is a 'provisional' morality: in particular, what form would a non-provisional morality take? Is Descartes suggesting that there is an 'absolute morality' for which his 'method', or the metaphysical system that he is about to construct, would provide the foundations? In Part VI, he talks about governing his conduct by principles learned from his method,[43] and he offers a strongly naturalistic account of human behaviour, telling us that 'even the mind depends so much on the temperament and the disposition of the bodily organs that if it is possible to find some means of making men in general wiser and more skilful than they have been up to now, I believe we must look for it in medicine'.[44] Would making men wiser make them correspondingly more moral? The term 'sagesse' (wisdom) had distinct moral connotations in writers like Charron, and consequently it is possible that Descartes is advocating some scientific basis for understanding morality.[45] If he is, this is hard to reconcile with his statement to Burman, where something much more pragmatic is suggested. Moreover, there is no trace of a new 'absolute morality' in Descartes' subsequent account of areas like moral psychology, where one might expect to find the consequences of morality being rebuilt on substantive foundations. It might be answered to both these objections that Descartes later changed his mind, abandoning the earlier medical model of morality, and that he not only provided quite a different account of moral psychology in his later writings, but also reinterpreted his earlier remarks on morality. But naturalistic as Descartes' approach is in Part VI of the *Discours*, I cannot find any evidence in the *Discours* that the provisional morality was 'to serve as a support for the attempt to integrate ethics into physical science', as one commentator has put it.[46] It seems more likely that what is at issue here is something quite different: the Church's attitude to Copernicanism. After all, the moral question at issue in the statement of a provisional morality is that of obedience. The provisional morality would then simply be the public commitment to social and religious mores and teachings, something to be abandoned when the truth of the matter can be established beyond question. Remember that Descartes' discussion takes place in the wake of his abandonment of *Le Monde*. This is a case where the question arose in a very striking way of whether one should follow one's own lights or follow the authorities, and the provisional morality in question is one that one follows until one has an indubitable demonstration of the truth of Copernicanism. This is in line with his later comment to Burman and with the context of his discussion.

Part III deals with the doctrines of the early *Regulae*, and Part V provides a summary of *Le Monde* and *L'Homme*, Part VI providing an introduction to the *Essais* that follow. Given this chronological sequence, we might expect Part IV to deal with the doctrines of the later *Regulae*, and perhaps the treatise on metaphysics. But in fact it offers a metaphysical doctrine which is completely different from anything to be found in the *Regulae*, and which I believe even postdates *Le Monde*, and therefore the treatise on metaphysics. It offers an account of cognition which is not only quite different from that of the later *Regulae*, but from that we find in chapter 1 of *Le Monde* also. Up to this point, Descartes has offered a naturalistic account of human cognition, supplemented by a linguistic model designed to help us understand what cognitive grasp consists in, to which is appended a promissory note about the contribution of the intellect. He now approaches the whole question in a completely different way. The new approach is not incompatible with the physiological details of the naturalistic account, but it shifts the focus of his account in an altogether different direction. The linguistic model, which constructs our cognitive relation with the world semantically, is never mentioned again, and this relation now becomes remodelled epistemologically. What Descartes seems to have done is to rewrite his views on cognition of the late 1620s and early 1630s in terms of a new account, which he presents in Part IV for the first time.

Scepticism and the Foundations of a New Metaphysics

In the short introductory remarks to the *Discours*, Descartes tells us that in Part IV the author sets out 'the arguments by which he proves the existence of God and the human soul, which are the foundations of his metaphysics'.[47] His argument to establish his foundations proceeds via hyperbolic doubt, to the realization that even doubting presupposes his own thinking, to an investigation of what this thinking thing is, namely an immaterial soul, and finally to an investigation of what is required for this thinking thing to exist, namely God. The doctrine of clear and distinct ideas plays a key role here, because the one thing that Descartes can find in his own cognitive experience to stand up against hyperbolic doubt is the *cogito ergo sum*—'I think therefore I exist'—and this thereby becomes the paradigmatic form of cognitive grasp, the model for all clear and distinct ideas. And applying this model to the contents of his thoughts, he discovers that he has a clear and distinct idea of something that has every perfection, God, whose own existence is not contingent and who is the source of the existence of everything else.

Of the stages in this argument, the first two—hyperbolic doubt and the *cogito*—have attracted the greatest attention. The general strategy behind them is clear. Descartes begins by showing that, provided one's doubt is sufficiently radical, there is nothing that cannot be doubted, except that one is doubting, and this requires that there be something which exists that is doing the doubting:

Since I wished to devote myself solely to the search for truth, I thought it necessary to . . . reject as if absolutely false everything in which I could imagine the least doubt, in order to see if I remained believing anything that was entirely indubitable. Thus, because our senses sometimes deceive us, I decided to suppose that nothing was such as they led us to imagine. And since there are men who make errors in reasoning, committing paralogisms in the simplest geometrical questions, and because I judged that I was as prone to error as anyone else, I rejected as false all the arguments that I had previously taken to be demonstrations. Lastly, considering that the very thoughts we have had while awake may also occur while we are sleeping without any of them being at that time true, I resolved to pretend that all the things that had ever entered my mind were no more true than the illusions of my dreams. But then I immediately noticed that while I was trying thus to think everything false, it was necessary that I, who was thinking this, was something. And observing that the truth 'I am thinking, therefore I exist' was so firm and sure that all the most extravagant suppositions of the sceptics were incapable of shaking it, I decided that I could accept it without scruple as the first principle of the philosophy I was seeking.[48]

In the *Meditationes*, Descartes will return to this argument and present it in a more elaborate form, and I shall postpone discussion of some of the detail until we come to the more elaborate version. For the moment, I want to concentrate on the radicalism of Descartes' doubt. It is radical both in comparison with his own thought up to this time, and in comparison with anything we find in his predecessors or contemporaries. The claim that no inspection of the perceptual images that we have will show whether they are the product of a dreaming or a waking state completely undermines his own earlier doctrine of clear and distinct ideas, where such an inspection is supposed to reveal something about the evidential value of the ideas. And none of his contemporaries or predecessors had advocated hyperbolic doubt, which I shall take to be that form of doubt which questions things that you can be (and may remain) absolutely certain about. As Descartes will put it later:

For what difference would it make to us if someone claimed that this truth, of which we are so strongly persuaded, appears false to God or to the angels, and hence is, in absolute terms, false? Why should we concern ourselves with this absolute falsity, when we neither believe it nor have the least suspicion of it? For we are supposing a belief or conviction so strong that nothing can remove it, and this conviction is in every respect the same as absolute certainty.[49]

For example, hyperbolic doubt about whether the external world exists is something you can take seriously without actually ever believing that there is in fact no external world: the challenge is to justify your belief in something that you can be absolutely certain about. It is a form of epistemological doubt, questioning whether our beliefs constitute knowledge, and it is driven by an apparent discrepancy between the stringent requirements that we place on knowledge and the kind of support that our knowledge-claims can receive. Such epistemological doubt leads one to question whether one's beliefs amount to knowledge, but it does not necessarily lead us to abandon those beliefs. One might still hold on to one's former beliefs, and judge that one was more justified in holding them than in holding any contrary beliefs. Such scepticism is usually idle, in the sense that it does not affect our behaviour or our mode of life. And even when it does result in a change of belief, as it may in the case of moral and theological scepticism for example, we still end up with beliefs: they are just different ones from those we had previously.

The kind of scepticism that we find in antiquity, and to some extent in Descartes' immediate predecessors, is different from this. Pyrrhonism, the paradigm form of systematic doubt in antiquity, had two distinctive features: it was a form of doxastic rather than epistemological doubt, and, secondly, it was driven by relativism rather than scepticism.[50] Epistemological doubt questions whether one's beliefs amount to knowledge, whereas doxastic doubt questions whether one is entitled to hold the beliefs one has. A sceptic is someone who holds that the world is determinately either in one state or another, that a thing has one property or another, and so on, but that there is no way we can tell which state it is in or which property it has. A relativist is someone who holds that what state the world is in, what properties something has, etc., is relative to features of the perceiver and the various circumstances under which perception occurs. Relativism drives doxastic doubt, scepticism drives epistemological doubt. Given the role of scepticism and epistemological doubt in Descartes' mature thought, it is important that we appreciate the differences between ancient and Cartesian doubt, especially since these have been largely obscured in the literature on the history of scepticism, Cartesian doubt being treated simply as a radical version of a traditional programme, whereas in fact it is quite different from Pyrrhonism.

In general, Pyrrhonism calls into question our ability to choose between different and perhaps conflicting appearances. The aim of the exercise is to show that the conditions for distinguishing veridical from non-veridical perception can never be met. Does this suggest a more precise target? I believe it does, namely the prevailing naturalistic construal of perception whereby there is, as it were, a natural way of functioning of sense organs which, provided the circumstances are right, will yield veridical perceptions. Aristotle, as we saw in Chapter 5, and to some extent the Stoics,[51] had relied on the idea that there is a natural way of functioning of sense organs which, provided the circumstances are right, will reveal the true nature of the world to us. The Pyrrhonists attempted to counter this view by showing that sense organs function in different ways. They pointed out, for example, that some animals have fur, some have spikes, some have scales, some have skin, and that as a result of these differences things will feel differently: none of these ways of feeling can be called veridical, or even more veridical than the others. There is no one way of functioning; and given the range of circumstances in which perception can occur, we cannot say that there is one set of circumstances which is the right one. It is not that there are such circumstances but that we cannot discover what they are: rather, it is simply that there exist no natural or even optimal conditions for sense perception, and hence no conditions under which they can be said to be veridical.

At this point we might ask why so many commentators tried to place a sceptical reading on the Modes. The answer lies partly in the fact that advocates of scepticism in the sixteenth and seventeenth centuries took their cue from Pyrrhonism, although this is quite compatible with their using Pyrrhonist techniques to new ends. More importantly, it has seemed unclear how the Pyrrhonist project is realizable unless one interprets it in terms of sceptical doubt. But the project is in fact realizable on the assumption of relativist doubt, and in establishing this we can incidentally bring to light the key Pyrrhonist technique that later scepticism, especially in its Cartesian version, will employ.

The ultimate point of the Pyrrhonist exercise is what is called *ataraxia* or *apatheia*—freedom from disturbance, tranquillity—and it is achieved by an intellectual journey. The journey begins when one investigates some question or field of enquiry and finds that opinions conflict as to where the truth lies. The usual hope of the investigation—for 'dogmatists' such as Epicureans and Stoics—is that *ataraxia* will be attained only if we can discover the rights and wrongs of the matter and give our assent to the truth. The difficulty is that, in any matter, things will appear differently to different people according to one or another of a variety of circumstances: these are what are catalogued in the Ten Modes of Aenesidemus, which provide ten basic ways of suspending judgement. Conflicting appearances cannot be equally true, so one needs a criterion of truth. But, the Pyrrhonist argues, no such criterion is available, with the result that we are left with conflicting appearances and the conflicting opinions based on them, unable to find any reason for preferring one to another and therefore bound to treat all of equal strength and equally worthy (or unworthy) of acceptance. But we cannot accept them all because they conflict, or make a choice between them for lack of a criterion, so we cannot accept any: we are forced to accept the equal strength of opposed assertions. So far as truth is concerned, we must suspend judgement. But can relativism yield the required suspension of judgement? The Pyrrhonist project relies on the existence of a conflict of opinions which admits of no resolution. It is the conflict of opinions that leads to the suspension of judgement, and it is this suspension of judgement, if accomplished satisfactorily, that leads the Pyrrhonist to the state of tranquillity that he seeks. The problem is whether relativistic doubt can lead to conflict of opinions, for how does the conflict itself arise? Surely the relativist cannot admit that the opinions conflict without assuming that there is some truth of the matter with respect to which they conflict.

But in fact the conflict of beliefs required for suspension of belief is possible on a relativistic basis. For while it is true that the Pyrrhonists require conflict of beliefs for suspension of judgement to occur, it does not follow from this that they themselves must produce the conflict of beliefs. The conflict of beliefs does not have to be *their* conflict, in the sense of a conflict between beliefs that they hold. This point is perhaps more familiar in the context of Descartes' setting out of epistemological scepticism. There, the sceptical procedure is to let the opponent make a knowledge claim and then show that the claim fails to meet the opponent's own requirements for knowledge, by showing that the requisite justification for the claim is not available. The sceptical argument has a distinctive dialectical structure, which requires the opponent to provide all the premisses of the argument, so that the sceptic can then show an inconsistency between them. The opponent must provide both the definition of knowledge and the knowledge claim, if the argument is to get off the ground. Similarly in the case of ancient doubt: it is crucial that the dogmatist provide all the premisses. The point is that the *Pyrrhonist* does not need to claim that the beliefs conflict, only to report the views of various 'dogmatists'. The dogmatists treat their own beliefs as being true and those of their opponents as being false, and this of course means that they treat them as conflicting. The Pyrrhonist then simply shows that, if we assume along with the dogmatists that there is a conflict, we can show, *contra* the dogmatists, that there cannot be any way of resolving it. Consequently, we must suspend our beliefs, or at least distance ourselves from all beliefs by withholding assent from any of them. The Pyrrhonist need make no claims about conflict himself except to report what dogmatists agree between themselves is a conflict: that is all he requires for his argument.

What is distinctive about Pyrrhonism is that, first, like scepticism but unlike relativism, it does not make any claims itself but merely questions the ability of others to make such claims; and second, like relativism but unlike scepticism, it does not accept that there is an undiscoverable truth of the matter but maintains rather that everything is relative. The first is a standard Pyrrhonist procedure, which perhaps originally derived from the Socratic stance of the questioner who knows nothing and systematically undermines the claims of his interlocutors, and it was subsequently taken up and developed, most notably by Descartes, in the context of seventeenth-century scepticism. Pyrrhonism is parasitic on the beliefs of dogmatists, and it is axiomatic to the Pyrrhonist method of proceeding that any assumptions, claims, or beliefs be those of the dogmatist, since the aim of the exercise is always a critical, negative one: to convince the dogmatists of the falsity of their beliefs, not to convince them of the truth of Pyrrhonism. The latter comes incidentally, as it were, just as the painter Apelles only achieved the effect he desired, namely foam on the horse's mouth, when he gave up trying to achieve it and flung his sponge at the canvas. The second feature, relativism, was something that pervaded Greek thought from Protagoras onwards. But ancient relativism is different from modern relativism of a 'conceptual schemes' variety, for example, which holds that the world is accessible only in so far as we are able to impose structure upon it, and that this structure is inevitably the product of cultures, languages, etc. On such a conception, there is indeed only truth relative to particular languages, cultures, theories, or whatever, rather than truth *per se*. Such relativism is not a form of doubt, however. The modern relativist will typically use relativism to try to establish something positive about the nature of knowledge: its dependence on conceptual schemes, for example, will not be taken to undermine knowledge, but to show its real character. But Pyrrhonism is not designed to reveal something about the nature of knowledge. It is designed to show the futility of the search for knowledge: it is the paradigmatic form of doubt.

With the revival of Pyrrhonism in the second half of the sixteenth century, we can find both a continuation of relativistically-driven doxastic doubt and the beginnings of a sceptically-driven epistemological doubt. This is true even of Montaigne's *Essais*, a point that has not been fully appreciated.[52] If one looks at the treatment of doubt in the *Essais*, one can find a clearly relativistic strain of thought. In the first chapter of Part II, for example, we are told that 'we change as does that animal that takes the colour of each place it visits' and that:

Not only does the wind of accidents move me at its will, but I am also moved and disturbed simply as a result of my own unstable posture, and anyone who observes carefully can scarcely find himself in the same state on two occasions. I give my soul now one face now another, depending on the direction in which I turn it. If I speak of myself in different ways, this is because I look at myself in different ways. All contradictions may be found in me by some twist and in some fashion.[53]

And even when we turn to the *Apologie de Raimond Sebond*, much of what Montaigne writes has a relativistic connotation: many of the examples he gives—what's true on one side of the mountain is false on the other; we hide away while engaging in sexual intercourse, whereas the Indians do it in public; and so on—stick closely to the relativist tone of his Pyrrhonist sources. And in Charron's *De la Sagesse* (1601), which, although it was little more than a compilation of the views of others, most notably Montaigne, was as influential as the *Essais*, this relativistic tone is reinforced. Charron tells us that human reason is a 'wandering, changeable, distorting, variable implement', there is 'no reason that does not have its opposite', that 'what is an abomination in one place is piety in another'.[54] And occasionally in the work of critics of such an approach we can find a return to the teleological justifications of our beliefs that ancient Pyrrhonism set out to destroy: Mersenne, in his *La vérité des sciences* (1625), for example, tries to meet systematic doubt with a revamped Aristotelian 'optimal-conditions' account of perceptual veridicality which stresses the actual success that scientific investigations have.[55]

Nevertheless, alongside this 'genuine' revival of Pyrrhonism, we can also find something new, and in Montaigne's *Apologie de Raimond Sebond* there is evidence of a sceptically-driven epistemological doubt. Montaigne's defence of Pyrrhonism rests on the fact that it shows that we cannot depend upon any of the beliefs about the world that we have formed by relying on our own resources; it 'presents man naked and empty, recognizing his natural weakness, able to receive from above some external power; stripped of human knowledge and consequently all the better able to lodge divine knowledge in himself, wiping out his judgement to make more room for faith; neither disbelieving nor setting up any doctrine against the common observances'.[56] The aim is not to establish the futility of the search for knowledge *per se*, but to establish the futility of the search for knowledge based entirely upon our own resources. Pyrrhonism was utilized in the sixteenth and seventeenth centuries, not primarily as a weapon of libertinage, but as a means of defending the faith against forms of Protestantism, as well as against certain kinds of scholastic natural theology.[57] It is not surprising that Descartes' first recorded brush with the question of scepticism, in his dispute with John Dury in the winter of 1634/5, should have been in the context of fideism, for scepticism largely turned around the question of the role of faith.[58] Indeed, fideism provides a key to the transformation of doxastic doubt into epistemological scepticism, for the theological context in which Pyrrhonism was revived guaranteed that there was an objective answer to questions about the nature and structure of the world. This gradually closed off the possibility of relativism, and although one can still find traces of it, these are increasingly rare exceptions, for relativism simply could not flourish in the theological context of seventeenth-century discussions of doubt. Even Charron, despite his relativist tone, has a decidedly equivocal commitment to the view that any set of beliefs is as good as any other. The problem was that of how we are to discover which set of beliefs is the correct one, and how we are to establish the truth of these beliefs; in other words, how we were to come to *know* the structure of the world. This problem was not straightforward, however, for as Montaigne's fideistic construal of scepticism indicates, while it is guaranteed that there is an objective answer to the question of what the world is like, because we know that God created the world in a particular way and that He has objective knowledge of what it is like, the possibility of our attaining this knowledge is not guaranteed. Indeed, the problem is even worse than that, for the distance between ourselves and God is so great that the way of bridging it does not seem to lie in rational enquiry at all but in faith.

At this point, we can begin to see how scepticism connects up with Descartes' concerns in natural philosophy and metaphysics. No mechanist in the first half of the seventeenth century could have accepted a fideist conception of understanding. This was partly because of the fact that traditional sources of faith, from the Bible to Christian teaching as set out by scholastic philosophers, were antithetical to the kind of natural-philosophical framework that mechanists—even mechanists like Mersenne, who was orthodox in matters of religion—were attempting to establish. But another factor is the rejection of any appeal to tradition, whether sympathetic or antagonistic, in natural philosophy. One thing that the condemnation of Copernicanism had brought to a head was the standing of natural philosophy; in particular, the issue at stake in the trials of Copernicans such as Foscarini and Galileo was whether one was to be guided in natural philosophy by the 'natural light of reason' or 'dogmas of the faith'.[59] For Descartes at least, there was an indissoluble connection between his mechanism and a commitment to Copernicanism, and even if he had not already had a commitment to the power of the 'natural light of reason', the question of the standing of Copernicanism would have forced such a commitment upon him. But here we hit the metaphysical problem that the natural light of reason, by itself, cannot yield an understanding of the ultimate nature of things, because the cognitive gulf between God and ourselves—expressed in its most radical form in Descartes' doctrine of eternal truths—means we cannot expect that our cognitive faculties can grasp the divine rationale behind the way things are. In his correspondence with Mersenne on the question of eternal truths, we saw that Descartes maintains that God's transcendence is such that He is not bound by empirical or even mathematical truths. He has created truths and could have created them differently, in a way that completely surpasses our understanding. Or, to put the matter in epistemological terms, He could have made all our beliefs false. It is just such an epistemological translation that we now find in the *Discours*. The epistemological correlate of the complete transcendence of God's powers takes the form of the introduction of hyperbolic doubt.

No demonstration that our beliefs are shaped by, or even a function of, subjective and environmental factors, which is the core of the Pyrrhonist attack on belief, could possibly yield hyperbolic doubt. On the other hand, if one has a sufficiently restrictive view of what can count as the justification required for genuine knowledge, then hyperbolic doubt is clearly a possibility, as an extrapolation from less radical forms of sceptical doubt. The kind of systematic doubt that Descartes employs in the *Discours* is like this, and it is distinctively different from Pyrrhonist doubt in a number of respects. In the first place, it is explicitly epistemological rather than doxastic. It does not affect our beliefs for, as Descartes admits, 'in practical life it is sometimes necessary to act upon beliefs that one knows are uncertain';[60] rather, it raises the question of what kind of certainty we require for our beliefs to be knowledge. Second, it is driven not by relativism but by a form of realist scepticism: realist in the sense that it is taken as given that there is a way the world is independently of us, that objects and events really have determinate properties independently of our impressions and judgements; and scepticism in the sense that we cannot know what the world is like, or what these properties are. The problem is not that we have no way of determining which of the various conditions under which perception occurs are those that secure veridicality, but rather that we have no access to the ultimate nature of reality. This is the epistemological analogue of the metaphysical problem of God's transcendence.

In fact, the doctrine of eternal truths does not appear again after the early 1630s in Descartes' writings, not because he has abandoned it, but because it is a metaphysical doctrine which has now been reformulated epistemologically, in terms of hyperbolic doubt: although hyperbolic doubt does retain clear traces of its origins, as we shall see when we look at the more elaborate version of the argument in the *Meditationes*. In its metaphysical version it is insoluble, for all one can do is point to the chasm dividing divine and human understanding: the doctrine of the divine creation of eternal truths is a dead end. The epistemological reformulation of the problem does yield a solution, however, and far from being a dead end it turns out to be the key to the defence of Cartesian natural philosophy. But we must not overlook the fact that the problem that Descartes is concerned with here—our lack of any direct access to reality—is initially generated metaphysically rather than epistemologically. Descartes has translated a metaphysical problem into an epistemological one, but it is still ultimately subordinated to metaphysical ends, namely the provision of metaphysical foundations for his natural philosophy, foundations required because of the onslaught against Copernicanism which (he believed) forced him to abandon *Le Monde*. Descartes uses scepticism, as did Montaigne, not as something problematic which needs to be answered, but as something that directs us inexorably towards the metaphysical question of how we bridge the gap between a transcendent God and human cognition. Indeed, hyperbolic doubt is in some ways constitutive of his epistemology, for it is only by means of hyperbolic doubt that we can be led to see the need for the kind of metaphysical foundations for natural philosophy that Descartes wants to provide.

In the first instance, what the doubt pushes us into is subjectivity, and indeed epistemological doubt centres on the perspective of the subject. Pyrrhonism had made constant reference to subjective states, and indeed, it made what one believes relative to a whole range of subjective states—anger, love, familiarity, habits, religious views, and so on—which Descartes never even mentions. Yet he manages to make the whole question of legitimation turn around the subject. Although he is concerned with such questions as that of what in perception is due to the perceiver and what is due to the world, this in itself would not generate a concern with subjectivity. The Epicureans were particularly concerned with this problem, for example, but they did not think of the perceiver as something separate from, or removed from, the world.[61] But just as important is the fact that naturalism pervades doubt in antiquity as well. Pyrrhonism is ultimately directed towards a state in which, by suspending all one's beliefs-cum-opinions-cum-judgements, one is finally completely at peace with the world. Pyrrhonism does not end up distancing us from the world: on the contrary, it shows that we are so integrated with the world that its very particular features shape our experience of it, making it impossible to transcend this particularity by trying to find optimal conditions for cognition.

Cartesian doubt pushes us in the other direction, and Descartes achieves this by developing and transforming Montaigne's conception of subjectivity. Montaigne probably initiated his project of self-exploration with the traditional aim of discovering a universal human nature, but what he ended up doing was something completely different.[62] He discovered himself, his thoughts, feelings, emotions: something cut off not just from the empirical world but from other subjects. It is not that subjectivity conceived as a universal human nature is separated from empirical nature, but rather that the self is cut off from empirical nature and indeed from other selves as well. Descartes deploys this view of the self—a self which has an identity in its own right, independent of the relation in which it stands either to the empirical world or other selves—in an epistemological context, so that the locus of knowledge of the empirical world is now something removed from that empirical world.[63] Because of the way in which he puts Montaigne's notion of subjectivity to use in this new context, subjective appearances are now not so much a feature of human cognition generally as a feature of *my* cognition. It is not that my cognition is significantly different from that of others, but rather that one experiences one's own cognition as a subjective process, whereas one experiences that of others quite differently. It is this that allows hyperbolic doubt, for a gap is opened up between the self and the empirical world, or, as it is now beginning to become, the 'external' world. We have seen that sceptical questions are absent from the discussions of cognition in the *Regulae* and *L'Homme*, and that these discussions are conducted in terms of a naturalized epistemology, supplemented by a linguistically modelled account of cognitive grasp in *Le Monde*. Where questions of legitimation are raised in this epistemology, as they are in the *Regulae*, they are raised in the context of a rhetorico-psychological theory about the vividness and particularity of the contents of our ideas. What now happens is we are forced to find a criterion by which to distinguish between (subjective) appearance and (external) reality, something which the earlier criterion, which was designed for different purposes, manifestly cannot provide. Yet what is sought in the notion of clarity and distinctness remains the same in one important respect, for in both cases self-conviction remains the primary aim. The difference arises from the fact that Descartes has moved from a naturalistic setting in which the task is to describe how cognition occurs (subject to the constraints of mechanism) to one in which the question is at issue of whether knowledge is even possible. Traditional metaphysics, or at least that part of it which we now refer to as ontology, had dealt with the question of how the world is; what Descartes manages to do is to transform, in a far more decisive way than any of his predecessors or contemporaries, the aim of metaphysics by making the question that of how the world is 'independently of us'. This makes an investigation of 'us' mandatory. By asking how the world is independently of us, rather than just how the world is, an epistemological ingredient is built into metaphysics that was not there previously. What Descartes does is to approach the question of how the world is independently of us by exploring the nature of the subject's experience and asking what features of that experience entitle us to make claims to knowledge.

The key question becomes that of determining whether there is anything extra-mental that corresponds to my ideas; and the idea that Descartes starts with is that of perfection: he realizes that he is not perfect because it is more perfect to know than to doubt, and he asks where his idea of something more perfect than he derives from. He can imagine having made up his ideas of things less perfect than he, but he cannot have made up his idea of something more perfect than himself, for 'it was manifestly impossible to get this from nothing'.[64] This is the argument for God's existence from His being the sole thing that could cause me to have that idea, which we looked at in chapter 6. God's existence and the nature of the mind are two things that we know clearly and distinctly when we reflect on them. What role does the *cogito* have in this? Descartes tells us that it is 'the first principle of the philosophy I was seeking',[65] but this cannot mean that it is the first principle in the sense of being a foundation, for, as we have seen, in summarizing Part IV of the *Discours*, he tells us explicitly that the nature of the human soul and the existence of God are the foundations of his metaphysics. Moreover, the clarity and distinctness that we experience when we reflect on the *cogito* itself requires grounding in God if it is to deliver the truth:

But if we did not know that everything real and true within us comes from a perfect and infinite being, however clear and distinct our ideas were, we would have no reason to be sure that they had the perfection of being true. But once the knowledge of God and the soul has made us certain of this rule, it is easy to recognise that the things we imagine in dreams should in no way make us doubt the truth of the thoughts we have when awake.[66]

The *cogito* presents us with a paradigmatic case of clarity and distinctness of the kind that Descartes is seeking, but it does not legitimate the use of clarity and distinctness as a criterion. That task rests ultimately with God, whose existence we can deduce from the idea that we have of Him. God then acts as the guarantor for knowledge, although how He acts in this way is not specified here.

Part IV of the *Discours* is a first stab at a foundational theory that will be developed much more fully in the *Meditationes*, and I shall put off more detailed discussion until we come to the *Meditationes*. But because of a prevalent misinterpretation of the *Discours* and the *Meditationes* as providing epistemological foundations for knowledge in the *cogito*, it will be helpful to summarize the reading that I am proposing. My reconstruction is as follows. The problem that Descartes started off with was that of building up a natural philosophy, mechanism, as a basis for a micro-corpuscularian, hydrostatically/hydrodynamically modelled physics whose fortunes were inextricably tied to those of Copernicanism. Mechanism on his interpretation required a particularly unyielding conception of God's transcendence, however, and this raised the question of what kind of relation we stand in to a transcendent God. Descartes realized that both these aspects of mechanism could be dealt with in terms of an epistemologized metaphysics. In the *Discours* he sets out the natural philosophy of *Le Monde*, which is summarized immediately after Part IV; in the *Meditationes* what is set out is a more metaphysical version of mechanism, presented in Meditation 6, which completely undermines the kind of common-sense beliefs about the natural world that one might naturally start off with before systematic doubt takes its toll. Systematic doubt is used as a prelude to legitimating a contentious natural philosophy, not to providing 'knowledge' with a firm foundation. We have seen why Descartes finds this necessary. Because of the nature of the problem, nothing short of indubitable metaphysical foundations will be sufficient to counter the threat posed by the Inquisition to Copernicanism. But how could a metaphysics do this; or, more precisely, what would a metaphysics have to do to accomplish this? Self-conviction is the key, just as it was in the earlier version of the doctrine of clear and distinct ideas, but our conviction cannot derive from the clarity or vividness of our ideas, since the basic problem is not the mind's cognitive relation to the empirical world, but our cognitive relation to a transcendent God who can create and change empirical truths at will. Note in this connection that in his summary of Part IV of the *Discours*, which covers the *cogito*, the nature of the mind, material extension, and the existence of God, Descartes does not tell us that the foundations of his metaphysics lie in the *cogito* and the nature of the material world, as an epistemological reading might lead us to expect, but in the nature of the mind and God's existence.

Publication and Critical Response

Some time early in 1636, Descartes moved to Leiden, the centre of Dutch publishing, to find a publisher for the *Discours* and the *Essais*. As he tells Mersenne in March 1636, 'I came here because the Elzeviers had earlier said that they would like to be my publishers'.[67] The Elzeviers were the greatest publishers of the time, and had used the liberal publishing laws of the Netherlands to produce editions of works—most famously Galileo's *Dialogue on Two Chief World Systems*—that could not be published elsewhere. The fact that Descartes should have first thought of a publishing house so closely associated with Galileo and Copernicanism contrasts strongly with his caution in other respects, for he not only had left cosmological theory out but wanted to publish the works anonymously.[68] This surely indicates a significant degree of indecision in Descartes' mind, which is hardly surprising. As it turns out, however, he was not to publish with the Elzeviers. He tells Mersenne that they had 'made difficulties' for him,[69] and he asks whether it might be more convenient to have it published in Paris. The trouble with this was that he thought there may be difficulties in interpreting his handwriting, his spelling and punctuation were careless, and the diagrams drawn by him were very rough. These difficulties seem to have put him off—there is no suggestion that he might go to Paris himself to supervise the printing—and he ended up taking his business to the Elzeviers' neighbour, Jan Maire, who subsequently became famous as the publisher of the *Discours*. The contract was signed on 2 December 1636 for an edition of 3,000 copies.[70] The manuscript was occasionally very technical, Descartes' handwriting was not especially legible, and the typesetter understood no French, so the typesetting possibly took longer than normal. It was ready for printing some time before 4 April,[71] but Mersenne was still waiting for clearance from the French censors, and it did not finally appear until 8 June, by which time a few people in Paris were already familiar with the contents from an early set of proofs, which Huygens had sent to Mersenne on 5 January so that he might apply for the *privilège* of the king. Descartes may have stayed in Douai from 1 May until the middle of June, possibly with a view to spreading a bit of advance publicity,[72] returning to collect and begin distributing the complementary 200 copies he had been promised by the printer as part of their contract.

What was the intended readership of the *Discours* and *Essais*? As well as the *ex officio* recipients, so to speak, such as Louis XIII, Richlieu, and the French ambassador at The Hague, who he would hardly have expected to read it, Descartes also sent out copies to three teachers at La Flèche, doubtless in the hope that the *Météors* at least might be adopted as a text. In a letter to one of these, Vatier, he says he has tried to write in such a way that even women might understand him,[73] and at the end of the *Discours*, Descartes tells us that he has written in French rather than Latin because 'I expect that those who use only their natural reason in all its purity will be better judges of my opinions than those who give credence only to the writings of the ancients'.[74] This suggests a lay audience, and perhaps one open to new ideas. It is true that the titles of the *Essais*—'Dioptrics' instead of 'The Telescope', and 'Meteors' instead of 'The Rainbow'—indicate technical works,[75] but other considerations may have been operative in choosing the titles: 'Dioptrics' and 'Meteors' suggest works with no ideological or theological significance, for example. It was clearly of importance to Descartes that the basics of his theory of matter, and his geometrical and physical optics, should get an airing, even if they had to be dissociated from his cosmology: although, showing some indecision, he makes sure the reader knows that he has developed a cosmology but had to suppress its publication,[76] and few at the time of the Galileo affair would have had any doubt as to what the source of the problem was. Although he summarizes *Le Monde* in Part V of the *Discours*, Descartes wrote to an unknown correspondent in 1637 refusing to publish the text itself (which he was still in the process of revising[77]), but saying that the *Discours* and the three essays were designed to 'prepare the way and test the waters'.[78] Such testing of the waters was clearly what he had in mind in sending complimentary copies to Cardinal De Bagni, whom Descartes knew as a papal nuncio while he was in Paris in the late 1620s, and Cardinal Barberini, nephew of Pope Urban VIII. A bookshop in Rome had written to the publisher accepting a dozen copies in 1637, on condition that the book did not mention the motion of the earth,[79] and Descartes was right to be circumspect in gauging the reaction of Rome, since his Copernican sympathies had been gleaned from the text without too much difficulty by some readers.[80]

Descartes was not always keen to receive responses, however, and on 1 March 1638 he wrote to Mersenne: 'As for M. B[eaugrand], I am amazed that you condescend to speak of him, . . . Treat the discourse written by him and those of his ilk with contempt, if you please, and make it clear to them that I have nothing but contempt for them'.[81] When he received Fermat's *Isagoge ad locos solidos* he returned it unread, believing it could only repeat what he had already said in the *Géométrie*.[82] He refers to the work of Fermat—possibly the greatest mathematician of the period, surpassing even Descartes—as dung or shit.[83] As Shea points out, those who took Descartes' request for responses at the end of the *Discours* at face value 'came in for contumely greatly at variance with his much-vaunted good breeding'.[84] He refers to the French mathematicians who criticized his *Géométrie* as 'two or three flies'. Roberval, a generally good mathematician and an innovator in the geometry of infinitesimals, is described as 'less than a rational animal'; Pierre Petit is described as 'some little dog who barks after me in the street'; Hobbes, no less, is 'extremely contemptible' for daring to criticize him; and the letters of Beaugrand are, we are told, only fit to be used as toilet paper.[85] Worse, some critics do not accept Descartes' replies to their criticisms, and have the temerity to continue in their original beliefs. They are 'so silly and weak that, once they have accepted a view, they continue to believe it, however false and irrational it may be, in preference to a true and well-grounded refutation which is subsequently put to them'.[86]

Many of the responses that Descartes received covered all of the essays, but it will be helpful in surveying them—a survey that will necessarily be very selective—to concentrate on the responses to each of them separately. This is justified not just because of the ease of presentation, but also because the essays elicited very different kinds of response. The *Discours* was the most generally contentious because it raised the widest range of issues: it hinted, however obliquely, at Copernicanism, set out the doctrine of animal automatism, and stepped into the dangerous area of metaphysics. Nevertheless, the odd respondent, like Ciermans, didn't even bother to read the *Discours*, confining his attention to the *Essais*. The *Météors* was generally regarded as by far the least interesting of the three accompanying essays, but since most of it was less technical than the other two, it attracted a fair amount of general criticism.[87] Discourse 8, however, was singled out for specific comment by a number of respondents. The *Dioptrique* was highly regarded and Descartes' success at a general level was not disputed. Nor was its practical importance: we have a report of what is described as 'an excellent telescope' constructed following Descartes' procedures by Ferrier in 1638, for example.[88] But it did attract some severe technical criticisms, notably from Fermat, and these were directed at its core account of refraction. The response to the *Géométrie* was exclusively technical because Descartes had written in such an abstruse way. Why he had done this is unclear. It wasn't as if he was trying to hide his 'method of discovery' in mathematics, or that he was writing in a theologically or ideologically contentious area. And in any case the treatment of optical ovals in Book II provided important mathematical backing for Discourses 8–10 of the *Dioptrique*, so there was some practical benefit to be gained from making a few concessions to the reader. He must later have regretted that he did not do so—although, defensive as always, he never explicitly admits this—for he ended up authorizing an introduction to be written setting out the material in a more elementary way.[89]

Responses to the *Discours* tended to focus on Cartesian physiology and the arguments for God's existence. The first criticisms that Descartes received were from Libertus Fromondus, who had been given a copy of Descartes' book by his colleague at the University of Louvain, Plempius. Fromondus was the pseudonym of Vincent Lenis, an arch-conservative and staunch defender of scholasticism, and his three objections to the *Discours* focused on Cartesian physiology.[90] Descartes' response to the first two are of some interest. Fromondus had objected that 'noble actions like sight cannot result from so ignoble and brutish a cause as heat'. Descartes replies:

He supposes that I think that animals see just as we do, that is, are aware or know that they see, which is said to have been Epicurus' view, and is still widely held. But . . . I explain quite explicitly that my view is that animals do not see as we do when we are aware that we see, but only when we do when our mind is elsewhere. In such a case the images of external objects are depicted on our retinas, and perhaps the impressions that they make in the optic nerves cause our limbs to make various movements, although we are quite unaware of them. In such a case we too move just like automata, but nobody thinks that the force of heat is sufficient to cause their movements.[91]

Descartes makes it clear here that he accepts that there are characteristically human cognitive states that cannot be explained reductively, but on the other hand he makes it just as clear that the cases of perceptual cognition that he does treat reductively are genuine cases of cognition: they simply lack the self-reflective or sense-conscious awareness that accompanies many human acts of cognition. The second objection questions why Descartes attributes 'substantive souls' (which Descartes treats as equivalent to sensitive souls) to animals, and asks how he would counter the 'atheist' suggestion that human beings have no rational souls. This is the problem of mechanism showing too much, and here Fromondus seems to have more traditional Epicurean reductions in mind. On this question Descartes is in fact on strong ground, as he is able to show that his own construal of the difference between the animal soul and the rational soul not only differentiates them more sharply than the Epicurean account, but also more sharply than the scholastic account, which construes them both as substantial forms.

Plempius himself sent his objections in two letters of January and March 1638, and Descartes provided detailed replies to both. They focus almost exclusively on the circulation of the blood, and the mechanism by which this is effected in the heart. Plempius ascribes a basically Aristotelian view to Descartes, quoting the *De respiratione*, where Aristotle maintains that 'the pulsation of the heart may be compared to ebullition, for ebullition takes place when a liquid expands by the action of heat'. While acknowledging that Descartes gives a more ingenious and economical explanation than Aristotle, Plempius opts for the Galenic theory, by which 'the heart is moved by some faculty' (a *vis pulsifica*, 'pulsational force') and he offers a number of observations which he believes provide empirical backing for this theory. As regards the circulation of the blood, he offers a number of observations against this.[92] Descartes is at pains to distinguish his account from Aristotle's, both as regards detail and because he sees the key thing as the kind of basis on which the view is supported rather than the view itself,[93] which lends credence to the idea that what Descartes has done is to shape traditional physiological accounts around a mechanical model. Nevertheless, one thing that is very evident from Descartes' replies to Fromondus is that he is easily able to hold his own in disputes over physiology, and there is evidence of significant experimental work on his part.[94]

In February 1638, Descartes responded to a number of points made by a teacher at La Flèche, Father Vatier. The letter begins with some very important indications about his idea of 'method', which I touched on earlier. He writes:

I must say first that my purpose was not to teach the whole of my Method in the discourse in which I propound it, but only to say enough to show that the new views in the *Dioptrique* and the *Météors* were not random notions, and were perhaps worth the trouble of examining. I could not demonstrate the use of this Method in the three treatises which I gave, because it prescribes an order of research which is quite different from the one I thought proper for exposition. I have however given a brief sample of it in my account of the rainbow, and if you take the trouble to re-read it, I hope it will satisfy you more than it did the first time; the matter is, after all, quite difficult in itself. I attached these three treatises to the discourse which precedes them because I am convinced that if people examine them carefully and compare them with what has previously been written on the same topics, they will have grounds for judging that the Method I adopt is no ordinary one and is perhaps better than some others.[95]

Next Descartes acknowledges that the treatment of God's existence, while the most important part of the *Discours*, is 'the least worked out section in the whole book'.[96] This was partly because he did not decide to include it until the last minute, and mainly because the full presentation and appreciation of the argument needs a fuller presentation of scepticism. He promises to set these and other matters out in more detail in a second edition: in effect, this will be done in the *Meditationes*,[97] which we know he was working on in late 1639,[98] and it is possible that he was at least considering the issues in some detail at this time. In the letter to Vatier he indicates that he is thinking about metaphysical questions, telling him that he has solved the problem of transubstantiation,[99] although references to metaphysical questions generally are surprisingly rare in his correspondence for this period. An important exception is his discussion of the *De Veritate* (Paris, 1624) of Herbert of Cherbury in a letter to Mersenne of 16 October 1639. Herbert had argued that the correct response to scepticism is to provide a general account of truth, on the grounds that if we understand what truth is we will be able to show that scepticism rests upon a misunderstanding of it. Descartes disagrees:

In general [the author] takes a very different path in his book from the one that I have followed. He examines what truth is; for my own part, I have never had any doubts about this, because it seems a notion so transcendentally clear that no one could be ignorant of it. There are many ways of examining a balance before using it, but there is no way to learn what truth is, if one does not [already] know its nature. For what reason could we have for accepting anything which could teach us the nature of truth if we did not know that it was true, that is to say, if we did not know truth? It is, of course, possible to tell the meaning of the word to someone who did not know the language, and tell him that the word *truth*, in its strict sense, denotes the conformity of thought with its object, and that when it is attributed to things outside thought, it means only that they can be the objects of true thoughts, whether in our minds or in God's. But we can give no definition of logic which will help anyone discover its nature. And I believe the same holds of many other things which are very simple and known naturally, such as shape, size, movement, place, time and so on. For if you try to define these things you only obscure them and cause confusion . . . The author takes universal consent as the criterion of his truths, whereas I have no criterion for mine except the light of nature.[100]

In other words, while we can define truth, such a definition could not be explanatory, for nothing can be clearer than truth. Unless we had a prior understanding of truth, we could not understand a definition of it, for we would have to be able to grasp that the definition itself was true if we were to understand it. Unless we already grasped the difference between truth and falsity, definition would be pointless.[101] Truth is not alone in this respect, however, and other basic notions—here Descartes lists those which he takes as basic in his natural philosophy, such as shape, size, and movement—are similarly primitive in the sense of being notions which could not require further elucidation. Secondly, the criterion by which we recognize truths is said to be 'the light of nature', although the *Discours* had made it clear that this light of nature, which takes the form of grasping things clearly and distinctly, is no longer self-legitimating, as I've argued it was earlier, but now requires a divine legitimation, because of hyperbolic doubt.

As regards the *Dioptrique*, Descartes was so much at the forefront of this area that it is only to be expected that he would be able to meet most objections with ease. Fromondus' objections, for example, did not engage Descartes' arguments so much as simply reaffirm the scholastic doctrine of intentional species, and Descartes dealt with them in a summary way.[102] But there were two respondents who raised key points: Fermat and Morin. Fermat had been developing his own geo-metrical optics, and he was able to challenge Descartes very much as an equal. He put forward objections to Descartes' account of reflection and refraction. His criticism of his account of reflection is directed against the principle of composition of motions, something crucial to his account of both reflection and refraction. Descartes had resolved the incident ray into a perpendicular component and one parallel to the reflecting surface. Since, in his tennis analogy, the latter was not opposed to the motion of the ball in that direction, he was able to argue that the horizontal motion was conserved, which gave him the result he wanted. But there are an infinite number of reference systems for resolution of motions into components, Fermat argues, and he provides another one, in which the horizontal and vertical components are oblique, which he believes to be consonant with Descartes' principles. This resolution does not lead to the result that Descartes wants, because the horizontal motion would now be opposed by the surface.[103] Descartes replies that the components of motion that he was talking about were real ones, not merely imaginary ones.[104] But we are given no idea of how we might distinguish 'real' motions, and if one is going to analyse reflection and refraction by resolving motion into true horizontal and vertical components, then one needs something that establishes real directions, such as forces. As regards the question of refraction, the dispute between Descartes and Fermat is inconclusive and the issue was pursued (conclusively in Fermat's favour) after Descartes' death between Fermat and Clerselier, who maintained a version of the Cartesian position.[105] The dispute, particularly at the stage to which Descartes was party, hinges on Descartes' problematic notion of 'determination'. Fermat assumes that Descartes means direction by 'determination', in which case how can he say that the perpendicular determination of the tennis ball is altered when it pierces the canvas and that its speed in that direction is thereby altered? If one sticks with Descartes' distinction, one is forced to say that 'since the motion of the ball is weakened, the determination which makes it move downwards from above has changed', which is clearly absurd. Moreover, if direction and speed are different things, how can Descartes deduce, from the conservation of horizontal determination, that the speed of the ball will be in the same direction after piercing the canvas as it was before?[106] But, as we have seen, Descartes does not understand 'determination' in this way, although Fermat can be forgiven for thinking he did.

Morin's queries cover the metaphysical aspects of the idea of 'tendency to motion'. He is understandably puzzled about the connection between motion, *action*, and tendency to motion, pointing out that Descartes maintains both that light is just 'a certain motion or *action*' received in the subtle matter that fills the pores of bodies, and that it is just 'the *action* or tendency to move of subtle matter'. But a tendency to move is not a motion, the two differing as 'potency and act'.[107] In his reply, Descartes avoids the terminology of potency and act, pointing out that when he has referred to motion he has always added the qualification 'or *action*', and that he understands by the term '*action*' something that includes both the power to move and motion.[108] One thing that Descartes does clearly believe is that the laws of motion and the laws of tendency to motion are the same,[109] that they are both, in effect, laws of *action*. Descartes will try to clear up these questions in the *Principia*, in terms of his metaphysical doctrine of modes, but in fact little clarification results, for the issue is fundamentally physical rather than metaphysical. Remember that the context of the discussion is the transmission of light, and that in considering light, Descartes does not 'consider motion but the action or tendencies to move'.[110] In keeping with his hydrostatic model, Descartes' concern is not with motions but with tendencies to motion.

As regards the *Météors*, Descartes clearly intended that it be adopted as a text in colleges. He writes to his friend Father Noël:

> There is no one, I think, who has a greater interest in examining the contents of this book than the members of [the Society of Jesus]. I already see that so many people are going to accept the contents of the book that, especially in the case of the *Météors*, I do not know how they will be able to teach these subjects from now on as they are taught year by year in most of your colleges, unless they either disprove what I have written or follow it.[111]

But it was never adopted as a text and discussion was restricted, although this did not stop it being plagiarized in the *Théorie et pratique de navigation* (1643) of the Jesuit Georges Fournier.[112] Fromondus, himself author of an Aristotelian text on meteorology, *Meteorologicorum Libri Sex* (1627), made a number of very traditional objections to the *Météors*, but his main reaction to Descartes was to ignore the *Météors* completely, and in the 1639 edition of his text he does not even mention it.[113] In his letter to Vatier, Descartes admits that he cannot prove the *a priori* assumptions (about the nature of matter) that he makes in the early chapters, and that he has foreseen that this would give rise to objections, but he says that he believed he could deduce them 'in due order from the first principles of my metaphysics', by which he presumably means his account of matter as corporeal extension, and that in any case 'it is not always necessary to have *a priori* reasons to convince people of the truth'.[114] Indeed, in his reply to Fromondus he goes further and gives a good general statement of the rationale underlying his use of micro-mechanical explanations. Fromondus criticizes his theory of matter as being excessively crude or crass, to which Descartes replies:

> If my philosophy seems excessively crude to him because, like mechanics, it deals with shapes, sizes, and motions, he is condemning what I hold its most praiseworthy

feature, and in which I take particular pride, namely, that I use no reasoning which is not mathematical and evident, and whose conclusions are confirmed by true experiments. Whatever I concluded could be done from the principles of my philosophy can in fact be done, whenever things in an active state were applied, as appropriate, to things in a passive state. I am surprised he has not noticed that the mechanics that has been in use up to now is nothing other than a small part of the true physics which, finding no refuge with the supporters of common philosophy, found one with the mathematicians. But this part of philosophy remains truer and less corrupt than other parts, because it relates to use and practice, and so those who make mistakes lose money.[115]

The most formidable objections that Descartes received to the *Météors* were, understandably, concerned with his account of the nature of light and the formation of colours in Discours 8. The key points were made independently by both Ciermans and Morin early in 1638. We have already mentioned Morin: Descartes had known him since his Paris days in the mid-1620s. Joseph Ciermans was a Jesuit mathematician who had been given a copy of the book by Plempius. Despite his remark to Vatier only two or three weeks earlier that his account of the rainbow was a sample of his method, Descartes tells Ciermans that 'if there is one place in the essay that is badly defended and exposed to the fire of the enemy' it is this.[116] Ciermans raises a problem about interference of light rays. If, for example, a ray of blue light crosses a ray of red light, and both are conceived as being made up of rotating corpuscles, then surely the faster rotating red corpuscles will be retarded by the slower rotating blue ones, and vice versa, so that an observer will perceive neither pure red nor blue light once the paths of the rays have crossed. It is no response to this to argue that light corpuscles are too small to interfere with anything, for light entering and leaving a prism is retarded or speeded up, and the only explanation for this is collision with the corpuscles of air.[117] Morin raised a similar problem about interference.[118] In replying, Descartes relies on a distinction that pervades *Le Monde*, but had not been made in the *Météors*, namely that between motion and tendency to motion. The thrust of the argument is that while it is true that a body cannot be conceived to act in various directions, or even in a straight line if there is an obstacle in its way, it can have a tendency to motion in different directions at the same instant, and this tendency to motion is not affected by obstacles to the realization of that tendency. Unfortunately, we are given no new elucidation of how exactly tendencies to motion are manifested. Descartes refers Ciermans to the vat-of-grapes example given in the *Dioptrique*, but reserves further explanation until he presents his full system of physics to the world.[119]

A second objection of Ciermans was also made independently by

Morin.[120] When Descartes accounts for the formation of colours by rays of light leaving a prism on a screen, in Discourse 8, he gets the order of colours wrong. In the *Dioptrique*, we are told that corpuscles of fine matter travel more swiftly through denser media because of the greater ease of passage that dense media offer (it is helpful to think in terms of sound waves in imagining how this happens). When he is explaining the formation of colours in Discourse 8, however, he assimilates the case of a corpuscle moving from glass to air (dense to rare, represented in Fig. 7.15) to the case of a corpuscle moving from air to water (rare to dense, represented in Fig. 7.16). As a consequence in his diagram (Fig. 7.15) he has red being produced by corpuscles that must be moving faster than the others, but he tells us that they are moving more slowly. That such confusions should have arisen is not surprising; after all, Descartes' controlling model, that of a tennis ball breaking the canvas, has the ball being retarded in what, intuitively, we think of as the analogue of the denser medium! His reply is unsatisfactory and, indeed, disingenuous: he shifts the argument away from corpuscles of fine matter and claims that in Fig. 7.16 the corpuscles are balls of wood, which obscures rather than clarifies what is at issue.[121]

As regards the *Géométrie*, it has to be admitted that things got off to a very bad start. When Mersenne applied, on Descartes' behalf, for a *privilège* for the *Discours* and *Essais* from the king at the beginning of 1637, the person who sifted through such applications was the secretary to the *Chancelier*, Jean Beaugrand. Beaugrand was also a keen mathematician, and he was familiar with two earlier attempts to develop algebra, that of Harriot, whose *Artis analyticae praxis* had appeared in 1631,[122] and that of Vieta,[123] whose pathbreaking *In Artem analyticem isagoge* and *Ad Logisticem speciosam notae priores* he published in a new edition with commentary in 1631. Beaugrand was a great admirer of Vieta and had introduced his protégé, Fermat, to Vieta's work. Descartes had made great claims about how he had relied wholly on his own resources in the *Discours*, yet Beaugrand thought he detected unacknowledged borrowings from Vieta and Harriot in the *Géométrie*. Descartes, of course, resisted such claims,[124] and they were indeed without foundation, but Beaugrand pursued them both in letters to Mersenne and in two anonymous pamphlets, and there is little doubt that he did Descartes' reputation some damage, not to mention hampering appreciation of Descartes' achievement in the *Géométrie*.[125]

A more substantive issue in the dispute between Descartes and Beaugrand was over the superiority of the method of deriving tangents employing circles set out in Book II of the *Géométrie*, over the procedure using lines devised by Fermat and supported by Beaugrand.[126]

Egmond aan Zee. Lottery ticket for the foundation of a new hospital, 1615.
Engraving by Claes Jansz Visscher.

Descartes' procedure was undeniably clumsy compared to the
streamlined procedure that had been developed by Fermat and taken
up by Beaugrand, but Descartes was extremely reluctant to admit this.
Nevertheless, later on, in correspondence, he was to make use of a
method in which a straight line turns about a point on the axis of the
curve, the points at which the line cuts the curve ultimately coinciding
as the line approaches or recedes from the axis. This procedure, which
is more straightforward than the circle method of the *Géométrie*,
follows Fermat in regarding the tangent as the limiting position of the
secant.[127]

An Indian Summer, 1637–1639

With the publication of the *Discours* and the *Essais* complete, Descartes
left Leiden for the coastal area around Haarlem in August 1637, staying either at Santpoort or nearby Egmond-Binnen. He remained in this
somewhat isolated, windswept, and rather bleak area, covered with
sand dunes and scrubby grass—captured in a contemporary engraving
of nearby Egmond aan Zee—until November 1639. Yet these two
years seem to have been amongst Descartes' happiest. Virtually the first
thing he did was to arrange for Francine and Hélène to join him. He
writes to a correspondent—who I suggested above may have been
Hogelande—about his 'niece', in fact Francine:

Everything here is going as well as one could wish. I spoke to my landlady yesterday, to find out if she would agree to have my niece here, and how much she would want me to pay. She said without hesitation that I could send for her whenever I liked and that we could easily agree upon a price, for one more child to look after didn't matter to her.[128]

As it turned out, the landlady needed a new maid, and Descartes asks his correspondent to help find her one, and for Hélène's views on the matter. The suggestion seems to be that Hélène might join the household as a maid. We do not know whether they joined him, but the circumstantial evidence suggests to me that they did. Descartes made plans for Francine's education in France in 1639/40, which suggests that he had formed a closer attachment to her than is evident in the period before August 1637. And Vrooman is quite correct in pointing out that the tone of Descartes' correspondence at this time 'reveals a concern for life, a certain enthusiasm and exuberance, and even a certain vanity'.[129] He shows concern that his hair is going grey, though he immediately and typically depersonalizes it by converting it into a scientific problem, telling Huygens in October 1637 that he is spending all his time trying to reverse the greying process, 'and I hope my efforts will succeed despite a lack of sufficient experiments'.[130] Even more indicative is a new-found sense of his own mortality, something experienced by many parents in raising young children. He writes, again to Huygens, that never has he taken such 'great care of myself as I am doing at the moment. I used to think that death could deprive me of only thirty or forty years at the most, it wouldn't surprise me now unless it were to deprive me of the prospect of a hundred years or more'.[131]

Descartes generally shuns visitors in this period, although intimate friends such as Huygens, Gillot, and Reneri did visit him on rare occasions, and Huygens occasionally brought others, such as Pollot, with him. The only local friends that he mentions are two Catholic priests, parish curates in Haarlem, Joan Albert Ban and Augustin Bloemert; his relationship with them seems to have been quite close, and he would occasionally have his mail directed to their addresses. We know very little about Bloemert, but Ban was a musical theorist whose work was evidently mathematically adept, although his practical musical skills apparently left much to be desired.[132] He was one of Mersenne's correspondents, although they seem to have disliked one another and Mersenne clearly regarded Ban as inept and self-satisfied, trying (successfully) to get him to embarrass himself in a musical 'contest' devised by Mersenne in 1640.[133] Since Huygens knew Ban before 1638,[134] it is possible that it was Huygens who first introduced him to Descartes. Ban reports to Huygens on 15 October 1639 that he has just spent 'half a day talking about music with the hero Descartes',[135] which gives an interesting insight into the kind of reputation that Descartes was getting for himself (and doubtless encouraging) at this time.

Descartes clearly spent a lot of time dealing with queries and objections to the *Discours* and the *Essais* in the three years after their publication. He spent a great deal of time answering letters: about one fifth to one quarter of his extant correspondence dates from this period. Mersenne literally showered him with letters, at times almost daily, and even though very few days went by without his composing a letter, he found himself answering up to 7 of Mersenne's letters in the one reply, sometimes responding to 20 or 30 different questions, often of a difficult and technical nature. But he also pursued other topics and interests. He seems to have had a great interest in gardening, for example, spending a lot of time cultivating a herb garden (for culinary rather than medicinal purposes). He seems to have spent considerable time dissecting animals: eels, fish, rabbits, and he even refers on one occasion to his dissections of live dogs.[136] Many of his results are recorded in his *Anatomica*, although the vivisections were needed, of course, for physiological rather than strictly anatomical purposes: mainly, it would seem, for the study of the circulation of the blood.[137]

His correspondence also deals with mathematical questions unrelated to the *Géométrie*, such as that of aliquot parts of numbers (integers smaller than the number into which it can be divided), amicable numbers (those numbers the sums of whose aliquot parts are equal to each other), and perfect numbers (numbers equal to the sum of their aliquot parts).[138] In 1638 Johan Stampioen published the first of a number of placards challenging mathematicians to solve mathematical problems, and announcing the imminent publication of his *Algebra ofte Nieuwe Stel-Regel* ('Algebra or New Method'). Evidently because of the word 'method' in the title, Descartes, true to form, took this as a personal challenge and was outraged, making an extended attack on Stampioen.[139] When Stampioen's book appeared at the end of 1638, Descartes helped Jacob van Wassenaer, a young surveyor from Utrecht, to write a review of it so damning that Stampioen challenged Wassenaer to solve a problem for a forfeit of 600 guilders. Wassenaer accepted, with Descartes providing the wager and solving the problem for him.[140] Independent judges, four local professors of mathematics, announced Wassenaer the winner in May 1639.

Amongst the projects not directly concerned with the *Discours* and the *Essais*, by far the most important is his account of simple machines, such as the pulley, inclined plane, wedge, cog-wheel, screw, and lever.[141] As well as scattered references, there are some detailed accounts in letters to Huygens and Mersenne. The exercise is similar to those we have seen him pursue since 1618, namely the explanation of something already well-established in more fundamental terms. In this case, what was already well-understood were the ratios between force and resistance. Descartes' aim is to set out the basic principle underlying these ratios, which is that 'the effect must always be proportional to the *action* that is required to produce it'.[142] In his discussion he relates three terms, *action*, *puissance* (power), and *force*. He tells Mersenne that when one says that 'less *force* must be employed for one effect than for another, this is not the same as saying that less *puissance* is needed—for even if there is more it will make no difference—but only that less *action* is needed. And I did not consider [in the letter of 13 July 1638] the *puissance* that is called the *force* of a man, but only the *action* by which a weight can be raised, whether the *action* comes from a man, or a spring, or another weight, etc.'.[143] *Force* and *action* are equated here, and what Descartes means by *force* is spelled out when he tells Huygens that the same *force* is required to lift a weight of 100 pounds to two feet as is required to lift a weight of 400 pounds to half a foot.[144] In other words, *force* is weight times vertical displacement, what we would now call 'work'. But as well as displacements, we can also think in terms of velocities. In the case of the lever, for example, the displacement of the lever on the depressed end is proportional to the displacement of the end which bears the load; and the speeds of the two ends are similarly proportional. Consequently it is not surprising to find that, in the standard accounts of the time, such as Galileo's, displacement and speed are treated interchangeably. Here Descartes perceives what he insists is a fundamental error in the standard account, for:

it is not the difference in speed [*vitesse*] that determines that one of these weights must be twice the other, but the difference in displacement [*espace*], as one can see, for example, from the fact that to raise a weight F by hand to G [a point vertically above it] it is not necessary, if you wish to raise it twice as quickly, to use a force exactly twice that which would otherwise be necessary; rather, one must use a force which is more or less than twice as much, depending on the varying proportion that speed can have to the factors that resist it. *Whereas to raise it with the same speed twice as high, that is to H, a force that is exactly double is needed; I say that is exactly double, just as one and one are exactly two: for a certain quantity of that force must be used to raise the weight from F to G and then as much again of the same force is needed to raise it from G to H.*[145]

It is the ratio of displacements, not the ratio of speeds, that explains why the proportion of force and resistance varies as it does. For Descartes, this means that before you can discuss speed, you need to understand weight. But weight is a functional relationship which Descartes explains reductively, as we have seen, so understanding weight involves an understanding of the basic principles of his physics, as becomes clear, for example, in his discussion of variations in the weight of a body as a function of its distance from the centre of the earth.[146] But he did not spell out these basic principles sufficiently to assuage criticism, and his treatment of speed was a feature of Descartes' account that even his staunchest supporters found difficult to accept.[147] Nevertheless, it is a key element in his account, and further reinforces the view that he does not regard kinematics as being a core discipline, in the way that Galileo and, later, Christiaan Huygens did. *A fortiori*, his attachment to mechanism does not take the form of an attachment to reducing physics to kinematics, as it does in the later Cartesian tradition.

Meditationes de Prima Philosophia

In late April or early May 1640, Descartes moved back to Leiden[148] to oversee the preliminary printing of his *Meditationes*, which had evidently been completed between 1638 and then. We have already seen that Descartes had admitted to Vatier that the weakest part of the *Discours* was the treatment of God's existence, and that a fuller presentation of scepticism was needed before the argument could be properly appreciated. This is just what we get in the *Meditationes*, which cover the ground already gone over in Part IV of the *Discours* in a much more elaborate way.

The *Meditationes* read like an account of a spiritual journey in which the truth is only to be discovered by a purging, followed by a kind of rebirth. The precedents for this seem to come from writers such as Ignatius Loyola, and more generally from the manuals of devotional exercises common at this time. The first two Meditations, in particular, are rather dramatic, and the sense of purging that one gets in the first Meditation endows scepticism with a quasi-religious imperative. But the main point of calling the *Meditationes* by that name seems to have been simply to focus the mind on the nature of the subject matter and to remind Descartes' audience that what he is doing is strictly within the bounds of orthodoxy: they do not draw in any way on the genre of devotional meditations for their content, or, indeed, for anything precise.[149]

Their full title is 'Meditations on First Philosophy, in which are demonstrated the existence of God and the distinction between the human soul and the body', and in the dedicatory letter to the Theology Faculty of the Sorbonne, the aims are said to be those of proving the existence of God by means of natural reason, and providing a philosophical demonstration of the immortality of the soul. Descartes points to the decree of the Lateran Council of 1513 attacking Alexandrian and Averroist heresies, telling us that he has attempted to meet the Council's command to Christian philosophers 'to refute their arguments and use all their powers to establish the truth'.[150] The claim that Descartes makes for his demonstrations is that 'they are as certain and evident as the proofs of geometry, if not more so'.[151] But the *Meditationes* also deal with the nature of the corporeal world, and the synopsis of Meditation 6 spells out the relative standing of this account, maintaining that his arguments show that our knowledge of the existence of corporeal things is 'not so solid or transparent as the arguments which lead us to knowledge of our own minds and of God, so that the latter are the most certain and evident of all possible objects of knowledge for the human intellect'.[152] This is somewhat puzzling at first sight. The aim of the last Meditation seems to be to establish a model of the corporeal world which does yield certainty, for it establishes the clarity and distinctness of the corporeal world when this corporeal world is grasped in mathematical terms.[153] Why the apparent hesitation then? I do not believe that it has anything to do with any hesitation that Descartes himself felt about the truth of his own mechanistic model: there is no independent evidence of such hesitation, quite the contrary. We must consider this question against the background of the controversy over Copernicanism. A core issue in dispute in both the 1616 and 1633 condemnations of Copernicanism was whether the heliocentric theory was 'a matter of faith and morals', which the second decree of the Council of Trent had given the Church the sole power to decide.[154] Both Foscarini and Galileo explicitly denied that it was, maintaining that the motion of the Earth and stability of the Sun were covered by the first criterion in Melchior Cano's handbook of post-Tridentine orthodoxy, *De locis theologicis*, namely that when the authority of the Church Fathers 'pertains to the faculties contained within the natural light of reason, it does not provide certain arguments but only arguments as strong as reason itself when in agreement with nature'.[155] Opponents of Foscarini and Galileo argued that the case was covered by different criteria, such as the sixth, which states that the Church Fathers, if they agree on something, 'cannot err on dogmas of the faith'. We have seen that Descartes asked Mersenne for full information on the 1633 condemnation, and he would have been well aware of at least the major issues in dispute in the 1616 condemnation. Indeed, given the importance of this matter for him, it is hard to believe that he would not have had detailed knowledge of the cases being made by both sides. In short, Descartes is prepared to defend the Church orthodoxy on God and the soul, but natural philosophy is an area to be guided by the natural light of reason, not the Church.

Now Copernicanism and mechanism are intimately tied for Descartes, since the mechanist physics of *Le Monde* provides the underpinning for and leads directly to the heliocentric theory. A defence of mechanism is therefore by extension a defence of Copernicanism for Descartes. And the *Meditationes* contribute to the defence of mechanism in three ways. If we look at the whole project from the point of view of mechanism, then Descartes can be seen as trying to realize three closely related aims. The first is to establish not just the existence of God but, more importantly, the transcendent nature of His existence, and thereby show that God cannot be immanent in nature. This explains why, despite having provided a causal proof of God's existence in Meditation 2 (and a variant on this at the end of Meditation 3[156]), Descartes needs to supply the ontological proof in Meditation 5: it alone can establish the transcendence of God in the fullest way, as we saw when looking at Descartes' early project for a treatise on metaphysics. And this transcendence is then not bridged—for this would defeat the point of the exercise—but rendered benign, as it were, in Meditation 6 through the doctrine of divinely guaranteed clear and distinct ideas. The second task is to establish the mutual exclusivity of the mind and the body, thereby showing that mind cannot be immanent in any way in nature. The third is to establish that the corporeal world can be characterized exhaustively in geometrical terms, and that such a characterization provides one with a clear and distinct grasp of its constituents and their behaviour. To achieve this last aim, Descartes begins by undermining the veridicality of our perceptual image of the corporeal world by means of systematic doubt, and the corporeal world is then reconstructed from first principles. The key to this transformation is the doctrine of clear and distinct ideas, and the general aim is to use the criterion to generate indubitably veridical notions of God and the mind, and then to show that the same criterion, when applied to the corporeal world, yields a mechanist model of the corporeal world. The first thing Descartes does is to establish the credentials of the criterion intuitively, and then establish what kind of criterion it is. The *cogito* provides a paradigm application of the criterion and shows its power: it is the only thing capable of ending hyperbolic doubt. Since the criterion is going to have to be guaranteed by God, Descartes has somehow to move from the *cogito* to God, and he does this by establishing that his idea of God is such that only God could be its source. So, having established the credentials of the criterion and its source of legitimacy, he applies it to corporeal nature.[157]

The first part of the exercise is to establish the general unreliability of our knowledge claims. As I indicated when we looked at Part IV of the *Discours*, the kind of doubt that Descartes engages in is quite different from that of traditional Pyrrhonism. Commentators have reconstructed the history of scepticism by reading back from Descartes, finding less radical forms of epistemological doubt in earlier times. But Descartes is not simply taking a traditional epistemological problem, radicalizing it, and providing a new solution. He is posing a new epistemological problem, quite different from anything that had gone before, one whose original motivation arises in a context that is more metaphysical than epistemological. There are three possible relations between the three substances introduced in the *Meditationes*—God, mind, and matter—and Descartes explores all three. The relation between God and corporeal nature, and that of the relation between mind and corporeal nature, are explored in straightforwardly metaphysical terms. But the third relation, between mind and God, is more problematic. Yet it is here, and not in the relation between mind and nature, that the epistemological questions arise. Indeed, in Meditation 6 our cognitive relation to the world turns out to be something ultimately subordinate to our cognitive relation to God:

There is no doubt that everything that I am taught by nature contains some truth. For if nature is considered in its general aspect, then I understand by the term nothing other than God himself, or the ordered system of created things established by God.[158]

The problem of our relation to God is the problem of what relation we can stand in to a completely transcendent God, a problem that had been raised in stark terms in the letters to Mersenne of 1630 in which the question of the standing of eternal truths was discussed. The discussion of hyperbolic doubt of Meditation 1 contains two traces of this issue. The first is the evil demon, who has the powers of a deceitful transcendent God. Here we have a direct attempt to translate the problem into epistemological terms. We are asked to imagine the evil demon deceiving us into thinking that the corporeal world exists, when in fact it does not. Note that the evil demon here has the powers of a *transcendent* God, for *ex hypothesi* we have neither the perceptual nor intellectual faculties to detect the deception. And lacking those faculties, we also lack the ability to understand in what the deception consisted in the first place. Descartes had raised an analogous problem in the *Regulae*, telling us that 'if someone is blind from birth, we should not expect to be able by force of argument to get him to have true ideas of colours just like the ones we have', and that, by the same token, 'if there is in the magnet some kind of nature which our intellect has never before perceived, it is pointless to hope that we will ever get to it by reasoning; for that, we should need to be endowed with a new sense, or with a divine mind'.[159] By analogy, we might argue that if the evil demon has access to a reality which our intellect has never before perceived it is pointless to hope that we will ever get to it by reasoning; for that, we should need to be endowed with a new sense, or with a divine mind. But Descartes' point is not that there is something unintelligible about hyperbolic doubt[160]—such an admission would clearly undermine his whole project—but rather that we cannot meet hyperbolic doubt by relying wholly on our own resources.

The second trace of the origins of hyperbolic doubt in the metaphysical question of our relation to God lies in the fact that mathematical truths are included. A useful and common epistemological way of thinking of hyperbolic doubt is as something that goes beyond that form of doubt which envisages states of affairs that are empirically possible to a form of doubt that envisages states of affairs which are merely logically possible, that is, which envisages states of affairs which, while not empirically possible, involve no logical contradiction. We might not grant that the empirical world is an illusion, for example that we are simply a brain in a vat whose neurones are stimulated in such a way as to make it appear that there is an external world; but there is no contradiction in envisaging such a state of affairs. But in Meditation 1 Descartes allows that mathematical truths such as '2 + 3 = 5' can be subjected to hyperbolic doubt, and here there may well be a logical contradiction. Completely epistemological versions of hyperbolic doubt tend to focus on the case of the existence of the external world, leaving the mathematical case to one side as unintelligible, but it is in fact no more or less intelligible than hyperbolic doubt about the existence of the external world. Indeed, the mathematical case more clearly reveals the metaphysical origins of Descartes' account. Descartes raised this question in his metaphysical discussion of eternal truths in the letters to Mersenne, as we have seen, well before any mention of hyperbolic doubt. It is hard to explain why it subsequently reappears in the context of hyperbolic doubt if this is not construed as being motivated metaphysically, for it makes no epistemological sense: how could the world be exactly as it is and yet 2 + 3 not equal 5? It is simply incomprehensible to us, and Descartes himself never claimed otherwise. What he did claim, as we have seen, was that what is comprehensible to us does not constrain God.

If Descartes' aim in introducing hyperbolic doubt was to show that we cannot legitimate our knowledge claims by relying wholly on our own resources, what role does the *cogito* play? It cannot act as a foundation for knowledge, and so far as I know Descartes nowhere suggests that it does. But it does serve two crucial functions: it blocks off the regress of doubt, and it acts as a paradigm application of the criterion of clear and distinct ideas. In introducing scepticism Descartes uses the traditional Pyrrhonist procedure. The sceptic lets the opponent make a knowledge claim and then shows that the claim fails to meet his opponent's own requirements for knowledge, by showing that the requisite justification for the claim is not available. The sceptical argument has a distinctive dialectical structure, which requires the opponent to provide all the premisses of the argument, so that the sceptic can then show an inconsistency between the premisses. The opponent must provide both the definition of knowledge and the knowledge claim if the argument is to get off the ground. But Descartes then turns the tables and uses this procedure against the sceptic himself. In order to be a sceptic in the first place the sceptic must engage in sceptical doubt, and Descartes uses the fact of sceptical doubt to show the sceptic that there is, after all, something that he cannot doubt, namely that he is doubting. The sceptic cannot resist this conclusion, because the argument form that secures it is the same as that employed by the sceptic himself to start off the sceptical process in the first place. Descartes makes the sceptic supply the material on which the argument works, the doubting from which the existence of the doubter follows. He makes the sceptic provide the materials for his own demise. This is a remarkably effective response to scepticism.[161]

The key feature of the *cogito* is that it is what, in earlier writings, Descartes had referred to as an *intuitus*, an instantaneous grasp. Descartes even uses the term *intuitus* in this context in the second set of Replies to the *Meditationes*:

When someone says *I am thinking therefore I am, or exist*, he does not deduce existence from thought by means of a syllogism, but recognizes it as something self-evident by a simple *intuitus* of the mind.[162]

Many commentators have been misled into thinking that Descartes is maintaining here that the *cogito* is not an inference. Quite the contrary, as we saw in Chapter 4, *intuitus* is the paradigm form of inference. If the *cogito* is an *intuitus*, then it is necessarily an inferential judgement of some kind. And what makes the *cogito* so important is that it is the paradigm form of *intuitus*, which is in turn the paradigm form of inference.

But what is it about the *cogito* that confers this status on it? We are given no explicit answer, but I am inclined to reconstruct an answer along the following lines. In the most general metaphysical terms, the distinctive feature of the *cogito*, compared to the items of purported knowledge that Descartes has rejected as being subject to hyperbolic doubt, is that this is a case where appearance and reality clearly coincide. There is a possible gap between it appearing to me that there is an external world and there really being an external world, and even between it appearing to me that 2 plus 3 equal 5 and their really equalling five. But there is no possible gap between it appearing to me that I am thinking and my really thinking. This is a self-evident, incorrigible truth. Descartes wants it to act as a model for other truths. But this is problematic, for in fact it is far from clear that we are dealing with a case in which reality and appearance self-evidently and indubitably coincide here. Rather, we seem to be dealing with a case in which the distinction between appearance and reality cannot be made because it is simply inappropriate. On the former reading of such cases, they are a paradigmatic form of knowledge. On the latter reading, they do not count as knowledge at all, as they would not have in the Aristotelian tradition, for example, where to know something is to have an explanation or at least an 'account' of that thing. And if they do not count as knowledge then *a fortiori* they cannot count as paradigm cases of knowledge.[163] As I have shown, it is crucial for Descartes that the *cogito* be a judgement. The problem is that it is difficult to see what exactly the judgement could consist in, but this is a general problem with his idea of cognitive grasp, not something specific to the *cogito*.

But whatever the difficulties here, it is clear that the criterion of clarity and distinctness plays the key role, and Descartes now uses it to establish the nature of the thinking subject (which I shall look at later), the nature of God, and the nature of the corporeal world. Before we consider these, however, we need to consider Descartes' notoriously problematic classification of ideas into those which are innate, those which are adventitious, and those invented by oneself.[164] The latter, which comprise such invented animals as 'sirens and hippogriffs', are relatively straightforward and need not detain us. In a letter to Mersenne of 23 June 1641 he gives as examples of innate ideas 'the idea of God, mind, body, triangle, and in general all those things which represent true, immutable, and eternal essences'.[165] Now the first mention of innate ideas in Descartes comes in his letter to Mersenne of 15 April 1630, in which he sets out his doctrine of the creation of eternal truths, where he tells Mersenne that eternal truths are 'inborn in our minds'.[166] This is instructive, for what these innate ideas seem to provide is immutable and eternal essences which would otherwise be unknowable, because we could not know by any other means what immutable and eternal essence God had willed mind, body, and triangles to have: remember here that God could have willed the sum of the internal angles of a triangle to be 179° if He had so wished, so the 'natural light of reason' would be of no help here. Adventitious ideas are those 'foreign to me and coming from outside', as the French version of the *Meditationes* puts it. The trouble is that it turns out in subsequent writings, most notoriously the *Notae in programma*, that these too are in some sense innate; but I believe the sense in which these are innate is very different: they are simply innate capacities with which corporeal cognitive organs are fitted, and which do not require a mind in the strict sense. We can defer consideration of them until later.

The one innate idea that we have already looked at in some detail is that of God. A notoriously problematic part of Meditation 3 is the establishment of the existence of God, for Descartes must use the doctrine of clear and distinct ideas to prove the existence of God, and then use God to provide a divine guarantee for these clear and distinct ideas. As Arnauld puts it in his objections to the *Meditationes*:

> How does the author avoid reasoning in a circle when he says that we are sure that what we clearly and distinctly perceive is true only because God exists. We can be sure that God exists only because we clearly and distinctly perceive this. Hence, before we can be sure that God exists, we must be able to be sure that whatever we perceive clearly and evidently is true.[167]

The problem here brings into focus a tension in his doctrine of clear and distinct ideas. As we have seen, this doctrine originally began life as a refinement of a traditional rhetorical-psychological theory about the evidential value of mental images, and it was transformed into a metaphysical doctrine about how we are to guarantee the veridicality of our cognition of the external world against hyperbolic doubt. The earlier doctrine was one which had some degree of common currency, in which clarity and distinctness had quite precisely defined meanings. The later version, while still directed towards the idea of self-conviction, sets out to achieve this in a very different way, and it operates with a notion of clarity and distinctness which is more contentious. What Descartes does is to trade on his readers' intuitions about clarity and distinctness and secure our agreement that we have a clear and distinct grasp in the *cogito*, and then proceeds to spell out in a novel way what this grasp must consist in, showing how it must be much more radical than we might have thought. Above all, it depends on a divine guarantee, something not at all evident when we first consider the nature of our grasp of the *cogito*. The price that Descartes pays for this is high, however, for, unlike the original version, the new notion of clarity and distinctness contains nothing intrinsic by which we might distinguish genuine clarity and distinctness from seeming clarity and distinctness. As Gassendi points out, 'everyone thinks that he clearly and distinctly perceives the truth that he champions'.[168]

Even more radical is Descartes' use of the criterion to establish the complete dependence of the corporeal world on God. In Meditation 3 he defends what is in effect a particularly strong form of mechanism, in which nature is stripped even of the power to persist from instant to instant.[169] The argument proceeds from three premisses. The first is the assumption that causation is instantaneous, that is, that cause and effect occur simultaneously: there is no temporal gap between cause and effect. The second premiss is that if something is to exist there must be some cause of its existence. By the first premiss this cannot be something in the past, for no past event can act now so as to cause a present event, so past existence cannot cause present existence. Hence, what causes the existence of the corporeal world now must be something that acts now. But (third premiss) the corporeal world cannot sustain itself—if I examine my own body, for example, I can discover in it no power by which it might sustain itself—so it must be something other than my body that sustains it. It cannot be my mind for, as we shall see below, the mind is subject to the same strictures. God is the only possibility remaining, and He must sustain the universe by recreating it at each instant.

The first premiss was quite traditional, and efficient causation had generally been regarded as instantaneous in scholastic philosophy.[170] It was an intuitively plausible and attractive view of causation,[171] something that fitted in closely with Descartes' hydrostatic model of *action*, upon which he had relied in his discussion of the instantaneous transmission of light, and which clearly has advantages if one thinks of collision in terms of incompressible bodies, where instantaneous changes of speed and direction are crucial. The third premiss is something that any mechanist would have to accept, given the first two premisses, but it would have been disputed by a naturalist, and it therefore begs the question somewhat. The second premiss is problematic in a number of ways: for example, if everything that exists must be caused to exist at the moment it exists, this means God's existence must have a cause. Descartes bites the bullet: God's essence is such that His existence is necessary, something the ontological argument will trade upon, so His essence causes Him to exist at every instant. This view puzzled Descartes' critics,[172] and it is indeed difficult to understand exactly how something can put itself into existence. But the way in which Descartes deals with God's existence is important as an indication of how he sees the question of existence. It draws a contrast between those things whose essence requires their existence and those whose essence does not. It is not the distinction as such that I wish to focus upon, however, but the way in which we move from the conception that we have of something to the question of its extra-mental existence.

This provides the model for Descartes' reconstruction of the corporeal world. We must start from our ideas, and discover whether there is any extra-mental reality that corresponds to them. But we can only start from those ideas that are clear and distinct, and in the case of the corporeal world Descartes wants to restrict our ideas to those that are mathematical:

It follows that corporeal things exist. But they may not all exist in a way that corresponds to how they appear in sense perception, for in many cases sensory grasp is obscure and confused. But at least they possess all the properties that I clearly and distinctly understand, that is, generally speaking, all those which come within the subject matter of pure mathematics.[173]

'Pure mathematics' here turns out, of course, to be geometry, for what Descartes means is that we have a clear and distinct grasp of corporeal bodies in so far as we grasp them under the category of extension. The strategy is, then, to start from ideas, to decide which of these are clear and distinct, and then to investigate the correspondence between these and reality. Since Descartes is effectively only prepared to allow that mathematical conceptions of corporeal reality are clear and distinct, he is able to establish (metaphysically) the unique legitimacy of a particular way of pursuing of natural philosophy without raising a single natural-philosophical question.

At this point, it is worth mentioning an especially problematic feature of Descartes' reconstruction of the corporeal world in mechanical terms. The primacy of shape, size, and motion in his account has often led to it being assimilated to the kind of account of primary and secondary qualities that Galileo offered in his *Assayer*,[174] whereby colours, for example, are merely psychic additions of the perceiving mind. Later Cartesians, most notably Malebranche, took this view, and it is not at all surprising that what is effectively an eliminativist reading of Descartes' account of colour has prevailed. Nevertheless, despite occasional statements that colours are just 'appearances', Descartes does not seem to have held an eliminativist account, but rather something closer to a dispositional one. In his replies to Arnauld's objections to the *Meditationes*, he tells Arnauld that he has been working on showing how 'colour, taste, heaviness, and all other qualities which stimulate the senses, depend simply on the exterior surface of bodies'.[175] The account he is working on is presumably that provided in the *Principia*, Part IV, art. 198, whose title reads: 'By means of our senses we apprehend nothing in external objects beyond their shapes, sizes and motions'.[176] In explanation, he writes: 'we have every reason to conclude that the properties in external objects to which we apply the terms "light", "colour", "odour", "flavour", "sound", "heat" and "cold" . . . are simply various dispositions in these objects which make them able to set up various kinds of motion in our nerves.'[177] This does not rule out the possibility, excluded by the eliminativist reading, that we perceive the colours of bodies in virtue of perceiving shapes, sizes, and motions. Indeed, the expression 'varias dispositiones' indicates that this is how we should take Descartes' account. Unfortunately, he does not elaborate, but the inclusion of heaviness in the list he gives to Arnauld is interesting, for in the reply to the sixth set of objections to the *Meditationes*, he does elaborate on the notion of heaviness, arguing that the heaviness of a body, while not itself corporeal or extended, 'could produce the full effect of which it was capable at any given point in that body', adding that the body's heaviness is not something 'distinct from the body'.[178] Of course, our cognitive apparatus needs to be 'fitted out' in the appropriate way if we are respond to various rotational motions in the requisite way, namely by having the sensation of colour, and this is presumably what Descartes is signalling when he writes in the *Notae in programma* that our ideas of colours are innate.[179] Innateness is construed there, as we shall see, very much as an innate capacity, and the claim seems to be that we have an innate capacity to respond visually to rotating light corpuscles by perceiving colour. But of course this is quite compatible with colour being a dispositional property of bodies, a view which makes colours something less than a real surface property of the body, but something more than merely a psychic addition of the perceiving mind. Although Descartes does not elaborate on this, we might perhaps think of colour along the lines of camouflage, something which is context-dependent and response-dependent for its effect, but which is nevertheless a real feature of the object camouflaged.

The other major question dealt with in the *Meditationes* is the nature of the thinking subject. This is something that will be developed at length in Descartes' subsequent writings, and I shall only draw attention to five of the more salient points of his conception here.

First, Descartes assumes that, even in doubting, I cannot doubt that there is something that is doing the doubting, and he proceeds to ask for the nature of this doubting subject. The key assumption here is that there is what we might refer to as a unified locus of subjectivity, a self, which is the origin or bearer of the particular doubt. Although this assumption has been questioned by many subsequent philosophers, it might seem anachronistic to press Descartes on this point. In fact it is not, for there was a relatively well-developed conception of the mind, proposed by Averroists, on which there can only be one intellect in the universe, which precludes the intellect being identified with an individual self, as Descartes maintains. A related point is in fact made by an unknown supporter of Gassendi in a letter of July 1641, who tells Descartes: 'you do not know whether it is you yourself who think or whether the world-soul in you does the thinking, as the Platonists believe'.[180] Although Descartes replies to the other objections made in the letter, he ignores this one.[181] In other words, he assumes the falsity of an Averroist-type view in Meditation 2, and when pressed ignores the issue. This is surprising in the light of the fact that the 1513 decree of the Lateran Council had singled this view out for criticism, and, as we have seen, in the dedicatory letter to the *Meditationes*, Descartes says that the Council 'expressly enjoined Christian philosophers to refute [Averroist] arguments and use all their powers to establish the truth, so I have not hesitated to attempt this task as well'.[182] On the Averroist conception of the mind, there is one intellect in the universe in which individual minds participate, but once the corporeal faculties die the individual mind dies with it, perhaps having made some contribution to the single intellect. As Zabarella describes it, 'the rational soul is thus like a sailor coming into a ship already constituted, and giving to man his outstanding operation, which is to contemplate and understand, just as a sailor steering a ship gives it the operation of navigation'; the intellect 'is not multiplied in accordance with the number of men but is only one in number in the whole human species. . . . When any man dies, this Intellect does not perish but remains the same in number in those that are left'.[183] The motivation behind this account of the mind derived from the Aristotelian doctrine that pure form cannot be individuated, and it was concluded from this that disembodied minds cannot be individuated and cannot be more than one in number. The theological problem with this is that, while it allows immortality, it does not allow personal immortality.

This brings us to the second issue, the question of Descartes' identification of the self with something intellectual, namely the mind. Descartes does two things here: he argues that the mind must be spiritual, and he assumes that having shown this he has also shown that the mind is identical with the self. Both of these are questionable. The way in which he establishes the first is a disaster. His argument is that I can doubt whether my body exists without doubting whether I exist, so the existence of my body cannot be the same as the existence of me. In the fourth set of objections to the *Meditationes*, Arnauld points out that this reasoning is quite invalid. For consider a parallel case. I may well be able to doubt that a right-angled triangle has the property of having a hypoteneuse whose square is equal to the sum of the squares of the other sides; but it does not follow from my being able to doubt that a right-angled triangle has this property that it does not really have it.[184] In a somewhat tortuous reply, Descartes effectively concedes the point, maintaining that the real demonstration of the distinctness of mind and body comes only in Meditation 6,[185] although the 'demonstration' given there simply states that I have a clear and distinct idea of mind, as something thinking and unextended, and I have a clear and distinct idea of body, as something non-thinking and extended, so the two cannot be the same.[186] Then, since he has already shown that he must be thinking, it follows that what he is essentially is a mind and not a body. But this demonstration has much more contentious premisses than the demonstration in Meditation 2, since it assumes that the nature of the mind and matter have already been established.[187] I do not want to dwell on these problems, however, for there is a deeper question at stake: to identify the mind with 'thought' is not automatically to identify it with the self. The key doctrines condemned by the Lateran Council had been Averroism and Alexandrism. Both of these had offered a doctrine on the question of the nature of the mind and had maintained that while the corporeal faculties were active the individual mind acted by means of those faculties. Alexandrians had argued that (at least as far as philosophical understanding was concerned) these corporeal faculties must be constitutive of the mind, because forms must always be instantiated in matter. Consequently, once the corporeal faculties ceased to be active, at death, the form of the body, its soul, also ceased to exist.[188] One way around this conclusion, for a Christian Aristotelian, was to stress the doctrine of the resurrection of the body at the Last Judgement. One's mind or form was then reunited with one's (revamped) body. There were metaphysical problems with this account, which centred on what happened between death and the Last Judgement: most notably, what happened to the form (which cannot exist uninstantiated) in the meantime, and whether the entity who reappeared at the Last Judgement could be said to be the same person as the one who had died earlier. And there were theological problems, as Ockham had shown in criticizing the Thomist version of this doctrine, for most medieval forms of prayer and worship were directed towards the saints, who interceded on one's behalf, rather than directly to God, but it was a consequence of the Thomist view that these saints did not come into existence again until the Last Judgement, so all the prayers and worship would have been useless. Tying the mind/soul to a body was clearly fraught with problems. On the other hand, to dissociate the mind from the body, as the Averroists did, was equally problematic, for it led to an inability to individuate minds, and to their identification with one another and perhaps even ultimately with God.[189] Alexandrism and Averroism are the Charybdis and Scylla through which Descartes must steer a passage in setting out his doctrine of the nature of the mind. In this, he faces insuperable difficulties.

Third, there is the question of what is included in the 'thinking' that the thinking subject, the *res cogitans*, engages in. In Meditation 2 we are given two descriptions of this thinking. First we are told that 'I am a thing that thinks; that is, I am a mind, an intelligence, or intellect, or reason'.[190] Then, on the next page, Descartes writes: 'But what am I? A thing that thinks. What is that? A thing that doubts, understands, affirms, denies, is willing, is unwilling, and also imagines and has sensory perceptions'.[191] The first remark suggests that thinking is rather narrowly defined, the second definition that it is very widely defined. If we think of the traditional distinguishing features of the mind as being intellect or judgement and volition, then the first characterization seems to exclude volition, whereas the second includes a variety of things, such as sense perceptions, which would not have been included in the traditional conception. Neither characterization can be taken at face value, however: the first seems to provide an open list, whereas the second must be heavily qualified. We have already seen that Descartes must allow some kind of thinking to animals in as much as they are capable of perceptual discrimination, but the 'thinking' that is at issue here in Meditation 2 is something in which the mind proper engages, and not something that animals are capable of. This raises the question of why corporeal faculties such as imagining and sense perception are included in the list, since animals are capable of these. Clearly, Descartes cannot mean imagining and sense perception *per se* here: he is referring to human imagining and sense perception. And because he includes these in a list of things characteristic of the thinking subject, which excludes animals, there must be some difference between human sense perception and animal sense perception, for example. It is not enough to say that one involves the mind whereas the other does not, because what we need to know is what difference the involvement of the mind makes. One possibility is that human sense-perception involves an awareness of one's perceptual states as perceptual states, whereas animal sense-perception does not. I think that there can be no doubt that Descartes believes that this is the case. The question is whether this in itself is all there is to it. What is so special about a simple awareness of one's own mental states? There is a widespread view that Descartes thought that awareness of one's own mental states was in fact constitutive of the uniqueness of human cognition, and this view has been reinforced by an interpretation of the *cogito* whereby my grasp of my own existence is an instantaneous act of self-consciousness, rather than an inference or judgement. We have seen that such an interpretation is mistaken: the *cogito* does involve inference and judgement. This prompts us to question whether consciousness of one's mental states is, in Descartes' view, constitutive of human mental life, or whether such consciousness is merely what is required if human mental life is to possess the features traditionally ascribed to it, namely will and judgement. Surely what makes human beings capable of judgement and volition is the fact that they can reflect on their own mental states, whereas animals cannot. Such traditional mental functions require awareness of one's own mental states, and this awareness is distinctive of human cognition and absent from animals, but it is not constitutive of them.[192] The most sensible reading of Descartes' claim is correspondingly that awareness of one's own mental states is the key to the difference between creatures with a mind and automata, and that without such awareness the characteristic features of human mental life would not be possible.[193]

Fourth, there is the question of the dependence of the self on God. When we looked at Mersenne's statement of the problem of naturalism in chapter 5, we saw that he considered the source of both naturalism and mortalism as lying in the construal of matter as being in some way active, and that his solution was to strip the corporeal world of all activity and powers, making it completely inert. But, as we also noted, the mechanist attempt to fill out the distinction between the supernatural and the natural in terms of that between the active and the inert, while it has a *prima facie* appeal in the case of naturalism, is not obviously relevant or appropriate to the question of mortalism. This problem intrudes with a vengeance in Meditation 3. There, as we have seen, Descartes strips nature even of the power to persist from instant to instant. The trouble is that this is not only lacking from corporeal things but from minds as well. After telling us that the distinction between preservation and creation is only a conceptual one, Descartes applies his doctrine of continuous creation to the mind:

I must therefore now ask myself whether I possess some power enabling me to bring it about that I who now exist will still exist a little while from now. For since I am nothing but a thinking thing . . . if there were such a power in me, I should undoubtedly be aware of it. But I experience no such power, and this very fact makes me recognise most clearly that I depend on some being distinct from myself.[194]

So not only the body, but the mind as well must be continually re-created by God at each instant if it is to persevere. This means that its cognitive and affective states—memories, sensations, imagination, judgements, and volitions—must also be recreated. The doctrine of the continual recreation of the mind only makes the existence of its mental states, not their content, dependent upon God, so there is some sense in which the mind's free will and independent judgement are preserved. But it cannot be denied that Descartes is sailing perilously close to the wind here. In particular, in making God the only active thing there is, it is difficult to see how the mind avoids becoming inert. Later on, in correspondence,[195] he will explicitly assert that the mind is active, but he makes no attempt to reconcile this claim with the present doctrine. The problem here arises because, by trying to model discussion of the mind along the lines elaborated for dealing with naturalistic construals of corporeal nature, Descartes ends up with no option but to put the mind on the inert side of the active/inert divide, because it comes within the natural and not the supernatural. The only benefit from this is that Averroism is ruled out, for the mind cannot be identical with God on this conception: but the doctrine of the continuous recreation of the mind might seem a high price to pay for this.

Fifth and finally, there is the question of the nature of the relation between the mind and the body. In Meditation 6, Descartes criticizes a form of Platonic dualism:

Nature teaches me through the sensations of hunger and thirst etc. that I am not merely present in my body as a sailor in present in a ship, but that I am very closely joined, and as it were intermingled, with it, so that I and the body form a unity. If this were not so, then I who am nothing but a thinking thing would not feel pain when the body was hurt, but rather the intellect would simply perceive the damage, just as a sailor perceives by sight whether anything in his boat is broken. Similarly, when the body needs food or drink, I should have an understanding of this fact as such, rather than having confused sensations of hunger and thirst. For these sensations of hunger, thirst, pain, etc., are nothing but confused modes of thinking which arise from the union and the intermingling, as it were, of the mind with the body.[196]

Sensory awareness is neither straightforwardly bodily nor straight-forwardly intellectual. Later, as we shall see, Descartes will maintain that there are three 'primitive' categories: extension, thought, and the 'substantial union of mind and body',[197] showing just how seriously he takes the question. When we looked at the question of perceptual cognition in animals in the context of chapter 1 of *Le Monde*, I raised the question whether the fact that one has a rational soul completely transforms the nature of one's experiences, rather than simply taking those experiences as given and reflecting on them. There was nothing to indicate what answer Descartes would give to this question in *Le Monde*. We can now begin to see what his answer is. It is not that we simply have sensory experiences, as animals do, but that then, unlike animals, we reflect on these experiences and make judgements about them. The fact that we are capable of reflection and judgement com-pletely transforms the nature of our experience, even when we are not reflecting and making judgements about it. And what the nature of our experience is like will inevitably have consequences for how we con-ceive of the 'I' that has these experiences, consequences that Descartes will devote the years from 1643 onwards drawing out.

We shall pursue a number of the topics raised here in the *Meditationes* in the context of the more detailed discussions that Descartes provides later, especially in the *Principia* and the *Passions*. But it is worth setting out the achievement of the *Meditationes* in terms of the development of Descartes' projects. It establishes the legitimacy of mechanism at a metaphysical level and in a more detailed way than is done in the *Discours*, and it does this by setting out to establish three things: that corporeal nature is both completely distinct from and completely dependent on God; that corporeal nature is completely distinct from mind; and that mind is both completely distinct from and completely dependent on God. The first two undermine any kind of naturalism about the corporeal world, whereas the second undermines Alexandrism and the third Averroism. All the work is done by metaphysically guaranteed clear and distinct ideas, which secure the veridicality of our cognition of the external world against hyperbolic doubt. By starting from those ideas of the corporeal world which are genuinely clear and distinct, Descartes arrives at a mechanistic picture of how the world is to be described at a most fundamental level, and he arrives at this not by natural-philosophical or empirical means, as he had done in earlier writings such as *Le Monde*, but by purely metaphysical ones. This is a remarkable achievement, but it is not, of course, a remarkable discovery, for the point of the exercise was never to discover metaphysically that mechanism provides the only true basis for a natural philosophy, but to legitimate mechanism, something which motivated Descartes' work long before it even occurred to him that metaphysical legitimation was needed. The question of metaphysical legitimation arose principally because Descartes took heliocentrism to be a direct consequence of the mechanistic cosmology of *Le Monde*, and the condemnations of 1616 and especially 1633 had indicated that no purely natural-philosophical argument was going to be decisive. The *Meditationes*, without completely revealing the aim of the exercise, provide an argument that Descartes hopes will be decisive, and to the extent that it proves to be so, the fuller project can be revealed in the *Principia*, how far he can go in the *Principia* being determined by the kind of reaction that the *Meditationes* elicit.

Public Brawl and Personal Grief, 1639–1640

Descartes' 'Indian Summer' came to an end with two events in the period between 1639 and 1640. The first was the beginning of an extremely acrimonious dispute, which turned into a long-drawn-out public brawl in which the theological implications of Descartes' work were questioned. The dispute began at the University of Utrecht. Reneri died in the middle of March 1639, and a friend of his, Anton Aemelius, delivered a funeral oration at the University which extolled the virtues of Cartesian natural philosophy over the philosophies of the traditional professors at Utrecht. The publication of the eulogy, which gave it an official stamp of approval, caused some consternation among these professors, and the situation was exacerbated when Henri le Roy, better known as Regius, took up the Cartesian cause in a polemical and abrasive manner. Regius had evidently visited Descartes in Santpoort with his friend Reneri, and he appears to have had Descartes' full confidence at this time. He was an extremely popular teacher and propagandist, and he had been elected a full professor of medicine at Utrecht in 1638. Unlike Descartes, he was not shy of public dispute, nor was he worried about becoming embroiled in theological quarrels with the authorities. On 10 June 1640 he proposed a number of Cartesian theses for public discussion, and Gisbert Voetius, a professor of theology at Utrecht, took up the cause of traditional philosophy and theology against him, and against the originator of these pernicious doctrines, Descartes himself. Sensing that Cartesianism posed an immense threat to traditional philosophy and theology, he set about exposing this threat in a systematic and personalized way. Voetius set out to destroy Descartes, and as well as his natural philosophical doctrines, his religion and his personal morality were thrown into the ring, in a public dispute that was to take its toll on Descartes over five years, and was to lay bare the life and beliefs of someone who had always been extremely jealous of his privacy.

The most momentous event of 1640, however, was the death of Francine. At the end of a letter to Mersenne of 12 September 1638, Descartes remarks that he is 'surrounded by fevers on all sides: everyone is ill in these parts, and up to now I alone in my house have avoided it'.[198] Plagues and epidemics were common at this time, and Leiden had suffered from a devasting epidemic only a few years earlier. Hélène and Francine recovered from their earlier illness, and Descartes made plans for Francine to study in France, presumably without her mother, under the tutelage of a Madame du Tronchet, someone who Baillet tells us was of the highest virtue, the mother of an ecclesiastic, and even a distant relative.[199] The journey to France was never to take place, however, for, as Baillet reports it, Francine 'died at Amersfort on the 7 September 1640, the third day of her illness, her body completely covered with sores'.[200] Descartes may have been at her bedside: although he had left for Leiden in late April or early May, we know he was 'unexpectedly' called away from Leiden between 1 September and some time between 8 and 15 September.[201] Baillet reports that Descartes said that her death left him 'with the greatest sorrow that he had ever experienced in his life'.[202]

9

The Defence of Natural Philosophy
1640–1644

Religious Controversy

Descartes left Santpoort for Leiden some time in April or May of 1640
to oversee the preliminary printing of his *Meditationes*, and that done,
he did not return to Santpoort. With Francine dead and Hélène simply
never mentioned again, an era in his life now comes to an end, and a
new one begins. He moved to a château at Endegeest, just outside
Leiden, where he was to stay until May 1643. The château was evidently well-equipped, having its own servants as well as a horse and
carriage, and was not far from the university and libraries. Descartes,
now in his late 40s, evidently began to enjoy a slightly less frugal life
than he had led up to this point. Less frugal, but certainly not more
peaceful, for although these are the years in which he wrote the *Principia*,
much of 1640 to 1644 are taken up by various disputes and polemics,
initially with replying to the objections solicited for the *Meditationes*,
and then with disputes with Voetius and Bourdin.

The first printing of the *Meditationes* was not to be a full one, but
rather a printing of proofs for distribution to various philosophers and
theologians. We have already seen, in the case of the *Discours* and the
Essais, that Descartes did not take kindly to objections, and was inclined to be dismissive of them. Moreover, in general terms, his response
to the objections to the *Meditationes*, although more polite than his
reaction to critics of the *Discours*, indicates no change of heart in this
respect. The simple fact is that Descartes did not like criticism. Why,
then, did he delay publication of the *Meditationes* until objections and
replies could be appended? It is perhaps an indication of the confidence
that Descartes felt about his metaphysics at this time; but such confidence could, of course, also be manifested by simply presenting the
work as it stood without worrying about how others might react. Here
we must take account of the fact that, although the objections are from
a range of views, and cover a wide spectrum, four of the first six sets
of objections are from critics designated as 'philosophers and theologians';[1] and the two sets that are from philosophers rather than theologians, the third (Hobbes) and fifth (Gassendi), are given relatively
short shrift, with a disproportionately small amount of space devoted

to replying to them. Descartes devotes a very large amount of space to responding to the seventh set of objections, published in the second edition of the *Meditationes*, by Bourdin, a Jesuit, even though these objections are exceptionally weak. And it is no surprise that the one critic whom he singles out for special praise is Arnauld, a theologian from the Sorbonne. Descartes is concerned with orthodoxy as much as anything else. Note in this connection that the *Meditationes* were published in Latin rather than French, despite the fact that the text is far less technical than the *Essais* that accompanied the *Discours*, and so apparently something with a wider appeal. Descartes says in the preface that he is only setting out his full arguments here, and had not done so in the *Discours* because, being in French, the *Discours* was designed to be read by anyone, and 'weaker intellects might believe that they ought to set out on the same path'.[2] This is somewhat disingenuous, for there is nothing potentially dangerous in the *Meditationes* that is not in the *Discours*, and in any case Descartes will sanction a French translation of the former in 1647, omitting the Preface referring to those 'weaker intellects' that cannot read Latin, of course.

Many of the objections and replies cover Descartes' incursions into scholastic philosophy or the relation of what he says to scholastic philosophy. In the first set of objections, for example, which were the only set Descartes himself solicited (the rest were solicited through Mersenne), Caterus, a local priest and friend of Ban and Bloemart, rakes over the doctrines of the objective reality of ideas, the proofs of God's existence and how they compare to those of Aquinas, and the nature of efficient causes. Similar concerns are raised in many of the other objections, particularly in the sixth and seventh sets, and the procedure of translating what Descartes says into scholastic terms is not confined to Caterus. Although Descartes is at pains to show that his project is very different from that pursued in scholastic philosophy, he does not want to give the impression of rejecting scholastic philosophy; and in the second set of replies he makes a remarkable concession, setting out his arguments for the existence of God and the distinction between mind and body axiomatically in 'a short exposition in synthetic form',[3] although he makes it clear that this serves merely to summarize his demonstrations.

I have argued that, by this stage, Descartes' project is ultimately directed towards metaphysical legitimation of his natural philosophy, which is resolutely Copernican. For this metaphysical legitimation to be successful, it was necessary to show that it was in line with the teachings of the Church, that it did not involve or lead to any theological unorthodoxy. Generally speaking, Descartes steers clear of theological questions, restricting his attention to showing that there is no incompatibility between his metaphysics and theological orthodoxy. He generally avoids trying to demonstrate theological dogmas metaphysically. When challenged that he has not established the immortality of the soul merely in showing that the soul and the body are distinct substances, for example, he replies that he 'does not take it upon myself to use the power of human reason to settle any of those matters which depend on the free will of God'.[4]

The fateful exception to this general approach is his account of the doctrine of transubstantiation, and in the letter to Dinet that accompanied the second edition of the *Meditationes* he throws his usual caution to the wind:

As far as theology is concerned, truths can never be in conflict with one another, and it would be impious to fear that any truths that philosophy discovers could be in conflict with those of the faith. Indeed, I maintain that there is no religious matter which cannot be equally well or even better explained using my principles than by using those commonly accepted. I believe I gave a very striking example of this at the end of my replies to the fourth set of objections, which dealt with a topic where it is notoriously difficult to reconcile philosophy with theology. I am ready to do the same for any other topic, if need be.[5]

The topic that Descartes refers to is transubstantiation. As early as November 1630, Descartes was concerned to reconcile his account of colour with 'the whiteness of the bread remaining in the blessed sacrament',[6] and he claimed to have solved the problem in a letter from the beginning of 1638.[7] The dogma of transubstantiation—the doctrine that, upon consecration, bread and wine become the body and blood of Christ—had been formulated by the Council of Trent in Thomist terms, as maintaining that the substance of the bread was transformed into that of Christ, while its form—*species*—remained the same. Clearly Descartes cannot accept this Thomist terminology, but translating the question into his own theory of matter does not leave the substantive issues untouched. On the orthodox Thomist account, the accidents of the bread, its non-essential qualities, inhere in the substance or substratum of the bread. Upon consecration, these accidents remain, but the substance or substratum changes into the body of Christ. But this is not because the body of Christ has taken on the accidents of bread; the key point is that the accidents do not inhere in this substratum, they are there by 'natural concomitance'.[8] As Arnauld puts it, 'we believe on faith that the substance of the bread is taken away from the bread of the Eucharist and only the accidents remain'.[9] These accidents are 'extension, shape, colour, smell, taste, and other qualities perceived by the senses'. The trouble is that, on Descartes' account of the nature of matter, shape, colour, taste, and smell are dependent upon extension; and extension cannot exist independently of something which is extended. Consequently it is impossible for any of them to persist if there is a change in the underlying substance to something unextended. Descartes' response is to maintain that the bread affects our sense organs in the same way before and after transubstantiation because it is its surface properties that cause us to have the sense perceptions we do, and these surface properties remain unchanged;[10] but this simply sidesteps the question of what they are the properties *of*.

The question of transubstantiation is a key one, for a natural philosophy that cannot account for it satisfactorily could not make any claim to orthodoxy. It was a question that was to plague discussions of Cartesianism in the seventeenth century,[11] and it was Descartes' account of this question, more than anything else, that resulted in his writings being put on the Index of Prohibited Books in 1663. Descartes himself becomes more and more guarded on the question. In 1648, Arnauld asks him to explain how the body of Christ can be contained within the same dimensions as that formerly occupied by the bread, when the essence of matter is extension and a body is just the dimensions of a particular region of matter: how can Christ's body be present without its own proper extension? Descartes replies that he cannot communicate his response in writing, and on being pressed further studiously ignores the issue.[12]

The letter to Dinet in which Descartes makes his unprecedented claim that there is no religious matter that cannot be explained using his principles needs to be put in context if we are to understand what lies behind this apparent entry into religious controversy. The point is that Descartes was already embroiled in religious controversy by this time, and in a sense was trying to fight his way out of it rather than provoke further controversy: the letter to Dinet is designed to lay bare what he regards as the orthodoxy of his metaphysics, and the injustice of criticism to the contrary. Dinet had taught at La Flèche, and was Bourdin's senior in the Jesuits, and so a potentially powerful ally. The letter to Dinet sets out the details of the disputes with Bourdin and Voetius, to some extent playing off the criticisms of the one, a Jesuit, against the other, a staunch Protestant, trying to show Descartes himself to be very much the offended party in the disputes. And on this occasion, this was a fair assessment, as neither Bourdin nor Voetius had much justification for the way in which they responded, the first with ridicule, the second with slander.

The dispute with Voetius arose in a context of religious conflict that conferred on Descartes' writings a politico-religious significance that Descartes could not have predicted, and which made them much more contentious than they might have been outside the Netherlands. At the beginning of the seventeenth century, the Netherlands had been divided by the question of Arminianism, which had offered an interpretation of the questions of predestination and election at odds with the prevailing Protestant orthodoxy. Various internal and external pressures (notably from James I of England) made the resolution of this question one on which the unity of the Netherlands hung, and interest in the questions correspondingly went far beyond theologians, although, correlatively, it gave theologians a political voice. Just how Descartes' doctrines became incorporated into this debate is a complex matter which we cannot pursue here,[13] but that it did become incorporated is beyond dispute, and the questions raised in the earlier Remonstrant controversy—such as doubt, scepticism, atheism, the unity and simplicity of God, freedom of the will, the relationship between mind and body— were raised again in much the same way in criticisms of Cartesianism. Remonstrants who had returned from exile following the death of Maurice, who had supported the orthodox line, tended to ally themselves politically with Cartesianism, even though most Dutch Cartesians were orthodox and there were significant doctrinal differences between Descartes and the Remonstrants (such as on the question of whether we have an innate idea of God). One of Descartes' fiercest critics, Revius, could write that 'Arminianism went but in its place came Cartesianism, which is much worse'.[14]

We have three histories of the dispute with Voetius from Descartes. In 1642 in the letter to Dinet he provides a twenty-page account;[15] by May 1643, in his *Epistola ad Voetium*, it runs to 200 pages;[16] and in the letter to the Magistrates of Utrecht of June 1645 to 70 pages.[17] This alone demonstrates its importance for Descartes, and important it was, for it was not just that his name had been slighted, but his future in the Netherlands, and certainly his future peace there, were thrown into doubt by the controversy. Moreover, in keeping with the political nature of the dispute and the question of public order that was raised in such controversies, he loses no opportunity to represent Voetius as a rabble-rouser, a man who was himself a threat to public order. The dispute had been initiated, as we have seen, not by something written by Descartes but by a number of theses which Regius had offered for public debate on 10 June 1640. Regius, who seems to have taken over from Reneri the role of Descartes' spokesman and defender of the Cartesian cause, assumed a growing importance in Descartes' life at this time, and the amount of correspondence with Regius begins to rival that with Mersenne. Regius not only corrected the manuscript of the *Meditationes*, but provided Descartes with his first objections,[18] and there can be no doubt that he had the support of Descartes in his polemics with Voetius. Regius' theses had focused on the circulation of the blood, and when an adversary of Harvey, Jacques Primerose,[19] replied, Regius had raised the stakes in his pamphlet entitled (in typical seventeenth-century polemical style) 'A Sponge to Wash Away the Filth of the Remarks published by Dr Primerose'. This inflamed the situation, unifying the conservative opposition and finally redirecting the controversy against Descartes himself, and pushing the nature of the controversy beyond physiology into theological questions. Descartes took no direct part in these disputes at first, preferring to advise Regius towards caution, something alien not just to Regius but seemingly to this generation of Dutch Cartesians, who, unlike Descartes, had been raised in a relatively liberal culture and were not going to be dictated to on matters of physiology and natural philosophy by ignorant and conceited theologians. As a consequence, a significant degree of polarization took place. Anna Maria van Schurmann, for example, a gifted linguist, feminist, and biblical scholar, with whom Descartes was on friendly terms and with whom he had discussed the only other strictly theological question in which we know him to have taken an interest—the Book of Genesis—eventually took Voetius' side in the dispute with Descartes, evidently accepting Voetius' claims that he was an 'atheist and libertine' and thanking God for 'separating her heart from that profane man'.[20]

In an effort to widen the dispute, Voetius wrote to Mersenne, who he clearly assumed would take his side, at the end of October 1640.[21] Mersenne not only did not rise to the bait, but sent his replies to Descartes to forward to Voetius, which he did, neglecting to pay postage so that Voetius himself would have to pay it.[22] On the Cartesian side, it was left once again to Regius to raise the stakes, which he did in April and May of 1641 by defending the thesis that the union of soul and body was one of two separate substances, and therefore not an actual unity. Voetius, now rector of the university, denounced the doctrine as heretical, and when Regius published his theses, Voetius had the book confiscated on the grounds that it had been published without official permission, getting his son Paul to publish additional theses attacking Regius and Cartesianism, and getting the senate of the university to prohibit Regius teaching anything other than medicine and forbidding him from mentioning any Cartesian doctrine in his courses. Descartes takes the matter lightly in his correspondence with Regius, advising him to have a good laugh at the idiocies of Voetius and son.[23] But despite the light-hearted tone of the letters, he was beginning to realize that he had to put up some public defence, and this is part of the rationale behind the letter to Dinet.

Descartes wrote to Huygens in 1642 that he asked 'for nothing but peace' from Bourdin and Voetius, 'but I realize that in order to get that I must wage war for a while'.[24] Like Voetius, Bourdin had offered a public refutation of Cartesianism. Bourdin was professor at the Jesuit *collège* at Clermont in Paris, where he held a public disputation in which three Cartesian theses were debated, and he published a short piece attacking Descartes as a result. His sarcastic dialogue attacking the *Meditationes* appeared as the seventh set of objections, which Descartes replies to in a relatively diplomatic and respectful way. Like Voetius, Bourdin had questioned the orthodoxy of Descartes' accounts, and it should be remembered that, transubstantiation apart, this orthodoxy was largely shared, resting on a similar version of late scholasticism in both cases.[25] Such unanimity from such opposing religious camps obviously presented a formidable front, one whose combined challenge Descartes could not hope to meet. Clearly his only option was to split the opposition by bringing out their differences with one another and playing on these. Vrooman gives a fair assessment of Descartes' Machiavellian ploy here. On the one hand, Descartes could cite his criticism of Bourdin as an answer to Voetius' charge that he was a Jesuit in disguise, and, at the same time, 'he appealed to Catholics and countrymen to judge his condition with compassion, for was he not being persecuted by Protestants and thus something of a matyr for the cause of his religion? To the Jesuits he would appear as a missionary and confessor in a land of heretics; to the Dutch Protestants he would play the role of censuring the Jesuits'.[26]

But no one could play such religious games with much success over any period of time; the manoeuvre was to have more success on the French Catholic side—he was eventually to be reconciled with Bourdin—than it was on the Dutch Protestant side, and Voetius was clearly not going to be deflected from his path. He instructed his son to draft a reply to Descartes and at the same time he wrote his own refutation, getting Martin Schoockius, a young professor at the University of Groningen, to put his name to it. What appeared under Schoockius' name was the *Admiranda methodus sive philosophia Cartesiana*, a libellous text which Descartes' friends were able to send him in proof so that his reply might appear simultaneously. In fact, however, the writing of it was delayed by Voetius' involvement in another campaign of persecution, this time against the members of a 'Society of the Holy Virgin' which, despite the connotations of its name, had ceased to be a Catholic group and had the burgher and thirteen prominent Protestant members of the local town as its members. Voetius accused the group of idolatry, and published a libellous pamphlet against the group anonymously. Descartes approached their spokesman, a French Protestant named Samuel Desmarets, to join in common cause against Voetius. Voetius managed to have the society condemned, however, and Descartes decided to attack him and defend himself at length in the *Epistola ad*

Voetium, published at the end of May 1643. Amongst other things, Descartes pointed out that Voetius and not Schoockius was the real author of the *Admiranda methodus*. Voetius reacted by presenting himself as a Protestant matyr hounded by a Jesuit spy, and Descartes was summoned before the Utrecht town council for slandering a clergyman, namely by maintaining that he was the author of the libellous pamphlet, on 16 June. This was a dangerous turn of events, and in September, after his claim that he lived outside their jurisdiction was rejected by the council, Descartes was threatened with expulsion and the public burning of his books. By this time he had travelled to the Hague, and with the help of the French ambassador and friends such as Huygens and Pollot, he got the Prince of Orange to intervene on his behalf with the magistrates of Utrecht. The council made no firm decision, however, and Descartes appealed for a judgement against Schoockius, who, on being arrested after church one Sunday and held for questioning over two days, finally admitted under oath that most of the *Admiranda methodus*, and all its worst invective, was in fact the work of Voetius. Voetius sued immediately, but was soon forced to withdraw his suit. Yet this cannot be regarded as a triumph for Descartes, for Voetius, through his son Paul, continued to write pamphlets against Descartes, giving rise to a general suspicion of Cartesianism and making Descartes' life in the Netherlands increasingly difficult.

Descartes had in fact shown some dissatisfaction with the Netherlands even before the Voetius affair took off in earnest, and early in 1640 he had contemplated moving to England, where he had been invited, probably by Sir Kenelm Digby.[27] What the attraction of England was is not clear, but he singles out the fact that Charles I was 'a Catholic by inclination', suggesting that he would feel happier in such an environment. But the political situation in England meant that it would have been rapidly losing its attractions for him in the 1640s, and having ruled out Italy, France seemed the obvious choice; but it would be 1646 before he made his first return trip to France, to be followed by two more in the next two years. As we shall see later, he may well have been inclined to return to France, but the political situation there rapidly approached a crisis, making it impossible to consider France as a place of retreat.

Recherche de la verité versus *Principia Philosophiae*

In looking at the *Meditationes*, I argued that the aim was to establish the credentials of Descartes' metaphysics, or at least to test the waters at a purely metaphysical level, before showing how his natural philosophy follows on from it. In this respect, I do not believe that the *Meditationes* should be read as a self-contained work, but rather as one which prepares the way for a full presentation of Descartes' metaphysically grounded natural philosophy. This is supported by the trajectory of Descartes' work both before the *Meditationes*—in the *Discours* and *Essais*, for example—and after it, in the *Principia*. And it will receive striking confirmation from Descartes himself, who, in conversation with Burman in 1649, tells him that: 'A point to note is that you should not devote so much attention to the *Meditationes* and to metaphysical questions, or give them elaborate treatment in commentaries and the like ... They draw the mind too far away from physical and observable things, and make it unfit to study them. Yet it is precisely these physical studies that it is most desirable for men to pursue'.[28] The *Meditationes* provide metaphysical foundations for a natural philosophy which is missing from that text. In the *Principia* the two are joined, and Descartes makes the move from metaphysics to natural philosophy in a way which, despite its overlay of scholastic terminology, reveals the overall structure of his project, a structure largely obscured in the *Meditationes*.

To help in understanding what Descartes was trying to achieve in the *Principia*, at least at the expository level, we should consider at this point an incomplete dialogue, *La Recherche de la verité par la lumière naturelle*, of very uncertain dating,[29] but which, on the balance of probabilities, should, I believe, be dated from around 1642. The manuscript was found amongst Descartes' papers after his death, but subsequently lost. We have a partial transcription by Leibniz and a 1701 Latin translation of the complete extant pages. Since the material we have ends in mid-sentence, we can assume that there is at least one page missing, but we do not know how far it continues. As for its contents, it goes through much of the material on hyperbolic doubt, the *cogito*, the nature of the mind, and the building up of knowledge, and its treatment of this material is much closer to the way in which it is covered in the *Meditationes* than in the *Discours*, although the exact order of presentation matches neither, nor indeed any other extant work.[30] It may have been composed after the *Discours*, possibly either as a draft of the *Meditationes* or as something written around the time that Descartes was concerned with replies to the objections to the *Meditationes*. To place the *Recherche* before the early 1630s, as a few commentators have done, is, I believe, completely out of the question, for Descartes tells us that he going to set out an account of cosmology, which he took no serious interest in before the early 1630s. On the other hand, to place it at the end of Descartes' life, as a greater number of commentators have done, cannot be ruled out, but it does not strike me as especially plausible. Since it sticks so closely to material covered in the *Meditationes*, we need some good independent reason if we are to date it significantly earlier or later than the *Meditationes*. It deals with a number of scholastically formulated questions, and many of the objections to the *Meditationes* were from the perspective of scholastic metaphysics and theology, which suggests the two exercises were contemporary. The parallels between Epistemon's objections and those made by Bourdin in the seventh set of objections in 1642 suggest this as the most likely date, and stylistic analysis also places it at this time,[31] although Descartes may have started work on it earlier.

As far as the actual substance of the *Recherche* is concerned, it adds to our understanding very little, for the material does not go beyond what we already have in the *Meditationes*. It may well represent a discarded attempt to present the whole of his thought, including his natural philosophy, on indubitable foundations. Eudoxus, who is the mouthpiece for Descartes in the dialogue, spells out what his project is in these terms:

We must begin with the rational soul, for all our knowledge resides in it; and having considered its nature and effects, we shall proceed to its author. And having come to know who He is, and how He has created all the things that are in the world, we shall be able to see whatever is most certain regarding the other creatures, and we shall examine in what way our senses receive their objects and how our thoughts are made true or false. Then I set out for you the works of men that involve corporeal things. After causing you to wonder at the most powerful machines, the most unusual automata, the most impressive illusions and the most subtle tricks that human ingenuity can devise, I shall reveal to you the secrets behind them, which are so simple and straightforward that you will no longer have reason to wonder at anything made by the hands of men. I shall then pass to the works of nature, and after showing you the cause of all her changes, the variety of her qualities, and how the souls of plants and animals differ from ours, I shall present for your consideration the entire edifice of the things that are perceivable by the senses. After giving an account of what we observe in the heavens and what we can judge with certainty about them, I shall pass on to the soundest conjectures concerning those things that cannot be determined by men, so as to explain the relation of things perceivable to the senses to things perceivable to the intellect, the relation of both these to the creator, the immortality of His creatures, and their state of being after the end of time. Then we shall come to the second part of this discussion, where we deal specifically with each of the sciences, picking out the most solid elements in them and putting forward a method to push them much further forward than has been possible up to now, a method which enables someone of middling intelligence to discover for himself everything that the most subtle minds can devise. Having thus prepared our understanding to make perfect judgements about the truth, we must also learn to control our will by distinguishing good things from bad, and by observing the true differences between virtues and vices.[32]

If the *Recherche* can indeed be dated to the early 1640s, then it may represent an alternative to the *Principia*. The project covers the same ground as that which Descartes had intended to cover in the originally projected six books of the *Principia*, and it might well have been a way of approaching the material that he discarded in favour of a textbook presentation. The first proposal for a textbook was to write what was in effect a parallel text, contrasting his own views with the *Summa philosophica* of Eustache of Saint Paul.[33] He tells Mersenne that 'in the same volume I intend to print a textbook of traditional philosophy, perhaps that of Father Eustache, with my own notes at the end of each proposition'.[34] Eustache's account covered dialectic, morals, physics, and metaphysics, and it is likely that Descartes' own account would likewise have covered these topics. But Descartes gave up the project in January 1641 on hearing of Eustache's death,[35] deciding to concentrate simply on presenting his own system instead of accompanying this with a criticism of the systems of others.

A Textbook of Natural Philosophy

After a couple of false starts, namely the *Recherche* and the commentary on Eustache, Descartes began work on the *Principia* at the beginning of 1641. Book I was completed in 1641, and he was up to the end of Book III in late April 1643; by the beginning of January 1644 he had reached the discussion of magnetism in Book IV, and he had his manuscript ready for the printer (Elzevier) by the middle of 1644. It was to be his last excursus into mechanics and cosmology of any significance. Originally designed as a systematic statement of the whole of his philosophy, Descartes did not get around to completing the last two sections on 'living beings and on man',[36] which would have included physiology and the passions, and perhaps morals. We do, however, have two works from the second half of the 1640s—*La Description du corps humain* and *Les Passions de l'âme*—which deal with these topics, and while the treatment of the passions in the latter probably post-dates the type of view that Descartes held in 1644 in some respects, it gives us a good general indication of how Descartes might have envisaged the *Principia* as a whole.

The *Principia* provides a systematic statement of Descartes' metaphysics and natural philosophy, and does not contain much material that is not in *Le Monde*, the *Essais*, and the *Meditationes*. Indeed in some ways it is a rewriting of *Le Monde*,[37] an attempt to reconstruct *Le Monde* on the basis of the foundations provided in the *Meditationes*. Despite the paucity of new material, there is some important restructuring of general arguments, as well as a spelling out of connections that have been made only implicitly in earlier writings. Part I—entitled 'Of the Principles of Human Knowledge'—is a relatively straightforward re-writing of the *Meditationes*, albeit with some rearrangement of the argument and an attempt to draw some methodological consequences. Descartes begins by introducing hyperbolic doubt, both with respect to mathematics and the existence of the external world, arguing that by an act of will we can withhold assent from anything of which we cannot form a clear and distinct idea,[38] although it will subsequently turn out that the will is not able to withhold assent from anything of which we can form a clear and distinct idea.[39] We have a clear and distinct idea of our own existence, as the *cogito* shows; the distinction between mind and body is secured simply by reflection on what is necessary to our existence, and this reflection shows that extension or shape 'does not belong to our nature'.[40] Our nature resides in 'think-ing', by which Descartes understands 'all those things that we are aware/conscious of as occurring in us, in so far as we are aware/con-scious of them'.[41] The distinction he wants to draw is that between the indubitability of my awareness and the dubitability of what it is that I am aware of. I might be aware of myself as walking, for example, but this might be by virtue of my dreaming that I am walking. Our judge-ment of our awareness is indubitable, 'for as long as our mind is only contemplating these ideas and neither affirming not denying that there is anything similar to them outside itself, it cannot err'[42]; the ultimate task is to make our judgement of the content of that awareness similarly indubitable. In order to do this we need to reflect upon the content of our ideas. We can recognize the truth of certain basic mathematical ideas, and also that the idea of necessary existence is contained in that of a supremely perfect being. This supremely perfect being must be the cause of our existence because endurance requires some maintaining cause, and we can find no such maintaining cause within ourselves.[43] Our explanations in philosophy must start with God, since He is the source of all things, but Descartes stresses God's transcendence: 'there is much, both in the boundless nature of God and in His creation, that goes beyond what we can comprehend'.[44] If we start from God, as Descartes recommends, and recognize that it would be contradictory for God, as the giver of understanding, to deceive us, we will see that 'it follows from this that all the things that we clearly perceive are true, and the doubts previously listed are removed'.[45]

So at a very early stage in the project, we have resolved hyperbolic doubt, and are able to proceed to an analysis of judgement. This in-volves the intellect and the will, the latter required because as well as grasping something we must assent to it. The intellect, guided by the natural light of reason, does not err when it grasps something clearly and distinctly, but the will can assent to anything, even something that is not presented to the intellect clearly and distinctly, and this, Descartes tells us, is the source of error.[46] We can tell simply by reflecting on our will that it is free, although we cannot understand in what way it is free because we cannot reconcile its freedom with divine preordination. Descartes presents this difficulty as deriving directly from God's transcendence: it is simply something that arises when a finite mind attempts to understand the infinite power of God.[47] This 'reconciliation'—as Descartes has the temerity to call it—of freedom of the will and divine preordination is clearly going to satisfy no one, and the problem was to dog the subsequent history of Cartesianism, especially in the writings of Malebranche. We shall look at Descartes' account of how the will acts when we come to his account of the passions. For present purposes, it is sufficient to note the general thrust of the account, which is that the intellect cannot act as a source of error.

Applying the criterion of clarity and distinctness to the question of what types of things we perceive, Descartes distinguishes his two fundamental categories, thought and extension, and a hybrid category of appetites, emotions, and passions (which he defers consideration of until the brief summaries of these questions in Part IV), as well as 'eternal truths' or 'common notions', among which he includes the principle of non-contradiction, the unalterability of the past, and the fact that existence is necessary for thought.[48] We are then provided with a rather complicated metaphysical apparatus to deal with thought and extension. The basic distinction is between substances and their properties, which are of three kinds: attributes, qualities, and modes.[49] Attributes are those properties of a substance without which it could not exist. Corporeal substance must be extended, for example, otherwise it simply could not be corporeal substance. Moreover, all other properties that a substance has presuppose its attributes, but not vice versa. Extension can be understood without shape and motion but not vice versa, for example, and thought can be understood without imagination and sensation but not vice versa. Shape and motion, and imagination and sensation, are merely 'modes' of their respective substances.[50] A mode is a property that does not alter the nature of the substance. Each substance, we are told, has one principal property (extension in the case of corporeal substance and thought in the case of mind), that is, one property which constitutes its nature and essence, and its other properties are merely modes. But having introduced his terminology, Descartes proceeds to use it in a loose and inconsistent way. So, on the one hand we are told that a substance may be known through any attribute at all, which suggests that bodies have more than one attribute, and on the other we are then told that anything other than the principal property of a body is a mode, which means nothing other than the principal property can be an attribute. And he then introduces a third, and somehow intermediate, category of 'quality', which is a property that, while not essential to a substance, would change its nature if it were changed.

What would an example of this be? One contender would be the impenetrability of corporeal bodies. Impenetrability cannot be the essence of corporeal substance because substances have only one essence, but nor can it be a mode, because to make corporeal substance penetrable would be to change its nature. Perhaps, then, it is a quality, although it could just as legitimately be thought of as a non-principal attribute. Anyway, what is of interest is not what we call it but what its status is in Descartes' schema. If we distinguish between impenetrability as a real property of corporeal things, as opposed to the sensory property of tangibility,[51] then impenetrability, Descartes believes, is a direct consequence of extension.[52] On the assumption that corporeal substance is a plenum, for one body to penetrate another it would have to occupy a region which was already occupied unless it annihilated the matter in that region, which is impossible. But the relation between extension and impenetrability is an especially intimate one, for as he tells us in the sixth set of replies to the *Meditationes*, 'the true extension of body is such that all interpenetrability of parts is excluded'.[53] In other words, whatever is extended is impenetrable and whatever is impenetrable is extended. And a moment's reflection shows that if Descartes wanted a physically viable plenum it could not be any other way. In identifying the classical notions of space and matter, he confers on corporeal extension all the properties of space except one. It becomes, for example, homogeneous, isotropic, continuous, infinitely divisible, and completely geometrical: this is what makes it so easily amenable to a completely mathematical treatment. But Descartes needs to provide an account of the structure of the corporeal world, not of empty space, so corporeal extension must differ from space. Impenetrability is the one property that makes corporeal extension *corporeal*. If we were to think of corporeal extension in terms of its two 'components'—space and matter—then it would be tempting to think of extension and impenetrability as its two principal attributes. How do we decide that one is the attribute and the other something essentially dependent upon and derivable from that attribute when the one involves the other for Descartes? We cannot derive impenetrability from extension without the assumption of the plenum, and what are we assuming when we assume a plenum if not the impenetrability of extension? I cannot see any metaphysical reason why the one should be regarded as prior to the other, although there is, of course, a perfectly good methodological-cum-epistemological reason why extension might be preferred to impenetrability. Descartes wants to provide a quantitative physics. Nothing, literally nothing, is easier to quantify than spatial extension. Impenetrability is, on the face of it, impossible to quantify, for it is a potentially infinite force: a completely solid body will always resist penetration no matter how great the body acting to penetrate it is.[54] So the obvious thing to do was to focus on spatially extended magnitudes, letting impenetrability, which Descartes studiously ignores, ride on the back of extension, as it were.

To add to the geometrical simplicity, Descartes effectively strips substance of temporal duration. The duration of things is simply 'a mode under which we conceive of the thing in so far as it continues to exist'.[55] Now this not only helps us account for physical processes geometrically but, much more importantly, it helps us account for them in terms of Descartes' hydrostatic model, where it is not motions but instantaneous tendencies to motion, not speeds but atemporal displacements, that matter. Of course, we perceive physical processes as temporal, but (leaving to one side the problems that continuous creation might pose for the continuity of motion[56]) Descartes needs only to invoke inertial states to account for this. It has often been thought that his principle of instantaneous causation has the consequence that different instants in the universe will be causally insulated from one another, so that no earlier state of affairs can have any effect on a later one. For if causation is instantaneous, how can an event at one time have any effect on an event at another time? But in fact a moment's reflection shows that this is quite possible. Take the case of the collision of two inelastic bodies. Assume that at t_1 they move with particular speeds in a particular directions, and that at t_2 they collide; as a result of this collision their speeds and direction of motion change, so we can imagine some later time t_3 at which they travel with their new speeds in new directions. Their velocities at t_1 and t_3 differ, and they differ because of the instantaneous causal process that happened at t_2. What has happened, of course, is that the causal process at t_2 has changed the inertial states of the bodies, and because of the principle of inertia, the bodies will persevere in their changed inertial states after the collision. At this fundamental mechanical level, then, an event at an earlier time can affect one at a later time, even if it produces its effect instantaneously.[57] The actual physical action, collision between corpuscles, takes place instantaneously, whereas the results of this action take the form of the continued inertial motions of the corpuscles. Once we have specified our inertial principles, as Descartes will do in Book II, the continued motion ceases to be of any physical interest: what matters is what happens at the instant at which the physical change is produced.

Another crucial move, which makes possible the construal of interactions between corpuscles in terms of equations, is the introduction of a law securing conservation of the total quantity of motion in a collision. In its general form the law states that God preserves the same amount of motion and rest in the material universe that He put there at the beginning. On the face of it, this seems to imply that nothing a mind does can initiate a new motion, in which case it is difficult to understand how it can act on the body. As Henry More put it in a letter to Descartes of 23 July 1649: 'I ask: when the human mind stirs the animal spirits by thinking more attentively and for a longer time and, moreover, rouses the body itself, doesn't it surely then increase the motion in the universe?'[58] Unfortunately, Descartes never responded to this point and makes no explicit mention of what his solution to this apparent dilemma is. A number of commentators have pointed to the fact that Descartes' claim is simply that God conserves the same amount of motion that He initially put into the universe, and that this does not preclude minds introducing new motion into the universe.[59] This is a questionable interpretation on textual grounds,[60] and since it is likely that the law was formulated in response to worries that Beeckman had about the total quantity of motion in the universe running down,[61] it is correspondingly unlikely that Descartes would contemplate anything but a causally closed system. The alternative is to take the principle of the conservation of motion as covering all motion. There can be no doubt that this is a more natural reading, and it has been the one traditionally taken. If one does this, one has to explain in what way the mind can influence corporeal bodies. One might argue that the speeds of bodies can be altered, but this would require some compensating alteration of speed in the body that effects the alteration, namely the pineal gland. This is clearly not going to work if we think simply in terms of motion, for the pineal gland would be responsible for transferring large amounts of motion, and this would require it to act in a way quite disproportionate to its size. Nor would it be of any help to point to the fact that total motion is conserved because total force of motion, or tendency to motion, is conserved, arguing that what the pineal gland does is to realize or actualize tendencies to motion; for quite apart from the fact that this would make force of, or tendency to, motion too close to Aristotelian potentialities, we do not have the faintest idea how the pineal gland could achieve this. This leaves us with the traditional interpretation, first proposed by Leibniz,[62] that although motion is conserved, *determinatio*, which for present purposes can be treated as being equivalent to direction, is not. While the pineal gland cannot alter the speed of a body in contact with it, it can alter the direction of its motion.[63] In short, conservation of motion is conservation of a scalar quantity.

What Descartes provides us with in Book I and the first part of Book II of the *Principia* is a metaphysical vocabulary, derived largely from scholasticism, and this metaphysical vocabulary is put to its greatest use in thinking through the nature of motion, rest, force, and *action*. This is a very problematic exercise, and in fact does little to illuminate the physical issues. Quite the contrary, it puts notions which are in need of clarification beyond any hope of such a thing. Indeed, it is difficult to believe that the aim could ever have been one of clarification: rather, it seems to have been that of showing the compatibility between his natural philosophy and traditional metaphysics by using the terminology of the latter to set out his theory of matter.

The notion that is called upon to do most of the work is that of a mode. The key passage here occurs in article 25 of Book II, designed to define what 'motion' in the strictest sense is. We have already seen that Descartes equates motion with translation in *Le Monde*, and here he spells out the difference between translation and the 'force or action that brings about this translation'. Motion, we are told, 'is always in the moving body as opposed to the body that brings about the motion'. Motion and the force or action that brings it about 'are not usually distinguished with sufficient care', and motion is 'only a mode of a moving body, not a substance, just as shape is a mode of the thing that has shape, and rest is a mode of the thing at rest'.[64] The French version talks of motion being a property of a body just as its shape and its being at rest are its properties.[65] The rejection of the contrast between motion on the one hand, and rest and shape on the other, indicates that motion is not bound up with the nature of the body, as it would be in a teleological construal of motion as in Aristotelian dynamics, but also that it is not something within the body, like the 'impressed' motion of *impetus* theory. Moreover, once it is put on a par with rest, there is no longer any intrinsic difference between motion and rest, in that rest can be taken as motion having the value of zero. Descartes treats rest as being genuinely on a par with motion. As he put it in *Le Monde*, 'I consider that rest is as much a quality which should be attributed to matter whilst it remains in the one place as motion is one which is attributed to it when it changes place'.[66] Consequently, as well as a 'force or action' which is responsible for motion there must also be a 'force or action' responsible for rest. In a letter to Mersenne paraphrasing the first law of motion, Descartes makes this clear:

It is quite wrong to take it as a principle that no body moves itself. From the fact that a body has started to move it is certain that it has within itself the force to continue to move; in the same way, the very fact that it is stationary in some place means that it has the force to continue to stay there.[67]

There are two questions that must be raised here: whether motion and rest are genuinely relative; and whether the force of motion and rest is a genuine physical force. On the first question, if motion—that is, translation—results from a force of motion, and if motion and rest are relative, does this mean that the force of motion and the force of rest are relative? In other words, is to say that a body has a force of motion the same as to say that it has a force of motion relative to contiguous bodies which have been chosen arbitrarily as providing one's reference frame? Take the case where I draw a straight line on a piece of paper by moving the nib of the pen across the paper, and compare this with the case where I draw the line by holding the pen still and moving the paper under it. Assuming I can always choose my reference frame in a way which preserves rectilinear inertia, can we allow that Descartes would have treated drawing the line as motion of the pen when looked at from one framework and motion of the paper when looked at from another? I do not believe we can: Descartes' motions are real motions, despite his talk of relativity of motion. He gives himself away in his reply to Fermat's objection to the principle of composition of motions, which we looked at in the last chapter. Descartes' principle had assumed a privileged reference system in which an incident ray is resolved into a perpendicular component and one parallel to the reflecting surface. When Fermat objects that there are an infinite number of reference systems for resolution of motions into components, offering another one in which the horizontal and vertical components are oblique, Descartes replies that the components of motion that he was talking about were real ones, not merely imaginary ones; but, as I said when we looked at this case, we are given no idea of how we might distinguish 'real' motions, and if one is going to use a parallelogram to resolve motion into true horizontal and vertical components then one needs something that establishes real directions, such as forces. Descartes clearly assumes real directions here. Similarly in his cosmology. The rotation of the planets around the sun is partly a result of the different sizes of corpuscle: heavier bodies are pushed outwards to the periphery of the solar system. Any attempt to impose an arbitrary reference system on this and determine direction and speed in relation to it would make a nonsense of the whole exercise, no less than the attempt to impose an arbitrarily chosen reference frame on the principle of the composition of motions would completely undermine his optics.

The principle of the relativity of motion is in blatant contradiction to these basic results of Descartes' physics. Why, then, does he advocate it? The first point to note is that *Le Monde* clearly proceeds on the assumption of the reality of motion. The examples that I have just given predate the *Principia*, so we must at least consider the possibility that Descartes changed his mind and that he came to accept the relativity of motion only around the time of composing the *Principia*. Now not only is relativity introduced in the *Principia*, it is introduced in terms which go well beyond the kind of thing that had been envisaged by other natural philosophers up to this point. Galileo, for example, in dealing with the question of why we were aware of none of the usual dynamic effects of motion if the earth moves, had pointed to the fact that bodies may move in the same way on a ship whether the ship is moving or not, so we cannot tell just from the behaviour of bodies whether our frame of reference is in motion or not. This is kinematic relativism. Descartes offers the much stronger dynamic relativism:

I further specified that the transfer occurs from the vicinity not of *any* contiguous bodies but only from the vicinity of *those that we consider to be at rest*. For the transference is reciprocal; and we cannot conceive of the body AB being transferred from the vicinity of the body CD without also understanding that the body CD is transferred from the vicinity of the body AB, and that exactly the same force and action is required for the one transference as for the other.[68]

But, Descartes explains, such dynamic relativity of motion conflicts with 'our ordinary way of speaking'. The reason for this is that we do not consider a body to have moved unless it has moved as a whole:

Let the body EFGH be the earth, [Fig. 9.1] and let the body AB upon its surface be transferred from E towards F, and simultaneously the body CD be transferred from H to G. Even though we know that the parts of the Earth contiguous to the body AB are transported from B towards A, and that the action employed in this transference must be neither different in kind from, nor less than, that in the body AB, yet we do not on that account understand the Earth to move from B to A or from [east to west]. For if this were so then the fact that the parts contiguous with CD were being transferred from C to D would, by the same reasoning, require us to understand the Earth to move in the opposite direction, that is from [west to east], which contradicts what we have already stated. So, to avoid departing from ordinary usage too greatly, we shall say in this case not that the Earth moves but simply that the bodies AB and CD move, and similarly in other cases. But meanwhile we will remember that whatever is real and positive in moving bodies, what it is in virtue of which we say they move, is also to be found in those contiguous to them, even though we consider these to be at rest.[69]

Such advocacy of relativism is new to the *Principia*, but I cannot believe that Descartes is genuinely committed to it. First, dynamic relativity undermines his reply to Fermat's objection to his principle of

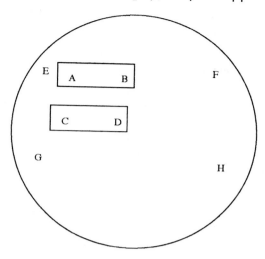

FIG. 9.1

composition. Secondly, we have just seen Descartes make a comparison between a body's state of motion and its shape. If a body's motion were relative to contiguous bodies, this would be a peculiar comparison to make, for its shape is not relative to anything. It is true that a body has shape simply by virtue of having boundaries which are formed through the motion of one region of the plenum relative to another, but what shape it has will not be a function of which regions we take to be stationary, whereas its motion would be on the relativistic reading.

Third, as with the principle of composition, his own laws of collision in fact presuppose the reality of motion. The rules are governed by Descartes' three laws of nature and the conservation law.[70] The conservation law both secures that the total quantity of motion is retained and allows collisions to be described in terms of equations relating the original sizes to the speeds of the corpuscles. The various permutations of same/different size, same/different speed, and same/different directions are described, excluding oblique collisions. Rules 1, 3, and 6 describe the behaviour of equal bodies with different initial speeds. Rule 1 deals with bodies whose speeds are equal and opposite, and tells us that on collision the bodies' speeds are reversed but undiminished, which we can represent as:

$$u, -u \rightarrow -u, u \qquad (I)$$

Rule 3 deals with the case where bodies of unequal speed collide. Assume that the difference in speed is a. Then the speed of the faster body is $u + 1/2a$, and the speed of the slower one will be $- (u - 1/2\ a)$. The faster body will, on Descartes' account, continue on its way, pushing the slower one in front of it:

$$u + 1/2a, \ -(u - 1/2\ a) \rightarrow u, \ u \qquad\qquad \text{(III)}$$

Rule 6 describes the case where one body has a speed of $2u$ and the other is at rest, and Descartes maintains that the motion is redistributed as follows:

$$2u, \ o \rightarrow -3/2u, \ 1/2u \qquad\qquad \text{(VI)}$$

Now if all motion is relative, it cannot make any difference to the collision what frame of reference it is observed in. But, as Barbour has pointed out, it does.[71] The relative speeds before the collisions are equal, and if we assume a frame of reference in uniform motion with respect to the frame chosen by Descartes, then, observed in the new frame, the collisions are:

$$2u, \ o \rightarrow o, \ 2u \qquad\qquad \text{(I$'$)}$$

$$2u, \ o \rightarrow 2u - 1/2a, \ 2u - 1/2a \qquad\qquad \text{(III$'$)}$$

$$2u, \ o \rightarrow -3/2u, \ 1/2u \qquad\qquad \text{(VI$'$)}$$

Since the outcomes here are different, then as Barbour points out, according to (I$'$), (III$'$), and (VI$'$) it is not possible to predict the outcome of a collision between equal bodies if only the relative speed of the two is known. But once the collisions have occurred we have no trouble specifying what transformation is necessary to go to Descartes' original frame of reference, and consequently the frame which yields (I$'$), (III$'$), and (VI$'$) provides a criterion of absolute rest.

I believe that it is difficult to explain Descartes' advocacy of the relativity of motion other than as an attempt to throw a smoke screen around his heliocentrism.[72] Indeed, in article 31 of Book II of the *Principia* we can see the smoke screen being put up:

Each body has only one motion of its own, for it is understood to move away from only one set of bodies, which are contiguous with it and at rest. But it can also share in countless other motions, namely in the cases where it is a part of other bodies which have other motions. For example, someone walking on a ship has a watch in his pocket: the wheels of the watch have only one motion of their own, but they also share in another motion because they are in contact with the walking man, and they and he form the one body. They also share in additional motions in virtue of being on a ship which is being tossed on the waves, in virtue of being in contact with the sea itself, and lastly, in virtue of their contact with the whole Earth, if indeed the whole Earth is in motion. Now all the motions really will exist in the motion of the watch, but we cannot easily comprehend all these motions at the one time, nor even know what they are.[73]

Note the throwaway line 'if indeed the Earth is in motion'. Clearly just about everything is in motion when we take into account those larger bodies of which a body forms part, so the motion of the Earth is of no consequence, and hardly even worth mentioning!

Once we begin to take the reality of motion seriously, we can start to take Descartes' account of the force of motion seriously, as he himself does. We have seen in Descartes' paraphrase of the first law of motion that moving bodies, even those undergoing rectilinear motion, are preserved in their motion by a force, bodies at rest likewise, and that this is a force within the body. But what does 'within the body' mean? Here we face the problem of what Descartes' commitment to mechanism amounts to as regards the existence of forces. One path he could take is the occasionalist one, whereby God is the sole source and the sole site of activity in the universe. Descartes certainly does not allow anything corporeal to be a source of activity in his metaphysics, and for present purposes this is tantamount to restricting such activity to God;[74] but one could only believe God was the sole site of activity if one concentrated exclusively on Descartes' metaphysics and supposed that his physics simply had to be reconciled to that. But this path, taken by many later Cartesians, most notably Clerselier and Malebranche, nevertheless gets matters the wrong way round; for all the fundamentals of Descartes' physics were worked out in *Le Monde*, and while there are a few improvements in questions of detail on this physics in the *Principia*—such as in the more elaborate rules of collision, in accounting for the speeds of rotation of the planets closer to the Sun than Saturn, and in the inclusion of half-yearly cycles in accounting for the tides, for example—there is nothing fundamental added, and nothing at all added that can be attributed to the metaphysical reformulation of doctrine. I shall return to this question below. For the moment, I simply want to draw attention to the fact that readings of Descartes' physics that construe it as being driven metaphysically are unlikely to throw any light on its own workings, and that there are no independent grounds for supposing that Descartes does not mean what he says when he tells Mersenne that the force of motion is in the body. That is to say, the force is sited in the body: he is not saying that it ultimately derives from the body. The question that now naturally arises is to what extent this force which God puts in bodies contravenes the key tenet of mechanism, namely the inertness of matter.

It is crucial here to determine in what form this force is present in matter. A body must always be in a state of motion or rest, so if there is a force responsible for this state, it will always be present in the body. In conserving a body, God conserves it in a particular state of motion (or rest), and He does this by conserving it with a particular force of motion (or rest). In other words, the very act of conserving corporeal nature involves imbuing the body with a particular force of motion or rest. Guéroult sums up the situation in these terms:

The principle of continuous creation implies that no created thing can exist unless it is sustained by a creative force, and that every force that inheres in a thing is nothing other than that by which God puts it in existence at each instant. Consequently, as distinct from rest and motion (which are modes of extension), force—whether it be the force of rest or the force of motion—cannot be a mode of extension any more than can duration or existence. In reality, force, duration, and existence are one and the same thing (*conatus*) under three different aspects, and the three notions are identified in the instantaneous action in virtue of which corporeal substance *exists* and endures, that is, possesses the force which puts it into existence and duration.[75]

In developing Guéroult's interpretation, Alan Gabbey[76] has distinguished between the force of motion *simpliciter* and the actual value that the force of motion takes in a particular body, the former being an attribute of the body, the latter being a mode. I am not convinced that the metaphysical categories fit quite so neatly here, but Gabbey is surely right on the more important point of the physical reality of forces when he maintains that, although God is the sole ultimate cause, 'at the "practical" level of physical investigation, forces—whether of motion or of rest—are real causes in their own right and distinct from motion and rest'.[77] If anyone doubts that Descartes treats these as being real forces, the most cursory glance at the role of centrifugal force in his cosmology will resolve such doubts immediately. But this raises the question of how easily such forces sit with mechanism. Here we have to face up to the real constraints under which Descartes' account works, and we have to recognize that these constraints are both physical and natural-philosophical or metaphysical. Descartes developed a statical notion of force, as something like instantaneous tendency to motion, which he saw as capturing physical action in a way consonant with mechanism, in as much as it does not violate the principle of the inertness of nature. This notion provided him with a way of modelling physical processes in a micro-mechanical way. The first point is that it is this concern, rather than the natural-philosophical or metaphysical one, which is dominant. Second, this physical concern is not reconcilable with a purely kinematic notion of physics—quite the contrary, the notion of instantaneous tendencies to motion actually prevents Descartes from dealing with the continuous motions required by kinematics, for he has no physical or mathematical way of translating the one into the other. Third, Descartes' natural philosophy does not restrict him to conceiving of natural processes purely in terms of matter in motion, so there is no conflict between his metaphysically conceived natural philosophy and his practical physics on these grounds. All it commits him to is the inertness of matter. And on a minimal reading of the inertness of matter, all Descartes needs to secure is that matter does not initiate any kind of activity. The conception of force as having its source in God but its site in matter clearly has no problem at all securing this. True, the exact metaphysical details, which Gueroult and Gabbey have done so much to spell out, do not fall into place very easily; but this, I believe, is because Descartes is trying to fill out a conception of force in the context of a physics which is completely contrary to Aristotelian physics, and in the context of a natural philosophy which is completely contrary to Aristotelian natural philosophy, in terms derived ultimately from Aristotelian metaphysics. No wonder he has troubles. The point is that we should not mistake these troubles, which arise from the attempt to reconcile what are in fact quite alien systems, for problems that affect his physics or his 'unreconstructed' natural philosophy.

The Task of Legitimation

Descartes' subsequent dispute with Regius throws some further light on these questions. In June 1645, less than a year after the publication of the *Principia*, Regius sent Descartes the manuscript of his own textbook on natural philosophy, his *Fundamenta Physice*. Descartes advised him strongly against publication, but Regius went ahead and published it in 1646, thereby precipitating a break with Descartes. In the preface to the French version of the *Principia*, the *Principes*, published in 1647, Descartes sets out his principal objections to the *Fundamenta* in these terms:

it appears that everything he wrote is taken from my writings, both from those I have published and also from a still imperfect work on the nature of animals which fell into his hands. But because he copied out the material inaccurately and changed the order and denied certain truths of metaphysics on which the whole of physics must be based, I am obliged to disavow his work entirely.[78]

The issue is less one of plagiarism (actually an unjust accusation[79]) than of the presentation of explicitly Cartesian doctrine in a form which Descartes did not approve of. The core of the problem is the way Regius 'changed the order and denied certain truths of metaphysics on which the whole of physics must be based'. Regius just could not see the point of metaphysical foundations, for any 'fool or fanatic' could justify whatever he liked on the basis of Descartes' first principles.[80] Regius himself starts with the basic principles of physics and moves through cosmology, astronomy, meteors, minerals, animals, and then the mind and the question of knowledge. This order of exposition mirrors not only the standard scholastic-textbook procedure, but also the order of material in the work of mechanists like Gassendi and Hobbes;[81] but it differs radically from Descartes' own, for not only does it not start with knowledge, it ignores God's role in the whole business. It divorces the legitimatory metaphysics from the natural philosophy and mechanics, and, worse, it presents the latter in a way in which it can be directly contrasted with traditional natural philosophy, and its very significant difference from this can be seen at a glance. If Descartes had just wanted to do this, then he could simply have published *Le Monde*. The problem with Regius' approach was not, however, that it showed Cartesian metaphysics, in its quasi-scholastic formulation, to be irrelevant to his natural philosophy, for Regius himself employs a number of scholastic distinctions in formulating his own account; rather, it divorces the question of legitimation from the treatment of natural philosophy. In his letter to Regius advising him not to proceed with publication, he tells Regius that his style of writing is suitable only for presenting theses, where one presents them in a paradoxical way so as to elicit objections to them. His own method of presentation is quite different:

As for myself, there is nothing I would more strenuously avoid than letting my opinions seem paradoxical, and I would never want them to be the subject of disputations. For I consider them so certain and evident that anyone who understands them correctly will have no occasion to dispute them.[82]

Descartes is concerned with legitimation not just because he wants his work to be accepted by the Church, but because he genuinely believes that the kind of novel metaphysical legitimation that he offers—one which proceeds via hyperbolic doubt, clear and distinct ideas, and God's guarantee—provides the key to reconstructing the whole of natural philosophy once and for all on firm foundations. As Regius presents Cartesian natural philosophy, it may be a better and truer natural philosophy than that offered in the scholastic textbooks; but then Galileo's astronomy was a better and truer astronomy than that offered in the scholastic textbooks, and that did not stop it being condemned. What was needed was something completely compelling, and Descartes' aim in the *Principia* was to present a completely compelling defence of his natural philosophy.

In understanding this aim, we must not misunderstand the deductive structure of the text. It is often assumed that Descartes' 'method' in the *Meditationes* and *Principia* consists of deduction of new truths from first principles, and that the model he uses is a geometrical one, where we start with definitions, axioms etc. and derive theorems from them. Such an assumption could not be more mistaken. For one thing, we have already seen that Descartes completely rejects the notion that deductive reasoning can lead to the discovery of new truths in the *Regulae*. Secondly, in accord with this, his own *Géometrie* does not begin with definitions and axioms, and proceed to demonstrate theorems deductively. As we have seen, his concern is not deductive demonstration but problem-solving, and the elaboration of new techniques for problem-solving. Third, in the letter to Vatier that we looked at in the last chapter, we saw that the only thing that Descartes refers to as a sample of his method is his account of the rainbow,[83] which could not be further from deduction from first principles. Where, then, does the idea of deduction from first principles derive from in Descartes? To answer this question properly, we need to distiguish between a method of presentation and one of discovery. Descartes explicitly denies that deduction can provide a method of discovery, but this does not prevent it from acting as a method of presentation. In the *Principia*, he builds up a general systematic natural philosophy from first principles, and the material is deductively arranged, but nowhere is it suggested that the very specific physical doctrines elaborated are to be, or have been, discovered from metaphysical foundations. Rather, the function of the deductive structure of the argument is to provide a systematic metaphysically grounded natural philosophy, into which specific results which have already been discovered can be incorporated. It is a means of imposing system on these results, and for most of his results Descartes claims little more than moral certainty. Regarding the results of the last Book of the *Principia*, for example, he tells us:

If one looks at the many properties relating to magnetism, fire, and the fabric of the entire world, which I deduced from first principles in this book, then even if one thinks my assumption of these principles to have been arbitrary and groundless, one will still perhaps acknowledge that it would hardly have been possible for so many items to fit into a coherent pattern if the original principles had been false.[84]

A few fundamental results can, he believes, be provided with a metaphysical guarantee—mathematical demonstrations, the knowledge that the material world exists, the basic principles of his physiology of perception, and his account of the transmission of light. The aim is, of course, to extend this guarantee to all physical truths in time.[85]

The model for the deductive mode of presentation in the *Principia* does not derive from geometry, where Descartes does not allow deductive proofs in the absence of the analytic problem-solving that produced those results in the first place; but rather, from the late scholastic textbooks from which Descartes learned his metaphysics at La Flèche.[86]

These textbooks, as we saw in Chapter 2, provide a metaphysical and natural-philosophical system in which Aristotle's thought was reconstructed from first principles as a means of securing orthodoxy. Once the important distinction between methods of discovery and methods of presentation is appreciated, the metaphysical reconstruction of the *Principia* can be seen for what it is: an attempt to provide a metaphysical guarantee for results that have already been discovered independently and, through this metaphysical guarantee, to establish not only the truth of his natural philosophy and cosmology, but also its compatibility with orthodoxy. And in this last respect, at least, he was successful, for the *Principia* was not put on the Index (or at least not for twenty years), which was quite an achievement, something that one cannot imagine happening in the case of *Le Monde*.

The Legacy of the *Principia*

The legitimatory apparatus of the *Principia* was abandoned by those of Descartes' successors—such as Rouhault and Régis—who followed up its arguments and defended Cartesian physics; and disputes over the *Principia*, of which there were many in the second half of the seventeenth century, simply ignored the legitimatory machinery. What Cartesians and others were interested in was the basic natural philosophy, and the key achievement or claim, depending upon how one looked at it, was the theory of vortices which was used to account for the planetary orbits, weight or gravity, tides, and magnetism in a completely mechanistic fashion. Descartes' account of these phenomena differs little from that he had provided in *Le Monde*, except in the case of magnetism, which is not dealt with in *Le Monde* and which he only seems to have taken a serious interest in around 1640, although he had made programmatic statements about how magnetism had to be accounted for in mechanist terms in the *Regulae*. In Book IV of the *Principia* he provides some details as to what form a mechanist account would take.[87]

Descartes' account of the magnet is interesting in a number of ways. First, magnetism was one of the most recalcitrant phenomena for a mechanist, and it had traditionally been marshalled as evidence for naturalism. Gilbert, for example, whose pioneering *De Magnete* appeared in 1600, had noted, on the basis of an extensive investigation of magnets, that magnetic effluxions were not only able to penetrate dense bodies, but could also magnetize a needle without apparently adding anything physical to it (its weight was not greater when it was magnetized, for example); and he had concluded from this that the form of a magnet

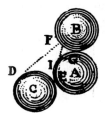

FIG. 9.2

is animate, and acts in a similar way to the human soul, which is the form of the body, and animates it, just as the soul animates the body.[88] Clearly the explanation of magnetism in mechanical terms provided the key to a successful mechanist natural philosophy which had any claim to be comprehensive. The second feature of interest is that, as Descartes notes,[89] if one scatters iron filings around a magnet—Descartes used a spherical loadstone—they form lines or 'tubes' shaped somewhat like vortices. These 'tubes', as Descartes thinks of them, are strongly reminiscent of the lines of motion that he had envisaged in his example of the wine in a vat, first developed in 1631, where 'whirlwinds' are formed in closed circuits.

The third feature of Descartes' account is that it is actually rather regressive, in that the micro-corpuscularian explanation offered relies on surface features of the postulated corpuscles, much in the tradition of classical atomism. He construes magnetic effluvia in terms of streams of corpuscles of the third element, and he considers that these streams of corpuscles move along the 'tubes' that we perceive when iron filings are aligned around a magnet. These corpuscles are channelled or grooved because they are squeezed through the interstices between contiguous spherical corpuscles made of the second element. That is, they are cylinders having three or four concave sides joined by rims, depending on whether they have been squeezed through three or four contiguous corpuscles (see Fig. 9.2).[90] Moreover, because they rotate on being squeezed through these interstices, the channels or grooves are rotated, forming a stream of diagonally grooved, cylindrical fragments of matter. The core of Descartes' explanation of the Earth's magnetic field (as we would call it) rests on the idea that some of these fragments will have a left-hand screw and some a right-hand screw. The fragments are initially expelled from the Sun along the plane of the equator, where the centrifugal force is greatest, and since the vortex that makes up our whole solar system rotates on its axis in one direction, the direction of the screw of those coming from the North Pole will be different from those coming from the South Pole. Consider Fig. 9.3, where ABCD

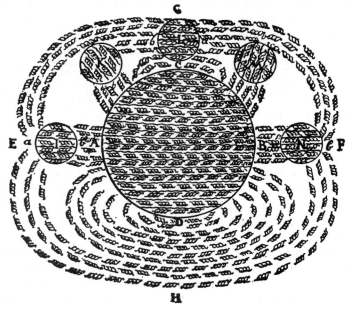

Fig. 9.3

represents the Earth and A and B the Poles. The fragments enter from one Pole and travel to the other along passages through the Earth, some of which allow fragments threaded in one and some in the opposite direction to pass through. When they emerge they return through the air to their point of origin 'forming a kind of vortex'.[91] This is the vortex seen when iron filings are sprinkled around a magnet. Descartes then goes on to explain why unlike poles attract and like ones repel, how iron is magnetized, and finally he indicates that the same kind of explanation can be applied to kindred phenomena such as static electricity, without providing details.[92]

This explanation is regressive, as I have said, but it would be wrong to think it is simply on a par with crude atomist explanations of magnetism. What marks it out is the fact that the Cartesian theory of vortices rests directly on the three laws of motion and the principle of the conservation of motion. The theory not only had a quantitative basis but, relying simply on the laws of motion and the tripartite division of matter, it provides an intuitively plausible account of the stability of planetary orbits, tides, and the nature of weight. To extend this theory into the realm of magnetic phenomena is simply an instance of what is sometimes described as 'spoils to the victor'. The theory of vortices is a much more powerful general theory than anything naturalists had advanced, and nothing remotely approaching it had been offered by other mechanists. If on the basis of such a theory an explanation of a phenomenon is offered which is no worse than that of any other account, it is entitled to be preferred: especially when vortex-like lines can actually be seen if one sprinkles iron filings around a magnet!

The resilience of the vortex theory, and the reluctance of Cartesians to give it up, should not be underestimated. Together with his laws of motion, Descartes' vortex theory was the starting point for all serious work in physical theory in the mid-seventeenth century, Newton's included.[93] It is not surprising that when Newton finally replaced it with a similarly general theory, that of universal gravitation, not everyone was immediately convinced that vortices had to go. Newton had examined the motion of bodies in fluids in Book II of his own *Principia*, arguing in some detail that it is the density of the medium, and not the subtlety of its parts, that is the principal factor in determining the resistance it offers. On the basis of this, he concluded both that the vortex theory was incompatible with Kepler's third law, and that vortices could not be self-sustaining: unless there were a constant imput of energy at the centre, motion would be diffused evenly throughout the whole vortex. Indeed, in the 'General Scholium' at the end of Book III he pointed out that in a Cartesian vortex, where the density of the medium is the same as the density of the body moving in it, the body would lose half its motion before it travelled a distance equal to twice its diameter.[94] But late seventeenth-century Cartesians such as Régis could not understand why Newton's advances should not be accommodated to the vortex theory, and they set out to show that vortices can be adapted to elliptical shapes if they are squeezed by neighbouring vortices, that the precessions of Mercury and Venus can be explained, that an improved account of the tides can be developed by correlating them with the position of the Moon by means of vortices, and so on,[95] and there were serious attempts to reconcile vortex theory with Newtonianism right into the eighteenth century, the last being Fontenelle's *Théorie des tourbillons* of 1752.[96] Even among those who, in the wake of Newton's *Principia*, rejected the vortex theory, there was a widespread feeling that at least it was the right *kind* of theory. Many mathematicians and physicists who recognized that Newton had done irremediable damage to the vortex theory were loath to accept his own account of gravitation, and eighteenth-century mathematical physicists such as D'Alembert and Euler were intent on pursuing what was a largely Cartesian programme, repudiating action at a distance and attempting to reshape Newtonian dynamics along mechanist lines.[97]

10
Melancholia and the Passions
1643–1650

'A Doctor of the Soul'

Over half of his extant correspondence dates from the last decade of Descartes' life, and it is much easier to build up a picture of his daily life in the period between the completion of the *Principia* and his move to Sweden than for any other period.[1] He evidently continued his practice of rising late, taking regular morning walks, in all probability with his dog 'Monsieur Grat',[2] and retained his generally frugal habits. Preferring fruit and vegetables to meat, he kept a well-stocked vegetable garden, as he had at Santpoort, as well as a garden for botanical experiments. There are even a couple of incidents with a bit of 'local colour' which have come down to us for this period. Baillet[3] reports the story of a local cobbler who came to visit Descartes on several occasions, only to be turned away twice by Descartes' servant because of his scruffy appearance. Descartes, on hearing of this, sent him some money and a note asking not to be disturbed any further. The cobbler, Dirck Rembrantsz van Nierop, returned the money, and his third attempt to see Descartes was successful. Descartes found him to have a talent for mathematics, and asked him to help him with some experiments; after receiving some tuition from Descartes, he subsequently went on to study navigation and astronomy, writing practical treatises in these areas. Descartes also, rather untypically, took some interest in local affairs, and when a local innkeeper, Meeus Jacobsz, killed a notoriously violent man in extenuating circumstances, Descartes wrote a long letter setting out the details of the case to one of his friends at court asking him to intercede on the man's behalf with the Prince of Orange.[4] These events seemed to have contributed to Descartes' reputation in the area. As a result of the first, Rembrantsz' village became something of a centre for those interested in Cartesianism, and as a result of the second Descartes evidently became someone to whom the locals felt that they could turn for advice, although there is no extant record of any requests for advice. But there does not seem to have been anyone local whom one could call a friend, as Ban and Bloemert had been in Santpoort, for example, and the most important relationship that he develops at this time is with someone he rarely meets, Princess Elizabeth.

The dedication to the *Principia* reads 'to the most serene Princess Elizabeth, eldest daughter of Frederick, King of Bohemia, Count Palatine, and Elector of the Holy Roman Empire'. Elizabeth was to play a key role in Descartes' life from 1643 onwards, though the nature of his relationship with her is extremely complex. Born in 1618, Elizabeth was a gifted linguist with a strong interest in theology, mathematics, philosophy, astronomy, and physics.[5] An intellectually precocious woman, she was evidently somewhat withdrawn and reclusive, as well as being frail and often unwell with apparently minor ailments. Various attempts were made to arrange a politically appropriate marriage for her in the 1630s, without success, and she was to remain unmarried. It is possible that she may have been introduced to Descartes as early as the winter of 1634/5, when he was at her mother's house, although the first mention of her in Descartes' correspondence is in a letter to Pollot, a mutual friend, of 6 October 1642.[6] Descartes probably knew her earlier in 1642, as it was evidently fashionable for young ladies of her class and acquaintance to travel up the river from the Hague or Leiden to Endergeest to visit Descartes, who had attained some fame and notoriety by this time.[7]

He was clearly very taken with Elizabeth. The pains he takes to explain his thought for her are quite unprecedented, as is the intimacy of his letters: his only reference to his mother is in a letter to Elizabeth, for example. He showed constant concern for her, and it has been suggested, not implausibly, that his move to Stockholm in 1649 was motivated partly by a desire to help the impoverished princess by soliciting Queen Christina's support.[8] He dedicated not only the *Principia* to her, but also, five years later, tells us in a dedicatory letter in the *Passions* that it was written for her. The second is not so surprising, since much of the material in the later part of the *Passions* was worked out in the correspondence with Elizabeth from 1643 onwards. But to dedicate the major systematic exposition of his natural philosophy to a 25-year-old woman whom he had known for not much over a year, and apparently had not met on very many occasions, does require some explanation. Gustave Cohen, an astute commentator on this period of Descartes' life, suggests that Descartes was in love with Elizabeth, but that the differences in age and social station (and, one might add, religion—Elizabeth was a staunch Protestant) effectively precluded him from forming any physical attachment to her.[9] Descartes' behaviour is certainly consistent with this. She occasionally visited him but, so far as we can tell, he reciprocated far less frequently, even though it would have been a short journey from Endergeest; and just as their acquaintance was beginning he unaccountably moved to Egmond, out of reach, as it were. Although he met her on a few occasions before she left the Netherlands in August 1646, he would apparently go out of his way to avoid her, and even when he visited the Hague he seems to have made sure that she would not be there.[10] This is hard to reconcile with the affection for her evident from the correspondence—an affection which is reciprocal, Elizabeth telling Descartes at a very early stage in the correspondence that she knows him 'to be the best doctor for her soul'[11]—and there can be little doubt that he felt disconcerted in some way by her physical presence.

Descartes' friendship with Elizabeth came at a time of some difficulty for him. The first letter from Elizabeth arrived in May 1643, at the height of the dispute with Voetius, a dispute that was to take up much of his time in the next two years. And just as this dispute was beginning to recede, a new one opened up at the University of Leiden.[12] A disciple of Descartes, Heereboord, had begun teaching a hybrid version of Cartesianism there in the early 1640s,[13] and in September 1646 the professor of theology, Trigland, and Revius, director of the Theological College—and someone who had tried to convert Descartes to Protestantism some years earlier—began a long dispute in which Descartes was condemned on various charges from Pelagianism (the standard charge in the attack on Arminians) to trying to convert the population to Catholicism (Heereboord was a Catholic convert). The situation was quite serious, and Descartes felt it necessary to apply for protection to a number of people, including the French ambassador.[14] Although the Leiden authorities were a good deal less aggressive than the Utrecht authorities had been,[15] and although Descartes had well-connected friends and, through them, support at court, he probably felt in a vulnerable position. Moreover, while he was gaining supporters in the Netherlands, he was losing some of the more able ones, such as Regius, who were presenting a form of Cartesianism which was increasingly out of Descartes' personal control. In France he had serious competitors, such as Roberval and Fermat, and although he managed to patch up his quarrel with Bourdin, he could not take Jesuit support for granted. As regards his French friends, during the 1640s many of these either died, became seriously ill, or became caught up in the worsening political situation in France. He travelled to France in May 1644, staying for four months, spending some time clearing up his father's affairs and visiting his brother and half-sister, Anne, and half-brother, Joachim. His father and sister had died four years earlier, and on this visit he was evidently not keen to spend much time with his family, preferring to be in Paris, where he spent August at the house of Picot, who undertook to translate the *Principia*, which had just appeared, into

French. Yet Descartes clearly had no intention of staying in France, returning in November to the peace of the Dutch countryside, where his mind 'was not wearied by the attention required by the bustle of life'.[16] On his return, the dispute with Voetius and Schookius came to a climax. His followers in the Netherlands were either being attacked or, in the case of Regius, following their own lights and bringing Cartesianism into disrepute and opening it up into theological censure. This took its toll on Descartes, and in May 1645 he wrote to Pollot:

Since my journey to France, I have aged twenty years, to the extent that it is now a greater effort for me to go to the Hague than it used to be to travel to Rome. It is not that I am sick, thank God, but I feel weak and more than ever I need comfort and rest.[17]

Although the correspondence with Elizabeth is interrupted between November 1643 and July 1644, when the dispute with Voetius and Schookius came to a head, his letters to Elizabeth show little evidence of such cares weighing down upon him. The correspondence provided an opportunity for writing about quite intimate matters in the context of a scientific theory of the passions, which in turn provided a form of emotional release. Nevertheless, the correspondence is a didactic one. Some time in the middle of 1643, for example, Descartes tested Elizabeth's knowledge of mathematics, setting her a famous problem about how one can find a fourth circle whose circumference touches those of three given ones. Elizabeth evidently learned her mathematics from Stampioen's textbook, which Descartes had attacked a few years earlier, but it stood her in good stead, and she had solved the problem before Descartes, worried that he might have set her a problem that was too difficult, sent the solution to Pollot.[18] Actually her solution involved more calculation than his, so Descartes spells out his own more elegant and economical procedure for her, introducing her to the basic principles of his *Géométrie*.[19] But despite her interest in metaphysics and mathematics, Elizabeth devotes little attention to these areas in her correspondence and the letters are, right from the start, principally concerned with the topic of the passions.

The correspondence brings to light a very significant change of focus in Descartes' thought, for the impact of the doctrine of substantial union of mind and body is considerable. When he dealt with the question of cognition in terms of this doctrine we saw that he was able to develop a notion of what it was that was distinctive about human cognition: not so much the presence of a will and an intellect, but the way in which having a will and an intellect shaped the perceptual process. He now begins to think through the question of the passions in terms of the substantial union, and the consequences are equally far-reaching.

Descartes had not corresponded with Elizabeth from November 1643 until after he had arrived in France in July 1644, and then, as far as we know, there is only one letter to Elizabeth. The correspondence resumes in earnest in the middle of 1645, and we can immediately detect a move from a somatopsychic account, in which the influence of bodily dispositions on the state of the soul is stressed, to a psychosomatic account in which are stressed the effects of the soul on bodily dispositions. Another way in which this might be described is in terms of a shift away from thinking of the passions in predominantly medical and physiological terms, to an approach which reflects (but does not simply reproduce) traditional humanist and moral thinking about them. The shift can be summed up symbolically by comparing Descartes' remark in the *Discours* that 'even the mind depends so much on the temperament and disposition of the bodily organs that if it is possible to find some means of making men in general wiser and more skilful than they have been up to now, I believe I must look for it in medicine',[20] with a comment to Chanut in 1646 that 'instead of finding ways to preserve life, I have found another, much easier and surer way, which is not to fear death'.[21] This shift can be seen to be a development brought about by reflection on the nature of the substantial union of mind and body; and Elizabeth's role in facilitating this shift is not insignificant, as we shall see, for she steers the discussion away from general metaphysical principles towards the question of practical consequences, both for general moral questions and for her particular condition of melancholia.

Mind in Body

In a letter to Pollot of 6 October 1642, Descartes tells his correspondent that he has heard of Elizabeth's interest in metaphysics, that she has read his own works, and that he will visit her at the Hague; but the first piece of correspondence dates from May 1643. This is a letter from Elizabeth, in which she raises a number of questions about the nature of the relation between mind and body, especially on the question of how something immaterial can move something extended, namely the pineal gland, if the laws of motion require physical contact between extended bodies for force of motion to be transferred.[22] In his reply, Descartes begins by setting out his general programme:

There are two things about the human soul on which the entire knowledge of its nature depends. The first is that it thinks, the second that, being united to the body, it can act and be acted upon with it. I have said almost nothing about the second, trying only to provide a proper understanding of the first, for my principal aim was to demonstrate the existence of a distinction between the soul and the body, and to this end only the first was needed, the second being a potential hindrance. But your Highness is so discerning that nothing can be hidden from her, so I shall now try to explain how I conceive of the union of the soul with the body, and how it has the power to move it.[23]

In explaining how the soul can act on the body, he argues that we should not confuse this with the question of how one body acts upon another. He refers Elizabeth back to the sixth set of replies to the objections to the *Meditationes*, where he uses the analogy of weight, which is distributed throughout a body, and while not itself corporeal or extended, 'could produce the full effect of which it was capable at any given point in the body'.[24] We have no difficulty in understanding how a body's weight acts to move it downwards, and we never think of this in terms of a real contact between two surfaces.[25] And just as a body's heaviness is not something 'distinct from the body', so the soul acts similarly. Earlier, Descartes had used a different image. In setting out for Regius a draft response to Voetius in a letter of January 1642, he calls the soul 'the true substantial form of man',[26] a remarkable way of describing the substantial union, for it suggests that Descartes is effectively treating the living body as a single substance, as a third kind of substance: something reinforced in a letter to Elizabeth of 28 June 1643, where he refers to 'three kinds of primitive notions', namely the mind, the body, and the union of the two.[27] The relevant sections of the *Principia*, probably composed around this time, reaffirm the substantial union of mind and body, and suggest distinctive properties of this 'third substance', namely sensations:

That there is a particular body that is more closely conjoined with our mind than any other body is obvious from the fact of our clear awareness that pain and other sensations come to us quite unexpectedly. The mind is aware that these sensations do not come from itself alone, and that they cannot belong to it simply in virtue of its being a thinking thing. Rather, they are able to belong to it only in virtue of its being joined to something other than itself which is extended and moveable, what we call the human body.[28]

In understanding why Descartes should make such a strong claim about the nature of the mind–body relation, it is important to place it in the context of what was an immense literature on the faculties which bore on this question.[29] In much of this literature, the distinction between mind and body was blurred at crucial points, and when it was not, various naturalistic 'sympathies' were invoked to explain the connection. In his influential *Tableau des Passions* of 1620, for example, Coëffeteau had maintained that the soul moves the heart in accordance with the movements of its sensitive appetite, something achieved not physically but in terms of some 'sympathy'.[30] And in one of the most comprehensive physiological accounts of the passions, Cureau de La Chambre's *Les caractères des passions*, which appeared in five volumes between 1640 and 1662—the first of which Descartes read, and remarked that he 'found in it nothing but words'[31]—the author wavers between a form of mechanism and a kind of vitalistic naturalism in which his version of animal spirits ('corps fluides') partake of the motion of the soul and the body indifferently, highlighting the almost irresistible tendency to think in naturalistic terms.[32] Clearly the whole point of a mechanist alternative to naturalism would be lost if the separation between mind and body that was thought necessary to mechanism was seen to require the postulation of 'sympathies' or vitalistically-conceived connections in order for the one to act on the other. One would have countered the naturalistic assimilation of mind and body, only to find oneself forced to allow a naturalistic account of the contact between the two. Descartes clearly has to prevent this, and the two ways in which he can go are either to sever the connection between mind and body, advocating a form of occasionalism, or to make the connection between operations of mind and body closer than one might otherwise have expected in a dualist account, through the doctrine of the substantial union.

There are traces of occasionalism in Descartes, but they occur when he is concerned with the relation between God's action and the motion of corporeal bodies. So, for example, Henry More takes Descartes to task on his metaphysical account of transfer of motion between bodies in impact. If motion is a mode of a body, that is, a determinate state of a body at a particular time, and if Descartes accepts the doctrine that properties cannot simply be alienated from a substance and transferred to another substance, how is it possible, he asks, for a substance to detach a mode from itself and give it to another?[33] In other words, if, as Descartes argues in the *Principes*,[34] motion is a property of a body just as its shape is, how can a body transfer its motion? Descartes replies that he has never maintained that modes are transmitted; rather, God simply conserves the same amount of motion in the universe, distributing it differently at different instants.[35] Now the extent to which Descartes' elaborate metaphysical account of motion is to be construed as occasionalist is a vexed question.[36] But there is no reason to conclude from his apparent advocacy of occasionalism in the case of divine action on the corporeal world either that the mind needs God as an intermediary to effect changes in the corporeal world,[37] or that he holds that the mind acts occasionally rather than causally on the body. Indeed, his doctrine of the substantial union, which he affirms consistently in the 1640s, indicates clearly that he would have rejected an occasionalist construal of the mind/body relation.

In proposing the doctrine of the substantial union of mind and body, Descartes is not, in fact, advocating a third substance; but embodied mind does have very distinctive features which mark it out from disembodied mind on the one hand, and body on the other.[38] What marks it out from mind *simpliciter* is the fact that it is essentially embodied; its characteristic properties depend on its being embodied. Note that the category of embodied mind does not in itself undermine dualism. For even if the mind were essentially embodied—something Descartes would completely reject—this would not, strictly speaking, prevent it being a separate substance: it is true that it would be dependent for its existence on something else, namely matter, but it is already dependent upon God for its existence, so being dependent does not rule out something being a substance in its own right. But while there may be no problem in this respect, there is in another, namely on the question of the identity of minds. Remember that if he is to secure personal immortality for a disembodied soul, and thereby avoid the Averroistic heresy, the disembodied soul needs an identity, something which distinguishes it from other disembodied souls. The traditional Thomist view had been that only a body could do this, which was why the theological doctrine of the resurrection of the body was stressed. There is no problem for Descartes in saying what makes *this* (embodied) mind *my* mind—my perceptions, memories, etc., all of which depend on corporeal organs, and hence a body, provide me with a continuing identity providing there is continuity in them.[39] But what makes *this* (disembodied) mind *my* mind? Disembodied minds would seem to have very little content, for perceiving, remembering, inferring, and even reasoning generally seem to be tied essentially to corporeal organs. They judge and exercise free will, but what do they judge, and what does it mean to talk about free will in this context? Focusing on the embodied mind certainly enables Descartes to give a more plausible account of cognition and the passions, but to neglect the disembodied mind is dangerous, not because one can ask whether one needs a disembodied mind at all—for it is a premiss of Descartes' whole project that the mind exists in a disembodied form after death—but rather because, in the absence of an account of what individuates it, his conception of the disembodied mind begins to look distinctly Averroistic.[40] Part of the problem is that Descartes' focus is generally on the self-evident indivisibility of the soul, something he emphasizes in Meditation 6 and in the *Passions*, as we shall see below. I think Descartes believed that this pre-empted any doubts one might have about identity: he certainly never raises the question explicitly. This does not meet the Averroist problem, however, which does not raise the question of whether the mind has parts but whether it is itself part of something.

It is true that Descartes insists on several occasions in his correspondence from 1640 onwards that there exists a purely intellectual
memory.[41] In a letter of condolence to Huygens on the death of his
wife, Descartes tells him that 'those who die pass to a sweeter and
more tranquil life than ours . . . We shall go to find them some day,
and we shall still remember the past; for I believe we have an intellectual
memory which is certainly independent of the body'.[42] But there is no
suggestion that he believes that this intellectual memory provides disembodied souls with an identity. It grasps universals rather than particulars,[43] which makes it unsuitable as a bearer of personal identity,
and indeed intellectual memory seems to bring the disembodied mind
closer to the Averroist 'one mind', which likewise grasps only universals.
Moreover, the respect in which it can be counted as genuine memory
is obscure, for Descartes tells Hyperaspites that 'where purely intellectual
things are concerned, memory in the strict sense is not involved; they
are thought of just as readily irrespective of whether it is the first or
second time they come to mind—unless, as often happens, they are
associated with particular names, in which case, since the latter are
corporeal, we do indeed remember them'.[44]

Intellectual memory is a peculiar and anomalous kind of memory
which Descartes never explains. His account of corporeal memory, on
the other hand, is something which is set out in some detail, most
notably in *L'Homme*. This prompts us to look at the other side of the
coin, Alexandrism. What distinguishes the 'substantial union' from a
mere human body, with all its corporeal faculties of reasoning, memory,
sensation etc.? What marks out the body as a 'substantial union' from
an automaton? After all, animal automata express fear, hope, and joy:

> If you teach a magpie to say good-day to its mistress when it sees her approach,
> this can only be because you are making the utterance of this word the expression
> of one of its passions. It will be an expression of the hope of eating, for example,
> if it has always been given a titbit when it says it. Similarly, all the things which
> dogs, horses, and monkeys are taught to perform are only expressions of their fear,
> their hope, and their joy; and consequently they can be performed without any
> thought.[45]

The difference lies in the fact that the behaviour of an automaton, no
matter how complex, can be explained in a completely reductive way:

> I am not disturbed by the astuteness and cunning of dogs and foxes, or all the
> things which animals do for the sake of food, sex, and fear; I maintain that I can
> easily explain the origin of all these things from the constitution of their organs.[46]

The behaviour of a human being, on the other hand, can be never be
explained reductively. A human being has the faculties of judgement and
will, and—something which is a precondition of these—consciousness

of her own mental states, whereas an automaton does not. The key point is that human sensations are quite unlike animal sensations, and the reason for this is now clear: it is not that human corporeal faculties are significantly different from animal ones, but that human corporeal faculties are largely regulated by and subordinate to the mind, and their content takes on a distinctly different kind of quality as a result.

This helps explain what is otherwise a very peculiar passage in a letter to Gibieuf written in 1642. Descartes tells Gibieuf that:

We observe in animals movements that are similar to those which result from our imaginations and sensations; but that does not mean that we observe imaginations and sensations in them. On the contrary, these same movements can take place without imagination, and we have arguments to demonstrate that they do so take place in animals, as I hope to show clearly by describing in detail the structure of their limbs and the causes of their movements.[47]

Descartes does not deny that we have to attribute sensations to animals to explain (at least some of) their movements, but he does appear to deny that we have to attribute imaginations to them to explain these movements. Yet in an earlier letter to Mersenne he talks about 'dissecting the heads of different animals in order to explain what imagination, memory, etc., consist of'.[48] And if animals did indeed have no imaginations, why do they have pineal glands? It makes no physiological sense. Moreover, if they have no imaginations, how can animals such as dogs, horses, and monkeys experience the fear, hope, and joy that he ascribes to them in the letter to the Marquess of Newcastle? Things become clearer when we read the immediately preceding paragraph in the letter:

I don't see any difficulty in understanding on the one hand that the faculties of imagination and sensation belong to the soul, because they are species of thought, and on the other hand that they belong to the soul only in so far as it is joined to the body, because they are kinds of thoughts necessary to conceive the soul in all its purity.[49]

Descartes has never treated the imagination as anything other than corporeal up to this point: now he suddenly ignores its corporeality. Why? Because conceiving of the imagination in terms of the substantial union and conceiving of it in terms of a piece of animal physiology are two different things.[50] Descartes is certainly overstating the case in saying that we do not have to attribute an imagination to animals in order to explain their behaviour, but the case he is overstating can be stated properly without difficulty. It is that the imagination functions very differently in the case of bodies and in the case of substantial mind/body unions, and despite the fact that the same organ is involved and, at a corporeal level, may even perform exactly the same functions, we cannot extrapolate from our own case to that of animals. The consciousness of mental states and the ability to exercise judgement and free will that the substantial union brings transforms the nature of our experience. Above all, it makes us responsible for our behaviour in a way in which mere automata are not. The doctrine of substantial union facilitates the understanding of how this responsibility arises, and this is a key question in Descartes' account of the passions.

A General Theory of the Passions

Discussions of the nature of the relation between mind and body in the seventeenth century generally occurred in the context of accounts of the passions, and even without Elizabeth's prompting Descartes would naturally have been drawn into the general question of the passions. They were associated with bodily conditions, bringing them under the purview of medicine and physiology, but they were also given ethical meanings (sadness—*tristitia*—was one of the cardinal sins for many centuries, for example), bringing them under the purview of moral psychology and theology. Treatises on the passions traditionally shared this combination of concerns, and Petrarch's *De remediis*, for example, a compendium of Stoic techniques for 'healing the passions', can be read as a treatise on morals or psychotherapy: the distinction is simply not there to be made.[51] Much the same can be said of the whole tradition of writing about the passions, including Descartes' *Passions de l'âme*, which takes us through the physiology of the passions and the nature of melancholia, as well as pointing out that 'all good and evil in this life depend on [the passions] alone'.[52] By the term 'morals', Descartes tells us in the 1647 Preface to the *Principes*, we are to understand 'the highest and most perfect moral system, which presupposes a complete knowledge of the other sciences [viz. medicine and mechanics] and is the ultimate level of wisdom'.[53] We clearly have to be extremely careful about how we characterize the boundaries of ethical discourse in the seventeenth century,[54] for the practical aim of treatises on the passions is, generally speaking, the 'healing of the soul', something which involves moral and psychotherapeutic considerations, and these require an understanding of the bodily conditions associated with various afflictions of the soul which may give rise to anything from immorality to madness. It is in this light that we must understand Descartes' remark in the *Discours*, quoted earlier, that if we seek to make men wiser we must look for the answer in medicine. There is undeniably an element of reductionism here, but it is not the crude reductionism it might at first seem; rather, it reflects what is in fact a complex nexus of considerations that make up an understanding of the nature of wisdom and goodness in this era.

The traditional disputes over the nature of the passions had a number of features, but one basic polarity pervading them is that between what can broadly be termed Stoic and Augustinian conceptions of the passions.[55] The Stoics treated the passions as false judgements and, following an already strong tradition of intellectualist ethics in Greek thought, they identified virtue and knowledge. Augustine was motivated by a number of theological problems that had concerned the Alexandrian Church Fathers generally; Christological problems about how Christ's 'agony in the garden' was possible if he was God, for example, had led to a study of the nature of the passions, with Athanasius attributing the agony in the garden to Christ's body alone, and Clement distinguishing between bodily passions, which are necessary for the preservation of life, and passions of the soul.[56] A problem which was not at first immediately related to this, but turned out to be a key question because of the nature of Augustine's answer to it, was how there could be evil in the world if God was good. His solution was to make human beings responsible for evil, and the philosophical tool that he uses to achieve this is the notion of free will. Earlier theories of moral behaviour had invoked the notion of responsibility for action, but had not introduced the notion of the will in this context. Augustine did, and thereby explained the existence of evil. But the theory of the will had ramifications for his views on the intellect and sensation, freedom and determination, and the moral evaluation of purpose and action.[57] In particular, the ethical consideration of the passions now comes to be formulated in terms of the action of the will. The affections, which he treats as the soul's motions, cannot simply be referred to a criterion of rationality, as the Stoics had urged, but must be assessed in terms of the act of will from which they arise, and 'if the will is wrongly directed the emotions will be wrong; if the will is right, the emotions will be not only blameless but praiseworthy'.[58] So, for example, a virtuous form of sadness or despair—*tristitia*—is ruled out on the Stoic view, but quite possible on Augustine's conception.[59] The fundamental character of the will, which guides its inclinations, is love, and virtuous affections are to be distinguished from vicious ones in terms of the moral quality of the love that rules in the will.

Once the topic of the affections had been formulated in terms of the action of the will, a long exercise of classification and categorization of them began, the most systematic account being that provided by Aquinas in Part II.i of the *Summa theologica*. Drawing extensively on Aristotle's *Rhetoric*, Aquinas' account was both comprehensive and ambitious. Like Augustine, he is opposed to the Stoic doctrine, although his criticisms of it are more systematic and penetrating, pointing out that the Stoics confuse sensitive and rational appetites, and hence the passions and the acts of will which alone are the seat of moral good and evil.[60] He begins by distinguishing 'passions of the body', such as physical suffering, which originate in the body and terminate in the soul, from 'passions of the soul', which originate in the soul and terminate in the body. The various passions of the soul generally recognized are then classified—following Plato's division of the soul into its rational, concupiscible, and irascible parts—into concupiscible affections (desires and appetites) and irascible affections (the passions strictly speaking), the former regarding good or evil absolutely and directly, the latter regarding them *'ratione ardui'*, that is, as something to be attained or avoided only with difficulty. The classification distinguishes between concupiscible affections directed towards a good object—love, desire, and pleasure or joy; concupiscible affections directed towards an evil object—hate, aversion, and pain or sorrow; irascible affections directed towards a good object—hope and despair; and irascible affections directed towards an evil object— fear, courage, and anger.[61] But the point of the exercise goes beyond mere classification of affective states. Aquinas' aim is to provide a genealogy for the passions whereby they can all be derived from four: pleasure, pain, hope, and fear. Pleasure and pain are the termini of all the passions, in that all the passions result in one or other of these, and hope and fear are the termini of the movements of the appetite: to take Aquinas' example, love passes through desire to hope, hate through aversion to fear.[62] This classification and genealogy of the passions provided the model for subsequent discussion, and despite the fact that the two most influential later writers on the passions, Vives and Descartes, rejected it, it continued well into the eighteenth century.[63]

Aquinas' account of the physiology of the passions reflects the traditional treatment, a treatment that was bequeathed to the seventeenth century. A passion arises when something good or evil is apprehended, exciting an appetite, which induces a bodily change. The passion is constituted by the dual movement of the appetite and the body.[64] Among the causes of the passion are the bodily 'complexion', which predisposes the body in various ways, and the particular bodily accompaniments of the passion which characterize that passion. But this does not mean that the resulting state of mind is no more than an effect of the bodily changes, a mere consciousness of them; for the bodily changes are merely an embodiment of the apprehension of good or evil seeking satisfaction. As Aquinas puts it, 'the affections of the soul are not caused by changes in the heart, but rather cause them . . . A man does not seek vengeance because the blood about the heart is inflamed; this is what disposes him to anger, but the anger itself comes from the appetite of vengeance'.[65] Gardiner sums up the doctrine well, noting that while Aquinas makes bodily changes essential to the constitution of a passion, the sensation of those changes is nowhere said to be essential to its psychical constitution. Aquinas' 'general representation is that of a process of apprehension and appetite on the one side resulting in expressive bodily movements on the other, the relation of the two being conceived in Aristotelian terms as one of "form" to "matter", so that the phenomenon may be described by either, but is best described, of course, by the determining factor, the form'.[66]

The most significant break with the Thomist account of the passions comes in the work of Vives.[67] Vives' conception of the passions differs significantly from that of Aquinas, for he considers only the more violent emotions to be passions, and the mind does not so much register the experience as share in it. In his *De anima et vita* (1538), Vives abandons the distinction between concupiscible and irascible passions and offers a different classification. But the key feature of Vives' account for our purposes is the way he makes the intellect and the will into autonomous faculties whose acts are mutually independent. As Levi has noted, 'behind his theory of the passions there is discernible a breakdown in the traditional scholastic psychology, a breakdown which was to be completed by the Neostoic moralists but which, as early as Vives, sets the stage for the debates of the moralists of the following century.'[68] Although the will should be guided by reason, which has as its object the rationally perceived good, the reason does not actually cause the will to choose in a particular way, for the will is essentially spontaneous in its liberty to choose. As Levi points out, what resulted was not only a blurring of the distinction between the passions and the virtues, but also a separation of the reason and the will 'such that it is difficult to see how an act can at the same time be both rational and free'.[69] The ultimate upshot of this was that the will and the reason were gradually prised further apart, so that in the neostoic revival of the sixteenth and seventeenth centuries (of which we may take Montaigne and Lipsius as early representatives)[70] it began to be urged that the reason could be relied upon to the exclusion of the will. One might expect disputes pursued along clear neostoic versus Augustinian/Thomist lines to follow from this, focusing on the question of whether the will did or did not play a part, but this is not what happened. The issue was complicated by the fact that, although he regarded them as mutually dependent, Aquinas had defended a 'real' distinction between the intellect and the will as two faculties of the soul, one having the true as its object, the other having the good. There is a fundamental instability or unclarity on the question of the relation between the will and reason, and what one tends to find on the anti-Stoic side in the late sixteenth- and early seventeenth-century literature on the passions, whether scholastic, devotional, or secular, is a basic adherence to a generally Augustinian/Thomist position tempered to a greater or lesser degree by elements drawn from Stoicism.

The deep problems in the literature can be glimpsed by considering Eustache's *Summa Philosophiae* (1609). Although this was not as influential as the *Tableau des passions* (1630) of Coëffeteau, Descartes does not mention Coëffeteau, whereas he had originally intended to print Eustache's textbook alongside his own *Principia* when that work was at an early draft stage. What we find in both Coëffeteau and Eustache is a sharp distinction between the higher and lower parts of the soul.[71] Eustache holds that the will is related to the intellect in the higher part of the soul as the imagination is related to the sensitive appetite in the lower part. Aquinas had treated reason, sense, and imagination as part of a single cognitive process, but the Stoic tendency to use the term 'imagination' pejoratively, combined with a move to think of imagination as being concerned with knowledge of material objects and reason as being concerned with knowledge of immaterial objects (universals, etc.), had a significant impact on later scholastic thinking; the imagination became insulated from reason and began to be treated as the source of error. This opens up the possibility of an act of will being at variance with the sensitive appetite and exercising no control over it. More generally, what results is an extremely unstable amalgam of elements taken from the Scholastic tradition and Stoicism, and the price paid is a fragmentation of the soul which has no obvious benefits. This opened the door to an abandonment of the Scholastic account in favour of Stoicism, notwithstanding the well-known difficulties with the Stoic account; for, as Levi remarks, 'as in antiquity, the great asset of Stoic theory is that it restores unity to a fragmented soul'.[72]

This, then, is the context within which Descartes was writing. Where the physiology of the passions was treated, there was an almost irresistible tendency to apply properly mental and corporeal attributes interchangeably, and even to conceive of animal spirits in a vitalistic fashion; and where the faculties were treated, there was an increasing fragmentation of the soul or mind with various 'lower' parts blending into the corporeal functions. And this occurred with no discernible improvement in our understanding of the nature of human affective states. Descartes' aim in producing a systematic account of the passions was more than anything else to restructure the whole question of the affective states around a clear understanding of the distinction between mind and body, and on the basis of such an understanding to formulate the appropriate notion of a substantial union needed to account for the source and nature of affective states.

We have three sources for Descartes' account. The first is his correspondence, that with Elizabeth being the most important, but that with Chanut, from 1646 onwards, also being of significance. Chanut usually acted as an intermediary between Descartes and Queen Christina of Sweden, although there is one letter of importance to Christina herself.[73] The second is his *Passions de l'âme*, written during the winter of 1645–6, but published only a few weeks before his death. The third is the preface to Picot's French translation of the *Principia*, the *Principes de Philosophie*, which appeared in 1647.

I indicated above that with the resumption of correspondence with Elizabeth in the middle of 1645 Descartes moves away from the somatopsychic account that he had favoured earlier to one in which psychosomatic factors are stressed. In the letters to Elizabeth that I quoted at the beginning of Chapter 1, for example, we saw him providing a psychosomatic treatment of melancholia, whereby the mind is forced to concentrate on agreeable things, this having the effect of relaxing the heart and allowing freer circulation of the blood. This may be a change in emphasis rather than a change in position, and he does not give up the idea that one's bodily disposition may aid or impede the will, pointing out that an indisposition in the body may prevent the will from acting freely.[74] Indeed, he makes it clear that what he has in mind is a reciprocal relation between mind and body:

Bodily health and the presence of agreeable objects greatly assist the mind by chasing from it all the passions which partake of sadness and making way for those which partake of joy. And, conversely, when the mind is full of joy, this helps greatly to cause the body to enjoy better health and to make the objects present to it appear more agreeable.[75]

In the *Passions*, which was evidently completed over the winter of 1645/6,[76] Descartes sets out to provide a comprehensive account of the various ways in which mind and body interact. The three parts of the text are designated by Descartes himself as providing a general account of the mind/body relation and the general nature of passions (Part I), a classification of the passions (Part II), and an account of particular passions (Part III), although from near the end of Part II the discussion shifts to the moral/therapeutic questions surrounding the passions.

The importance of beginning the *Passions* with an account of the general questions surrounding the mind/body relation is brought out rather well by a comment to Chanut in 1646 that the *Principia* does not in fact get one very far as regards morals.[77] One should remember that the projected fifth and sixth parts of the *Principia* were supposed to be 'on living beings and on man' respectively. Descartes now realizes that there is a big gap between the metaphysically grounded natural philosophy that he had set out in the *Principia* and the kind of things that one needs to establish to provide an account of human behaviour. Certainly the idea of a medically based ethics, which would have connected the natural philosophy of Parts II, III, and IV with the account of human beings in the projected Part VI, via a consideration of physiology in the projected Part V, no longer looks viable, and in the 1647 Preface to the *Principes*, morals is listed along with mechanics and medicine as one of the three fundamental sciences.[78] The foundations of morals no longer lie in medicine (if they ever did), but rather in an account of the substantial union of mind and body.

A clue to the orientation of Descartes' whole approach is given in his statement at the beginning of the *Passions* that he writes not as 'an orator, nor as a moral philosopher, but as a physicist [*physicien*]'.[79] This means two things. First, his treatment of the passions is dependent upon the metaphysical foundations of natural philosophy set out in the *Principia* and, in this respect, the passions have the same ultimate foundation as the two other basic sciences, mechanics and medicine. As I have already argued, it is an egregious error to imagine that Descartes is maintaining that one could actually discover substantive truths by deriving them from first principles, and this holds for the passions just as much as for natural philosophy generally. The first principles provide a framework within which the exposition of doctrine must proceed if any systematic certainty is to attach to one's conclusions. So, the first point is that, writing as a '*physicien*', Descartes is providing an account of the passions which aspires to some degree of certainty, in contrast to rival accounts. Secondly, as Rodis-Lewis points out, in saying he does not write as a moral philosopher, Descartes is setting himself against 'those for whom this is the point of departure: the Stoics saw in *pathos*, passion, a *pathological* phenomenon, which the sage was required to quash in aspiring to *apatheia*'.[80] It is not just that Descartes disagrees with this account of the passions, but with this whole approach to them. Unless one has a proper understanding of the faculties of the mind, bodily physiology, and how the substantial union of mind and body functions, one cannot even begin to investigate the nature of the passions. Even if such an understanding yielded the conclusion that the passions are something that must be overcome, the Stoics would not be vindicated because they have approached the question in a completely wrong-headed fashion. It is tempting to draw an analogy with Descartes' rejection of the Aristotelian account of perception here: Aristotle simply assumed that our perceptual image must resemble the object perceived, and built his account of the transmission of light and the physiology of perception around this assumption, instead of investigating the optics and physiology first. Similarly, the Stoics can be accused of attempting to provide a moral theory of the passions without any investigation of their psychological and especially their physiological basis.

Descartes begins Part I of the *Passions* by noting that whether something is called an action or a passion depends simply on whether it is considered with respect to the mind or the body, so the crucial thing is to start with the difference between the soul and the body.[81] As we have seen, contemporary accounts of the passions were very vague on the key question of what the relation between the mind and the body is, and in this context Descartes places himself on firm ground by arguing that any serious discussion of the passions must begin with this question: and, of course, on home ground, for his account of both physiology and the functions of the mind were far more elaborate than anything available in the contemporary literature. Above all, he can avoid the common error of thinking of the action of the mind on the body as being like the action of one body on another.[82] Articles 7 to 16 set out in a summary way the mechanistic physiology of *L'Homme*, and the *Passions* contain the only exposition of his physiology published in his lifetime. We are then provided with a division of the functions of the soul into two: actions and passions. Actions comprise volitions which either terminate in the soul, as 'when we will to love God', or in the body, as when we move our legs by willing to walk. They also include those perceptions which have their origin in the soul, as when we reflect upon our own existence. Perceptions which have their origin in the body, on the other hand, are passions. The treatment of the passions then proceeds, from article 21 onwards, in terms of functions of the soul which depend on its union with the body. Perceptions which do not derive from the soul itself can be caused either by external bodies acting upon us, or from natural appetites of the body, such as hunger, which we sense through bodily organs, or they can be felt 'as in the soul itself', in which case no immediate cause is evident.[83] These last are the 'passions of the soul' to which Descartes' account is devoted, and he is concerned with their phenomenology rather than their causes; for while we may be deceived about their causes—they may be experienced whether we are awake or asleep, for example—we cannot be deceived about their existence or specific nature.[84] They are defined as being 'caused, maintained, and strengthened by a movement of the spirits', and take the form of 'excitations of the soul', as do volitions; but, unlike volitions, they do not have their source in the soul. Articles 30 to 47 then provide a psychophysiology of the soul in terms of Descartes' doctrine that the pineal gland is the seat of the soul, much along the lines of *L'Homme*. Two features of this account are worth noting. First, in article 36 he explains how different passions can arise in different people who are apparently stimulated in the same way. Clearly any treatment of the passions is going to have to account for what we might call differences in temperament. But the explanatory value of his account is minimal, to say the least, for he simply translates differences in response into differences in the disposition of the brain. The idea is that the spirits are reflected differently in different people depending on the initial disposition of their brain, and hence pineal gland, something which results in different responses.[85] Here, the poverty of Descartes' tennis-racquet account of the action of the pineal gland, whereby it acts simply by redirecting animal spirits at different angles depending on its disposition, is clear.

Second, in article 47 he uses the doctrine of the pineal gland being the seat of the soul to undermine the prevalent account of the passions in terms of a conflict between higher and lower parts of the soul:

All the struggles that people customarily imagine between the lower part of the soul, which is called sensitive, and the higher or 'rational' part, or between the natural appetites and the will, just consist in the opposition between the movements which the body, by its spirits, and the soul, by its will, tend to excite simultaneously in the gland. For there is only a single soul in us, and this soul has within itself no diversity of parts; one and the same soul is sensitive and rational, and all its appetites are volitions.[86]

The conflicts that we experience are, then, conflicts between the soul and the body, for there is no sense in which they can be either conflicts between higher and lower parts of the soul, or conflicts between different powers of the soul. The spirits can move the pineal gland in a particular way, stimulating a desire for something, and while the will cannot halt this directly, it can represent objects to itself so vividly that, by the principle of association, the course of the spirits will gradually be halted. In these circumstances the soul will be impelled 'almost simultaneously' both to desire and not to desire the same thing; but the 'almost' is important, and this will not be a genuine conflict in the soul. A parallel case occurs in the body, when the passions cause the organs or limbs to act in a certain way, and the soul attempts to stop this, causing conflict in the body. What is required in both cases is mastery of one's passions, which derive from 'firm and determined judgements'.[87] There is no question of using one passion to offset another, and even less of trying to live without passions: they are crucial for fortifying and sustaining individual acts of will, and those who have no inclination for the passion of wonder, for example, are 'usually very ignorant'.[88]

Part II of the *Passions* deals with their classification. The basis for this is different from that of a writer like Aquinas, who attempts to provide a systematic genealogy in terms of an account of primitive passions from which others can be derived. Moreover, rejecting any distinction between parts of the soul, Descartes rejects the distinction between concupiscible and irascible appetites which depends on this, thereby removing the basis of the traditional classifications.[89] Although he lists six primitive passions—wonder, love, hate, desire, joy, and sadness— and although, except for the first, these are part of the standard scholastic listing, Descartes takes a thoroughly functional approach, for the basis for identifying passions is in terms of the importance their perceivable objects have for us, how much difficulty we have in obtaining them, whether they are harmful or of benefit to us, and so on. Moreover, the full listing—as opposed to the six primitive passions—is explicitly open-ended, for there are, Descartes tells us, an indefinite number of passions.

In the course of his discussion of joy and sadness in the *Passions*, Descartes introduces an important distinction between joy and intellectual joy, and sadness and intellectual sadness. Intellectual joy and sadness are not passions properly speaking, for they 'come into the soul by the action of the soul itself'[90] and not by the action of the body. In the *Principia*, Descartes had mentioned that, when we hear good news, 'it is first of all the mind that makes a judgement about it and rejoices with that intellectual joy which occurs without any bodily disturbance and which, for that reason, the Stoics allowed the wise man to experience'.[91] Such 'inner excitations',[92] as Descartes calls them, come to play an increasingly important role as the *Passions* progresses, and at the end of Part II he introduces a fuller account of their nature:

Here I shall merely add one further consideration which, I believe, helps to prevent us from suffering any discomfort from the passions. This is that our well-being depends principally upon inner excitations which are excited in the soul only by the soul itself. In this respect they differ from the passions of the soul, which invariably depend on some movement of the spirits. Although these excitations of the soul are often joined with those passions which are similar to them, they may also frequently be found with others, and they may even originate in those to which they are opposed. For example, when a husband mourns his dead wife, it sometimes happens that he would be sorry to see her brought to life again. It may be that his heart is constricted by the sadness excited in him by the funeral display and by the absence of a person to whose company he was accustomed. And it may be that some remnants of love or pity occur in his imagination and draw genuine tears from his eyes, in spite of the fact that he feels at the same time a secret joy in his innermost soul, and the excitation of this joy has such a power that the concomitant sadness and tears can do nothing to diminish its force. Again, when we read of strange adventures in a book, or see them represented on stage, this sometimes arouses sadness in us, sometimes joy, or love, or hatred, and generally any of the passions, depending on which objects are presented to our imagination. But along with this we have pleasure of feeling them aroused in us, and this pleasure is an intellectual joy which can just as easily originate in sadness as in any of the other passions.[93]

Here Descartes begins to show some influence of neostoicism, for he goes on to tell us that such inner excitations affect us more intimately than the passions, and hence, so long as our soul always has the means of happiness within itself, anything external is powerless to harm it.[94] At this point, considerations of the physiology of the passions recede into the background, as ethical questions are construed in terms of the true worth of things, which the passions exaggerate in one direction or the other. The traditional contrast between reason and passion now appears as a contrast between an inner excitation and a passion. So, for example, in a letter to Chanut of 1 February 1647, Descartes distinguishes between 'the love which is purely intellectual or rational and the love which is a passion'.[95] The former consists in the movement of the will that accompanies the knowledge that a good is possessed, the latter in the experience of possessing the good. Intellectual love is clear, love as a passion confused.[96] Our judgement of the worthiness of the object determines the degree of our intellectual emotion, whereas the extent of the passion depends on our degree of esteem for the object. Since the second must be proportional to the first, it is the intellectual or rational version of the emotion, the 'inner excitation', that provides the key to how we should behave.

The direction and regulation of the passions enables us to live a good life: 'good' both in the sense of being ethical and in the sense of being fulfilling, for the two are inseparable in Descartes' account. Consider, for example, his discussion of generosity, probably the most important concept in Descartes' ethics. Although the word *generosité* had much the same core meaning in ordinary seventeenth-century French as it has for us, the French moralists had added a connotation of nobility, and *generosité* is very close to the notion of *gloire* defended in the personalist ethics of Balzac, Corneille, and others, in part as an attempt to elaborate a true *gentilhomme* morality. Descartes defines generosity as follows:

I believe that true generosity, which causes a man to esteem himself to the greatest degree which is legitimate, consists solely in this: partly in his understanding that there is nothing which truly belongs to him except his free control of his volitions, and the only grounds for praise or blame are that he uses it well or badly; and partly in his feeling within himself a firm and constant resolution to use it well—that is, never to ask the will to undertake and carry out whatever he judges to be the best. To do this is to pursue virtue perfectly.[97]

In other words, it is ultimately our degree of self-esteem which will determine the worth of what we do. Hence the importance of the therapeutic aspects of Descartes' moral programme, such as those set out in the letter to Elizabeth in the letter of the middle of 1645, which recommends exercises for ridding oneself of melancholia—the affliction of those drawn to intellectual reflection—by 'directing the imagination'.[98]

In Search of Peace, 1646–1649

Descartes' closest correspondent from the middle of 1644 onwards was Elizabeth, and it is with her that he shared the results in many of his intellectual endeavours: indeed, it is to some extent because of her great interest in the matter that he pursues the passions so assiduously. As we have seen, he suffered greatly from tiredness after returning from Paris in 1644, and his rate of work seems to have slowed considerably. After the completion of the *Principia* in the middle of 1644, much of Descartes' intellectual efforts were directed towards developing a theory of the passions, but he did continue to pursue research in botany, anatomy, and physiology at least up until 1648, this material presumably forming the basis for the projected Part V of the *Principia*.

The beginning of his interest in botany can be dated to 1639, when he wrote to Mersenne thanking him for the offer of some seeds, adding that he knew they would be available at the Leiden botanical gardens but that the seeds had not ripened there and the time to sow them had arrived; he also asks for a plant catalogue of the Jardin Royal in Paris, saying he could send the catalogue of the Leiden botanical gardens in exchange.[99] Unfortunately, we have no record of his work in botany, and it is unclear how far his interest extended. The study of anatomy is something he pursued from 1629 onwards, and we have some records of his anatomical observations between 1629 and 1648.[100] This indicates extensive dissection of cows, calves, sheep, and to a lesser extent fish. For obvious reasons, he had a great interest in the heart and vascular system, seeking, amongst other things, a connection between the pulmonary artery and the aorta, which he failed to find.[101] There is also evidence of extensive work on the oesophagus, stomach, and intestines.[102] As regards physiology, as well as some writings of doubtful provenance,[103] we have a short unfinished treatise called *La Description du Corps Humain*.[104] This was written in the winter of 1647/8, and Descartes tells Elizabeth that it is a rewriting of work he had started twelve or thirteen years ago—that is, *L'Homme*—and that the original work fell into the hands of 'others, who transcribed it badly', a clear reference to Regius.[105] The *Description* was abandoned early in 1647, because of the detailed research that would have been needed to develop an adequate account of the early development of animals,[106] but five parts are extant: an introduction, a section on the heart and the circulation of the blood, a section on nutrition, a section on the formation of blood, heart, lungs, and nerves in the foetus, and finally a section concentrating on the formation of veins and arteries. Only the last two parts contain material that goes beyond *L'Homme*, for although Descartes had had a long-standing interest in the formation of the foetus, he had not attempted to incorporate any material in *L'Homme*. He was certainly familiar with Fabricius' treatise on the formation of the egg and the chick, *De formatione ovi et pulli* (1621), and in a letter to Mersenne of 2 November 1646 he tells him that he first read it 'more than fifteen years ago'.[107] The records of his anatomical research record quite extensive experiments on the evolution of the chick in the egg,[108] with Descartes opening thirty eggs at various stages after incubation and noting the stage of development. His embryological research would seem to have been confined exclusively to chick embryos, however, and it is not surprising that he felt overwhelmed by the amount of research he would have to do if he was to present an account of foetal development that had any claims to being comprehensive.

This work was done against the background of tiredness, continuing attacks from Protestant theologians and, in August 1646, the permanent departure of Elizabeth from the Netherlands. Elizabeth's family suffered a blow in November 1645 when her brother Edward married Anne de Gonzague, a sister of the Queen of Poland, and converted to Catholicism as a precondition of the marriage. Her mother was, as I have already mentioned, a symbol of the Protestant cause in Europe, and Princess Elizabeth took the matter very much to heart, writing to Descartes in impassioned tones.[109] Descartes' reply is undiplomatically diplomatic: that is to say, while she wrote to Descartes for sympathy and (perhaps unreasonably) support in this time of need, his reply coolly considers the pros and cons of conversion, telling her not to take the matter so seriously, and giving the strong impression that it actually matters very little whether one espouses the Protestant cause or the Catholic one.[110] And it is just possible that this is not merely his way of trying to take the heat of the issue, but his considered view of denominational quarrels. In any event, she was not to write to him for another five months, which may have reflected her annoyance with his response. By the time she did start corresponding again, her family, no stranger to turmoil, was in one of the greatest that it ever faced. A French officer named L'Espinay had boasted that he had seduced both her mother and her sister, Louise-Hollandine, and her brother Philip impulsively challenged him to a duel. The duel was in fact called off at the last minute, but the next day Philip stabbed L'Espinay to death in the market place. Elizabeth took Philip's side, but her mother would not listen and even suspected her of complicity. The family effectively came apart, Philip fleeing The Hague never to return, and Elizabeth being banished to Berlin.[111] At her request, Descartes visited her immediately before her departure on 15 August 1646, the last time they were ever to see each other. They continued to correspond regularly, and the letters discuss a range of thinkers from Socrates to Machiavelli, for whom Descartes shows a grudging respect, conceding that the constraints of justice are different in the cases of sovereigns and private individuals.[112]

The period after Elizabeth's departure was a difficult one for Descartes, and in May 1647 he wrote to her saying that he was travelling to France and may have to remain there for some time, but he would definitely return before the winter. He continues:

For the letter that I have received from your highness leads me to hope that you will return to The Hague towards the end of the summer. Indeed, I may tell you that this is the chief reason why I would prefer to live in this country than any other. As for the peace I had previously sought here, I foresee that from now on I may not get as much of that as I would like. For I have not yet received all the satisfaction that is due to me for the insults I suffered at Utrecht, and I see that further insults [from Revius and others] are on the way. A troop of theologians, followers of scholastic philosophy, seem to have formed a league in an attempt to crush me by their slanders.[113]

The 'further insults' Descartes mentioned had been catalogued in a letter to the Curators of the University of Leiden only six days earlier,[114] where he complains of being accused of 'atheism' in a public disputation held there.

Descartes' stay in France was marred by the death of Mydorge and the illness of Mersenne, but he met with Gassendi and Hobbes, probably at the Paris home of the Marquess of Newcastle, and since he subsequently became reconciled with both of them it is possible that this meeting was beneficial. He was also introduced to the young prodigy, Pascal, with whose essay on conic sections (written at the age of 16) Descartes was familiar. Unfortunately Descartes' old adversary Roberval was present at the meeting, and since Pascal had a high fever, Roberval did most of the talking, much to Descartes' fury. A second meeting was more successful, however, and it was probably at this meeting that Descartes suggested to Pascal an experiment to decide between Torricelli's theory of atmospheric pressure, which postulated the possibility of a vacuum, and his own plenum account.[115] Pascal carried out the experiment with his brother-in-law on 19 September 1648, carrying up the Puy du Dome two glass tubes of mercury inverted in baths of mercury, and noting the fall of the mercury with increased altitude.

Descartes returned to the Netherlands in September 1647, accompanied by his old friend Picot, who stayed with Descartes at Egmond-Binnen throughout the winter. During the winter he must have worked on his response to Regius, the *Notae in Programma*, which appeared at the beginning of 1648. Descartes had dissociated himself from Regius' *Fundamenta* in the preface to the *Principes*, and Regius responded swiftly by publishing a broadsheet setting out in the form of numbered theses the points of disagreement. This broadsheet appeared towards the end of 1647, and Descartes responded immediately, reprinting it alongside his own replies to each of the theses. I have already indicated that the central issue in dispute is the need for a metaphysical grounding of natural philosophy, Regius' *Fundamenta* representing the kind of presentation of natural philosophy that Descartes had pursued before the 1633 condemnation of Galileo, and the *Principia* representing the kind of presentation that he thought necessary in the wake of that condemnation. The main thrust of the *Notae* is consequently taken up with showing how, lacking the requisite metaphysical grounding, it is impossible to avoid confusion. One question that was at issue was that of innate ideas, and Descartes offers an interesting gloss on this doctrine.

In looking at Meditation 3, I said that Descartes would subsequently treat what he refers to as 'adventitious' ideas as being in some sense innate. Such a treatment is offered in the *Notae*. Regius' twelfth thesis had been that 'the mind has no need of ideas, or notions, or axioms which are innate; its faculty of thinking is all it needs for performing its own acts'.[116] Descartes' response is interesting: he almost seems to concede the point, although he represents the matter as being a confusion on Regius' part, maintaining that

the author's disagreement with me seems to be merely verbal. When he says that the mind has no need of ideas, or notions, or axioms which are innate, while admitting that the mind has the power of thinking (presumably natural or innate), he is plainly asserting the same thing as I, though verbally denying it. I have never written or judged that the mind requires innate ideas *qua* something distinct from its faculty of thinking. I did, however, observe that there were certain thoughts within me which neither came to me from external objects nor were determined by my will, but which came solely from the power of thinking within me; and I applied the term 'innate' [to these]. . . . The sense here is the same as that in which we say that generosity is innate in certain families, or that certain diseases such as gout or stones are innate in others; it is not that the babies of such families suffer from these diseases in their mother's womb, but just that they are born with a certain disposition or faculty to contract them.[117]

Then he proceeds to rebut the conclusion that Regius had drawn from his twelfth thesis, namely that 'all common notions that the mind has engraved in it originate from observation of things or verbal instruction'.

It is in his response to this that Descartes advocates a much broader conception of what is innate:

If we bear in mind fully the scope of our senses, and what it is precisely that reaches our faculty of thinking by way of them, we must admit that in no case are the ideas of things presented to us by the senses just as we form them in our thinking. So much so that there is nothing in our ideas which is not innate to the mind, or faculty of thinking, except only those circumstances which pertain to experience, such as the fact that we judge that this or that idea which we now have present to our thought is to be referred to certain extraneous things. This is not because these extraneous things transmitted the ideas themselves to our minds through the organs of sense, but because they transmitted something which gave the mind, at that very moment, occasion to form these ideas, by means of a faculty innate to it. For nothing reaches our mind from external objects through the organs of sense except certain corporeal motions, as our author himself asserts in article nineteen, in accordance with my own principles. But neither the motions themselves nor the figures arising from them are conceived by us exactly in the shape they take in the sense organs, as I have explained at length in my *Dioptrique*. Hence it follows that the very ideas of the motions and shapes are themselves innate in us. The ideas of pains, colours, sounds, and the like must be all the more innate if, on the occasion of certain corporeal motions, our mind is to be capable of representing them to itself, for there is no similarity between these ideas and the corporeal motions.[118]

The context is rather important here. Descartes does not seem to be talking in this passage about innate ideas so much as an innate capacity or disposition to have certain ideas. Some of these ideas that we have an innate capacity for may be innate ideas, but some seem to be what he had called adventitious ideas in Meditation 3 and elsewhere. Descartes is notoriously imprecise about how we should conceive of ideas— whether they themselves are dispositions or acts, how we distinguish them from their propositional content, even whether they are mental or physical. He simply does not seem much bothered by these questions, questions which for his successors were often the key ones.[119] But there does seem to be a crucial distinction to be made here between our innate disposition to have innate ideas and our innate disposition to have adventitious ideas. Actually, the latter is something of a misnomer, for what it seems to amount to is an innate disposition to respond to sensory stimuli in a particular way—by perceiving a colour, hearing a sound, experiencing a pain, etc. Clearly one could have such innate sensory dispositions without innate ideas of God, or of the essence of matter, mind, and triangles. Indeed, the mind proper does not seem to be at all relevant to the exercise of these dispositions or capacities: if I see something as being red, this is not because of some voluntary act of the will or some intellectual act on my part. I can, of course, exercise my judgement and ask whether the surfaces of bodies are really overlaid with colour, as they appear, but this is a quite separate matter. Innate sensory dispositions seem to be part of our cerebral physiology, and I cannot see any reason why animals should not have such dispositions, in Descartes' view. There is no reason, from anything Descartes says, to think that they do not hear sounds or see colours, but in order to do this they would need to be 'fitted out' in the requisite way. And here we are back with the theme of the first chapter of *Le Monde*, where the question was raised of the relation between the causal-mechanical process that occurs in perception and the cognition that results from it: that is, the question of how perceptual information can be grasped and represented such that perceptual cognition results from this causal-mechanical process. In the earlier account of this question, we saw that there is a need for the person or automaton to be fitted out with appropriate physiology if it is to respond to a sensory stimulus in any way that can be called cognitive; and we also saw that, provided questions of one's awareness of one's cognitive states is not raised, nothing more than the appropriate physiology is needed.

The other main source on Descartes' thought at this time is a record of an interview with Franz Burman, a 20-year-old student active in the circle of young Cartesians at Leiden[120] who, on 16 April 1648, came to dine with Descartes, eliciting a response on various passages in his writings and noting down Descartes' comments. Four days later he solicited the help of his friend Johannes Clauberg[121]—a 'third-generation' Cartesian, being a pupil of Johannes de Raey, who was in turn a pupil of Regius—in writing out a full record of the interview. Despite the fact it was to remain unpublished and indeed unknown for 250 years, the document is invaluable, for Descartes is very forthcoming and very concerned to clarify his general position, and Burman came along well-prepared and shows no hesitation in pressing Descartes on a number of points. Consequently, while no new material is presented in the conversation, we do get Descartes' own overview of his published writings. The principal topic of discussion is metaphysics, although Descartes pointedly avoids any theological topics and makes it clear that metaphysics is really only a prelude to the really important business, natural philosophy.[122]

Almost immediately after the interview with Burman, Descartes travelled to France again.[123] It was becoming increasingly clear that Elizabeth was not going to return to the Netherlands, and Descartes' thoughts were turning to France. During his previous visit his friends had put in train a petition to the king to grant Descartes a royal pension of 3,000 livres. Hearing he had been granted the pension, he returned in May 1648, perhaps expecting the kind of recognition that he believed due to him, a recognition not forthcoming in the Netherlands. He did not stay with Picot, but took a grander and more central residence, indicating perhaps that he now intended remaining in Paris. His timing could not have been worse, however, for the Fronde was beginning, and the city was in a state of near-revolution. He wrote to Chanut shortly after arriving in Paris that he would soon return 'to the innocence of the desert that I left, where I was much happier'.[124] He had himself to put up a considerable sum for the document granting him the pension,[125] which he never received—something he may have predicted, if only because of the huge government financial deficit that was one of the factors behind the Fronde. He was fully reconciled with Gassendi during this trip, but his old friend Mersenne was on his death bed, and Roberval was hounding him. Picot entreated him to stay on a little longer, and he moved into Picot's house for a short time, but the barricades went up in the streets on 26 August and he returned to the Netherlands the next day. Six months later he wrote in a bitter letter to Chanut that he went to Paris as someone whose friends had invited him to dinner, but 'on arriving I found their kitchen in chaos and the kettle overturned; this is why I left without saying a word so as not to increase their grievance',[126] and shortly afterwards he tells Chanut:

But what disgusted me most is that none of them showed any sign of wishing to know any part of me other than my face. So I came to think that they only wanted to have me in France as one would an elephant or a panther, because of its rarity, not as something that might be of use.[127]

In the twelve months between his return to Egmond and his departure for Sweden in August 1649, Descartes caught up with his correspondence, and as well as letters on the passions between Descartes, Elizabeth, Chanut, and Christina, there is a particularly important set of exchanges with Henry More on topics in metaphysics and natural philosophy which, as we have already seen, raise problems with Descartes' identification of matter and extension. More's account is interesting because at this time he was very attracted to Cartesianism, and what he tries to do is to reformulate Cartesian natural philosophy in more intuitively plausible metaphysical terms. The thrust of More's objection to Descartes' dualism is that it is impossible to understand how a purely spiritual soul—something which by Descartes' account has no extension whatsoever—can be joined to a purely material body, that is, to something that is nothing but extension. Is it not better to assume, More asks, that the soul, though immaterial, is also extended; indeed that everything, even God, is extended?[128] How otherwise could He be present in the world? Having argued that the concept of extension cannot be used for the definition of matter, since it is too wide and embraces both body and spirit, both of which are extended, albeit in a different manner, More suggests secondly that matter, being necessarily sensible, should be defined only by its relation to sense, that is, by tangibility. But if Descartes insists, as he does, on avoiding all reference to sense perception, then matter should be defined by the impenetrability which it possesses and which marks it out from spirit. Spirit, though extended, is freely penetrable and cannot be touched. Thus spirit and body can co-exist in the same place, and of course two—or any number of—spirits can have the same identical location and 'penetrate' each other, whereas for bodies this is impossible. The key thing that More wants to avoid here is the Cartesian geometrization of being, and to maintain the classical distinction between *space* and *things in space*. These latter are things actually moving in space and not merely relatively to one another; they are things that occupy space in virtue of a special and proper quality or force—impenetrability—by which they resist each other and exclude each other from their 'places'.

Descartes cannot accept such a metaphysical reconstruction because of his hydrodynamic model of the cosmos, which requires solid bodies, such as planets, to be embedded in a fluid which carries them along in a vortical motion. The doctrine of the plenum is designed to secure this at a metaphysical level, and the heliocentrism that Descartes' model brings with it is disguised by a correlative metaphysical doctrine, that of the relativity of motion, which constrains us to maintain that contiguous bodies, rather than purely spatial co-ordinates, provide the reference frame for motion. What is interesting about More's response is that it is an example of one form of rapprochement between Cartesian physics and doctrines of matter and space that one associates more with traditional atomism (compare More's criticisms, for example, with those of Gassendi in the fifth set of objections to the *Meditationes*). And what is important about traditional atomist conceptions here is not so much their metaphysical credentials, but the ease with which atomism fits into the kinematic approach to physics which Galileo, Huygens, and Newton pursued so brilliantly, but which Descartes has so much difficulty in coming to terms with.

The Move to Sweden

At the end of June 1648, Elizabeth wrote to Descartes that she had been planning to make a trip to Sweden with the Dowager Queen of Sweden, Marie-Eleonora, but the proposal had come to nothing.[129] This was not the first time the topic of Sweden had come up in Descartes' letters, and Elizabeth refers rather cryptically to 'your friend' (Chanut) and 'the person to whom he gives your letters' (Queen Christina). By this time Descartes had established firm relations with the Swedish court. Chanut had been appointed as a minister of France to the Swedish court in 1645—he was to become the French ambassador to Sweden in October 1649[130]—and Descartes had known him since 1644, probably through his brother-in-law, Clerselier, who was at work on the French translation of the *Meditationes* at this time. Chanut quickly became a fervent admirer of Descartes, as well as a close friend (the two were usually inseparable for Descartes). He had been instrumental in trying to obtain a pension for Descartes in France, and on arriving in Sweden he starting lobbying on Descartes' behalf with Christina.[131] At this time, Christina was a mere 20 years old, although she had already been on the throne for 14 years, and had been educated very much as a monarch, providing her with a remarkable grasp of classical literature. Intelligent, gifted, a libertine, fiercely independent and wilful, she was single-handedly converting the Swedish court from a far-flung province into a centre for learning, attracting humanists of the calibre of Isaac Vossius into her circle. She converted to Catholicism in 1652 and abdicated in 1654, and her personality and career were the talk of European salons. Having alienated Protestants with her conversion, her behaviour at Mass—conspicuously reading Virgil during the sermons and cursing indiscriminately—caused consternation among Catholics. The Pope himself warned her several times about her behaviour in Rome in 1656, although it is unlikely that she paid his warnings much heed: Gilbert Burnet reported that in 1687 she told him that God's providential care of the Church was evident from the fact that 'among the four Popes I have known there has not been one with common sense'.[132] Throughout her life—icily captured by Greta Garbo in her famous screen portrayal of Christina—she showed no trace of fear or favour, and no exception was made for Descartes, somewhat to his regret.

The most remarkable feature of Descartes' acceptance of Christina's offer to travel to Sweden was that it was effectively acceptance of patronage, although a provisional one,[133] and in making the first move in seeking it, he wrote to Chanut in 1646 that, because of the persecution to which he was subject in the Netherlands, he had 'good reason to wish to be known by persons of greater distinction, whose power and virtue might protect me'.[134] In his last letter before the offer finally came, he wrote: 'I hereby declare to your majesty that there is nothing so difficult that she might command me to do that I should not always be ready to do my utmost to accomplish it, and that if I had been born a Swede I could not be more devoted'.[135] As we have seen, Descartes had shown no interest in patronage up to this point. The closest that he had ever come to patronage previously was in his relationship with

Huygens, and through him the Prince of Orange, but there is no sense in which he was ever a 'client' of either, his relation to the Prince being too remote, and his relation to Huygens being, at a personal level, effectively one of equals. It goes without saying that his relationship with Elizabeth was hardly one of patronage, as she and her family were in no position to offer patronage to anyone. Indeed, Descartes' journey to Sweden might have been made at least in part with the intention of trying to secure Queen Christina's patronage for Elizabeth.[136] Another motive may have been to pursue experiments on the existence of a vacuum: Chanut had written to Mersenne on 21 March 1648 in an attempt to get Descartes to carry out such experiments,[137] and he and Descartes made a number of barometrical experiments, of the kind that Pascal was undertaking at the same time, after Descartes' arrival there. There was a special reason for carrying out the experiments in a northerly region, for while Descartes accepted the basic premiss of Torricelli's account that a change in atmospheric pressure caused the fall of mercury in the tube, he also believed that the air above the earth is at the centre of a vortex, and that it is therefore of an oval shape, so that as one travelled further north there should be a detectable difference in barometric pressure.[138] But there can also be little doubt that he believed that he would escape the kind of persecution to which he had been subject in the Netherlands since the beginning of the Voetius affair, as well as receiving something like the recognition he believed due to him. At least in the first instance, he cannot have been disappointed in this latter respect, for Christina sent a full admiral and a warship to take him to Sweden, although because of a complete misunderstanding about whether he had received a formal invitation, Admiral Flemming left empty-handed. When he did finally leave, on 1 September, he had put his affairs in order, leaving his papers with Hogelande in Leiden, giving Picot control of his financial matters, and making out a will. He borrowed Picot's valet for the journey, and turned up at the boat with his hair in ringlets, wearing long pointed shoes and fur-trimmed gloves, much to the surprise of acquaintances, who evidently thought of him as a more casual dresser.[139]

On arrival in Stockholm on 1 October, Descartes settled into an apartment at Chanut's ambassadorial residence. Chanut himself was not able to return until the end of December, but Christina welcomed him cordially the day after his arrival, and Baillet records that, in a long interview two days later, she enthusiastically spelled out to Descartes what her plans for him were: he would join the court, take out Swedish nationality, and she would incorporate him into the Swedish nobility. Descartes evidently replied that he had not ruled out returning to the Netherlands, or even to France when the troubles there had ceased.[140]

Christina gave Descartes time to acclimatize himself. She had instructed her librarian, Freinsheim—on whose 1647 lecture on the sovereign good Descartes had commented to Christina at the time—to introduce Descartes into Swedish customs and life, and he acted as an intermediary between Descartes and the Queen. He evidently enjoyed the company of Freinsheim, as he did that of the French ambassador to Poland, the Comte de Brégy, but the closeness of Brégy and Descartes to the Queen was viewed with suspicion in court circles, and Christina's ambivalent religious sentiments undoubtedly contributed to this, her Protestant courtiers fearing her conversion to Catholicism. Court intrigues were almost certainly not to Descartes' liking, and although Christina later claimed that she was thankful to Descartes for making it easier for her to overcome certain difficulties in the Catholic religion, it is actually rather unlikely that he had any influence in this respect.[141] In fact his general intellectual influence on the Queen was probably rather minimal. It was Vossius, thirty years Descartes' junior, who would appear to have exercised the real intellectual influence, and shortly after his arrival Descartes complained to Elizabeth about Christina's 'great passion for scholarly knowledge', which was 'driving her at the present time to learn Greek and to collect many ancient books; but perhaps this will pass'.[142]

At first Descartes' duties were virtually non-existent: he was not required to attend court, and Christina did not require any lessons before mid-January. In December he is supposed to have written the libretto to the ballet La Naissance de la paix, but the text we have is in fact almost certainly not the work of Descartes.[143] He was given two tasks, though. The first was to put his numerous papers (which included Le Monde and L'Homme, as well as many drafts of letters) in order, and he evidently completed this task before his death, if to little avail, for they were nearly lost when the ship that carried them from Sweden to France sank. The trunk containing them was recovered, however, and Clerselier had to order them afresh as an army of servants dried them out.[144] The second task was to set up an academy for scholars, and he did consult with the Queen on a number of occasions on this, even drawing up a set of rules governing the conduct of debates. These were undemanding tasks, however, and it was not until Christina's return from the country on 14 January 1650 that he was required to give her lessons. These she insisted should be conducted at five o'clock in the morning, three days a week. The lessons lasted about five hours, and evidently focused on the passions, ethics, and perhaps some theology; in the tradition of Roman thought in which Christina had been raised and on which she thrived, these topics were pursued very much with a view to the practical consequences.

The winter was an exceptionally harsh one, evidently the worst in sixty years. Chanut fell ill on 18 January with a condition that rapidly turned into pneumonia, and Descartes helped to nurse him back to health, but on 1 February, just as he was presenting the statutes for the newly proposed academy to Christina, he himself fell ill, possibly having contracted his condition from Chanut, who was recovering by this time.[145] Descartes, now in his mid-fifties, his daily routine completely disrupted, and quite unused either to rising early—he was required to take a regular 4.30 a.m. coach ride to the palace—or to the severe winter conditions, was not to be so fortunate, and soon became seriously ill. He refused to have anything to do with the Queen's own doctor, Johan van Wullen, a physician from Amsterdam who had taken the side of Revius in the Leiden affair and remained antagonistic to him, and preferred to rely on his own cure, wine flavoured with tobacco, to make him vomit up the phlegm. Coming out of a delirious state on the seventh day of his fever, his condition seemed to improve slightly, but he suffered a fatal turn on the ninth day, and died at 4.00 a.m. the next morning, 11 February.

Death and Dismemberment

A number of rumours soon sprang up about Descartes' last days and death. In an anonymous satire published in 1692, called *Nouveaux mémoires pour servir à l'histoire du cartesianisme*, Daniel Huet spread the story that Descartes had made a fool of himself in a public speech at the Swedish court by forgetting the original Greek of Procopius, the historian of the Barbaric wars, and inventing a Procopian philosophy which his audience, who were familiar with the text, knew could not possibly have been genuine. In shame, he fled northwards to Lapland, where his physiognomy enabled him to pass for a Lapp, and the Lappish Shamans admitted him to their rites of drum beating. Huet, who had visited Christina's court in 1652, maintained that Chanut had revealed to him that it was during these events that Descartes caught pneumonia and died.[146] Even more common are stories of Descartes' poisoning by enemies at the court. There were certainly rumours of death threats against Brégy,[147] and Descartes and Chanut were strongly suspected by the Swedish Lutherans of trying to draw Christina to Catholicism. Whether these suspicions were well-founded—and I doubt if they were, at least in the case of Descartes—they were certainly widespread, and one cannot rule out the possibility that certain courtiers would have wished for his demise. There may have been some suspicion of poisoning at the time, but there is no evidence of this, and the symptoms that are reported do not indicate poisoning. We have no reason to doubt that Descartes died of pneumonia in Stockholm, as indicated in all contemporary accounts.[148]

To leave to one side the clearly mythological accounts in no way dispels the web of intrigue surrounding Descartes' death, however. In 1666 his remains were exhumed to be returned to France.[149] At the exhumation the French ambassador was allowed to cut off the forefinger of his right hand, and the body was placed in a copper coffin. On their arrival in Paris in January 1667, the remains were placed in the chapel of St. Paul, and transferred to the Abbey of St. Étienne-du-Mond on 24 July 1667. When the Abbey was closed in 1792, the body was reburied in a sarcophagus at the Jardin Elysée des Monuments Français, only to be removed again in 1819 to be reburied in the church of St. Germain-des-Prés, where it now lies in the chapel of the Sacré Coeur, evidently between the remains of two Benedictines, although the original tombstone was lost, found, and then mislaid again, and one may entertain some doubts as to which of the remains are those of Descartes. But these are insignificant compared to the doubts one might entertain about the skull that is in with the remains, for that, it would seem, is certainly not Descartes'[150]. It seems that a captain in the Swedish guards who was present at the original exhumation removed the skull and replaced it with another, and the skull was resold several times before coming into the hands of Berzelius, who in 1821 offered it to Cuvier, and this skull is now to be found in the Musée de l'Homme in the Palais de Chaillot.[151] Various attempts have been made to authenticate the skull, including comparing its measurements with those of a drawing of Descartes' skull based on the portrait by Frans Hals, an unfortunate choice since Descartes almost certainly never sat for Hals[152] so the comparison is of little use. Where Descartes' forefinger has gone, no one knows, but relics tend to multiply rather than disappear, so we need have no fear that it is lost.

Notes

Abbreviations

The titles of six works cited extensively in these notes are abbreviated as follows:

Adam: Charles Adam, *Vie et œuvres de Descartes* (Paris, 1910). This work appeared as vol. xii of the first edition of AT, but was not reprinted in the second edition.

AT: *Œuvres de Descartes*, ed. Charles Adam and Paul Tannery, 2nd edn., 11 vols. (Paris, 1974–86).

Baillet: Adrien Baillet, *La Vie de Monsieur Descartes*, 2 vols. (Paris, 1691; facsimile repr., 2 vols. in 1, Geneva, 1970).

Écrivains: Gustave Cohen, *Écrivains français en Hollande dans la première moitié du XVIIᵉ siècle* (Paris, 1920; facsimile repr. Geneva, 1976).

JIB: *Journal tenu par Isaac Beeckman de 1604 à 1634*, ed. Cornelius de Waard, 4 vols. (The Hague, 1939–53).

M: *Correspondance du P. Marin Mersenne, religieux minime*, ed. Cornelius de Waard, R. Pintard, B. Rochot, and A. Baelieu, 17 vols. (Paris, 1932–88).

Abbreviations of classical titles follow those in Liddell and Scott's *Greek–English Lexicon*, 9th edn. (Oxford, 1978) and Lewis and Short's *Latin Dictionary* (Oxford, 1980).

Introduction

1. I first came across this story in print in a recent book on the history of robotics, where it is presented as fact, although no references are given. Investigation showed the story to have had a wide currency between the late eighteenth century and the early decades of this century. For the different versions of the story and their sources see Leonora G. Rosenfield, *From Beast-Machine to Man-Machine*, rev. edn. (New York, 1968), 202–3, and the accompanying notes on p. 236. Descartes is not the first philosopher reputed to have constructed a mechanical companion. Albertus Magnus was said to have had a robot that could move and greet visitors with the salutation *Salve!* ('How are you!'). Thomas Aquinas, his pupil at the time, is reported to have attacked and broken the gregarious android when he came across it unexpectedly in the night. The story is reported, with references I have not followed up, in G. A. Lindeboom, *Descartes and Medicine* (Amsterdam, 1979), 62.
2. See Aram Vartanian, *La Mettrie's L'Homme Machine* (Princeton, NJ, 1960), 191.
3. But see Hiram Caton, *The Origin of Subjectivity* (New Haven, Conn., 1973), and Richard B. Carter, *Descartes' Medical Philosophy* (Baltimore, 1983), where he is construed as a materialist. I do not think such a reading is plausible, but I do not believe it is as ridiculous as some critics have made out.
4. Genevieve Lloyd, *The Man of Reason* (London, 1984), 50. This view trades on a caricature of Descartes' position—cf. Amélie Rorty, 'Descartes on Thinking with the Body', in J. Cottingham (ed.), *The Cambridge Companion to Descartes* (Cambridge, 1992), 371–92, for a concise corrective to this reading—although it is only fair to say that it is a caricature that has been current since the seventeenth century.

5. The suggestion is made in Julian Jaynes, 'The Problem of Animate Motion in the Seventeenth Century', *Journal of the History of Ideas* 31 (1970), 219–34: 224. It is pure speculation.

6. Sir John Pentland Mahaffy, *Descartes* (Edinburgh, 1880), 63.

7. Richard Ryder, *Animal Revolution* (Oxford, 1989), 56–7. I owe this reference to Peter Harrison, 'Descartes on Animals', *Philosophical Quarterly* 42 (1992), 219–27, who points out (p. 220 n. 9) that Ryder has evidently confused Descartes with Claude Bernard.

8. See e.g. the representation of Descartes as Faust in the frontispiece to the 1701 edition of his works (reproduced at the beginning of this chapter).

9. Even the Port-Royal was not the bastion of Cartesianism it is sometimes thought to be. See Steven Nadler, 'Arnauld, Descartes, and Transubstantiation: Reconciling Cartesian Metaphysics and Real Presence', *Journal of the History of Ideas* 49 (1988), 229–46: 229–30; and more generally Henri Gouhier, *Cartésianisme et Augustinisme au XVIIe siècle* (Paris, 1978).

10. In spite of its age, Francisque Boullier, *Histoire de la philosophie cartésienne*, 2 vols. (Paris, 1868) remains the best comprehensive account of the influence of Descartes in the seventeenth and eighteenth centuries, especially on philosophical thought.

11. See Trevor McClaughlin, 'Censorship and Defenders of the Cartesian Faith in France (1640–1720)', *Journal of the History of Ideas* 60 (1979), 563–81. Christopher Allen has drawn my attention to a lovely satirical sketch by Boileau on the resistance of the universities to Descartes and Gassendi, which first appeared in 1671: Nicholas Boileau, *Œuvres complètes*, ed. F. Escal (Paris, 1966), 327–30, with an informative note on p. 1066.

12. Both quotes are from Caton, *The Origin of Subjectivity*, 11. Note also that on 2 Oct. 1793 the National Convention decreed that Descartes' remains be placed in the Pantheon, such was his importance to the French revolutionaries, although the decision was never carried out.

13. The text appears in translation with a good introduction as Desmond Clarke (ed. and trans.), *François Poulain de la Barre: The Equality of the Sexes* (Manchester, 1990).

14. See Erica Harth, *Cartesian Women* (Ithaca, NY, 1992), ch. 2. By the end of the century, the attitude of this group to Descartes had become more critical.

15. See Peter Schouls, *Descartes and the Enlightenment* (Edinburgh, 1989).

16. See Rensselaer W. Lee, *Ut pictura poesis* (New York, 1967), 27–8, 72–3; Stephanie Ross, 'Painting the Passions: Charles LeBrun's *Conférence sur l'expression*', *Journal of the History of Ideas* 45 (1984), 25–47.

17. See Christopher Allen, 'La Tradition du classicisme', Ph.D. dissertation (University of Sydney, 1990), 264–72.

18. See the account of the influence of Cartesianism on the architectural writings of the Perrault brothers in ch. 1 of Alberto Pérez-Gómez, *Architecture and the Crisis of Modern Science* (Cambridge, Mass., 1983).

19. 'Music is a science which should have definite rules; these rules should be drawn from an evident principle; and this principle cannot really be known to us without the aid of mathematics. . . . I must confess that only with the aid of mathematics did my ideas become clear and did light replace a certain obscurity of which I was unaware before.' Jean-Philippe Rameau, *Treatise on Harmony* (New York, 1971), p. xxxv.

20. See Ernestine van der Wall, 'Orthodoxy and Scepticism in the early Dutch Enlightenment', in R. Popkin and A. Vanderjagt (eds.), *Scepticism and Irreligion in the Seventeenth and Eighteenth Centuries* (Leiden, 1993), 121–42.

21. See Desmond Clarke, *Occult Powers and Hypotheses* (Oxford, 1989), and Eric Aiton, *The Vortex Theory of Planetary Motions* (London, 1972). Even Descartes' account of the formation of the earth, the most unlikely part of his natural philosophy, had

an influence: see Jacques Roger, 'The Cartesian Model and its Role in Eighteenth-Century "Theory of the Earth" ', in T. M. Lennon, J. M. Nicholas, and J. W. Davis (eds.), *Problems of Cartesianism* (Kingston, Ont., 1982), 95–112.

22. See e.g. Larry Laudan, *Science and Hypothesis* (Dordrecht, 1981), esp ch. 4.
23. See e.g. my 'The Metaphysics of Impenetrability: Euler's Conception of Force', *British Journal for the History of Science* 15 (1982), 132–54, and Alan Gabbey, 'The Mechanical Philosophy and its Problems: Mechanical Explanation, Impenetrability, and Perpetual Motion', in J. Pitt (ed.), *Change and Progress in Modern Science* (Dordrecht, 1985), 9–84.
24. The literature in this area is vast. Robert E. Schofield, *Mechanism and Materialism* (Princeton, NJ, 1970), and Enrico Bellone, *A World on Paper* (Cambridge, Mass., 1980), can be strongly recommended on the eighteenth and nineteenth centuries respectively.
25. Michael Foster, *Lectures on the History of Physiology during the 16th, 17th, and 18th Centuries* (New York, 1970), 278. See the account in John Sutton, 'Connecting Memory Traces', Ph.D. dissertation (University of Sydney, 1993), ch. 2. For more negative assessments of Descartes' contribution see Annie Bitbol-Hespériès, *Le Principe de vie chez Descartes* (Paris, 1990), 23–5.
26. On Malebranche's 'epistemologization' of Descartes see Richard Watson, *The Breakdown of Cartesian Metaphysics* (Atlantic Highlands, NJ, 1987), and his 'Foucher's Mistake and Malebranche's Break: Ideas, Intelligible Extension and the End of Ontology', in S. Brown (ed.), *Nicolas Malebranche* (Assen, 1991), 22–34. On Malebranche's influence see Charles J. McCracken, *Malebranche and British Philosophy* (Oxford, 1983).
27. Voltaire, *Lettres philosophiques*, ed. R. Naves (Paris, 1964), 63.
28. It is true that the extent of this kind of sceptically driven epistemological approach has often been overestimated, and naturalistic and interpretational conceptions of perceptual cognition were offered by philosophers in the seventeenth and eighteenth centuries, from Arnauld up to Reid—see John Yolton, *Thinking Matter* (Oxford, 1983) and *Perceptual Acquaintance* (Oxford, 1984)—but none the less, that it was the dominant approach up until the twentieth century is beyond question.
29. Kuno Fischer, *Geschichte der neueren Philosophie*, 6 vols. (Berlin, 1852–77). The volume on Descartes is translated as *Descartes and his School* (London, 1887).
30. On historiographical aspects of the rationalism/empiricism issue, see Louis E. Loeb, *From Descartes to Hume* (Ithaca, NY, 1981), ch. 1, and Bruce Kuklick, 'Seven Thinkers and How They Grew: Descartes, Spinoza, Leibniz; Locke, Berkeley, Hume; Kant', in R. Rorty, J. B. Schneewind and Q. Skinner (eds.), *Philosophy in History* (Cambridge, 1984), 125–40. On the historiography of philosophy in the period between Descartes and Kant see Giovanni Santinello (gen. ed.), *Storia della storie generali della filosofia, ii: Dall'età cartesiana a Brucker* (Brescia, 1982).
31. There were admirers of Descartes, such as Spinoza, who not only rejected the need for a sceptical challenge to get one's foundations going but also stuck to a very naturalistic construal of the mind. But Spinoza was an exception.
32. Cf. Michael Dummett, *Frege: Philosophy of Language*, 2nd edn. (London, 1981), p. xxxiii: 'Descartes' revolution was to make epistemology the most basic sector of the whole of philosophy.... [His] perspective continued to be that which dominated philosophy until this century, when it was overthrown by Wittgenstein, who in the *Tractatus* reinstated philosophical logic as the foundation of philosophy, and relegated epistemology to a peripheral position.' This is not an uncontroversial view, but the rearguard nature of modern sceptically driven epistemology is perhaps evident in Bernard Williams' attempt to continue the Cartesian project, an attempt which he characterizes as being like Stravinsky's 'neoclassical' project of reharmonizing Pergolesi's *Il Fratello Innamorato* (1732) in his *Pulcinella*. See Bernard Williams, *Descartes* (Hassocks, 1978), 10.

33. See e.g. Daniel Dennett, *Consciousness Explained* (London, 1991).
34. Werner Jaeger, *Aristotles, Grundlegung einer Geschichte seiner Entwicklung* (Berlin, 1923).
35. An interesting exception to this trend is Norman Kemp Smith, *New Studies in the Philosophy of Descartes* (London, 1952), where a British philosopher offers a powerful account of Descartes' intellectual development, only to be mauled (somewhat clawlessly in my view) in an anonymous review by a French philosopher, Martial Guéroult, for daring to question the monolithic structure of Descartes' thought. See the comments in Gregor Sebba, *Bibliographia Cartesiana* (The Hague, 1964), 53.
36. Martial Guéroult, *Descartes selon l'ordre des raisons*, 2 vols. (Paris, 1953). This is an astonishing claim. Cf. Descartes' remark to Burman: 'A point to note is that you should not devote so much attention to the *Meditationes* and to metaphysical questions, or give them elaborate treatment in commentaries and the like. . . . They draw the mind too far away from physical and observable things, and make it unfit to study them. Yet it is precisely these physical studies that it is most desirable for men to pursue' (AT v. 165) This was not an isolated remark: see e.g. Descartes to Elizabeth, 28 June 1643; AT iii. 695.
37. This is not to say that Huygens was a Cartesian as regards the details of his physics. That he was not is evident from his comment to Bayle in 1693 that he could find 'almost nothing I can approve of as true in all the physics, metaphysics, and *météors*' of Descartes. *Œuvres complètes de Christiaan Huygens*, ed. La Société Hollandaise des Sciences, 22 vols. (The Hague, 1888–1950), x. 403.

Chapter 1

1. Descartes to Elizabeth, 18 May 1645; AT iv. 201.
2. Elizabeth to Descartes, 24 May 1645; AT iv. 207–10.
3. Descartes to Elizabeth, May or June 1645; AT iv. 219–20.
4. Ibid. 220–1.
5. See Descartes to Schooten, 9 Apr. 1649; AT v. 338.
6. Stanley W. Jackson, *Melancholia and Depression* (New Haven, Conn., 1986), 5. Although Jackson only mentions the English words here, he is referring to a general phenomenon.
7. Ibid. 103.
8. Lawrence Babb, *Elizabethan Malady* (East Lansing, Mich., 1951), 175.
9. See Jackson, *Melancholia and Depression*, 78–115 for a good summary of the variations in this period.
10. See Michael A. Screech, *Montaigne and Melancholy* (London, 1991).
11. The detailed account given in ch. 1 of Adam can still be taken as the standard one, although the detail covers Descartes' lineage rather than his upbringing.
12. La Haye was renamed La Haye-Descartes in 1802, and simply Descartes in 1967.
13. By the standards of the time, the gap between the death of his wife and Joachim's remarriage was lengthy. As Micheline Baulant points out, 'in the sixteenth, seventeenth, and early eighteenth centuries, in the majority of cases in the Parisian region . . . the spouse remarried very rapidly. As a general rule, the men—sometimes saddled with children—remarried after several months or even after several weeks' ('The Scattered Family: Another Aspect of Seventeenth-Century Demography', in R. Foster and O. Ranum (eds.), *Family and Society* (Baltimore, 1976), 104–16: 104).
14. They were: Joachim (1602–1680?), Claude (b. 1604), François (b. 1609), and Anne (b. 1611).
15. Adam 11.
16. On holidays in Jesuit schools generally, see Gabriel Compayré, *Histoire critique des doctrines de l'éducation en France*, 2 vols. (Paris, 1879), i. 181–2.

17. See Descartes to Clerselier, 2 Mar. 1646; AT iv. 372, line 6, and the corresponding note to the new edition on p. 373.
18. This letter is not included in AT. It first appeared, together with a facsimile of the original, in Maxime Leroy, *Descartes, le philosophe au masque*, 2 vols. (Paris, 1929), ii. 167–73. It is not known whether the author is Descartes himself or his elder brother Pierre. They were both at La Flèche (Pierre graduated in 1612), and their handwriting is indistinguishable at this time. See the informative discussion in Charles Adam and Gérard Milhaud (eds.), *Descartes: Correspondance publiëe avec un introduction et des notes*, 8 vols. (Paris, 1936–63), i. 473–4.
19. The date on the letter does not include a year, but it would have been written in 1609 at the latest, as Jeanne Sain died in late 1609 or early 1610.
20. Descartes' paternal grandmother was a Ferrand, so the Ferrand mentioned here would probably not have been closer than a second cousin.
21. See Stephen Ozment, *When Fathers Ruled* (Cambridge, Mass., 1983) for an argument that there is a significant degree of exaggeration in the currently popular view that little genuine affection existed in the early modern family.
22. This correspondence is no longer extant, but the contents of a couple of letters from René to Pierre are reported on by Baillet, who had seen the letters. See Baillet i. 118. Adam and Tannery unaccountably reverse the order of passages in their version of these letters: cf. AT i. 3.
23. Descartes to [Pollot], mid-Jan. 1641; AT iii. 278–9.
24. I cannot understand on what basis, the confident assertion is made in AT iv. 373 (first note added in the new edition) that it was his father and his sister whom Descartes is mourning. The claim seems to me to be quite implausible.
25. See Adam 433–44 note. On why Descartes' father should have been so disappointed in his son, see John Cole, *The Olympian Dreams and Youthful Rebellion of René Descartes* (Urbana, Ill., 1992) ch. 5, esp. pp. 104–13.
26. Elizabeth Wirth Marvick, 'Nature versus Nurture: Patterns and Trends in Seventeenth-Century French Child-Rearing', in L. de Mause (ed.), *The History of Childhood* (London, 1976), 259–301: 288.
27. Baillet was the first to write a comprehensive biography of Descartes, but there had been earlier brief accounts of Descartes' life on which Baillet drew: Daniel Lipstorp, *Specimena Philosophiae Cartesianae* (Leiden, 1653), Pierre Borel, *Vitae Renati Cartesii summi philosophi compendium* (Paris, 1656), as well as three more derivative works: Johannes Tepelii, *Historia Philosophiae Cartesianae* (Nuremberg, 1674), Gerardus De Vries, *De Renati Cartesii meditationibus . . .* (Utrecht, 1691), and Gabriel Daniel, *Voyage du monde de M. Descartes* (Paris, 1693). On these earlier sources see Adam v–xi. The general reliability of Baillet's account is a matter of dispute: see the judicious and cautious assessment in Gregor Sebba, 'Adrien Baillet and the Genesis of his *Vie de Monsieur Descartes*', in T. Lennon, J. M. Nicholas, and J. W. Davis. (eds.), *Problems of Cartesianism* (Kingston, Ont., 1982), 9–60.
28. The University of Paris was an exception to the rule here, as one could enter it as young as 12, with grammar being the only requirement, so it operated as a kind of *collège* in some of its functions. Paris was the only significant town or city in France not to have a municipal *collège* in the sixteenth century.
29. See George Huppert, *Public Schools in Renaissance France* (Chicago, 1984).
30. Jean Delumeau, *Le Péché et la peur* (Paris, 1983), 24; and p. 271, where the monastic origins of the phenomenon are discussed in terms of what was included in the seven deadly sins. See also Delumeau's *La Peur en Occident* (Paris, 1978).
31. As well as the works of Delumeau cited above, see his 'Prescription and Reality', in E. Leites (ed.), *Conscience and Casuistry in Early Modern Europe* (Cambridge, 1988), 134–58. See also Philippe Ariès, *Religion populaire et réforme liturgique* (Paris, 1975).

32. Part of the rationale given was that earlier ages had been less sinful and hence less danger had resulted from songs, farces etc. which dealt with religion, but by the sixteenth and seventeenth centuries the world had become so thoroughly sinful and corrupt that such things could no longer be tolerated. See Delumeau, *Le Péché et la peur*, 129–62.

33. Delumeau, 'Prescription and Reality', 144; and see *Le Péché et la peur*, 517–35 on the problems of obligatory confession. But cf. Aemon Duffy, *The Stripping of the Altars* (New Haven, Conn., 1992), who argues that the schism between the religion of the élite and the religion of the people has been exaggerated.

34. The problems can ultimately be traced back to the practice of early Christianity, which found it far easier to develop substitutes for pagan practices, especially magical and superstitious ones, rather than trying straightforwardly to repress them. On this see Valerie Flint, *The Rise of Magic in Early Modern Europe* (Oxford, 1991), esp. pt. iii.

35. Keith Thomas, *Religion and the Decline of Magic* (Harmondsworth, 1978), 54.

36. See e.g. Thomas Hobbes, *Leviathan* (London, 1651; facsimile repr. Menton, 1969), 366 (last para. of ch. 45).

37. Thomas, *Religion and the Decline of Magic*, passim.

38. Carolly Erickson, *The Medieval Vision* (New York, 1976), 75–6. It was not unknown for prostitutes to come to church in search of customers, and there seems to have been a trade in obscene pictures in some churches: see Johan Huizinga, *The Waning of the Middle Ages* (Harmondsworth, 1965), 156.

39. Delumeau, *Le Péché et la peur*, 48, and ch. 2 generally. See also see Philippe Ariès, *L'Homme devant la mort* (Paris, 1977).

40. Cf. Philippe Ariès, *Centuries of Childhood* (New York, 1962), 81–2.

41. Thomas, *Religion and the Decline of Magic*, 35.

42. Ibid. 51.

43. Delumeau, 'Prescription and Reality', 147–8.

44. See Arthur D. H. Adkins, *Merit and Responsibility* (Oxford, 1960), chs. 3 and 4.

45. On these questions see Jean-Pierre Vernant, *The Origins of Greek Thought* (Ithaca, NY, 1982), 6–8.

46. Cf. Adkins, *Merit and Responsibility*, ch. 14 on Plato, and ch. 16 on Aristotle on the 'quiet' virtues. On later developments see James Hankinson, 'Actions and Passions: Affection, Emotion, and Moral Self-Management in Galen's Philosophical Psychology', in J. Brunschwig and M. Nussbaum (eds.), *Passions and Perceptions* (Cambridge, 1993), 184–222.

47. These questions are discussed in Peter Brown, *The Body and Society* (London, 1989).

48. See ibid. 126 ff. for a summary and discussion.

49. The standard works on the Brethren of the Common Life are Albert Hyma, *The Brethren of the Common Life* (Grand Rapids, Mich., 1950), and R. R. Post, *The Modern Devotion* (Leiden, 1968).

50. Quoted in Franz Bierlaire, 'Erasmus at School: The *Civilitate Morum Puerilium Libellus*', in R. L. DeMolen (ed.), *Essays on the Works of Erasmus* (New Haven, Conn., 1978), 239–51: 239. The next quotation is from p. 240 of this valuable essay. See also Herman de la Fontaine Verwey, 'The First "Book of Etiquette" for Children', *Quaerendo* 1 (1971), 19–30.

51. Marvin B. Becker, *Civility and Society in Western Europe, 1300–1600* (Bloomington, Ind., 1988), 2.

52. *Regulae Societatis Iesu* (Rome, 1580), 127: 'Gestus corporis sit modestus, et in quo gravitas quaedam religiosa praecipue eluceat.' Cited in Dilwyn Knox, 'Ideas on Gestures and Universal Languages, c.1550–1650', in J. Henry and S. Hutton (eds.), *New Perspectives on Renaissance Thought* (London, 1990), 101–36: 114.

53. Norbert Elias, *Über den Prozess der Zivilisation*, 2 vols. (Basle, 1939). As important, for our purposes, is his *The Court Society* (Oxford, 1983). See also the assessment

of Elias' work in Jeffrey Minson, 'Men and Manners: Kantian Humanism, Rhetoric and the History of Ethics', *Economy and Society* 18 (1989), 191–220, to which I am indebted.

54. Elias, *The Court Society*, 221. See also the comments on the shift in the focus of penitence from external sanction to internal contrition as early as Abelard's work in the twelfth century in Jacques Le Goff, *Time, Work, and Culture in the Middle Ages* (Chicago, 1980), 38–41. Cf. Delumeau, *Le Péché et la peur*, 337–8.

55. The passage is given at AT i. 2. We should not be taken in by the title 'seigneur de . . .', however, as such appellations were easy to pick up, and did not even have to be attached to a fief, or indeed any land at all. Evidently it was common practice in Poitou, Descartes' own region, for successful merchants to avail themselves of a noble title simply by taking the name of their shop: e.g. in a contract of 1603, a Loys Micheau, proprietor of 'L'Écu', apparently something like a general store, is referred to as 'Seigneur de l'Écu'. See George Huppert, *Les Bourgeois Gentilshommes* (Chicago, 1977), 37.

56. The issue of who was and was not exempt from taxation was the source of severe unrest, as can be imagined. On this and related political and social issues see Roland Mousnier, *La Vénalité des offices sous Henri IV et Louis XIII* (Paris, 1971), and his *The Institutions of France under the Absolute Monarchy, 1598–1789*, 2 vols. (Chicago, 1979–84).

57. Huppert, *Les Bourgeois Gentilshommes*, 100–2.

58. Nannerl O. Keohane, *Philosophy and the State in France* (Princeton, NJ, 1980), 19.

59. This is noted ibid. 138. We shall examine the question of the passions below.

60. Cited in Compayré, *Histoire critique des doctrines de l'éducation en France*, i. 174.

61. Cf. Ariès, *Centuries of Childhood*, 155–7.

62. Cf. ibid. 241–68.

63. François de Dainville, *L'Éducation des jésuites* (Paris, 1978), 267–78.

64. Huppert, *Les Bourgeois Gentilshommes*, *passim*.

65. Ibid. 77–8.

66. See the discussion in Donald R. Kelley, *The Beginning of Ideology* (Cambridge, 1981), 238–44.

67. Huppert, *Les Bourgeois Gentilshommes*, 166.

68. The Jesuits had their own colleges in France in the second half of the sixteenth century, but they were not very successful for a number of reasons, amongst which was the difficulty experienced by the Society in retaining members. See A. Lynn Martin, *The Jesuit Mind* (Ithaca, NY, 1988), esp. ch. 1.

69. See Aldo Scaglione, *The Liberal Arts and the Jesuit College System* (Amsterdam, 1986), 23.

70. 'Propositum a nobis est, sapientem atque eloquentem pietatem finem esse studiorum' (we propose a learned and eloquent piety as the goal of study); Jean Sturm, *De literarum ludis recte aperiendis liber* (Strasburg, 1543), 15^r; cited in Scaglione op. cit., 43.

Chapter 2

1. We know that Descartes spent nine years at La Flèche, but we cannot be certain which years. Four possibilities have been suggested in the literature: 1604–12, 1605–13, 1606–14, 1607–15. The first and last of these are certainly incorrect, and the third seems the most likely. See the discussion in Henri Gouhier, *Les Premières Pensées de Descartes* (Paris, 1958), 158–9. I shall follow the usual practice of accepting 1606 as the date of entry.

2. Baillet i. 28, giving Lipstorp as his source; the relevant passage in Lipstorp's *Specimena Philosophiae Cartesianae* (Leiden, 1653), 74–5, is reproduced in Adam 20, n. b.

3. Adam 19–20.

4. Descartes to Charlet [9 Feb. 1645], AT iv. 156: 'vous, qui m'auez tenu lieu de Pere pendant tout le temps de ma ieunesse.'
5. Baillet i. 20–2.
6. Chauveau, who became a Jesuit and subsequently taught at La Flèche, is mentioned in passing once by Descartes, in a letter to Mersenne of 28 Jan. 1641; AT iii. 296.
7. What I shall have to say about the details of the educational system in Jesuit schools derives from four main sources: Gabriel Codina Mir, *Aux sources de la pédagogie des jésuites* (Rome, 1968), Gabriel Compayré, *Histoire critique des doctrines de l'éducation en France*, 2 vols. (Paris, 1879), François de Dainville, *La Naissance de l'humanisme moderne* (Paris, 1940), and *L'Éducation des jésuites* (Paris, 1978); and information specifically on La Flèche is derived from Camille de Rochemonteix, *Un collège des jésuites au XVIIe et XVIIIe siècles*, 4 vols. (Le Mans, 1889). The text of the *Ratio Studiorum* governing Jesuit teaching is given in G. Michael Pachtler (ed.), 'Ratio Studiorum et Institutiones scholasticae S. J. per Germanium diu vigentes', *Monumenta Germaniae Paedagogica* ix (Berlin, 1890) and in Ladislaus Lukács (ed.), *Monumenta atque Institutio Studiorum Societatis Iesu (1589, 1591, 1599)* (Monumenta Paedagogica Societatis Iesu 5; Monumenta Historica Societatis Iesu 129, Rome, 1986). I shall not give detailed references, as my aim is limited to presenting a general picture.
8. Dainville, *L'Éducation des jésuites*, 16.
9. Quoted in Aldo Scaglione, *The Liberal Arts and the Jesuit College System* (Amsterdam, 1986), 96.
10. Dainville, *La Naissance de l'humanisme moderne*, 19–20.
11. Ibid. 21.
12. On the Catholic apologists for tyrannicide of the last two decades of the sixteenth century, see Quentin Skinner, *The Foundations of Modern Political Thought*, 2 vols. (Cambridge, 1978), ii. 345–8.
13. See Scaglione, *The Liberal Arts and the Jesuit College System*, 113.
14. See the very illuminating account of Jesuit architecture in ch. 8 of Joan Evans, *Monastic Architecture in France from the Renaissance to the Revolution* (Cambridge, 1964).
15. This seems to have been a later development, however, for there are reports from the 1570s of students from Jesuit colleges roaming the streets unsupervised, knocking on doors at dawn shouting 'go to confession', breaking up fights, intervening in domestic disputes, and lying in wait at the entrance to brothels to intercept corrupt members of the clergy. See A. Lynn Martin, *The Jesuit Mind* (Ithaca, NY, 1988), ch. 3.
16. Cf. Jean Delumeau, *Le Péché et la peur* (Paris, 1983), ch. 11.
17. The hearts of Henri and his wife Marie were burnt by the Republicans in 1793 but the intermingled ashes are still there, kept in a niche above the gallery in the north transept.
18. Dainville, *L'Éducation des jésuites*, 175. Until the dormitories at La Flèche were completed in 1609 there were severe constraints on the number of students and classes would have been smaller, but thereafter the class sizes were standard.
19. Dainville, *La Naissance de l'humanisme moderne*, 138 ff.
20. Ibid. 64.
21. Ibid. 26–7.
22. Peter Brown, *The Body and Society* (London, 1989), 124.
23. On this whole question see Stephen Gaukroger (ed.), *The Uses of Antiquity* (Dordrecht, 1991). See also Anthony Grafton, *Defenders of the Text* (Cambridge, Mass, 1991), ch. 1, esp. 31–3 on recent scholarship on the allegorical reading of antiquity in the Renaissance and the seventeenth century.
24. See Jerome Friedman, *The Most Ancient Testimony* (Athens, Oh., 1983), on the use of the rabbinic tradition in the sixteenth century.

25. See Dainville, *La Naissance de l'humanisme moderne*, 45 ff.
26. Compayré, *Histoire critique*, i. 189.
27. The list of texts differs very little from that of the Protestant educational reformer, Sturm: cf. R. R. Bolgar, *The Classical Heritage and its Beneficiaries* (Cambridge, 1954), 350–1. See also Bolgar's discussion of the texts prescribed in the *Ratio*, 358–60.
28. Marc Fumaroli, *L'Âge de l'éloquence* (Geneva, 1980), 223–423.
29. For a good, succinct discussion of the main figures in the second Sophistic, see G. M. A. Grube, *The Greek and Roman Critics* (Toronto, 1965), ch. 20. For details of the characteristics of this form of rhetoric, see Charles S. Baldwin, *Rhetoric and Poetry to 1400* (Gloucester, Mass., 1959), ch. 1.
30. For details see Marcia L. Colish, *The Stoic Tradition from Antiquity to the Early Middle Ages*, 2 vols. (Leiden, 1985).
31. Fumaroli, *L'Âge de l'éloquence*, 227–30.
32. AT vi. 7.
33. Descartes to Mersenne [end of Dec. 1637?], AT i. 479.
34. Mario Biagioli, *Galileo Courtier* (Chicago, 1993), 111–2. The author cites the case of Cosimo I's marriage, where spectators complained about the excessively intricate nature of the symbolism.
35. See Scaglione, *The Liberal Arts and the Jesuit College System*, 122.
36. Fumaroli, *L'Âge de l'éloquence*, 96 ff., 206 ff., 257 ff., 394 ff.
37. Scaglione, *The Liberal Arts and the Jesuit College System*, 89.
38. For further discussion of these problems see my *Cartesian Logic* (Oxford, 1989), ch. 1.
39. See ibid. 45–7.
40. It is now known that the *De Mundo* is not by Aristotle; it is thought to date from the first century AD, drawing on Aristotle and the Stoic writer Posidonius. Unlike the genuine works of Aristotle, in which God is merely a 'mover' in the cosmos, the God of the *De Mundo* is a God who creates and sustains the cosmos (*Mu.* 397^{b}13–24): hence its importance for later Christian writers who wished to reconcile Aristotelianism and Christianity.
41. Change of place has something of a special status, in that Aristotle maintains that it is involved in every other kind of change (e.g. *Ph.* 208^{a}32 and 260^{b}22), but nowhere does he maintain, as atomists did, that the other forms of change are reducible to local motion. Cf. Pierre Gassendi, *Opera omnia*, 6 vols. (Lyons, 1658; facsimile rep. Stuttgart–Bad Cannstatt, 1964), i. 338b, who tries to assimilate Aristotle's view to the cause of atomism on these grounds. See Barry Brundell, *Pierre Gassendi* (Dordrecht, 1987), 58–9.
42. See J. Sirven, *Les Années d'apprentissage de Descartes* (Albi, 1928), 35.
43. On the use of Clavius in Jesuit colleges, and on Descartes' mathematical education at La Flèche, see Geneviève Rodis-Lewis, 'Descartes et les mathématiques au collège: Sur une lecture possible de J.-P. Camus', in N. Grimaldi and J.-L. Marion (eds.), *Le Discours et sa méthode* (Paris, 1987), 187–211. More generally, see G. Cosentino, 'Le matematiche nella *Ratio Studiorum* della Compagnia di Gesù', *Miscellanea storica ligure* 2 (1970), 171–213, and 'L'insegnamento delle matematiche nei collegi Gesuitici nell'Italia settentrionale', *Physis* 13 (1971), 205–17.
44. Compayré, *Histoire critique*, i. 194.
45. The sonnet is given in Rochemonteix, *Un Collège des Jésuites*, i. 147.
46. The existence of the moons of Jupiter was interpreted by Jesuit mathematicians and astronomers not in Copernican terms but rather in terms of Tycho Brahe's system. See Scheiner's remarks quoted in William Shea, 'Galileo, Scheiner, and the Interpretation of Sunspots', *Isis* 61 (1970), 498–519: 502. The full defence of a Tychonic system by the Jesuits only came in 1620, however: see Biagioli, *Galileo Courtier*, ch. 5.

47. See the selection of poems in Dudley Wilson (ed.), *French Renaissance Scientific Poetry* (London, 1974), which includes René Bretonnayau's medical epic 'Des Hemorrhoides, & leur cure'.

48. See Richard S. Westfall, 'Scientific Patronage: Galileo and his Telescope', *Isis* 76 (1985), 11–30. The discovery of the satellites of Jupiter also contributed to the political mythology of the Medicis: Jupiter was an emblem for the founder of the Medici dynasty, Cosimo I, and the satellites—the 'Medicean stars' as Galileo called them—were represented as emblems of Cosimo I's dynastic progeny, acting as a confirmation of the naturalness of the Medici rule. See Biagioli, *Galileo Courtier*, 88–9.

49. AT x. 215–16.

50. Cf. Adam 31–2.

51. On the question of Jesuit commentaries on the *Metaphysics* I am indebted to Charles H. Lohr, 'Jesuit Aristotelianism and Sixteenth-Century Metaphysics', in G. Fletcher and M. B. Scheute (eds.), *Paradosis* (New York, 1976), 203–20; 'Metaphysics', in C. B. Schmitt, Q. Skinner, E. Kessler, and J. Kraye (eds.), *The Cambridge History of Renaissance Philosophy* (Cambridge, 1988), 537–638; 'The Sixteenth-Century Transformation of the Aristotelian Natural Philosophy', in E. Kessler *et al.*, *Aristotelismus und Renaissance* (Wiesbaden, 1988), 89–99; 'The Sixteenth-Century Transformation of the Aristotelian Division of the Speculative Sciences', in D. Kelley and R. Popkin (eds.), *The Shapes of Knowledge from the Renaissance to the Enlightenment* (Dordrecht, 1991), 49–58; and to J. F. Courtine, 'Suárez et la tradition aristotélicienne de la métaphysique', in Kessler *et al.*, *Aristotelismus und Renaissance*, 101–26.

52. For details see Lohr, 'The Sixteenth-Century Transformation of the Aristotelian Division of the Speculative Sciences'; and esp. Lohr, 'Metaphysics', 605 ff., where the ordering of the contents of Aristotle's *metaphysics* is compared with those of Cobos' *Expositio in libros metaphysicae* (1583), Mas' *Disputatio metaphysica* (1587), Zúñiga's *Philosophiae prima pars* (1597), and Suárez' *Disputationes metaphysicae* (1597).

53. See Joaquim F. Gomez, 'Pedro da Fonseca: Sixteenth Century Portugese Philosopher', *International Philosophical Quarterly* 6 (1966), 632–44: 633–4. In the case of at least some Protestant theologians, a sharp distinction is made between the post-reformation scholasticism of Suárez, Fonseca, Toletus, and the Coimbra commentators, which is highly praised, and the earlier scholasticism of Aquinas, which is completed rejected! Descartes' Dutch critic Voetius is a case in point. See Theo Verbeek, *Descartes and the Dutch* (Carbondale, Ill., 1992), 7.

54. Cf. José F. Mora, 'Suárez and Modern Philosophy', *Journal of the History of Ideas* 14 (1952), 528–47: 530. Suárez was the dominant influence in seventeenth-century scholasticism: see B. Jansen, 'Die scholastische Philosophie des 17. Jahrhunderts', *Jahrbuch der Görresgesellschaft* 50 (1937), 401–44.

55. A fact noted in Sirven, *Les Années d'apprentissage*, 15.

56. See the very illuminating account of these questions in Albert R. Jonsen and Stephen Toulmin, *The Abuse of Casuistry* (Berkeley, Calif., 1988).

57. Baillet i. 35–6.

58. See, e.g. the corrections offered to Baillet's account in Adam 34–40.

59. Julian Jaynes, 'The Problem of Animate Motion in the Seventeenth Century', *Journal of the History of Ideas* 31 (1970), 219–34: 223.

60. Michael McDonald, *Mystical Bedlam* (Cambridge, 1981), 160.

61. Engravings of a number of these hydraulic devices appeared in Salomon de Caus, *Les raisons des forces mouvantes avec diverses machines tant utiles que plaisantes ausquelles sont adjoints plusiœurs desseigns de grotes et fontaines* (Frankfurt, 1615), with which Descartes was familiar.

62. Jaynes, 'Animate Motion', 223–4. Georges Houdard, *Les Châteaux royaux de Saint*

Germain-en-Laye (Saint Germain, 1912) evidently has details but I have not been able to consult it. The grottoes had begun to deteriorate by the middle of the seventeenth century.

63. AT xi. 120.
64. AT vi. 6.
65. AT i. 4.
66. Quoted in Thomas M. Carr, *Descartes and the Resilience of Rhetoric* (Carbondale, Ill., 1990), 1. I have used Carr's translation. For the original text and the background to this document, see J.-R. Armogathe and V. Carraud, 'Texte original et traduction français d'un inédit de Descartes', *Bulletin cartésien* 15 (1988), 1–4, and J.-R. Armogathe, V. Carraud, and R. Feenstra, 'La Licence en droit de Descartes: Un placard inédit de 1616', *Nouvelles de la République des Lettres* (1988), 123–45.
67. Baillet provides details of Descartes' life of gambling and debauchery in Paris during this period, but the account looks fanciful and gets wrong some of the few details we actually do know. While it cannot be dismissed, it looks to me more like a stylized account of what the typical gentleman would have done at this age, rather than an account of what Descartes did.
68. On what was effectively the French pilgrimage to Holland in this period, see *Écrivains passim.*
69. Gerhardt Oestreich, *Neostoicism and the Early Modern State* (Cambridge, 1982), 34–5.
70. Ibid. 50.
71. J. R. Hale, 'The Military Education of the Officer Class in Early Modern Europe', in C. Clough (ed.), *Cultural Aspects of the Italian Renaissance* (Manchester, 1976), 440–61: 440.
72. See Oestreich, *Neostoicism and the Early Modern State*, 54.
73. See ibid. 29–30.
74. AT x. 151.
75. See e.g. his remarks on mathematical vocabulary in *On the Theory of the Art of Singing*, in *The Principal Works of Simon Stevin*, ed. Ernst Cronie, E. J. Dijksterhuis, R. J. Forbes, M. G. J. Minnaert, and A. Pannekeok, 5 vols. (Amsterdam, 1955–66), v. 426–9. For a more directly political Lipsian influence, see his *On Civic Life*, ibid. 465–81.
76. AT x. 141.
77. Maximilian was a staunch follower of Lipsius, drawing heavily on him in his own political testament, *Monita Paterna* (1639); see Oestreich, *Neostoicism and the Early Modern State* 100.

Chapter 3

1. JIB i. 228.
2. Baillet i. 43.
3. JIB i. 237. See also the editor's comment in n. 4 on that page: the problem of the nature of geometrical points was one that had exercised a few minds in the late sixteenth and early seventeenth centuries.
4. JIB iv. 202.
5. JIB i. 244 (Dec. 1619).
6. JIB iii. 221.
7. The Netherlands were distinctive in that mathematics and mechanics were taught in universities at the end of the sixteenth century, whereas elsewhere the teaching of these was largely outside these institutions. See Klaas van Berkel, 'A Note on Rudolphus Snellius and the Early History of Mathematics in Leiden', in C. Hay (ed.), *Mathematics from Manuscript to Print, 1300–1600* (Oxford, 1988), 156–61.

8. See e.g. Beeckman to Mersenne, 1 Oct. 1629; M i. 283.
9. A qualification (which incidentally points to Beeckman's physical sophistication) is needed here. Klaas van Berkel, in his 'Beeckman, Descartes, et la philosophie physico-mathématique', *Archives de philosophie* 46 (1983), 620–6, while recognizing the importance of micro-corpuscularianism in Beeckman's account of hydrostatics, for example, notes that Beeckman did not always reason in such a way, pointing to his treatment of isoperimetric figures (JIB iv. 122–6). Here, in explaining why larger bodies retain their motion longer than smaller ones, Beeckman offers a geometrical and macroscopic account because it is an important feature of the problem that large bodies can have a large mass (which keeps them in motion) and a relatively small surface area (the size of which is directly proportional to the air resistance that they meet). Micro-corpuscles have a relatively large surface area for their mass, so one cannot extrapolate from the behaviour of micro-corpuscles to the behaviour of macroscopic bodies which they compose. But this isolated instance in Beeckman's work does not invalidate the general point not only that Beeckman developed micro-corpuscularianism but that it remained his preferred mode of explanation. What it does show is that his commitment to this model did not lead him to overlook problems of scaling.
10. John A. Schuster, *Descartes and the Scientific Revolution, 1618–1634*, 2 vols. (Ann Arbor, Mich., 1977), i. 59–60. On the importance of picturability in Beeckman's approach, see also Klaas van Berkel, *Isaac Beeckman (1588–1637) en de mechanisierung van het wereldbeeld* (Amsterdam, 1983), 155–216.
11. See Robert Lenoble, *Mersenne ou la naissance du mécanisme* 2nd edn. (Paris, 1971), chs. 9–11.
12. It should be noted that this holds true only of the use of atoms in purely mechanical contexts, such as collision. Even Descartes, in the more traditional context of meteorological phenomena, will invoke the shapes of atoms/corpuscles in his explanations.
13. Schuster, *Descartes and the Scientific Revolution*, i. 62.
14. A slight qualification is needed here. For Epicurus, atoms themselves seem to be composed of 'minima', and so are not strictly the smallest entities, nor are they even the smallest physically significant ones, on some interpretations, as the distance travelled in an instant is a function of the size of the minima (which is the same for all minima); and not of the atom. But the crucial points are that atoms cannot actually be divided, are the smallest naturally occurring entities, and determine all physical properties, with the possible exception of the distance an atom will travel in an instant of time.
15. No explanation is forthcoming as to how the congeries acquire the property of elasticity that their parts lack, and a moment's reflection shows that simply having spaces between the parts will not solve the problem, for it is the inelastic parts themselves that will actually meet on collision.
16. AT x. 219.
17. See AT x. 60, n. d.
18. In a letter to Beeckman of 26 Mar. 1619, Descartes asks Beeckman to let him know what he thinks of his 'Mechanics' (AT x. 159). This may be a reference to the hydrostatics manuscript.
19. It was not published until 1650, just after Descartes' death. Details of its publishing history are given in AT x. 79–88, and the Latin text is given at AT x. 89–141, with variant readings, 142–50. An English translation was published in 1653 and a French one followed in 1658. The fullest treatment of the *Compendium Musicae* remains André Pirro, *Descartes et la musique* (Paris, 1907).
20. Descartes tells Mersenne that the treatise was written in 1618 (Descartes to Mersenne, Oct. or Nov. 1631; AT i. 229). The treatise ends with the comment that it has been written in 'the midst of turmoil and uneducated soldiers', which

indicates it dates from no earlier than summer 1618, assuming that this was when Descartes joined Maurice's army. Descartes adds it was written in haste, which suggests, given it was a present, that it was written just before it was presented to Beeckman.

21. See the exemplary account of Beeckman's musical doctrines in H. Floris Cohen, *Quantifying Music* (Dordrecht, 1984), 116–61.

22. François de Dainville, *La Naissance de l'humanisme moderne* (Paris, 1940), 201.

23. See the discussion in Claude V. Palisca, *Humanism in Italian Renaissance Musical Thought* (New Haven, Conn., 1985), 244–50.

24. AT x. 89.

25. AT x. 91.

26. Ibid. What is most satisfying to the senses must not be confused with what is most satisfying to the soul; the soul is satisfied with something that is 'neither that which is perceived most easily nor that which is perceived with the greatest difficulty' (ibid. 92).

27. An arithmetic 'proportion' (or progression, as we would now say) is one in which each term except the first differs from the previous one by a constant amount, as when we add a fixed term to each number, such as in the series 1, 3, 5, 7. A geometric 'proportion' is one in which the ratio of each term to the preceding one (again, an exception being made for the first term) is a constant, as when we multiply each term by a fixed number, such as in the series 1, 2, 4, 8, 16.

28. AT x. 91–2. As a quick calculation shows, the last claim is strictly speaking false, as the ratio between AB and BC is not exactly 2 : 3, although it is a close approximation to it.

29. AT x. 113.

30. AT x. 125.

31. Cohen, *Quantifying Music*, 164. The observant reader may have noticed that in the list correlating notes (pitches) and numbers, given just above, D is given, not a single number, but a range: it is 320 or 324, 160 or 162, 80 or 81. This 'mobilization', as it is called, is a response to the problem of chromatic alteration in scales with just intonation, and the problem is one that Descartes never really comes to terms with.

32. AT x. 102.

33. It happens, we now know, because naturally produced notes comprise several pitches, the lowest (the fundamental) being what we hear as the pitch of the note, the others (the partials) being the principal factors in determining the timbre of the note. The partials are at pitches of an octave, an octave plus a fifth, two octaves, two octaves plus a major third, two octaves plus a fifth, two octaves plus a slightly flattened major seventh, and so on, above the fundamental. Strings at the same pitches as the lower partials, in particular, will resonate sympathetically.

34. AT x. 110.

35. JIB i. 269. Cf. the discussion in Cohen, *Quantifying Music*, 188–90.

36. See David P. Walker, *Studies in Musical Science in the Late Renaissance* (London, 1978), ch. 4.

37. Huygens, in his *Nouveau cycle harmonique*, will later treat the augmented fourth (10 : 7) and the diminished fifth (7 : 5) as consonances, because he can see no good physical or mathematical reason for excluding them. See *Œuvres complètes de Christiaan Huygens*, ed. La Société Hollandaise des Sciences, 22 vols. (The Hague, 1888–1950), xx. 162–4.

38. On late sixteenth- and early seventeenth-century accounts see Alexandre Koyré, 'A Documentary History of the Problem of Free Fall from Kepler to Newton', *Transactions of the American Philosophical Society* 45 (1955), 329–95. Koyré's very influential discussion of the contributions of Galileo and Descartes to this problem are developed in more detail in his *Études galiléennes*, now translated as

Galilean Studies (Hassocks, 1978). I argued that his assessment of the nature of Galileo's contribution is mistaken in my *Explanatory Structures* (Hassocks, 1978), ch. 6. Since then, I have been convinced by John Schuster that his treatment of Descartes is also mistaken, and my account in what follows is heavily influenced by Schuster, *Descartes and the Scientific Revolution*, i. 72–93.

39. We have three rather fragmentary sources for Descartes' treatment of free fall. The first is Beeckman's statement of the problem and his comments on Descartes' solution in his diary (given in full at AT x. 58–61); the second is the second of the two essays entitled *Physico-Mathematica* (AT x. 75–8); the third is an entry in the *Cogitationes Privatae* (AT x. 219–22).

40. *Lapis cadens in vacuo cur semper celerius cadat*, AT x. 58–61.

41. See William Shea, *The Magic of Numbers and Motion* (Canton, Mass., 1991), 22–4.

42. AT x. 219.

43. See the discussion in Schuster, *Descartes and the Scientific Revolution*, i. 74 ff.

44. See J. Sirven, *Les Années d'apprentissage de Descartes* (Albi, 1928), 95–100.

45. In 1614, for example, Beeckman had written: 'A stone thrown in a void therefore moves perpetually; but the air obstructs it and continually strikes it, causing its motion to diminish. But the Philosophers' claim that a force is implanted in the stone seems to have no basis. For who can conceive what this is, or how it keeps the stone in motion, or in what part of the stone it lies? It is easier to imagine that, in a void, a moved body will never come to rest because nothing that would cause it to change [*causa mutans*] meets with it: nothing changes without there being some cause of the change' (JIB i. 24–5).

46. The text, which derives from Beeckman's diary, is given at AT x. 67–74, as the first part of the *Physico-Mathematica*. See also the related manuscript in the *Cogitationes Privatae*, AT x. 228.

47. Schuster, *Descartes and the Scientific Revolution*, i, 94.

48. Stevin's statical works are translated in *The Principal Works of Simon Stevin*, ed. Ernst Cronie, E. J. Dijksterhuis, R. J. Forbes, M. G. J. Minnaert, and A. Pannekeok, 5 vols. (Amsterdam, 1955–66), i. 375–501.

49. Ibid. 415.

50. AT x. 70–1.

51. AT x. 68.

52. AT x. 70.

53. AT x. 71.

54. Schuster, *Descartes and the Scientific Revolution*, i. 101.

55. The deficiencies are spelled out clearly in Shea, *The Magic of Numbers and Motion*, 27–33.

56. AT x. 151.

57. AT x. 153.

58. AT x. 158. Vlessingen was the port of embarkation for Breda and Dordrecht. It is worth remembering that this part of the Netherlands had not been reclaimed from the sea to any great extent at this time, and was a network of islands.

59. AT x. 159.

60. AT x. 162–3.

61. Something like this view is also taken in John Cole, *The Olympian Dreams and Youthful Rebellion of René Descartes* (Urbana, Ill., 1992), but Cole reads much more into Descartes' correspondence with Beeckman than the evidence warrants, and makes Beeckman figure prominently in Descartes' later reported dreams, which is at best speculative.

62. AT x. 158–9. Descartes actually refers to France (Galliae), but I am assuming, along with Adam and Tannery, that this is a slip of the pen, since there were no troubles in France at this time, but there were in Germany, following the death

of the Emperor Matthias on 20 Mar. It is, of course, a peculiar slip to make, and if one thinks such slips require explanation, as a psychoanalytically orientated account would, one might wonder whether Descartes is in fact referring to trouble of a personal kind which he associates with France, perhaps with his family. But if this is in fact the case, we have no information about what such trouble might be.

63. AT x. 162.
64. Virgil, *Aeneid*, 3. 7. The original has *incerti* whereas Descartes substitutes the singular. Otherwise the quotation is exact.
65. Descartes to Beeckman, 26 Mar. 1619, AT x. 159–60.
66. AT x. 227, Leibniz' decipherment at 227–8, n.d.
67. In fact, although the computation of lunar tables as a navigational aid became a thriving industry in the seventeenth and eighteenth centuries, it was not until the nineteenth century that a set of tables was compiled which was sufficiently accurate to allow navigation by the moon with any confidence.
68. See AT x. 163, n. c.
69. The first three classes of cubic actually yield sixteen equations, but Descartes disallows those equations which lack positive roots, namely $x^3 = -a - bx$, $x^3 = -a - bx^2$, $x^3 = -a - bx - cx^2$.
70. The cossic notation here derives from Clavius, where N stands for a whole number, κ a root, and ʒ a square. The O is Descartes' innovation, and it stands for any known quantity, although this quantity is not necessarily the same in the ON and in the Oκ, which is something of a drawback in the notation.
71. That is to say, Descartes is looking for a way of extracting roots of the form a + √b + √c.
72. The Latin reads '*alia denique imaginari quidem possunt*'. That Descartes is not referring to imaginary roots here is clear from the fact that he has just excluded negative roots: he would hardly be likely to accept the former, which are much more abstract and counterintuitive, without the latter.
73. AT x. 154–8.
74. I am indebted, in what follows, to the clear exposition of Descartes' early mathematical writings in ch. 3 of Chikara Sasaki, *Descartes' Mathematical Thought* (Ann Arbor, Mich., 1989).
75. Galileo, *Operations of the Geometric and Military Compass*, trans. Stillman Drake (Washington, DC, 1978).
76. I am distinguishing the various compasses functionally rather than structurally: Descartes' mesolabe compass, which I shall discuss below, can in fact be modified to give a trisection compass.
77. AT x. 240–1.
78. AT x. 232–3.
79. AT x. 241.
80. Shea, *The Magic of Numbers and Motion*, 38–40.
81. This is misleading only if one were to assume, wrongly, that Descartes' cossic notation was powerful enough to allow him to think in terms of an analytic theory of equations, as he will do later in the *Géométrie*.
82. AT vi. 391–2.
83. See Charles B. Boyer, *History of Analytic Geometry* (Princeton, NJ, 1988), 64.
84. Schuster, *Descartes and the Scientific Revolution*, i. 146.
85. I shall deal with the vexed question of the dating of the various parts of the *Regulae* in the next chapter. For the present it is sufficient to point out that I am following the 'Weber thesis' that Rule 4 is a composite rule comprising two parts (AT x. 371 line 1–374 line 15, referred to as 4A, and 374, line 16 to the end of the Rule, referred to as 4B) written at different times.
86. AT x. 376.

87. AT x. 376–9.
88. For details see chs. 6 and 7 of Sasaki, *Descartes' Mathematical Thought*.
89. On these questions generally see Giovanni Crapulli, *Mathesis Universalis: genesi di un'idea nel XVI secolo* (Rome, 1969).
90. AT x. 214.
91. On the Brotherhood, see Frances Yates, *The Rosicrucian Enlightenment* (London, 1972).
92. Baillet i. 107.
93. See AT vi. 17.
94. The original has *Ars parvis*, but Descartes is almost certainly referring to the *Ars brevis* mentioned in the earlier letter of 26 Mar., quoted at the beginning of the last section.
95. i.e. the 'topics', which, as we saw in the last chapter, were aids to finding the right form of argument or premisses for a position that one wants to defend.
96. AT x. 164–5.
97. On this aspect of Lull's work, which she treats as a contribution to the development of the art of memory, see Frances Yates, *The Art of Memory* (London, 1966), ch. 8.
98. AT x. 168.
99. For parallels other than the ones I am concerned with here, and for an overall assessment of the relations between Descartes and the Rosicrucians, see Shea, *The Magic of Numbers and Motion*, ch. 5.
100. See Paolo Rossi, 'The Legacy of Ramon Lull in Sixteenth-Century Thought', *Medieval and Renaissance Studies* 5 (1961), 182–231.
101. See my *Cartesian Logic* (Oxford, 1989), 33–8.

Chapter 4

1. On Descartes' meeting with Faulhaber see the extract from Lipstorp's *Specimina Philosophiae Cartesianae*, given at AT x. 252–3.
2. See ibid. for a list of Faulhaber's writings.
3. Johannes Faulhaber, *Nouae Geometricae & Opticae Inventiones, aliquot peculiarium Instrumentorum* (Frankfurt, 1610). See Stillman Drake's short account in Galileo, *Operations of the Geometric and Military Compass*, trans. Drake (Washington, DC, 1978), 26, 34.
4. AT vi. 11.
5. AT vi. 12–13.
6. Baillet i. 80–6.
7. *Corpus* is of course also the Latin term for the human body, and if there is a sexual content to the dream, which seems likely, then the 'double meaning' here is surely significant. Similarly with the reference to the 'seeds' of wisdom.
8. The fact that the melon is said to be from a foreign land, thereby adding to its exoticism, possibly has sexual connotations, and certainly suggests more than the commonsensical idea that Descartes was merely thirsty and was dreaming of something that would quench his thirst. The melon was treated as a counteractive to the passions in Galenic medicine, as noted in Richard Kennington, 'Descartes' "Olympica" ', *Social Research* 28 (1961), 171–204: 197 n. 13. Whether Descartes would have been aware of this (at this time) is another matter.
9. The resemblances were set out in the 1950s by Paul Arnold—see e.g. his *Histoire des Rose-Croix et les origines de la franc-maçonnerie* (Paris, 1955), 273–99—but Arnold's thesis is riddled with problems: see John Cole, *The Olympian Dreams and Youthful Rebellion of René Descartes* (Urbana, Ill., 1992), 214–26. See also the account in Henri Gouhier, *Les Premières Pensées de Descartes* (Paris, 1958), 140, and the response in William Shea, *The Magic of Numbers and Motion* (Canton, Mass., 1991), ch. 5.

10. See Maxime Leroy, *Descartes, le philosophe au masque*, 2 vols. (Paris, 1929), i. 89–90.

11. I am very pessimistic about what can be achieved by trying to interpret Descartes' dreams, not merely because so many attempts to interpret them have been ignorant beyond belief but because, even when a well-informed and plausible interpretation is offered, it is never remotely compelling (I say this as someone sympathetic to Freudian analysis). The best account known to me is that offered in chs. 7 and 8 of Cole, *Olympian Dreams*. Cole sets the scene for his interpretation in ch. 6 by reading much into Descartes' correspondence with Beeckman in 1619, seeing in the last two letters a perception on Descartes' part of lack of support from Beeckman, who has settled down to a comfortable family life as a schoolteacher while Descartes is out on his great search. The first dream is then read as a search for Beeckman through 'the Acquaintance, the Other person, and the mysterious Mr. N'. Cole's general account is thorough and fits in quite well with my own reading of the Descartes/Beeckman relationship. Indeed, in a sense I would quite like it to be true, as it would genuinely throw light on some aspects of their relationship which I have left open; but I just find myself unconvinced of its truth, because the question is so overdetermined.

12. Freud cautiously suggests that the melon may 'represent a sexual picture which occupied the lonely young man's imagination'. Cole (*Olympian Dreams*, 15) reads Freud's comments as suggesting homosexual thoughts, but the theme is not pursued. Many psychoanalytic readings of the dreams have discovered latent homosexuality, especially in the first, but these readings are so mechanical that it is difficult to imagine how they could find any dream at all not to have homosexual content. For an example of this kind of reading see Stephen Schönberger, 'A Dream of Descartes: Reflections on the Unconscious Determinants of the Sciences', *International Journal of Psychoanalysis* 30 (1939), 43–57, who finds the first dream to centre around masturbation and homosexuality, and the sparks of light in the second to represent the sight of the sexual act. Lacking free associations on Descartes' part, Schönberger simply seems to have provided his own.

13. AT x. 186.

14. Andreas Laurentius, *A Discourse of the Preservation of the Sight: of Melancholike Diseases: of Rheumes, and of Old Age*, trans. Richard Sulphet (London, 1599), 82. Cited in Stanley W. Jackson, *Melancholia and Depression* (New Haven, Conn., 1986), 187.

15. AT x. 187.

16. They were published in a Dutch translation in 1684, the first Latin edition appearing in 1701. The *Regulae* have now appeared in a critical edition with both Dutch and Latin texts: *Descartes: Regulae ad directionem ingenii: Texte critique établi par Giovanni Crapulli avec la version hollandaise du XVIIᵉ siècle* (The Hague, 1966).

17. The essentials of Weber's position are set out in Jean-Paul Weber, 'Sur la composition de la Regulae IV de Descartes', *Revue philosophique de la France et de l'étranger* 154 (1964), 1–20. A more elaborate account, in many ways too elaborate, basing details of dating on the finest nuances in the text, is given in his *La Constitution du texte des Regulae* (Paris, 1964). A different reconstruction of the *Regulae*, which equates the universal mathematics and universal method of Rule 4, is given in Jean-Luc Marion, *Sur l'ontologie grise de Descartes*, 2nd edn. (Paris, 1981), but the reconstruction is unconvincing: see Pamela A. Kraus, 'From Universal Mathematics to Universal Method: Descartes' "Turn" in Rule IV of the *Regulae*', *Journal of the History of Philosophy* 27 (1983), 159–74. On the disputes over the authenticity and dating of the *Regulae* prior to the modern debates, see Alexandre Tillman, *L'Itineraire du jeune Descartes* (Lille, 1976), 916–54.

18. See John A. Schuster, *Descartes and the Scientific Revolution, 1618–1634*, 2 vols.

(Ann Arbor, Mich., 1977), i. 216. Schuster argues convincingly that Rule 8 comprises material from both 1619–20 and 1626–8.

19. The other developed theory of scientific demonstration in antiquity was that of the Stoics, but this had a minimal (and for our purposes non-existent) influence on later logical thinking. On its influence see Calvin G. Normore, 'Medieval Connectives, Hellenistic Connections: The Strange Case of Propositional Logic', in M. J. Osler (ed.), *Atoms, Pneuma, and Tranquillity* (Cambridge, 1991), 25–38.

20. For a full discussion of these questions see my *Cartesian Logic* (Oxford, 1989), ch. 1.

21. We must not neglect the possible influence of Francis Bacon here. Descartes praises Bacon on a number of occasions (e.g. AT i. 109, 195, 251), and Marion has drawn attention to some parallels between Bacon's work and the *Regulae*: see the index entries in Jean-Luc Marion, *Règles utiles et claires pour la direction de l'esprit dans la recherche de la vérité* (Paris, 1977).

22. AT x. 361.

23. AT x. 381–2.

24. Cf. Weber, *La Constitution du texte des Regulae*, 80–93.

25. The words Descartes uses are *deducere* and *demonstrare*, and their French equivalents *déduire* and *démontrer*.

26. Desmond Clarke, *Descartes' Philosophy of Science* (Manchester, 1982), 63–74 and 207–10.

27. AT x. 365. Cf. the beginning of Part I of the *Discours*: 'The power of judging well and of distinguishing the true from the false—which is properly called "good sense" or "reason"—is naturally equal in all men' (AT vi. 2). Cf. also Arnauld, who in the introduction to the Port-Royal *Logique* tells us that 'conceiving, judging, reasoning, and ordering are all done quite naturally', and that logic cannot teach us *how* to perform these acts 'for nature, in giving us reason, gave us the means to perform them' (*Logique de Port Royal*, ed. C. Jourdain (Paris, 1846), 44–5). Arnauld had access to the unpublished manuscript of the *Regulae* while writing the *Logique*.

28. AT x. 372–3.

29. AT x. 370.

30. AT x. 387–8.

31. See the texts collected in Anthony A. Long and David Sedley (eds. and trans.), *The Hellenistic Philosophers*, 2 vols. (Cambridge, 1987), ii. 243–54, translations at i. 241–53.

32. Michael Frede, 'Stoics and Skeptics on Clear and Distinct Impressions', in M. Burnyeat (ed.), *The Skeptical Tradition* (Berkeley, Calif., 1983), 65–93: 66. Frede argues that the Stoic position has in fact been misinterpreted, that the Stoics do not in fact assert that we can tell from an introspection whether an impression is a cognitive impression, and that the causal features of such impressions are the crucial factor.

33. Aristotle is, of course, aware of the fact that different approaches are needed in different areas. As he tells us in the *Nicomachean Ethics*, 'it is equally unreasonable to accept merely probable conclusions from a mathematician and to demand strict demonstration from an orator' (1094^{a}25 ff.). But what is at issue in the present context is whether logic, in practical circumstances, can ever be either necessary or sufficient to induce conviction.

34. There is an interesting modern discussion of these questions in Gilbert Harman, *Change in View* (Cambridge, Mass., 1986).

35. See the discussion in ch. 3 of Anthony Grafton and Lisa Jardine, *From Humanism to Humanities* (London, 1986).

36. *Passions de l'âme*, arts. 43–8; AT xi. 361–7.

37. Of the many accounts of this, see esp. Malcolm Schofield, 'Aristotle on the Imagination', in G. E. R. Lloyd and G. E. L. Owen (eds.), *Aristotle on the Mind and the Senses* (Cambridge, 1978), 99–140.
38. *De An.* 432ᵃ7–10.
39. Quintilian, *Institutio Oratoria*, trans. H. E. Butler, 4 vols., Loeb Classical Library (London, 1920–2), VI. ii. 27–35.
40. Kathy Eden, *Poetic and Legal Fiction in the Aristotelian Tradition* (Princeton, NJ, 1986), 91.
41. Note e.g. his remark to Mersenne in a letter of 25 Nov. 1630: 'I will test, in the treatise on dioptrics, whether I am able to explain my thoughts and persuade others of a truth after I have persuaded myself of it—something I am not sure of' (AT i. 172).
42. Quintilian, *Institutio Oratoria*, VIII. iii. 61.
43. Ibid. VI. ii. 27–9.
44. AT x. 217.
45. This is pointed out in Dennis L. Sepper, 'Descartes and the Eclipse of the Imagination, 1618–1630', *Journal of the History of Philosophy* 27 (1989), 379–403: 383–4.
46. AT x. 373.
47. I have taken the details of Clavius' account from Chikara Sasaki, *Descartes' Mathematical Thought* (Ann Arbor, Mich., 1989), 75–6.
48. Cf. Adam 60–1.
49. AT x. 216.
50. The text is given, together with an introduction, at AT x. 257–76. A definitive edition, together with very useful notes, is provided in Pierre Costabel, *René Descartes: Exerciées pour les eléments des solides: Essai en complément d'Euclide—Progymnasmata de solidorum elementis* (Paris, 1987). See also the English translation, again with useful notes, in Pasquale Federico, *Descartes on Polyhedra: A Study on the Solidorum Elementis* (New York, 1982).
51. On the question of dating, see Sasaki, *Descartes' Mathematical Thought*, 196–201.
52. AT x. 267.
53. See Imre Lakatos, *Proofs and Refutations* (Cambridge, 1976), 6, n. 1.
54. A polygon is a closed plane figure formed by three or more points joined by three or more lines, none of which intersect.
55. For a full account of these calculations, consult Federico, *Descartes on Polyhedra*.
56. See the account in Gaston Milhaud, *Descartes savant* (Paris, 1921), 86–7, and the discussion in Sasaki, *Descartes' Mathematical Thought*, 188–91.
57. See the discussion in ch. 5 of Judith V. Field, *Kepler's Geometrical Cosmology* (London, 1988).
58. See A. I. Sabra, *Theories of Light from Descartes to Newton* (London, 1967), 97 ff.
59. Milhaud, *Descartes savant*, ch. 5; Sirven, *Les Années d'apprentissage*, 325–30.
60. Sabra, *Theories of Light*, 78 ff.
61. Recent detailed accounts of Descartes' discovery of the sine law—such as Schuster, *Descartes and the Scientific Revolution*, A. Mark Smith, 'Descartes' Theory of Light and Refraction: A Discourse on Method', *Transactions of the American Philosophical Society* 77/3 (1987), 1–92, and William Shea, *The Magic of Numbers and Motion* (Canton, Mass., 1991)—all reject such an early dating.
62. The text can be found at AT x. 253, lines 25–30.
63. The text can be found at AT x. 344–6.
64. AT x. 344.
65. Schuster, *Descartes and the Scientific Revolution*, i. 127–49. See also Shea, *The Magic of Numbers and Motion*, 48–54.
66. A circle is strictly speaking a conic section (a limiting case of an ellipse), because it can be formed by a plane cutting a cone parallel to its base, but the term conic

section is usually reserved for the more complex sections, namely the ellipse (formed by cutting the cone from one side to another with a plane not parallel to the base), parabola (formed by cutting from the base to the side with a plane parallel to one side), and hyperbola (formed by cutting from the base to the side with a line perpendicular to the base).

67. Schuster, *Descartes and the Scientific Revolution*, i. 146.
68. AT x. 346.
69. Cf. Baillet i. 104.
70. AT i. 1.
71. AT i. 2.
72. For the background to the somewhat complex questions of inheritance lying behind these two letters, see Baillet i. 116–17 and ii. 459–60. There is a good summary in Adam 42–3.
73. Baillet ii. 406.
74. See Sirven, *Les Années d'apprentissage*, 290–311.
75. See Robert Lenoble, *Mersenne ou la naissance du mécanisme*, 2nd edn. (Paris, 1971), pp. xv–xvii, for bibliographic details.
76. AT i. 3.
77. Adam 63.
78. Baillet i. 117–22.
79. Cf. Adam 64.
80. AT ii. 388.
81. AT ii. 636.
82. Descartes to Balzac [5 May 1631], AT i. 202–4; and, more briefly, to Mersenne [13 Nov. 1639], AT ii. 623. See Eugenio Garin, *Vita e opere di Cartesio* (Rome, 1984), 277–33.
83. On this episode see Richard J. Blackwell, *Galileo, Bellarmine, and the Bible* (Notre Dame, Ind., 1991), which contains translations of Foscarini's treatise and related materials.
84. The decline was complete by 1667, when the Accademia del Cimento stopped being active. On Italian science in the seventeenth century after the condemnation of Galileo, see Michael Segre, *In the Wake of Galileo* (New Brunswick, NJ, 1991), 127–42.

Chapter 5

1. The information that follows derives from a letter, now lost, from Descartes to his father, written from Poitiers and dated 24 June 1625. Its contents are reported by Baillet; see AT i. 4–5.
2. Baillet i. 118.
3. See Balzac to Descartes, 30 Mar. 1628: 'I forgot to tell you that your butter has triumphed over that of Mme the Marquise. To my taste it is hardly less perfumed than the marmalades of Portugal, which came to me via the same messenger. I think you feed your cows marjoram and violets. It may even be that sugar cane grows in your meadow, to fatten these excellent milk producers' (AT i. 571).
4. Baillet i. 130–1, 152–4.
5. Amongst other things, Viau was suspected of being a Rosicrucian. For details of the famous trial and the background to it see Frédéric Lachèvre, *Le Procès du poète Théophile de Viau*, 2 vols. (Paris, 1909).
6. On this whole episode see René Pintard, *Le Libertinage érudit dans la première moitié du XVIIe siècle*, 2nd edn. (Geneva, 1983), ch. 1, and, on Descartes' possible association with this group, Adam 75–85. Extracts from some of these libertine texts can be found in Antoine Adam (ed.), *Les Libertins au XVIIe siècle* (Paris, 1964).

7. François Garasse, *La doctrine curieuse des beaux esprits de ce temps ou prétendus tels* (Paris, 1623), [v–vi] and 267–8. Charron is singled out for special mention (27–34). There is a useful set of short extracts from Garasse's interminable book in Adam, *Les Libertins an XVIIe Siècle*. See also the discussion of Garasse in J. S. Spink, *French Free-Thought from Gassendi to Voltaire* (London, 1960), 9–12.

8. See Lynn Thorndike, *A History of Magic and Experimental Science*, 8 vols. (New York, 1923–58), vii. 186–8.

9. Charles Jourdain, *Histoire de l'université de Paris au XVIIe et au XVIIIe siècle*, 2 vols. (Paris, 1888), i. 195.

10. See François Garasse, *Les recherches des recherches et autres œuvres de M. Étienne Pasquier* (Paris, 1622) and *La doctrine curieuse des beaux esprits . . .* (Paris, 1623).

11. See Marin Mersenne, *L'Impiété des déistes, athées et libertins de ce temps*, 2 vols. (Paris, 1624; facsimile repr. of vol. i, Stuttgart, 1975).

12. Nannerl O. Keohane, *Philosophy and the State in France* (Princeton, NJ, 1980), 120.

13. AT vi. 22–3.

14. See Olivier Bloch, *La Philosophie de Gassendi* (The Hague, 1971) for a forceful statement of Gassendi's materialism, qualified in Lynn Sumida Joy, *Gassendi the Atomist* (Cambridge, 1987) and Barry Brundell, *Pierre Gassendi* (Dordrecht, 1987).

15. AT i. 5.

16. On Descartes' relations with Silhon, see Adam 463–6, n. b.

17. See the account of Silhon's writings in Richard H. Popkin, *The History of Scepticism from Erasmus to Spinoza* (Berkeley, Calif., 1979), 161–71, and of Descartes' response in Geneviève Rodis-Lewis, *L'Anthropologie cartésienne* (Paris, 1990), 136–41.

18. Baillet i. 137.

19. Descartes to Mersenne, 20 Nov. 1629; AT i. 76–7.

20. Pintard, *Le Libertinage érudit*, 91.

21. See the letter of Balzac to Descartes, 30 Mar. 1628; AT i. 570.

22. A. Mark Smith, 'Descartes' Theory of Light and Refraction: A Discourse on Method', Transactions of the American Philosophical Society, 77/3 (1987), 1–92: 11–12, points out that he was certainly familiar with Witelo's *Perspectiva*, Kepler's *Ad vitellionem*, probably with Alhazen's *De aspectibus,* and possibly with Pecham's *Perspectiva communis* and Roger Bacon's *Perspectiva*.

23. Neither Descartes nor Baillet mentions the Christian name of this Ferrier, and there were three manufacturers of scientific instruments of this name active in Paris in the first four decades of the seventeenth century—Antoine (active around 1608), Guillaume (active 1620–40), and Jean (active around 1641). I follow Daumas in assuming it was Guillaume who was most likely Descartes' friend and correspondent, and not Jean, as has been commonly assumed. See Maurice Daumas, *Les Instruments scientifiques aux XVIIe et XVIIIe siècles* (Paris, 1953), 97–9.

24. See e.g. the discussion in ch. 2 of Smith, 'Descartes' Theory of Light and Refraction'.

25. John A. Schuster, *Descartes and the Scientific Revolution, 1618–1634*, 2 vols. (Ann Arbor, Mich., 1977), i. 304–54.

26. M i. 404–15, where the letter is dated to 1626. Schuster relies on this dating in his reconstruction, plausibly suggesting that Mydorge is reporting work done jointly with Descartes. However, it is now accepted by the editors of Mersenne's correspondence (M xvii. 71, n. 310), following Costabel, that Mydorge's reference to his 'work on conics' is to his book on conic sections published in 1631, which would date the letter to 1631 at the earliest; and while this would not rule out the possibility that Mydorge was reporting earlier work he had done with Descartes in the letter, it would make it far less likely. The later dating does not undermine the general thrust of Schuster's reconstruction, however, and the discovery of the sine law via the cosecant version still remains a strong contender, if only because

it fits so well with the materials that Descartes had to hand and with what others did with similar materials. It should, perhaps, also be pointed out that it cannot be established beyond doubt that Mydorge is referring to a published work, in which case the original Schuster reconstruction would go through. I must say I am a little surprised that the Mersenne editors are so certain of the Costabel reading, but their judgement is so impeccable on just about everything else that I am inclined to follow them on this, if not with quite their degree of confidence.

27. 'De Refractione', AT xi. 645–6, assuming this to be by Descartes.

28. Schuster, *Descartes and the Scientific Revolution*, i. 310.

29. There remain two difficulties with this interpretation. The first is that we also find a sine version of the law in Mydorge's account; the second is that there is no mention of the image principle in the account. As regards the first difficulty, far from being a problem, it in fact supports Schuster's interpretation by showing the primacy of the cosecant over the sine version of the law at this stage of the development of the law. Propositions II–V of Mydorge's report deal with the theory of lenses. Proposition II uses the cosecant form of the law, even though the sine law would have been easier to handle, but in a corollary to Proposition II, and in Proposition V, Mydorge finds it necessary to move from the cosecant version to the sine version of the law. In order to show that the hyperbola is an anaclastic surface, he has to make the shift from the cosecant to the sine version, not for any reason to do with how he conceives of the path of real rays—he clearly takes the path of real rays to be captured in the constant radii of the two unequal circles illustrated in Fig. 5.2—but rather because the geometry of the demonstration requires this shift from one form of the relation to its trigonometrically equivalent form. Then in Proposition III (on hyperbolas), which offers a synthetic proof effectively following on from Proposition V, the sine version of the law is taken over, as it is in Proposition IV (on ellipses). But the way in which the sine version of the law is introduced in Mydorge's report gives it every appearance of being a variant on the core form of the law, the cosecant version, this being the one that represents the path of real rays. Secondly, if the proposed reconstruction does capture the actual means by which the law was discovered, why does Mydorge not mention the image principle? Here Schuster points out that, once stated in its cosecant form, the law takes on a life of its own, as it were, and can be considered independently of the image principle. The image principle is not strictly necessary for the actual proof of the law, and Kepler had in any case shown that it breaks down in certain cases, such as where the ray approaches the surface at a very oblique angle.

30. See William Shea, *The Magic of Numbers and Motion* (Canton, Mass., 1991), 156–7, and Pierre Costabel, *Démarches originales de Descartes savant* (Paris, 1982), 68–70.

31. e.g. AT x. 395.

32. Beeckman's diary entry is given at AT x. 336.

33. See Schuster, *Descartes and the Scientific Revolution*, i. 349–52.

34. Marin Mersenne, *Quaestiones celeberrimae in Genesim* (Paris, 1623), and *Observationes et emendationes ad Francisci Georgii Veneti problemata* (Paris, 1623). See the exemplary treatment of Mersenne's response to naturalism in ch. 3 of Robert Lenoble, *Mersenne ou la naissance du mécanisme*, 2nd edn. (Paris, 1971).

35. On the general idea of attachment to the occult in the seventeenth century being above all a form of heresy, see George MacDonald Ross, 'Occultism and Philosophy in the Seventeenth Century', in A. J. Holland (ed.), *Philosophy, its History and Historiography* (Dordrecht, 1983), 95–115, and Simon Schaffer, 'Occultism and Reason', ibid. 117–43.

36. William L. Hine, 'Marin Mersenne: Renaissance Naturalism and Renaissance

Magic', in B. Vickers (ed.), *Occult and Scientific Mentalities in the Renaissance* (Cambridge, 1984), 165–76: 174, criticizing Lenoble.

37. On the various forms of magic in this era, see David P. Walker, *Spiritual and Demonic Magic from Ficino to Campanella* (London, 1958).

38. See Étienne Gilson, 'Autour de Pomponazzi: Problématique de l'immortalité de l'âme en Italie au début du XVIᵉ siècle', *Archives d'histoire doctrinale et littéraire du moyen âge* 18 (1961), 163–279, and Harold Skulsky, 'Paduan Epistemology and the Doctrine of One Mind', *Journal of the History of Philosophy* 6 (1968), 341–61. Ficino was complaining as early as 1492 that orthodox Aristotelianism had degenerated into either Alexandrism or Averroism: see his *Opera omnia Plotini*, ed. F. Creuzer, 3 vols. (Oxford, 1835), vol. i, p. xviii.

39. Keith Hutchison, 'Supernaturalism and the Mechanical Philosophy', *History of Science* 21 (1983), 297–333, shows that this kind of ground for adhering to mechanism was a general seventeenth-century phenomenon and not at all restricted to Mersenne.

40. e.g. in J. E. McGuire, 'Boyle's Conception of Nature', *Journal of the History of Ideas* 33 (1972), 523–42.

41. Galileo defends something akin to mechanism in *The Assayer*, but it plays no role in his astronomy or kinematics; see my *Explanatory Structures* (Hassocks, 1978), ch. 6.

42. For details see Katherine Park and Eckhard Kessler, 'The Concept of Psychology', in C. B. Schmitt, Q. Skinner, E. Kessler, and J. Kraye (eds.), *The Cambridge History of Renaissance Philosophy* (Cambridge, 1988), 455–63; Katherine Park, 'The Organic Soul', ibid. 464–84; and Eckhard Kessler, 'The Intellective Soul', ibid. 485–534.

43. See J. Peghaire, *Intellectus et ratio selon S. Thomas d'Aquin* (Paris, 1936).

44. Jean-Paul Weber, *La Constitution du texte des Regulae* (Paris, 1964), 80 ff. Cf. Schuster, *Descartes and the Industrial Revolution*, ii. 449 ff.

45. Cf. Descartes to Hogelande, 8 Feb. 1640: 'No one will ever emerge as a truly self-sufficient mathematician unless his mind has a great natural aptitude for the subject, and he has then refined it by a long course of study' (AT iii. 724).

46. Presumably they do not have to be in conscious conformity with the Rules, either in the sense that explicit knowledge of the Rules is required or in the sense that one cannot hit upon the kind of discoveries under discussion here by chance, provided both can be reconstructed in terms of the move from the simple to the more complex.

47. AT x. 394–5.

48. This is noted in Schuster, *Descartes and the Scientific Revolution*, ii. 452 ff., to which I am indebted here.

49. AT x. 410–11.

50. AT x. 411.

51. For a more much detailed account of this question see my 'Aristotle on the Function of Sense Perception', *Studies in History and Philosophy of Science* 11 (1980), 75–89.

52. *De An.* 418ᵇ32 ff.

53. Cf. *De An.* 418ᵃ13.

54. AT x. 412–13.

55. AT x. 413.

56. Later on, in Meditation 6, Descartes himself will deny that we can distinguish the number of sides in a chiliagon (a thousand-sided figure): AT vii. 72.

57. One could, perhaps, tell some (inevitably very complicated) story about the motion of rigid bodies in a plenum, and Descartes is already thinking in terms of a plenum (see Rule 14; AT x. 442–4), but the argument as presented makes no reference to a plenum and must be taken on its own merits.

58. AT x. 415.

59. i.e. any two points in the visual field stand in the same spatial relation relative to one another as do corresponding points in the retinal image.
60. AT x. 415.
61. The view that Descartes considers animals as simple machines in the *Regulae*—as maintained e.g. in Ferdinand Alquié, *La Découverte métaphysique de l'homme chez Descartes* (Paris, 1950), 66–7—does not have textual support. We shall return to the question of automata in ch. 7.
62. Cf. Gordon P. Baker and Katherine J. Morris, 'Descartes Unlocked', *British Journal for the History of Philosophy* 1/1 (1993), 3–21.
63. AT x. 365.
64. AT x. 417.
65. AT x. 419.
66. AT x. 440–1.
67. AT x. 439.
68. AT x. 438.
69. AT x. 442–3.
70. AT x. 444.
71. AT x. 445.
72. The traditional conception of ancient mathematics as an abstract and powerful 'geometrical algebra' is criticized in Arpád Szabó, *Anfänge der griechischen Mathematik* (Freiburg, 1969), and Sabetai Unguru, 'On the Need to Rewrite the History of Greek Mathematics', *Archive for History of Exact Sciences* 15 (1975/6), 67–114. On the idea of arithmetic as a form of metrical geometry, see my 'Aristotle on Intelligible Matter', *Phronesis* 25 (1980), 187–97.
73. This constraint is only ever overlooked once in the whole of Greek and Alexandrian mathematics, in Heron's *Metrica* (1.8), where two squares (areas) are multiplied together, and this may well simply have been an oversight. One scholiast on Heron treats it as such, and there is no way in which Heron could have justified the procedure.
74. Towards the end of the Alexandrian period, most notably in Diophantus' *Arithmetica,* we do begin to find a search for problems and solutions concerned with general magnitudes, but these procedures never represent anything more than auxiliary techniques forming a stage preliminary to the final one, where a determinate number must be computed. For details see Jacob Klein, *Greek Mathematical Thought and the Origin of Algebra* (Cambridge, Mass., 1986).
75. AT x. 455–6.
76. AT x. 456–7.
77. AT x. 458.
78. Alexander Boyce Gibson, 'The *Regulae* of Descartes', *Mind* 7 (1898), 143–58 and 332–63; Schuster, *Descartes and the Scientific Revolution*, ii. 491–3.
79. I have used the standard English translation of Heath.
80. Schuster, *Descartes and the Scientific Revolution*, ii. 492–3. Schuster sees in this process as an example of the ontological grounding or legitimation of mathematics, something that plays a very important role in his interpretation. This part of his interpretation I cannot accept, and what he treats as the ontological legitimation of mathematics I am treating in terms of an appeal to a notion of representation derived from the rhetorical-psychological tradition.
81. AT x. 464.
82. AT x. 466.
83. AT vi. 374.
84. AT x. 334–5. Schuster, *Descartes and the Scientific Revolution*, ii. 531 ff., draws attention to the importance of this case; I am indebted to his account but not to his interpretation, which gives Descartes' project a metaphysical gloss that I do not believe represents his motivation at this period. See n. 80 above.

85. Reported separately by Beeckman: see AT x. 342–6.
86. Sextus Empiricus, *Adversus mathematicos*, III. For a very rare discussion of the arguments, see Ian Mueller, 'Geometry and Scepticism', in J. Barnes, J. Brunschwig, M. Burgneat, and M. Schofield (eds.), *Science and Speculation* (Cambridge, 1982), 69–95.
87. AT x. 331.
88. Descartes to Mersenne, 15 Apr. 1630 (AT i. 139). However, on 27 June of the same year Descartes will register at the University of Leiden as 'Renatus Descartes Picto, studiosus matheseos'—René Descartes from Poitou, student of mathematics.
89. AT i. 137–8.
90. I cannot agree with Schuster, *Descartes and the Scientific Revolution*, ii. 590, that Descartes may also have been referring to the tentative early draft chapters of the *Dioptrique* here, for Descartes' interest in optics will not diminish in intensity, as is shown in the correspondence with Ferrier of 1629, which we shall look at in the next chapter.
91. In a letter to Descartes dated 30 Mar., Balzac tells him that he will send a parcel to him via someone who is visiting Brittany: AT i. 570.
92. AT i. 7–11.
93. On these disputes see Marc Fumaroli, *L'Âge de l'éloquence* (Geneva, 1980), 695–706, and Bernard Tocanne, *L'Idée de nature en France dans la seconde moitié du XVIIᵉ siècle* (Paris, 1978), 371–7.
94. AT i. 10.
95. This view is most firmly expressed in the second of his *Dissertations critiques*, 'De la grande eloquence': *Œuvres de Monsieur de Balzac*, ed. Valentin Conrart, 2 vols. (Paris, 1665; facsimile repr. Geneva, 1971), ii. 519–30, esp. 519–20.
96. Thoms M. Carr, *Descartes and the Resilience of Rhetoric*, (Carbondale, Ill., 1990), 15.
97. See ibid. ch. 2.
98. On the place of 'attentiveness' in Descartes' account see ibid. ch. 3.
99. Baillet. ii. 501.
100. See the references given in Pintard, *Le Libertinage érudit*, 606 (text for p. 203 n. 2).
101. See M ii. 117, 163–4, 178, for details.
102. But see Geneviève Rodis-Lewis, *L'Œuvre de Descartes*, 2 vols. (Paris, 1971), ii. 478–9, where the earlier date is supported.
103. Bagni was not even familiar with Charron's *La Sagesse*. See Popkin, *The History of Scepticism*, 90.
104. On Bérulle see Henri Bremond, *Histoire littéraire du sentiment religieux en France depuis la fin des guerres de religion jusqu'à nos jours,* iii: *La Conquête mystique, l'école française* (Paris, 1925), 3–279.
105. See Popkin, *The History of Scepticism*, 174. On the early seventeenth-century French debates on chemistry, which centred on the nature of base metals and iatrochemistry, see Hélène Metzger, *Les Doctrines chimiques en France du début du XVIIᵉ à la fin du XVIIIᵉ siècle* (Paris, 1969), chs. 2 and 3.
106. See Descartes to Villebressieu, summer 1631, AT i. 213.
107. Popkin, *The History of Scepticism*, 175.
108. Ibid. 174, quoting the *Discours* (AT vi. 32).
109. See Lenoble, *Mersenne ou la naissance du mécanisme*, 275 ff.
110. See Peter Dear, 'Jesuit Mathematical Science and the Reconstitution of Experience in the Early Seventeenth Century', *Studies in History and Philosophy of Science* 19 (1987), 133–75, and Nicholas Jardine, *The Birth of the History and Philosophy of Science* (Cambridge, 1984), 225–57. This lower status was reflected in the social standing and salaries of mathematicians compared to philosophers, and Galileo, for example, went to great lengths to have himself considered as a

philosopher (he and Benedetti were the only mathematicians to achieve this status in court society). See Mario Biagioli, *Galileo Courtier* (Chicago, 1993), ch. 1.

111. AT i. 271.

112. AT i. 271–2.

113. Baillet i. 164–6. Descartes *may* have known Bérulle as early as 1624, when the latter was in Rome: cf. M i. 436.

114. Cf. Descartes' much later statement in his conversation with Burman that people devote too much attention to his metaphysics and not enough to his physics, and that 'it is just these physical studies that it is most desirable for men to pursue, since they would yield abundant benefits for life' (AT v. 165).

115. Henri Gouhier, *La Pensée religieuse de Descartes*, 2nd edn. (Paris, 1972), 60–4.

116. See Descartes to Mersenne, 15 Apr. 1630; AT i. 144.

Chapter 6

1. On the vexed question of whether Descartes spent the winter of 1628/9 in France or in the Netherlands, see the summary in Geneviève Rodis-Lewis, *L'Œuvre de Descartes*, 2 vols. (Paris, 1971), i. 102–4. I am inclined to accept the argument in *Écrivains* 431–5 that he spent the time in the Netherlands.

2. See Descartes to Mersenne, 25 Dec. 1639: 'I have a *Summa* of St. Thomas and a Bible which I brought here from France' (AT ii. 630). We do not know which *Summa* of Aquinas Descartes is referring to here, but Gilson has identified a passage in the *Summa contra Gentiles*, which Descartes *may* have had in mind in his discussion of eternal truths in the letters to Mersenne of 1631. See Étienne Gilson, *La Liberté chez Descartes et la théologie* (Paris, 1913), 99–100.

3. Certainly very little furniture: see Descartes to Ferrier, 18 June 1629 (AT i. 15).

4. One such attempt is reported in Adam 345, n. a, and *Écrivains* 475. Descartes evidently maintained he would not change his religion because it was that of the King, but when pressed said that he would hold to the religion in which he had been brought up.

5. Cf. Adam 102–5.

6. e.g. AT vi. 31.

7. Descartes had spent the winter of 1628/9 in the countryside of Brittany, and had had some difficulty finding the peace he required there (see Descartes to [Pollot] [1648]: AT v. 556). Also, France had a serious over-population problem, its twenty million inhabitants making it as large in population terms as the rest of Europe put together. But it is not clear exactly what Descartes' problem with the French countryside was.

8. See Simon Schama, *The Embarrassment of Riches* (Berkeley, Calif., 1988), on seventeenth-century Dutch culture. Remember, however, that France also had some claims in this respect, and as Fumaroli reminds us, Grotius describes France in his *De jure belli et pacis* (1625) as 'the most beautiful kingdom after the kingdom of heaven'. See Marc Fumaroli, 'Des leurres qui persuadent les yeux', in P. Rosenberg, *France in the Golden Age* (New York, 1982), 1–33, for a good, concise summary of France's claims to cultural primacy.

9. See Gassendi's comment to Peiresc, on travelling through the Netherlands in July 1629, that 'everyone here is for the movement of the Earth'; Nicolas-Claude Fabri de Peiresc, *Correspondance*, 7 vols. (Paris, 1888–98), iv. 202.

10. Descartes to Mersenne [18 Mar. 1630]; AT i. 130.

11. On this episode see William Shea, *The Magic of Numbers and Motion* (Canton, Mass., 1991), 191–201.

12. Descartes tried to cast Ferrier in a bad light to people on whom the latter relied, and showed a clear fear that Ferrier would succeed in his attempt to grind a perfect anaclastic lens without Descartes' guidance. Indeed, in general Descartes'

attitude to his craftsmen left something to be desired. When it was reported to Descartes that Florimond de Beaune had injured his hand trying to cut a lens to Descartes' specification, he wrote: 'You might think I am saddened by this, but in fact I am proud that the hands of the best craftsman do not extend as far as my reasoning' (Descartes to Huygens, 12 Mar. 1640; AT iii. 747). See Shea, *The Magic of Numbers and Motion*, 197–201.

13. On French cuisine see Descartes to Mersenne, 18 Mar. 1630 (AT i. 129), and on furniture see Descartes to Ferrier, 18 June 1629 (AT i. 15). On the advantages of the French over the Dutch educational system, see Descartes to *** [12 Sept. 1638] (AT ii. 378). Descartes had evidently intended to take his daughter Francine to France to give her a good education in 1640, but she died before the journey had begun.

14. Descartes to Ferrier, 18 June 1629; AT i. 14.

15. Descartes to Balzac, 5 May 1631; AT i. 203.

16. See the account in *Écrivains* 243–310.

17. Lisa T. Sarasohn, 'Nicolas-Claude Fabri de Peiresc and the Patronage of the New Science in the Seventeenth Century', *Isis* 84 (1993), 70–90: 72.

18. See ibid. *passim*, and on patronage in France more generally, Sharon Kettering, *Patrons, Brokers, and Clients in Seventeenth-Century France* (Oxford, 1986).

19. See e.g. the detailed account of Galileo's very complex relation to his patrons in Mario Biagioli, *Galileo Courtier* (Chicago, 1993).

20. Descartes to *** [Aug./Sept. 1629]; AT i. 21.

21. AT i. 25.

22. Descartes to *** [Aug./Sept. 1629]; AT i. 19–20. This is a problematic letter in terms of composition and dating: cf. AT i. 18–19 and M ii. 250–1.

23. Descartes to Mersenne, 8 Oct. 1629; AT i. 26–7.

24. An over-optimistic claim, as it turns out.

25. Descartes to Ferrier, 18 June 1629; AT i. 13–16.

26. Ferrier to Descartes, 26 Oct. 1629; AT i. 38–52.

27. Descartes to Ferrier, 13 Nov. 1629; AT i. 53–69.

28. AT i. 50–1. The burning point of a lens referred to here is the point at which rays refracted through a convex lens converge. The distance between the burning point and the geometrical centre of the lens is its focal length.

29. AT i. 62–3.

30. Descartes to Mersenne, 25 Nov. 1630; AT i. 180.

31. See Shea, *The Magic of Numbers and Motion*, 155–9.

32. Descartes to Ferrier, 13 Nov. 1629; AT i. 62.

33. AT i. 255.

34. See Baillet, i. 170–1.

35. Descartes to Gibieuf, 18 July 1629; AT i. 17 We must beware of reading too much into Descartes' term 'little' here, and it is possible that the treatise was quite substantial: cf. Rodis-Lewis, *L'Œuvre de Descartes*, ii. 484–5, n. 22.

36. Descartes to Mersenne, 25 Nov. 1630; AT i. 182.

37. AT i. 181–2.

38. Marin Mersenne, *L'Impiété des déistes, athées et libertins de ce temps*, 2 vols. (Paris, 1624; facsimile repr. of vol. i, Stuttgart, 1975), vol, i, p. [xii].

39. See the discussion in Michael J. Buckley, *At the Origins of Modern Atheism* (New Haven, Conn., 1987), 56–64.

40. Cf. the remark of the other great writer against atheism in this period, the Jesuit Leonard Lessius, who in his *De providentia Numinis et animae immortalitate* (1613) writes: 'Although at this day, there may be many who deny in their secret judgments all divine power and Deity, yet are they not much knowne to the world; since the feare of the laws doth impose silence to these kind of men, and only secretly among their familiars do they vomit out their Atheisme' (quoted in Buckley,

At the Origins of Modern Atheism, 44). It is also worth remembering the famous—and to my mind still compelling—argument in Lucien Febvre, *Le Problème de l'incroyance au XVIe siècle* (Paris, 1942), that there was simply no conceptual space for atheism (in the strict sense) in the sixteenth century. Cf. Buckley, *At the Origins of Modern Atheism*, *passim*.

41. AT v. 153.
42. AT vi. 33.
43. See Jean Delumeau, *Le Péché et la peur* (Paris, 1983), 102–7, and the literature cited there.
44. AT i. 143–4.
45. Its authorship has not been established with certainty, but the most likely candidate is a 'des Vallées' mentioned by two seventeenth-century writers, Charles Sorel and Tallement de Réaux, as having discovered a *langue matrice* or primitive mother tongue. Contrary to the more widely held view that such a language, if one existed, was Hebrew, des Vallées maintained that it was in fact a secret and mysterious language that only he and the angels had access to. See Charles Sorel, *La Science universelle*, 4 vols. (Paris, 1637–43), iv. 32. There were others who made similar claims at this time, and one of Mersenne's editors, de Waard, thought a more likely candidate for the authorship was Claude Hardy (M iv. 332; M v. 140), but a more recent editor, Bernard Rochot, has shown convincingly that such an attribution cannot be right (M x. 271–3). On universal language schemes in the seventeenth century, a number of which were influenced by Descartes' views, see James Knowlson, *Universal Language Schemes in England and France, 1600–1800* (Toronto, 1975) and M. M. Slaughter, *Universal Language and Scientific Taxonomy in the Seventeenth Century* (Cambridge, 1982).
46. AT i. 80–2.
47. The open letter to Balzac presents a hypothetical reconstruction—one with decidedly political overtones—of language, in which the original language has features rather like those Descartes' project for a universal language is designed to capture: 'In primitive times, before civilization, before there were any quarrels in the world, and when language was the naïve and spontaneous expression of the emotions of the transparent soul, the eloquence of superior minds was like a divine force, whose source lay in the zeal for truth and abundant good sense. It is this that drew semi-savage men from the forests, established laws, founded cities and had the power of ruling as well as that of persuasion. But a little later, with the Greeks and the Romans, the disputes of the courts and the frequency of political speeches corrupted it when it was used excessively. For it was handed down to the common people who, having no desire to secure the conviction of the audience by honest combat armed only with the truth, reverted to sophisms and traps, with words empty of meaning. It was not uncommon for them to mislead ingenuous people in this way, but despite this they had no more claim to argue for the glory of eloquence with the Ancients than traitors can rival soldiers in bravery' (AT i. 9). An important thing that Balzac and Descartes share is a commitment to language which shows its truth on its face, so to speak, even though they conceive differently of how this is to be achieved. The political overtones of Descartes' account mirror the close links between the history of eloquence and the development of politics to be found throughout Balzac's writings: see e.g. his 'Dissertations politiques', in *Œuvres de Monsieur de Balzac*, ed. Valentin Conrart, 2 vols. (Paris, 1665; facsimile repr. (Geneva, 1971), ii. 419–506.
48. Mersenne took a more optimistic approach in his *Harmonie universelle*. Basing himself on Descartes' idea of building up such a language from 'simple ideas', and ordering these on analogy with mathematics, he examined the mathematical possibility of creating new words sufficient to name all those species of things we need to name if we are to classify them scientifically. See Marin Mersenne, *Harmonie*

universelle, 3 vols. (Paris, 1636–7; facsimile repr. Paris, 1975), pt. i, props. 47–50.

49. See my *Cartesian Logic* (Oxford, 1989), ch. 4.
50. AT i. 145–6.
51. See Jean-Luc Marion, *Sur la théologie blanche de Descartes* (Paris, 1981), 27–159.
52. Suárez, *Disputationes metaphysicae* xxviii, s. 3, paras. 2–9.
53. AT i. 149.
54. The passage is given in Marion, *Sur la théologie blanche de Descartes*, 28.
55. Descartes to [Mersenne], 27 May 1630; AT i. 152.
56. Ibid.
57. For detailed discussion of these questions see my *Cartesian Logic*, ch. 2.
58. There are of course various reductive accounts of morality, whether theological, where acting morally is equated with acting out of a blind love of God, or naturalistic, where acting morally is e.g. ultimately to be explicated in terms of self-interest. But if either of these kinds of reduction is to have any claim to success, it must at least explain the phenomenology of moral behaviour.
59. See the discussion in Henri Gouhier, *La Pensée religieuse de Descartes*, 2nd edn. (Paris, 1972), 260–2.
60. See Marion, *Sur la théologie blanche de Descartes*, 140–59.
61. AT i. 152.
62. AT i. 145.
63. In my account of these questions I am indebted to J. M. Bos, 'On the Representation of Curves in Descartes' *Géométrie*', *Archive for History of Exact Sciences* 24 (1981), 295–338; and 'Arguments on Motivation in the Rise and Decline of Mathematical Theory: The Construction of Equation, 1637–ca. 1750', *Archive for History of Exact Sciences* 30 (1984), 331–80; Shea, *The Magic of Numbers and Motion*, 58–67; and Jules Vuillemin, *Mathématique et métaphysique chez Descartes* (Paris, 1960), 77-98.
64. Descartes sent his solution to the problem to Golius in Jan. 1632 (cf. AT i. 232) and later told Mersenne that it had taken him 'five or six weeks to find the solution' (AT i. 244), so we can take it that he began working on it some time around Nov. 1631.
65. On Pappus' problem see especially Bos, 'Arguments on Motivation'; Emily Grosholz, *Cartesian Method and the Problem of Reduction* (Oxford, 1991), 25–35; George Molland, 'Shifting the Foundations: Descartes' Transformation of Ancient Geometry', *Historia Mathematica* 3 (1976), 21–49; Chikara Sasaki, *Descartes' Mathematical Thought* (Ann Arbor, Mich., 1989), 296–321.
66. AT vi. 378.
67. Here I follow the very helpful treatment in Richard S. Westfall, *Never at Rest* (London, 1980), 24–7.
68. AT vi. 382–7.
69. I draw here on the useful summary in Shea, *The Magic of Numbers and Motion*, 46–7.
70. Descartes was not familar with procedures for rectifying algebraic curves, which were only developed around the middle of the seventeenth century.
71. AT vi. 166.
72. Ibid.
73. AT vi. 443.
74. I don't think it too anachronistic to see Wittgenstein as trying to flesh out a similiar idea when he urges that mathematical proofs are above all 'perspicuous representations'. Cf. e.g. Ludwig Wittgenstein, *Remarks on the Foundations of Mathematics*, ed. G. H. von Wright and R. Rhees, 3rd edn. (Oxford, 1978), 233 ff., where a set of five rows of four vertical lines of dots is taken as a paradigm case

of something that might convince one of the commutative law for multiplication (in this case, $5 \times 4 = 4 \times 5$).

75. In October Descartes tells Mersenne that he has had to interrupt what he has been working on, which is almost certainly a reference to the treatise on metaphysics. See Descartes to Mersenne, 8 Oct. 1629; AT i. 23.
76. Ibid. The allusion is to the painter Apelles (4th cent. BC), who is said to have hidden behind one of his paintings in order to listen to the comments of his critics.
77. Descartes to Mersenne, 13 Nov. 1629; AT i. 70.
78. AT vi. 231.
79. Mydorge had in fact provided the notes to the third edition of 1626, so Descartes could hardly have failed to be familiar with the work, on these grounds alone.
80. Quoted in Charles B. Boyer, *The Rainbow* (Princeton, NJ, 987), 207–8.
81. See John A. Schuster, *Descartes and the Scientific Revolution, 1618–1634*, 2 vols. (Ann Arbor, Mich., 1977), ii, 566–79.
82. JIB iii. 66–9.
83. AT i. 25.
84. See AT i. 665.
85. Sebastian Basso, *Philosophiae naturalis adversus Aristotelem, Libri XII* (Amsterdam, 1649), 300 ff.
86. AT i. 71–4. The discussion of free fall is written in Latin whereas the rest of the letter is in French, and it is highly likely that Descartes is simply copying out a fragment of something he had written earlier, perhaps as early as 1618, when he replied to Beeckman on this question.
87. AT vi. 41–2.
88. AT i. 137.
89. AT i. 140–1.
90. Descartes to Mersenne, 23 Dec. 1630; AT i. 194.
91. AT i. 136.
92. JIB iv. 142.
93. AT i. 24.
94. This is pointed out in H. Floris Cohen, *Quantifying Music* (Dordrecht, 1984), 196.
95. See de Waard's introductory essays to JIB i. i–xxiv and xxv–xxxiv.
96. Only a fragment of this letter survives: JIB iv. 195. See the exemplary account of these questions in Cohen, *Quantifying Music*, 192–7.
97. AT i. 154–5.
98. Descartes to [Beeckman] 17 Oct. 1630; AT i. 157–67.
99. Cohen, *Quantifying Music*, 196.
100. See his remark in Descartes to Colvius, 14 June 1637; AT i. 379–80.

Chapter 7

1. See Adam 123.
2. So Golius tells Huyghens in a letter of 1 Nov. 1632, cited in *Écrivains* 476.
3. Cf. ibid. 475.
4. Ibid. 472–7 and Paul Mouy, *Le Développement de la physique cartésienne, 1646–1712* (Paris, 1934), 8–10, give details of Reneri's career.
5. See ibid. 9–10.
6. AT i. 216–7. The terminology here derives from the alchemical distinction between 'noble' and 'base' metals.
7. AT vi. 41–60.
8. But cf. Part V of the *Discours*, where, in describing *Le Monde*, Descartes says 'after that', that is, *L'Homme*, 'I described the rational soul'. AT vi. 59.
9. Descartes to Mersenne, 25 Feb. 1630; AT i. 119–20.

10. Descartes to Mersenne [10 May 1632]; AT i. 250–1.
11. AT i. 102. Cf. Descartes to Mersenne [20 Feb. 1639]; AT ii. 525.
12. Descartes to Mersenne [13 Nov 1639]; AT ii. 621.
13. Descartes to Mersenne [Nov. or Dec. 1632], AT i. 263.
14. AT xi. 6.
15. The specific sources here seem to be Suárez and Eustache de Saint Paul rather than Aristotle himself, suggesting that Descartes is thinking of the kind of material he had studied at La Flèche. See Étienne Gilson, *Index scolastico-cartésien*, 2nd edn. (Paris, 1979), items 211 and 392. This is confirmed earlier in the first chapter, where he tells us that 'most philosophers'—a term usually reserved for scholastic philosophers—'agree that sound is nothing but a certain vibration of air which strikes our ears'. This is a view to be found in the Coimbra commentaries, from which Descartes learned his physics at La Flèche: see Gilson, *Index scolastico-cartésien*, items 424 and 425.
16. AT xi. 8–9.
17. AT vi. 94.
18. See the setting out of the arguments for and against the idea of a *quies media*—an interval of rest between successive motions in different directions—in Marin Mersenne, *Harmonie universelle*, 3 vols. (Paris, 1636–7; facsimile repr. Paris, 1975), iii. 163–5.
19. There is a comprehensive discussion of 'determination' in Alan Gabbey, 'Force and Inertia in the Seventeenth Century: Descartes and Newton', in Stephen Gaukroger (ed.), *Descartes: Philosophy, Mathematics and Physics* (Brighton, 1980), 230–320: 247–62. Gabbey's definition of 'determination' in Descartes' usage as 'the directional mode of motive force' (p. 258) fits with the account of *Le Monde*, although the metaphysical apparatus which Gabbey uses to fill out the distinction is a later development on Descartes' part.
20. See Rule 5 of the rules of collision: *Principia* Part II, art. 50; AT viii$_1$. 69.
21. AT xi. 10.
22. AT xi. 11.
23. Ibid.
24. It turns metals into liquids because the constitutive parts of metals are equal and are all affected equally, whereas it separates out the unequal parts of wood and causes the smaller parts of the wood to fly away in the form of smoke, the larger ones remaining as ash.
25. AT xi. 15.
26. AT xi. 16.
27. There were a number of such experiments from the Middle Ages onwards, culminating the famous dispute between Boyle and Hobbes in 1660s. For details see Edward Grant, *Much Ado about Nothing* (Cambridge, 1981).
28. AT xi. 19.
29. AT xi. 20.
30. Descartes to [Reneri], 2 June 1631; AT i. 205–8. Reneri's original letter has not survived.
31. See John A. Schuster, *Descartes and the Scientific Revolution, 1618–1634*, 2 vols. (Ann Arbor. Mich., 1977), ii. 594–601.
32. The correlation between the properties of light and three different kinds of matter is made explicitly at AT xi. 29–30, and repeated later in *Principia* III, art. 52; AT viii$_1$. 152.
33. AT xi. 31. The procedure he follows here may be like what he has in mind in Rule 10 of the *Regulae*, when he tells us that 'when we want to read something written in an unfamiliar cipher which lacks any apparent order we invent an order so as to test every conjecture that we can make about individual letters, words, or

sentences, arranging the characters in such a way that by an enumeration we may discover what can be deduced from them. Above all, we must guard against wasting time by guessing in a random and unmethodical way about similarities' (AT x. 405).

34. Descartes to Mersenne, 18 Dec. 1629; AT i. 86.
35. AT v. 167.
36. See Steven J. Dick, *Plurality of Worlds* (Cambridge, 1982), 35–6.
37. AT xi. 33.
38. See the discussion in William Charlton, *Aristotle's Physics Books I and II* (Oxford, 1970), 129–45.
39. AT xi. 33.
40. AT xi. 36. Note, however, that at the beginning of his discussion (pp. 32–3) Descartes talks of the space being there first, and God creating matter in it (or perhaps transforming it from empty space into corporeal extension). This may be due to the exigencies of exposition, or to a lack of clarity on Descartes' part about his own doctrine.
41. See e.g. Galileo's brilliant kinematic analysis of falling bodies in terms of motion in a void, in the second half of the 'First Day' of his *Two New Sciences*, published in 1638. The case is discussed in detail in my *Explanatory Structures* (Hassocks, 1978), ch. 6.
42. AT xi. 45.
43. Ibid.
44. AT xi. 38.
45. David M. Balme, 'Greek Science and Mechanism I', *Classical Quarterly* 33 (1939), 129-38.
46. For the details of these questions see Richard Sorabji, *Necessity, Cause, and Blame* (London, 1980) and Sarah Waterlow, *Nature, Change and Agency in Aristotle's Physics* (Oxford, 1982).
47. See Michael Frede, 'The Original Notion of Cause', in M. Schofield, M. Burnyeat, and J. Barnes (eds.), *Doubt and Dogmatism* (Oxford, 1980), 217–49; and Sorabji, *Necessity, Cause, and Blame*.
48. AT xi. 39.
49. AT xi. 41.
50. JIB i. 24–5.
51. Descartes to Mersenne [13 Nov. 1629]; AT i. 73–4.
52. Galileo Galilei, *Two New Sciences*, trans. Stillman Drake (Madison, Wis., 1974), 65–108.
53. AT xi. 42.
54. Gabbey, 'Force and Inertia', 243.
55. AT xi. 43.
56. See Martial Guéroult, 'The Metaphysics and Physics of Force in Descartes', in Gaukroger (ed.), *Descartes: Philosophy, Mathematics and Physics*, 196–229, and Gabbey, 'Force and Inertia', 234–9. Since Descartes provides no elaboration of this question either in *Le Monde* or in other writings of this period, we shall postpone consideration of it.
57. AT xi. 85–6.
58. AT ii. 74.
59. See e.g. the discussions in Westfall, *Force in Newton's Physics* (London, 1971), ch. 2, and William Shea, *The Magic of Numbers and Motion* (Canton, Mass., 1991), 279–82.
60. Here I agree with Schuster, *Descartes and the Scientific Revolution*, ii. 635, that: 'operationally speaking, in terms of the application and practice of Descartes' mechanics, the enunciation of a "Beeckman-like", fully kinematic principle of

inertia would have been irrelevant, whereas it was important to be able to deploy a principle specifying the instantaneous "determination" (or quantity or direction of the tendency to motion) of a moving body'.

61. See e.g. to cite popular accounts, E. J. Dijksterhuis, *The Mechanization of the World Picture* (New York, 1961), 403–18, and Bernard Williams, *Descartes* (Hassocks, 1978), 261–2.
62. This is especially problematic in the light of Descartes' negative theology, in which, as we saw in the last chapter, almost nothing can be said about God.
63. AT xi. 46–7.
64. Ibid.
65. Descartes to Mersenne [10 May 1632]; AT i. 250–1. When Descartes says that we can discover all the different forms and essences a priori, he means that we can discover them from their causes, not that there is some non-empirical way of discovering them.
66. AT xi. 50.
67. AT xi. 51.
68. AT xi. 52.
69. AT xi. 53.
70. It is possible that Descartes would have revised this attempt to save the phenomena had *Le Monde* appeared as planned—he will do so for the *Principia*—and it has the appearance of a stop-gap measure here.
71. AT xi. 59.
72. AT xi. 64–5.
73. Towards B and not towards D because it has a natural inclination to continue its motion in a straight line, and so must go to the outside of the circle ACZN rather than towards the centre S. AT xi. 70.
74. AT xi. 70–1.
75. AT xi. 72–3.
76. AT x. 68.
77. Shea, *The Magic of Numbers and Motion*, 289. See also the general discussion of the problem of the tides in William Shea, *Galileo's Intellectual Revolution*, 2nd edn. (New York, 1972), 172–89.
78. AT xi. 81.
79. These will be covered in the *Principia*, however.
80. AT xi. 82.
81. AT xi. 82–3.
82. Descartes to Mersenne, [Nov. or Dec.] 1632; AT i. 261.
83. AT xi. 89–90.
84. AT xi. 95. On Descartes' conception of pressure in this context see Alan E. Shapiro, 'Light, Pressure, and Rectilinear Propagation: Descartes' Celestial Optics and Newton's Hydrostatics', *Studies in History and Philosophy of Science* 5 (1974), 239–96.
85. AT xi. 97.
86. AT xi. 98.
87. Beeckman had shown experimentally in 1629 that the speed of light is finite, but Descartes advances astronomical observations which contradict Beeckman's results. In fact, however, Descartes' proposed astronomical observations are flawed in that they would not show what he thinks they do. See Spyros Sakellariadis, 'Descartes' experimental Proof of the Infinite Velocity of Light and Huygens' Reply', *Archive for History of Exact Sciences* 26 (1982), 1–12.
88. Descartes to Beeckman, 22 Aug. 1634; AT i. 307.
89. AT xi. 99.
90. AT xi. 101.
91. AT vi. 97–8.

92. AT vi. 98–9.
93. AT vi. 100.
94. Descartes' account of refraction is, needless to say, not wholly satisfactory, and Fermat, in particular, was later to point out a number of problems with it. See the discussion in A. I. Sabra, *Theories of Light from Descartes to Newton* (London, 1967), 107–35.
95. Descartes was certainly not the first to suggest this, but his knowledge of earlier work on the rainbow is hard to gauge. On this earlier work see the survey in Charles B. Boyer, *The Rainbow* (Princeton, NJ., 1987).
96. AT vi. 326–7.
97. The number of rainbows does not stop at two. Tertiary rainbows are occasionally visible in nature, particularly against a dark background, but despite the odd possible sighting of quintic bows, after that it seems that they can only be seen under laboratory conditions. Up to nineteen bows have been identified under laboratory conditions. See Boyer, *The Rainbow*, 271, 309.
98. AT vi. 331.
99. Descartes unaccountably assumes that what holds for a ray moving from air to water also holds for a ray moving from glass to air, as in the case of the ray leaving the prism.
100. AT vi. 332–3.
101. Because Descartes has mistakenly used a ray travelling from air to water as his example (see n. 99 above), his account of the colours gives them in the inverse order to that which we would expect. Two of Descartes' correspondents pointed this out to Descartes when the *Météors* was published. See Morin to Descartes, 22 Feb. 1638 (AT i. 546–7); and Ciermans to Descartes [Mar. 1638] (AT ii. 59–61). His reply to Morin is completely inadequate: see AT ii. 208, and Morin's reponse, AT ii. 293–4. See also the discussion in Alan E. Shapiro, 'Kinematic Optics: A Study of the Wave Theory of Light in the Seventeenth Century', *Archive for History of Exact Sciences* 11 (1973), 134–266: 155–9.
102. The trouble is that once the corpuscles have entered the second medium they all seem to rotate clockwise, and if they are adjacent to one another this will be problematic, for a body adjacent to a corpuscle which rotates clockwise will tend to be moved in an anti-clockwise direction. On the other hand, perhaps Descartes would allow rotation in different directions.
103. For references see Shea, *The Magic of Numbers and Motion*, 211.
104. AT vi. 335.
105. AT vi. 335–6.
106. AT vi. 337–41. I have found the expositions in Boyer, *The Rainbow*, 212–18, and Shea, *The Magic of Numbers and Motion*, 219–22, very helpful.
107. It was standard practice before the employment of decimals to choose a large round figure in order to avoid fractions in the calculation.
108. Descartes to [Vatier], [22 Feb. 1638]; AT i. 559. Cf. AT vi. 325.
109. I am not counting Galileo's account of free fall as mechanist as it has no bearing on mechanism, and I am treating Fermat's account of refraction *at this time* as being directed by mathematical considerations.
110. Descartes to Mersenne, 20 Feb. 1639; AT ii. 525.
111. AT xi. 201–2.
112. *Anatomica*; AT xi. 549–634.
113. Descartes to Mersenne [early June 1637]; AT i. 378.
114. See Gilson, *Index scolastico-cartésien*, items 171, 173, and 174.
115. The most detailed treatment of Descartes' physiology and its sources is Annie Bitbol-Hespériès, *Le Principe de vie chez Descartes* (Paris, 1990). See also the invaluable notes to his translation of *L'Homme* in Thomas Steele Hall, *René Descartes: Treatise of Man* (Cambridge, Mass., 1972).

116. See the discussion of the development of Cartesian physiology in Leonora Cohen Rosenfield, *From Beast-Machine to Man-Machine*, rev. edn. (New York, 1968), 28–37, 241–64. See also Albert Balz, *Cartesian Studies* (New York, 1951), 106–57; and Bitbol-Hespériès, *Le Principe de vie chez Descartes*, 22.

117. See G. A. Lindeboom, *Descartes and Medicine* (Amsterdam, 1979), 62, and Thomas Steele Hall, *Ideas of Life and Matter*, 2 vols. (Chicago, 1969), i. 218–29.

118. Descartes to Mersenne, 23 June, 1641; AT ii. 386.

119. AT xi. 120.

120. On Descartes' reaction to Harvey see Étienne Gilson, *Études sur le rôle de la pensée médiévale dans la formation du système cartésien*, 5th edn. (Paris, 1984), 51–101.

121. See the detailed discussion in Bitbol-Hespériès, *Le Principe de vie chez Descartes*, 55–102.

122. AT xi. 123. In the *Anatomica* Descartes mentions three forms of fire, one in the heart, one in the brain ('as from vinous spirit'), and one in the stomach ('as from green wood'): AT xi. 538.

123. Gary Hatfield, 'Descartes' Physiology and its Relation to his Psychology', in J. Cottingham (ed.), *The Cambridge Companion to Descartes* (Cambridge, 1992), 335–70: 343.

124. AT xi. 128.

125. AT xi. 132.

126. AT xi. 133. If, as I shall suggest below, in reflex action the pineal gland is bypassed, then in reflex action the discharge of animal spirits will be independent of the action of the pineal, and it will be the cerebral ventricles that direct the animal spirits. I am grateful to John Sutton for pointing this out to me.

127. AT xi. 166–7.

128. AT xi. 174–5, 197–9.

129. AT xi. 178.

130. In the early *Cogitationes Privatae* (AT x. 230) Descartes is generally critical of mnemonic techniques, although Paolo Rossi, *Clavis universalis* (Milan, 1960), 175, and Frances Yates, *The Art of Memory* (London, 1966), 373–4, try to connect Descartes' thought with the tradition of mnemonics. Cf. Dennis L. Sepper, '*Ingenium*, Memory Art, and the Unity of Imaginative Knowing in the Early Descartes,' in S. Voss (ed.), *Essays on the Philosophy and Science of René Descartes* (Oxford, 1993), 142–61.

131. See John Sutton, 'Connecting Memory Traces', Ph.D. dissertation (University of Sydney, 1993), ch. 2, to which I am indebted here.

132. AT xi. 178–9.

133. AT xi. 179.

134. AT xi. 151–63.

135. I don't include here a possible fifth criterion: the degree of deflection of the pineal gland and the changes in flow patterns of the animal spirits resulting from this. See AT xi. 183–5.

136. AT xi. 159–60.

137. See Rudolph E. Siegel, *Galen on Sense Perception* (Basle, 1970) for details of Galen's account, and Friedrich Solmsen, 'Greek Philosophy and the Discovery of the Nerves', *Museum Helveticum* 18 (1961), 150–67 and 169–97, for earlier thinking about the structure of the nerves.

138. Traditionally, following Galen, three kinds of spirit had been distinguished: animal spirits, which control motor activity, sense perception, and a few lower psychic activities such as appetite, common sense, and imagination; natural spirits, centring on the liver; and vital spirits, centring on the heart. Descartes ignores vital and natural spirits.

139. See David P. Walker, 'Medical Spirits in Philosophy and Theology from Ficino to

Newton', in *Arts du spectacle et histoire des idées* (Tours, 1984), 287–300, from
which I have drawn some details in what follows.

140. See e.g. Walter Pagel, 'Medieval and Renaissance contributions to Knowledge of
the Brain and its Functions', in W. Pagel *et al.*, *The History and Philosophy of
Knowledge of the Brain and its Functions* (Oxford, 1958), 95–114.

141. AT vii. 413.

142. Hobbes comes close to such a view but it is questionable whether he holds it:
see Jamie C. Kassler, 'The Paradox of Power: Hobbes and Stoic Naturalism',
in Stephen Gaukroger (ed.), *The Uses of Antiquity* (Dordrecht, 1991), 53–78.

143. AT vi. 58.

144. AT vi. 57. Cf. AT vi. 2: 'reason or [good sense] . . . is the only thing that makes
us men or distinguishes us from beasts'.

145. Descartes did not distinguish these, although it should be noted that the distinction between the two is not straightforward. On some of the problems with
ascribing the discovery of the reflexes unreservedly to Descartes, see Georges
Canguilhem, *La Formation du concept du réflexe aux XVIIe et XVIIIe siècles*
(Paris, 1955).

146. AT xi. 142–3.

147. AT xi. 165–6.

148. I am indebted to John Sutton for drawing this possibility to my attention.

149. AT xi. 176–7.

150. AT i. 413–14.

151. See David C. Lindberg, *Theories of Vision from al-Kindi to Kepler* (Chicago, 1976),
202–5.

152. See e.g. Richard S. Peters (ed.), *Thomas Hobbes: Body, Man, Citizen* (New York,
1962), 175–181.

153. AT xi. 4.

154. See Robert Lenoble, *Mersenne ou la naissance du mécanisme*, 2nd edn. (Paris,
1971), 108.

155. See Catherine Wilson, 'Constancy, Emergence, and Illusions: Obstacles to a Naturalistic Theory of Vision', in S. Nadler (ed.), *Causation in Early Modern Philosophy* (University Park, Penn., 1993), 159–77. Wilson mistakenly claims that
Descartes 'does not think that brains can reason or calculate' (p. 164), but her
paper brings out clearly just how easy the slide down the Malebranchian path is
if one does hold this view.

156. The nature of the overtone series attracted many researchers in the seventeenth
century. For details see Sigalia Dostrovsky, 'Early Vibration Theory: Physics and
Music in the Seventeenth Century', *Archive for History of Exact Sciences* 14 (1975),
169–218.

157. Descartes to Mersenne [Oct. 1631]; AT i. 223.

158. Descartes to Mersenne, 4 Mar. 1630; AT i. 126.

159. See the exemplary discussion in Claude V. Palisca, 'Scientific Empiricism in Musical
Thought', in H. H. Rhys (ed.), *Seventeenth-Century Science and the Arts* (Princeton,
NJ, 1961), 91–137.

160. H. Floris Cohen, *Quantifying Music* (Dordrecht, 1984), 170 ff., argues otherwise,
but his argument seems to me beside the point. The question is whether the
overtone series can be used to explain the harmonic structure in polyphonic and
triadic-tonal systems. I shall not argue this question here, but for a concise summary
of the problems with the reductionist overtone view see Milton Babbitt, 'Past and
Present Concepts of the Nature and Limits of Music', in B. Boretz and E. T. Cone
(eds.), *Perspectives of Contemporary Music Theory* (New York, 1972), 2–9.

161. As John Yolton tends to do in his *Perceptual Acquaintance* (Oxford, 1984), 22–
31.

162. John Cottingham, 'A Brute to the Brutes?', *Philosophy* 53 (1978), 551–9: 553.
163. Here I part company with naturalist/materialist readings of Descartes' account of human cognition, such as that offered in Hiram Caton, *The Origins of Subjectivity* (New Haven, Conn., 1973).
164. Williams, *Descartes*, 282.
165. Williams cites in favour of his interpretation a passage in a letter from Descartes to Mersenne, 30 July 1640; AT iii. 121. But all Descartes says there is: 'As for brute animals, we are so used to believing that they have feelings just like us/just like ours [*ainsi que nous*] that it is hard to rid ourselves of this opinion.' The passage is ambiguous, and does not make Williams' interpretation 'certain', as he claims. In fact, Descartes' usual practice is to qualify his statements that animals lack reason by saying that they lack thought *of the kind that we have*: see the letter to the Marquess of Newcastle, 23 Nov. 1646, where he responds to the idea that animals may have some thoughts such as we experience in ourselves with the remark that if they were 'to think as we do' then they would need an immaterial soul (AT i. 576); and the letter to More of 5 Feb. 1649, where his concern is specifically whether animals 'have sensations like ours' (AT v. 276–7). Occasionally he neglects to add the qualification, as in the sixth set of Replies to the Objections to the *Meditationes*, where he agrees that he has claimed that 'animals possess no thought at all' (AT vii. 426), but here he is reporting an objection made to his account and he does not set out his own argument. The distinction between the claim that animals have no thoughts and the claim that they have no thoughts like the ones we have seems a central one to us, and Descartes can be criticized for carelessness in not always making clear which he means; but the point remains that he sometimes unambiguously claims that animals have no thoughts *like ours*, and so far as I can tell he never (when context is taken into account) unambiguously claims that they have no thoughts at all.
166. Descartes to Plempius for Fromondus, 3 Oct. 1637; AT i. 413.
167. Cf. ibid.
168. Reply to fifth set of objections to the *Meditationes*; AT vii. 358. Cf. *Discours* Part V; AT vi. 57–9.
169. Descartes to More, 5 Feb. 1649; AT v. 259.
170. Peter Harrison, 'Descartes on Animals', *Philosophical Quarterly* 42 (1992), 227.
171. AT vi. 60.
172. AT i. 270–1.
173. There are many good accounts of these events available. See, e.g. Stillman Drake, *Galileo at Work* (Chicago, 1978), and, for a closer assessment of the politics involved, Mario Biagioli, *Galileo Courtier* (Chicago, 1993), ch. 6. The doctrine of the Earth's motion only ceased to be a heresy with the decree of Pius VII in 1820: see Joseph Turmel, *Histoire des dogmes*, 6 vols. (Paris, 1931), iv. 40–1, on the later history of the controversy. It is only relatively recently that the truth of the doctrine has been publicly acknowledged by the Church.
174. See Descartes to Mersenne, 14 Aug. 1634; AT i. 303–4.
175. See R. Hookyaas, 'The Reception of Copernicanism in England and the Netherlands', in C. Wilson *et al.*, *The Anglo-Dutch Contribution to the Civilization of Early Modern Society* (Oxford, 1976), 33–44.
176. See Adam 165–77.
177. For some, it was purely an Italian affair. See e.g. the letter of Ismaël Boulliau to Gassendi of 21 June 1633 in Gassendi, *Opera omnia*, 6 vols. (Lyons, 1658), vi. 412; and his letter to Mersenne of 16 Dec. 1644 in M xiii. 20. The complex theological background to Galileo's trial is discussed fully in Richard J. Blackwell, *Galileo, Bellarmine, and the Bible* (Notre Dame, Ind., 1991), but I am convinced by Biagioli, *Galileo Courtier*, ch. 6, that political considerations seem to have been the paramount ones.

178. Descartes to Mersenne [Feb. 1634]; AT i. 281.
179. See Adam 169. See also Descartes' own comments: AT i. 281, 285; AT v. 544, 550.
180. Descartes to Mersenne [Apr. 1634]; AT i. 286.
181. See the passage in the conversation with Burman, given at AT v. 165, where Descartes warns against devoting too much time to metaphysical questions, especially to his *Meditationes*. These are just preparation for the main questions, which concern physical and observable things. Cf. Descartes to Elizabeth, 28 June 1643; AT iii. 695.

Chapter 8

1. There is some detail on Thomas Sargeant in *Écrivains* 481–2.
2. Descartes to Huygens, 20 May 1637; AT i. 631–4.
3. For details, see *Écrivains* 493–6.
4. See G. H. Turnbull, *Hartlib, Dury and Comenius* (London, 1947), 167.
5. Jack R. Vrooman, *René Descartes–A Biography* (New York, 1970), 137. On the relationship with Hélène, see *Écrivains* 483–90.
6. The document is reproduced in Baillet ii. 89–90.
7. 'Presumably', because she may, of course, have procured the services of a letter-writer, although Descartes does talk about her writing to him (AT i. 394: marginal note in letter of 30 Aug. 1637) in a way that suggests that she can write.
8. Baillet ii. 91.
9. See Descartes to ***, 30 Aug. 1637; AT i. 393.
10. See AT i. 580–1.
11. See Paul Mouy, *Le Développement de la physique cartésienne, 1646–1712* (Paris, 1934), 9–10.
12. Descartes' account covers most of the phenomena that had traditionally fallen under the topic of meteorology, although some are left out: he does not deal with earthquakes and, since he does not consider them sublunary phenomena, nor does he deal with comets.
13. AT vi. 233–4.
14. AT vi. 237–8.
15. AT vi. 235–6.
16. AT vi. 82–3.
17. AT vi. 148.
18. AT vi. 148–9.
19. Descartes to *** [Oct. 1637]; AT i. 458.
20. Cf. J. F. Scott, *The Scientific Work of René Descartes* (London, 1952), 86–8. In fact, Fermat's work on analytic geometry was only published posthumously in 1679.
21. AT vi. 369.
22. AT vi. 370. In other words, what Descartes has realized is that line lengths form an algebraic field. See the discussion in Michael S. Mahoney, 'The Beginnings of Algebraic Thought in the Seventeenth Century', in Stephen Gaukroger (ed.), *Descartes: Philosophy, Mathematics and Physics* (Brighton, 1980), 141–55.
23. AT vi. 370–1.
24. AT vi. 373–4.
25. The importance of this development is spelled out succinctly by Scott in his detailed account of Book II (*The Scientific Work of René Descartes*, ch. 8) and I follow Scott's account here.
26. Ibid. 114.
27. AT vi. 413.
28. This simplified version of Descartes' account borrows from Charles B. Boyer, *History of Analytic Geometry* (Princeton, NJ, 1988), 94–5.

29. See Michael S. Mahoney, 'Infinitesimals and Transcendent Relations: The Mathematics of Motion in the Late Seventeenth Century', in D. Lindberg and R. Westman (eds.), *Reappraisals of the Scientific Revolution* (Cambridge, 1990), 461–92: 465.

30. See Richard H. Popkin, *The Third Force in Seventeenth-Century Thought* (Leiden, 1992), 95–6, for an account of the meeting.

31. See Gilbert Gadoffre, *Descartes: Discours de la méthode* (Manchester, 1941); 'Sur la chronologie du *Discours de la méthode*', *Revue d'histoire de la philosophie et de la civilisation* 2 (1943), 45–70; 'Réflexions sur la genèse du *Discours de la méthode*', *Revue de synthèse* 65 (1948), 11–27; 'La Chronologie des six parties', in N. Grimaldi and J. L. Marion (eds.), *Le Discours et sa méthode* (Paris, 1978), 19–40. See also the evidence presented in Constantino Láscaris Comneno, 'Análisis del *Discurso del método*', *Revista de filosofía* 14 (1955), 293–351, where a very similar view is developed. A number of revisions to Gadoffre's account are proposed in the first section of Élie Denissoff, *Descartes, premier théoricien de la physique mathématique* (Louvain, 1970).

32. See Edwin M. Curley, 'Cohérence ou incohérence du *Discours?*' in Grimaldi and Marion (eds.), *Le Discours et sa méthode*, 41–64.

33. AT vi. 4. This is not merely false modesty on Descartes' part: as we saw when we looked at the early *Regulae*, Descartes is opposed to the provision of 'rules for thinking', such as those provided by the Jesuits, because he thought that the natural light of reason provided us with all we needed in this respect. The point of 'imitation' in the present context would presumably be to make better use of the natural light of reason.

34. AT vi. 4.

35. AT vi. 10–11.

36. AT vi. 11. As we saw in Ch. 4, his account of his state of mind here conflicts with his earlier account.

37. AT vi. 15.

38. AT vi. 22.

39. AT v. 178. Étienne Gilson—*René Descartes: Discours de la méthode, texte et commentaire*, 4th edn. (Paris, 1975), 234—believes that this might be a later rationalization on Descartes' part, but this seems to me a wholly implausible view.

40. AT vi. 23.

41. *Œuvres de Monsieur de Balzac*, ed. Valentin Conrart, 2 vols. (Paris, 1665; facsimile repr. Geneva, 1971), ii. 308.

42. AT vi. 27.

43. AT vi. 61.

44. AT vi. 62.

45. Certainly there is a long tradition of reading him in this way. In chronological order, some of the principal discussions are to be found in Pierre Mesnard, *Essai sur la morale de Descartes* (Paris, 1936); Gilson, *René Descartes: Discours de la méthode*; Ferdinand Alquié, *La Découverte métaphysique de l'homme chez Descartes* (Paris, 1950); Anthony Levi, *French Moralists* (Oxford, 1964); and Nicholas Grimaldi, 'Morale provisoire et découverte métaphysique', in Grimaldi and Marion (eds.), *Le Discours et sa méthode* (Paris, 1987), 303–19.

46. Levi, *French Moralists*, Richard B. 248. Carter, *Descartes' Medical Philosophy* (Baltimore, 1983), tries to develop such a reading, defending a 'medical ethics' in detail, as part of a more general materialist interpretation of Descartes, but the interpretation is just not plausible.

47. AT vi. 1.

48. AT vi. 31–2.

49. Reply to the second set of objections to the *Meditationes*; AT vii. 145.

50. This reading is defended in detail in my 'The Ten Modes of Aenesidemus and the Myth of Ancient Scepticism', *British Journal for the History of Philosophy* 3 (1995), forthcoming.
51. See Michael Frede, 'Stoics and Skeptics on Clear and Distinct Impressions' in M. Burnyeat (ed.), The *Skeptical Tradition* (Berkeley, Calif., 1983).
52. See e.g. the influential discussion in Richard H. Popkin, *The History of Scepticism from Erasmus to Spinoza* (Berkeley, Calif., 1979), chs. 2–3, where all forms of doubt in Montaigne are assimilated to sceptical doubt.
53. Michel de Montaigne, *Essais*, ed. Maurice Rat, 2 vols. (Paris, 1962), i. 369–70.
54. All quotes are from bk. i, ch. 14 of Pierre Charron, *De la Sagesse*, 2nd. edn. (Paris, 1604).
55. Marin Mersenne, *La Vérité des Sciences, contres les Septiques ou Pyrrhoniens* (Paris, 1625; facsimile repr. Stuttgart, 1969), 194–5.
56. Montaigne, *Essais*, ii. 562.
57. See the essays, and esp. the editor's introduction, to Richard H. Popkin (ed.), *Scepticism and Irreligion in the Seventeenth and Eighteenth Centuries* (Leiden, 1993).
58. Popkin has done more than anyone to show this. See his introduction to ibid. and his *The Third Force in Seventeenth-Century Thought*.
59. See Richard J. Blackwell, *Galileo, Bellarmine, and the Bible* (Notre Dame, Ind., 1991), ch. 1. We shall return to this question below.
60. AT vi. 31.
61. As one commentator has pointed out, Epicurus' approach to the study of perception 'neither starts with nor centres on the perspective of the subject. The subject is treated from the start as a part of the natural world, whose perceptions and cognitions are to be explained—by reference to the action and interaction of atoms' (Stephen Everson, 'Epicurus on the Truth of the Senses', in Everson (ed.), *Companions to Ancient Thought*, i: *Epistemology* (Cambridge, 1990), 161–83: 181). Galileo had also raised this question in his *Il Saggiatore* of 1623, and he had distinguished primary and secondary qualities, the latter being additions of 'consciousness' (Galileo, *Discoveries and Opinions of Galileo*, ed. and trans. Stillman Drake (Garden City, NY, 1957), 274–9), but no question about the nature of subjectivity is raised thereby.
62. See the discussion in Charles Taylor, *Sources of the Self* (Cambridge, 1989), ch. 10.
63. In a very different context, Plotinus, in the third century AD, had conceived of cognition as involving an ontological gulf between subject and object. See Eyjólfur Emilsson, *Plotinus on Sense-Perception* (Cambridge, 1988).
64. AT vi. 34.
65. AT vi. 32.
66. AT vi. 39.
67. AT i. 338.
68. AT i. 340.
69. The nature of Descartes' quarrel with the Elzeviers is not known, but it was evidently serious, as he tells Mersenne that he 'would prefer to employ somebody who has no connection with Elzevier, who will probably have warned his correspondents because he knows that I am writing to you' (AT i. 340).
70. *Écrivains* ch. 13 provides full details of the agreement with Maire as well as a facsimile of the contract.
71. Saumaise writes on 4 Apr., 'le liure de sieur des Cartes est acheué d'imprimer' (AT x. 554).
72. See Adam 243–5.
73. Descartes to [Vatier], 22 Feb. 1638; AT i. 560.

74. AT vi. 77.
75. Cf. Adam 185.
76. AT vi. 41.
77. See Descartes to Huygens, 5 Oct. 1637; AT i. 434.
78. Descartes to *** [27 Apr. 1637]; AT i. 370.
79. Descartes to Mersenne, 19 June 1639; AT ii. 565.
80. e.g. by Ciermans; see Ciermans to Descartes [Mar. 1638]; AT ii. 59.
81. AT ii. 24.
82. Descartes to Mersenne, 9 Feb. 1639; AT ii. 495.
83. Descartes to Mersenne [Dec. 1638]; AT ii. 463–4: 'ie vous diray, entre nous, que ie les compare aux vers d'Ennius, desquels Virgile tiroit de l'or, i'entens *de scercore Ennij*'.
84. William Shea, *The Magic of Numbers and Motion* (Canton, Mass., 1991), 292, n. 37.
85. References are given ibid. 292–3, n. 37.
86. Preface to the *Meditationes*; AT vii. 8.
87. See e.g. the remark in a letter of Chapelain to Balzac, 29 Dec. 1637, quoted at AT i. 485–6: 'His *Dioptrique* and his *Géométrie* are his two masterpieces in the judgement of the masters. The *Météors* is arbitrary and problematic, but admirable nevertheless.'
88. Adam 188.
89. 'Calcul de Mons. des Cartes' [1638]; AT x. 659–80. The authorship is unknown, but Godefroid de Haestrecht and Florimond Debeaune have been suggested as possibilities.
90. We do not have Fromondus' objections, but we do have Descartes' replies. See Descartes to Plempius for Fromondus, 3 Oct. 1637. The replies to his objections to the *Discours* are to be found at AT i. 413–16.
91. AT i. 413–14.
92. Plempius to Descartes [Jan. 1638]; AT i. 497–9.
93. Descartes to Plempius, 15 Feb. 1638; AT i. 522.
94. e.g. AT i. 523–34.
95. Descartes to [Vatier] [22 Feb. 1638]; AT i. 559–60.
96. AT i. 560.
97. A Latin translation of the *Discours*, *Dioptrique*, and *Météors* appeared in 1664 (AT vi. 517–720), but no new material was added.
98. Descartes to Mersenne [13 Nov. 1639]; AT ii. 622.
99. AT i. 564–5.
100. AT ii. 596–7.
101. For further discussion of this point, see my *Cartesian Logic* (Oxford, 1989), 51–60.
102. Descartes to Plempius for Fromondus, 3 Oct. 1637; AT i. 416–20.
103. Fermat to Mersenne [Apr. or May 1637]; M vi. 250–2.
104. Descartes to Mersenne [5 Oct. 1637]; AT i. 452–3.
105. See A. I. Sabra, *Theories of Light from Descartes to Newton* (London, 1967), ch. 4.
106. Fermat to Mersenne [Nov. 1637?]; M vi. 322–31.
107. Morin to Descartes, 22 Feb. 1638; AT i. 542–3.
108. Descartes to Morin, 13 July 1638; AT ii. 204.
109. See Descartes to Mersenne, 5 Oct. 1637; AT i. 450–1.
110. Descartes to Mersenne, 30 Sept. 1640; AT iii. 183.
111. Descartes to [Noël], Oct. 1637; AT i. 455.
112. See Adam 200.
113. See Charles B. Boyer, *The Rainbow* (Princeton, NJ, 1987), 219.
114. Descartes to [Vatier] [22 Feb. 1638]; AT i. 563.

115. Descartes to Plempius for Fromondus, 3 Oct. 1637; AT i. 421.
116. Descartes to Ciermans [23 Mar. 1638]; AT ii. 71.
117. Ciermans to Descartes [Mar. 1638]; AT ii. 58–9.
118. Morin to Descartes, 22 Feb. 1638; AT i. 556.
119. Descartes to Ciermans [23 Mar. 1638]; AT ii. 74.
120. Ciermans to Descartes [Mar. 1638]; AT ii. 59–61; Morin to Descartes, 22 Feb. 1638; AT i. 546–9.
121. See the discussion in Shea, *The Magic of Numbers and Motion*, 216–18.
122. On Harriot's contribution to the development of algebra see J. A. Lohne, 'Dokumente zur Revalidierung von Thomas Harriot als Algebraiker', *Archive for History of Exact Sciences* 3 (1976), 185–205.
123. On the early development of algebra generally, and esp. Vieta's contribution to it, see Jacob Klein, *Greek Mathematical Thought and the Origin of Algebra* (Cambridge, Mass., 1986).
124. Descartes to Mersenne [end of Dec. 1637?]; AT i. 478–80.
125. On this whole episode see Chikara Sasaki, *Descartes' Mathematical Thought* (Ann Arbor, Mich., 1989), 335–79.
126. The documents, including Beaugrand's original accusation to Mersenne, are given at AT v. 503–12. See also the detailed account in Gaston Milhaud, *Descartes savant* (Paris, 1921), 149–75.
127. See Scott, *The Scientific Work of René Descartes*, 114–15.
128. Descartes to ***, 30 Aug. 1637; AT i. 393.
129. Vrooman, *René Descartes*, 141.
130. Descartes to Huygens, 5 Oct. 1637; AT i. 434–5.
131. Descartes to Huygens, 4 Dec. 1637; AT i. 649.
132. See Huygens to Boësset, 19 Jan. 1641; M x. 416–17.
133. On the relation between Mersenne and Ban see David P. Walker, *Studies in Musical Science in the Late Renaissance* (London, 1978), ch. 6.
134. See M vii. 1–2.
135. Letter quoted at AT ii. 586.
136. Descartes to Mersenne [30 July 1640]; AT iii. 139 and 141. See the references given for both his dissections and his gardening in Adam 233.
137. See e.g. Descartes to Plempius, 15 Feb. 1639; AT i. 523–8.
138. See Descartes to Mersenne [13 July 1638]; AT ii. 250–5; see also AT v. 563–7.
139. See the account of these events in Adam 272–80.
140. See the discussion in Pierre Costabel, *Démarches originales de Descartes savant* (Paris, 1982), 121–40.
141. I am indebted in what follows to the careful discussion in Westfall, *Force in Newton's Physics*, 72–8.
142. Descartes to Mersenne [13 July 1638]; AT ii. 228.
143. Descartes to Mersenne, 15 Nov. 1638; AT ii. 432–3.
144. Descartes to Huygens, 5 Oct. 1637; AT i. 435–6.
145. Descartes to Mersenne, 12 Sept. 1638; AT ii. 354.
146. This is the dominant theme of the letter to Mersenne [13 July 1638]; AT ii. 222–45.
147. See e.g. Debeaune to Mersenne, 25 Sept. 1638; M viii. 86–90 (also at AT v. 515–17).
148. On 11 Mar. he tells Mersenne that he will be in Leiden in five or six weeks; AT iii. 35–6. The letter to Pollot of 7 May is the first addressed from Leiden; AT iii. 59.
149. This is established decisively in Bradley Rubidge, 'Descartes' *Meditations* and Devotional Meditations', *Journal of the History of Ideas* 51 (1990), 27–50.
150. AT vii. 3. Cf. ibid. 153–4.
151. AT vii. 4.

152. AT vii. 16.
153. '[Corporeal things] possess all the properties which I grasp clearly and distinctly, that is, all those which, viewed in general terms, come under the subject matter of pure mathematics' (AT vii. 80).
154. The decision was made on the basis of the doctrines of the Church Fathers. See Blackwell, *Galileo, Bellarmine, and the Bible*, ch. 1.
155. Quoted ibid. 18.
156. AT vii. 48–52.
157. Many interpretations have been proposed of the *Meditationes*, and this is not the place to go through them. Instead, I am offering what I believe to be the most plausible reading, which will be supported where necessary both by the text itself and by what I have tried to reconstruct as to the genesis of particular arguments. For what is still the best statement of an approach diametrically opposed to the one that I am taking, one which assumes that the *Meditationes* is completely self-contained, see Martial Guéroult, *Descartes selon l'ordre des raisons*, 2 vols. (Paris, 1953). Implausible as I believe it is, such a line of interpretation is still commonly favoured among Descartes commentators.
158. AT vii. 80.
159. AT xi. 439.
160. As many modern commentators have argued. The most famous argument for the unintelligibility of hyperbolic doubt is Ludwig Wittgenstein, *On Certainty* (Oxford, 1969).
161. In this all-important respect Descartes' argument goes well beyond Augustine's argument, at the beginning of pt. ii of bk 3 of *De libero arbitrio voluntatis*, that in order to be deceived one must exist.
162. AT vii. 140.
163. For further discussion of this point see my 'Vico and the Maker's Knowledge Principle', *History of Philosophy Quarterly* 3 (1986), 29–44: 37–40.
164. AT vii. 37–8. Cf. AT iii. 303.
165. AT iii. 383.
166. AT i. 145.
167. AT vii. 214.
168. AT vii. 278.
169. See the discussions in J. Vigier, 'Les Idées de temps, de durée et d'éternité dans Descartes', *Revue philosophique* 89 (1920), 196–233 and 321–48; Jean Wahl, *Du rôle de l'idée de l'instant dans la philosophie de Descartes* (Paris, 1920); and Daniel Garber, *Descartes' Metaphysical Physics* (Chicago, 1992), 263–73.
170. See J. E. K. Secada, 'Descartes on Time and Causality,' *Philosophical Review* 94 (1990), 45–72: 49–52.
171. At least in classical mechanics. In Relativity theory, physical-causal processes must always take time, as there can be no instantaneous transmissions or propagations.
172. e.g. AT vii. 210–14.
173. AT vii. 80.
174. *Discoveries and Opinions of Galileo*, ed. and trans. Stillman Drake (Garden City, NY, 1957), 275–9.
175. AT vii. 254.
176. AT viii₁. 321.
177. AT viii₁. 323. The French version talks of 'various dispositions in the shapes, sizes, positions, and movements of the parts of the body' (AT ix₂. 317).
178. AT vii. 411–12.
179. AT viii₁. 359.
180. *** to Descartes [July 1641]; AT iii. 403.
181. Descartes to *** [Aug. 1641]; AT iii. 426.
182. AT vii. 3.

183. Quoted in Ernst Cassirer, Paul Kristeller, and John Herman Randall (eds.), *The Renaissance Philosophy of Man* (Chicago, 1949), 261.

184. AT vii. 201–2. Despite being shown the invalidity of this argument form by Arnauld, Descartes will use it again in the *Principia* II, art. 4, in his attempt to demonstrate that hardness cannot be an essential property of matter because we can imagine matter not having the property of being hard! (AT viii$_1$. 42.)

185. AT vii. 226.

186. AT vii. 78.

187. Cf. his objection to the idea that the body can think in the second set of replies: 'whatever can think is a mind, or is called a mind; but since mind and body are in reality distinct, no body is a mind; therefore no body can think' (AT vii. 132). Incidentally, we must note that the 'thinking' here is characteristically human thought (involving judgement and will).

188. Something like this doctrine could be offered as a basis for what Arnauld mentions as the commonly held view that 'the souls of brute animals are distinct from their bodies, but nevertheless perish along with them' (AT vii. 204).

189. The problem of my distinctness from my thinking, brought up in the third set of objections to the *Meditationes* (AT vii. 177), and that of the similarity between Descartes's account and the Platonic view that nothing corporeal belongs to my essence, raised in the fourth set (AT vii. 203), both bear on the question of how far Descartes has managed to avoid Averroism. In his set of objections, Gassendi also raises such problems: see AT vii. 259 ff., and esp. 262.

190. AT vii. 27.

191. AT vii. 28.

192. Cf. Gordon P. Baker and Katherine J. Morris, 'Descartes Unlocked', *British Journal for the History of Philosophy* 1/2 (1993), 3–21, who are more inclined to see the issue as being one of a choice between consciousness of one's own mental states versus judgement and volition; they opt for the latter. That awareness does play an important role is, however, evident from e.g. the later correspondence with More.

193. On the face of it, this reading looks incompatible with Descartes' remarks towards the end of the replies to the seventh set of objections to the *Meditationes*, where he says that it is wrong to argue that mind, as a separate substance, not only be required to think, but also 'that it should think that it is thinking, by means of a reflexive act, or that it should have awareness of its own thought' (AT vii. 559). But what this rules out is not the need for the mind to have the capacity to be aware of 'thoughts', in the sense of its own mental states (perceptions, etc.), but the need for the mind to have the capacity to be aware of 'thoughts' in the sense of its judgements. The fact that Descartes uses the example that an architect does not need to reflect on the skill he has to possess in order to be an architect surely indicates that this is what he has in mind. In short, we need to be aware of our mental states if we are to make judgements about them, but the judgements themselves do not have to be reflexive.

194. AT vii. 49.

195. e.g. Descartes to Arnauld, 29 July 1648 (AT v. 222) and Descartes to More [Aug. 1649] (AT v. 403–4).

196. AT vii. 81.

197. Descartes to Elizabeth, 21 May 1643; AT iii. 665.

198. AT ii. 361.

199. Baillet ii. 90.

200. Ibid. 90. The circumstances and symptoms suggest scarlet fever, although there were other epidemics with symptoms similar to scarlet fever, such as the 'English sweats', which produced a high mortality rate in the middle of the sixteenth century. It is often very difficult to identify exactly the nature of the epidemics in

this period, for not only are symptoms not always described adequately but diseases themselves change through mutation of viruses and bacteria, and seventeenth-century diseases and modern ones may be quite different.

201. See Adam 288.
202. It should be said, however, that we have no direct evidence of grief on his part. His letter to Mersenne of 15 Sept. 1640 shows that he had already thrown himself back into work. And in a letter to Pollot written only four months after Francine's death, consoling him on the death of his brother in very similar circumstances, he refers to Francine's death and writes that 'it would be barbarous to feel no sorrow at all when one has sufficient cause, but it would be cowardly to abandon oneself wholly to one's grief' (Descartes to [Pollot] [mid-Jan. 1641]; AT iii. 279).

Chapter 9

1. Cf. Arnauld's comment in his objections: 'It could be claimed that the work under discussion belongs entirely to philosophy; yet since the author has ... submitted himself to the tribunal of theologians, I propose to play a dual role here' (AT vii. 197).
2. AT vii. 7.
3. AT vii. 160–70.
4. AT vii. 153.
5. AT vii. 581.
6. Descartes to Mersenne [25 Nov. 1630]; AT i. 179.
7. Descartes to [Vatier] [22 Feb. 1638]; AT i. 564–5.
8. See the detailed and invaluable discussion in J.-R. Armogathe, *Theologia cartesiana: L'Explication physique de l'Eucharistie chez Descartes et Dom Desgabets* (The Hague, 1977), 10 ff.
9. AT vii. 217.
10. AT vii. 248–56.
11. See Richard A. Watson, 'Transubstantiation among the Cartesians', in T. M. Lennon, J. M. Nicholas, and J. W. Davis (eds.), *Problems of Cartesianism* (Kingston, Ont., 1982), 127–48, and Steven Nadler, 'Arnauld, Descartes, and Transubstantiation: Reconciling Cartesian Metaphysics and Real Presence', *Journal of the History of Ideas* 49 (1988), 229–46.
12. See the account ibid. 234–5.
13. Theo Verbeek, *Descartes and the Dutch* (Carbondale, Ill., 1992), provides the best account to date of this question, and my account in this paragraph relies exclusively on this account.
14. Cited ibid. 5.
15. AT vii. 582–601.
16. AT viii₂. 1–194.
17. AT viii₂. 201–73.
18. See Descartes to Regius [24 May 1640]; AT viii. 63–70, and the fragments of Regius to Descartes, 5 May 1640; AT iii. 60–1.
19. Primerose was a French-trained physician of Scottish parents, active mainly in England. His anti-Harvey tract *De vulgi erroribus in medicina* had been published in Amsterdam in 1638. See M viii. 648, n. 4.
20. See Jack R. Vrooman, *René Descartes: A Biography* (New York, 1970), 153–7, on the Descartes–Voetius–Schurmann relationship.
21. Voetius to Mersenne [second half of Oct. 1640]; M x. 164. Voetius will in fact write about five letters to Mersenne on this theme, and Descartes gives extracts from some of them in his letter to the Magistrates of Utrecht. See AT iii. 602–4.
22. Descartes to Mersenne, 11 Nov. 1640; AT iii. 231.
23. Descartes to Regius [Apr. 1642]; AT iii. 558–60.

24. Descartes to Huygens, 26 Apr. 1642; AT iii. 784.
25. Voetius criticized scholasticism extensively, but he accepted the post-Reformation scholasticism of Suárez, Fonseca, Toletus, and the Coimbra commentators. See Verbeek, *Descartes and the Dutch*, 7.
26. Vrooman, *René Descartes*, 160. Vrooman's account of these episodes manages to distil the essence from the detailed account in *Écrivains* 547–79 and 595–602, and I have relied on both these sources in what follows.
27. Descartes to Mersenne, 1 Apr. 1640; AT iii. 50. On the possibility that Digby made the invitation, see AT iii. 89–90. Digby was to write the first exposition of Cartesian philosophy in English, in his *Two Treatises* (Paris, 1644; facsimile repr. New York, 1978).
28. AT v. 165.
29. See Geneviève Rodis-Lewis, *L'Œuvre de Descartes*, 2 vols. (Paris, 1971), i. 420, n. 1. Proposed dates vary from 1629 to 1650.
30. See Ferdinand Alquié (ed.), *Œuvres philosophiques de Descartes*, 3 vols. (Paris, 1963–73), ii. 1114 n. 2.
31. See Pierre-Alain Cahné, *Un autre Descartes: Le Philosophe et son langage* (Paris, 1980), 56–62.
32. AT x. 505–6.
33. On the relation between Eustache and Descartes see Leslie Armour, 'Descartes and Eustachius a Sancto Paulo', *British Journal for the History of Philosophy* 1/2 (1993), 3–21.
34. Descartes to Mersenne, 11 Nov. 1640; AT iii. 233.
35. Descartes to Mersenne, 21 Jan. 1641; AT iii. 286.
36. *Principia* IV, art. 188; AT viii₁. 315.
37. See the comparisons in AT xi. 698–706.
38. *Principia* I, art. 6; AT viii₁. 6.
39. *Principia* I, art. 43; AT viii₁. 21.
40. *Principia* I, art. 8; AT viii₁. 7.
41. *Principia* I, art. 9; AT viii₁. 7.
42. *Principia* I, art. 13; AT viii₁. 9.
43. *Principia* I, art. 21; AT viii₁. 13.
44. *Principia* I, art. 25; AT viii₁. 14.
45. *Principia* I, art. 30; AT viii₁. 16.
46. *Principia* I, arts. 42–4; AT viii₁. 20–1.
47. *Principia* I, art. 41; AT viii₁. 20.
48. These are, of course, very different kinds of proposition, but presumably what Descartes intends to draw attention to is merely what he considers to be their indubitability, not what this indubitability derives from.
49. *Principia* I, art. 56; AT viii₁. 26. Cf. Descartes to *** [1645 or 1646?]; AT iv. 348–50.
50. *Principia* I, art. 53; AT viii₁. 25.
51. See Descartes to More, 15 Apr. 1649; AT v. 341–2.
52. See the account of these questions in Daniel Garber, *Descartes' Metaphysical Physics* (Chicago, 1992), 144–8.
53. AT vii. 422.
54. See my 'The Metaphysics of Impenetrability: Euler's Conception of Force', *British Journal for the History of Science* 15 (1982), 132–54.
55. *Principia* I, art. 55; AT viii₁. 26.
56. It is far from clear that it does actually pose problems for the continuity of motion. See Garber, *Descartes' Metaphysical Physics*, 266–73.
57. At the metaphysical level things are more complicated, for Descartes wants to maintain both that causation is instantaneous and that nothing past can be the cause of the present existence of anything. The physical interpretation of instantaneous

causation that I have just given does allow that past events can affect future ones, so long as it is just a case of something continuing in the absence of anything occurring which would change it. But of course the same consideration applies to existence. The problem is compounded when we come to the question of what exactly God creates when He puts a body into existence, for it seems that in bringing something into existence He thereby also creates something like its inertial state. I cannot think of any way in which the physics and metaphysics can be reconciled here.

58. AT v. 385.
59. Garber, *Descartes' Metaphysical Physics*, 273–93, and Peter Remnant, 'Descartes: Body and Soul', *Canadian Journal of Philosophy* 9 (1979), 377–86.
60. See Alan Gabbey, 'The Mechanical Philosophy and its Problems: Mechanical Explanation, Impenetrability, and Perpetual Motion', in J. Pitt (ed.), *Change and Progress in Modern Science* (Dordrecht, 1985), 9–84, and Peter McLaughlin, 'Descartes on Mind–Body Interaction and the Conservation of Motion', *Philosophical Review* 102 (1993), 155–82.
61. JIB i. 266–7. Motion also runs down in Newton's universe, without the intervention of 'active principles'. See Alan Gabbey, 'Force and Inertia in the Seventeenth Century: Descartes and Newton', in Stephen Gaukroger (ed.), *Descartes: Philosophy, Mathematics and Physics* (Brighton, 1980), 241 and 305, n. 61.
62. Leibniz, *Die philosophischen Schriften*, ed. C. I. Gerhardt, 7 vols. (Berlin, 1875–90), vi. 620–1 (*Monadology* §80). Note that Leibniz speaks of conservation of the force of motion, rather than conservation of motion. This fits my own reading of the Principle, but, as I have just indicated, it does not help with the present question to think in terms of force of motion rather than motion.
63. There is a good defence of this traditional reading in McLaughlin, 'Descartes on Mind–Body Interaction'.
64. *Principia* II, art. 25; AT viii$_1$. 54.
65. AT ix$_2$. 76.
66. AT xi. 40.
67. Descartes to Mersenne, 28 Oct. 1640; AT iii. 213.
68. *Principia* II, art. 29; AT viii$_1$. 55–6.
69. *Principia* II, art. 30; AT viii$_1$. 56–7. Both the Latin and French texts unaccountably transpose 'east' and 'west'.
70. *Principia* II, arts. 36–44; AT viii$_1$. 61–7.
71. Julian B. Barbour, *Absolute or Relative Motion?* i: *The Discovery of Dynamics* (Cambridge, 1989), 460–1.
72. Cf. Koyré: 'It is, by the way, extremely probable that Descartes thought it out not for purely scientific reasons, but in order to escape the necessity of asserting the motion of the earth and to be able to affirm—with his tongue in his cheek—that the earth was at *rest* in its vortex' (Alexander Koyré, *From the Closed World to the Infinite Universe* (Baltimore, 1957), 143). See also the similar assessment in Eric Aiton, *The Vortex Theory of Planetary Motions* (London, 1972), 33.
73. *Principia* II, art. 31; AT viii$_1$. 57.
74. As I indicated in the last chapter, Descartes occasionally allows that the mind can set bodies in motion, e.g. Descartes to Arnauld, 29 July 1648 (AT v. 222), and Descartes to More [Aug. 1649] (AT v. 403–4).
75. Martial Guéroult, 'The Metaphysics and Physics of Force in Descartes', in Stephen Gaukroger (ed.), *Descartes: Philosophy, Mathematics and Physics* (Brighton, 1980), 197. Garber, *Descartes' Metaphysical Physics*, 297, draws a distinction between God's sustaining activity and His activity in conserving the total quantity of motion, and argues that Guéroult (and, following him, Gabbey) is wrong to treat these as the same thing. This seems to me to be quite mistaken, although I do concede that this is a grey area.

76. Gabbey, 'Force and Inertia in the Seventeenth Century: Descartes and Newton', 234–9.
77. Ibid. 238. Gabbey also unaccountably refers to God as 'the only true substance' for Descartes, a peculiar claim that would make him at best an Averroist and at worst a Spinozist.
78. AT ix$_2$. 19.
79. See Verbeek, *Descartes and the Dutch*, 54.
80. See Regius to Descartes, 23 July 1645; AT iv. 255.
81. See Garber, *Descartes' Metaphysical Physics*, 62 and 327, n. 68.
82. Descartes to Regius [July 1645]; AT iv. 248.
83. AT i. 559–60.
84. *Principia* IV, art. 205; AT viii$_1$. 328.
85. See my 'Descartes: Methodology', in G. Parkinson (ed.), *The Renaissance and Seventeenth-Century Rationalism* (London, 1993), 167–200.
86. See my 'The Sources of Descartes' Procedure of Deductive Demonstration in Metaphysics and Natural Philosophy', in J. Cottingham (ed.), *Reason, Will and Sensation* (Oxford, 1994), 47–60.
87. *Principia* IV, arts. 133–83; AT viii$_1$. 275–311.
88. William Gilbert, *On the Magnet* (New York, 1958), 65–71.
89. *Principia* IV, art. 179; AT viii$_1$. 307–8.
90. See *Principia* III, arts. 87–93; AT viii$_1$. 143–7.
91. *Principia* IV, art. 133; AT viii$_1$. 276.
92. *Principia* IV, art. 184–6; AT viii$_1$. 311–14.
93. See Alexander Koyré, *Newtonian Studies* (London, 1965), ch. 3.
94. *Sir Isaac Newton's Mathematical Principles of Natural Philosophy and his System of the World*, trans. Andrew Motte, rev. Florian Cajori, 2 vols. (New York, 1971), ii. 543. See the discussions in Richard S. Westfall, *Force in Newton's Physics* (London, 1971), 510–12, and Alan E. Shapiro, 'Light, Pressure, and Rectilinear Propagation: Descartes' Celestial Optics and Newton's Hydrostatics', *Studies in History and Philosophy of Science* 5 (1974), 239–96.
95. See Desmond M. Clarke, *Occult Powers and Hypotheses* (Oxford, 1989), 158–9 and 186–7.
96. There is a detailed account of these later attempts in Aiton, *The Vortex Theory of Plantary Motions*, chs. 7–10.
97. See my 'The Metaphysics of Impenetrability: Euler's Conception of Force', Gabbey, 'The Mechanical Philosophy and its Problems', and more generally Clifford Truesdell, *Essays in the History of Mechanics* (New York, 1968).

Chapter 10

1. See the summary accounts in *Écrivains* 585–94 and Jack R. Vrooman, *René Descartes: A Biography* (New York, 1970), 194–7.
2. 'Monsieur Grat' is mentioned in Baillet ii. 456.
3. Ibid. 553–5.
4. Descartes to [Huygens?] [1648?]; AT v. 262–5.
5. I know of no recent biography of Elizabeth. The principal sources on her life are Gottschalk Guhrauer, 'Elizabeth, Pfalzgräfin bei Rhein, Äbtissin von Herford', *Raumers Historisches Taschenbuch*, pt. iii (1850), ser. 1: 1–150; ser. 2: 417–554; Louis Foucher de Careil, *Descartes, la princesse palatine et la reine Christine*, 2nd edn. (Paris, 1909); and Elizabeth Godfrey, *A Sister of Prince Rupert* (New York, 1909). Adam 401–31 and *Écrivains* 603–39 provide more recent and more accessible accounts. Vrooman, *René Descartes*, ch. 6, presents an engaging portrait of Elizabeth based on these sources. See also Marguerite Néel, *Descartes et la princesse Elizabeth* (Paris, 1946).

6. AT iii. 577–8.
7. *Écrivains* 604.
8. Susanna Åkerman, *Queen Christina of Sweden and her Circle* (Leiden, 1991), 45–6.
9. *Écrivains* 606.
10. Ibid. 607.
11. Elizabeth to Descartes [16] May 1643; AT iii. 662.
12. On the Leiden dispute see Theo Verbeek, *Descartes and the Dutch* (Carbondale, Ill., 1992), 34–51.
13. Heereabord cannot have known much about the details of Descartes' philosophy in the early stages of his teaching, and probably owed more to Bacon and Ramus. See ibid. 35.
14. See ibid. 47.
15. Verbeek (ibid. 61–70) argues that their attitude was actually quite even-handed.
16. Descartes to Elizabeth, 28 June 1643; AT iii. 693.
17. Descartes to Pollot, 18 May 1645; AT iv. 204–5.
18. See Descartes' letter to Pollot of 21 Oct. and [Nov.] 1643; AT iv. 26 and 43.
19. Descartes to Elizabeth [Nov. 1643]; AT iv. 38–42.
20. AT vi. 62.
21. Descartes to Chanut, 15 June 1646; AT iv. 441–2.
22. Elizabeth to Descartes [16] May 1643: AT iii. 661.
23. Descartes to Elizabeth, 21 May 1643; AT iii. 664–5.
24. AT vii. 441–2.
25. Descartes to Elizabeth, 21 May 1643; AT iii. 667.
26. AT iii. 505.
27. AT iii. 691.
28. *Principia* II, art. 2; AT viii$_1$. 41.
29. See Anthony Levi, *French Moralists* (Oxford, 1964), esp. ch. 9, and H. M. Gardiner, Ruth Clarke Metcalf, and John Beebe-Center, *Feeling and Emotion* (New York, 1937), ch. 5.
30. Nicolas Coëffeteau, *Tableau des passions humaines, de leurs causes et de leurs effets* (Paris, 1630), 12.
31. Descartes to Mersenne, 18 Jan. 1641: AT iii. 296.
32. On Cureau see Levi, *French Moralists*, 248–56.
33. More to Descartes, 23 July 1649: AT v. 382.
34. AT ix$_2$. 76.
35. Descartes to More [Aug. 1649]; AT v. 403–4.
36. See Daniel Garber, *Descartes' Metaphysical Physics* (Chicago, 1992), 299–305.
37. Cf. Descartes to Arnauld, 29 July 1648: 'That the mind, which is incorporeal, can set a body in motion is shown to us every day by the most certain and most evident experience, without the need of any reasoning or comparison with anything else' (AT v. 222).
38. See John Cottingham, 'Cartesian Trialism', *Mind* 95 (1985), 218–30.
39. I don't mean that there are literally no problems here—the question of criteria for personal identity is riddled with problems—merely that the kind of thing one should look to in order to provide such criteria is reasonably clear. In the case of disembodied minds it is not. For a discussion of the philosophical problem of disembodied minds see Terence Penelhum, *Survival and Disembodied Existence* (London, 1968).
40. This is in fact the direction that Malebranche, inadvertently but unavoidably, will take Cartesianism, although the doctrine of the substantial union cannot be blamed in Malebranche's case because the union begins to look distinctly insubstantial in Malebranche.
41. The first mention is in Descartes to Mersenne [1 Apr. 1640]; AT iii. 48. On

intellectual memory see J. J. MacIntosh, 'Perception and Imagination in Descartes, Boyle, and Hooke', *Canadian Journal of Philosophy* 13 (1983), 327–52, and John Sutton, 'Connecting Memory Traces: Studies of Neurophilosophical Theories of Memory, Mental Representation, and Personal Identity from Descartes to New Connectionism', Ph.D. dissertation (University of Sydney, 1993), 84–101.

42. Descartes to [Huygens] [13 Oct. 1642]; AT iii. 580.
43. Conversation with Burman; AT v. 150.
44. Descartes to *** [Aug. 1641]; AT iii. 425.
45. Descartes to the Marquess of Newcastle, 23 Nov. 1646; AT iv. 574–5.
46. Descartes to More, 5 Feb. 1649; AT v. 278.
47. Descartes to [Gibieuf] [19 Jan. 1642]; AT iii. 479.
48. Descartes to Mersenne [Nov. or Dec. 1632]; AT i. 263.
49. Descartes to [Gibieuf], [19 Jan. 1642]; AT iii. 479.
50. Cf. *Principia* I, art. 9; AT viii. 7–8. There Descartes points to what he considers an ambiguity in the expression 'I see', distinguishing between mere vision and the 'actual sense or awareness of seeing'.
51. See Letizia A. Panizza, 'Stoic Psychotherapy in the Middle Ages and Renaissance: Petrarch's *De remediis*', in M. Osler (ed.), *Atoms, Pneuma, and Tranquillity* (Cambridge, 1991), 39–66.
52. *Passions*, art. 212; AT xi. 488.
53. AT ix$_2$. 14.
54. We have to begin by asking the Socratic question that Bernard Williams urges us to ask: 'what part might be played by knowledge of the sciences; how far purely rational enquiry might take us; how far the answer to the question might be expected to be different if it is asked in one society rather than another; how much, at the end of all that, must be left to personal decision': *Ethics and the Limits of Philosophy* (London, 1985), 3. Were more historians of ethics sensitive to such questions, there would not be such a hiatus in histories of ethics between the Stoics and Kant's immediate predecessors in the eighteenth century. Indeed, more attention to this period might teach us something about the nature of our own dominant narrow ethical discourse, so effectively criticized by Williams.
55. The Stoic/Augustinian polarity extends beyond the question of the passions, and is a key one in Renaissance thought. See William J. Bouwsma, 'The Two Faces of Humanism: Stoicism and Augustinianism in Renaissance Thought', in H. Oberman and T. Brady (eds.), *Itinerarium Italicum* (Leiden, 1975), 3–60.
56. See Levi, *French Moralists*, 15–19.
57. On the difference between Augustine's account of moral responsibility and that of his predecessors, see the exemplary account in Albrecht Dihle, *The Theory of the Will in Classical Antiquity* (Berkeley, Calif., 1982).
58. Augustine, *Civ. Dei.*, XIV, ch. 6.
59. Ibid., ch. 8.
60. Aquinas, *Summ. theol.*, Qu. XXIV, arts. 1–2.
61. Ibid., Qu. XXIII, art. 4.
62. Ibid., Qu. XXV, art. 4.
63. Gardiner *et al.*, *Feeling and Emotion*, 110.
64. Aquinas, *Summ. theol.*, Qu. XLV, art. 3.
65. Quoted in Gardiner *et al.*, *Feeling and Emotion*, 115.
66. Ibid. 116.
67. The most comprehensive account of Vives' contribution is Carlos G. Noreña, *Juan Luis Vives and the Emotions* (Carbondale, Ill., 1989).
68. Levi, *French Moralists*, 26.
69. Ibid. 27.
70. On this revival see Léontine Zanta, *La Renaissance du stoïcisme au XVIe siècle* (Paris, 1914).

71. What follows is derived largely from the exemplary discussion in Levi, *French Moralists*, ch. 6.
72. Ibid. 155.
73. This correspondence is collected in English translation, with a very useful introductory essay, in John J. Blom, *Descartes: His Moral Philosophy and Psychology* (Hassocks, 1978).
74. Descartes to Elizabeth, 1 Sept. 1645; AT iv. 282.
75. Descartes to Elizabeth [Nov. 1646]; AT iv. 529.
76. See Descartes to Chanut, 15 June 1646; AT iv. 442.
77. Descartes to Chanut, 15 June 1646; AT iv. 441.
78. AT ix$_2$. 14, 17.
79. *Passions*, reply to second letter; AT xi. 326. I am especially indebted in my account of the *Passions* to the introduction and notes in Geneviève Rodis-Lewis (ed.), *Descartes: Les Passions de l'âme* (Paris, 1970), and to Levi, *French Moralists*, chs. 9 and 10.
80. In her introduction to Stephen Voss (ed. and trans.), *René Descartes: The Passions of the Soul* (Indianapolis, 1989), pp. xvi–xvii.
81. *Passions*, art. 2; AT xi. 328.
82. See Descartes to Elizabeth, 21 May 1643; AT iii. 666.
83. *Passions*, art. 25; AT xi. 347.
84. *Passions*, art. 26; AT xi. 348–9.
85. *Passions*, art. 36; AT xi. 357–8.
86. *Passions*, art. 47; AT xi. 364.
87. *Passions*, art. 48; AT xi. 367.
88. *Passions*, art. 75; AT xi. 384
89. *Passions*, art. 68; AT xi. 379.
90. *Passions*, art. 91; AT xi. 397.
91. *Principia* IV, art. 190; AT viii$_1$. 317.
92. I follow Voss in translating 'émotions intérieures' as inner *excitations* rather than inner *emotions*: see Voss, *René Descartes*, 138.
93. *Passions*, art. 147; AT xi. 440–1. The first example suggests to me a low view of women on Descartes' part: I cannot imagine him putting the example the other way round, so that it is the wife who feels a secret joy at her husband's death.
94. *Passions*, art. 148; AT xi. 441–2.
95. AT iv. 601.
96. AT iv. 603–4.
97. *Passions*, art. 153; AT xi. 445–6.
98. Descartes to Elizabeth, May or June 1645; AT iv. 219–20.
99. Descartes to Mersenne, 13 Nov. 1639; AT ii. 619.
100. *Anatomica quaedam ex M^{to} Cartesii*; AT xi. 549–634.
101. *Anatomica*; AT xi. 551.
102. e.g. AT xi. 587.
103. The most important of these is the *Primae cogitationes circa generationem animalium et nonnulla de saporibus*, given at AT xi. 505–42 (with an introduction covering questions of dating and authenticity on 501–4) and various anatomical excerpts taken by Leibniz and edited by Foucher de Careil which Adam and Tannery refer to as *Excerpta anatomica*, the text being given at AT xi. 549–634.
104. The text is given at AT xi. 223–86.
105. Descartes to Elizabeth, 31 Jan. 1648; AT v. 112.
106. See the conversation with Burman, AT v. 170.
107. AT iv. 555.
108. AT xi. 614–21.
109. Elizabeth to Descartes [30 Nov. 1645]; AT iv. 335–7.
110. Descartes to Elizabeth [January 1646]; AT iv. 351–2. Cf. his remark in his *Notae*

in Programma that he 'does not wish to appear to be assuming the right to question someone else's religion' (AT viii₁. 353).

111. The generally accepted view is that Elizabeth was banished by her mother, but it is possible that she made her journey to represent the family's interest to the Elector of Brandenburg: cf. Adam 424.
112. See Descartes to Elizabeth [Sept. 1646]; AT iv. 486–93.
113. Descartes to Elizabeth [10 May 1647]; AT v. 15–16.
114. AT v. 2–12.
115. For the details of the meeting see *Écrivains* 637–8.
116. AT viii₁. 345.
117. AT viii₁. 357–8.
118. AT viii₁. 358–9.
119. Indeed, he is not even always particularly concerned to make a sharp distinction between the mind or soul and the brain. In Discourse 4 of the *Dioptrique*, for example, he tells us that 'we know for certain that it is the soul (*l'âme*) that has sensations, not the body'. This passage strongly suggests the widely accepted (but incorrect) view that for Descartes sensations are something that are peculiar to the incorporeal. But it turns out that what he means is that sensations occur in the brain and not in the sense organs (a view held by the Epicureans, for example). For he goes on to say that it is not, strictly speaking, because of the presence of the soul in the sense organs that it has sensations, 'but because of its presence in the brain, where it exercises the faculty of common sense. For we observe injuries and disease which just attack the brain and impede all the senses generally, even though the rest of the body continues to be animated' (AT vi. 109). That is, the soul is in the sense organs as well as in the brain, but it is its presence in the brain that is responsible for sensation, for brain injuries impede sensation. The question whether sensation takes place in a corporeal organ or in an incorporeal substance is just not an issue for Descartes, just as whether 'ideas' are corporeal or incorporeal is not an issue. For the later Cartesians such as Malebranche, these are the pivotal questions, and almost all contemporary commentators have tried to read this concern back into Descartes.
120. See Verbeek, *Descartes and the Dutch*, 70–7, on this circle.
121. Clauberg was to be the first Cartesian of note in Germany, becoming professor of philosophy and theology at Duisberg in 1651. Elizabeth had a hand in ensuring that Cartesianism was well represented at the new University of Duisberg through her cousin, Frederick William, Elector of Brandenberg, who was the driving force behind setting up the university.
122. AT v. 165.
123. On this trip see *Écrivains* ch. 25.
124. Descartes to Chanut [May 1648]; AT v. 183.
125. 'I went to Paris to buy a parchment—the most expensive and useless I have ever received': Descartes to Chanut [31 Mar. 1649]; AT v. 326.
126. Descartes to Chanut, 26 Feb. 1649; AT v. 292.
127. Descartes to Chanut [31 Mar. 1649]; AT v. 328–9.
128. More to Descartes, 11 Dec. 1648; AT v. 238–9. See the discussion in Alexandre Koyré, *From the Closed World to the Infinite Universe* (Baltimore, 1957), ch. 5.
129. Elizabeth to Descartes, 30 June [1648]; AT v. 195–7.
130. On Chanut's life see Adam 512–14, n. *a*.
131. There may have been political reasons behind this. Åkerman notes: 'The Sveo-Gallic alliance had lately been threatened by the presence of anti-royalist libertines at the Swedish court and Chanut wanted to provide a more orthodox French influence on the Queen' (*Queen Christina*, 45).
132. Quoted ibid. 259.
133. Descartes told Christina that he did not necessarily intend staying in a permanent

capacity, and he wrote to Elizabeth on 9 Oct. 1649 that he might not stay beyond the summer: AT v. 431.

134. Descartes to Chanut, 1 Nov. 1646; AT iv. 535.

135. Descartes to Christina [26 Feb. 1649]; AT v. 294.

136. *Écrivains* 643, n. 2, points out that it is remarkable how many references there are to Elizabeth in Descartes' correspondence with Chanut. Note e.g. his otherwise gratuitous mention of Elizabeth in his first letter to Chanut of 1 Nov. 1646; AT iv. 534.

137. M xvi. 195.

138. See Åkerman, *Queen Christina*, 46–7.

139. See the bemused description by Brasset, secretary of the French embassy at The Hague: AT v. 411.

140. Baillet ii. 388.

141. See Åkerman, *Queen Christina*, 44–69, and esp. her discussion (pp. 55–69) of the thesis in Ernst Cassirer, *Descartes: Lehre—Persönlichkeit—Wirkung* (Stockholm, 1939), that Christina's conversion was helped by her embracing a Cartesian methodology.

142. Descartes to Elizabeth [9 Oct. 1649]; AT v. 430.

143. See Richard A. Watson, 'René Descartes n'est pas l'auteur de *La Naissance de la paix*', *Archives de philosophie* 53 (1990), 389–401.

144. The letters began to appear in various editions from 1663 onwards, although there were gaping lacunae in what was published: e.g. the letters to Elizabeth were not published until 1879, and a large part of the correspondence between Descartes and Huygens was not discovered until this century. Moreover, standards of editing were often poor. Roth, who discovered and published the correspondence with Huygens in 1926, noted numerous errors and omissions in Clerselier's edition when he compared this with the newly discovered originals.

145. For the details of Descartes' last days see Baillet ii. 414–23.

146. I have followed the summary in Åkerman, *Queen Christina*, 51–2. Huet's report that he got the story from Chanut is implausible, because Baillet worked from Chanut's memoirs and would surely have drawn attention to such an odd episode.

147. See AT v. 468–9.

148. These sources are reproduced at AT v. 470–500.

149. I follow the summary in G. A. Lindeboom, *Descartes and Medicine* (Amsterdam, 1979), 13–14.

150. If indeed there is a skull in with the remains. Berzelius reports that no skull was found among the bones when the remains were moved to St. Germain-des-Prés in 1819.

151. See E. Weil, 'The Skull of Descartes', *Journal of the History of Medicine and Allied Sciences* 11 (1956), 220–1.

152. See Johan Nordström, 'Till Descartes' ikonografi', *Lychnos* (1957–8), 194–250, which I have not been able to consult, but whose argument is reported in Gregor Sebba, *Bibliographia Cartesianà: A Critical Guide to the Descartes Literature, 1800–1960* (The Hague, 1964), 3.

Biographical Sketches

The name entries in the Index contain very brief biographical information, but there is some need for rather longer entries on a selection of some of the more obscure or more important figures. I have concentrated on Descartes' contemporaries and two of his early biographers, and I have included very little bibliographical material. Bibliographies of philosophers (broadly construed) in France and the Netherlands in the seventeenth century can be obtained from the exhaustive surveys in Jean-Pierre Schobinger (ed.), *Die Philosophie des 17. Jahrhunderts, ii: Frankreich und Niederlande*, 2 vols. (Basle, 1993). For bibliographical material on scientists, as well as more extensive biographical detail, the reader should begin by consulting Charles Coulston Gillispie (ed.), *Dictionary of Scientific Biography*, 16 vols. (New York, 1970–80).

ARNAULD, Antoine (1612–94), was born into a family closely associated with Jansenism, his sister Angélique reforming the Port-Royal along Jansenist lines after becoming Abbess. He studied theology at the Sorbonne, and was ordained a priest and awarded a doctorate in theology in 1641. At the invitation of Mersenne, he contributed a set of objections to the *Meditationes* which show remarkable philosophical depth. Descartes held him in high regard, and he was to develop a particularly sophisticated, realist version of the Cartesian doctrine of ideas in his *Des vrais et fausses idées* (1683). His earlier *La Logique, ou l'art de penser* of 1662 (better known as the *Port-Royal Logic*) was an extremely influential account of the kind of psychologized logic/method that flourished at that time. His collected writings, mostly on theological questions but containing a lot of material on philosophy, and some on mathematics, make up 43 volumes. A fierce and able opponent of the Jesuits on philosophical and theological matters, Arnauld was expelled from the Sorbonne in 1655 and spent much of his life in exile, first in the Netherlands and then in Belgium.

BAILLET, Adrien (1649–1706), was author of the first comprehensive biography of Descartes. Born into a peasant family, he was noted for his unkempt and ascetic appearance. After studying theology, he spent some years as a schoolmaster and was appointed in 1680 as librarian in the house of Lamoignon, the *avocat général*, who had inherited a magnificent collection of books from his father, first president of the *parlement* of Paris. Within six months Baillet had reclassified and reshelved the entire collection, and in the next two years he had compiled a classified index of the collection which filled thirty-two folio volumes. Once he had finished this, however, he began to think how much more valuable a comprehensive classification of the whole of knowledge would be, and he began on his project of publishing a catalogue covering authors' contributions, and critical assessments by other authors, in every area of knowledge from botany to philology, poetry to law, mathematics to theology. From the 'general plan' of the *Jugements des savants*, it appears that the project was to comprise around 130 large folio volumes, although only nine appeared before the project was abandoned in 1694. It brought him significant controversy, not least because of the attacks on the French etymologist Gilles Ménage contained therein; and the situation was exacerbated by Baillet's association with the Jansenists and Ménage's association with the Jesuits at a time of fierce controversy between the two. Baillet's life of Descartes went to press in 1691. Drawing on the full range of published and unpublished sources, he was able to compile an account of Descartes' life that went far beyond anything that had been put together up to that time. He seems to have been somewhat reluctant to take on the task, for he evidently had no great liking for Descartes, except for the last ten years of his life, in which he saw Descartes as leading an ascetic existence (Francine notwithstanding) which he himself coveted (his early ambition had been to become a Trappist monk). It was his collaborator, the Abbé Jean-Baptiste Legrand, who had initially intended to write the work, and he had been given Chanut's (q.v.) memoires by Clerselier (q.v.) for that purpose, but it was Baillet—who, it should be noted, was engaged in another major project, discovering the true identities of authors who wrote under pseudonyms—who was left to produce the biography, the first volume (of two) apparently appearing within a year of his starting serious work on it. In 1691 a royal ban on the teaching of Cartesianism was in place in France, and Baillet's biography was politically explosive: not only Baillet but his patron, Lamoignon, came under pressure. Despite its flaws, Baillet's biography remains far and away the single most important source of our knowledge of Descartes' life after his own writings.

BALZAC, Jean-Louis Guez de (c.1595–1654), had attended Jesuit colleges in Angoulême, Poitiers, and Paris, and like Descartes had travelled in Italy and the Netherlands. He was one of the great French stylists of his day, instrumental in shifting the French language away from an exuberant renaissance style to the neo-classical style that came to dominate French letters in the seventeenth century. His *Lettres* of 1624 immediately raised him to a prominent position in the literary-political world of the French court, although he was disappointed in his political aspirations at an early stage, and retreated to his family château at Angoulême. Balzac and Descartes were of the same age and had rather similar backgrounds, and they seem to have been friends throughout the 1620s. In March 1628 Descartes wrote a long open letter in defence of Balzac's literary style, and he kept up an affectionate correspondence into the 1630s.

BEAUGRAND, Jean (c.1595–1640), French lawyer and mathematician, author of a treatise on geostatics (1636). He was one of a select few familiar with the writings of Vieta (q.v.), and edited some of his works for publication. Friendly with Fermat (q.v.) and Mersenne (q.v.), he was highly regarded in French mathematical circles. He became mathematician to Gaston d'Orléans in 1630, and he was charged, as the secretary to the *Chancelier*, with looking through applications for the King's *privilège*. In this capacity he came across Mersenne's application for a *privilège* for Descartes' *Discours* and *Essais* at the beginning of 1637. Believing that Descartes had plagiarized his mathematical material from Vieta and Harriot, he engaged in a very acrimonious dispute with Descartes, pursued at times through anonymous pamphlets.

BEECKMAN, Isaac (1588–1637), began by studying for the Dutch Reformed ministry first at Leiden, then at Saumur, until 1612, although he had learned mathematics, nautical science, and Hebrew privately at the same time. He did not take up a ministry but entered his father's factory making candles and water conduits, subsequently laying water conduits in Zeeland, but also carrying out experiments in combustion, hydraulics, and hydrodynamics, and working through a number of fundamental questions in mechanics and acoustics. By 1613 he had formulated a theory of inertia which went beyond the standard *impetus* account, and had an advanced understanding of collision. At the same time he was completing a degree in medicine, graduating from the University of Caen in 1616, although he never practised medicine. From 1618 onwards he made a living as an educational administrator, setting up a Collegium Mechanicum for craftsman and scholars to study mechanics and its technological applications, and in 1628 he set up the first meteorological station in Europe. At the end of 1618 he met Descartes, and although there was some degree of mutual collaboration in their relationship, Descartes learned from Beeckman the basics of a micro-corpuscularian approach

Biographical Notes

to mechanics. After Descartes left the Netherlands in 1619, the two corresponded regularly at first, a correspondence which shows the very extensive degree of personal and intellectual indebtedness on Descartes' part. They met again in 1628, but the relation soured when Descartes unjustly accused Beeckman of boasting about what Descartes had learned from him. Although subsequently reconciled, their relationship never had its former warmth. Beeckman published nothing other than his MD thesis, but kept an invaluable diary recording all his experiments, correspondence, theories, etc. This diary was edited by Cornelius de Waard and appeared in four volumes between 1939 and 1953 (the original was lost in a bombing raid in the war). Because of the very unsystematic way in which he pursued and reported on his researches, Beeckman's contribution to seventeenth-century science has been largely neglected, but his diary reveals him to have been a key figure.

BÉRULLE, Pierre de (1575–1629), was ordained a priest in 1599; in 1611, with five other priests from the Sorbonne, he founded the Oratory. He was very active in the reform of the religious orders and the priesthood generally, and was made a cardinal in 1627. Bérulle took an active role in Parisian political and intellectual life, and in October 1628 Descartes had an audience with him at which he encouraged Descartes to pursue his researches. Bérulle was instrumental in the Augustinian revival in France, a movement which was to have great success in theology and philosophy, e.g. in the work of Malebranche (q.v.), who managed to put an Augustinian gloss on Descartes' writings.

BURMAN, Frans (1628–79), matriculated in theology at the University of Leiden in 1643. He belonged to an early network of Dutch Cartesians active in the 1640s which included Clauberg. On 16 April 1648 he interviewed Descartes, and the record of the interview survives. He subsequently went on to become professor of theology at Utrecht, founding a Cartesian club there, the 'College der Sçavanten'.

CHANUT, Hector-Pierre (1601–62), began his career as a financial controller in the town of Riom, near Clermont-Ferrand, moving to Sweden in 1645 to take up a diplomatic post there, and becoming French ambassador to Sweden in 1649. He married Marguerite Clerselier, sister of Claude (q.v.), in 1626, and through Claude came to know Descartes. He acted as an intermediary between Descartes and Queen Christina (q.v.), and was instrumental in getting Descartes to move to Sweden in 1649. Descartes stayed with the Chanut family while in Sweden. After Descartes' death Chanut became ambassador to the Netherlands. He was consulted for information about Descartes in the 1650s, and his memoirs were passed on to Clerselier at his death, who passed them on to the Abbé Legrand in order that a biography of Descartes might be written, although this task was in fact completed by Legrand's collaborator Baillet (q.v.).

CHARLET, Étienne (1570–1652), was the second Jesuit Rector of La Flèche, appointed in 1607. He was from Poitou and was closely related to the Brochard line of Descartes' family, as well as having cousins in the Rennes *parlement* where Descartes' father was a parliamentarian. In a letter of 1645 Descartes wrote to Charlet that he had been a second father to him while he was at La Flèche. Charlet was appointed one of the five assistants to the Jesuit superior in Rome in 1627, a position he held until 1646.

CHARRON, Pierre (1541–1603), was born in Paris, one of twenty-five children. He studied Greek, Latin, and philosophy at the Sorbonne, then law, and finally theology. He was a prominent theologian and preacher until he met Montaigne (q.v.) in 1589; thenceforth he devoted himself to developing what he saw as the key elements in Montaigne's thought. His *De La Sagesse* of 1601 was to eclipse even Montaigne's own essays in the seventeenth century, even though it is really a rather derivative amalgam of elements taken from Montaigne and others. He was regarded as an incorrigible sceptic/relativist, and *De La Sagesse* was widely criticized throughout the seventeenth century.

Biographical Notes

CHRISTINA, Queen of Sweden (1626–89), was daughter of King Gustav II and Maria Eleonora of Brandenburg, and was crowned when she came of age in 1644. She made great efforts to transform the Swedish court into a centre of learning, and although she shows some enthusiasm for Descartes' philosophy, her interest really lay in the areas of classical philology represented by humanists such as Isaac Vossius. She converted to Catholicism in 1654 and abdicated as a result, but remained embroiled in various political intrigues throughout the rest of her life, and seems to have shunned religious orthodoxy of any kind.

CLAVIUS, Christoph (1537–1612), entered the Jesuit order at Rome in 1555, later studying at the University of Coimbra in Portugal, one of the principal centres of Jesuit thought. He was professor of mathematics at the Collegio Romano in Rome from 1565 until his death. He wrote comprehensive works on geometry, arithmetic, and algebra, as well as a defence of the Ptolemaic system against Copernicus, but he remained a close friend of Galileo. He played a key role in the improvement of the Julian calendar, and while not an innovator was one of the ablest mathematicians of his generation. His textbooks were used extensively in mathematics and mechanics courses in Jesuit colleges, and it is largely due to his influence that such subjects figured in the curriculum at these colleges.

CLERSELIER, Claude (1614–84) was a French government officer and one of the first (and one of the staunchest) supporters of Descartes in France. Although he made a contribution to the development of Cartesian philosophy his importance derives from his publication of various writings of Descartes. As well as bringing out *Le Monde* (1677) and *L'Homme* (1664), he may also have been responsible for the publication of the *Passions* in 1649. When the ship carrying Descartes' letters back to France after his death sank, Clerselier set an army of servants drying out the rescued documents, and he set to work classifying and dating them, bringing out the first edition of Descartes' correspondence in three volumes between 1657 and 1667.

DELLA PORTA, Giambattista (1535–1615) was a Neapolitan natural philosopher and mathematician. Probably self-taught, he published in a wide range of areas including cryptography, mnemonics, human and plant physiognomy, horticulture, military fortification, distillation, meteorology, hydraulics, and astronomy. His writings on natural magic and optics were very popular in the first decades of the seventeenth century, and seem to have been available at La Flèche, where Descartes read them. His fascination with optical illusions gave the books a broad appeal, and they were instrumental in cultivating an interest in optics in Descartes.

DIGBY, Sir Kenelm (1603–65), was one of Descartes' early English admirers. From a staunchly Catholic and Royalist family, he spent much of the years 1635–1660 in exile in Paris. It was probably Digby who invited Descartes to England in 1640, an invitation Descartes apparently considered seriously. In 1644 he published in Paris his *Two Treatises*, the first exposition of Cartesian philosophy in English, although it is actually an eclectic mix of Cartesianism and Aristotelianism.

ELIZABETH, Princess of Bohemia (1618–80), was the eldest daughter of Elizabeth Stuart and Frederick V. The family were forced into exile in the Netherlands in 1620, and were dogged by lack of funds and a number of family tragedies. Elizabeth and Descartes had an immensely fruitful correspondence, principally on the passions, in the 1640s, and Descartes showed great concern for her welfare. She left the Netherlands in 1646, and although he visited her rarely when she was living there, he was clearly at a loss when she left: indeed, it is likely that he had a very strong personal attachment to her. He dedicated both his *Principia* and his *Passions* to her, and it is possible that his move to Sweden in 1649 was motivated partly by an attempt to secure Queen Christina's (q.v.) patronage for her. After Descartes' death, Elizabeth played a role in establishing

Cartesianism in Germany. She ended her days as Abbess of a Lutheran monastery at Herford in Westphalia.

FAULHABER, Johannes (1580–1635) was born at Ulm, where he lived throughout his life, probably teaching at the military engineering college there. He began publishing mathematical treatises in 1604, and in the earlier writings he seems to have been especially interested in arithmetic and scientific instruments. From 1613 onwards his writings took on Rosicrucian turn, as he became interested in biblical prophesy, the Cabbala, and the work of Agrippa. He was the first to publish a work addressed to the Rosicrucians, the *Mysterium Arithmeticum* of 1615. In late 1619 and early 1620, he and Descartes struck up a friendship, which does not seem to have continued after Descartes left Ulm.

FERMAT, Pierre de (1601–65), was a Toulouse lawyer and parliamentarian, classical scholar and philologist. Above all, he was one of the most imaginative and brilliant mathematicians of the seventeenth century, making crucial contributions to most areas of mathematics in his day, including analytic geometry, number theory, and probability theory. His researches in analytic geometry overlapped with those of Descartes, and in 1637 he subjected Descartes' geometrical optics to a number of profound criticisms, subsequently going on to develop his own general optics. Descartes refused to read Fermat's works, believing (incorrectly) that he could have nothing to learn from them.

FERRIER, Guillaume [or Jean?] (fl. 1620–40), French maker of optical instruments. Descartes, Mydorge (q.v.), and others worked with a Ferrier in the mid-1620s, although there were a number of Ferriers active in optical manufacturing in Paris between 1620 and 1640, and it is unclear which of these was Descartes' collaborator. When Descartes moved to the Netherlands he invited Ferrier to join him, offering to pay his fares and put him up in his house, treating him like a brother. Ferrier, who seems to have been in some financial difficulty, was desperate for a patron, but prevaricated for a while; and when he finally did decide to join Descartes, the latter already had Villebressieu (q.v.) with him and wanted nothing to do with Ferrier. Descartes showed some concern that Ferrier would reveal his methods of calculating focal lengths and grinding various kinds of aspherical lenses, and treated him rather badly.

GALILEI, Galileo (1564–1642), Italian astronomer, mathematician, and natural philosopher. I shall confine myself to Galileo's direct relevance to Descartes. Descartes probably first came across the name of Galileo in the context of his discovery of the moons of Jupiter, which were celebrated at La Flèche in 1611, and Descartes himself composed some verses in their honour. Galileo was very much in favour with the Jesuits at this time, but after his first condemnation by the Inquisition in 1616 they began to take a different attitude. Galileo's interests and those of Descartes overlapped in numerous areas, from proportional compasses to musical theory, but the key areas were to be those of astronomy and mechanics. As the foremost defender of the Copernican model of the solar system, Galileo played a key role in dictating the terms of the debate around Copernicanism—the importance of an understanding of inertia, and of accounting for the tides, for example, were a crucial part of his defence—and his second condemnation in 1633 was a very significant blow to the Copernican cause, for it effectively closed off the possibility that examination of such questions was compelling as far as the Church was concerned. Descartes had developed a full mechanical defence of the heliocentric theory by this stage, and he was devastated by the 1633 condemnation. His whole approach to questions in natural philosophy was significantly altered as a result. As regards mechanics, Galileo's approach to mechanical questions was very different from that of Descartes. He concentrated on kinematics, and in particular on accounting for the motion of isolated bodies in a void, with a view to building up from this an account of their behaviour in resisting media. Descartes, by contrast, did not see the medium through which a body moves in terms of resistance at all, but in terms of the

Biographical Notes

system of constraints which determines the body's physical behaviour. His approach pictured the planets being carried around the sun by the celestial fluid, for example, something which initially (before the appearance of Newtonian dynamics) appeared much more plausible, simpler, and much less mysterious than Galileo's approach. Descartes apparently never met Galileo, even though he passed through Florence while Galileo was living there.

GARASSE, François (1585–1631), was a French Jesuit who, shocked by the *libertinage* of his age, which he tended to trace back to Charron (q.v.), set about attacking all forms of *libertinage* in an ideological and polemical (some might say demented) way in the 1620s. His attempt to counter virtually any form of unorthodox thought by means of interminably long polemical diatribes against various 'Troglodytes' and 'village rats' was not an intellectual success, but had some influence in reinforcing the repressive climate of Paris in the 1620s.

GASSENDI, Pierre (1592–1655), received his doctorate in theology from Avignon in 1614 and was ordained a priest in 1616. In the 1620s he moved in the Mersenne (q.v.) circle, and carried out a number of astronomical observations with Mydorge (q.v.). His work of the 1620s is characterized by a radical anti-Aristotelianism, and he began a detailed study of Epicureanism, believing that it had been completely misrepresented in earlier times, and that it provided a more secure foundation for Christian theology than Aristotelianism. He is probably the most famous advocate of atomism in the first half of the seventeenth century, and he did a good deal to rehabilitate atomism, even though his own writings on this topic, which all derive from the 1640s, are wordy and incomplete. He contributed a set of objections to Descartes' *Meditationes* and, unhappy with Descartes' response, subsequently set out his disagreement with him in more elaborate terms.

GIBIEUF, Guillaume (*c.*1591–1650), was a French theologian who graduated from the Sorbonne. He joined the Oratory at its founding in 1612. Throughout the 1920s he was working on a book on freedom of the will, and Descartes, who knew him at this time, was familiar with his thinking on the subject. Gibieuf took a sympathetic but critical interest in Descartes' philosophy in subsequent years, and Descartes seems to have respected his opinion.

HOBBES, Thomas (1588–1679). In the first stage of his career, Hobbes' interests were very much in line with late renaissance humanism: his interest in politics, for example, took the form of a translation of Thucydides, a favourite republican text. Around 1630, however, he began to take a serious interest in geometry, natural philosophy, and optics. In the mid-1630s he spent some time with Mersenne (q.v.), who introduced him to developments in French natural philosophy, and it was Mersenne who solicited a set of objections to Descartes' *Meditationes* from Hobbes. Although Descartes gave these relatively short shrift, and although they disagreed fundamentally in their optics (Descartes treating the speed and direction of a light ray as completely separate, whereas Hobbes saw them as part of the same thing), there was no significant animosity in their relationship, and they apparently met on friendly terms during Descartes' last trip to Paris in 1649. Hobbes always held Descartes in very high regard, although his interests overlapped to the greatest extent with those of Gassendi (q.v.).

HUYGENS, Constantijn (1596–1687), statesman and poet, was secretary to the Prince of Orange. He was a deeply cultured man, intensely interested in science, and he was one of Descartes' staunchest and most devoted admirers in the Netherlands. More important, he was someone of real influence who could offer some degree of protection to Descartes, although the relationship was never one of patron and client. They had a warm personal friendship, and Descartes took an interest in the education of his son Christiaan, who was to become one of the greatest natural philosophers and mathematicians of the seventeenth century.

476

Biographical Notes

KEPLER, Johannes (1571–1630), made crucial contributions to astronomy and optics. Descartes was not so much interested in the mathematical details of planetary orbits as in the structural features of the planetary system that guaranteed the stability of such orbits, and he seems to have taken no notice of Kepler's famous laws showing that the planets travelled in ellipses, although Beeckman (q.v.), who was studying Kepler at the time, probably brought this to Descartes' attention. Descartes himself seems to have made no study of Kepler's astronomical writings. The situation in optics, however, is quite the reverse, Descartes apparently having made a careful study of Kepler's pathbreaking *Ad Vitellionem* at an early stage.

LIPSTORP, Daniel (1631–84), was the first to publish a biography of Descartes—*Specimena Philosophiae Cartesianae* (Leiden, 1653)—although we know little of the author except that he was born in, and died in, Lübeck, and that he was registered as a 'student of philosophy' at the University of Leiden in 1652.

MALEBRANCHE, Nicolas (1638–1715), studied philosophy and theology at the Collège de La Marche and the Sorbonne, and was ordained and entered the Oratory in 1664. In the same year he read *L'Homme*, which Clerselier (q.v.) had just published, and reports that he was so excited that he suffered from palpitations of the heart. Through his *Recherche de la vérité* (1st edn. 1674/5) he quickly became the most influential Cartesian philosopher, and indeed before Locke the most influential philosopher of any kind in his era, eclipsing even Descartes. He mixed elements of Cartesianism and Augustinianism to produce a doctrine among whose distinctive features were a commitment to an occasionalist account of the mind/body relation and an anti-realist view of perception in which we are perceptually aware not of the external world but of reified 'representations'. Since it was through Malebranche that many subsequent philosophers—especially British philosophers—learned their Descartes, his reading of Cartesian epistemology in particular, which was very different from what was in many ways the more subtle reading of Arnauld (q.v.), came to be the received view.

MERSENNE, Marin (1588–1648), was the son of a labourer, receiving a scholarship to La Flèche in 1604. He went on to study theology at the Sorbonne and classics at the Collège de France. He joined the Order of Minims in 1611, and was based at Nevers until 1619, when he returned to the Minim convent in Paris. He was remarkably erudite, having a command of many languages, including Hebrew, and just about every area of scientific research being pursued in his time. Between 1623 and 1625, around the time that Descartes first got to know him, he completed, after a couple of devotional works, four large comprehensive books attacking various forms of heresy. In the course of these works he made it clear that traditional Aristotelianism could not readily withstand the onslaught from various forms of naturalism, mortalism, and magic, and he elaborated a form of mechanism which was a formative ingredient in Descartes' thinking about mechanism. Later in the 1620s he compiled a large collection of mathematical writings, and began to publish in the one area of science to which he made a lasting contribution, acoustics. Mersenne was an indefatigable correspondent (the modern edition of his correspondence runs to nearly 10,000 pages), and his correspondence forms the best guide to scientific thought in the years 1629–48. His access to an unparalleled range of correspondents was due in no small part to his sure grasp of a vast range of scientific matters. He was Descartes' principal correspondent, as well as his main point of contact with French intellectual life from 1630 onwards, and it was Mersenne who elicited the objections to the *Meditationes* on Descartes' behalf.

MONTAIGNE, Michel Eyquem de (1533–92), was born near Bordeaux, and was a member of the Bordeaux *parlement* for thirteen years. His *Essais*, which began to appear in 1580, represented the quintessence of French *gentilhomme* culture, and exercised an immense influence on French intellectual life right through to the end of the seventeenth

Biographical Notes

century. His revival of ancient Pyrrhonism was to provide a crucial ingredient in Descartes' formulation of a sceptically driven epistemology in the 1630s.

MORE, Henry (1614–87), was, with Ralph Cudworth, the leading member of the Cambridge Platonists, a group based at Emmanuel and Christ's College, Cambridge, who sought to counter various forms of naturalism and mechanism by a return to a Platonically inspired natural philosophy. Although in his later work he became increasingly hostile to Cartesianism, in the late 1640s More was an enthusiastic, if critical, admirer of Descartes, and there was an important exchange of letters between the two.

MORIN, Jean-Baptiste (1583–1656), French physician, mathematician, natural philosopher, astronomer, and astrologer. He was professor of mathematics at the Collège Royal and a member of Mersenne's (q.v.) circle. An indefatigable polemicist, he stridently opposed both Galileo (q.v.) and Descartes, and by the late 1630s, after a lengthy debate over the determination of longitudes, had managed to alienate just about everyone, continuing his research after that time in isolation from other scientists. He is reputed to have made a very lucrative career through his astrological work.

MYDORGE, Claude (1585–1647), was a lawyer and government official, although he was able to devote himself to his real interests, mathematics and optics, from the early 1620s onwards. He worked with Descartes and Ferrier (q.v.) on optical questions in the mid-1620s, devoting himself particularly to the study of mirrors. Building on the work of Apollonius, he developed the study of conic sections in a number of new ways, with very extensive coverage of ellipses, which played the major role in his geometrical optics. Although there was an element of competition in Descartes' relation with him in the late 1620s and early 1630s, he took Descartes' side in the dispute with Fermat in 1638.

PEIRESC, Nicolas-Claude Fabri de (1580–1637), was one of the best-connected scientific patrons of his time, having extensive connections with scientists in Italy and France. After reading Galileo's *Sidereus Nuncius* in 1610 he carried out a number of fundamental astronomical observations; and he continued to organize astronomical observations into the 1630s, when he put his extensive diplomatic and religious contacts in different parts of the world to use to make precise measurements of longitude. From 1624 onwards he was Gassendi's (q.v.) chief patron. Descartes never moved directly in Peiresc's circle, but he was indirectly obliged to him through Mersenne (q.v.) and others, especially for information on the parhelion observed at Frascati on 20 March 1629.

POLLOT, Alphonse (c.1604–68), was a French Protestant refugee to the Netherlands, an administrator in the house of Orange. His contact with Descartes began in 1638, when he sent him, through Reneri (q.v.), some objections to the *Discours*. He subsequently became a friend of Descartes and acted as an intermediary between Descartes and Elizabeth (q.v.).

REGIUS [Henri le Roy] (1598–1679), a Dutch physician and natural philosopher, was one of the principal representatives of Cartesianism in the Netherlands. He occasionally accompanied Reneri (q.v.) on his visits to Descartes at Santpoort, and became a staunch supporter of Cartesian physiology and natural philosophy. He was appointed professor of medicine at the University of Utrecht in 1638, and his polemical style and refusal to tolerate interference from theologians led him into clashes with Voetius (q.v.), clashes which were soon to embroil Descartes himself, who encouraged Regius in the early stages of the dispute. In 1646 Regius published his own version of Cartesian natural philosophy which stripped it of the legitimatory metaphysical apparatus that Descartes had supplied in the *Principia*, and highlighted some of the more radical elements in Cartesianism. From this point onwards Descartes and Regius entered into an acrimonious public dispute. Regius was, however, instrumental in the establishment of Cartesianism in Dutch intellectual life in the 1650s.

Biographical Notes

RENERI [Régnier, Reniersz], Henricus [Henri] (*c*.1593–1639), was a Walloon Belgian, the first disciple of Descartes. He had originally studied theology at the Catholic University of Louvain, only to convert to Protestantism on reading Calvin, and then studied medicine. He was the first to provide institutional teaching of Cartesian natural philosophy, and he and Descartes were close during the period from 1632 until Reneri's untimely death in 1639. Descartes moved to Deventer in 1632 to teach him his physics, and joined him in Utrecht 1635. There was an overt element of hero-worship in Reneri's relationship to Descartes, and his Cartesianism was evidently never as critical as that of his friend Regius (q.v.).

ROBERVAL, Gilles Personne de (1602–75), came from a simple French farming family and was a largely self-taught mathematician. He mixed with Mersenne's (q.v.) circle on his arrival in Paris in 1628 and showed himself to be an able mathematician. It is at this time that he would first have met Descartes. After a short period as a professor of philosophy, he was appointed professor of mathematics at the Collège Royale in 1634. His main contributions lay in the area of the geometry of infinitesimals, but he had wide interests. Descartes' relations with him were never especially cordial, and on his return to Paris in 1647 Roberval evidently provoked Descartes' ire by constantly trying to monopolize the conversation.

SUÁREZ, Francisco (1548–1617), was the most important of the Jesuit metaphysicians active in the second half of the sixteenth century. Born in Granada, he taught at various Spanish and Portuguese universities and at the Collegio Romano. His contributions were in the areas of jurisprudence and political philosophy, and metaphysics. His books on metaphysics underlay courses in Jesuit colleges, and although his position was broadly Thomist he introduced a number on innovations. Descartes knew his work well, and various formulations of his own metaphysics are almost literal negations of passages in Suárez.

VIETA [Viète], François (1540–1603), was a brilliant French mathematician with interests in cryptography, astronomy, and cosmology, but whose outstanding contribution was to algebra. His *In artem analyticem isagoge* (1591) was the first contribution to algebra as we now understand it. Beaugrand (q.v.) brought out an edition of his works in 1631, and saw what he considered 'borrowings' in Descartes' *Géométrie* when it appeared in 1637. But Descartes seems to have been ignorant of Vieta's work at the time he was developing his own algebra, and his clumsy notation shows beyond reasonable doubt that his starting-point was the relatively elementary work of Clavius (q.v.) rather than Vieta.

VILLEBRESSIEU (or VILLE-BRESSIEU), Étienne de (d. 1653), French chemist, natural philosopher, and engineer to the King of France. He was principally an experimentalist specialising in hydraulics, but with interests in the theory of matter and especially metallurgy, although he seems never to have published anything. He shared with Descartes an active interest in questions in natural philosophy. He was evidently one of Descartes' closest friends in the 1620s and early 1630s. They were both part of the Paris circle of natural philosophers in the mid-1620s, and he and Descartes may have shared accommodation in Amsterdam in 1630 and 1631. The life of Descartes by Pierre Borel, published in 1653 (or perhaps 1656: the date of publication is a matter of dispute), draws on Villebressieu's unpublished memoirs, which are no longer extant.

VOETIUS [Voët], Gisbert [Gysbert] (1588–1676), was a Dutch theologian, professor of theology and later rector at the University of Utrecht. He seems to have spent all his spare time conducting campaigns against Catholics, Jesuit spies, heretics, and Cartesians. He waged a campaign against Regius, trying to have him removed from his chair in 1641, and Descartes was drawn into the dispute in 1642. Indeed, much of his time between 1642 and late 1644 was devoted to a very acrimonious and public dispute with

Biographical Notes

Voetius. Although Voetius succeeded in making life in the Netherlands difficult for Descartes in the 1640s, in the long run his campaign was to no avail: it was his own university, Utrecht, that became the most Cartesian of the Dutch universities in the 1650s.

Select Bibliography

Editions of Descartes' Works

The standard edition of Descartes' works, and that from which I have worked, is:

ADAM, CHARLES, and TANNERY, PAUL (eds.), *Œuvres de Descartes,* 2nd edn., 11 vols. (Paris, 1974–86). This is abbreviated to AT in the notes.

The best single-language selection of Descartes' works, which contains invaluable notes, is the French edition of Alquié:

ALQUIÉ, FERDINAND (ed.), *Œuvres philosophiques de Descartes,* 3 vols. (Paris, 1963–73).

Among the various other editions of particular works which are of special importance are:

ADAM, CHARLES, and MILHAUD, GÉRARD (eds.), *Descartes: Correspondance publiée avec une introduction et des notes,* 8 vols. (Paris, 1936–63).
ARMOGATHE, J.-R., and CARRAUD, V., 'Texte original et traduction français d'un inédit de Descartes', *Bulletin cartésien* 15 (1987) (supplement to *Archives de philosophie* 50), 1–4.
COSTABEL, PIERRE, *René Descartes: Exercices pour les éléments des solides: Essai en complément d'Euclide—Progymnasmata de solidorum elementis* (Paris, 1987).
CRAPULLI, GIOVANNI, *Descartes: Regulae ad directionem ingenii: Texte critique établi par Giovanni Crapulli avec la version hollandaise du XVIIe siècle* (The Hague, 1966).
GADOFFRE, GILBERT (ed.), *Descartes: Discours de la méthode* (Manchester, 1941).
GILSON, ÉTIENNE (ed.), *René Descartes: Discours de la méthode, texte et commentaire,* 4th edn. (Paris, 1975).
MARION, JEAN-LUC (ed. and trans., with the collaboration of Pierre Costabel), *Règles utiles et claires pour la direction de l'esprit dans la recherche de la vérité* (Paris, 1977).
RODIS-LEWIS, GENEVIÈVE (ed.), *Descartes: Les Passions de l'âme,* 2nd edn. (Paris, 1970).

Modern English Translations of Descartes' Works

The most comprehensive and most reliable translation of Descartes' writings into English is:

COTTINGHAM, JOHN, STOOTHOFF, ROBERT, MURDOCH, DUGALD, and KENNY, ANTHONY, *The Philosophical Writings of Descartes,* 3 vols. (Cambridge, 1984–91).

Except where otherwise mentioned, the following works contain full translations of texts which do not appear, or appear only in an abbreviated form, in Cottingham *et al.* Many of these editions have quite detailed notes.

BLOM, JOHN J., *Descartes: His Moral Philosophy and Psychology* (Hassocks, 1978). This is a translation of the correspondence with Elizabeth and others on the passions, and although the letters translated are all to be found in vol. iii of Cottingham *et al.*, the introductory material makes the collection especially valuable.

Bibliography

COTTINGHAM, JOHN, *Descartes' Conversation with Burman* (Oxford, 1976).

FEDERICO, PASQUALE, *Descartes on Polyhedra: A Study on the Solidorum Elementis* (New York, 1982).

HALL, THOMAS STEELE (ed. and trans.), *René Descartes: Treatise of Man* (Cambridge, Mass., 1972).

MAHONEY, MICHAEL S., *René Descartes: Le Monde, ou traité de la lumière* (New York, 1979).

MILLER, VALENTINE RODGER, and MILLER, REESE P., *René Descartes: Principles of Philosophy* (Dordrecht, 1983).

OLSCAMP, PAUL J. (trans.), *René Descartes: Discourse on Method, Optics, Geometry, and Meteorology* (Indianapolis, 1965).

ROBERT, WALTER (trans.), *René Descartes: Compendium of Music*, Musicological Studies and Documents 8 (American Institute of Musicology, 1961).

SMITH, DAVID EUGENE, and LATHAM, MARCIA L., *The Geometry of René Descartes* (Chicago, 1925; repr. New York, 1954).

VOSS, STEPHEN H. (trans.), *René Descartes: The Passions of the Soul* (Indianapolis, 1989). This text of the *Passions* is translated in vol. i of Cottingham *et al.*, but the Voss edition has detailed notes.

Biographies

The three principal biographical sources are, in chronological order:

BAILLET, ADRIEN, *La Vie de Monsieur Descartes*, 2 vols. (Paris, 1691; facsimile repr. Geneva, 1970). This is abbreviated to Baillet in the notes.

ADAM, CHARLES, *Vie et œuvres de Descartes* (Paris, 1910). This is abbreviated to Adam in the notes.

COHEN, GUSTAVE, *Écrivains français en Hollande dans la première moitié du XVIIᵉ siècle* (Paris, 1920; facsimile repr. Geneva, 1976). This is abbreviated to *Écrivains* in the notes.

Valuable as an account of the development of Descartes' thought (although there are many differences between the readings offered there and those offered in the present work) is:

RODIS-LEWIS, GENEVIÈVE, *L'Œuvre de Descartes*, 2 vols. (Paris, 1971).

As far as material in English is concerned, there is an engaging portarit of Descartes in:

VROOMAN, JACK R., *René Descartes: A Biography* (New York, 1970).

Bibliographies

For material up to 1960, the reader should consult the magnificent critical survey in:

SEBBA, GREGOR, *Bibliographia Cartesiana: A Critical Guide to the Descartes Literature, 1800–1960* (The Hague, 1964).

After 1960, the only comprehensive single-volume work simply lists sources, with some basic classification of topics:

CHAPPELL, VERE and DONEY, WILLIS, *Twenty-Five Years of Descartes Scholarship, 1960–1984* (New York, 1987).

For critical accounts of material after 1960, and for all material after 1984, the *Bulletin cartésien*, which appears regularly as a supplement to the *Archives de philosophie*, should be consulted. On seventeenth-century thought in France and the Netherlands more generally, the reader should consult the comprehensive bibliographical surveys in:

Bibliography

SCHOBINGER, JEAN-PIERRE (ed.), *Die Philosophie des 17. Jahrhunderts, ii: Frankreich und Niederlande*, 2 vols. (Basle, 1993).

Dictionaries and Indexes

COTTINGHAM, JOHN, *A Descartes Dictionary* (Oxford, 1993).
MORRIS, JOHN, *Descartes Dictionary* (New York, 1971).

On the details of Descartes' indebtedness to scholastic sources, the following has never been bettered:

GILSON, ÉTIENNE, *Index scolastico-cartésien*, 2nd edn. (Paris, 1979).

Other Primary Sources

ADAM, ANTOINE (ed.), *Les Libertins au XVIIe siècle* (Paris, 1964).
BALZAC, JEAN-LOUIS GUEZ DE, *Œuvres de Monsieur de Balzac*, ed. Valentin Conrart, 2 vols. (Paris, 1665; facsimile repr. Geneva, 1971).
BASSO, SEBASTIAN, *Philosophia naturalis adversus Aristotelem, Libri XII* (Amsterdam, 1649).
BEECKMAN, ISAAC, *Journal tenu par Isaac Beeckman de 1604 à 1634*, ed. Cornelius de Waard, 4 vols. (The Hague, 1939–53). This is abbreviated to JIB in the notes.
BÉRULLE, PIERRE DE, *Œuvres complètes*, 2 vols. (Paris, 1644; facsimile repr. Montsoult, 1960).
BOILEAU, NICHOLAS, *Œuvres complètes*, ed. F. Escal (Paris, 1966).
CAUS, SALOMON DE, *Les raisons des forces mouvantes avec diverses machines tant utiles que plaisantes ausquelles sont adjoints plusioeurs desseigns de grotes et fontaines* (Frankfurt, 1615).
CHARRON, PIERRE, *De la Sagesse*, 2nd edn. (Paris, 1604).
COËFFETEAU, NICOLAS, *Tableau des passions humaines, de leurs causes et de leurs effets* (Paris, 1630).
[Coimbra commentators], *Commentarii collegii Conimbricensis e societate iesu: in universaram dialecticam Aristotelis Stagiritae* (Cologne, 1607; facsimile repr. Hildesheim, 1976).
—— *Commentarii collegii Conimbricensis [. . .] in octo libros physicorum Aristotelis* (Coimbra, 1594; facsimile repr. Hildesheim, 1984).
CUREAU DE LA CHAMBRE, MARIN, *Les Caractères des passions*, 5 vols. (Amsterdam, 1658–63).
DIGBY, KENELM, *Two Treatises* (Paris, 1644; facsimile repr. New York, 1978).
DUPLEIX, SCIPION, *La Physique, ou science des choses naturelles*, ed. Roger Ariew (Paris, 1990).
EUSTACHE DE SAINT-PAUL, *Summa philosophiae quadripartita*, 2 vols. (Lyons, 1626).
FAULHABER, JOHANNES, *Nouae Geometricae & Opticae Inventiones, aliquot peculiarium Instrumentorum* (Frankfurt, 1610).
FICINO, MARSILIO, *Opera omnia Plotini*, ed. F. Creuzer, 3 vols. (Oxford, 1835).
FONSECA, PETRUS, *Commentariorum Petri Fonsecae [. . .] in Libros metaphysicorum Aristotelis* (Cologne, 1615; facsimile repr. Hildesheim, 1964).
GALILEO GALILEI, *Discoveries and Opinions of Galileo*, ed. and trans. Stillman Drake (Garden City, NY, 1957).
—— *Two New Sciences*, trans. Stillman Drake (Madison, Wis., 1974).
—— *Operations of the Geometric and Military Compass*, trans. Stillman Drake (Washington, DC, 1978).
GARASSE, FRANÇOIS, *Les recherches des recherches et autres œuvres de M. Étienne Pasquier* (Paris, 1622).
—— *La doctrine curieuse des beaux esprits de ce temps ou prétendus tels* (Paris, 1623).

Bibliography

GASSENDI, PIERRE, *Opera omnia*, 6 vols. (Lyons, 1658; facsimile repr. Stuttgart, 1964).

GILBERT, WILLIAM, *On the Magnet*, trans. S. P. Thompson *et al.*, ed. D. J. Price (New York, 1958).

HOBBES, THOMAS, *Leviathan* (London, 1651; facsimile repr. Menston, 1969).

—— *Thomas Hobbes: Body, Man, Citizen*, ed. Richard S. Peters (New York, 1962).

HORN, GEORG, *Historiae philosophicae* (Leiden, 1655).

HUYGENS, CHRISTIAAN, *Œuvres complètes de Christiaan Huygens*, ed. La Société Hollandaise des Sciences, 22 vols. (The Hague, 1888–1950).

KEPLER, JOHANNES, *Johannes Kepler Gesammelte Werke*, ed. Walther von Dykk, Max Caspar *et al.* (Munich, 1938–).

LEIBNIZ, GOTTFRIED WILHELM, *Die philosophischen Schriften*, ed. C. I. Gerhardt, 7 vols. (Berlin, 1875–90).

LIPSTORP, DANIEL, *Specimena Philosophiae Cartesianae* (Leiden, 1653).

LUKÁCS, LADISLAUS (ed.), *Monumenta atque Institutio Studiorum Societatis Iesu (1589, 1591, 1599)* (Monumenta Paedagogica Societatis Iesu 5; Monumenta Historica Societatis Iesu, 129) (Rome, 1986).

MERSENNE, MARIN, *Observationes et emendationes ad Francisci Georgii Veneti problemata* (Paris, 1623).

—— *Quaestiones celeberrimae in Genesim* (Paris, 1623).

—— *L'Impiété des déistes, athées et libertins de ce temps*, 2 vols. (Paris, 1624; facsimile repr. of vol. i, Stuttgart, 1975).

—— *La Vérité des sciences, contres les sceptiques ou Pyrrhoniens* (Paris, 1625; facs. repr. Stuttgart, 1969).

—— *Harmonie universelle*, 3 vols. (Paris, 1636–7; facsimile repr. Paris, 1975).

—— *Correspondance du P. Marin Mersenne, religieux minime*, ed. Cornelius de Waard, R. Pintard, B. Rochot, and A. Baelieu, 17 vols. (Paris, 1932–88). This is abbreviated to M in the notes.

MONTAIGNE, MICHEL DE, *Essais*, ed. Maurice Rat, 2 vols. (Paris, 1962).

PACHTLER, G. MICHAEL (ed.), 'Ratio Studiorum et Institutiones scholasticae S. J. per Germanium diu vigentes', *Monumenta Germaniae Paedagogica*, ix (Berlin, 1890).

PEIRESC, NICOLAS-CLAUDE FABRI DE, *Correspondance*, 7 vols. (Paris, 1888–98).

SILHON, JEAN DE, *Les deux veritez de Silhon: l'une de dieu et de sa providence, l'autre de l'immortalité de l'ame* (Paris, 1626).

SOREL, CHARLES, *La science universelle*, 4 vols. (Paris, 1637–43).

STEVIN, SIMON, *The Principal Works of Simon Stevin*, ed. Ernst Cronie, E. J. Dijksterhuis, R. J. Forbes, M. G. J. Minnaert, and A. Pannekeok, 5 vols. (Amsterdam, 1955–66).

SUÁREZ, FRANCISCO, *Metaphysicarum disputationem, in quibus et universa naturalis theologia ordinate traditur . . .* (Paris, 1866; facsimile repr. Hildesheim, 1965).

TOLETUS, FRANCISCUS, *Opera omnia philosophica*, 5 vols. (Cologne, 1615–16; facsimile repr. Hildesheim, 1985).

VOLTAIRE, FRANÇOIS-MARIE AROUET DE, *Lettres philosophiques*, ed. R. Naves (Paris, 1964).

WILSON, DUDLEY (ed.), *French Renaissance Scientific Poetry* (London, 1974).

Selected Secondary Sources (Books and Collections)

AITON, ERIC, *The Vortex Theory of Planetary Motions* (London, 1972).

ÅKERMAN, SUSANNA, *Queen Christina of Sweden and her Circle* (Leiden, 1991).

ALQUIÉ, FERDINAND, *La Découverte métaphysique de l'homme chez Descartes* (Paris, 1950).

ARMOGATHE, J.-R., *Theologia cartesiana: L'Explication physique de l'Eucharistie chez Descartes et Dom Desgabets* (The Hague, 1977).

BALZ, ALBERT G. A., *Cartesian Studies* (New York, 1951).

BARBOUR, JULIAN B., *Absolute or Relative Motion? i: The Discovery of Dynamics* (Cambridge, 1989).

BECK, LESLIE JOHN, *The Method of Descartes* (Oxford, 1952).

Bibliography

BERKEL, KLAAS VAN, *Isaac Beeckman (1588–1637) en de mechanisierung van het wereldbeeld* (Amsterdam, 1983).

BIAGIOLI, MARIO, *Galileo Courtier* (Chicago, 1993).

BITBOL-HESPÉRIÈS, ANNIE, *Le Principe de vie chez Descartes* (Paris, 1990).

BLACKWELL, RICHARD J., *Galileo, Bellarmine, and the Bible* (Notre Dame, Ind., 1991).

BLOCH, OLIVIER RENÉ, *La Philosophie de Gassendi* (The Hague, 1971).

BOUILLIER, FRANCISQUE, *Histoire de la philosophie cartésienne*, 2 vols. (Paris, 1868).

BOYER, CHARLES B., *The Rainbow* (Princeton, NJ, 1987).

—— *History of Analytic Geometry* (Princeton, NJ, 1988).

BREMOND, HENRI, *Histoire littéraire du sentiment religieux en France depuis la fin des guerres de religion jusqu'à nos jours, iii: La Conquête mystique, l'école française* (Paris, 1925).

BROWN, PETER, *The Body and Society* (London, 1989).

BRUNDELL, BARRY, *Pierre Gassendi* (Dordrecht, 1987).

BUCKLEY, MICHAEL J., *At the Origins of Modern Atheism* (New Haven, Conn., 1987).

CANGUILHEM, GEORGES, *La Formation du concept du réflex e aux XVIIe et XVIIIe siècles* (Paris, 1955).

CARR, THOMAS M., Jr., *Descartes and the Resilience of Rhetoric* (Carbondale, Ill., 1990).

CASSIRER, ERNST, *Descartes: Lehre—Persönlichkeit—Wirkung* (Stockholm, 1939).

CATON, HIRAM, *The Origin of Subjectivity* (New Haven, Conn., 1973).

CLARKE, DESMOND M., *Descartes' Philosophy of Science* (Manchester, 1982).

—— *Occult Powers and Hypotheses* (Oxford, 1989).

CODINA MIR, GABRIEL, *Aux sources de la pédagogie des jésuites* (Rome, 1968).

COHEN, H. FLORIS, *Quantifying Music* (Dordrecht, 1984).

COLE, JOHN R., *The Olympian Dreams and Youthful Rebellion of René Descartes* (Urbana, Ill., 1992).

COMPAYRÉ, GABRIEL, *Histoire critique des doctrines de l'éducation en France*, 2 vols. (Paris, 1879).

COSTABEL, PIERRE, *Démarches originales de Descartes savant* (Paris, 1982).

COTTINGHAM, JOHN (ed.), *The Cambridge Companion to Descartes* (Cambridge, 1992).

—— (ed.), *Reason, Will and Sensation* (Oxford, 1994).

CRAPULLI, GIOVANNI, *Mathesis universalis: genesi di un'idea nel XVI secolo* (Rome, 1969).

DAINVILLE, FRANÇOIS DE, *La Naissance de l'humanisme moderne* (Paris, 1940).

—— *L'Éducation des jésuites* (Paris, 1978).

DAUMAS, MAURICE, *Les Instruments scientifiques aux XVIIe et XVIIIe siècles* (Paris, 1953).

DELUMEAU, JEAN, *La Peur en occident* (Paris, 1978).

—— *Le Péché et la peur* (Paris, 1983).

DENISSOFF, ÉLIE, *Descartes, premier théoricien de la physique mathématique* (Louvain, 1970).

DIHLE, ALBRECHT, *The Theory of the Will in Classical Antiquity* (Berkeley, Calif., 1982).

DIJKSTERHUIS, E. J., *The Mechanization of the World Picture* (New York, 1961).

EDEN, KATHY, *Poetic and Legal Fiction in the Aristotelian Tradition* (Princeton, NJ, 1986).

ELIAS, NORBERT, *Über den Prozess der Zivilisation*, 2 vols. (Basle, 1939).

—— *The Court Society* (Oxford, 1983).

FISCHER, KUNO, *Geschichte der neueren Philosophie*, 6 vols. (Berlin, 1852–77).

FUMAROLI, MARC, *L'Âge de l'éloquence* (Geneva, 1980).

GARBER, DANIEL, *Descartes' Metaphysical Physics* (Chicago, 1992).

GARDINER, H. M., METCALF, RUTH CLARK, and BEEBE-CENTER, JOHN, *Feeling and Emotion* (New York, 1937).

GAUKROGER, STEPHEN, *Explanatory Structures* (Hassocks, 1978).

—— (ed.), *Descartes: Philosophy, Mathematics and Physics* (Brighton, 1980).

—— *Cartesian Logic* (Oxford, 1989).

GILSON, ÉTIENNE, *La Liberté chez Descartes et la théologie* (Paris, 1913).

485

Bibliography

GILSON, ÉTIENNE, *Études sur le rôle de la pensée médiévale dans la formation du système cartésien*, 5th edn. (Paris, 1984).

GOUHIER, HENRI, *Les Premières Pensées de Descartes* (Paris, 1958).

—— *La Pensée religieuse de Descartes*, 2nd edn. (Paris, 1972).

—— *Cartésianisme et augustinisme au XVIIe siècle* (Paris, 1978).

GRIMALDI, NICOLAS, and MARION, JEAN-LUC (eds.), *Le Discours et sa méthode* (Paris, 1987).

GROSHOLZ, EMILY, *Cartesian Method and the Problem of Reduction* (Oxford, 1991).

GUÉROULT, MARTIAL, *Descartes selon l'ordre des raisons*, 2 vols. (Paris, 1953).

HARTH, ERICA, *Cartesian Women* (Ithaca, NY, 1992).

HUPPERT, GEORGE, *Les Bourgeois Gentilshommes* (Chicago, 1977).

—— *Public Schools in Renaissance France* (Chicago, 1984).

JONSEN, ALBERT R., and TOULMIN, STEPHEN, *The Abuse of Casuistry* (Berkeley, Calif., 1988).

JOURDAIN, CHARLES, *Histoire de l'université de Paris au XVIIe et au XVIIIe siècle*, 2 vols. (Paris, 1888).

JOY, LYNN SUMIDA, *Gassendi the Atomist* (Cambridge, 1987).

KETTERING, SHARON, *Patrons, Brokers, and Clients in Seventeenth-Century France* (Oxford, 1986).

KLEIN, JACOB, *Greek Mathematical Thought and the Origin of Algebra* (Cambridge, Mass., 1986).

KNOWLSON, JAMES, *Universal Language Schemes in England and France, 1600–1800* (Toronto, 1975).

KOYRÉ, ALEXANDRE, *From the Closed World to the Infinite Universe* (Baltimore, 1957).

—— *Newtonian Studies* (London, 1965).

—— *Galilean Studies* (Hassocks, 1978).

LENNON, THOMAS M., NICHOLAS, J. M., and DAVIS, JOHN W. (eds.), *Problems of Cartesianism* (Kingston, Ont., 1982).

LENOBLE, ROBERT, *Mersenne ou la naissance du mécanisme*, 2nd edn. (Paris, 1971).

LEROY, MAXIME, *Descartes, le philosophe au masque*, 2 vols. (Paris, 1929).

LEVI, ANTHONY, *French Moralists* (Oxford, 1964).

LINDEBOOM, G. A., *Descartes and Medicine* (Amsterdam, 1979).

MARION, JEAN-LUC, *Sur la théologie blanche de Descartes* (Paris, 1981).

—— *Sur l'ontologie grise de Descartes*, 2nd edn. (Paris, 1981).

McCRACKEN, CHARLES J., *Malebranche and British Philosophy* (Oxford, 1983).

MILHAUD, GASTON, *Descartes savant* (Paris, 1921).

MOUSNIER, ROLAND, *La Vénalité des offices sous Henri IV et Louis XIII* (Paris, 1971).

—— *The Institutions of France under the Absolute Monarchy 1598–1789*, 2 vols. (Chicago, 1979–84).

MOUY, PAUL, *Le Développement de la physique cartésienne, 1646–1712* (Paris, 1934).

NÉEL, MARGUERITE, *Descartes et la princesse Elizabeth* (Paris, 1946).

OESTREICH, GERHARD, *Neostoicism and the Early Modern State* (Cambridge, 1982).

PEGHAIRE, J., *Intellectus et ratio selon S. Thomas d'Aquin* (Paris, 1936).

PENELHUM, TERENCE, *Survival and Disembodied Existence* (London, 1968).

PINTARD, RENÉ, *Le Libertinage érudit dans la première moitié du XVIIe siècle*, 2nd edn. (Geneva, 1983).

PIRRO, ANDRÉ, *Descartes et la musique* (Paris, 1907).

POPKIN, RICHARD H., *The History of Scepticism from Erasmus to Spinoza* (Berkeley, Calif., 1979).

—— *The Third Force in Seventeenth-Century Thought* (Leiden, 1992).

—— (ed.), *Scepticism and Irreligion in the Seventeenth and Eighteenth Centuries* (Leiden, 1993).

ROCHEMONTEIX, CAMILLE DE, *Un collège des jésuites au XVIIe et au XVIIIe siècles*, 4 vols. (Le Mans, 1889).

RODIS-LEWIS, GENEVIÈVE, *La Morale de Descartes*, 3rd edn. (Paris, 1970).

Bibliography

—— *L'Anthropologie cartésienne* (Paris, 1990).

ROSENFIELD, LEONORA COHEN, *From Beast-Machine to Man-Machine*, rev. edn. (New York, 1968).

ROSSI, PAOLO, *Clavis universalis* (Milan, 1960).

SABRA, A. I., *Theories of Light from Descartes to Newton* (London, 1967).

SASAKI, CHIKARA, *Descartes' Mathematical Thought*, 1989 Princeton University Ph.D. thesis (University Microfilms repr., Ann Arbor, Mich. [1989]).

SCAGLIONE, ALDO, *The Liberal Arts and the Jesuit College System* (Amsterdam, 1986).

SCHOULS, PETER A., *Descartes and the Enlightenment* (Edinburgh, 1989).

SCHUSTER, JOHN A., *Descartes and the Scientific Revolution, 1618–1634*, 1977 Princeton University Ph.D. thesis (University Microfilms repr., 2 vols., Ann Arbor, Mich. [1977]).

SCOTT, J. F., *The Scientific Work of René Descartes* (London, 1952).

SCREECH, MICHAEL A., *Montaigne and Melancholy* (London, 1991).

SHEA, WILLIAM R., *The Magic of Numbers and Motion* (Canton, Mass., 1991).

SIRVEN, J., *Les Années d'apprentissage de Descartes* (Albi, 1928).

SMITH, NORMAN KEMP, *New Studies in the Philosophy of Descartes* (London, 1952).

SPINK, J. S., *French Free-Thought from Gassendi to Voltaire* (London, 1960).

SZABÒ, ARPÁD, *Anfänge der griechischen Mathematik* (Freiburg, 1969).

TAYLOR, CHARLES, *Sources of the Self* (Cambridge, 1989).

THOMAS, KEITH, *Religion and the Decline of Magic* (Harmondsworth, 1978).

THORNDIKE, LYNN, *A History of Magic and Experimental Science*, 8 vols. (New York, 1923–58).

TILLMAN, ALEXANDRE, *L'Itinéraire du jeune Descartes* (Lille, 1976).

TOCANNE, BERNARD, *L'Idée de nature en France dans la seconde moitié du XVIIe siècle* (Paris, 1978).

TRUESDELL, CLIFFORD, *Essays in the History of Mechanics* (New York, 1968).

VARTANIAN, ARAM, *La Mettrie's L'Homme Machine* (Princeton, NJ, 1960).

VERBEEK, THEO, *Descartes and the Dutch* (Carbondale, Ill., 1992).

VOSS, STEPHEN H. (ed.), *Essays on the Philosophy and Science of René Descartes* (Oxford, 1993).

VUILLEMIN, JULES, *Mathématique et métaphysique chez Descartes* (Paris, 1960).

WAHL, JEAN, *Du rôle de l'idée de l'instant dans la philosophie de Descartes* (Paris, 1920).

WALKER, DAVID P., *Spiritual and Demonic Magic from Ficino to Campanella* (London, 1958).

—— *Studies in Musical Science in the Late Renaissance* (London, 1978).

WATSON, RICHARD A., *The Breakdown of Cartesian Metaphysics* (Atlantic Highlands, NJ, 1987).

WEBER, JEAN-PAUL, *La Constitution du texte des Regulae* (Paris, 1964).

WESTFALL, RICHARD S., *Force in Newton's Physics* (London, 1971).

—— *Never at Rest* (Cambridge, 1980).

WILLIAMS, BERNARD, *Descartes* (Hassocks, 1978).

—— *Ethics and the Limits of Philosophy* (London, 1985).

WITTGENSTEIN, LUDWIG, *On Certainty*, ed. G. E. M. Anscombe and G. H. von Wright (Oxford, 1969).

YATES, FRANCES, *The Art of Memory* (London, 1966).

—— *The Rosicrucian Enlightenment* (London, 1972).

YOLTON, JOHN, *Thinking Matter* (Oxford, 1983).

—— *Perceptual Acquaintance* (Oxford, 1984).

ZANTA, LÉONTINE, *La Renaissance du stoïcisme au XVIe siècle* (Paris, 1914).

Index

Index

Index

Index

Index

epistemology, 14, 119, 160, 184, 249, 289; Descartes' 11, 55, 160–1, 304–21 *passim*, 336–52 *passim*; philosophy reduced to 5–6, 420 n. 32

Erasmus, Desiderius (1469–1536, Dutch humanist and reformer) 30–1, 42, 48

Eratosthenes (*c*.284–192 BC, Greek mathematician, astronomer, and geographer) 95–7

eternal truths, doctrine of 197, 203–10, 316–18, 340

ethics, 25, 65, 305, 307–8, 364, 388, 394–5, 399–400, 413, 467 n. 54; teaching of 52, 61; *see also* casuistry; provisional moral code

Euclid (*fl.* 300 BC, Greek mathematician) 125, 138, 173, 175, 299

Euler, Leonhard (1707–83, Swiss mathematician and physicist) 127, 383

Eustache de Saint Paul [Eustachius a Sanct Paulo] (d. 1640, professor of theology at the Sorbonne) 364, 398, 448 n. 15

extension 4, 167–8, 170–2, 240, 329, 345, 347–8, 356–7, 366, 367, 411–2; limits to 237–8

Fabricius [Fabrici *or* Fabrisio] ab Aquapendente, Girolamo (1533–1619, Italian physician and anatomist) 406

*Faulhaber, Johannes 105, 128, 130

Ferdinand II (1578–1637, Holy Roman Emperor) 104

*Fermat, Pierre de 297, 299, 323, 324, 327–8, 331–2, 371, 372, 386, 451 n. 109

*Ferrier, Guillaume [or Jean?] 139, 144, 187–9, 191–5, 299, 324, 443–4 n. 12; identity of 438 n. 23

Ficino, Marsilio (1433–99, Neoplatonic philosopher) 19

fideism 315, 316

fire 228–9, 232–3, 271, 379

Fischer, Kuno (1824–1907, German neo-Kantian/Hegelian historian of philosophy) 6

La Flèche, college of, 20, 21, 24, 38–61 *passim*, 62, 66, 67, 74, 84, 90–1, 98, 104, 123, 129, 138, 139, 204, 322, 357, 379

Fludd, Robert (1574–1637, English occultist philosopher and physician) 136

foetus, formation of 2, 405–6

Fonseca, Pedro (1528–99, Portuguese Jesuit scholastic philosopher and theologian) 53–4, 60, 116, 427 n. 53

Fontenelle, Bernard le Bouvier de (1657–1757, French essayist and poet) 383

force 5, 13, 83–4, 86–9, 154, 220, 244–7, 376

form, Aristotle's doctrine of 55–8, 238–40, 348, 356, 380–1

Foscarini, Paolo Antonio (*c*.1580–1616, Italian Carmelite friar, defender of Copernicanism) 53, 133–4, 316, 337

foundations of knowledge 309–21

Francis I (1494–1541, King of France) 36

Franeker, University of 195

Frederick V (1596–1632, Elector Palatine, then briefly King of Bohemia, later exiled in the Netherlands) 101–2, 104, 293–4

Frederick Henry of Nassau, Prince of Orange (1584–1647) 293, 361, 414

free fall, Aristotle on 55–6; Beeckman on 73, 80–4; Descartes on 70, 73, 80–4, 221; Galileo on 80

Frege, Gottlob (1848–1925, German mathematician and logician) 7

Freinsheim [Freinshemius], Johann (1608–60, German scholar, librarian at the Swedish court) 415

Freud, Sigmund (1856–1939, founder of psychoanalysis) 109

Fromondus, Libertus [Libert Froidmont] pseudonym of Vincent Lenis (1587–1653, Dutch theologian and natural philosopher) 288, 324–5, 326, 327, 329

Fronde, the 411

Galen [Claudius Galenus] (*c*.130–*c*.201, Greek physician, physiologist and philosopher) and Galenism 225, 270, 277, 325, 452 n. 138

*Galilei, Galileo 14, 150, 164, 184, 189, 209, 223, 269, 316, 321, 335, 337, 378, 442–3 n. 110; condemnation of 11, 13, 134, 185, 190, 290–2, 304, 323, 408; discovery of the moons of Jupiter 59, 129; kinematics 80, 288, 336, 412, 449 n. 41, 451 n. 109; longitude, determination of 92; primary and secondary qualities 345; proportional compasses 94; relativity of motion, principle of 372; tides, theory of the 254

Galilei, Vincenzo (*c*.1520–91, Italian musical theorist, father of above) 79

*Garasse, François 136

gardening 334

Index

494

Index

Index

mechanism 12, 71, 112, 139, 146–52, 158–81 *passim*, 183, 184–6, 196–7, 200, 220–1, 226–92 *passim*, 320–1, 325, 337–8, 343–4, 352, 380–3, 390, 401

Medici family 59, 427 n. 48

medicine 17–19, 20, 54, 64, 158, 270, 388, 394–5, 400

melancholia 18–20, 62, 110, 388, 394, 399

Melanchthon [Schwarzerd], Philip (1497–1560, German Protestant reformer) 45

memory 157, 166, 270, 273–4, 281, 282, 391, 433 n. 97, 452 n. 130; intellectual memory 392

Menaechmus (4th century BC, Alexandrian mathematician, discoverer of the geometry of conic sections) 131

*Mersenne, Marin, 50, 181, 183, 184, 185, 188, 189, 194, 217–19, 227, 243, 249, 255, 271, 286–7, 290–1, 321–2, 326, 331, 333–5, 337, 342, 355, 358, 364, 375, 393, 405, 406, 407, 411, 414; acoustics, contribution to 139, 191; Descartes' early acquaintance with 38, 132, 136–9; instrumentalism of 71, 185; language, theory of 284, 445–6 n. 48; mathematics, surveys of 132, 139; mathematics as a model for knowledge 184; mechanism, formulation of 146–52, 195–200, 269; musical 'contest' with Ban, 333; role in the Descartes/ Beeckman dispute 22–4; scepticism, response to 315; theological orthodoxy, defence of 136–7, 146–52, 195–7, 316; Voetius and 359

Merton School 80

mesolabe 95–9, 130–1, 210, 214

metaphysics 12, 52, 59–61, 158, 186, 202, 227, 247, 355–83 *passim*, 387; Descartes' 11, 106, 190, 195–210, 292, 304–21 *passim*, 336–52 *passim*, 355–83 *passim*, 410

meteorology 58, 218–20, 295–6, 329–31, 378

method 92, 101–3, 104–34 *passim*, 152–7, 158, 324, 326, 378–80

microscope 298–9

military training 55, 65–6

mind 6, 347–51, 348–51; and the brain 469 n. 119; *see also* intellect; reason

mind/body, dualism 2, 7, 277–8, 338, 358, 359, 365; psychosomatic and somatopsychic processes 17–20, 388, 399; substantial union of 351, 387, 388–94

modes 329, 366–7, 370, 390

*Montaigne, Michel de 20, 25, 33, 34, 36, 133, 137, 188, 306, 314–16, 318–19, 397

*More, Henry 288, 369, 390, 411–12

*Morin, Jean-Baptiste 138, 183, 188, 327, 328, 330–1

mortalism, *see* naturalism; soul, immortality of

motion, conservation of 231–2, 244–5, 369–70, 373, 390; composition of 328, 371; definition of 370–7; direction of, *see* determination; force of, 244–5, 248, 369–77, 388; laws of, *see* nature, laws of; relativity of 371–7, 412; tendency to 87–8, 154, 246, 247, 248, 328–9, 330, 369, 376; *see also* action, inertia

music 4, 74–80, 96–7, 222, 223; Descartes' theory of 67, 70, 73, 74–80, 91, 123–4, 191, 286–7; teaching of 52, 58

*Mydorge, Claude 59, 132, 138–9, 141–4, 193, 211, 225, 407, 438–9 n. 26, 439 n. 29

Napier, Richard (1559–1634, English clergyman and physician) 62

natural philosophy, teaching of 52

naturalism 7, 115, 136, 147–52, 156, 185–6, 195, 207, 275, 289, 308–9, 319, 351, 383, 390; *see also* Alexander of Aphrodisias and Alexandrism

nature, laws of 240–9, 329, 373–5, 388

Naudé, Gabriel (1600–53, French physician and libertine) 138, 183

Newton, Isaac (1642–1727, English natural philosopher and mathematician) and Newtonianism 4, 5, 82, 246, 254, 383, 412

Nifo, Agostino (1469/70–1538, Italian philosopher and physician) 52

Noël, Étienne (1581–1660, French Jesuit, rector of various colleges, natural philosopher) 329

novelties, teaching of science by means of 58–9

number, early spatial conceptions of 173–4; representation in the intellect and the imagination 171–2

numbers, types of: amicable 334; figurate 127–8; perfect 75, 334

occasionalism 390

Ockham [Occam], William of (c.1285–c.1349, English philosopher, theologian, and political theorist) 52, 348

496

Index

optics 72, 105, 139–46, 158, 190, 283, 296–9, 322–3, 327–30, 371, 401; geometrical 129, 139–46, 153–5, 261–2, 297–9; physical 115, 144–6, 221–2, 229–31, 237–76 *passim*, 297–9; optical illusions 59, 129, 191; speed of light 258, 450 n. 87

Oresme, Nicholas (*c.*1320–82, French theologian and natural philosopher) 238

Ovid [Publius Ovidius Naso] (43 BC–17 AD, Roman poet) 49

Pappus (late 4th century, Alexandrian mathematician) 97, 99, 125, 126, 211, 214, 215, 301, 302

parhelia 217–19, 296

Paris, University of 24, 34, 40, 136, 422 n. 28

Pascal, Blaise (1623–62, French mathematician, philosopher, and theologian) 61, 407, 414

Pasquier, Étienne (1529–1615, French historian and constitutional theorist) 34, 36

passions, 15, 33; Descartes' theory of 4, 18, 25, 120, 132, 364, 366, 384–405 *passim*, 415

patronage 189–90, 413–14

*Peiresc, Nicolas-Claude Fabri de 189, 218

Pelagianism 386

perception, *see* cognition; vision

Pereira, Gomez (16th century Spanish physician and physiologist) 271

Peter of Spain [Petrus Hispanus Portugalensis] (*c.*1200–77, Portuguese scholastic philosopher, Pope John XXI from 1276–1277) 103

Petit, Pierre (*c.*1594–1677, French engineer and mathematician, pioneer of observational astronomy) 323

Petrarch [Petrarca], Francesco (1304–74, Italian humanist) 394

Philoponus, John (6th century Christian Neoplatonist philosopher) 57

Philostratus, Flavius (*c.*170–245, Greek rhetorician) 51, 123

physiology 5, 60, 64, 158, 167, 190, 227–8, 269–90, 324–26, 359, 364, 379, 400, 401, 405

Picot, Claude (*c.*1601–68, French cleric, member of the Mersenne circle) 138, 386–7, 408, 411, 414

Pindar (*c.*522–*c.*440 BC, Greek poet) 49

pineal gland 272–4, 281, 369–70, 388, 393, 401–2, 452 n. 126

planets, constitution of 228–56 *passim*; orbits of 5, 249, 250–4, 371, 375, 380–3; *see also* Copernicus and Copernicanism

Plato (*c.*428–*c.*348 BC, Greek philosopher) 10, 28, 46, 49, 121, 198, 220, 242, 270, 346, 351, 398

Platonism and Neoplatonism 6, 10, 147, 148, 204, 275, 346, 404

Plempius [Plemp] Vopiscus (1601–71, Dutch Galenist physician, professor of medicine and then rector of the University of Louvain) 225, 324, 325, 330

plenum, *see* void

Poitiers, University of 24, 62, 64

*Pollot, Alphonse 333, 361, 385, 387, 388

Pomponazzi, Pietro (1462–1525, Italian Aristotelian philosopher) 52, 60; *see also* Alexander of Aphrodisias and Alexandrism

Porphyry (*c.*232–*c.*305, Neoplatonist philosopher, pupil of Plotinus) 53

Port-Royal 61, 419 n. 9

Poulain de la Barre, François (1647–1723, Cartesian social philosopher) 4

prime matter, doctrine of 56, 240

Primerose, Jacques (d. 1659, physician, opponent of Harvey) 358–9

problem solving 124–6, 127, 169, 174–5

Proclus (410–85, Greek Neoplatonist philosopher) 100

proof (demonstration) 112, 180, 217; *see also* analysis and synthesis; deduction

proportions 75–9; theory of 92–99, 130–1, 180, 304; *see also* compasses, proportional

Protagoras (*c.*490–*c.*420 BC, Greek philosopher) 314

Protestantism 23, 25, 26, 27–8, 29, 45, 48, 55, 65, 104, 126, 187, 196, 294, 357, 358, 360, 385, 386, 406, 413, 415

'provisional moral code' 137, 307–8

psychoanalysis 9, 109, 434 n. 11 and 12

psychologism 9

psychology 10, 51, 54, 112, 120–4, 147, 180, 191

Ptolemy [Claudius Ptolemaeus] (*c.*90–168, Egyptian astronomer and geographer) 142–3

Pyrrhonism 311–16, 339, 341; *see also* scepticism

Pythagoreans 75, 79, 108

quadrivium 52, 53

Quintilian [Marcus Fabius Quintillanus] (*c.*35–*c.*100, Roman rhetorician) 42, 49, 51, 119–23

497

Index

Index

Stevin, Simon (1548–1620, Dutch mathematician and engineer) 66, 67, 70, 85–6

Stoics and Stoicism 18, 29, 61, 65, 118–19, 120, 137, 148, 242–3, 305, 311, 312, 394, 395–8, 400, 404, 435 n. 32

Sturm, Johannes (1507–89, German educationalist) 37, 45

*Suárez, Francisco 52–3, 60, 204–5, 427 n. 53, 448 n. 15

subjectivity, nature of 318–19, 342, 346–51

substance 12, 242, 356, 366, 390, 391

sun, constitution of the 250

syllogism 54; see also dialectic

Tacitus, Publius [Gaius Cornelius] (c.55–120, Roman historian) 50

tangents to curves, procedures for finding 217, 302–3, 331–2

Tasso, Torquato (1544–94, Italian poet and essayist) 20

telescope 298–90, 322, 324

Telesio, Bernadino (1509–88, Italian natural philosopher and physician) 149, 277–8, 289–90

Tibullus, Albius (c.54–19 BC, Roman poet) 49

tides, theory of the 58, 249, 254–5, 292, 375, 382, 383

time 80–3, 118, 368, 380

Toletus [Toledo, Tolet], Francisco (1532–96, Spanish Jesuit, scholastic philosopher, and theologian) 39, 53–4, 60, 61, 84, 116, 427 n. 53

topics (topoi) 53, 103, 113, 120

Torricelli, Evangelista (1608–47, Italian mathematician and natural philosopher) 407, 414

transubstantiation 326, 356–7, 360

Trent, Council of, and Tridentine reform 41, 48, 337, 356

Trigland [Triglandius], Jacques [Jacob] (1583–1654, Dutch theologian) 386

Trinity, doctrine of the 101

trivium 52, 53

truth, nature of 326–7

Turnebus, Adrien (1512–65, French humanist) 112

Turing machines 7

universals 392, 398

Utrecht, magistrates of 358–9, 361; University of 295, 352–3, 359, 386, 407

Valla, Lorenzo (c.1405–57, Italian humanist) 48

Vanini, Lucilio (1584–1619, Italian philosopher) 136

Vatier, Antoine (1596–1659, French Jesuit, teacher at La Flèche) 322, 326, 329, 379

Veronese [Paolo Caliari] (1528–88, Italian painter) 31

Vesalius, Andreas (1514–64, Belgian anatomist) 278

Viau, Théophile de (1590–1626, Parisian libertine) 136

*Vieta [Viète], François 98–9, 331

*Villebressieu, Étienne de 138, 139, 183, 188, 225–6

Virgil [Publius Vergilius Maro] (70–19 BC, Roman poet) 49, 91, 413

vision 159–67, 228, 258, 273, 274–90 passim, 296–9, 400–1; see also cognition

Vitoria, Francisco de (1483/92–1546, Spanish theologian and jurist) 61

Vives, Juan Luis (1492–1540, Spanish humanist philosopher) 45, 396, 397

*Voetius [Voët], Gisbert [Gysbert] 189, 353, 354, 357–61, 386, 387, 389, 414

Voetius [Voët], Paul (1619–67, son of the above) 360, 361, 427 n. 53

void and plenum, theory of 81, 82, 88–9, 230, 234–6, 240, 241, 247–8, 257, 367, 407

Voltaire, François Marie Arouet de (1694–1778, French essayist) 5

vortex theory 4–5, 249–69 passim, 383, 414; magnetic vortices 380–3

Vossius, Gerard Jan (1577–1649, Dutch humanist) 65

Vossius, Issac (1618–1689, Dutch humanist, son of the above) 413, 415

Wassenaer, Jacob [Jan] van (fl. 1639, surveyor from Utrecht) 334

weight, Descartes' theory of 86–7, 89, 249, 253–4, 335–6, 346, 380, 382, 389

will, the 166, 199, 208, 248, 270, 365, 366, 387, 395–8, 409; freedom of 147, 166, 278, 350, 358, 366, 391, 392, 394, 395, 397–8, 399, 401

Witelo (1230/35–c.1275, Polish natural philosopher) 143

Wittgenstein, Ludwig (1889–1951, Austrian/British philosopher) 7, 10, 420 n. 32, 446 n. 74

Zabarella, Jacopo (1533–89, Italian Aristotelian philosopher) 52, 347

Zarlino, Giossefo (1519–90, Italian musical theorist) 74–5, 78–9, 96–7

499